LOEB CLASSICAL LIBRARY
FOUNDED BY JAMES LOEB 1911

EDITED BY
JEFFREY HENDERSON

SELECT PAPYRI
I

LCL 266

SELECT PAPYRI

PRIVATE DOCUMENTS

WITH AN ENGLISH TRANSLATION BY

A. S. HUNT

AND

C. C. EDGAR

HARVARD UNIVERSITY PRESS
CAMBRIDGE, MASSACHUSETTS
LONDON, ENGLAND

First published 1932

ISBN 978-0-674-99294-8

Printed on acid-free paper and bound by The Maple-Vail Book Manufacturing Group

CONTENTS

PREFACE

This volume represents the first stage in the fulfilment of a long-standing undertaking to edit for the Loeb Library a selection of non-literary Graeco-Roman papyri. Its appearance has been expedited by the assistance of Mr. C. C. Edgar, who recently took upon himself the bulk of the work; to him belongs a corresponding share of any credit that may attach to the production of this book.

The documents here edited are concerned exclusively with private affairs; a second volume contains official papers. An endeavour has been made to avoid, so far as possible, papyri which have previously been utilized in other selections; a certain amount of repetition was, however, unavoidable. Where English translations were already available, as in the case of texts taken from the publications of the Egypt Exploration Society or the Amherst or the Rylands Papyri, these have been revised, but are often used with a minimum of change. We are furthermore indebted to Professor A. E. R. Boak for permission to print a Michigan papyrus [before its publication] No. (184).

A. S. H.

May 1932

INTRODUCTION

The papyri edited in this volume cover a period of approximately one thousand years. With the establishment of the Ptolemaic dynasty in Egypt Greek became the official language of the country, and maintained that position throughout the period of Roman rule and down to, and indeed some time after, the Arab invasion. The earliest dated Greek papyrus so far recovered is a marriage contract of the year 311 B.C. (No. 1 in this selection). At the beginning of the eighth century A.D. Greek was still freely employed by the newly appointed Arab officials, and bilingual receipts written in Greek and Arabic persisted for a further century or more.

A scientific pursuit of Greek papyri has been in progress for little longer than [two generations]. The older collections, those of London, Paris, Berlin and Vienna—to name the more important—were based entirely on purchase from dealers, and it was not till the winter of 1895–1896 that an expedition was organized from this country for the express purpose of the discovery of papyri. Spectacular finds made the following season on the site of the ancient Oxyrhynchus drew general attention to this method of research, and since then excavations have been carried on at a number of Graeco-Roman sites by French, German, Italian, American, as well as British, explorers. Native diggers, moreover, con-

tinued to make discoveries both in the course of their agricultural operations and in less legitimate ways. A very large output has been the combined result: the old collections have been enlarged and many new ones formed, both in Europe and across the Atlantic.

The sources of papyri and the conditions of their recovery from the soil of Egypt are consequently now well known. Most have come from the ruins of ancient towns or villages, either from the remains of houses or from the rubbish-heaps which surrounded them. All the Oxyrhynchus papyri, for instance, were found in the extensive mounds of rubbish, some of these being as much as thirty feet in height and the product of several centuries. The second main source is tombs, which may be productive in more ways than one. Occasionally, though rarely, treasured papyri accompanied their owners to the grave. In the Ptolemaic period, discarded sheets of papyrus were often used in making painted cartonnage for the embellishment of mummies, and many valuable texts have been extracted from these. Sometimes too they were included in the wrappings of mummified sacred animals: a cemetery of crocodiles at the ancient Tebtunis provided material for a large volume.

Literary papyri, whether representing lost or extant works, of course form but a fraction of what has been found. Of the non-literary or documentary kind those already edited now run into [thousands]. These documentary papyri may conveniently be divided into two classes, the official and the private. The latter is the class exemplified in the following pages. It consists chiefly of wills, agreements,

receipts, letters, accounts, lists and other memoranda, and religious relics both Christian and pagan. Of agreements there are many varieties—for marriage and divorce, for adoption and alienation, manumission, apprenticeship, labour, surety, sale, lease, gift, division of property, abandonment and settlement of claims, indemnity, appointment of representatives and arbitrators, loan and repayment.

A fertile field is here opened for research in various subjects. For the historian there is a plentiful harvest. Some gleanings for dynastic and political history may be obtained even from private papers. It is, however, in regard to economic and social conditions that these are more commonly instructive. Such subjects as the forms of land tenure, methods of cultivation, organization and development of trade and handicrafts, fluctuation of prices, have abundant evidence. Its significance moreover is not always merely local. For instance, the economic decline which set in towards the close of the third century and contributed to the eventual collapse of the Roman Empire is clearly reflected in the papyri. Here may be traced the gradual replacement of free labour and small holdings by serfdom and overgrown estates supporting semi-independent communities, here too the prodigious fall in currency-values comparable to that recently witnessed in Central Europe. Individual provinces no doubt had their peculiar problems, but they were stricken by the same disease, and a study of the symptoms in Egypt, where the data are so plentiful, assists the comprehension of the general process.

For the illustration of the common life of the time, popular culture, religious ideas, habits and

amusements, there is a wealth of information. The quantities of correspondence passing between persons of various stations in life and of widely different degrees of education afford many intimate glimpses and amusing details; and nowhere perhaps are the special qualities and significance of the documentary papyri more evident. One such quality is their unconscious and ephemeral character. Herein they differ markedly from inscriptions, which were designed for public view and for posterity, and whose candour is not always above suspicion. The figures in the papyri, on the other hand, are as a rule off their guard; they are to be seen following their ordinary daily pursuits, with a refreshing absence of pose and advertisement. They neither make nor possess any claim to fame, and therein lies their interest. For such people are seldom to be met with in the pages of the ancient historians, where the limelight is commonly focussed upon outstanding personalities, while the multitudes of humbler folk, the material which the supermen worked with and set their mark upon, are left to lurk in obscurity. In Graeco-Roman Egypt this dark background has been illumined and faint outlines made clearer by the papyri.

Another science which has profited largely is that of law. In dealing with papyri there are three legal systems to be reckoned with, the native Egyptian and the imported Greek and Roman; for though the Greek element predominates, the other two are often in evidence. With regard to Roman law in particular, a supply of concrete cases has proved an instructive supplement to the literary authorities. Upon certain subjects, notably marriage, the registra-

tion and sale of real property, and mortgage, there is quite an accumulation of learned comment. For a general study of the juristic side of the papyri, in the absence of any work in English, reference may be made to the *Grundzüge* of L. Mitteis.

The linguistic contribution of these spontaneous products of ordinary life is also of importance. In those of the later period, especially in the letters, frequent deviations will be noticed from classical usage, and the reader who is familiar with the Greek of the New Testament can hardly fail to be struck by similarities of idiom. This resemblance is natural: the writers of the New Testament and the papyri alike employed the vernacular of the day. But recognition of this simple fact is comparatively recent. So-called Biblical Greek was but lately regarded as a peculiar speech largely influenced by Semitic modes of expression. Many of the words and phrases formerly explained as Hebraistic are, however, now seen to be no more than current vulgarisms. Scriptural interpretation may also be assisted in other ways. For instance in the papyri are found the actual legal conditions and formulae which coloured the ideas, and are often echoed in the language, of St. Paul. Abundant illustration of the value of such data to the student of the New Testament can be seen in, *e.g.*, the works of Professor Deissmann of Berlin, who has been the pioneer-in-chief in this department, or in Moulton-Milligan's *Vocabulary of the Greek Testament.*

1969. Some principal editions of non-literary papyri are given here:

B. P. Grenfell and A. S. Hunt, and others, *The Oxyrhynchus Papyri*, 24 vols., 1896– ; *The Tebtunis Papyri*, 3 vols.,

1907, 1933 and 1938; F. G. Kenyon and H. I. Bell, *Greek Papyri in the British Museum*, 5 vols., 1893– ; J. P. Mahaffy and J. G. Smyly, *The Flinders Petrie Papyri*, 3 vols., 1893–1905; U. Wilcken, F. Zucker, W. Schubart and others, *Aegyptische Urkunden aus den Museen zu Berlin*, 11 vols., 1893–1968, *Griechische Urkunden*; P. Jouguet and others, *Papyrus grecs de Lille*, 2 vols., 1907– ; G. Vitelli and others, *Papiri greci e latini della Società Italiana*, 14 vols., 1912– ; C. C. Edgar, *Catalogue des antiquités égyptiennes du Musée du Caire, Zenon Papyri*, 5 vols., 1925–1940; J. Maspero, *Catalogue*, etc., . . ., *Papyrus grecs d'époque byzantine*, 3 vols., 1911–1916 (cp. *Traité d'études byz.*, II, *Les Papyrus*, A. Bataille, 1955); H. A. Sanders and others, *University of Michigan Papyri*, 14 vols.; F. Preisigke, F. Bilabel, and E. Kiessling, *Sammelbuch griechischer Urkunden aus Aegypten*, 5 vols., 1915– ; U. Wilcken, *Urkunden der Ptolemäerzeit*, 2 vols., 1927, 1957. Some series are still in progress. Other publications are cited in the list of sources on pp. xix-xx. New publications are noted in *Archiv für Papyrusforschung*; *Aegyptus*; *Chronique d'Égypte*; *Études de Papyrologie*; *Journal of Juristic Papyrology*; *L'Année Philologique* (J. Marouzeau). Note also F. Preisigke and others, *Wörterbuch der griechischen Papyrusurkunden . . . aus Aegypten* (1925); *Namenbuch* (1922); *Berichtigungsliste* (1922–). U. Wilcken and L. Mitteis, *Grundzüge und Chrestomathie der Papyruskunde*, 1912 (a masterly survey); W. Schubart, *Einführung in die Papyruskunde*, 1918; M. David and B. A. van Groningen, *Papyrological Primer*, 1946. Finally, M. Rostovtseff, *A Large Estate in Egypt*, 1922; Claire Préaulx, *Les Grecs en Égypte d'après les Archives de Zénon*, 1947; and *Économie royale des Lagides*, 1939; J. C. Winter, *Life and Letters in the Papyri*, 1933; A Bouché-Leclercq, *Histoire des Lagides*, 4 vols., 1903–1907; E. Bevan, *A History of Egypt under the Ptolemaic Dynasty*, 1927; J. C. Milne, *A History of Egypt under Roman Rule*, 1924; A. G. Johnson, *Roman Egypt*, 1936; H. I. Bell, *Egypt from Alexander the Great to the Arab Conquest*, 1948.

EXPLANATORY NOTES

EGYPTIAN DATES

THE Egyptian civil year consisted originally of twelve 30-day months and five intercalary days. It was therefore about a quarter of a day shorter than the natural year. Thus at the beginning of the Ptolemaic period Thoth 1 fell on November 13 (Julian calendar) and at the beginning of the Roman period had moved back to August 30. But in the reign of Augustus the calendar was stabilized by the addition of a sixth intercalary day in every fourth year, so that thereafter the Egyptian months corresponded permanently with the Roman months as tabulated below.

The Macedonian months, by which many papyri are dated, were originally lunar. In the earlier Ptolemaic period their relation to the Egyptian months is, except at certain intervals, somewhat obscure, but they seem to have gradually lost their lunar character, and before the end of the second century B.C. they were finally assimilated to the Egyptian months in the order shown.

Thoth 1	= Dius 1	= August 29 (or after a leap-year 30).
Phaophi 1	= Apellaeus 1	= September 28 (29).
Hathur 1	= Audnaeus 1	= October 28 (29).
Choiak 1	= Peritius 1	= November 27 (28).
Tubi 1	= Dystrus 1	= December 27 (28).
Mecheir 1	= Xandicus 1	= January 26 (27).

Phamenoth 1	= Artemisius 1	= February 25
Pharmouthi 1	= Daesius 1	= March 26
Pachon 1	= Panemus 1	= April 26.
Pauni 1	= Loius 1	= May 26.
Epeiph 1	= Gorpiaeus 1	= June 25
Mesore 1	= Hyperberetaeus 1	= July 25.
Intercalary 1	= Intercalary 1	= August 24.

In the Imperial age various months received honorific titles, more or less ephemeral, such as Germaniceus, Domitianus. Where such names occur in the following texts their Egyptian equivalents are noted.

According to the Egyptian method of dating, the first year of a reign was the period, however short, between the accession and the following 1st of Thoth. In the fourth and third centuries B.C. the Greeks in Egypt used different starting-points in reckoning the years of the king, but after a time they adopted the Egyptian system together with the Egyptian calendar. The same system continued to be used under the Roman emperors. In the later papyri the Roman practice of dating by consulships (see No. 9) becomes increasingly common; sometimes too an era is employed (see No. 21); and very often we find a reference to the indiction, which was a period of one year in a 15-year cycle originally introduced for fiscal purposes.

Egyptian Money

In the earlier Ptolemaic papyri the unit by which sums of money are generally reckoned is the silver drachma (= 6 obols). But in the second and first centuries B.C. it became more common to reckon by

copper drachmae. It is supposed that when the copper standard was introduced one drachma of silver was worth 60 of copper, but the ratio soon rose, and in the texts reprinted here it may be assumed to be about 1:500. A tetradrachm = 4 drachmae, a mina = 100 drachmae, and a talent = 6000 drachmae.

In Roman times the silver drachma (= 7 obols) was the ordinary unit of reckoning, one Alexandrian tetradrachm being normally equal to a denarius. The purchasing power of this drachma was much less than that of the Ptolemaic and gradually diminished down to the time of Diocletian. Though called silver, the coinage was actually of very base alloy.

In the Byzantine texts the only stable unit is the gold solidus. The inferior currency had depreciated to such an extent that by the middle of the fourth century a solidus was worth about 2000 myriads of denarii, and by the end of the sixth about 7000 myriads. The purchasing power of a solidus was, at a rough estimate, about twenty times that of a Ptolemaic silver drachma.

Method of Publication and List of Abbreviations

The texts are printed in running form, though for convenience of reference the lines of the scribe are numbered according to the numbering of the *editio princeps*. Accents, punctuation, and marks of diaeresis are added in conformity with modern usage. Interpolations and corrections are incorporated in the text and not specially marked or recorded. Faults of orthography and grammar, if likely to

cause any difficulty, are corrected in the critical apparatus. Approved restorations and emended readings, most of which have been published or republished in Preisigke's *Berichtigungslisten*, are adopted without remark. Iota adscript has been printed where so written, otherwise iota subscript is employed. Square brackets [ ] indicate a lacuna, round brackets ( ) the resolution of a symbol or abbreviation, angular brackets ⟨ ⟩ a mistaken omission in the original, braces { } a superfluous letter or letters, double square brackets ⟦ ⟧ a deletion. Dots placed within brackets represent approximately the number of letters lost or deleted; dots outside brackets indicate mutilated or otherwise illegible letters. It has not been thought necessary, for the purpose of this edition, to follow the usual practice of placing dots under such letters as are doubtful; but questionable readings, if of any importance, are duly noted.

In the Greek text (2nd hand), (3rd hand), etc., indicate that the following words were not written by the same hand as the preceding part of the document. The numbers in the critical notes refer to the lines of the text, and *l.* stands for *lege*. To prevent a possible misunderstanding it may be well to emphasize the fact that the translation gives the sense of the Greek as corrected in the critical apparatus. For instance, when a scribe, as often happens, misspells ἡμᾶς as ὑμᾶς, we reproduce his spelling in the text, correct it in the notes, and translate in accordance with the correction.

Abbreviations used in this volume for series, as far as they were published by 1931, and for other publications (cp. also vol. ii, pp. xxxv-xxxvii):

EXPLANATORY NOTES

B.G.U. = *Ägyptische Urkunden aus den Museen zu Berlin: Griechische Urkunden.*

B.S.A.A. = *Bulletin de la Société archéologique d'Alexandrie.*

Class. Phil. = *Classical Philology.*

J.E.A. = *Journal of Egyptian Archaeology.*

P. Amh. = *The Amherst Papyri*, vols. i.-ii., by B. P. Grenfell and A. S. Hunt.

P. Bour. = *Les Papyrus Bouriant*, by Paul Collart.

P. Cairo Masp. = *Catalogue des antiquités égyptiennes du Musée du Caire : Papyrus grecs d'époque byzantine*, vols. i.-iii., by J. Maspero.

P. Cairo Zen. = *Catalogue des antiquités égyptiennes du Musée du Caire : Zenon Papyri*, vols. i.-iv., by C. C. Edgar.

P. Columbia = *Memoirs of the American Academy in Rome*, vol. vi. : " A Lease from the Estate of Apollonius," by W. L. Westermann.

P. Cornell = *Greek Papyri in the Library of Cornell University*, by W. L. Westermann and C. J. Kraemer, Jr.

P. Eleph. = *Elephantine-Papyri* (*B.G.U.*, Sonderheft), by O. Rubensohn.

P. Fay. = *Fayûm Towns and their Papyri*, by B. P. Grenfell, A. S. Hunt, and D. G. Hogarth.

P. Flor. = *Papiri Fiorentini*, vols. i. and iii. by G. Vitelli, vol. ii. by D. Comparetti.

P. Giess. = *Griechische Papyri zu Giessen*, vol. i., by E. Kornemann, O. Eger, and P. M. Meyer.

P. Giess. bibl. = *Mittheilungen aus der Papyrussammlung der Giessener Universität*, iii., by H. Büttner.

P. Grenf. = *Greek Papyri*, series i. and ii., by B. P. Grenfell and A. S. Hunt.

P. Hamb. = *Griechische Papyrusurkunden der Hamburger Bibliothek*, vol. i., by P. M. Meyer.

P. Hib. = *The Hibeh Papyri*, part i., by B. P. Grenfell and A. S. Hunt.

P. Lond. = *Greek Papyri in the British Museum*, vols. i.-v., by Sir F. G. Kenyon and H. I. Bell.

P. Oslo = *Papyri Osloenses*, by S. Eitrem and L. Amundsen.

P. Oxy. = *The Oxyrhynchus Papyri*, vols. i.-xvii., by B. P. Grenfell and A. S. Hunt.

P. Par. = *Les Papyrus grecs du Musée du Louvre*, published in *Notices et Extraits*, t. xviii. 2, by W. Brunet de Presle and E. Egger.

P. Petr. = *The Flinders Petrie Papyri*, parts i.-iii., by J. P. Mahaffy and J. G. Smyly.

P. Ryl. = *Catalogue of the Greek Papyri in the Rylands Library*, vol. i. by A. S. Hunt, and vol. ii. by J. de M. Johnson, V. Martin, and A. S. Hunt.

P.S.I. = *Papiri della Società Italiana*, vols. i.-ix., by G. Vitelli and others.

P. Tebt. = *The Tebtunis Papyri*, parts i. and ii., by B. P. Grenfell, A. S. Hunt, J. G. Smyly, and E. J. Goodspeed.

Rev. Ég. = *Revue égyptologique*.

Stud. Pal. = *Studien zur Paläographie und Papyruskunde*, by C. Wessely and others.

U.P.Z. = *Urkunden der Ptolemäerzeit (ältere Funde)*, vol. i., by U. Wilcken.

M.Chrest. = L. Mitteis, *Chrestomathie*.

W. Chrest. = U. Wilcken, *Chrestomathie*.

SELECT PAPYRI

I. AGREEMENTS

1. MARRIAGE CONTRACT

P. Eleph. 1, ll. 1-18. 311 B.C.

[1]Ἀλεξάνδρου τοῦ Ἀλεξάνδρου βασιλεύοντος ἔτει ἑβδόμωι, Πτολεμαίου σατραπεύοντος ἔτει τεσαρε-[2]σκαιδεκάτωι, μηνὸς Δίου. συγγραφὴ συνοικισίας Ἡρακλείδου καὶ Δημητρίας. λαμβάνει Ἡρακλείδης [3]Δημητρίαν Κώιαν γυναῖκα γνησίαν παρὰ τοῦ πατρὸς Λεπτίνου Κώιου καὶ τῆς μητρὸς Φιλωτίδος ἐλεύθερος [4]ἐλευθέραν προσφερομένην εἱματισμὸν καὶ κόσμον (δραχμῶν) (χιλίων), παρεχέτω δὲ Ἡρακλείδης Δημητρίαι [5]ὅσα προσήκει γυναικὶ ἐλευθέραι πάντα, εἶναι δὲ ἡμᾶς κατὰ ταὐτὸ ὅπου ἂν δοκῆι ἄριστον εἶναι βουλευομένοις κοινῆι [6]βουλῆι Λεπτίνηι καὶ Ἡρακλείδηι. εἰὰν δέ τι κακοτεχνοῦσα ἁλίσκηται ἐπὶ αἰσχύνηι τοῦ ἀνδρὸς Ἡρακλείδου Δημητρία, [7]στερέσθω ὧμ προσηνέγκατο πάντων, ἐπιδειξάτω δὲ Ἡρακλείδης ὅ τι ἂν ἐγκαλῆι Δημητρίαι ἐναντίον ἀνδρῶν τριῶν, [8]οὓς ἂν δοκιμάζωσιν ἀμφότεροι. μὴ ἐξέστω δὲ Ἡρακλείδηι γυναῖκα ἄλλην ἐπεισάγεσθαι ἐφ' ὕβρει Δημητρίας μηδὲ [9]τεκνοποιεῖσθαι ἐξ ἄλλης γυναικὸς μηδὲ κακοτεχνεῖν μηδὲν παρευρέσει μηδεμιᾶι Ἡρακλείδην εἰς Δημητρίαν· [10]εἰὰν δέ τι ποῶν τούτων

I. AGREEMENTS

1. MARRIAGE CONTRACT

311 B.C.

In the 7th year of the reign of Alexander son of Alexander, the 14th year of the satrapship of Ptolemy,[a] in the month Dius. Marriage contract of Heraclides and Demetria. Heraclides takes as his lawful wife Demetria, Coan, both being freeborn, from her father Leptines, Coan, and her mother Philotis, bringing clothing and ornaments to the value of 1000 drachmae, and Heraclides shall supply to Demetria all that is proper for a freeborn wife, and we shall live together wherever it seems best to Leptines and Heraclides consulting in common. If Demetria is discovered doing any evil to the shame of her husband Heraclides, she shall be deprived of all that she brought, but Heraclides shall prove whatever he alleges against Demetria before three men whom they both accept. It shall not be lawful for Heraclides to bring home another wife in insult of Demetria nor to have children by another woman nor to do any evil against Demetria on any pretext. If Heraclides is discovered doing any of these things

[a] Ptolemy Soter, who, though practically an independent sovereign, retained the title of satrap till 305 B.C.

ἁλίσκηται Ἡρακλείδης καὶ ἐπιδείξηι Δημητρία ἐναντίον ἀνδρῶν τριῶν, οὓς ἂν δοκιμάζωσιν [11]ἀμφότεροι, ἀποδότω Ἡρακλείδης Δημητρίαι τὴμ φερνὴν ἣν προσηνέγκατο (δραχμὰς) (χιλίας) καὶ προσαποτεισάτω ἀργυρί-[12]ου Ἀλεξανδρείου (δραχμὰς) (χιλίας). ἡ δὲ πρᾶξις ἔστω καθάπερ ἐγ δίκης κατὰ νόμον τέλος ἐχούσης Δημητρίαι καὶ τοῖς μετὰ [13]Δημητρίας πράσσουσιν ἔκ τε αὐτοῦ Ἡρακλείδου καὶ τῶν Ἡρακλείδου πάντων καὶ ἐγγαίων καὶ ναυτικῶν. ἡ δὲ συγγραφὴ [14]ἥδε κυρία ἔστω πάντηι πάντως ὡς ἐκεῖ τοῦ συναλλάγματος γεγενημένου, ὅπου ἂν ἐπεγφέρηι Ἡρακλείδης κατὰ [15]Δημητρίας ἢ Δημητρία τε καὶ τοὶ μετὰ Δημητρίας πράσσοντες ἐπεγφέρωσιν κατὰ Ἡρακλείδου. κύριοι δὲ ἔστωσαν Ἡρακλεί-[16]δης καὶ Δημητρία καὶ τὰς συγγραφὰς αὐτοὶ τὰς αὑτῶν φυλάσσοντες καὶ ἐπεγφέροντες κατ' ἀλλήλων. μάρτυρες [17]Κλέων Γελῶιος, Ἀντικράτης Τημνίτης, Λύσις Τημνίτης, Διονύσιος Τημνίτης, Ἀριστόμαχος Κυρηναῖος, Ἀριστόδικος [18]Κῶιος.

[a] Coins struck in Egypt with the head of Alexander on the obverse.

2. MARRIAGE CONTRACT

P. Tebt. 104. 92 B.C.

[1](Ἔτους) κβ Μεχ(εὶρ) ια. ὁμο(λογεῖ) Φιλίσκο(ς) Ἀπολλω(νίου) Πέρσης τῆ[ς ἐπιγο(νῆς)] Ἀπολλωνίαι τ(ῆι) καὶ Κελλαύθε<ι> [2]Ἡρα(κλείδου) Περσ(ίνηι) μετὰ κυ(ρίου) τοῦ [ἀδελφοῦ] α[ὐτ(ῆς) Ἀ]πολ[λωνί]ου ἔχειν παρ' α(ὐτῆς) εἰς χα(λκοῦ) νομ(ίσματος) λό(γον) (τάλαντα) β καὶ (δραχμὰς)

and Demetria proves it before three men whom they both accept, Heraclides shall give back to Demetria the dowry of 1000 drachmae which she brought and shall moreover forfeit 1000 drachmae of the silver coinage of Alexander.[a] Demetria and those aiding Demetria to exact payment shall have the right of execution, as if derived from a legally decided action, upon the person of Heraclides and upon all the property of Heraclides both on land and on water. This contract shall be valid in every respect, wherever Heraclides may produce it against Demetria, or Demetria and those aiding Demetria to exact payment may produce it against Heraclides, as if the agreement had been made in that place. Heraclides and Demetria shall have the right to keep the contracts severally in their own custody[b] and to produce them against each other. Witnesses: Cleon, Gelan; Anticrates, Temnian; Lysis, Temnian; Dionysius, Temnian; Aristomachus, Cyrenaean; Aristodicus, Coan.

[b] The contract was usually deposited with one of the witnesses, called the συγγραφοφύλαξ; but in the present case a valid copy was kept by each of the principals.

2. MARRIAGE CONTRACT

92 B.C.

(Summary) Year 22, Mecheir 11. Philiscus son of Apollonius, Persian of the Epigone,[a] acknowledges to Apollonia also called Kellauthis, daughter of Heraclides, Persian, having with her as guardian her brother Apollonius, that he has received from her in copper money 2 talents 4000 drachmae, the

[a] See note *b* on p. 7.

'Δ [3]τὴν διωμο(λογημένην) αὐτῶι φερνὴ(ν) [ὑπ]ὲρ [αὐ]τῆ[ς] 'Απ[ο]λλω(νίας), ἐὰν ε[. . .] τὴν φερνὴ(ν) . ανεκικ( ) [4]οτολ( ).

[συ(γγραφοφύλαξ)] Διονύ(σιος).

(2nd hand) [5]Βασιλεύοντος Πτολεμαίου τοῦ [καὶ 'Αλεξ]άν[δρου θεοῦ Φι]λομήτορος ἔτους δευτέρου [6]καὶ εἰκοστοῦ, ἐφ' [ἱε]ρ[έως 'Αλεξάνδρου κα]ὶ τῶ[ν] ἄλλ[ω]ν τῶν [γρ]αφομένων ἐν [7]'Αλεξανδρείαι, μηνὸς Ξανδικ[ο]ῦ ἑνδεκάτηι Μ[εχεὶ]ρ ἑνδεκάτηι, [8]ἐν Κερκεοσίρει τῆς Πολέμωνος μερίδος τοῦ 'Αρ[σινοΐ]του νομοῦ. ὁμολογεῖ [9]Φιλίσκος 'Απολλωνίο[υ] Π[έρσ]ης τῆς ἐπιγονῆς 'Απολλωνίαι τῆι [10]καὶ Κελλαύθει 'Ηρακλε[ίδου] Περσίνηι μετὰ κ[υρί]ου τοῦ ἑαυτῆς [11]<ἀ>δαλφοῦ 'Απολλωνίου ἔ[χει]ν παρ' [α]ὐτῆς εἰς χαλκοῦ νομίσ-[12]ματος λόγον τάλαντα δύο καὶ δραχμὰς τετρακισχιλία[ς] τὴν διω-[13]μολογημένην αὐτῶι φερνὴν ὑπὲρ αὐτῆς 'Απολλωνίας. [ἔ]στω δὲ [14]'Απολλωνίαι π[α]ρὰ Φιλίσκωι πειθαρχοῦσα α[ὐ]τοῦ ὡς προσῆ[κό]ν ἐστιν [15]γυναῖκα ἀνδρός, κυρ<ι>εύουσαν μετ' αὐτοῦ κοινῇ τῶν ὑπαρχόντων αὐτοῖς. [16]τὰ δὲ [δ]έοντα π[ά]ντα καὶ τὸν [ἱμ]ατισμὸν καὶ τἆλλα ὅσα προσήκει γυναικὶ [17]γαμετῆι παρεχέσθω Φιλίσκος 'Απολλωνίαν ἐνδημῶν καὶ ἀποδημῶν [18]κατὰ δύναμιν τῶν ὑπαρχόντων αὐτοῖς, καὶ μὴ ἐξέστω Φιλίσκωι [19]γυναῖκα ἄλλην ἐπ[α]γ[α]γέσθαι ἀλλὰ 'Απολλωνίαν μηδὲ παλλακὴν μηδὲ [20]π[αιδ]ικὸν ἔχειν μηδ[ὲ τεκνο]ποιεῖσθαι ἐξ ἄλλης γυναικὸς ζώσ[η]ς [21]'Απ[ο]λλωνίας μηδ' ἄλλην [οἰκία]ν οἰκεῖν ἧς οὐ κυριεύσει 'Απολλωνίαι [22]μηδ' ἐγβάλλειν μηδὲ ὑβ[ρίζ]ε[ι]ν μηδὲ κακουχεῖν αὐτὴν μηδὲ τῶν ὑπαρ-[23]χόντων μηθὲν ἐξαλλοτ[ρ]ιοῦν ἐπ' ἀδικίαι τῆι

dowry for herself, Apollonia, agreed upon with him . . . Keeper of the contract: Dionysius.

(Text of contract) In the 22nd year of the reign of Ptolemy also called Alexander, the god Philometor, the priest of Alexander and the other priests being as written in Alexandria,[a] the 11th of the month Xandicus, which is the 11th of Mecheir, at Kerkeosiris in the division of Polemon of the Arsinoite nome. Philiscus son of Apollonius, Persian of the Epigone,[b] acknowledges to Apollonia, also called Kellauthis, daughter of Heraclides, Persian, having with her as guardian her brother Apollonius, that he has received from her in copper money 2 talents 4000 drachmae,[c] the dowry for herself, Apollonia, agreed upon with him. Apollonia shall live with Philiscus, obeying him as a wife should her husband, owning their property in common with him. All necessaries and clothing and whatever else is proper for a wedded wife Philiscus shall supply to Apollonia, whether he is at home or abroad, in proportion to their means. It shall not be lawful for Philiscus to bring in another wife besides Apollonia, nor to keep a concubine or boy, nor to have children by another woman while Apollonia lives, nor to inhabit another house over which Apollonia is not mistress, nor to eject or insult or ill-treat her, nor to alienate any of their property to the detriment

[a] The scribes often used such formulae to avoid the labour of writing out the list of eponymous priests.

[b] Literally "Persian of the next generation," denoting a certain civil status; but it is hard to say what the term originally meant and what it eventually came to imply.

[c] Equivalent to about 35 drachmae of silver.

---

11. *l.* <ἀ>δελφοῦ. 17. *l.* Ἀπολλωνίαι.

Ἀπολλωνίαι. ἐὰν δέ τι 24τούτων ἐπιδειχθῆι ποιῶν ἢ τὰ δέοντα ἢ τὸν ἱματισμὸν ἢ τἆλλα 25μὴ παρέχῃ αὐτῆι καθὰ γέγραπται, ἀποτεισάτωι Φιλίσκος Ἀπολλωνίαι 26παραχρῆμα τὴν φερνὴν τὰ δύο τάλαντα καὶ τὰ[ς] τετρακισχιλίας δραχμὰς 27τοῦ χαλκοῦ. κατὰ τὰ αὐτὰ δὲ μηδὲ Ἀπολλωνίαι ἐξέστω ἀπόκοιτον μη[δὲ] 28ἀφήμερον γίνεσθαι ἀπὸ τῆς Φιλίσκου οἰκίας ἄνευ τῆς Φιλίσκου γνώ[μ]ης μηδ' ἄλλω[ι] 29ἀνδρ[ὶ] συνεῖναι μηδὲ φθε[ί]ρειν τὸν κοινὸν οἶκον μηδὲ αἰσχύνεσθ[αι] 30Φιλίσκον ὅσα φέρει ἀνδρὶ αἰσχύνειν. ἐὰν δὲ Ἀπολλωνία ἑκοῦσα βούλη[ται] 31ἀπαλλάσσεσθαι ἀπὸ Φιλίσκου, ἀποδότω αὐτῆι Φιλίσκος τὴν φερνὴν ἁπ[λῆν] 32ἐ[ν] ἡμέραις δέκα ἀφ' ἧς ἐὰ[ν ἀπ]αιτηθῆι. ἐὰν δὲ μὴ ἀπ[ο]δῷ καθὰ γέγραπ[ται, 33ἀπ]ο[τ]εισάτω αὐτῆι παραχρῆμα ἣν εἴληφεν ἡμι[όλ]ιον τὴ[ν] φερνήν. 34μάρτυρες Διονύσιος Πάτρωνος, Διονύσιος Ἑρμαΐσκου, Θέων Πτολεμαίου, 35Δίδυμος Πτολεμαίου, Διονύσιος Διονυσίου, Ἡράκλειος Διοκλ[έους,] οἱ ἓξ Μακεδόνες 36τῆς ἐπιγονῆς. συγγραφοφύλαξ Διονύσιος. (3rd hand) 37Φιλίσκ[ος] Ἀπολλωνίου Πέρσης τῆς ἐπιγονῆς ὁμολογῶ ἔχειν τὴν φερνὴν τὰ δύο τάλαντ[α] 38κ[αὶ τὰς τε]τρακισχιλίας δραχμὰς τοῦ χαλκοῦ καθότι προγέγραπται καὶ τέθιμαι 39[τὴν συγγρα]φὴν κυ[ρία]ν παρὰ Διο[νυ]σίωι. ἔγραψεν ὑπὲρ αὐτοῦ Διονύσιος Ἑρμαΐσκ[ου 40ὁ προγεγραμμένος διὰ τ]ὸ αὐτὸν μὴ ἐπίστασθ[αι γρά]μματα. (4th hand) 41Διονύσιος ἔχω κυρίαν. (1st hand) 42ἔτους κβ Μεχεὶρ ια. πέπ(τωκεν) εἰς ἀναγρ(αφήν).

Verso: 43Ἀπ[ολ]λωνίας [πρὸ]ς Φι[λ]ίσκον 44ὁμο(λογία) γάμου κεχ . [. . . . . .] . . κοιν . Below, names of the principals and of the witnesses.

of Apollonia. If he is proved to be doing any of these things or fails to supply her with necessaries or clothing or other things as stated, Philiscus shall forthwith forfeit to Apollonia the dowry of 2 talents 4000 drachmae of copper. In like manner it shall not be lawful for Apollonia to spend the night or day away from the house of Philiscus without Philiscus's consent or to consort with another man or to dishonour the common home or to cause Philiscus to be shamed by any act that brings shame upon a husband. If Apollonia chooses of her own will to separate from Philiscus, Philiscus shall repay her the bare dowry within ten days from the date of the demand. If he does not repay as stated, he shall forthwith forfeit to her one and a half times the amount of the dowry which he has received. Witnesses: Dionysius son of Patron, Dionysius son of Hermaiscus, Theon son of Ptolemaeus, Didymus son of Ptolemaeus, Dionysius son of Dionysius, Heraclius son of Diocles, all six Macedonians of the Epigone. Keeper of the contract: Dionysius. (Acknowledgement) I, Philiscus son of Apollonius, Persian of the Epigone, acknowledge that I have received the dowry of 2 talents 4000 drachmae of copper as is stated above, and I have deposited the contract, being valid, with Dionysius. Dionysius son of Hermaiscus, the aforesaid, wrote for him, as he is illiterate. (Receipt) I, Dionysius, have received the contract, being valid. (Docketed) Deposited for registration on Mecheir 11 of year 22. (Endorsed) Marriage compact of Apollonia with Philiscus. . . .

30. *l.* αἰσχύνην.

3. MARRIAGE CONTRACT

B.G.U. 1052. **13 B.C.**

[2]Πρωτάρχωι [3]παρὰ Θερμίου τῆς Ἀπίωνος μετὰ κυρίου [4]τοῦ < > Ἀπολλωνίου τοῦ Χαιρέου καὶ παρὰ Ἀπολ-[5]λωνίου τοῦ Πτολεμαίου. συνχωροῦσιν Θέρμιον [6]καὶ Ἀπολλώνιος Πτολεμαίου συνεληλυ-[7]θέναι ἀλλήλοις πρὸς βίου κοινωνίαν, ὁ δὲ αὐ-[8]τὸς Ἀπολλώνιος Πτολεμαίου εἰληφέ-[9]ναι παρὰ τῆς Θερμίου διὰ χιρὸς ἐξ οἴ-[10]κου φερνάριον ἐνωτίων χρυσῶν ζεῦ-[11]γος τεταρτῶν τριῶν καὶ ἀργ(υρίου) (δραχμὰς) . . . [12]ἀπὸ τοῦ νῦν τὸν Ἀπολλώνιον Πτολεμαίου [13]χο[ρηγ]ε[ῖ]ν τῇ Θερμίῳ τὰ δέοντα πάντα [14]καὶ τὸν ἱματισμὸν ὡς γυναικὶ γαμετῇ [15]κατὰ [δ]ύναμιν τῶν ὑπαρχόντων καὶ μὴ [16]κακ[ουχ]ῖν αὐτὴν μηδὲ ἐγβάλλειν μηδὲ [17]ὑβ[ρί]ζιν μηδ' ἄλλην γυναῖκαν ἐπισάγειν [18]ἢ ἐκτίν[ειν] παραχρῆμα τὸ φερνάριον [19]σὺν ἡμ[ιολίᾳ], τῆς πράξεως γινομένης [20]ἔκ τε [αὐτο]ῦ Ἀπολλωνίου τοῦ Πτολεμαίου [21][καὶ] ἐκ τῶν ὑπαρχόντων αὐτῷ πάν-[22][των κα]θάπερ ἐγ δίκης, καὶ τὴν δὲ Θέρ-[23][μιον . . .]τιλιν τὰ πρὸς τὸν ἄνδρα καὶ [24][τὸν κοι]νὸν βίον δίκαια καὶ μήτε ἀ-[25][πόκοι]τον μήτε ἀφήμερον γίνεσθαι [26][ἀπὸ τῆ]ς οἰκίας ἄνευ τῆς Ἀπολλωνί-[27][ου] το[ῦ Π]τολεμαίου γνώμης μηδὲ φθίρε<ι>ν [28][μηδὲ] καταβλάπτειν τὸν κοινὸν οἶκον [29][μηδ' ἄλ]λῳ ἀνδρὶ συνεῖναι ἢ καὶ αὐτὴν [30]τούτ[ω]ν τι διαπραξαμένην κριθῖσαν [31]στέρεσθαι τοῦ φερναρίου χωρὶς τοῦ [32]τὸν παραβαίνοντα ἐνέχεσθαι καὶ τῷ [33]ὡρισμένῳ προστίμῳ. [34](ἔτους) ιζ Καίσαρος Φαρμοῦθι κ̄.

4. *e.g.* ⟨συγγενοῦς⟩, **or cancel the first** τοῦ.

3. MARRIAGE CONTRACT

13 B.C.

To Protarchus [a] from Thermion daughter of Apion, with her guardian Apollonius son of Chaereas, and from Apollonius son of Ptolemaeus. Thermion and Apollonius son of Ptolemaeus agree that they have come together to share a common life, and the said Apollonius son of Ptolemaeus acknowledges that he has received from Thermion by hand from the house a dowry of a pair of gold earrings weighing 3 quarters and . . . silver drachmae ; and from now Apollonius son of Ptolemaeus shall furnish to Thermion as his wedded wife all necessaries and clothing in proportion to his means and shall not ill-treat her nor cast her out nor insult her nor bring in another wife, or he shall straightway forfeit the dowry increased by half, with right of execution upon both the person of Apollonius son of Ptolemaeus and all his property as if by legal decision, and Thermion shall fulfil her duties towards her husband and their common life and shall not absent herself from the house for a night or a day without the consent of Apollonius son of Ptolemaeus nor dishonour nor injure their common home nor consort with another man, or she again if guilty of any of these actions shall, after trial, be deprived of the dowry, and in addition the transgressing party shall be liable to the prescribed fine. The 17th year of Caesar,[b] Pharmouthi 20.

[a] The head of an Alexandrian tribunal to whom agreements were submitted in order to receive legal sanction.

[b] In dates and official documents the name Caesar, when standing alone, means the Emperor Augustus.

4. MARRIAGE CONTRACT

P. Ryl. 154. A.D. 66.

[1][’Αν]τίγραφον [συγγραφῆ]ς. (ἔτους) ιγ Νέρωνος Κλαυδίου Καίσαρος Σεβαστοῦ Γερμανικοῦ Αὐτοκράτορο(ς), [2][μη]νὸς ’Απελλα[ίου κβ Φαῶ]φι κβ, ἐν Βακχ[ι]άδι τῆ[ς ‘Ηρ]ακλείδου μερί[δο]ς τοῦ ’Αρσινοΐτου ν[ο]μοῦ. [ὁμ]ολογεῖ [3][Χαι]ρήμων ’Απολ[λωνίου Π]έρσης τῆς ἐπιγονῆ[ς] ὡς (ἐτῶν) λδ οὐλῆι ῥινὶ μ[έ]σηι Σισόιτι Πετεήσ[ι]ος [ὡς] (ἐτῶν) οα [4][οὐλ]ῆι ὀφρύι ἀριστε[ρᾶι ἔχειν] παρ’ αὐτοῦ ἐπὶ τῆ[ι αὐ]τοῦ θυγατρὶ προούση[ι] κ[αὶ] συνούσηι τοῦ Χα[ιρήμονος] γυναικὶ [5][Θαϊ]σαρίωι φερνῆς [ἀργυ]ρί[ο]υ ἐπισήμου δραχμὰς [ἑκατὸ]ν καὶ παραφέρνων ἐν[ωτ]ίων χρυσῶν ζε[ῦγος τετα]ρτῶν [6][τεσσ]άρων καὶ μη[νίσκο]ν [χρυ]σοῦν τεταρτῶν [τριῶ]ν καὶ δακτύλια χ[ρυσᾶ] δύο τεταρτῶν [δ]ύ[ο καὶ] ψελ[ί]ων [7][ἀργ]υρῶν ζεῦγος ὁ[λκῆς] ἀσήμου δραχμῶν τεσσ[αρ]άκοντα τεσσάρων καὶ κ[λ]άλ[ι]α δύο ὁλκῆς ἀσ[ή]μ[ου δρα]χμῶν [8][δε]καὲξ καὶ ἱμα[τίω]ν σ[τ]ολὰ[ς] δύο, λευκὴι μία [ναρ]κ[ι]σσίνη μία, καὶ πάλλ[ι]α πέντε καὶ χαλκώμ[ατ]α καὶ [9][ἐκ]λουτρίδιον, ἐ[πὶ τ]ὸ αὐτὸ μνῶν τεσσάρων, [κ]α[ὶ] ἄνευ σταθμοῦ εδρυσ . α[ι] χαλκαῖ δύο καὶ κασσι[τέρο]υ μναῖ [10][πέν]τε, καὶ ἄνευ δι[ατε]ιμήσ[ε]ως εἰς καρπίαν κ[α]ὶ ἐν πρ[οσφ]ορᾷ ἀπ[ὸ] τοῦ ἐνεστῶτος ιγ (ἔτους) [Ν]έρων[ος Κλ]α[υδίου [11]Καί]σαρος Σεβασ[το]ῦ Γερμανικοῦ Αὐτοκράτορος τὸν ὑπάρχοντα αὐτῶι Σισ[όι]τι περὶ Βακχιάδα κ[λῆρ]ον [12][κατ]οικικὸν ἀρο[υ]ρῶν δέκα ἡμίσους τετάρτου ἐν δυσὶ σφραγεῖσι, ἀφ’ ὧν ἐν τῶι λεγομέν[ωι] Σάδηι [κλ]ήρ[ο]υ [13][ἄρο]υραι ἑπτὰ ἥμισ[υ

4. AGREEMENTS

4. MARRIAGE CONTRACT

A.D. 66.

Copy of contract. The 13th year of Nero Claudius Caesar Augustus Germanicus Imperator, the 22nd of the month Apellaeus or 22nd of Phaophi, at Bacchias in the division of Heraclides in the Arsinoite nome. Chaeremon son of Apollonius, Persian of the Epigone, aged about 34 years, with a scar on the middle of the nose, acknowledges to Sisois son of Peteesis, aged about 71 years, with a scar on the left eyebrow, that he has received from him as a dowry on his daughter Thaisarion, who has previously been living with Chaeremon as his wife,[a] a hundred drachmae of coined silver and as *parapherna* a pair of gold earrings weighing four quarters, a gold crescent of three quarters, two gold rings of two quarters, a pair of silver armlets weighing 44 drachmae of uncoined metal, two bracelets weighing 16 drachmae of uncoined metal; clothing consisting of two robes, one white and one narcissus, and five mantles; copper vessels and a basin, weighing in all four minae, two copper . . . unweighed, and five minae of tin; and without valuation in usufruct and as a gift from the current 13th year of Nero Claudius Caesar Augustus Germanicus Imperator the catoecic holding of 10¾ arurae owned by Sisois in the area of Bacchias in two plots, one of them consisting of 7¾ arurae of a holding in the place called Sade, the boundaries of which are,

[a] Without a written contract, but in a recognized form of union.

8. *l.* λευκὴν μίαν κτλ.

τ]έτ[α]ρτον, ὧν γείτονες τούτ[ω]ν νότου πρότε[ρ]ον Ἡρα[κλεί]δου τοῦ Ζωί[λο]υ κλῆρ[ος, βορρᾶ [14]Ἀπολ]λωνίου τοῦ Στράτωνος κλῆρος, λιβὸς διῶρυξ λεγομένηι Ἀρχείου δι' οὗ ἀποχεῖ{ε}ται ὁ κλῆρ[ο]ς, ἀπ[η-[15]λιώ]του Πεθεῦτο[ς] τοῦ Πτόλλιδος κλῆρος, ἀνὰ μέσον ὄντος κοινοῦ ὑδραγώγου δι' οὗ ποτίζεται [ὁ] κλῆ[ρος, [16]τῆ]ς δὲ δευτέρας σφ[ρ]αγεῖδος τῶν λοιπῶν ἀρουρῶν τριῶν ἐν τῶι λεγομένωι Πιενηούιος, γε[ί]τονε[ς [17]δὲ καὶ τούτων νό[του] Βακχί[ο]νος τοῦ Ἀμμω[νίου] κλῆρος, β[ορρ]ᾶ Πα[. . . .]εῦτος τ[οῦ . .] . ιν[. . . . . [18]κλ]ῆρος, λιβὸς διῶρυξ εἰς ὃν εἰσχεῖτα[ι] ὁ κλῆρ[ος], ἀπηλίωτος Π[ι]σιστρά[το]υ κλήρου. συμ[β]ιούτω[σαν ο]ὖν [19][ἑα]υτοῖς ἀλλήλο[ις ο]ἱ γ[α]μοῦντες ἥ τε Θαϊσάριον καὶ ὁ Χα[ι]ρήμων ἀμεμψιμοιρήτως καθότι π[ρότ]ερον [20][συ]νεβίουν, τοῦ Χ[αιρ]ήμονος ἄγοντος τὰ κατ' ἔ[το]ς γεωργικὰ ἔργα πάντα τῶν τῆς προσφορᾶς κλή[ρ]ου [21][ἀρο]υρῶν δέκα ἡμίσ[ο]υς τετάρτου καὶ κατασπείροντας καὶ ἀποφέροντας τὰ περιεσόμεν[α] ἐκ τ[ού-[22]τω]ν κατ' ἔτος γενήματα καὶ ἐπιγενήματα ἀπ[ὸ] τοῦ αὐτοῦ ἐνεστῶ[τος] ἔτους καὶ ε[ἰ]σφέρ[ον]τος [23][εἰς] τὸν κοινὸν τῆς [σ]υμβιώσεως οἶκον κα[ὶ τ]ελοῦντας τὰ ὑπὲρ τούτων κατ' ἔτ[ο]ς δημόσια [πά]ντα [24][σι]τικά τε καὶ ἀργυρι[κ]ὰ ἀπὸ τοῦ αὐτοῦ ἐνεστῶτος ἔτους. ἐὰν δὲ διαφορᾶς αὐτοῖς γεναμένης [25][χ]ωρίζονται ἀπ' ἀλλήλων, ἤτοι τοῦ Χαιρήμονος ἀποπέμποντος τ[ὴ]ν Θαϊσάριον ἢ καὶ αὐτῆς ἑκουσίω[ς [26]ἀ]παλλασσομέν[η]ς [ἀ]π' αὐτοῦ, ἔστωι τοῦ τῆ[ς] Θα[ϊ]σαρ[ί]ου πατρὸς Σισόιτος, ἐὰ[ν] δὲ [ο]ὗτος μὴ περιῆι, αὐ[τῆς] Θ[α]ϊσαρί[ου [27]ὁ] σημαινόμενο[ς κλῆρ]ος τῶν ἀρουρῶν δ[έκα] ἡμίσους τετάρτου καθὼ[ς] πρόκειται· ἔτι δὲ καὶ προ[σα]πο-

on the south the holding formerly belonging to Heraclides son of Zoilus, on the north the holding of Apollonius son of Straton, on the west the canal called that of Archias by which the holding is drained, on the east the holding of Petheus son of Ptollis, separated by a common water-channel by which the holding is irrigated, and the second plot comprising the remaining three arurae in the place called after Pieneouis, the boundaries of which are, on the south the holding of Bacchion son of Ammonius, on the north the holding of . . . son of . . ., on the west the canal into which the holding drains, on the east the holding of Pisistratus. Wherefore let the parties to the marriage, Thaisarion and Chaeremon, live together blamelessly as they have previously been doing, Chaeremon conducting all the agricultural work of each year on the 10¾ arurae of the holding which forms the gift, sowing and harvesting the yearly crops and after-crops grown thereon from the said current year and carrying them to the common home of their wedded life, and paying thereon all the yearly public dues both in corn and in money from the said current year. If on a difference arising between them they separate from each other, whether Chaeremon sends Thaisarion away or she voluntarily leaves him, the above-mentioned holding of 10¾ arurae shall belong to Thaisarion's father Sisois or, if he be no longer alive, to Thaisarion herself; and

14. *l.* δι' ἧς. 18. *l.* εἰς ἣν, ἀπηλιώτου, κλῆρος. 21. *l.* καταστείροντος καὶ ἀποφέροντες. 23. *l.* τ]ελοῦντος. 25. *l.* [χ]ωρίζωνται.

[28]δώσιν αὐτῆι ὁ Χ[αιρ]ήμων καὶ τὴν προγ[εγρα]μμένην φερνὴν καὶ τὰ παράφερνα οἷα ἐὰν ἐκ τῆς τρί-[29]ψεως ἐγβῆι, ἐπ[ὶ μὲν] τῆς ἀποπομπῆς πα[ραχρῆ]μα, ἐπὶ δὲ {του} τῆς ἑκουσ[ίο]υ ἀπαλλαγῆς ἐν ἡμέρα[ι]ς τριά-[30][κο]ντα ἀφ' ἧς ἐὰ[ν ἀπαι]τηθῆι. ἐν ὧι δ' [ἄ]ν ἔτι [τὰ κατὰ] τὸν ἀπ' ἀλλ[ή]λων τῶν [γα]μούντω[ν χ]ωρ[ι]σμὸ[ν] γέ[νη-[31]τ]αι, ἀπ[ο]μερισθ[ήσεται] τὰ ἐκφόρια τοῦ κλήρ[ο]υ [εἰς] τὴν δωδε[κά]μην[ο]ν τὴν τοῦ τῆς [ἀ]ποπλοκῆς ἔ[τους [32]κα]ὶ ἕξε[ι] ὁ μὲν Χα[ιρήμω]ν κατὰ τὸ ἀνὰ λόγον τ[ῶν μ]ηνῶν ὧν ἐὰν ἦι ἡ Θαϊσ[άριο]ν μεμενηκυῖα ἐν τῶ[ι κ]οινῶι [33][οἴκω]ι, ὁ δὲ Σισόις τὸ ἐπίλοιπον, πρ[ό]τερον ἀνταναιρεθ[έ]ντων τῶν τοῦ κλήρου δημοσίων καὶ σπερμά[τω]ν, γει-[34][νο]μένης τῆς πράξ[ε]ως τῶν κατὰ τὴν συνγραφὴν τῶι Σισόιτι ἤ, μὴ περιόν[το]ς, τῆι Θαϊσαρί[ωι] καὶ τοῖς [παρ' α]ὐτῆς [35][ἐκ] τοῦ Χαιρήμ[ονο]ς καὶ ἐκ τῶν ὑπαρχόντων αὐτοῖς πάντων καθάπερ ἐγ δίκης. ὑπογραφεὺς τοῦ Σ[ι]σόιτος [36][. . . .]ν Ἑρμᾶτος ὡς (ἐτῶν) μα οὐλ(ὴ) μετώπωι ἐγ δεξιῶν, τοῦ Χαιρήμονος εἰδότος γ[ρά]μματα.

28. *l.* δώσει. 30. *l.* ἔτει.

5. MARRIAGE CONTRACT

P. Oxy. 1273. A.D. 260.

[1]Ἀγαθῇ τύχῃ. ἐξέδετο Αὐρηλία Θαῆσις Εὐδαίμονος μητρὸς Ἡρα-[2]ΐδος ἀπ' Ὀξυρύγχων πόλεως μετὰ συνεστῶτος Αὐρηλίου Θέωνος [3]τοῦ καὶ Νεπωτιανοῦ καὶ ὡς χρημα(τίζει) τὴν ἑαυτῆς θυγα-

1. *l.* ἐξέδοτο.

Chaeremon shall moreover return to her the aforesaid dowry and the *parapherna* in whatever state they may eventually be through wear, in the case of dismissal immediately, and in the case of her voluntary departure within thirty days from the date of the demand. In whatever year the separation of the parties to the marriage takes place, the proceeds of the holding for the twelve months of the year of the divorce shall be divided, and Chaeremon shall receive a share proportionate to the number of months during which Thaisarion shall have remained in their common home and Sisois the remainder, the public dues on the holding and loans of seed having first been deducted. To enforce the terms of the contract Sisois or, if he is no longer alive, Thaisarion and her assigns shall have the right of execution upon Chaeremon and all his propety as if by legal decision. The signatory for Sisois is . . . son of Hermas, aged about 41 years, with a scar on the right side of the forehead, Chaeremon being literate.

5. MARRIAGE CONTRACT

A.D. 260.

For good fortune. Aurelia Thaesis daughter of Eudaemon and of Herais, of Oxyrhynchus, acting with Aurelius Theon also called Nepotianus and however he is styled,[a] has given her daughter

[a] A common formula, used either because the parentage and domicile were not known to the scribe or merely for the sake of brevity.

τέραν Αὐρηλίαν [4]Ταϋσεῖριν πρὸς γάμον ἀνδρὶ Αὐρηλίῳ Ἀρσινόῳ Τρύφωνος μητρὸς Δη-[5]μητρίας ἀπὸ τῆς αὐτῆς πόλεως, ᾧ προσφέρει ἡ αὐτὴ ἐκδότις ἐπὶ τῇ [6]αὐτῇ θυγατρὶ αὐτῆς καὶ γαμουμένῃ ἐν φερνῇ χρυσοῦ κοινοῦ σταθμῷ [7]Ὀξυρυγχιτικῷ περιτραχήλιον μανιάκην καλούμενον ἔχον λίθον [8]ὁλκῆς χωρὶς τοῦ [λί]θ[ο]υ τεταρτῶν δεκατριῶν, ἁπτώδιον ἔχον [9]λίθους πέντε περικεχρυσωμένους ὁλκῆς χωρὶς τῶν λίθων τεταρτῶν [10]τεσσάρων, ἐνωτίων ζεῦγος ἔχον πείνας δέκα ὁλκῆς χωρὶς τῶν πει-[11]νῶν τεταρτῶν τριῶν, δακτυλίδιον μεικρὸν τετά[ρ]ταις ἥμισυ, [12]καὶ ἐν ἱματίοις ἐν συντειμήσει δελματικομαφόρτην ἀργέντινον [13]ἔνσημον δραχμῶν διακοσίων ἑξήκοντα, χιτώνιον λευκὸν μονα-[14]χὸν κροσ<σ>ωτὸν ἔνσημον δραχμῶν ἑκατὸν ἑξήκοντα, δελματι-[15]κομαφόρτην καλλάινον δραχμῶν ἑκατόν, ἕτερον δελματικομα-[16]φ[ό]ρ[τ]ην λευκὸν προπόρφυρον δραχμῶν ἑκατόν, ὡς εἶναι ἐπὶ τὸ αὐ-[17]τὸ τὴν ὅλην φερνὴν χρυσοῦ κοινοῦ μναγιαῖον ἓν τετάρτας τέσσαρας [18]ἥμισυ καὶ συντειμήσεως ἱματίων δραχμὰς ἑξακοσίας εἴκοσι, [19]πάντα κεφαλαί[ο]υ οἷς οὐδὲν προσεγράφη, περὶ ἧς προκειμένης φερνῆς [20]ἐπ[ε]ρωτηθεὶς ἡ ἐκδότις Αὐρηλία Θαῆσις ὡμολόγησεν ὁ γαμῶν [21]Αὐρή[λιος] Ἀρσίνοος ἐσχηκέναι ἀριθμοῦ πλήρεις ἐπὶ τοῦ προκειμένου [22]σταθμ[οῦ κ]αὶ συντειμήσεως. συνβιούτωσαν οὖν ἀλλήλοις οἱ γαμοῦν-[23]τες ἀμέμπτως φυλάσσοντες τὰ τοῦ γάμου δίκαια, ὁ δὲ γαμῶν [24]ε . [. .] . χορηγεί[τω] τῇ γυναικὶ τὰ δέοντα πάντα κατὰ δύναμιν. [25]ἐ[ὰν δ]έ, ὃ [μὴ ε]ἴη, ἐκ διαφορᾶς

11. *l.* τετάρτης ἡμίσους. 17. *l.* μναϊαῖον. 20. *l.* ἐπερώτησεν.

Aurelia Tausiris in marriage to Aurelius Arsinous son of Tryphon and of Demetria, of the said city, as husband, to whom the said giver brings as the dowry of her said daughter the bride in common gold on the Oxyrhynchite standard a necklace of the kind called *maniaces* with a stone, weighing without the stone 13 quarters, a brooch (?) with 5 stones set in gold, weighing without the stones 4 quarters, a pair of earrings with 10 pearls, weighing without the pearls 3 quarters, a small ring of half a quarter, and in clothing, of which the value is estimated, a silvery, striped Dalmatian shawl worth 260 drachmae, a white, single tunic, tasselled and striped, worth 160 drachmae, a turquoise-coloured Dalmatian shawl worth 100 drachmae, another Dalmatian shawl, white with purple border, worth 100 drachmae, making the total of the whole dowry 1 *mnaiaion*,[a] 4½ quarters in common gold and 620 drachmae in estimated value of clothes, a sum total to which no addition has been made ; and questioned concerning the aforesaid dowry by the giver of the bride, Aurelia Thaesis, the bridegroom Aurelius Arsinous acknowledged that he had received the full number at the aforesaid weight and valuation. Wherefore let the parties to the marriage live together blamelessly, observing the duties of marriage, and let the bridegroom supply his wife with all things necessary in proportion to his means. But if—which heaven forbid—owing to disagreement a separation takes

[a] Properly, the amount of gold worth a mina of silver, which was probably about an octadrachm. See Segrè, *Metrologia*, p. 428.

ἀπα[λλαγὴ τῶν γ]αμούντων γένηται, 26 ἀπ[οδότω] ὁ γαμῶν τῇ ἐκδότιδι, [ἐὰν περιῇ, εἰ δ]ὲ μή, τῇ γαμουμένῃ, 27 τὴ[ν π]ρ[οκει]μένην φερνὴν π[λήρη ἐν ἡμέρ]αις ἑξήκοντα ἀφ' ἧς ἐὰν 28 α[ἴτη]μα γένηται, τὰ μὲν χρυσία κατ' ἀ[ρ]ι[θμη]σιν τοῦ ἐφ' ἑκάστου σταθμοῦ, 29 ἐπὶ δὲ τῶν ἐπὶ συντειμήσεως ἱματίων αἵρεσις ἔσται περὶ τοὺς περὶ τὴν 30 γαμουμένην ἔχειν αὐτὰ τῆς τότε ἐσομένης αὐτῶν συντειμήσεως 31 καὶ λαβεῖν [τ]ὸ ἐνδέον ἐν ἀρ[γ]υρίῳ ἢ αὐτὴν τὴν προκειμένην συντείμη- 32 σιν, καὶ [τ]ὴν τούτων πάντων τρίψιν καὶ ἀπουσίαν εἶναι πρὸς τὸν γαμοῦν- 33 τα. [ἐὰ]ν [δὲ] καὶ ἐπὶ τῆς ἀπαλλαγῆς ἔγκυος ᾖ{ν} ἡ γαμουμένη, δότω αὐτῇ 34 ὁ γαμῶν εἰς λόγον δαπάνης λοχείας δραχμὰς τεσσαράκοντα. ἐπὶ δὲ τῆς 35 ἀπαιτήσεως τῆς πρ[ο]κειμένης φερνῆς ἡ πρᾶξις ἔσται τοῖς περὶ τὴν γα- 36 μουμένην παρά τε τοῦ γαμοῦντος καὶ ἐκ τῶν ὑπαρχόντων αὐτῷ πάντων. 37 κυρία ἡ συνγραφὴ δισσὴ [γρα]φεῖσα πρὸς τὸ ἑκάτερον ἔχειν μοναχόν, ἥνπερ ὁπη- 38 νίκα ἐὰν αἱρῶνται ἢ καί τις αὐτῶν δημοσιώσει διὰ τοῦ καταλογείου 39 οὐ προσδεόμενος τῆς τοῦ ἑτέρου μεταλήμψεως οὐδὲ ἑτέρας εὐδοκήσεως 40 διὰ τὸ ἐντεῦθεν εὐδοκεῖν τῇ ἐσομένῃ δημοσιώσει, περὶ δὲ τοῦ ταῦτα 41 ὀρθῶς καλῶς γείνεσθαι ἀλλήλους ἐπερωτήσαντ[ε]ς ὡμολόγησαν. 42 (ἔτους) ζ Αὐτοκρατόρων Καισάρων Πουπλίου Λικιννίου Οὐαλεριανοῦ καὶ Πουπλίου 43 Λικι[νν]ί[ο]υ Οὐαλεριανοῦ Γαλλιηνοῦ Γερμανικῶν Μεγίστων Εὐσεβῶν Εὐτυχῶν 44 καὶ Π[ο]υπλ[ίο]υ Λικιννίου Κορνηλίου Σαλωνείνου Οὐαλεριανοῦ τοῦ ἐπιφανεστάτου 45 Καίσ[αρ]ος Σεβαστῶν Μεχεὶρ β. (2nd hand) Αὐρηλία Θαῆσις ἐξεδόμην 46 τὴν θυγατέρα μου

place between the parties, the bridegroom shall restore to the giver of the bride, if still alive, or, if not, to the bride, the aforesaid dowry in full within sixty days from the date of the demand, the gold objects in accordance with the count of their several weights, while for the clothes of which the value is estimated the bride's representatives shall have the choice of taking them at a valuation to be then made and receiving the balance in silver or of accepting the amount of the aforesaid valuation, and the wear and waste of all these objects shall be debited to the bridegroom. If at the time of the separation the bride is pregnant, the bridegroom shall give her for the expenses of her confinement 40 drachmae. In demanding restoration of the aforesaid dowry the bride's representatives shall have the right of execution upon the bridegroom and upon all his property. This contract is valid, being written in duplicate so that each party may have a copy, and whenever they choose or either of them chooses, he or she shall make it public through the bureau[a] without requiring the concurrence of the other or any further approval, because the future publication is herewith approved, and to each other's questions whether this is done rightly and fairly they have given their assent. The 7th year of the Emperors and Caesars Publius Licinnius Valerianus and Publius Licinnius Valerianus Gallienus, Germanici Maximi Pii Felices, and Publius Licinnius Cornelius Saloninus Valerianus, the most noble Caesar, Augusti, Mecheir 2. (Signed) I, Aurelia Thaesis, have given my daughter in marriage

[a] The bureau of the archidicastes in Alexandria.

πρὸς γάμον τῷ προτεταγμένῳ [47]Ἀρσινόῳ καὶ προσήνεγκα αὐτῷ τὴν προκειμένην φερ-[48]νὴν ὡς πρόκειται καὶ ἐπερωτηθεῖσα ὡμολόγησα. Αὐρήλιος [49]Θέων ὁ καὶ Νεπωτιανὸς συνέστην αὐτῇ καὶ ἔγραψα ὑπὲρ [50]αὐ[τ]ῆς μὴ εἰδυίης γράμματα. (3rd hand) Αὐρήλιος Ἀρσίνοος [51][ἔσ]χον τὴν {την} προκειμένην φερνήν, [52]καὶ ἐάν, ὃ μὴ εἴη, ἀπαλλαγὴ γένη-[53]ται, ἀποδώσω ὡς πρόκειται καὶ ἐπ-[54]ε[ρ]ωτηθεὶς ὡμολόγησα.

6. DEED OF DIVORCE

B.G.U. 1103. 13 B.C.

[2]Πρωτάρχωι [3]παρὰ Ζωΐδος τῆς Ἡρακλείδου μετὰ κυ-[4]ρίου τοῦ ἀδελφοῦ Εἰρηναίου τοῦ Ἡρακλείδου [5]καὶ παρὰ Ἀντιπάτρου [τ]οῦ Ζήνωνος. συ[νχω-][6]ροῦσιν Ζωῒς καὶ Ἀντίπατρος κεχωρίσ[θ]αι [7]ἀπ' ἀλλήλων τῆς συστάσης αὐτοῖ[ς συμ-][8]βιώσεως κατὰ συγχώρησιν διὰ τοῦ [αὐ-][9]τοῦ κριτηρίου τῷ ἐνεστῶτι ιζ (ἔτει) Καίσαρ[ος] [10]Ἁθύρ, ἡ δὲ Ζωῒς ἀπεσχηκέναι παρὰ τοῦ [11]Ἀντιπάτρου διὰ χιρὸς ἐξ οἴκου ὃ εἶχεν εἰς [12]φερνάριον ἱματίδια ἐν ἀργυ[ρί]ου δρα[χμαῖς] [13]ἑκατὸν εἴκοσι καὶ ἐνωτίων [χ]ρυσῶν [14]ζεῦγος· εἶναι μὲν αὐτόθεν ἄκυρον [15]τὴν τοῦ γάμου συνχώρησιν, μὴ ἐπε-[16]λεύσεσθαι δὲ τὴν Ζωΐδα μηδ' ἄλ-[17]λον ὑπὲρ αὐτῆς ἐπὶ τὸν Ἀντίπατρον [18]περὶ ἀπαιτήσεως τοῦ φερναρίου, ἀμφο-[19]τέρους δὲ ἐπ' ἀλλήλους μήτε περὶ [20]συνβιώσεως μηδὲ περὶ ἄλλου μηδε-[21]νὸς ἁπλῶς τῶν ἕως τῆς ἐνεστώσης [22]ἡμέρας, ἀφ' ἧς καὶ ἐξεῖναι τῇ μὲν [23]Ζωΐδι συναρμόζεσθαι ἄλλῳ ἀνδρὶ [24]καὶ

to the above-mentioned Arsinous and have presented to him the aforesaid dowry as stated, and in answer to the formal question I have given my consent. I, Aurelius Theon also called Nepotianus, acted with her and wrote on her behalf, as she is illiterate. I, Aurelius Arsinous, have received the aforesaid dowry, and if—which heaven forbid—a separation takes place, I will restore it as stated above, and in answer to the formal question I have given my consent.

6. DEED OF DIVORCE

13 B.C.

To Protarchus [a] from Zois daughter of Heraclides, with her guardian her brother Irenaeus son of Heraclides, and from Antipater son of Zenon. Zois and Antipater agree that they have separated from each other, severing the union which they had formed on the basis of an agreement made through the same tribunal in Hathur of the current 17th year of Caesar, and Zois acknowledges that she has received from Antipater by hand from his house the material which he received for dowry, clothes to the value of 120 drachmae and a pair of gold earrings. The agreement of marriage shall henceforth be null, and neither Zois nor other person acting for her shall take proceedings against Antipater for restitution of the dowry, nor shall either party take proceedings against the other about cohabitation or any other matter whatsoever up to the present day, and hereafter it shall be lawful both for Zois to marry another

[a] See No. 3, note *a*.

τῷ δὲ Ἀντιπάτρῳ ἄλλῃ γυναι-[25]κὶ ἀμφοτέροις ἀνυπευθύνοις οὖσι, [26]καὶ χωρὶς τοῦ κύρια εἶναι τὰ συνκε-[27]χωρημένα ἔτι καὶ ἐνέχεσθαι τὸν [28]παραβαίνοντα τοῖς τε βλάβεσ{σ}ι [29]καὶ τῷ ὡρισμένῳ προστίμῳ. [30](ἔτους) ιζ Καίσαρος Φαρμοῦθι β̄.

7. DEED OF DIVORCE

P. Oxy. 266. A.D. 96.

[1]Ἔτους ἑκκαιδ[ε]κάτου Αὐτοκράτορος Καίσαρος Δομιτιανοῦ Σεβαστοῦ [2]Γερμανικοῦ μη(νὸς) Γε[ρμ]ανικοῦ   ἐν Ὀξ(υρύγχων) πόλ(ει) τῆς Θηβαΐδος. [3]ὁμολογεῖ Θαῆσις Θώνιος τοῦ Ἀμιθώνιος μητρὸ<ς> Σινθεῦ-[4]τος μετὰ κυρίου τοῦ πατρωοῦ Ὀννώφρις Ὀννώφριο[ς] τοῦ Παμ-[5]μένους μητρὸς Τααρθώνιος τῷ γενομένῳ αὐτῆς ἀνδρὶ [6]Πετοσαράπι Θομπεκύσιος τοῦ Σαραπίωνος μητρὸ<ς> Σινθώ-[7]νιος, πάντες ἀπ' Ὀξυρύγχων πόλεως, ἐν ἀγυι[ᾷ], ἀπέχειν [8]παρ' αὐτοῦ ἀργυρίου Σεβαστοῦ νομίσματος δραχμὰς τετρα-[9]κοσίας κεφαλαίου ἃς προσηνέγκατο αὐτῷ ἐφ' ἑαυτῇ ἐν φερνῇ [10]μ[ε]τ' ἐγγύου [τ]ῆς μητρὸς αὐτοῦ Σινθώνιος Πετοσαράπιος τοῦ [11][.]βι[. . . .] κα[τὰ συ]νγραφὴν συνοικισίου διὰ τοῦ ἐν Ὀξυρύγχων [12][πόλει ἀγορανο]μίου ταῖς ἐπαγομέναις τοῦ τεσσαρασκαιδε-[13][κάτου ἔτους Αὐ]τοκράτορος Καίσαρος Δομιτιανοῦ Σεβαστοῦ [14][Γερμανικοῦ, ἣ]ς τὴν ἐπίφορον αὐτόθεν ἀναδεδωκέναι αὐτῷ [15][κεχιασμένην ε]ἰς ἀκύρωσιν ἕνεκα τοῦ [δι]αζυγὴν τοῦ γάμου [16][γενέσθαι, καὶ]

15. [δι]αζυγήν E.-H.: [ἀν]αζυγήν Edd.

[a] The date has not been filled in. Germanicus, to be distinguished from Germaniceus, = Thoth.

man and for Antipater to marry another woman without either of them being answerable. In addition to this agreement being valid, the one who transgresses it shall moreover be liable both to damages and to the prescribed fine. The 17th year of Caesar, Pharmouthi 2.

7. DEED OF DIVORCE

A.D. 96.

The 16th year of the Emperor Caesar Domitianus Augustus, on the of the month Germanicus,[a] at Oxyrhynchus in the Thebaid. Thaesis daughter of Thonis son of Amithonis, her mother being Sintheus, having with her as guardian her step-father Onnophris son of Onnophris son of Pammenes, his mother being Taarthonis, acknowledges to her late husband Petosarapis son of Thompekusis son of Sarapion, his mother being Sinthonis, all parties inhabitants of Oxyrhynchus, by agreement executed in the street,[b] that she has received from him the capital sum of 400 silver drachmae of the Imperial coinage which she brought him as a dowry on herself, his mother Sinthonis daughter of Petosarapis son of . . . being guarantee, in accordance with a contract of marriage drawn up through the office of the agoranomi in Oxyrhynchus on the intercalary days of the 14th year of the Emperor Caesar Domitianus Augustus Germanicus, and that she has herewith returned to him the authoritative document crossed and cancelled because the marriage is dissolved, and that she neither makes

[b] Literally "in the street," a phrase characteristic of Oxyrhynchite contracts, implying that the agreement was made before the public notary.

μὴ ἐγκαλεῖν αὐτῷ μηδὲ ἐγκαλέσειν μηδὲ ἐπε-[17][λεύσεσθαι μη]τὲ περὶ τῶν προκειμένων μηδὲ περὶ παρα-[18][φέρνων διὰ ? τ]ὸ ἀπεσχηκέναι μηδὲ περὶ ἄλλου μηδε-[19][νὸς πράγματος] μεχρὶ τῆς ἐνεστώση[ς ἡ]μέρας. κ[αὶ] αὐτὸς δὲ [20][ὁ Πετοσάραπ]ις ὁμολογεῖ ἐν ἀγυιᾷ [τ]ῇ αὐτῇ μὴ [ἐ]νκαλεῖν [21][μηδὲ ἐνκαλέ]σειν μηδὲ ἐπ[ελεύσεσθ]αι τῇ Θαήσ[ει [22]μηδὲ τοῖς πα]ρ' αὐτῆς π[ε]ρὶ μηδεν[ὸς ἁπλ]ῶς μέχρι [τῆς [23]ἐνεστώσης ἡμέρας - - -

8. DEED OF DIVORCE

P. Grenf. ii. 76. A.D. 305–306.

[1]. . . . . ς Σοῦλις νεκροτάφος τοπαρχίας Κύσε[ως] [2]Σενψάις θυγατρὸς Ψάιτος ἐκ μητρὸς Τεοῦς νεκροτάφις [3]ἀπὸ τῆς αὐτῆς χαίρειν. ἐπὶ ἔκ τινος πονηροῦ δαίμο-[4]νος συνέβη αὐτοὺς ἀπεζεῦχθαι ἀλλήλων τὴν κοι-[5]νὴν αὐτῶν συνβίωσιν, ἐντεῦθεν ὁμολογῶ [6]ὁ μὲν ὁ προκείμενος Σοῦλ πεπληρωμένος πάν-[7]των τῶν παραδοθέντων αὐτῇ [π]αρ' [ἐμοῦ οἱῳδή-][8]ποτε τρόπῳ εἰδῶν ἀποπέμπεσθαι αὐτὴ[ν καὶ μη-][9]κέτι μετελεύσεσθαι μηδὲ περὶ συνβιώ[σεως μή-][10]τε περὶ ἕδνου, ἀλλ' ἐξεῖναι αὐτῇ ἀποστῆ[ναι καὶ] [11]γαμηθῆναι ᾧ ἐὰν βουληθῇ, ἡ δὲ προκειμ[ένη Σεν-][12]ψάις πεπληρῶσθαι παρ' αὐτοῦ τοῦ προκει[μένου] [13]Σοῦλ πάντων τῶν ἐπιδοθέντων αὐ[τῷ εἰς λό-][14]γον πρ[οι]κός, ἅμα [τ]ε ἄλλων [τιν]ῶν ὄ[ντων] [15]αὐτῆς σκευῶν, καὶ ἄλλῳ οἱῳδήποτε τ[ρόπῳ], [16]καὶ μὴ μετελεύσεσθαι ἀλλήλους [ἐντεῦ-][17]θεν περὶ μηδενὸς ἁπαξαπλῶς

2. *l.* Σενψάιτι θυγατρί, νεκροτάφῃ. 3. *l.* ἐπεί. 9. *l.* μήτε.

nor will make any claim nor will proceed against him on account of the aforesaid sum or of the *parapherna*, since she has received them back, or of anything else up to the present date. Petosarapis likewise acknowledges, in the street as said, that he neither makes nor will make any claim nor take proceedings against Thaesis or her assigns about any matter whatsoever up to the present day. . . .

8. DEED OF DIVORCE

A.D. 305-306.

. . . Soulis, grave-digger, of the toparchy of Kusis,[a] to Senpsais daughter of Psais and of Tees, grave-digger, of the same toparchy, greeting. Since through some evil spirit it has come about that we have separated from each other in respect of our common wedded life, I, the aforesaid Soul, herewith acknowledge that before sending her away I have received in full all the objects given to her by me in any manner whatsoever and that I will not hereafter take proceedings against her about cohabitation or wedding-gift,[b] but that she is free to depart and marry whom she chooses; and I, the aforesaid Senpsais, acknowledge that I have received in full from him, the aforesaid Soul, all that was given to him by way of dowry, including certain separate objects of my own, or in any other way whatsoever; and we will not henceforth take proceedings against each other about any matter at all of any kind,

[a] A locality in the Great Oasis.

[b] The gift from bridegroom to bride, not found in pre-Byzantine contracts.

ἐ[γγράφου ἢ] 18ἀγράφου παντὸς πράγματος τὸ σύ[νολον] 19διὰ τὸ τελείαν ἀποζυγήν. ἡ ἀπο[ζυγὴ ἥδε] 20δισσὴ γραφεῖσα ἐφ' ὑπογραφῆς κ[υρία] 21ἔστω καὶ βεβαία ὡς ἐν δημοσί[ῳ κατακει-] 22μένη, καὶ ἐπερωτηθεὶς ὡμολ[όγησα]. 23(ἔτους) ιδ καὶ (ἔτους) β [τ]ῶν κυρίων ἡ[μῶν 24Κωνστ]α[ν-τίου] καὶ Μαξι[μια-25νοῦ Σεβαστῶν καὶ - - -

9. REPUDIATION OF A MARRIAGE

P. Oxy. 129. 6th cent. A.D.

1.[. . . . .] . . [. .] ἰνδ(ικτίονος) ἑνδε-κ[ά]της. τὸ παρὸν τῆς διαλύσεως ῥεπούδιον διαπέμπομαι 2ἐγ[ὼ] Ἰωάννης πατὴρ Εὐφημίας τῆς ἐμῆς ὑπεξουσίου θυγατρὸς σοὶ Φοιβάμμωνι τῷ εὐδοκ(ιμω)τ(άτῳ) μου 3γαμβρῷ, διὰ Ἀναστασίου τοῦ λαμπρο(τάτου) ἐκδίκου ταύτης τῆς Ὀξυρυγχιτῶν πόλε(ως), περιέχων 4ὡς ὑποτέτακται. ἐπειδὴ εἰς ἀκοὰς ἐμὰς ἦλθεν ὅτι εἰς ἔκθεσμα πράγματά τινα παρεμβάλλεις 5ἑαυτόν, ἅπερ οὐδὲ θεῷ οὐδὲ τοῖς ἀνθρώποις ἀρέσκουσιν, καὶ οὐ δέον ἐστὶν ταῦτα ἐγ γράμμασιν 6ἐντεθῆναι, καλὸν ἡγησάμην τὴν μεταξὺ σοῦ καὶ αὐτῆς τῆς ἐμῆς θυγατρὸς Εὐφημίας διαλυθῆναι 7συνάφιαν διὰ τὸ ἐμέ, ὡς εἴρηται, ἀκηκοέναι σε παρεμβάλλοντα ἑαυτὸν ἐν τοῖς αὐτοῖς 8ἀθέσμοις πράγμασιν καὶ βούλεσθαί με εἰρηνικὸν καὶ ἡσύχιον βίον διάξαι τὴν ἐμὴν θυγατέρα. 9τούτου οὖν ἕνεκεν τὸ παρὸν τῆς μεταξὺ σοῦ καὶ αὐτῆς τῆς ἐμῆς θυγατρὸς Εὐφημίας 10συναφίας ῥεπούδιον διαπεμψάμην σοι διὰ τοῦ

3. *l.* περιέχον. 10. *l.* διεπεμψάμην (so in l. 13).

written or unwritten, because the separation is absolute. This deed of separation, written in duplicate and signed, shall be valid and guaranteed as if deposited in a public record-office, and in answer to the formal question I have given my assent.[a] The 14th year of our lords Constantius and Maximianus Augusti and the 2nd year of . . .[b]

[a] The present copy was the one signed by Soul and given to Senpsais.

[b] Second year of the Caesars Severus and Maximinus.

---

19. *l.* τελείαν ⟨εἶναι τὴν⟩ ἀποζυγήν.

9. REPUDIATION OF A MARRIAGE

6th cent. A.D.

. . . 11th indiction. I, John, father of Euphemia my unemancipated daughter, transmit this present deed of repudiation and divorce to you, Phoebammon, my most honourable son-in-law, through Anastasius the most illustrious *defensor* of this city of Oxyrhynchus, couched as follows. Forasmuch as it has come to my ears that you are giving yourself over to lawless deeds, which are pleasing neither to God nor man and are not fit to be put into writing, I have thought it well that the marriage between you and her, my daughter Euphemia, should be dissolved, because, as already said, I have heard that you are giving yourself over to these same lawless deeds and I wish my daughter to lead a peaceful and quiet life. I therefore have sent you the present repudiation of the marriage between you and her, my daughter Euphemia, through the aforesaid most illustrious

εἰρημένου λαμπρο(τάτου) ἐκδίκου μεθ᾽ ὑπογραφῆς [11]ἐμῆς, οὗ τὸ ἴσον ἔλαβον ἐνυπόγραφον χειρὶ τοῦ αὐτοῦ λαμπρο(τάτου) ἐκδίκου. πρὸς οὖν ἀσφάλειαν [12]τῆς αὐτῆς μου θυγατρὸς Εὐφημίας τὸ παρὸν τῆς περιλύσεως ῥεπούδιον [13]διαπεμψάμην σοι γραφὲ(ν) μηνὶ Ἐπεὶφ ια ἰνδ(ικτίονος) ἑνδεκάτης. + (2nd hand) + Ἰωάννης πατὴρ Εὐφημίας [14]τῆς ἐμῆς θυγατρὸς ὁ προγεγραμμένος διεπεμψάμην τὸ παρὸν τῆς περιλύσεως ῥεπούδιον [15]σοὶ Φοιβάμμωνι τῷ εὐδοκιμωτάτῳ γαμβρῷ ὡς πρόκ(ειται). +

10. DEED OF ADOPTION

P. Oxy. 1206. A.D. 335.

[1]Ὑπατείας Ἰουλίου Κωνσταντίου πατρικίου ἀ[δ]ελφοῦ τοῦ δε[σ]πότου ἡμῶν [2][Κ]ωνσταντίνου Αὐγούστου καὶ Ῥουφίου Ἀλβίνου τῶν λαμπ(ροτάτων). [3]Αὐρήλιοι Ἡρακλῆς Ἁράσιος τὸ ἐφέστιον ἔχω[ν ἐν] τ[ῇ] λαμπ(ρᾷ) καὶ λαμπ(ροτάτῃ) Ὀξυρυγ[χ(ιτῶν)] [4]πόλει καὶ ἡ συνοῦσα γυνὴ Ἀσάριον Ἀγάθωνος ἀπὸ τ[ῆ]ς αὐτῆς πόλεως [5]καὶ Αὐρήλιος Ὡρίων Ὡρίωνος ἀπ[ὸ τῆ]ς [αὐ]τῆς πόλεως ἀλλήλοις [6]χαίρειν. ὁμολογοῦμεν ἡμῖς [μὲν ὅ τ]ε Ἡρακλῆς καὶ ἡ γ[υ]νὴ Εἰσάριον ἐκδε-[7]δωκέναι σοὶ τῷ Ὡρίωνι τὸν ἐξ [ἡμ]ῶν υἱὸν Πατερ[μοῦθ]ιν ὡς ἐτῶν [8]δύο εἰς υεἱοθεσίαν, ἐμὲ δὲ τὸν [Ὡρίων]α ἔχειν το[ῦτ]ον γνήσιον [9]υἱὸν πρὸς τὸ μένειν αὐτῷ τὰ ἀπ[ὸ τ]ῆς διαδοχῆς τῆς κληρονομίας [10]μου δίκαια, καὶ οὐκ ἐξέστε μοι τοῦτον ἀπώσασθαι οὔτε εἰς [11]δουλαγωγείαν ἄγειν διὰ τὸ εὐγενῆ αὐτὸν εἶν[α]ι κ[αὶ] ἐξ εὐγενῶν [12]γονέων ἐλευθέρων, ὥσπερ

defensor with my own signature, and I have taken a copy of this document, written by the hand of the same most illustrious *defensor*. Wherefore for the security of my said daughter Euphemia I have sent you the present deed of repudiation and dissolution written on Epeiph 11, 11th indiction. (Signed) I, John, the aforesaid, father of Euphemia my daughter, have sent the present deed of repudiation and dissolution to you, Phoebammon, my most honourable son-in-law, as stated above.

10. DEED OF ADOPTION

A.D. 335.

In the consulship of Julius Constantius, patrician, brother of our master Constantinus Augustus, and Rufius Albinus, the most illustrious. Aurelius Heracles son of Harasis, whose home is in the illustrious and most illustrious city of Oxyrhynchus, and his wife Aurelia Isarion daughter of Agathon, of the said city, and Aurelius Horion son of Horion, of the said city, mutual greetings. We acknowledge, Heracles and his wife Isarion on the one side, that we have given away to you, Horion, for adoption our son Patermouthis, aged about two years, and I, Horion, on the other side, that I have taken him as my true son so as to establish for him the rights of succession to my estate, and it shall not be lawful for me to disavow him or reduce him to slavery, because he is well-born and of well-born and free parents, and like-

4. *l.* Ἰσάριον; *cf.* ll. 6, 13. 10. *l.* ἐξέσται; so in ll. 13, 15.

οὐδὲ καὶ ἡμῖ[ν τῷ τ]ε Ἡρακλείῳ καὶ [13]τῇ γυνεκὶ Εἰσαρίῃ ἐξέστε τὸν παῖδα ἀποσπᾶν ἀπ[ὸ σο]ῦ τοῦ Ὡρίωνος [14]διὰ τὸ ἁπαξαπλῶς εἰς υειοθεσίαν ἐκδεδωκέναι [σοι α]ὐτόν, οὐδ᾽ αὖ [15]μετὰ ταῦτα ἐ[ξέστ]ε τινὶ παραβένειν τὰ ἐνγε[γ]ραμμένα διὰ [16]τὸ ἐπὶ τούτοις συνπεπῖσθαι καὶ συντετῖσθαι. κύρια τὰ τῆς υειο-[17]θεσίας γράμματα [δισσ]ὰ γραφέντα πρὸς τὸ ἑκάτερον μέρος [18]ἔχειν μοναχόν, καὶ ἐπερωτηθέντες ὑπ᾽ ἀλλήλων ὡμολογήσα(μεν). [19]ὑπατείας τῆς προκ(ειμένης) Φαρμοῦθι [. (2nd hand) [20]Αὐρ]ήλιος Ὡρίων παρείληφα τὸν παῖδα εἰ[ς υἱοθεσίαν [21]καὶ] ἀπογράψομαι αὐτὸν εἰς ἐμαυτοῦ γνήσιο[ν υἱὸν πρὸς τὸ [22]μέ]νιν αὐτῷ τὰ ἀ[πὸ τῆ]ς διαδοχῆς ἐκ κληρ[ο]ν[ομίας μου [23]ὡς] πρόκιται, καὶ ἐπ[ερ]ωτηθ(εὶς) ὡμολόγησα. Α[ὐρήλιος . . . . . [24]ἔγρ]αψα ὑπ(ὲρ) αὐτοῦ γράμμ(ατα) μὴ εἰδότος.

11. ALIENATION OF A DAUGHTER

P. Oxy. 1895. A.D. 554.

[1][+ Βασιλείας τοῦ θειοτάτου καὶ εὐσεβ(εστάτου) ἡμῶν δεσπότου Φλ(αουίου) Ἰουστινιανοῦ τοῦ αἰωνίου Αὐγούστου καὶ [2]Αὐτοκράτο]ρος ἔτους κη τοῖς τὸ ιγ´ μετὰ τὴν ὑπατίαν Φλ[(αουίου) Βασιλίου τοῦ λαμπρ(οτάτου) . . . . . . ἰνδ(ικτίονος) . [3]?Αὐρηλία Ἡρα]ἶς θυγάτηρ Ἰωάννου μητρὸς Σωσάννας ἀπὸ [. . . . . [4]. . . . .]απώλῃ υἱῷ Μηνᾷ καὶ Μαξίμᾳ τῇ σῇ γαμετῇ, θ[υγατρὶ . . . . ἀπὸ . . . . . . χαίρειν. [5][πρὸ . . . . ἐνι]αυτῶν πλέον ἔλαττον ὁ ἐμὸς σύμβιος ἐτελ[εύτησεν, ἐγὼ δὲ ἀπελείφθην [6]ὑπὲρ

wise it shall not be lawful for us, Heracles and his wife Isarion, to remove the boy from you, Horion, because we have once for all given him away to you for adoption, nor shall it hereafter be lawful for anyone to transgress the terms of the deed, because on these we have consented and agreed. This deed of adoption, written in duplicate so that each party may have a copy,[a] is valid, and on being formally questioned by each other we have given our consent. In the consulship aforesaid, Pharmouthi . . . (Signed) I, Aurelius Horion, have received the boy for adoption, and I will register him with my household as my true son so as to establish for him the rights of succession to my estate as aforesaid, and in answer to the formal question I have given my consent. I, Aurelius . . ., have written for him, as he is illiterate.

[a] The present copy is the one given to the parents and signed by Horion.

12. *l.* Ἡρακλεῖ. 13. *l.* γυναικὶ Εἰσαρίῳ. 15. *l.* παραβαίνειν. 16. *l.* συντεθεῖσθαι.

11. ALIENATION OF A DAUGHTER

A.D. 554.

In the 28th year of the reign of our most godlike and pious master Flavius Justinianus the eternal Augustus and Imperator, the 13th year after the consulship of Flavius Basilius the most illustrious . . . in the . . . indiction. Aurelia Herais daughter of John and Susanna, of . . ., to . . . -seller, son of Menas, and Maxima your wife, daughter of . . ., greeting. . . . years ago, more or less, my husband died, and I was left toiling and suffering hardship

τῆς ἐμῆ]ς ἐξ αὐτοῦ θυγατρὸς κάμνουσα καὶ δυστηχο[ῦσα εἰς τὸ χορηγεῖν αὐτῇ τὰς [7]δεούσας τρο]φάς, καὶ τανῦν μὴ εὐποροῦσα ἀποθρέψαι [αὐτὴν . . . . [8] . . . . . οὖσα]ν ἐτῶν ἐννέα πλέον ἔλαττον ἠξίωσα ὑ[μᾶς . . . . ταύτην [9]παραλαβεῖ]ν παρ' ἐμοῦ εἰς θυγατέρα, καὶ ὁμολογῶ παρα[δεδωκέναι αὐτὴν ὑμῖν ἀπὸ τοῦ [10]νῦν εἰς τὸν ἑξ]ῆς ἅπαντα χρόνον εἰς θυγατέρα νομίμην, [ὥστε ὑμᾶς χορηγοῦντας τὰ δέον-[11]τα χώραν γον]έων εἰς θυγατέρα ἀποπληρῶσαι εἰς α[ὐτήν, καὶ ἐντεῦθεν μὴ δύνασθαί [12]με ταύτην ἀ]ποσπάσαι ἀφ' ὑμῶν. εἰ δὲ τοῦτο ποιήσ[ω, ὁμολογῶ ὑμῖν ἀποτίσειν [13]ἅπαντα τὰ ἀ]ναλώματα λόγῳ τῶν αὐτῆς ἀποτρο[φῶν . . . . [14]. . . . . . ὑποθ]εμένη εἰς τὸ δίκαιον ταύτης τῆς ὁμολο[γίας πάντα τὰ ἐμοῦ ὑπάρχοντα [15]καὶ ὑπά]ρξ[ον]τα ἰδικῶς καὶ γενικῶς ἐνεχύρου λόγῳ [καὶ ὑποθήκης δικαίῳ. [16]κυρία] ἡ [ὁμο]λογία ἁπλῆ γραφεῖσα, καὶ ἐπερωτ[ηθεῖσα ὡμολόγησα. (2nd hand) [17][? Αὐρηλία Ἡ]ραῒς θυγάτηρ Ἰωάννου . . . . . . [

12. EMANCIPATION OF A SLAVE

P. Oxy. 722. A.D. 91 or 107.

[1]῎Ετους δεκάτου Αὐτοκράτορ[ος Καίσαρος Δομιτιανοῦ] [2]Σεβαστοῦ Γερμανικοῦ Ὑπε[ρβερεταίου] [3]ἐπαγο(μένων) (2nd hand) ϛ Σεβα(στῇ) (1st hand) μη(νὸς) Καισαρείου ἐ[παγο(μένων) (2nd hand) ϛ Σεβα(στῇ) (1st hand) ἐν Ὀ-][4]ξυρύγχων πόλει τῆς Θηβαΐδ[ος ἐπ' ἀγορανό-][5]μων Ψαμμίων τριῶν.

for my daughter by him, in order to provide for her the necessary sustenance ; and now, not having the means to maintain her . . ., she being nine years old, more or less, I have asked you . . . to receive her from me as your daughter, and I acknowledge that I have handed her over to you from now for all succeeding time as your legal daughter, so that you shall supply her needs and fill the place of parents to daughter, and I have no power henceforth to take her away from you. If I do so, I agree to pay you for all the expenses of her maintenance . . ., pledging for the rights of this agreement all my property present and future, specifically and as a whole, by way of security and by right of mortgage. This agreement, written in one copy only, is valid, and in answer to the formal question I have given my consent. (Signed) I, Aurelia Herais . . .

6. *l.* δυστυχο[ῦσα.

12. EMANCIPATION OF A SLAVE

A.D. 91 or 107.

The 10th year of the Emperor Caesar Domitianus Augustus Germanicus, on the 6th intercalary day of Hyperberetaeus,[a] *dies augustus*, which is the 6th intercalary day of the month Caesareus,[b] *dies augustus*, at Oxyrhynchus in the Thebaid, before three agoranomi, all called Psammis. Achilleus, aged about

[a] The extra intercalary day of the leap-year observed as an Imperial holiday.

[b] = Mesore.

6 ἀφεῖκαν ἐ{υ}λευθέραν ὑπὸ Δία Γ[ῆν Ἥλιον Ἀχιλλεὺς] 7 ὡς (ἐτῶν) κ μέσος μελίχρως μ[ακροπρόσωπος 8 οὐ(λὴ) μ]ετώπῳ μέσῳ καὶ Σαραπ[ᾶς ὡς (ἐτῶν) . μέσος 9 μ]ελ[ίχρως μακροπρόσωπος οὐ(λὴ) . . . . 10 . . ἀ]ριστερ[. , ἀμφότεροι . . . . τοῦ 11 Ἀμ]μωνίου μητρὸς Σαραποῦτος [. . . . . 12 τῶ]ν ἀπ' Ὀξυρύγχων πόλεως, [ἐν ἀγυιᾷ τὸ ὑ- 13 πάρ]χον αὐτοῖς ἐξ ἴσου τρίτον μέ[ρος τῆς ἐξαπη- 14 λευ]θερωμένης κατὰ τὸ ἄλλο δ[ίμοιρον δού-] 15 λης Ἀπολλωνοῦτος ὡς (ἐτῶν) κϛ μέσ[ης μελίχρωτος 16 μα]κροπροσώπου οὐλὴ ποδὶ δ[εξιῷ . . . .] 17 ἐξαπηλευθερωμένης (ταλάντων) δ[. . . . . 18 . .]ν τῶν τοῦ ἀπελευθερουμέ[νου . . . . τρίτου 19 μέρου]ς ἀργυρίου ἐπισήμου δρα[χμῶν . . . . 20 τ]ε[τ]ρωβόλου καὶ ὧν τέτακται [. . . . Ἀχιλλεῖ] 21 καὶ Σαραπᾷ Ἡρακλᾶς Τρύφωνο[ς τοῦ . . . .] 22 μητρὸς Ταοννώφριος Πανεσι[είους ἀπὸ τῆς 23 α]ὐτῆς πόλεως ὡς (ἐτῶν) λα μέσο[ς μελίχρως] 24 μακροπρόσωπος οὐ(λὴ) ὑπὲρ γό(νυ) δεξ[ιὸν λύτρων] 25 ἀργυρίου Σεβαστοῦ νομίσμα[τος δραχμῶν] 26 διακοσίων χαλκοῦ ταλάντω[ν . . . .] 27 χιλίων, οὐκ ἐξόντος τῷ Ἀχ[ιλλεῖ οὐδ' ἄλλῳ 28 ὑ]πὲρ αὐτοῦ ἀπαίτησιν ποιε[ῖσθαι παρὰ τῆς Ἀπολ- 29 λ]ωνοῦτος οὐδὲ τῶν π[αρ' αὐτῆς τῶν προκει- 30 μ]ένων λύτρων οὐδ' ἐπιε[. . . . .] 31 γνωστὴρ τῆς ἐλευθερώ[σεως . . . .] 32 τοῦ Πετεήσιος μητρὸς [. . . . . . . ἀπὸ τῆς αὐτῆς] 33 πόλεως ὡς (ἐτῶν) μ μ[έσος μελίχρως μακρο-] 34 πρόσωπος οὐ(λὴ) ἀντικ[νημίῳ . . . . . ἐν ἀγυιᾷ] 35 τῇ αὐτῇι. (2nd hand) Ἀχιλλ[εὺς . . . .] 36 πεπύημε σ[ὺν

36. *l.* πεποίημαι

20 years, of medium height, with fair complexion, long face, and a scar in the middle of his forehead, and Sarapas, aged about . . . years, of medium height, with fair complexion, long face, and a scar on his left . . ., both sons of . . . son of Ammonius, their mother being Sarapous daughter of . . ., all of Oxyrhynchus, have set free under sanction of Zeus, Earth, and Sun, by deed drawn up in the street, the third part which they jointly own of the female slave who has already been freed as regards the other two thirds, namely Apollonous, aged about 26 years, of medium height, with fair complexion, long face, and a scar on the right foot; and whereas she has already been freed to the extent of two thirds for . . . talents, the sum payable in respect of the third part now being freed consists of a fee of . . . drachmae 4 obols of coined silver and of the ransom paid to Achilleus and Sarapas by Heraclas son of Tryphon son of . . ., his mother being Taonnophris daughter of Panesies, of the said city, aged about 31 years, of medium height, with fair complexion, long face, and a scar above the right knee, namely 200 drachmae of Imperial silver coin and . . . talents 1000 drachmae of copper[a]; and it shall not be lawful for Achilleus or anyone else on his behalf to demand the aforesaid ransom from Apollonous or her assigns or to . . . Certifier of the manumission: . . . son of . . . son of Peteesis, his mother being . . ., of the said city, aged about 40 years, of medium height, with fair complexion, long face, and a scar on the . . . shin, in the street as said. (Signed) I, Achilleus, with my brother Sarapas, have emanci-

[a] At this period a drachma of silver usually = 450 of copper.

τῷ ἀδελφῷ] [37]Σεραπᾶτι τὴ[ν ἐλευθέρωσιν] [38]τοῦ τρίτου [μέρους δούλης] [39]Ἀπολονοῦτ[ος καὶ ἀπέχω] [40]τὰ λύτρα ἀ[ργυρίου δραχ(μὰς)] [41]διακοσία[ς χαλκοῦ [42]. .]υ[

Verso: ἐπαγο(μένων) ς [

13. APPRENTICESHIP TO A WEAVER

P. Oxy. 275. A.D. 66.

[1]Ὁ[μ]ο[λ]ογοῦσιν ἀλλή[λ]οις Τρύφων Διονυ[σίου] [2]τοῦ Τρύφωνος μητρὸς [Θ]αμούν[ιο]ς τῆ[ς] [3]Ὀννώφριος καὶ Πτολεμαῖο[ς] Παϋσιρίωνος [4]τοῦ Πτολεμαίου μητρὸς Ὠφελοῦτος τῆς [5]Θέωνος γέρδιος, ἀμφότεροι τῶν ἀπ' Ὀξυ-[6]ρύγχων πόλεως, ὁ μὲν Τρύφων ἐγδεδόσ-[7]θαι τῷ Πτολεμαίῳ τὸν ἑαυτοῦ υἱὸν Θοῶ-[8]νιν μητρὸς Σαραεῦτος τῆς Ἀπίωνος οὐδέ-[9]πω ὄντα τῶν ἐτῶν ἐπὶ χρόνον ἐνιαυτὸν [10]ἕνα ἀπὸ τῆς ἐνεστώσης ἡμέρας, διακονοῦ(ν)-[11]τα καὶ ποιο[ῦ]ντα πάντα τὰ ἐπιτασσόμε-[12]να αὐτῷ ὑπὸ τοῦ Πτολεμαίου κατὰ τὴν [13]γερδιακὴν τέχνην πᾶσαν ὡς καὶ αὐτὸς [14]ἐπίστα<τα>ι, τοῦ παιδὸς τρεφομένου καὶ ἱμα-[15]τισζομένου ἐπὶ τὸν ὅλον χρόνον ὑπὸ [16]τοῦ πατρὸς Τρύφωνος, πρὸς ὃν καὶ εἶναι [17]τὰ δημόσια πάντα τοῦ παιδός, ἐφ' ᾧ [18]δώσει αὐτῷ κατὰ μῆνα ὁ Πτολεμαῖος [19]εἰς λόγον διατροφῆς δραχμὰς πέντε [20]καὶ ἐπὶ συνκλεισμῷ τοῦ ὅλου χρόνου [21]εἰς λόγον ἱματισμοῦ δραχμὰς δεκαδύο, [22]οὐκ ἐξόντος τῷ Τρύφωνι ἀποσπᾶν τὸν [23]παῖδα ἀπὸ τοῦ Πτολεμαίου μέχρι τοῦ [24]τὸν χρόνον πληρωθῆναι, ὅσας δ' ἐὰν ἐν [25]τούτῳ ἀτακτήσῃ ἡμέρας, ἐπὶ τὰς [26]ἴσας αὐτὸν παρέξεται [με]τὰ τὸν χρό-

pated the third part of the slave Apollonous, and I have received the ransom, 200 drachmae of silver . . . (Endorsed) The 6th intercalary day . . .

---

39. *l.* Ἀπολλωνοῦτ[ος.

13. APPRENTICESHIP TO A WEAVER

A.D. 66.

Tryphon son of Dionysius son of Tryphon and of Thamounis daughter of Onnophris, and Ptolemaeus son of Pausirion son of Ptolemaeus and of Ophelous daughter of Theon, weaver, both being inhabitants of Oxyrhynchus, mutually acknowledge that Tryphon has apprenticed to Ptolemaeus his son Thoonis, whose mother is Saraeus daughter of Apion, and who is not yet of age, for a period of one year from the present day, to serve and to follow all the instructions given to him by Ptolemaeus in the art of weaving as far as he himself knows it, the boy to be fed and clothed for the whole period by his father Tryphon, who will also be responsible for all the taxes on him, on the condition that Ptolemaeus will pay to him monthly on account of food 5 drachmae and at the close of the whole period on account of clothing 12 drachmae, nor shall Tryphon have the right to remove the boy from Ptolemaeus until the completion of the period, and for whatever days therein the boy plays truant, he shall send him to work for

27νον ἢ ἀ[πο]τεισάτω ἑκάσ[τ]ης ἡμέρας 28ἀργυρίου [δρ]αχμὴν μίαν, [τ]οῦ δ' ἀποσπα<σ>-29θῆναι ἐντὸς τοῦ χρόν[ου] ἐπίτειμον 30δραχμὰς ἑκατὸν καὶ εἰς τὸ δημόσιον 31τὰς ἴσας. ἐὰν δὲ καὶ αὐτὸ[ς ὁ] Πτολεμαῖος 32μὴ ἐγδιδάξῃ τὸν παῖ[δ]α, ἔνοχος 33ἔστω τοῖς ἴσοις ἐπιτε[ί]μοις. κυρία 34ἡ διδασκαλική. (ἔτους) ιγ Νέ[ρ]ωνος Κλαυδίου 35Καίσαρος Σεβαστοῦ Γερμανικοῦ 36Αὐτοκράτορος μηνὸς Σεβαστοῦ κᾱ. (2nd hand) 37Πτολεμαῖος [Πα]ϋσιρίωνος 38τοῦ Πτολεμαίου μητρὸς Ὠφε-39λοῦτος τῆς Θέωνος ἕκαστα 40ποιήσω ἐν τῷ ἐνιαυτῷ ἑνί. 41Ζωίλος Ὥρου τοῦ Ζωίλου μητρὸς 42Διεῦτος τῆς Σωκέως ἔγραψα 43ὑπὲρ αὐτοῦ μὴ ἰδότος γράμματα. 44ἔτους τρισκαιδεκάτου 45Νέρωνος Κλαυδίου Καίσαρος 46Σεβαστοῦ Γερμανικοῦ 47Αὐτοκράτο[ρο]ς μη(νὸς) Σεβαστοῦ κᾱ.

14. APPRENTICESHIP TO A WEAVER

P. Oxy. 725. A.D. 183.

1[Ὁμολογοῦσιν ἀλλήλοις Ἰσ]χυρίων Ἡραδίωνος 2[μητρὸς . . . . ἀπ' Ὀξυ]ρύγχων πόλεως καὶ 3[Ἡρακλᾶς Σαραπίωνος το]ῦ καὶ Λέοντος Ἡρακλεί-4δ[ο]υ μ[ητρὸς . . . . ἀπὸ] τῆς αὐτῆς πόλεως 5[γέρ]διο[ς, ὁ μὲν Ἰσχυρίων ἐγ]δεδόσθαι τῷ Ἡρα-6[κλᾷ] τὸν το[ῦ. . . . .] . . [. . .] ἀδελφοῦ 7. [.] . ον Θῶν[ιν ἀ]φήλ[ικα π]ρὸς [μ]άθησιν τῆς δη-8λ[ο]υμένης [τέ]χνης ἀπὸ νεομη[νίας τοῦ] ἑξῆς 9μ[η]νὸς Φαῶφ[ι] ἐπὶ χρόνον ἔτη πέ[ντε, κ]αὶ παρ-10έξει αὐτὸν προσεδρεύοντα τῷ διδασκάλῳ 11ἐπὶ τὸν δηλο[ύμε]νον χρ[ό]νον καθ'

the like number at the end of it or else forfeit one drachma of silver for each day, and for removing him within the period he shall pay a penalty of 100 drachmae and the like sum to the Treasury. If Ptolemaeus fails to instruct the boy fully, he shall be liable to the same penalties. This contract of apprenticeship is valid. The 13th year of Nero Claudius Caesar Augustus Germanicus Imperator, the 21st of the month Sebastus.[a] (Signed) I, Ptolemaeus son of Pausirion son of Ptolemaeus and of Ophelous daughter of Theon, will do everything in the one year. I, Zoilus son of Horus son of Zoilus and of Dieus daughter of Sokeus have written for him, as he is illiterate. The 13th year of Nero Claudius Caesar Augustus Germanicus Imperator, Sebastus 21.

[a] =Thoth.

14. APPRENTICESHIP TO A WEAVER

A.D. 183.

Ischyrion son of Heradion and of . . ., of Oxyrhynchus, and Heraclas son of Sarapion also called Leon son of Heraclides and of . . ., of the same city, weaver, make this mutual acknowledgement. Ischyrion agrees that he has apprenticed to Heraclas the . . . of . . ., Thonis, a minor, to learn the art referred to from the 1st of next month, Phaophi, for a period of five years, and he will deliver him to attend his teacher

ἑκάστην [12]ἡμέραν ἀπὸ ἀν[ατολῆς] ἡ[λίου] μέχρι δύσεως, [13]ποιοῦντα πάντ[α τὰ ἐπιταχθ]ησόμενα [α]ὐτῷ [14]ὑπὸ τοῦ αὐτοῦ δ[ιδασκάλ]ου ὡς ἐπὶ τῶν ὁμοί-[15]ων μαθητῶν, [τρεφόμ]ενον ὑπὸ τοῦ Ἰσχυ-[16][ρί]ωνος. κ[αὶ τὰ μὲν] πρῶτα ἔτη δύο [17]καὶ μῆνας ἑπτὰ τοῦ τρίτου ἐνιαυτοῦ [18]οὐδὲν δώσει ὑπὲρ μισθοῦ τοῦ παιδὸς ὁ Ἡρα-[19]κλᾶς, τοῖς δὲ λοιποῖς μησὶ πέντε τοῦ αὐ-[20]τοῦ τρίτου ἐνιαυτοῦ χορηγήσει ὁ Ἡρα-[21]κλᾶς ὑπὲρ μισθῶν τοῦ αὐτοῦ μαθητοῦ [22]κατὰ μῆνα δραχμὰς δεκαδύο κ[α]ὶ τῷ τε-[23]τάρτῳ ἐνιαυτῷ ὁμοίως κατὰ μῆνα [24]ὑπὲρ μισθῶν δραχμὰς δεκαὲξ καὶ τῷ [25]πέμπτῳ ἐνιαυτῷ ὁμοίως κατὰ μῆ-[26]να δραχμὰς εἴκοσι τέσσαρας, καὶ κατασκευ-[27]άσει ὁ Ἡρακλᾶς τῷ αὐτῷ μαθητῇ τῷ μὲν [28]ἐνεστῶτι τετάρτῳ καὶ εἰκοστῷ ἔτει [29]χ[ι]τῶνα ἄξιον δραχμῶν δεκαέξ, τῷ [δὲ] [30]ἰσιόντι κε (ἔτει) ἕτερον χιτῶνα ἄξιον δ[ρα-][31]χμῶν εἴκοσι, καὶ [τ]ῷ κϛ (ἔτει) ὁμοίως ἄλλο[ν] [32]χιτῶ[ν]α ἄξιον δραχμῶν εἴ[κ]οσι τε[σσάρων], [33]κ[α]ὶ τῷ κζ (ἔτει) ἄλλον χιτῶνα [ἄ]ξιον δ[ραχμῶν] [34]εἴκοσι ὀκτώ, καὶ τῷ κη (ἔτει) ὁμοίως ἄλλ[ον] χιτῶ-[35]να ἄξιον δραχμῶν τριάκοντα δύο. ἀρ-[36]γήσει δὲ ὁ παῖς εἰς λόγον ἑορτῶν κατ' ἔτος [37]ἡμέρας εἴκοσι, οὐδενὸς ἐκκρουομένου [38]τ[ῶ]ν μισθῶν τούτων ἀφ' οὗ χρόνου ἐὰν [39]χορηγηθῇ μισθός, ἐὰν δὲ πλείονας τού-[40]των ἀργήσῃ [ἢ ἀσ]θενήσῃ ἢ ἀτακτήσῃ ἢ [41]δι' ἄλλην τιν[ὰ αἰ]τίαν ἡμέρας, ἐπὶ τὰς [42][ἴσ]ας ἐπάναγκε[ς] παρέξει αὐτὸν ὁ Ἰσχυρί-[43]ων τῷ διδασκά[λ]ῳ ἡμέρας παραμένον-[44]τα καὶ ποιοῦντ[α] πάντα καθὼς πρόκειται [45]χωρὶς μισθοῦ, τρεφόμενον ὑπὸ τοῦ αὐτοῦ [46]Ἰσχυρίωνος, διὰ τὸ ἐπὶ τούτοις ἑστάσθαι. [47]ὁ [δ]ὲ Ἡρακλᾶς εὐδοκῶν τούτοις πᾶσι

for the stated period every day from sunrise to sunset, doing everything that he is ordered by the said teacher like other such apprentices, and being fed by Ischyrion. And for the first two years and for seven months of the 3rd year Heraclas shall pay no wages for the boy, but in the remaining five months of the said 3rd year Heraclas shall pay as wages of the said apprentice 12 drachmae a month, and in the 4th year likewise for wages 16 drachmae a month, and in the 5th year likewise 24 drachmae a month; and Heraclas shall furnish to the said apprentice in the current 24th year a tunic worth 16 drachmae, and in the coming 25th year a second tunic worth 20 drachmae, and in the 26th year likewise another tunic worth 24 drachmae, and in the 27th year another tunic worth 28 drachmae, and in the 28th year likewise another tunic worth 32 drachmae. The boy shall have twenty holidays a year on account of festivals without any deduction from his wages after the payment of wages begins; but if he is idle for longer than this or is absent through illness or insubordination or for any other reason, Ischyrion shall be bound to deliver him to his teacher for an equivalent number of days, to remain with him and perform all his duties as aforesaid without wages, being fed by Ischyrion, because the contract has been made on these terms. Heraclas on the

καὶ ἐκ-[48]δειδάξειν τὸν μαθητὴν τὴν δηλουμέ-[49]νην τέχνην ἐν τῷ πενταετῖ χρόνῳ [50]καθὼς καὶ αὐτὸς ἐπίσταται καὶ χορηγήσειν [51]τοὺς μηνιαίους μισθοὺς καθὼς πρόκει-[52]τα[ι] ἀπὸ τοῦ ὀγδόου μηνὸς τοῦ τρίτου ἐνιαυ-[53]τοῦ. καὶ μὴ ἐξεῖναι μηδενὶ αὐτῶν παρα-[54]βαίνειν τι τῶν προκειμένων ἢ ὁ παραβὰς [55]ἐκτείσι τῷ ἐνμένοντι ἐπίτειμον δραχμὰς [56]ἑκατὸν καὶ εἰς τὸ δημόσιον τὰς ἴσας. κύριον [57]τὸ ὁμολόγημα. (ἔτους) κδ Αὐτοκράτορος Καίσαρος [58]Μάρκου Αὐρηλίου Κομμόδου Ἀντωνίνου [59]Σεβαστοῦ Ἀρμενιακοῦ Μηδικοῦ Παρθικοῦ [60]Σαρματικοῦ Γερμανικοῦ Μεγίστου Θὼθ κε. (2nd hand) [61]Ἡρακλᾶς Σαραπ(ίωνος) τοῦ κ(αὶ) Λέοντος τέθειμαι τὸ [62]ὁμολόγημα καὶ εὐδοκῶ πᾶσι τοῖς προκ(ειμένοις). [63]Θῶνις ὁ κ(αὶ) Μωροῦς Ἁρθώνιος ἔγραψ[α] [64]ὑπὲρ αὐ(τοῦ) μὴ εἰδ(ότος) γράμμ(ατα).

15. APPRENTICESHIP TO A SHORTHAND WRITER

P. Oxy. 724. A.D. 155.

[1]Πα[ν]εχώτης ὁ καὶ Πανάρης τῶν κεκοσμητευκότων τῆς Ὀξυρυγχειτῶν [2]πόλεως διὰ Γεμέλλου φίλου Ἀπολλωνίῳ σημιογράφῳ χαίρειν. συνέστησά σοι [3]Χαιράμμωνα δοῦλον πρὸς μάθησιν σημείων ὧν ἐπίσταται ὁ υἱός σου [4]Δι[ο]νύσιος ἐπὶ χρόνον ἔτη δύο ἀπὸ τοῦ ἐνεστῶτος μηνὸς Φαμενὼθ τοῦ [5]ὀκτωκαιδεκάτου ἔτους Ἀντωνίνου Καίσαρος τοῦ κυρίου μισθοῦ τοῦ συμπεφω-[6]νημένου πρὸς ἀλλήλους ἀργυρίου δραχμῶν ἑκατὸν εἴκοσι χωρὶς ἑορτι-[7]κῶν, ἐξ ὧν ἔσχες τὴν πρώτην δόσιν ἐν δραχμαῖς τεσσαράκοντα, τὴν δὲ [8]δευτέραν λήψῃ τοῦ

other side consents to all these provisions and agrees to instruct the apprentice fully in the aforesaid art in the space of five years as far as he knows it himself and to pay the *monthly wages as aforesaid*, beginning from the 8th month of the 3rd year. Neither of them shall be permitted to violate any of the aforesaid provisions, and the one who violates them shall forfeit to the one who observes them a penalty of 100 drachmae and to the Treasury the like amount. This agreement is valid. The 24th year of the Emperor Caesar Marcus Aurelius Commodus Antoninus Augustus Armeniacus Medicus Parthicus Sarmaticus Germanicus Maximus, Thoth 25. (Signed) I, Heraclas son of Sarapion also called Leon, have made this agreement and consent to all the aforesaid provisions. I, Thonis also called Morous son of Harthonis, have written for him, as he is illiterate.

15. APPRENTICESHIP TO A SHORTHAND WRITER

A.D. 155.

Panechotes also called Panares, ex-cosmetes of Oxyrhynchus, through his friend Gemellus, to Apollonius, writer of shorthand, greeting. I have placed with you my slave Chaerammon to learn the signs which your son Dionysius knows, for a period of two years from the present month Phamenoth of the 18th year of Antoninus Caesar the lord, for the fee agreed upon between us of 120 silver drachmae, with exception of feast-days; and of this sum you have had a first instalment of 40 drachmae, and you

παιδὸς ἀνειληφότος τὸ κομεντάρ[ι]ον ὅλον ἐν δρα-
[9]χ[μ]αῖς τ[εσσ]αράκοντα, τὴν δὲ τρίτην λήψομαι
ἐπὶ τέλει τοῦ χρόνου τοῦ [10]παιδὸς ἐκ παντὸς λόγου
πεζοῦ γράφοντος καὶ ἀναγεινώσ[κον]τος ἀμέμπτως
[11]τὰς {δὲ} λοιπὰς δραχμὰς τεσσαράκοντα. ἐὰν
δὲ ἐντὸς τοῦ χ[ρ]όνου αὐτὸν [12]ἀπαρτίσῃς, οὐκ ἐκ-
δέξομαι τὴν προκειμένην προθεσμ[ί]αν, οὐκ ἐξόντος
[13]μοι ἐντὸς τοῦ χρόνου τὸν παῖδα ἀποσπᾶν, παρα-
μενεῖ δέ σ[ο]ι μετὰ [τὸ]ν χρό[νον ὅσας] [14]ἐὰν ἀργήσῃ
ἡμέρας ἢ μῆνας. (ἔτους) ιη Αὐτοκράτορος Καίσαρος
Τίτου Αἰλίου Ἁδριανοῦ [15]Ἀντωνείνου Σεβαστοῦ
Εὐσεβοῦς Φαμενὼθ ε.

9. *l.* λήψει.

16. ENGAGEMENT OF A WET-NURSE

B.G.U. 1107. 13 B.C.

[2]Πρωτάρχ[ω]ι [3]παρὰ Ἰσιδώρας τῆς Κομ[. . . .
. . . .] μετὰ κυρίου τοῦ ἀ[δελφοῦ Εὐ-
τυχίδου [4]το]ῦ Κομ[. . . .] καὶ παρ[ὰ Δ]ιδ[ύ]μης
[τῆς] Ἀπολ[λωνίου Περ]σείνης [μετὰ κυρίου] [5]τοῦ
ἀδελφοῦ Ἰσχυρίωνος τοῦ Ἀπολλων[ίου Πέρσου τῆς
ἐπιγονῆς. συνχωρεῖ ἡ [6]Διδύ]μη τροφεύσειν καὶ
θηλάσειν ἔξω [πα]ρ' ἑα[τῆι κατὰ πόλιν τῶι ἰδίωι]
[7]αὐτῆς γάλακτι καθαρῶι καὶ ἀφθόρωι ἐπὶ χρ[όνον
μῆ]νας [δεκαὲξ] ἀπὸ Φαρ-[8]μοῦθι τοῦ ἐνεστῶτος
ἑπτακαιδεκάτου (ἔτους) [Καίσαρος] ὃ ἐγδ[έδοται
αὐτῇ ἡ Ἰσιδώρα] [9]δουλικὸν αὐτῆς παιδίον [ἀ]ν-
αίρε[τον] ὑποτ[ίτθιον - - - ὧι ὄνομα - - -]
[10]λαμβάνουσα παρ' αὐτῆς Ἰσιδώρας μισθ[ὸν τοῦ τε
γάλακτος καὶ τῆς τροφείας κατὰ] [11]μῆνα ἕκαστον

3-4. suppl. E.-H. 6. *l.* ἑαυτῆι.

will receive a second instalment of 40 drachmae when the boy has learned all the commentary[a] by heart, and the third instalment, the remaining 40 drachmae, you will receive at the end of the period when the boy can write and read from prose of all kinds without fault. If you make him perfect within the period, I will not await the aforesaid date, though I shall have no right to remove the boy within the period, and he shall remain with you after the period for as many days or months as he may have been absent from work. The 18th year of the Emperor Caesar Titus Aelius Hadrianus Antoninus Augustus Pius, Phamenoth 5.

[a] A collection of the tachygraphic signs.

16. ENGAGEMENT OF A WET-NURSE

13 B.C.

To Protarchus[a] from Isidora daughter of . . ., having with her as guardian her brother Eutychides son of . . ., and from Didyma daughter of Apollonius, Persian, having with her as guardian her brother Ischyrion son of Apollonius, Persian of the Epigone.[b] Didyma agrees to nurse and suckle, outside at her own home in the city, with her own milk pure and untainted, for a period of 16 months from Pharmouthi of the current 17th year of Caesar, the foundling infant slave child . . . called . . . which Isidora has given out to her, receiving from her, Isidora, as wages for milk and nursing ten silver

[a] See No. 3, note *a*. [b] See Glossary.

ἀργυρίου δραχμὰς δέκα καὶ ἐλαίου κοτύλας δ[ύ]ο· οἷς [εὐτα-]12κτουμένην αὐτὴν ποιεῖσθαι τήν τε ἑατῆς καὶ τοῦ παιδίου ἐπιμέλῃαν 13μὴ φθείρουσαν τὸ γάλα μηδ' ἀνδροκοιτοῦσαν μηδ' ἐπικύουσαν [μηδ' ἕτερον] 14παραθηλάζουσαν παιδίον, ἅ τε ἐὰν λάβῃ ἢ πιστευθῇ τῶν τούτου, ταῦτα σῶα συν-15τηρήσειν καὶ ἀποδώσειν ὅταν ἀπαιτῆται ἢ ἐκτείσειν τὴν [ἑκάστου ἀξίαν πλὴν] 16συνφανοῦς ἀπωλείας, ἧς καὶ φανερᾶς γενηθίσης [ἀπο]λελύσ[θω· αὐτόθεν] 17δ' ἀπέσχηκεν ἡ Διδύμη παρὰ τῆς Ἰσιδώρας διὰ χειρὸς ἐξ οἴκου ἔλαιον τῶν πρώτων 18μηνῶν τριῶν τοῦ τε Φαρμοῦθι καὶ Παχὼν καὶ Παῦνι· καὶ μὴ ἐγλείπειν τ[ὴν τροφείαν ἐντὸς] 19τοῦ χρόνου, ἐὰν δέ τι παραβαίνῃ ἐκτίνιν αὐτὴν ἅ τε [εἴληφεν τροφεῖα καὶ] 20ἃ ἐὰν προσλάβῃ σὺν ἡμιολίαι καὶ τὰ βλάβη καὶ δα[παν]ήματα, [ἐκτί]σειν δ' ἔτι [(δραχμὰς)] 21πεντακοσίας καὶ τὸ ὡρισμένον [πρόστιμον, τῆς πράξεως γεινομένης τῇ Ἰσιδώρᾳ] 22ἔκ τε αὐτῆς Διδύμης καὶ [ἐκ τῶν] ὑπαρχόντων αὐτῆς πάν(των) καθ[ά]περ ἐγ δίκ[ης], 23ἀκύρων οὐσῶν καὶ ὧν ἐὰν ἐπενένκῃ πίστεων πασῶν, σκέπης [πάσης]· 24ἕκαστα δὲ αὐτῆς ἐπιτελούσης καὶ τὴν Ἰσιδώραν [χο]ρηγήσειν αὐτῇ 25τὰ κατὰ μῆνα τροφεῖα ὡς πρόκειται ἐπὶ τοὺς λοιποὺς [μῆνας] 26δεκατρεῖς καὶ μὴ ἀποσπάσειν τὸ παιδίον ἐντὸς τοῦ χρόνου [ἢ καὶ αὐτὴν] 27ἐκτίνιν τὸ ἴσον ἐπίτιμον· παραβαλεῖ δὲ ἡ Διδύμη πρὸς [τὴν Ἰσιδώραν] 28κατὰ μῆνα ἕκαστον ἀεὶ διὰ ἡμερῶν τεσσάρων ἄγουσα [καὶ τὸ παιδίον πρὸς τὸ] 29ἐπιθεωρεῖσθαι ὑπ' αὐτῆς. ἀξιοῦ(μεν). (2nd hand) 30⟦Ἰσιδώρα συνχωρῶ κατὰ τὰ προγε[γραμμένα]. 31Εὐτυχίδης ἐπιγέγραμμαι κύριος τῆς ἀδελφ[ῆς]

11. οἷς E.-H. 12. l. ἑαυτῆς, ἐπιμέλειαν. 17. πρώτων E.-H.

drachmae and two cotylae[a] of oil every month. So long as she is duly paid she shall take proper care both of herself and of the child, not injuring her milk nor sleeping with a man nor becoming pregnant nor suckling another child, and whatever things of the child she receives or is entrusted with she shall keep safe and shall give back when demanded or else forfeit the value of each except in the case of manifest loss, on proof of which she shall be exempted. Didyma has forthwith received from Isidora by hand from the house oil for the first three months, Pharmouthi, Pachon, and Pauni. She shall not cease nursing before the end of the time, and if she breaks the agreement in any way she shall forfeit the wages which she has already received and those which she may have received besides, increased by one half, with damages and expenses, and shall moreover pay 500 drachmae and the prescribed fine, Isidora having the right of execution upon the person of Didyma and all her property as if by legal decision, all assurances which she may produce and all resort to protection being invalid. If she fulfils every condition, Isidora shall deliver to her the monthly wages as stated above for the remaining 13 months and shall not remove the child before the end of the time, or she herself shall pay the like penalty. Didyma shall visit Isidora every month regularly on four separate days bringing the child to be inspected by her. We request (ratification). (Signed) I, Isidora, agree on the above terms. I, Eutychides, have professed myself guardian of my sister and have

[a] A cotyla contained about ¼ litre.

<καὶ γέγραφα> 32ὑπὲρ αὐτῆς γρά(μματα) μὴ ἰδυίας.⟧ (3rd hand) 33⟦Διδύμη συνχωρῶ κατὰ τὰ πρ[ογεγραμμένα]. 34Ἰσχυρίων ἐπιγέγραμμαι [τῆς ἀδελφ-]35ῆς μου κύριος καὶ γέγρα[φα ὑπὲρ αὐτῆ-]36ς γράμ<μ>ατα μὴ εἰδυίας.⟧ (1st hand) 37Ἰσιδώ(ρας). (ἔτους) ιζ 38Καίσαρος . . . . .

17. CONTRACT FOR LABOUR IN AN OIL-PRESS

P. Fay. 91. A.D. 99.

1Φαῶ(φι) ιη. ὁμολ(ογία) Θενετκούει<το>ς πρὸ(ς) Λούκιο(ν). 2Ἔτους τρίτου [Α]ὐτοκράτορος Καίσαρος Νερούα 3Τραϊανοῦ Σε[β]αστοῦ Γερμανικοῦ Φαῶφι ὀκ-4τωκαι[δ]εκάτηι, ἐ[ν Εὐ]ημερείᾳ τῆς Θεμίστου 5μερίδος τοῦ Ἀρ[σινο]είτου νομοῦ. ὁμολογεῖ 6Θενετκοῦεις Ἥρ[ω]νος παρεμβάλλουσα Περ-7σείνη ὡς ἐτῶν εἴκοσι ἓξ οὐλὴ ἀντικνημίῳ 8δεξιῶι, μετὰ κυρίου το[ῦ] συνγενοῦς Λεοντᾶ τοῦ 9Ἱππάλου ὡς ἐτῶν πεντήκοντα τεσσάρων 10οὐλὴ μετόπωι ἐγ δεξιῶν, Λουκίωι Βελλήνῳ 11Γεμέλλωι ἀπολυσ[ί]μωι ἀπὸ στρατείας ἐγ λε<γε>ῶνο(ς) 12ὡς ἐτῶν ἑξήκον[τα] ἑπτὰ οὐλὴ ἀντίχιρει ἀριστ(ερᾷ) 13ἔχειν παρ' αὐτ[οῦ] π[αραχρῆμα διὰ] χ[ι]ρ[ὸς ἐ]ξ οἴκ(ου) 14ἀργυρίου δραχ[μὰς] δεκαὲξ ἀρραβῶνα ἀναπόρι-15φον. ἐπάνα[γ]κον οὖν παρεμβαλεῖν τὴν Θεν-16ετκοῦειν ἐν [τ]ῶι ὑ[πά]ρχοντι τῷ Λουκίωι Βελ-17λήνωι Γεμέλ[λ]ῳ [ἐν] Εὐημερείᾳ ἐλαιουργίωι 18ἀφ' ἧς ἡμέρας [ἐ]ὰν [α]ὐτῆι παρανγε[ίλῃ ἐ]λαικοὺς 19καρποὺς ἐκπεπ{π}τωκότας εἰς τὸ ἐνεστὸ(ς) 20τρίτον ἔτος, ποιοῦσαν πάντα ὅσα καθήκει 21παρεμβαλλού[σ]ῃ μέχρει ἐγβάσεως πάσης 22ἐλαιουργίας,

written for her as she is illiterate. I, Didyma, agree on the above terms. I, Ischyrion, have professed myself guardian of my sister and have written for her, as she is illiterate. (Docketed) Isidora's (agreement). The 17th year of Caesar . . .

17. CONTRACT FOR LABOUR IN AN OIL-PRESS

A.D. 99.

Phaophi 18. Agreement of Thenetkouis with Lucius. The third year of the Emperor Caesar Nerva Trajanus Augustus Germanicus, Phaophi 18, at Euhemeria in the division of Themistes in the Arsinoite nome. Thenetkouis daughter of Heron, olive-carrier,[a] Persian, aged about 26 years, with a scar on the right shin, having with her as guardian her kinsman Leontas son of Hippalus, aged about 54 years, with a scar on the right side of the forehead, acknowledges to Lucius Bellenus Gemellus,[b] discharged legionary, with a scar on the left wrist, that she has received from him directly by hand from his house 16 drachmae of silver as irrepudiable earnest-money. Thenetkouis is thereby bound to carry at the olive-press belonging to Lucius Bellenus Gemellus at Euhemeria from whatever day he orders her the olive crop included in the current third year, doing all that is required of a carrier until the completion of the entire oil-manufacture, and receiving from

[a] Probably "one who feeds the press with olives."
[b] See No. 109.

14. *l.* ἀρραβῶνα; so in l. 30.

λαμβάνουσα‹ν› παρὰ τοῦ Λουκίου [23]Βελλήνου τὸν ἡμερήσιον μισθὸν ὡς [24]ἐπὶ τῶν ὁμοίων παρεμβαλλουσῶν ἐν [25]τῇ κώμηι, ὑπολογήσιν δὲ τὸν Λούκιον [26]τὰς τοῦ ἀργ[υ]ρίου δραχμὰς δεκαὲξ κατὰ [27]μέρος ἐκ τῶν ἐσομένων μισθῶν. ἐὰν [28]δὲ μὴ ποιῇ ἡ Θενετκοῦεις κατὰ τὰ προ-[29]γεγραμμένα, ἀποδώσιν αὐτὴ(ν) τῷ Λουκίωι [30]τὸν ἀρραβôνα διπλοῦν, γεινομένης τῷ [31]Λουκίωι Βελλήνωι τῆς πράξεως ἔκ [32]τε τῆς ὁμολ(ογούσης) καὶ ἐκ τῶ(ν) ὑπαρχ(όντων) αὐτῇ πάντω(ν) [33]καθάπερ ἐγ δίκης. ὑπογραφεὺς τῆς Θενε-[34]τκούειτο(ς) Λεοντᾶς ὁ προγεγραμμένος. (2nd hand) [35]Θενετκοῦις Ἥρων[ο]ς Περσίνη μετὰ κυ-[36]ρίου τοῦ συνγε[νοῦ]ς Λεοντᾶ τοῦ Ἱππάλου [37]ὁμολογῶι ἔχειν παρὰ τοῦ Λουκίου τὰς [38]τοῦ ἀραβῶνος ἀργυρίου δραχμὰς δεκα-[39]έξ, καὶ παρεμβαλ[ῶ]ι ἐν τῷ ἐλαιουργίῳ [40]ἀφ' ἑᾶς ἡμέρας [ἐάν] μοι παρανγίλῃς [41]λαμβάνουσα παρὰ σοῦ Λουκίου τοὺς μισθοὺς ‹ὡς› [42]ἐπὶ τῶν ὁμοίων παρανβαλλουσῶν καὶ ἕ-[43]καστα ποιήσω καθὼς πρόκιται. Λεοντᾶς [44]γέγραφα καὶ ὑπὲρ τῆς [Θ]ενεκτούιτος [45]μὴ ἰδότος γράμματα. (1st hand) [46]ἐντέτακτ[αι γ] (ἔτους) Φαῶφι ιη, διὰ Ἥρωνος [47]τοῦ πρὸς τῷ γραφείῳ Εὐημερείας. (3rd hand) [48]Λούκιος Βελλῆνος Γέμελλος δι(ὰ) [49]Ἐπαγάθου ἀπέχω τὰς προκιμέ(νας) [50]καὶ οὐθὲν ἐνκαλῶι [51]ἀργυρίου δραχμὰς δεκαέξ. (ἔτους) πέμ‹π›του Αὐτοκράτορος Καίσαρος Νερούα Τραϊανοῦ Σεβαστοῦ Γερμανικοῦ Τῦβ(ι) ιβ.

40. *l.* ἧς. 42. *l.* παρεμβαλλουσῶν. 45. *l.* εἰδυίας.

Lucius Bellenus her daily wage at the same rate as the similar carriers in the village; and Lucius shall deduct the 16 drachmae of silver by instalments from the wages to be paid. If Thenetkouis does not act in accordance with the conditions above written, she shall pay back to Lucius double the earnest-money, Lucius Bellenus having the right of execution upon the acknowledging party and upon all her property as if by legal decision. Signatory on behalf of Thenetkouis: Leontas the aforesaid. (Subscribed) I, Thenetkouis daughter of Heron, Persian, having with me as guardian my kinsman Leontas son of Hippalus, acknowledge that I have received from Lucius the 16 drachmae of silver forming the earnest-money, and I will carry at the olive-press from whatever day you order me, receiving from you, Lucius, my wages at the same rate as similar carriers, and I will do everything as stated above. I, Leontas, have written for Thenetkouis also, as she is illiterate. (Docketed) Registered in the 3rd year, Phaophi 18, by Heron, keeper of the record-office of Euhemeria. (Receipted) I, Lucius Bellenus Gemellus, have received through Epagathus the aforesaid 16 drachmae of silver and am satisfied. The 5th year of the Emperor Caesar Nerva Trajanus Augustus Germanicus, Tubi 12.[a]

[a] The acknowledgement of the repayment of the earnest-money is dated two years later than the contract.

18. CONTRACT FOR LABOUR IN A VINEYARD AND LEASE OF A FRUIT-GARDEN

P. Oxy. 1631. A.D. 280.

[1]Αὐ[ρηλίῳ Σερήνῳ τῷ καὶ] Σαραπίων[ι Ἀγα]θείνου μητρὸς Ταποσειριάδο[ς] ἀπὸ τῆς λαμπρᾶς καὶ λαμ-[2][προτάτης Ὀξυρυγχιτῶν] πόλεω[ς] [3]π[αρὰ Αὐρηλίων Κτιστ]οῦ Ῥ[ο]ύφου [μητρ]ὸς Διονυσίας καὶ τοῦ υἱοῦ Πτολεμαίου μητρὸς Ταύριος ἀμφοτέρων [4]ἀπὸ [τῆς λαμπρᾶς καὶ λ]αμπροτά[της] Ὀξυρυ[γ]χ[ιτ]ῶν πόλεως καὶ Πελωίου Ἡρακλήου μη(τρὸς) Ταπονθεῦτος [5]ἀπὸ κ[ώμης Τανάεως?]. ἑκου[σί]ω[ς ἐπι]δεχόμεθα μισθώσασθαι ἐφ' ἐνιαυτὸν ἕνα ἔτι ἀπὸ α Ἁθὺρ τοῦ [6]ἐνεσ[τῶτος ἕκτου? ἔτους] τὰ ἀμπελουργ[ι]κὰ ἔργα πάντα το[ῦ] ὑπάρχοντός σοι περὶ κώμην Τανάειν [7]ἀμπε[λικοῦ κτήματος κα]ὶ τῆς πρ[ο]σ[ούσ]ης [καλ]αμείας ὅσ[ο]ν ἕκαστ[ό]ν ἐστιν ἀρουρηδοῦ, ἡμεῖς μὲν οἱ πε-[8]ρὶ τὸν [Αὐρήλιον Κτιστὸν] κατὰ τὸ ἥμ[ισυ], ἐγὼ δὲ ὁ Πελώιος κατὰ τὸ λοιπὸν ἥμισυ, ἅπερ ἔργα ἐστὶν [9]τῆς ἀ[μπέλου τ]ιλμὸς καλάμου, συλλο[γὴ] καὶ μεταφ[ο]ρὰ τούτου, ξυλοτομία δικαία, ἀνκαλισμὸς καὶ δέσις, [10]ἀ[π]οκ[οπὴ καὶ ? πρ]οσφ[ορὰ] φύλλων καὶ ἐμβολὴ ἐκτὸ[ς] πλαστῶν, ἀπωρυγισμὸς ὅσων δεῖ ἀπωρύγων, σκαφη-[11]τός, γ[ύ]ρ[ω]σις κ[αὶ π]αρα[γρ]αφή, τῆς δὲ καλ[α]μουργίας οὔσης πρὸς σὲ τὸν γεοῦχον, τῆς δὲ ταύτης ὑπουργίας [12]οὔσης πρ[ὸ]ς ἡμᾶς, τῶν δὲ λοιπῶν ἔργω[ν] μετὰ τὰ προκείμενα ὄντων πρὸς ἡμᾶς, ἅπερ ἐστὶν σκαλ-[13]μός, βλαστολογία, [π]αραμυθιακὴ ἐργασία, διάστασις,

5. For ἐπ' ἐνιαυτόν: so in l. 21. 10. ἐκβολή possible.

18. CONTRACT FOR LABOUR IN A VINE-YARD AND LEASE OF A FRUIT-GARDEN

A.D. 280.

To Aurelius Serenus also called Sarapion son of Agathinus and Taposirias, of the illustrious and most illustrious city of Oxyrhynchus, from the Aurelii Ctistus son of Rufus and Dionysia and his son Ptolemaeus, whose mother is Tauris, both of the illustrious and most illustrious city of Oxyrhynchus, and Peloius son of Heracleus and Tapontheus, of the village of Tanais (?). We voluntarily undertake to lease for one year more from Hathur 1 of the present 6th (?) year all the vine-tending operations in the vineyard owned by you in the area of the village of Tanais and the adjoining reed-plantation, whatever be the acreage of each, we, the party of Aurelius Ctistus, undertaking half and I, Peloius, the remaining half, which operations are, concerning the vineyard, plucking of reeds,[a] collection and transport of them, proper pruning, making into bundles and binding, stripping and transport of leaves and throwing them outside the mud-walls, layering as many vine-shoots as are necessary, digging, scooping hollows round the vines and trenching, you, the landlord, being responsible for the arrangement of the reeds and we for assisting you in the work, we being responsible for the remaining operations after those mentioned, namely, breaking up the ground, picking off shoots, keeping the vines well tended, giving

[a] For training the vines. As Egypt grew very little wood, reeds were in great request for this purpose.

ἀνάλημψις, φυλλολογίαι αἱ ἐνχρῄζουσαι, τῶν δὲ [14]καλαμίων διτομία καλαμίου ἑκατέρου, ἐπάρδευσις καὶ βοτανισμὸς διηνεκής, ἔτι δὲ καὶ στῆναι ἡμᾶς [15]π[αρ]ὰ σοὶ ἐ[ν τῷ] κτήματι καὶ ἐν τῇ καλαμείᾳ πρὸ τῶν ὄνων χωφορούντων πρὸς τὸ ὅπου δεῖ τὸν χοῦν βάλλε-[16]σθαι, καὶ πο[ι]ησόμεθα τὴν τῶν χωρούντων εἰς τὸν οἶνον κ[ο]ύφων κομπασίαν, καὶ ταῦτα λαβόντα τὸν [17]οἶνον [σ]υνθήσομεν ἐν τῷ ἡλιαστηρίῳ καὶ ἐπαλείψομεν καὶ κεινήσομεν καὶ μεταδιαιράσομεν καὶ πα-[18]ραφυλάξομεν ἐς ὅσον ἐν ἡλιαστηρίῳ ἀπόκ[ε]ιται, μισθοῦ τῶν προκειμένων ἔργων πάντων ἀργυρίου δρα-[19]χμῶν τετρακισχειλίων πεντακοσίων καὶ πυροῦ ἀρταβῶν δέκα καὶ οἴνου παρὰ ληνὸν κεραμίων [20]τεσσάρ[ω]ν, οὕσπερ μισθοὺς ἀπολημψόμεθα κατὰ μέρος κατὰ προκοπὴν τῶν ἔργων. καὶ ὡσαύτως ἐπι-[21]δ[ε]χόμεθα μισ[θώ]σασθαι ἐφ' ἐνιαυτὸν [ἕνα καρποὺς] τῶν ὄντων ἐν τῇ παλ[α]ι[ᾷ ἀ]μ[πέ]λῳ φοινείκων καὶ ἀκρο-[22]δρύων πάντων, ὑπὲρ ὧν τελέσομεν ἐκ[φόρια] ἔκτακτα φοίνικος χλωρο[ῦ ἀ]ρτάβην μίαν ἥμισυ, πατητοῦ [23]ἀρτάβην μίαν ἥμισυ, καρ[υ]ωτοῦ ἀρτάβην μίαν ἥμισυ, ἐλαι[ῶ]ν μελαινῶν ἀρτάβης ἥμισυ, περσικῶν [24]ἐκλε[κτ]ῶν πεντακοσίων, κιτρίων δεκα[πέ]ντε, σύκων θερινῶν μέχρι ἀναβάσεως τετρακοσίων, [25]χειμερινῶν πε[ν]τακ[οσί]ων, [σικύ?]δια λευκοπε[ίο]να μεγάλα τέ[σσ]αρα. ἔτι δὲ κ[α]ὶ τὸ προσὸν πωμάρι-[26]ον ἐξ νότου τοῦ [χ]ωρίου [ὁμοίως ? ἐπὶ] τοῖ[ς ἐ]πάνω μ[ι]σθοῖς ἀρώ[σο]μεν [καὶ] ποιήσομε[ν] τὴν ἐπάρδε[υσιν], βοτα-[27]νολογ[ία]ν καὶ τὰ ἄλλα [τὰ κατὰ] καιρὸν ἔρ[γ]α πάντα, τῆς τού[του] καλαμουργίας μόνης καὶ τῆς στρώσεως [28]τοῦ χοῦ ὄντων πρὸς σὲ τ[ὸ]ν [γεοῦ]χον, ἀκινδύνων παντὸς

space to the growths, cutting back, needful thinnings of foliage; and concerning the reed-plantations (?), the bisection of each of the two,[a] watering and continual weeding; and further we agree to assist you in the vineyard and the reed-plantation in superintending the asses which bring earth, in order that the earth may be thrown in the proper places, and we will perform the testing of the jars intended for the wine, and will put these, when they have been filled with wine, in the open-air shed, and plaster them, and move the wine, and strain it from one jar into another, and watch over them as long as they are stored in the open-air shed, the wage for all the aforesaid operations being 4500 silver drachmae, 10 artabae of wheat, and 4 jars of wine at the vat, which wages we are to receive in instalments according to the progress of the operations. And we likewise undertake to lease for one year the produce of all the date-palms and fruit-trees which are in the old vineyard, for which we will pay as a special rent 1½ artabae of fresh dates, 1½ artabae of pressed dates, 1½ artabae of walnut-dates, ½ artaba of black olives, 500 selected peaches, 15 citrons, 400 summer figs before the inundation, 500 winter figs, 4 large white fat melons (?). Moreover we will in consideration of the above wages likewise (?) plough the adjoining fruit-garden to the south of the vineyard, and will do the watering, weeding, and all the other seasonal operations, only the arrangement of reeds in it and the strewing of earth being left to you, the landlord, the rent being

[a] The meaning is obscure.

17. *l.* μεταδιεράσομεν. 26. *l.* ἐκ νέου.

κινδύνου. βεβαιουμένης δὲ ἡμῖν τῆς ἐπιδο-[29]χῆς ποιήσομεν τὰ τῆς ἀμπέλου καὶ πωμαρίου καὶ καλαμείας κατὰ καιρὸν ἔργα πάντα εὐκαίρως καὶ εὐ-[30]αρέστως, τῶν σῶν ἐπακολουθούντων ἅπασι, καὶ ἀποδώσομεν τὰ ἔκτακτα τῷ δέοντι καιρῷ [31]ἀνυπερθέτως, καὶ μετὰ τὸν χρόνον παραδώσομεν τὰ μισθούμενα σύμφυτα, ἐπιμεμελημέ-[32]να τοῖς ἔργοις καὶ ἀπὸ θρύων καὶ βοτάνης καὶ ἀγρώστεως πάσης, γεινομένης σοι τῆς πράξεως [33]παρὰ ⟦λλ⟧ ἡμῶν ἀλληλ[εγ]γύων [ὄ]ντ[ων] εἰς ἔκτεισιν, ὡς καθήκει. κυρία ἡ ἐπιδοχή, καὶ ἐπερωτη-[34]θέντες ὡμολο[γ]ήσαμεν. [(ἔτους) ἕκ?]του Α[ὐτ]οκράτορος Καίσαρος Μάρκου Αὐρηλίου Πρόβου Περσικοῦ Μεγίστ[ο]υ [35]Γοθθικοῦ Μεγίσ[το]υ Εὐσεβοῦς Εὐτυχοῦς Σεβαστοῦ Χοίακ κε. (2nd hand) Αὐρήλ(ιοι) Κτιστὸς κι ὁ υἱὸς [36]Πτολεμα[ῖος] κ[αὶ] Πελώιος ἐπεδεξάμεθα εἰς μίσθωσιν τὰ [37]ἀμπελου[ργικὰ ἔ]ργ[α] πά[ν]τα ἐπὶ τοῖς ἐπάνω μισθοῖς, καὶ ἀποδώ-[38]σομεν τὰ [ἔκτακ]τα ὡς π[ρ]όκειται, [κ]αὶ ἐπερωτηθέν[τες] ὡ-[39]μολογή[σαμεν. Τιβ]έριος Κλαύδιος Ὡρίων ἔγρα(ψα) ὑπὲρ [α]ὐτῶν [40]μὴ ἰδότ[ων γρά]μματα.

Verso: (1st ? hand) [41][ἐπ]ιδ[οχ]ὴ [Α(ὐρηλίου Κτισ]τοῦ ἀλλαγεῖσα.

19. CONTRACT WITH STONE-CUTTERS

P. Oxy. 498. 2nd cent. A.D.

[1]Ἀντίγραφον. Ἀντωνίᾳ Ἀσκληπιάδι [2]τῇ καὶ Κυρίᾳ διὰ Ἀπολλωνίου ἐπιτρό-[3]που παρὰ Ἀσκλᾶτος Ἀλεξάνδρου [4]καὶ Ἀπολλωνίου Ἀμόιτος μητρὸς

secured against all risks. If our undertaking is guaranteed to us, we will perform all the seasonal operations of the vineyard and fruit-garden and reed-plantation at the proper times and to your satisfaction, your agents keeping a check on everything, and we will pay the special rent at the required time without delay, and at the end of the period we will deliver the objects of the lease under cultivation, well cared for by our operations, and free from rushes, weeds, and all coarse grass, you having the right of execution upon us, who are mutual securities for the payment of the rent, as is fitting. This undertaking is valid, and in answer to the formal question we have given our consent. The 6th (?) year of the Emperor Caesar Marcus Aurelius Probus Persicus Maximus Gothicus Maximus Pius Felix Augustus, Choiak 25. (Signed) We, the Aurelii Ctistus and his son Ptolemaeus and Peloius, have undertaken under a lease all the vine-tending operations on promise of the above wages, and we will pay the special rent as aforesaid, and in answer to the formal question we have given our consent. I, Tiberius Claudius Horion, have written for them, as they are illiterate. (Endorsed) Undertaking of Aurelius Ctistus replacing the previous one.

19. CONTRACT WITH STONE-CUTTERS

2nd cent. A.D.

Copy. To Antonia Asclepias also called Cyria, through her guardian Apollonius, from Asclas son of Alexander and Apollonius son of Amois and of

[5]Ταῦριος ἀμφοτέρων ἀπ' Ὀξυρύγχων [6]πόλεως. ἐπιδεχόμεθα λαξείαν [7]τῶν οἰκοδομουμένων λίθων κύ-[8]βων καμηλικῶν ἀπὸ βορινῆς λατο-[9]μίας εἰς οἰκίαν σου τῆς Ἀντωνίας [10]ἐπ' ἀμφόδου Παμμένους Παραδεί-[11]σου μισθοῦ τῆς λαξείας τῶν μὲν [12]ἐξωτέρω λίθων κύβων καμηλι-[13]κῶν ὡς τῶν δεκαὲξ δραχμῶν τεσσ[ά-][14]ρων, [τ]ῶν δὲ ἐ[σ]ωτεριαίων ὡς τῶν [15]τρ[ιάκ]οντ[α δρα]χμῶν τεσσάρων, καὶ [16]τῶν [ἀ]ντιβλημάτων ὡς τῶν ἑκατὸν [17]λίθων κύβων καμηλικῶν δραχμῶν τρι-[18]ῶν, καὶ κεφαλειτοπαραμηκῶν ἐξωτ[ε-][19]ριαίων λίθων κύβων καμηλικῶν ὡς [20]τῶν δεκαὲξ δραχμῶν ὀκτὼ καὶ ἐσω-[21]τεριαίων λίθων κύβων καμηλικῶν [22]κεφαλειτοπαραμηκῶν ὡς τῶν τρι-[23]άκοντα δραχμῶν ὀκτώ, πελεκημά-[24]των λίθων [κ]ύβων καμηλικῶν ὡς τῶ[ν] [25]πεντήκον[τα δ]ραχμῶν τεσσάρων κα[ὶ] [26]πελεκημάτ[ων] κεφαλε[ι]τοπαραμηκῶν [27]λίθω[ν κύ]βων [κα]μηλικῶν ὡς τῶν πεν-[28]τήκ[ο]ντα δρ[α]χ[μῶ]ν ὀκτώ. τὰ δὲ προκεί-[29]μενα πάντα ἀ[πολα]ξ[εύσο]μεν οὐδε-[30]μιᾶς πρὸς ἡμ[ᾶς] οὔσης κ[ο]σμοπ[ο]ιήσε-[31]ως, λήμψεται δὲ ἕκαστος ἡμῶν ἑκ[άσ-][32]της ἡμέρας ἧς ἐὰν ἐργάζηται κα[ὶ ἄρ-][33]τον ἕνα καὶ προσφάγιον. ἐὰν δὲ χρε[ί-][34]αν ἔχωσι οἱ οἰκοδόμοι ὑπουργίας λαξι-[35]κῆς, ἡμεῖς ὑπουργήσομεν ἢ καί τις ἡ-[36]μῶν, ἕκαστος λαμβάνων ἑ[κ]άστης [37]ἡμέρας μισθοῦ ὑπουργίας δραχμὰς [38]τέσσαρας καὶ ἕκαστος ἡμῶν ὁμοίως [39]ἑκάστης ἡμέρας ἄρτον ἕνα καὶ προσ-[40]φάγι[ον. μ]έχρι δὲ δευτέρας καὶ εἰκάδος [41]{μ[έχρι] δὲ δευτέρας καὶ εἰκάδος} τοῦ [42][ὄντος μ]ην[ὸς] Ἐπεὶφ ἐξόντος σοι ἑτέροις [43][μεταμισθοῦ]ν τὴν αὐτὴν λαξείαν [44][τὴν τῶν προκει]μένων λίθων κύβων [45][καμηλικῶν ἀπὸ

Tauris, both of Oxyrhynchus. We undertake to cut the squared building-stones transportable[a] by camel, to be taken from the northern quarry for the house of you, Antonia, in the quarter of Pammenes' Garden, at the following rate of payment: the outer squared camel stones at 4 drachmae for 16, the inner ones at 4 drachmae for 30, the *antiblemata*[b] at 3 drachmae for 100 squared camel stones, oblong corner-stones at 8 drachmae for 16 outer squared camel stones and at 8 drachmae for 30 inner ones, axe-hewn squared camel stones at 4 drachmae for 50 and axe-hewn squared camel corner-stones at 8 drachmae for 50. All the aforesaid stones we will cut, but no ornamentation shall be required of us. Each of us shall also receive for each day that he works one loaf and relish. If the builders need assistance from stone-cutters, we or one of us will assist them, each man receiving 4 drachmae as wages for each day's assistance and each of us likewise one loaf and relish for each day. Until the 22nd of the present month of Epeiph you have the right to transfer to others this contract for cutting the aforesaid squared camel stones from the northern

[a] Literally "camel stones"; but probably the meaning is that they were carried by camel.

[b] Stones inserted in gaps in the masonry.

βο]ρινῆς λατομίας 46[. . . . .] αν σου μεθ[. . 47. . . . .]ς εἰς ἡμέ[ρας 48. . . . . κυρία ἡ ἐπι]δοχή. ἔτου[ς - - -

20. ENGAGEMENT OF CASTANET DANCERS

P. Cornell 9. A.D. 206.

1Ἰσιδώρᾳ κροταλι[στ]ρίᾳ 2παρὰ Ἀρτ[ε]μι[σί]ας ἀπὸ κώ-3μης Φιλαδελφείας. βούλομαι 4παρ[α]-λαβεῖν σε σὺν ἑτέραις κρο-5ταλ[ισ]τρίαις β λιτουρ-γῆ{σα}σαι 6παρ' ἡμῖν ἐπὶ ἡμ[έρ]ας ἓξ ἀπὸ 7τῆς κδ τοῦ Παῦ[ν]ι μηνὸς κατ' ἀρ-8χαίους, λαμβαν[ό]ν-των ὑμῶν 9ὑπὲρ μισθοῦ καθ' [ἡμ]έραν ἑκάσ-10την (δραχμὰς) λϛ καὶ ὑ[πὲ]ρ πασῶν τῶν 11ἡμε[ρ]ῶν κριθῆς [(ἀρτάβας)] δ καὶ ἄρ-12των ζεύγη κ̄, ὅσ[α] δὲ ἐὰν κα-13τενέγκηται ἱμά[τ]ια ἢ χρυσᾶ 14κόσμια, ταῦτα σ[ῶ]α παραφυ-15λάξομεν, παρ[εξ]όμεθα δὲ 16ὑμῖν κατερχομέ[νο]ις ὄνους 17δύο καὶ ἀνερχο[μ]έ-νοις 18τοὺς ἴσους. 19ἔτους ιδ Λουκίου Σεπτι[μ]ίου Σεουήρου 20Εὐσεβοῦς Περτίνακος [καὶ] Μάρκου 21Αὐρηλίου Ἀντωνί[νο]υ Εὐσεβοῦς 22Σεβαστῶν καὶ Που[βλί]ου Σεπτιμίου 23Γέτα Καίσαρος Σεβ[α-στο]ῦ, Παῦνι ιϛ̄.

21. ENGAGEMENT OF MUSICIANS

P. Oxy. 1275. 3rd cent. A.D.

1[Ὁ]μολογοῦσιν ἀ[λλήλοις (2nd hand) Αὐ]ρήλιοι Ὀν-2νῶφρις Ἀμμω[νίου] (1st hand) μητρὸς 3[Θα]-ϊσοῦτος καὶ Ἀφῦγχ[ις Ἡ]ρα[κ]λᾶτος μητ(ρὸς) 4Τ[α]ϋσείριος καὶ Ἑρμ[ογ]ένης Διονυσίου 5μητ(ρὸς)

quarry. . . . . The engagement is valid. Year . . .

20. ENGAGEMENT OF CASTANET DANCERS

A.D. 206.

To Isidora, castanet dancer, from Artemisia, of the village of Philadelphia. I wish to engage you with two other castanet dancers to perform at my house for six days from the 24th of the month Pauni according to the old reckoning,[a] receiving between you for wages 36 drachmae for each day and for the whole six days 4 artabae of barley and 20 pairs of loaves, and whatever garments or gold ornaments you bring down we will safely guard, and we will provide two donkeys for you when you come down[b] and the same when you return. The 14th year of Lucius Septimius Severus Pius Pertinax and Marcus Aurelius Antoninus Pius, Augusti, and Publius Septimius Geta Caesar Augustus. Pauni 16.

[a] The old Egyptian year, *annus vagus*, not entirely driven out of use by the introduction of the Julian year.
[b] From Arsinoe, the metropolis of the nome.

2. Ἀρτεμισίας uncertain; Westermann reads -ης. 12. *l.* κατενέγκητε.

21. ENGAGEMENT OF MUSICIANS

3rd cent. A.D.

The Aurelii Onnophris son of Ammonius and of Thaisous, Aphunchis son of Heraclas and of Tausiris, Hermogenes son of Dionysius and of Heraclous,

Ἡρακ[λο]ῦτος καὶ [. . . . . .]σις Φ[ι]λώτου 6μητρ[ὸ]ς Ἀριστοῦτος κ[αὶ . . . . . .] Ἀμμ[ω]νίου, 7οἱ πέντε π[ρο]στάται κώμης Σούεως, 8καὶ Κοπρεὺς Σαραπάμμων[ος] ὁ προεσ-9τὼς συμφωνίας αὐλητῶν καὶ μουσικῶν, 10οἱ μὲν περὶ τὸν Ὀννῶφριν παρειλη-11φέναι τὸν Κοπρέα μετὰ τῆς ἑαυτοῦ 12συμφωνίας λειτουργήσοντας τοῖς 13ἀπὸ τῆς προκιμένης κώμης ἐφ' ἡμέ-14ρας ἑορτῶν πέντε ἀπὸ δεκάτης Φαμε-15νὼθ τοῦ ἐνεστῶτ(ος) β (ἔτους) μισθοῦ ἡμε-16ρησίως δραχμῶν ἑκατὸν τεσσαράκοντα 17καὶ ἄρτων ζευγῶν τεσσαράκοντα, 18ἐλαίου ῥαφανίνου κοτυλῶν ὀκτώ, καὶ 19ὅλων τῶν ἡμερῶν οἴνου κεραμίου ἑνός, 20ὄξους κεραμίου ἑνός, ἐνδεῦθεν δὲ 21ὁμολογῖ ὁ Κοπρεὺς ἐσχηκέναι εἰς λό-22[γο]ν ἀραβῶν[ος] δραχμὰς εἴκοσι. παρα-23λήμψ[ον]ται δὲ οἱ περὶ τὸν Ὀννῶφριν 24[τ]ὸν Κ[οπρ]έα μετὰ τῆς ἑαυτοῦ συμφωνίας 25ἀπὸ τοῦ Ὀ[ξ]υρυγχείτου διὰ ὄνων δέκα καὶ ἀπο-26κα[ταστήσ]ουσι εἰς τὴν προκιμένην κώμην - - -

22. ENGAGEMENT OF A FLUTE-PLAYER

Stud. Pal. xiii. p. 6. A.D. 322.

1[Ὑπατεία]ς [τ]ῶν δεσποτῶν ἡμῶν 2[Λικινίου Σεβαστοῦ] τὸ [ϛ]" καὶ [Λικ]ινίου τοῦ 3[ἐπιφανεστάτου Καίσ]αρος τὸ β". 4Α[ὐρηλίῳ Εὐγε]νίῳ γυμνασιάρχῳ βουλευτῇ 5Ἑρμοῦ πόλεως 6Αὐρήλιος [Ψενῦμις Κ]ολλούθου μητρὸς Μελιτί-7νης α[ὐλητ]ὴ[ς ἀ]πὸ Ἑρμοῦ πόλεως χαίρειν. 8ὁμολο[γῶ συντ]ετῖ[σθαι κα]ὶ συνπεπῖσθαι 9πρὸς σὲ τὸν γεοῦχον ὥστε με ἀπαντήσιν 10πρ[ὸς κώμη]ν . . . . ριν

8. *l.* συντ]εθει[σθαι.

. . . sis son of Philotas and of Aristous, and . . . son of Ammonius, all five presidents of the village of Souis, and Copreus son of Sarapammon, head of a company of flute-players and musicians, mutually acknowledge that Onnophris and his associates have engaged Copreus with his company to perform for the inhabitants of the aforesaid village for five feast-days from the 10th of Phamenoth of the current 2nd year, at a daily wage of 140 drachmae, 40 pairs of loaves and 8 cotylae of coleseed oil and an allowance for the whole time of one jar of wine and one jar of sour wine [a]; and Copreus acknowledges herewith that he has received as earnest-money 20 drachmae. Onnophris and his associates shall send ten donkeys to meet Copreus and his company coming from the Oxyrhynchite nome and transport them to the aforesaid village . . .

[a] The "vinegar" of the New Testament (Matt. xxvii. 48).

---

20. *l.* ἐντεῦθεν.

22. ENGAGEMENT OF A FLUTE-PLAYER

A.D. 322.

In the consulship of our masters Licinius Augustus for the 6th time and Licinius the most eminent Caesar for the 2nd time. To Aurelius Eugenius, gymnasiarch and senator of Hermopolis, from Aurelius Psenumis son of Colluthus and Melitina, flute-player, of Hermopolis, greeting. I acknowledge that I have contracted and agreed with you the landlord to present myself at the village of . . . at

καὶ τρύγας τῶν ὄντων [11][ἐκεῖ ἀμπελικῶ]ν χωρί[ω]ν μ[ε]τὰ τῶν [12]συν[τ]ετα[γμ]ένων ληνοβατῶν καὶ ἀμέμπτως [13]ὑ[πηρετήσ]ασθαι τοῖς ληνοβάταις καὶ τοῖς ἄλλοις [14]ἐν τῇ αὐλήσει καὶ [μὴ] ἀπολειφθῆναι τῶν ληνο-[15]βατῶν μέχρι τάξεως αὐτῆς τῆς τρύγης [16]τῆς προ[σ]αγούσης {τρύγης} εὐτυχοῦς δεκάτης [17]ἰνδικτί[ονος, ἐπ]ὶ δὲ τ[ῇ α]ὐλήσει καὶ τῇ τέρψει [18]λήμψ[ομαι] τὰ ἑσταμένα παρὰ τῶν ὑπευ-[19]θύνων. [τὸ σύ]μφωνον κύριον, ὃ καὶ [20]μοναχ[ῶς ἐ]ξεδόμην, καὶ ἐπερωτ(ηθεὶς) ὡμολόγ(ησα). [21]ὑ[πατείας τῆς] προκ(ειμένης) Χοίακ κ̅δ̅. (2nd hand) [22]Αὐ[ρ(ήλιος) Ψε]ν[ῦμις] ἀποπληρώσω [23]τὰ ἐ[γγεγρ]αμμένα ὡς πρόκειται. Αὐρ(ήλιος) [Πιν]ουτίων βοηθ(ὸς) Ἀνικήτου [25]ἔ[γρ(αψα)] ὑ[πὲ]ρ α(ὐτοῦ) γρ(άμματα) μὴ εἰδ(ότος).

Verso: [σύμφωνον Αὐρηλί]ου Ψε[ν]ύμι[ος εἰ(ς) Εὐγ]ένει[ον].

23. CONTRACT WITH PURPLE-DYERS

P. Grenf. ii. 87. A.D. 602.

[1]+ Ἐν ὀνόματι τοῦ κυρίου [κ]αὶ δεσπότου Ἰησοῦ [2]Χριστοῦ τοῦ θεοῦ καὶ σω[τ]ῆρος ἡμῶν, [3]βασιλείας τοῦ θειοτάτου [ἡ]μῶν δεσπότου [4]Φλ(αουίου) Μαυρικίου Τιβερίου τοῦ αἰωνίου Αὐγούστου [5]Αὐτοκράτορος ἔτους εἰκοστοῦ Παχὼν εἰκὰς ὀγδόη, [6]ἀρχ(ῇ) ἕκτης ἰνδ(ικτίονος), ἐν Ἑρμοῦ πόλει τῆς Θηβαΐδος. + [7]Αὐρήλιοι Ἰωάννης υἱὸς Φοιβάμμονος ἐκ [8]μητρὸς Στεφαν[ῶ]τος καὶ Μηνᾶ καὶ Ψᾶ [9]οἱ ἐμοὶ υἱοὶ κογχισταὶ ἀπὸ τῆς Ἑρμουπολιτῶν [10]+ κύρῳ τῷ θεοφιλεστάτῳ πρεσβυτέρῳ καὶ αὐθέντῃ [11]στιππουργῷ υἱῷ Βίκτο[ρ]ος ἀπὸ τῆς αὐτῆς

the vintage of the vineyards which are there along with the appointed grape-treaders and without fault assist the grape-treaders and the other workers by my flute-playing and not leave the grape-treaders until the completion of the vintage of the approaching auspicious 10th indiction; and for the flute-playing and the entertainment I shall receive the prescribed fee from those responsible. This agreement, which I have issued in a single copy, is valid, and in answer to the formal question I have given my consent. The aforesaid consulship, Choiak 24. (Signed) I, Aurelius Psenumis, will fulfil the terms of the engagement as stated above. I, Aurelius Pinution, assistant of Anicetus, have written for him, as he is illiterate. (Endorsed) Agreement of Aurelius Psenumis with Eugenius.

23. CONTRACT WITH PURPLE-DYERS

A.D. 602.

In the name of our Lord and Master Jesus Christ, our God and Saviour, in the 20th year of the reign of our most godlike master Flavius Mauricius Tiberius the eternal Augustus and Imperator, on the 28th of Pachon, beginning of the 6th indiction, at Hermopolis in the Thebaid. The Aurelii John son of Phoebammon and of Stephanos and my sons Menas and Psa, purple-dyers, of Hermopolis, to my lord [a] the most pious elder and master flax-worker, son of Victor, of the said city, greeting. We acknowledge

[a] The omission of the name is unusual, but as it is given below as Colluthus, we are obliged to read κύρῳ rather than Κύρῳ, "Cyrus."

12 πόλεως χαίρειν. ὁμολογοῦμεν ἀδιαιρέτως 13 ἐσχηκέναι καὶ δεδέχθαι παρ' αὐτῆς λόγῳ 14 προχρείας τῆς ἡμῶν κογχιστικῆς 15 τέχνης χρυσοῦ νομισμάτ[ια π]έντε παρὰ 16 κεράτια ἓξ ἕκαστον ζυγῷ Ἑρμοῦ πόλεως, 17 γί(νεται) χρ(υσ.) νο(μ.) ε π(αρὰ) κερ(άτ.) λ, ἐφ' ᾧ ἡμᾶς παραμεῖναί 18 σοι καὶ προσεδρεῦσαί τῷ σ[ῷ ἐ]ργαστηρίῳ 19 καὶ ἐργάσασθαί σοι εἰς τὴν ἡμῶν κογχιστικ(ὴν) 20 τέχνην ἐπὶ τοῦ ἔργου τῆς παρούσης ἕκτης ἰνδ(ικτίονος) 21 ἀπὸ κατάρξεως τῆς τέχνης μέχρι καταλύσεως 22 αὐτῆς, καὶ κογχίσαι σοι ἀπὸ δεσμιτίων διακοσίων 23 εἴκοσι πέντε ὑπὲρ ἑκάστου νομισματίου 24 ἑνὸς παρὰ κεράτια ἕξ, ἡμῶν μέντοι γε 25 παρεξομένων τὰ τούτων ἐργα[λί]τια, χωρίς τινος 26 ὑπερθέσεως καὶ ἀντιλογίας καὶ κρί[σ]εως καὶ δίκης, 27 καὶ μὴ δύνασθαι ἡμᾶς ἀποστῆναι τοῦ ἐργαζομένου 28 σοι ἄχρι καταλύσεως τῆς σῆς τέχνης· εἰ δὲ τοῦτο 29 ποιήσομεν, παρέξομεν λόγῳ καταδίκης 30 τοῦ νομίσματος ἑνὸς παρὰ κεράτια ἓξ κεράτια 31 ἓξ πρὸς τῇ ἀποδόσει τῆς αὐτῆς προχρείας, 32 λαμβάνοντες μέντοι γε παρὰ σοῦ ἡμέραν μίαν 33 καθ' ἑβδομάδα ἀπὸ φόλλεων δύο ἑκάστου 34 δεσμιτίου, κινδύνῳ ἡμῶν καὶ πόρῳ τῆς 35 ἡμῶν παντοίας ὑποστάσεως. τὸ παρὸν γραμματεῖον 36 κύριον καὶ βέβαιον καὶ ἐπερωτηθέντες ὡμολο(γήσαμεν). (2nd hand) 37 + Αὐρήλιοι Ἰωάννης Φοιβάμμονος καὶ Μηνᾶ 38 καὶ Ψᾶ οἱ ἐμοὶ υἱοὶ οἱ προκ(είμενοι) ἐθέμεθα τοῦτο 39 τὸ γραμματεῖον ὡς πρόκ(ειται). + Αὐρ(ήλιος) Ἰωάννης Θεοδώρου 40 ἀπὸ Ἑρμοῦ (πόλεως) ἀξ(ιωθεὶς) ἔγραψα ὑπὲρ αὐτῶν γραμμ(άτα) μὴ εἰδότων. (3rd hand) 41 + Κόλλουθος Βίκτορος σὺν θεῷ 42 [. . . . . ὡς πρό]κ(ειται ?) [

that we have jointly received and accepted from your worship by way of advance for our craft of purple-dyeing five gold solidi less six carats[a] each on the Hermopolitan standard, total 5 gold sol. less 30 car., on condition that we remain with you and be attached to your factory and work for you at our craft of purple-dyeing on the work of the present 6th indiction from the commencement to the completion of the process and that for every solidus less six carats we dye for you the contents of 225 bundles, ourselves providing the tools for these, without any delay or dispute or lawsuit or judgement, and that we cannot leave the work being done for you until the completion of your business; if we do so, on each solidus less six carats we shall pay you by way of fine six carats in addition to the repayment of the said advance, though in any case we receive from you on one day each week two folles for each bundle,[b] and this at our own peril and out of our own property of every kind. The present deed is valid and guaranteed, and in answer to the formal question we have given our consent. (Signed) We, the Aurelii John son of Phoebammon and Menas and Psa my sons, the aforesaid, have made this deed as above. I, Aurelius John son of Theodorus, of Hermopolis, have written for them at their request, as they are illiterate. I, Colluthus son of Victor, by the grace

[a] A solidus contained nominally 24 carats.

[b] This parenthetical clause refers to the regular payment of the dyers apart from the question of the advance. A follis at this period was roughly worth about $\frac{1}{200}$ of a solidus.

---

18. σ[ου Edd. 22. *l.* δεσμιδίων. 25. *l.* ἐργαλεί-δια: ἐργα[λ]εῖα Crönert. 32. *l.* ἡμέρᾳ μιᾷ.

Verso: [43] + χ(ειρογραφία) π[ρ]οχρ(είας) ϛ ἰνδ(ικτίονος) χρ(υσοῦ) νο(μισματίων) ε π(αρὰ) κ(εράτια) λ γενομέ(νης) ὑ(πὲρ) Ἰωάννου Φοιβάμμωνος καὶ Μηνᾶ κ[αὶ Ψᾶ] [44] ἀπὸ Ἑρμοῦ πόλε(ως).

24. CONTRACT FOR THE CHARGE OF A STABLE

P. Oxy. 138. A.D. 610–611.

[1] Ἐν ὀνόματι τοῦ κυρ[ίο]υ κ[αὶ δεσπότου Ἰησοῦ Χριστοῦ, θεοῦ καὶ σωτῆρος] [2] ἡμῶν, βασιλείας τοῦ θειοτάτου καὶ εὐσεβ(εστάτου) ἡμῶν δ[εσπότου μεγίστου] [3] εὐεργέτου Φλαουίου Ἡρακλείου τοῦ αἰωνίου Αὐγούστου καὶ Α[ὐτοκρ(άτορος) ἔτους α . . . [4] ἰνδ(ικτίονος) ιδ, (ἔτους) σπζ σνϛ. + [5] Φλαουίῳ Ἀπίωνι τῷ πανευφήμῳ καὶ ὑπερφυεστάτῳ ἀπὸ ὑπάτων [6] καὶ πατρικίῳ, γεουχοῦντι καὶ ἐνταῦθα τῇ λαμπρᾷ Ὀξυρυγχ(ιτῶν) πόλ(ει), διὰ Μηνᾶ [7] οἰκέτου τοῦ ἐπερωτῶντος καὶ προσπορίζοντος τῷ ἰδίῳ δεσπό(τῃ) [8] τῷ αὐτῷ πανευφήμῳ ἀνδρὶ τὴν ἀγωγὴν καὶ ἐνοχήν, ἐγὼ Ἰωάννης [9] σὺν θεῷ πακτάριος τοῦ ὀξέως δρόμου τοῦ ἐνδόξου ὑμῶν οἴκου καὶ [10] τοῦ βαδιστικοῦ στάβλου τοῦ αὐτοῦ ἐνδόξου ὑμῶν οἴκου, υἱὸς τοῦ μακαρίου [11] Θεοδώρου, ὁρμώμενος ἐκ τῆς Ὀξυρυγχ(ιτῶν) πόλ(εως), ὁμολογῶ τὰ ὑπογ[εγραμμ]ένα. [12] βουλόμενος ἀντέχεσθαι καὶ τῆς χρείας τοῦ βαδιστικοῦ στάβλου τοῦ ἐνδόξου [13] ὑμῶν οἴκου μετὰ τὸν ὑπ᾽ ἐμὲ ὀξὺν δρόμον ἐπὶ ἕνα ἐνιαυτόν, λογιζόμενον [14] ἀπὸ πεντεκαιδεκάτης τοῦ Χοίακ μηνὸς τῆς παρούσης τεσσαρασκαιδεκάτης [15] ἰνδ(ικτίονος) μέχρι πεντεκαιδεκάτης τοῦ

of God . . . (Endorsed) Acknowledgement of an advance in the 6th indiction of 5 gold solidi less 30 carats made on behalf of John son of Phoebammon and Menas and Psa, of Hermopolis.

24. CONTRACT FOR THE CHARGE OF A STABLE

A.D. 610–611.

In the name of our Lord and Master Jesus Christ, our God and Saviour, in the 1st year of the reign of our most godlike and pious master and greatest benefactor, Flavius Heraclius the eternal Augustus and Imperator, . . ., 14th indiction, year 287 = 256.[a] To Flavius Apion[b] the all-honoured and most magnificent, of consular rank and patrician, landowner at this illustrious city of Oxyrhynchus, through Menas his servant, who is acting on his behalf and assuming for his master, the said all-honoured personage, the rights and obligations of the agreement, I, John, by the grace of God contractor for the express post belonging to your honourable house and for the riding stable belonging to your said honourable house, son of the late Theodorus, of the city of Oxyrhynchus, make the following acknowledgement. Wishing to undertake the business of the riding stable belonging to your honourable house in addition to the express post which is under my care, for one year reckoned from Choiak 15 of the present 14th indiction to Choiak 15 of the (D.V.)

[a] Dated by the two local eras employed at Oxyrhynchus.

[b] Many of the Byzantine papyri from Oxyrhynchus come from the archives of the distinguished family of which this Apion and two ancestors of the same name were members.

Χοίακ μηνὸς τῆς σὺν θ(εῷ) πεντεκαιδεκάτης [16]ἐπινεμή(σεως), ἐκείνησα λόγον πρὸς τὴν ὑμετέραν ὑπερφύειαν διὰ τῶν αὐτῇ [17]προσηκόντων καὶ τοῦτο τὸ βαδιστικὸν στάβλον καταθαρηθῆναί μοι [18]παρὰ τῆς ὑμετέρας ὑπερφυείας· καὶ δὴ κατεπίστευσάν μοι οἱ προσήκοντες [19]τῇ ὑμετέρᾳ ὑπερφ(υείᾳ) αὐτὸ τὸ βαδιστικὸν στάβλον ἐπὶ τὸν προγεγραμμέ(νον) [20]ἕνα ἐνιαυτόν, λογιζόμε(νον) ἀπὸ πεντεκαιδεκάτης τοῦ Χοίακ μη(νὸς) τῆς [21]παρούσης τεσσαρασκαιδεκάτης ἰνδ(ικτίονος). ὁμολογῶ ὑπεισελθεῖν τοῦτο [22]καὶ εἰς τὰς ἀνακυπτούσας πάσας γεουχικὰς χρείας, καὶ στρῶσαι [23]τοῖς τε περιβλέπτοις διοικηταῖς καὶ λαμπροτάτοις χαρτουλαρίοις καὶ παισὶν [24]ἀπερχομένοις εἰς οἱανδήποτε γεουχικὴν χρείαν, καὶ μὴ συγχωρῆ[σα]ι [25]μέμψιν τινὰ γενέσθαι κατ' ἐμοῦ, ἀνενδοιάστως κινδύνῳ ἐμῷ [26]καὶ τῆς ἐμῆς ὑποστάσεως, καὶ δέξασθαί με παρ' αὐτῆς λόγῳ [27]πάκτου τῆς αὐτῆς χρείας τοῦ αὐτοῦ ἐνιαυτοῦ χρυσίου λίτραν [28]μίαν ζυγῷ Ἀλεξανδρ(είας), ὁμολογῶν, ὡς εἴρηται, πᾶσαν χρείαν τοῦ [29]εἰρημένου στάβλου ποιεῖν, καὶ χορηγῆσαι ἄλογα εἰς τὰς [30]γεουχικὰς χρείας κινδύνῳ ἐμῷ, ὡς εἴρηται, καὶ τῆς ἐμῆς [31]ὑποστάσεως, καὶ στρῶσαι τοῖς τε περιβλέπτοις διοικηταῖς καὶ [32]λαμπρο(τάτοις) χαρτουλαρίοις καὶ παισὶν ἀπερχομένοις, ὡς προείρηται, [33]εἰς γεουχικὰς χρείας. καὶ ἐπὶ τούτοις πᾶσιν ἐπωμο{υ}σάμην [34]πρὸς τοῦ θεοῦ τοῦ παντοκράτορος καὶ νίκης καὶ σωτηρίας καὶ διαμονῆς [35]τῶν εὐσεβ(εστάτων) ἡμῶν δεσποτῶν Φλαουίου Ἡρακλείου καὶ Αἰλίας [36]Φλαβίας τούτοις ἐμμένειν, ταῦτα διαφυλάττειν, ἐν μηδενὶ [37]παραβῆναι τρόπῳ, καὶ ὑπεθέμην εἰς τὸ δίκαιον ταύτης

coming 15th indiction, I proposed to your magnificence through your representatives that this riding stable also should be entrusted to me by your magnificence; and accordingly the representatives of your magnificence gave me the charge of it for the aforesaid one year reckoned from Choiak 15 of the present 14th indiction. I agree to undertake this duty and all the services that may arise in connexion with the estate, and to find mounts for the noble superintendents and the most illustrious secretaries and the servants who go forth on business of the estate of whatsoever kind, without giving any ground for dissatisfaction, at the risk, uncontestedly, of myself and of my property; and I agree to accept from you as stipulated fee for the said services during the said year one pound of gold on the Alexandrian standard, undertaking for my part, as aforesaid, to perform all the business of the said stable and to furnish horses for the needs of the estate at the risk, as already said, of myself and my property, and to find mounts for the noble superintendents and the most illustrious secretaries and the servants who go forth, as aforesaid, on business of the estate. To all this I swear by Almighty God and by the supremacy, security, and permanence of our most pious sovereigns Flavius Heraclius and Aelia Flavia [a] that I will abide by and observe these conditions and in no way infringe them, and I pledge for the rights of this agreement

[a] Perhaps a mistake for Fabia.

τῆς [38]ὁμολογίας πάντα μου τὰ ὑπάρχοντα καὶ ὑπάρξοντα ἰδικῶς καὶ [39]γενικῶς, ἐνεχύρου λόγῳ καὶ ὑποθήκης δικαίῳ. κυρ(ία) ἡ ὁμολογία [40]δισσὴ γραφ(εῖσα) καὶ ἐπερ(ωτηθεὶς) ὡμολ(όγησα). (2nd hand) + Ἰωάννης. (3rd hand) + Ἰωάννης πακτάριος [41]τοῦ ὀξέως δρώμου τοῦ ἐνδόξου οἴκου τῆς ἡμῶν ὑπερφεοίας καὶ τοῦ βαδεστικοῦ [42]ὁ πρωγεγραμμένος πεποίημοι καὶ τὴν παροῦσαν ὁμωλογίαν τοῦ βαδεστικοῦ [43]στάβλου ἐπὶ τὸν ἕνα ἐνιαυτὸν ἀπὸ πεντεκαιδεκάτης τοῦ Χοίακ μη(νὸς) [44]τῆς παρούσης τεσσαρασκαιδεκάτης ἰνδ(ικτίονος), ἐπὶ τῷ πάκτῳ τῆς μιᾶς [45]λείτρας τοῦ χρυσίου Ἀλεξανδρίας, ὡς πρόκ(ειται). Φοιβάμμων μίσθιος αὐτοῦ, [46]υἱὸς τοῦ μακαρίου Παπνουθίου, ἔγραψα ὑπὲρ αὐτοῦ κατ' ἐπιτρωπὴν αὐτοῦ, [47]πρωτέξαντός μου τῷ ἴδιον ὄνωμα. + [48]+ δι' ἐμοῦ Παπνουθίου συμβολαιογράφ(ου) ἐτελειώθη. [49]* *di em*(*u*) *Papnut*(*hiu*) *etelioth*(*e*). . . ἰνδ(ι)κ(τίονος) ιδ, (ἔτους) σπζ σνϛ.

Verso: [50][+. . . . .] . . [. . . . .]ωμ( ) πακταρ(ίου) τοῦ ὀξέως δρόμου [51]καὶ τοῦ βαδιστικοῦ.+

25. PROMISE TO BE HONEST

P. Oxy. 139. A.D. 612.

[1][+ Ἐν ὀνόματι τοῦ κυρίου καὶ δεσπότου Ἰησοῦ [2]Χριστοῦ τοῦ θεοῦ καὶ σωτῆρος ἡμῶν, [3]βασιλείας τοῦ θειοτάτου καὶ εὐφήμου [4]δεσπότου μεγίστου εὐεργέτου Φλ(αουίου) Ἡρακλείου [5]τοῦ αἰωνίου Αὐγούστου] καὶ Αὐτοκρ(άτορος) [6]ἔτ[ους γ], Φ[αῶ]φι κθ ἰνδ(ικτίονος) α. [7]Φλ(αουίῳ) Ἀπίωνι τῷ πανευφήμῳ καὶ ὑπερφ(υεστάτῳ) [8]ἀπὸ ὑπάτων καὶ

all my property present and future, in its separate parts and as a whole, by way of security and by right of mortgage. This agreement, written in duplicate, is valid, and in answer to the formal question I have given my consent. (Signed) John. (Signed by deputy) I, John, the aforesaid, contractor for the express post of the honourable house of your magnificence and for the riding stable, have made the present agreement also concerning the riding stable for the one year from Choiak 15 of the present 14th indiction, at the stipulated fee of one pound of gold on the Alexandrian standard, as aforesaid. I, Phoebammon, his hired assistant, son of the late Papnouthius, have written for him by his authorization, he having first signed his own name. (Subscribed) Executed by me, Papnouthius, notary. (Repeated in Latin characters) Executed by me, Papnouthius. . . . indiction 14, year 287 = 256. (Endorsed) . . . contractor for the express post and the riding stable.

41. *l.* *δρόμου, ὑμῶν ὑπερφυείας, βαδιστικοῦ.* 42. *l.* *προγεγραμμένος πεποίημαι, ὁμολογίαν, βαδιστικοῦ.* 46. *l.* *ἐπιτροπήν.* 47. *l.* *προτάξαντος αὐτοῦ τὸ ἴδιον ὄνομα.*

25. PROMISE TO BE HONEST

A.D. 612.

In the name of our Lord and Master Jesus Christ, our God and Saviour, in the 3rd year of the reign of our most godlike and honoured master and greatest benefactor, Flavius Heraclius the eternal Augustus and Imperator, Phaophi 29, 1st indiction. To Flavius Apion [a] the all-honoured and most magni-

[a] See No. 24, note *b*.

πατρικίῳ, γεουχοῦντι καὶ 9ἐνταῦθα τῇ λαμπρᾷ Ὀξυρ(υγχιτῶν) πόλ(ει), διὰ Μηνᾶ 10οἰκέτου τοῦ ἐπερωτῶντος καὶ προσπορ(ίζοντος) 11τῷ ἰδίῳ δεσπότῃ τῷ αὐτῷ πανευφ(ήμῳ) 12ἀνδρὶ τὴν ἀγωγὴν καὶ ἐνοχήν, 13Αὐρήλιος Μηνᾶς πρωτοφύλαξ, υἱὸς 14Ὧρ μητρὸς Ἡραΐδος, ἀπὸ κώμης 15Ἀδαίου τοῦ Ὀξυρ(υγχίτου) νομοῦ παγαρχουμέ(νης) 16παρὰ τῆς ὑμετέρας ὑπερφ(υείας). ὁμολογῶ 17τῇ ὑμετέρᾳ ὑπερφ(υείᾳ) διὰ τῶν αὐτῇ 18προσηκόντων, ὡς εἴ ποτε καιρῷ 19ἢ χρόνῳ φανῶμεν κλέψαντες 20μηχανικὰ σκεύη ἢ βοίδια, 21ἢ οἱανδήποτε κλοπὴν 22ποιήσαντες, ἢ ὑποδέξασθαι 23λιστάς, ἐπὶ τῷ ἐμὲ παρασχεῖν 24τῇ ὑμετέρᾳ ὑπερφ(υείᾳ) ὑπὲρ 25ἑκάστου ἐγχειρήματος χρυσίου 26νομίσμ(ατα) εἴκοσι τέσσαρα, ἔργῳ καὶ 27δυνάμει ἀπαιτούμ(ενα) κινδ(ύνῳ) ἐμῷ καὶ 28τῆς ἐμῆς ὑποστάσεως. κυρ(ία) 29ἡ ὁμολ(ογία) ἁπλ(ῆ) γραφ(εῖσα) καὶ ἐπερ(ωτηθεὶς) ὡμολ(όγησα).+ 30Μηνᾶς υἱὸς Ὧρ στοιχεῖ μοι 31αὕτη ἡ ὁμολ(ογία) ὡς πρ(όκειται). Ἰωάν[ν]ης 32ἔγρ(αψα) ὑ(πὲρ) αὐτοῦ ἀγρ(αμμάτου) ὄντος. 33+ *di em(u) Ioannu eteliothh.*

Verso: 34[+ὁμολ(ογία)] Μηνᾶ πρωτοφύλακ(ος), υἱοῦ Ὧρ, ἀπὸ κώμ(ης) Ἀδαίου τοῦ Ὀξυρυγχ(ίτου) νομοῦ.+

26. DEED OF SURETY FOR A SERF

P. Oxy. 135. A.D. 579.

1+Βασιλείας τοῦ θειοτάτου καὶ εὐσεβεστάτου ἡμῶν δεσπότου μεγίστου εὐεργέτου 2Φλ(αουίου) Τιβερίου Κωνσταντίνου τοῦ αἰωνίου Αὐγούστου

ficent, of consular rank and patrician, landowner at this famous city of Oxyrhynchus, through Menas his servant who is acting on his behalf and assuming for his master, the said all-honoured personage, the rights and obligations of the agreement, from Aurelius Menas, head-watchman, son of Hor and of Herais, of the village of Adaeus in the pagarchy of your magnificence in the Oxyrhynchite nome. I acknowledge to your magnificence through your representatives that if at any season or time I shall be found to have stolen mechanical implements or cattle, or to have committed any theft whatsoever, or to have harboured thieves, I am bound to deliver to your magnificence for each infraction 24 gold solidi, to be really and truly exacted at the risk of my person and my property. This acknowledgement, made in a single copy, is valid, and in answer to the formal question I have given my assent. (Signed) I, Menas son of Hor, agree to this acknowledgement as above. I, John, have written for him, as he is illiterate. (Subscribed) Executed by me, John. (Endorsed) Acknowledgement of Menas, head-watchman, son of Hor, of the village of Adaeus in the Oxyrhynchite nome.

---

19. *l.* φανῶμεν. 23. *l.* λῃστάς.

26. DEED OF SURETY FOR A SERF

A.D. 579.

In the 4th year[a] of the reign of our most godlike and pious master and greatest benefactor Flavius Tiberius Constantinus the eternal Augustus and

[a] Probably a mistake for 5th year.

καὶ Αὐτοκράτορος 3ἔτους δ̅ Φαμενὼθ κε̅ ἰνδ(ικτίονος) ιβ. 4τοῖς ὑπερφυεστάτοις κληρονόμοις τοῦ {τῆς} ἐν εὐκλεεῖ τῇ μνήμῃ 5Ἀπίωνος γενομένου πατρικίου, γεουχοῦσιν καὶ ἐνταῦθα τῇ λαμπρᾷ 6Ὀξυρυγχ(ιτῶν) πόλει, διὰ Μηνᾶ οἰκέτου τοῦ ἐπερωτῶντος καὶ προσ-7πορίζοντος τοῖς ἰδίοις δεσπόταις τοῖς αὐτοῖς πανευφήμοις 8ἀνδράσιν τὴν ἀγωγὴν καὶ ἐνοχήν, Αὐρήλιος Παμούθιος μολυβουργός, 9υἱὸς Γεωργίου μητρὸς Ἀννιανῆς, ὁρμώμενος ἀπὸ τῆς Ὀξυρυγχ(ιτῶν) 10πόλεως. ὁμολογῶ ἑκουσίᾳ γνώμῃ, ἐπομνύμενος τὸν θεῖον 11καὶ σεβάσμιον ὅρκον, ἐγγυᾶσθαι καὶ ἀναδέχεσθαι παρὰ τῆς ὑμῶν 12ὑπερφυείας διὰ τῶν αὐτῇ προσηκόντων Αὐρήλιον Ἀβρ[α]άμιον 13υἱὸν Ἑρμίνου μητρὸς Ἡραΐδος, ὁρμώμενον ἀπὸ κτήματος 14μεγάλης Ταρουθίνου διαφέροντος τῇ ὑμῶν ὑπερφυείᾳ τοῦ 15Ὀξυρυγχ(ίτου) νομοῦ ἐναπόγραφον αὐτῆς γεωργόν, ἐφ᾽ ᾧ τε αὐτὸν 16ἀδιαλείπτως παραμεῖναι καὶ διάγειν ἐν τῷ αὐτοῦ κτήματι 17μετὰ τῶν αὐτοῦ φιλτάτων καὶ γαμετῆς καὶ κτηνῶν καὶ πάσης 18τῆς αὐτοῦ ἀποσκευῆς ἀποκρινόμενον εἰς ἅπαντα τὰ ὁρῶντα 19τὸ αὐτοῦ πρό[σ]ωπον ἤτοι τὴν τοῦ ἐναπογράφου τύχην, 20καὶ μηδαμῶς αὐτὸν καταλεῖψαι τὸ αὐτὸ κτῆμα μήτε μὴν 21μεθ⟦ε⟧ίστασθαι εἰς ἕτερον τόπον, ἀλλὰ καὶ ἐπιζητούμενον 22αὐτὸν πρὸς ἐμὲ παρὰ τῆς ὑμῶν ὑπερφυείας διὰ τῶν αὐτῇ 23προσηκόντων ἐν οἱᾳδήποτε ἡμέρᾳ οἱασδηποτοῦν ἕνεκεν 24προφάσεως, τοῦτον παραφέρω καὶ παραδώσω ἐν δημοσίῳ 25τόπῳ ἐκτὸς παντὸς τόπου προσφυγῆς καὶ λόγου, ἔνθα αὐτὸν 26καὶ παρείληφα, ἐν τῇ φυλακῇ τοῦ αὐτοῦ ἐνδόξου οἴκου, 27ἢ [εἰ] μὴ τοῦτο{υ} ποιήσω, ὁμολογῶ καταβαλεῖν ὑπὲρ

Imperator, Phamenoth 25, 12th indiction. To the most magnificent heirs of Apion [a] of glorious memory, patrician, landowners in this illustrious city of Oxyrhynchus, through their servant Menas who is acting on their behalf and assuming for his masters, the said all-honoured persons, the rights and obligations of the agreement, from Aurelius Pamouthius, lead-worker, son of George and Anniana, of the city of Oxyrhynchus. I acknowledge of my free will, swearing the divine and imperial oath,[b] that I accept from your magnificence, through your representatives, the charge of and responsibility for Aurelius Abraham son of Herminus and Herais, who comes from the estate of Great Tarouthinas belonging to your magnificence in the Oxyrhynchite nome and is enrolled as your farmer, engaging that he shall uninterruptedly remain and abide on his proper estate along with his family and wife and animals and all his household gear, I being answerable for all that regards his person or his status as your bondsman, and that he shall in no wise leave the said estate or remove to another place; and if he is required of me by your magnificence through your representatives at any date and for any reason whatsoever, I will bring and deliver him in a public place debarred from every sanctuary and subterfuge, even where I received him, in the guard-room of your said honourable house. If I fail to do this, I agree to pay down for his desertion and my failure

[a] Grandfather of the Apion of No. 24.
[b] That is, swearing by the Emperor.

18. *l.* ἀποκρινόμενος.

τῆς αὐτοῦ [28]ἀπολείψεως καὶ μὴ γινομένης παρ' ἐμοῦ παραδόσεως [29]χρυσοῦ νομίσματα ὀκτὼ ἔργῳ καὶ δυνάμει ἀπαιτούμενα. [30]κ[υρ]ία ἡ ἐ[γγύ]η ἁπλῆ γραφεῖσα καὶ ἐπερωτηθ(εὶς) ὡμολ(όγησα). [31]* *di em(u) Anastasiu eteliothh.*

Verso: ἐγγύη Παμουθίου μολυβουργ(οῦ) υἱοῦ Γεωργίου ἀπὸ [τῆς 'Οξυρυγχ(ιτῶν) πόλ(εως)] ἀναδεχομ(ένου) 'Αβραάμ[ιο]ν υἱὸν 'Ερμίνου ἀ[πὸ κτήμ(ατος)] Τ[α]ρ[ο]υθί[νου.+]

27. SALE OF LAND

P. Grenf. ii. 23 (*a*). 107 B.C.

(Col. 1) [1]Ἔτους ια τοῦ καὶ η [2]Φαῶφι κη̅. [3]ἀπέδο-(το) Ταοῦς [4]καὶ Σεννῆ(σις) καὶ [5][Σ]ιεφμοῦς [6]Πετε-αρσ(εμθεῖ) καὶ [7]τοῖς ἀδελ(φοῖς) γῆς [8](ἀρούρας) γ (ἥμισυ) χα(λκοῦ) (ταλάντων) θ. (Col. 2) [1]Βασι-λευόντων Κλεοπάτρας καὶ Πτολεμαίου ἐπικα-λουμένου 'Αλεξάνδρου τοῦ υἱοῦ θεῶν Φιλομητόρων ἔτους ια τοῦ καὶ ὀγδόου, ἐφ' ἱερέων καὶ ἱερειῶν [2]καὶ κανηφόρου τῶν ὄντων καὶ οὐσῶν, μηνὸς Φαῶφι ὀγδόηι καὶ εἰκάδι, ἐν Κροκοδίλων πόλει ἐπὶ Πανίσκου ἀγορανόμου τῆς ἄνω τοπαρχίας τοῦ Παθυρίτου. [3]ἀπέδοτο Ταοῦς 'Αρπῶτος ὡς ἐτῶν μη μέση μελίχρ(ως) στρογγυλοπρόσω(πος) εὐθύρ(ιν) οὐλὴ μετώπωι καὶ αἱ ταύτης ἀδελφαὶ Σεννῆσις ἡ καὶ Τατοῦς 'Αρπῶτος ὡς (ἐτῶν) μβ [4]μέση μελί-χρ(ως) στρογγυλοπρόσω(πος) εὐθύριν οὐλὴ μετώπωι καὶ Σιεφμοῦς Παχνούμιος ὡς ἐτῶν κ μελί(χρως) στρογγυλοπρόσωπος εὐθύριν ἄσημος, αἱ τρεῖς

to deliver him 8 gold solidi, to be really and truly exacted. This deed of surety, made in a single copy, is valid, and in answer to the formal question I have given my assent. (Subscribed) Executed by me, Anastasius. (Endorsed) Deed of surety of Pamouthius, lead-worker, son of George, of Oxyrhynchus, accepting responsibility for Abraham son of Herminus of the estate of Tarouthinas.

27. SALE OF LAND

107 B.C.

(Summary) The 11th which is also the 8th year,[a] Phaophi 28. Taous and Sennesis and Siephmous have sold to Peteharsemtheus and his brothers 3½ arurae of land for 9 talents of copper. (Text) In the 11th which is also the 8th year of the reign of Cleopatra and her son Ptolemy surnamed Alexander, gods Philometores, the priests and priestesses and canephorus being those now in office,[b] on the 28th of the month Phaophi, in Crocodilopolis, before Paniscus, agoranomus of the upper toparchy of the Pathyrite nome. Taous daughter of Harpos, aged about 48 years, of medium height, fair-skinned, round-faced, straight-nosed, with a scar on her forehead, and her sisters Sennesis also called Tatous, daughter of Harpos, aged about 42 years, of medium height, fair-skinned, round-faced, straight-nosed, with a scar on her forehead, and Siephmous daughter of Pachnoumis, aged about 20 years, fair-skinned, round-faced,

[a] That is, the 11th year of Cleopatra III. and the 8th of Ptolemy Alexander, deified under the name of "mother-loving gods" (Philometores).

[b] See No. 2, note *a*.

Πέρσιναι, μετὰ κυρίου [5]τοῦ τῆς προγεγραμμένης Ταοῦτος ἀνδρὸς Ψεννήσιος τοῦ καὶ Κρούριος τοῦ Ὥρου Πέρσου τῆς ἐπιγονῆς τῶν ἐκ Γοτνὶτ κώμης τῆς κάτω τοπαρχίας τοῦ [6]Λατοπολίτου ὡς (ἐτῶν) με μέσου ἢ ἐλ(άσσους) μελανχρόου ὑποκλαστοῦ μακροπροσώ(που) εὐθυρίνου οὐλὴ χείλη̣ι τῶι κάτω, τὴν ὑπάρχουσαν αὐταῖς ἐν τῶι ἀπὸ βορρᾶι πεδίωι [7]Παθύρεως γῆν ἤπειρον σιτοφόρον ἀδιαίρετον ἐν σφραγῖσι δυσὶ ἀρουρῶν τριῶν ἡμίσους καὶ τοῦ προσόντος χαλάσματος ἀπὸ (ἀρουρῶν) ζ τῶν ἐν (ἀρούραις) μ, ὧν γείτονες [8]τῆς μὲν μιᾶς σφραγῖδος νότου γῆ Πατοῦτος τοῦ Ὥρου καὶ τῶν ἀδελφῶν, βορρᾶ γῆ Χεσθώτου τοῦ Μελιπάιτος, ἀπηλιώτου γῆ Ἀέους καὶ τῶν ἀδελ(φῶν), λιβὸς περίχωμα, [9]τῆς δ' ἄλλης νότου γῆ Χεσθώτου τοῦ προγεγραμμένου, βορρᾶ γῆ Χεσθώτου τοῦ Πανεμγέως, ἀπηλιώτου γῆ Θράσωνος καὶ τῶν ἀδελφῶν, λιβὸς τὸ περίχωμα, ἢ οἳ [10]ἂν ὦσι γείτονες πάντων πάντοθεν. ἐπρίατο Πετεαρσεμθεὺς Πανεβχούνιος ὡς (ἐτῶν) λϛ μέσος μελί(χρως) ὑποκλαστὸς μακροπρόσω(πος) εὐθύριν καὶ οἱ τούτου ἀδελ(φοὶ) [11]Πετεσοῦχος καὶ Φαγῶνις καὶ Ψεννῆσις, οἱ δ̄ Πέρσαι τῆς ἐπιγονῆς τῶν ἐκ Παθύρεως, ἑκάτερος κατὰ τὸ ἴσον μέρος χαλκοῦ (ταλάντων) ἐννέα. προπωλήτριαι καὶ (Col. 3) [1]βεβαιώτριαι τῶν κατὰ τὴν ὠνὴν ταύτην πάντων Ταοῦς καὶ Σεννῆσις ἡ καὶ Τατοῦς καὶ Σιεφμοῦς αἱ ἀποδόμεναι, ἃς ἐδέξαντο Πετεαρσεμθεὺς καὶ Πετεσοῦχος καὶ Φαγῶνις καὶ Ψεννῆσις οἱ πριάμενοι. [2]Πανίσκος κεχρη(μάτικα).

(Col. 2) 6. *l.* χείλει and βορρᾶ.

[a] The nature of this surplus, which is mentioned in other documents, has not yet been clearly explained.

straight-nosed, without distinctive mark, all three being Persians, with their guardian the husband of the aforesaid Taous, Psennesis also called Krouris son of Horus, Persian of the Epigone, of the village of Gotnit in the lower toparchy of the Latopolite nome, aged about 45 years, of medium height or under, dark-skinned, rather curly-haired, long-faced, straight-nosed, with a scar on the under lip, have sold the land, lying inland, corn-bearing, and undivided, which belongs to them in the northern plain of Pathyris and contains three and a half arurae in two plots with the attached surplus[a] out of the 7 in the 40 arurae. The boundaries of the one plot are, on the south the land of Patous son of Horus and his brothers, on the north the land of Chesthotes son of Melipais, on the east the land of Aes and his brothers, on the west an embankment, and of the other plot, on the south the land of the above-mentioned Chesthotes, on the north the land of Chesthotes son of Panemgeus, on the east the land of Thrason and his brothers, on the west the embankment, or whatever the boundaries may be all round. Peteharsemtheus son of Panebchounis, aged about 36 years, of medium height, fair-skinned, rather curly-haired, long-faced, straight-nosed, and his brothers Petesouchus, Phagonis, and Psennesis, all four Persians of the Epigone, inhabitants of Pathyris, have bought the land for nine talents of copper, each paying an equal share. Negotiators and guarantors of all the terms of this deed of sale: Taous and Sennesis also called Tatous and Siephmous, the vendors, who have been accepted by Peteharsemtheus, Petesouchus, Phagonis, and Psennesis, the purchasers. (Subscribed) Registered by me, Paniscus.

28. SALE OF A HOUSE

P. Amh. 51. — 88 B.C.

(Col. 1) [1](Ἔτους) κϛ Μεσορὴι [3]κη̄. ἀπέδοτο Πετεῆσις [4]Πατῆτος [5]Πελαίαι Εὐνόου [6]τὴν ὑπάρχου-[7]σαν αὐτῶι [8]ἐν τῶι ἀπὸ [9]ἀπηλιώτου [10]μέρει Παθύ(ρεως) [11]οἰκίαν ᾠκο-[12]δομημένην [13]καὶ δεδοκω-[14]μένην καὶ τε-[15]θυρωμένην, [16]ὧν αἱ γειτνίαι [17]δεδήλωνται [18]διὰ τῆς ὠνῆς. (Col. 2) [19]Βασιλευόντων Πτολεμαίου τοῦ ἐπικαλουμένου Ἀλεξάνδρου καὶ Κλεοπάτρας τῆς ἀδελφῆς θεῶν [20]Φιλομητόρων Σωτήρων ἔτους ἕκτου καὶ εἰκοστοῦ, ἐφ᾽ ἱερέων καὶ ἱερειῶν καὶ κανηφόρου τῶν ὄντων [21]καὶ οὐσῶν, μηνὸς Μεσορὴι κη̄, ἐν Παθύρει ἐφ᾽ Ἑρμίου ἀγορανόμου τῆς ἄνω τοπαρχίας τοῦ Παθυρίτου. [22]ἀπέδοτο Πετεῆσις Πατῆτος Πέρσης ὡς (ἐτῶν) μ μέσος μελίχρως τετανὸς μακροπρόσωπος [23]εὐθύριν οὐλὴ ὑπ᾽ ὀφρύι ἀριστερᾷ τὴν ὑπάρχουσαν αὐτῶι οἰκίαν ᾠκοδομημένην καὶ δεδο-[24]κωμένην καὶ τεθυρωμένην τῆς οὔσης ἐν τῶι ἀπὸ ἀπηλιώτου μέρει Παθύρεως [25]λεγομένης κρήνης, ἧς γείτονες νότου οἰκία Πελαίου τοῦ ὠνουμένου, βορρᾶ οἰκία [26]Ταενούτιος τῆς Ψενποήριος ἧς κρ[α]τεῖ Τοτοῆς Πανεχάτου, ἀπηλιώτου καὶ λιβὸς [27]ῥύμη βασιλική, ἢ οἳ ἂν ὦσι γείτονες πάντοθεν. ἐπρίατο Πελαίας Εὐνόου χα(λκοῦ) (ταλάντου) α. [28]προπωλητὴς καὶ βεβαιωτὴ[ς] τῶν κατὰ τὴν ὠνὴν ταύτην πάντων Πετεῆσις [29]ὁ ἀποδόμενος, ὃν ἐδέξατ[ο] Πελαίας ὁ πριάμενος. [30]Ἑρμίας κεχρη(μάτικα).

16. *l.* ἧς.

28. SALE OF A HOUSE

88 B.C.

(Summary) The 26th year, Mesore 23. Peteesis son of Pates has sold to Pelaeas son of Eunous the house belonging to him in the eastern part of Pathyris, built and raftered and furnished with doors, the boundaries of which are given in the deed of sale. (Text of deed) In the 26th year of the reign of Ptolemy surnamed Alexander and of Cleopatra the sister,[a] gods Philometores Soteres, the priests and priestesses and the canephorus being those now in office, the 28th of the month Mesore, at Pathyris, before Hermias, agoranomus of the upper toparchy of the Pathyrite nome. Peteesis son of Pates, Persian, aged about 40 years, of medium height, fair-skinned, smooth-haired, long-faced, straight-nosed, with a scar under the left eyebrow, has sold the house belonging to him, built and raftered and furnished with doors, at the so-called fountain in the eastern part of Pathyris, of which the boundaries are, on the south the house of Pelaeas the purchaser, on the north the house of Taenoutis daughter of Psenpoeris, of which Totoes son of Panechates has possession, on the east and west a royal street, or whatever the boundaries may be all round. Pelaeas son of Eunous has bought it for 1 talent of copper. Negotiator and guarantor of all the terms of this deed of sale: Peteesis the vendor, who has been accepted by Pelaeas the purchaser. (Subscribed) Registered by me, Hermias.

[a] Cleopatra IV., called sister but actually niece and wife of Ptolemy Alexander. The two bore the title of "mother-loving and saviour gods" (Philometores Soteres).

29. SALE OF A HOUSE AND RENUNCIATION OF OWNERSHIP

B.G.U. 998. 101 B.C.

(Col. 1) [1][Βα]σιλεύοντος Πτολεμαίου τοῦ καὶ ἐπικαλουμένου Ἀλεξάνδρου θεοῦ Φιλομήτορος ἔτους ιδ, [2][ἐφ'] ἱερείων καὶ ἱερειῶν καὶ κανηφόρου τῶν ὄντων καὶ οὐσῶν, μηνὸς Χοίαχ β̄, ἐν Παθύρει [3][ἐφ'] Ἑρμίου τοῦ παρὰ Πανίσκου ἀγορανόμου. ἀπέδοτο Ψενμεγχῆς Πανεχάτου Πέρσης [4][τῆς] ἐπιγονῆς ὡς (ἐτῶν) νε μέσος μελίχρω(ς) τετανὸς ἀναφάλακρος μακροπρόσω(πος) εὐθύριν οὐλὴ μήλῳ [5][ἀρισ]τερὸν ἐπισ[κάζω]ν τὸν πόδα δεξιόν, συνεπικελεύοντος τῷ τούτου υἱοῦ Ἁρπαήσιος [6][τοῦ] Ψενμεγχῆ[τος Πέ]ρσου ὡς (ἐτῶν) λ μέσος μελίχρω(ς) ὑπόκλαστος μακροπρόσω(πος) εὐθύριν ἄσημος [7][τὴν] ὑπάρχουσα[ν οἰ]κίαν ᾠκοδομημένην καὶ κεκαμαρωμένην καὶ τεθυρωμένην καὶ [8][τῆς] προσούση[ς αὐλῆς] τῆς οὔσης ἐν τῷ ἀπὸ βορρᾶ μέρει Παθύρεως, ἧς γείτονες νότου οἰκία Νεχού(του) [9][τοῦ] Πανεχά[του, βορρ]ᾶ οἰκία Κεφάλωνος, ἀπηλιώ(του) ῥύμη, λιβὸς οἰκία Πόρτιτος τοῦ Πετεσούχου [10][ἧς ἀν]ὰ μέσον ῥ[ύ]μη, ἢ οἳ ἂν ὦσι γείτονες πάντοθεν. ἐπρίατο Πετεῆσις Ὀνηοῦς Πέρσης ὡς (ἐτῶν) μ [11][μέσος] μελίχρω(ς) ὑπόκλαστος οὐλὴ μετώπῳ, χαλκοῦ τάλαντα τέσσαρες. προπωλητὴς καὶ [12][βεβαιω]τὴς τῶν κατὰ τὴν ὠνὴν ταύτην πάντων Ψενμεγχῆς ὁ ἀποδόμενος, ὃν ἐδέξατο [13][Πετεῆ]σις ὁ πριάμενος. Ἑρμίας ὁ παρὰ Πανίσκου κεχρη(μάτικα).

(Col. 2) [1]Ἔτους ιδ Χοίαχ β̄ ἐν Παθύρει ἐφ' Ἑρμίου

(Col. 1) 2. *l.* ἱερέων. 5. *l.* [ἀρισ]τερῷ, τοῦ. 6. μέσου, etc. 8. [τὴν] προσοῦσα[ν, etc. 11. *l.* ταλάντων τεσσάρων.

29. SALE OF A HOUSE AND RENUNCIATION OF OWNERSHIP

101 B.C.

The 14th year of the reign of Ptolemy surnamed Alexander, god Philometor, the priests and priestesses and canephorus being those now in office, Choiach 2, at Pathyris, before Hermias agent of Paniscus, agoranomus. Psenmenches son of Panechates, Persian of the Epigone, aged about 55 years, of medium height, fair-skinned, smooth-haired, bald in front, long-faced, straight-nosed, with a scar on the left cheek, limping on the right foot, with the concurrence of his son Harpaesis son of Psenmenches, Persian, aged about 30 years, of medium height, fair-skinned, rather curly-haired, long-faced, straight-nosed, without distinguishing mark, has sold the house belonging to him, built and furnished with vaults and doors, with the attached courtyard, situated in the northern part of Pathyris, its boundaries being, on the south the house of Nechoutes son of Panechates, on the north the house of Cephalon, on the east a street, on the west the house of Portis son of Petesouchus with a street between, or whatever the boundaries may be all round. Peteesis, son of Ones, Persian, aged about 40 years, of medium height, fair-skinned, rather curly-haired, with a scar on the forehead, has purchased it for 4 talents of copper. Negotiator and guarantor of all the terms of this deed of sale : Psenmenches the vendor, whom Peteesis the purchaser has accepted. Registered by me, Hermias agent of Paniscus.

Year 14, Choiach 2, at Pathyris, before Hermias

τοῦ παρὰ Πανίσκου ἀγορανόμου. [2]ὁμολογεῖ Ψενμεγχῆς Πανεχάτου Πέρσης τῆς ἐπιγονῆς ἀφίστασθαι ἀπὸ [3]τῆς πεπραμένης οἰκίας ᾠκοδομημένης καὶ τεθυρω(μένης) καὶ τῆς προσούσης [4]αὐλῆς τὴν οὖσαν ἐν τῷ ἀπὸ βορρᾶ μέρει Παθύρεως, ἧς γείτονες νότου οἰκία [5]Νεχούτου τοῦ Πανεχάτου, βορρᾶ οἰκία Κεφάλωνος, ἀπηλιώ(του) ῥύμη, λιβὸς οἰκία [6]Πόρτιτος τοῦ Πετεσούχου ἧς ἀνὰ μέσον ῥύμη, ἢ οἳ ἂν ὦσι γείτονες, ἥ<ς> ἔθετο [7]ὠνὴν Πετεήσι ἐπὶ τοῦ αὐτοῦ ἀρχείου πρὸς χαλκοῦ (τάλαντα) δ, καὶ μὴ ἐπελεύ-[8]σασθαι μήτ' αὐτὸς Ψενμεγχῆς μηδ' ἄλλον μηδένα τῶν παρ' αὐτοῦ ἐπὶ τὸν [9]Πετεῆσιν μηδ' ἐπ' ἄλλον μηδένα τῶν παρ' αὐτοῦ· εἰ δὲ μή, ἥ τ' ἔφοδος τῶι ἐπι-[10]πορευομένωι ἄκυρος ἔστω καὶ προσαποτεισάτω ὁ ἐπελθὼν ἐπίτι(μον) παραχρῆμα [11]χαλκοῦ τάλαντα ὀκτὼ καὶ ἱερὰ βασιλεῦσι ἀργυρίου ἐπισήμου δραχμὰς ρξ [12]καὶ μηθὲν ἧσσον ἐπάναγκον αὐτῷ ἔστω ποιεῖν κατὰ <τὰ> προγεγραμμένα. [13]ἡ δὲ ὁμολογία ἥτε κυρία ἔστω πανταχῆ οὗ ἂν ἐπιφέρηται. Ἑρμίας ὁ παρὰ Πανίσκου κεχρη(μάτικα).

30. SALE OF A HOUSE

P. Lond. 1722. A.D. 573.

☧ [1]Μετὰ τὴν ὑπατείαν τοῦ δ[εσπότου ἡμῶν Φλ(αουίου) Ἰουστίνου] Φαμεν[ὼ]θ ῑ. [τ]ῆ[ς] ἕκ[τ]η[ς] [2]ἰνδικτίονος, ἐν Συήνῃ. [3]Αὐρήλιοι Ἰακὼβ ἐκ πατρὸς Πάειτος Ῥωβὴν μητρὸς [end of line lost] [4]τὸ ἐπιτήδευμα καὶ ἡ τούτου γαμετὴ Τσενδία ἐκ πατρὸς Σούρτ[ου μ]ητρὸς Τουῶτε, [5]ἀμφότεροι καταμένοστες ἐν Συήνῃ, παρέχοντες

5. *l.* καταμένοντες.

agent of Paniscus, agoranomus. Psenmenches son of Panechates, Persian of the Epigone, acknowledges that he abandons possession of the house which he has sold, built and furnished with doors, with the attached courtyard, situated in the northern part of Pathyris, its boundaries being, on the south the house of Nechoutes son of Panechates, on the north the house of Cephalon, on the east a street, on the west the house of Portis son of Petesouchus with a street between, or whatever the boundaries may be, of which house he has made a deed of sale to Peteesis at the same record-office for 4 talents of copper, and that neither Psenmenches himself nor any of his assigns shall take proceedings against Peteesis or any of his assigns; and if anyone does so, the proceedings shall be invalid and in addition the aggressor shall straightway forfeit a penalty of 8 talents of copper and a fine, consecrated to the Crown, of 160 drachmae of coined silver, and he shall be none the less bound to conform to the above terms. This agreement shall be valid wherever produced. Registered by me, Hermias agent of Paniscus.

(Col. 2) 4. *l.* τῆς οὔσης. 13. *l.* ἤδε.

30. SALE OF A HOUSE

A.D. 573.

The year after the consulship of our master Flavius Justinus, Phamenoth 1[.], 6th indiction, at Syene. Aurelius Jacob, whose father is Pais son of Reuben and his mother . . ., being a . . . by trade, and his wife Aurelia Tsendia, whose father is Sourtus and her mother Touote, both dwelling in Syene, bringing

ὑπὲρ αὐτῶν ὑπογραφέα καὶ [6]μάρτυρας τοὺς ἑξῆς ὑπογράφοντας, Φλαουίῳ Ἰακώβῳ υἱῷ Ἰσακίου [7]μητρὸς Τλοῦδος τυμπανάρ(ιῳ) τοῦ ἀριθμοῦ Συήνης καὶ ἀπὸ Συήνης χαίρειν. ὁμολογοῦμεν ἑκουσίῳ καὶ ἀμετανοήτῳ γνώμῃ καὶ ἀδόλῳ προαιρέσει [9]καὶ εἰλικρινεῖ συνειδήσει κατὰ τήνδε τὴν ἁπλῆν ἔγγραφον ἀσφάλειαν [10]πεπρακέναι σοι σήμερον καὶ καταγεγραφέναι ἀπὸ τοῦ νῦν ἐπὶ τὸν ἀεὶ καὶ [11]ἑξῆς ἅπαντα χρόνον τὴν ὑπάρχουσαν ἡμῖν οἰκίαν ἐξ ὁλοκλήρου ἀπὸ [12]ἐδάφους ἕως ἀέρος διακειμένην ἐπὶ τῆς αὐτῆς Συήνης περὶ τὸ νότινον [13]μέρος τοῦ φρουρίου καὶ περὶ λαύραν τῆς παρεμβολῆς καὶ τῆς οἰκίας Παπνουθίου [14]Μαύρου καὶ τοῦ καμηλôνος τῆς βασταγῆς τῶν <ἀπὸ> Φιλῶν, ἐλθοῦσαν εἰς ἡμ[ᾶ]ς ἀπὸ [15]δικαίου ἀγορασίας παρὰ Ἀβρααμίου καὶ Ἀλάμμονος υἱῶν Παύλου Οὐρανίου [16]καὶ εἰς αὐτοὺς ἀπὸ κληρονομικοῦ δικαίου τοῦ ἀναπαυσαμένου πατρ[ὸ]ς αὐτῶν Παύλου [17]Οὐρανίου καὶ εἰς αὐτὸν ἀπὸ δικαίου κληρονομίας τῶν γονέων αὐτοῦ, ἐν ᾗ τῇ ἁπάσῃ [18]οἰκίᾳ ἐν μὲν πρώτῃ στέγῃ κέλλια δύο, ἓν μὲν νότινον μέγα νεῦον εἰς βορρᾶ [19]εἰς τὸ προσπαρακείμενον πυλôνα, ἄλλο δὲ ἀπηλιωτικὸν νεῦον εἰς λίβα εἰς τὸ [20]πυλôνα, καὶ τὸ ὑποπέσσιον ἤτοι τχρηρε, ἐν δὲ τῇ δευτέρᾳ στέγῃ συμπόσια δύο, [21]ἓν μὲν νεῦον εἰς βορρᾶ, ἄλλο δὲ νεῦον εἰς λίβα εἰς τὸ πέσσον, μετὰ καὶ τῶν [22]ἐπάνω αὐτῶν δύο συμπόσια ἀσκέπαστα ἐν τῇ τρίτῃ στέγῃ ἕως ἀέρος, καὶ [23]ὁ πέσσος ἀπὸ ἐδάφους ἕως ἀέρος, εἰσὶ δὲ γείτονες αὐτῆς νότου ῥύμη δημοσία [24]μεθ' ἣν οἰκία Δίου Ταγαρίας, βορρᾶ οἰκία νῦν

14. *l.* καμηλῶνος. 19. *l.* τὸν πυλῶνα. 21. *l.* τόν.
22. *l.* συμποσίων ἀσκεπάστων.

a signatory on their behalf and witnesses who sign below, to Flavius Jacob son of Isaac and of Tlous, drummer of the *numerus*[a] of Syene and himself belonging to Syene, greeting. We acknowledge that with free and fixed purpose and guileless intention and pure conscience, in accordance with this unduplicated written bond, we have sold to you today and conveyed to you from now to all succeeding time the house belonging to us in its entirety from basement to house-top, which house is situated in the said Syene within the northern part of the fortress and the quarter containing the Camp and the house of Papnouthius son of Maurus and the camel-yard of the carriers from Philae and came to us by right of purchase from Abraham and Alammon sons of Paul son of Uranius and to them by right of inheritance from their deceased father Paul son of Uranius and to him by right of inheritance from his parents. The contents of the whole house are: on the first floor two store-rooms, one large one on the south facing north towards the subsidiary gateway and another on the east facing west towards the main gateway, and the space below the stair or *techerere*,[b] on the second floor two dining-rooms, one facing north, another facing west towards the staircase, and above these two uncovered dining-rooms on the third floor forming the house-top, and the stair from basement to house-top. Its boundaries are: on the south a public street and beyond this the house of Dius son of Tagaria, on the north the house now belonging to Dius son of Isaac also called

[a] A military force.
[b] The Egyptian word for this part of the house.

Δίου Ἰσακίου τοῦ καὶ Ποσίου, [25]ἀπηλιώτου οἰκία Πετεροοῦτος Μαρτυρίου καὶ Τήρου Τήρονος γαμετῆς αὐτοῦ, λιβὸς [26]ῥύμη δημοσία εἰς ἣν νεύει ἡ αὐθεντικὴ αὐτῆς θύρα, ἁπαξαπλῶς ἀκολούθως [27]τῇ γεγενημένῃ ἡμῖν περὶ τούτου πράσει ἥνπερ σοι ἐξεδόμεθα {σοι} εἰς πλεω-[28]τέραν σου ἀσφάλειαν, ἢ οἳ ἐὰν ὦσι γείτονες πάντῃ πάντοθεν, καθὼς [29]ὑπηγορεύσαμεν ἡμεῖς οἱ ἀποδόμενοι, καὶ οὐδὲν ἡμῖν ὑπολέλειπται ἄπρατον [30]ἐν τῇ προδεδηλουμένῃ οἰκίᾳ, τιμῆς τῆς πρὸς ἀλλήλους συμπεφωνημένης [31]καὶ συναρεσάσης χρυσοῦ δοκίμου νομισματίων παλαιοχαράκτων [32]εὐστάθμων δεκαοκτώ, γί(νεται) χρ(υσ.) νο(μ.) ιη, ἥνπερ τελείαν τιμὴν αὐτόθι [33]ἀπεσχήκαμεν παρὰ σοῦ τοῦ ὠνουμένου ἡμεῖς οἱ πεπρακότες ἐν τῇ ἐνεστώσῃ [34]ἡμέρᾳ διὰ χειρὸς εἰς χεῖρα ἡμῶν ἐπὶ τῆς αὐτῆς Συήνης ἀριθμῷ καὶ σταθμῷ [35]πλήρη πρὸς τὸ ἐντεῦθεν σὲ τὸν ὠνούμενον τῆς προδεδηλουμένης [36]οἰκίας ἐξ ὁλοκλήρου ἀπὸ ἐδάφους ἕως ἀέρος κυριεύειν καὶ δεσπόζειν [37]καὶ διοικεῖν καὶ οἰκονομεῖν καὶ οἰκοδομεῖν καὶ πωλεῖν καὶ χαρίζεσθαι καὶ τέκνοις [38]καὶ ἐγγόνοις διατάσσειν καὶ ἐπιτελεῖν τὰ περὶ αὐτῆς τρόπῳ ᾧ ἐὰν αἱρῇ [39]ἀκωλύτως καὶ ἀνεμποδίστως καὶ μὴ ἐγκαλεῖν σοι μήτ' ἐγκαλέσειν μήθ' [40]ἕτερόν τινα τῶν ἐξ ἡμῶν ὀνόματος ἐν μηδενὶ καιρῷ κατὰ μηδένα τρόπον [41]ἀφορμῇ μηδεμιᾷ διὰ τὸ ὡς προείπομεν ἀπεσχηκέναι ἡμᾶς παρὰ σοῦ τελείαν [42]τὴν προγεγραμμένην τιμήν, τὸν δὲ ἐγκαλέσοντά σοι ἢ καὶ ἀντιποιησόμενον [43]περὶ τῆς προδεδηλουμένης οἰκίας ἐξ ὁλοκλήρου ἀπὸ ἐδάφους ἕως ἀέρος [44]ἢ μέρους αὐτῆς ἡμεῖς οἱ πεπρακότες ἀποστήσομεν καὶ καθαροποιήσομέν [45]σοι ἰδίοις ἡμῶν ἀναλώμασι,

Posius, on the east the house of Peteroous son of Martyrius and his wife Terou daughter of Teron, on the west a public street into which its principal door opens, absolutely in conformity with the deed of sale made for us about this property, which deed we have delivered to you for your greater security, or whatever the boundaries may be on every side, according to the statement of us the vendors. And we have left nothing unsold in the aforesaid house. The price mutually agreed upon and approved is eighteen solidi of assayed gold, of old mintage and correct weight, total 18 gold sol., the whole of which price we the vendors have received on the spot from you the purchaser on the present day from hand to hand in the said Syene, complete in number and weight, so that henceforth you the purchaser may own and be master of the aforesaid house in its entirety from top to bottom and administer and manage it and build or sell or give it away or bequeath it to your children and descendants or dispose of it in whatever manner you choose without let or hindrance, and neither we nor any other acting in our name may make, now or in future, any claim against you on any occasion in any manner on any pretext, because, as we said before, we have received from you the above-mentioned price in full. And if any person makes a claim against you or disputes the possession of the aforesaid house in its entirety from top to bottom or of part of it, we the vendors will repel him and make clear your title at our own expense. And we

---

30. *l.* προδεδηλωμένῃ; so in ll. 35, 43.

καὶ ἐξεδόμεθά σοι τήνδε τὴν πρᾶσιν [46]κυρίαν οὖσαν καὶ βεβαίαν ἐφ᾽ ὑπογραφῆς τοῦ ὑπὲρ ἡμῶν ὑπογράφοντος καὶ ἐπερ(ωτηθέντες) [47]ὡμολογήσαμεν καὶ ἀπελύσαμεν. (2nd hand) ⳨ Αὐρήλιοι Ἰακὼβ Πάειτος Ῥωβὴν καὶ ἡ τούτου [48]γαμετὴ Τσενδία Σούρτου οἱ προκ(είμενοι) πεπράκαμεν τὴν προκειμένην οἰκίαν ἐξ ὁλο-[49]κλήρου ἀπὸ ἐδάφους ἕως ἀέρος καὶ ἀπεσχήκαμεν παρὰ σοῦ τὴν προγεγραμ-[50]μένην τιμὴν ἐ<ν> νομισματίοις δεκαοκτὼ καὶ βεβαιοῦμεν τὴν πρᾶσιν ὡς πρόκ(ειται). [51]Φλ(αούιος) Φῶτις Θαλασίου Ἀγουσταλι(ανὸς) λεγ(εῶνος) Συήνης ἀξιωθεὶς ἔγραψα ὑπὲρ αὐτῶν [52]γράμματα μὴ εἰδότων. (3rd hand) ⳨ Αὐρήλιος Ἰακὼβ Ψεννησίου ἀπὸ Συήνης μαρτηρῶ. (4th hand) [53]⳨ Φλ(αούιος) Δίδυμος Σιλβανοῦ ἀπὸ βικαρ(ιανῶν) μαρτυρῶ. (5th hand) [54]+Φλ(αούιος) Παπνοῦθις Δίου στρ(ατιώτης) λεγ(εῶνος) Συήνης μαρτυρῶ. (6th hand) [55]Φλ(αούιος) Ἰωάννης Παὰμ στρ(ατιώτης) λεγ(εῶνος) Συήνης μαρτυρῶ. (7th hand) [56]Φλ(αούιος) Μακάριος Ἰσακίου στρ(ατιώτης) λεγ(εῶνος) Συήνυς μαρτυρῶ. (8th hand). [57]⳨ Φλ(αούιος) Ἀβραὰμ Στεργορίου ἀπὸ ἀκτουαρ(ίων) λεγ(εῶνος) Φιλῶν μαρτυρῶ. ⳨ (9th hand) [58]Φλ(αούιος) Μακάριος Ποσίου στρατιώτης λεγεῶνος Συήνης μαρτυρῶ. (10th hand) [59]⳨ Φλ(αούιος) Παείων Ψαχῶτος στρ(ατιώτης) λεγ(εῶνος) Συήνης μαρτυρῶ. (1st hand) [60]⳨ Φλ(αούιος) Ἀβραάμις Παμὴτ κεντυρ(ίων) λεγ(εῶνος) Συήνης ἐσωμάτισα.

52. l. μαρτυρῶ. 56. l. Συήνης.

have issued to you this deed of sale which is valid and guaranteed over the signature of our signatory, and in answer to the formal question we have given our consent and delivered the deed. (Signed) We the aforesaid, Aurelius Jacob son of Pais son of Reuben and his wife Aurelia Tsendia daughter of Sourtus, have sold the aforesaid house in its entirety from ground to air and have received from you the above-mentioned price of eighteen solidi and guarantee the sale as aforesaid. I, Flavius Photis son of Thalasius, *Augustalianus* [a] of the legion of Syene, have written for them at their request, as they are illiterate. I, Aurelius Jacob son of Psennesius, from Syene, witness. I, Flavius Didymus son of Silvanus, of the *vicariani*,[a] witness. I, Flavius Papnouthis son of Dius, soldier of the legion of Syene, witness. I, Flavius John son of Paam, soldier of the legion of Syene, witness. I, Flavius Macarius son of Isaac, soldier of the legion of Syene, witness. I, Flavius Abraham son of Stercorius, of the *actuarii* [a] of the legion of Philae, witness. I, Flavius Macarius son of Posius, soldier of the legion of Syene, witness. I, Flavius Paion son of Psachos, soldier of the legion of Syene, witness. I, Flavius Abraham son of Pamet, centurion of the legion of Syene, have drawn up the deed.

[a] See Glossary.

31. SALE OF A SLAVE

P. Cairo Zen. 59003, ll. 11-22. 259 B.C.

11 [Βασιλεύοντος Πτολε]μαίου τοῦ Πτολεμαίου καὶ τοῦ υἱοῦ Πτολεμαίου ἔτους ἑβδόμου 12 [καὶ εἰκοστοῦ, ἐφ' ἱερέως Ἀλ]εξάνδρου καὶ θεῶν Ἀδελφῶν, κανηφόρου Ἀρσινόης Φιλαδέλφου 13 [τῶν ὄντων ἐν Ἀλε]ξανδρείαι, μηνὸς Ξανδικοῦ, ἐν Βίρται τῆς Ἀμμανίτιδος. 14 [ἀπέδοτο Νικάνωρ Ξ]ενοκλέους Κνίδιος τῶ[ν] ⟦Τουβίου ἱππέων κληροῦχος⟧ περὶ Τουβίαν 15 [Ζήνωνι Ἀγρεοφῶντ]ος Καυνίωι τῶν περὶ Ἀπολλώνιον τὸν διοικητὴν 16 [παιδίσκην Βαβυλώ]νιον ἧι ὄνομα Σφραγὶς ὡ[ς ἐτ]ῶν ἑπτὰ δραχμῶν πεντήκοντα. 17 [βεβαιωτὴς . . .]ος Ἀνανίου Πέρσης [τῶ]ν Τουβίου ⟦ἱππέων⟧ κληροῦχος. 18 [μάρτυρες ⟦ . . . . .] . ος Ἀγάθωνος Πέρσης⟧ [ὁ δεῖνα] . ωνα δικαστής, Πολέμων Στράτωνος Μακεδὼν 19 [⟦οἱ δύο⟧ τῶν Τουβίου ἱ]ππέων κληροῦχοι, Τιμ[όπολις Βοτέω Μιλήσιος, 20 [Ἡράκλειτος Φιλίππου Ἀθηναῖος,] Ζήνων Τιμάρχου [Κο]λοφώνιος, Δημόστρατος 21 [Διονυσίου Ἀσπένδιος, οἱ] τέσσαρες τῶν περὶ Ἀπολλώνιον τὸν διοικητήν. Verso: ὠνὴ παιδίσκη[ς.

19. *l.* κληροῦχος.

32. SALE OF A SLAVE

P. Oxy. 95. A.D. 129.

1 Ἔτους τρισκαιδεκάτου Αὐτοκράτορος 2 Καίσαρος Τραϊανοῦ Ἁδριανοῦ Σεβαστοῦ Παῦνι 3 κθ, ἐν

31. SALE OF A SLAVE

259 B.C.

In the 27th year of the reign of Ptolemy [a] son of Ptolemy and of his son Ptolemy, the priest of Alexander and of the gods Adelphi [b] and the canephorus of Arsinoe Philadelphus being those in office in Alexandria,[c] in the month Xandicus, at Birta [d] in the land of Ammon. Nicanor son of Xenocles, Cnidian, in the service of Tobias, has sold to Zenon [e] son of Agreophon, Caunian, in the service of Apollonius the dioecetes, a Babylonian girl named Sphragis, about seven years of age, for fifty drachmae. Guarantor . . . son of Ananias, Persian, of the troop of Tobias, cleruch. Witnesses : . . . judge ; Polemon son of Straton, Macedonian, of the cavalrymen of Tobias, cleruch ; Timopolis son of Botes, Milesian, Heraclitus son of Philippus, Athenian, Zenon son of Timarchus, Colophonian, Demostratus son of Dionysius, Aspendian, all four in the service of Apollonius the dioecetes. (Endorsed) Deed of sale of a girl.

[a] Ptolemy Philadelphus.

[b] The deified king and queen, Ptolemy II. and Arsinoe.

[c] Compare No. 2, note *a*. Probably the names of the new priests were still unknown in Transjordania, where the contract was written.

[d] A stronghold of the Ammonite chief Tobias.

[e] See No. 88, note *a*.

32. SALE OF A SLAVE

A.D. 129.

The 13th year of the Emperor Caesar Trajanus Hadrianus Augustus, Pauni 29, at Oxyrhynchus in

Ὀξυρύγχων πόλει τῆς Θηβαΐδος. [4]ὁμολογεῖ Ἀγαθὸς Δαίμων ὁ καὶ Διονύσιο[ς] [5]Διονυσίου τοῦ Διονυσ[ί]ου μητρὸς Ἑρμιόνης [6]ἀπ' Ὀξυρύγχων πόλεω[ς Γ]αΐῳ [Ἰο]υλίῳ Γερμα-[7]νῷ υἱῷ Γαΐῳ Ἰουλίου Δομε[τιανο]ῦ ἐν ἀ[γυ]ιᾷ, [8]ἐκμαρτυρεῖσθαι δ[ι]ὰ τ[αύτης τῆς] ὁμολο-[9]γίας ἣν πεποίηται ὁ ὁμολογῶν Ἀγαθὸς Δαί-[10]μω[ν] ὁ καὶ Διονύσιος τῷ Ἰουλίῳ Γερμανῷ [11]τῇ πέμπτῃ καὶ εἰκάδι μηνὸς Τῦβι τοῦ [12]ἐνεστῶτος τρισκαιδεκάτου ἔτους [13]ἰδιόγραφον πρᾶσιν τῆς ὑπαρξάσης αὐτῷ [14]ἀγοραστῆς, πρότερον Ἡρακλείδου τοῦ [15]καὶ Θέωνος Μάχωνος Σωσικοσμείου [16]τοῦ καὶ Ἀλθαιέως, δούλης Διοσκοροῦτος [17]ὡς (ἐτῶν) κε ἀσήμου, ἣν ἔκτοτε παρεί<λη>φεν [18]παρ' αὐτοῦ ὁ Ἰούλιος Γερμανὸς ταύτην [19]τοιαύτην ἀναπόριφον πλὴν ἱερᾶς [20]νόσου καὶ ἐπαφῆς, τειμῆς ἀργυρίου [21]δραχμῶν χειλίων διακοσίων, ἃς [22]ἔκτοτε ἀπέσχεν ὁ Ἀγαθὸς Δαίμω[ν] [23]ὁ καὶ Διονύσιος παρ[ὰ] τοῦ Ἰουλίου Γερμα-[24]νοῦ ἐκ πλήρους ἅμα τῇ ἰδιογράφῳ πράσ[ι], [25]ἀφ' ἧς ἐτάξατο ὁ Ἰούλιος Γερμανὸς [26]τὰ εἰς τὸ ἐνκύκλιον τῆς αὐτῆς δούλη[ς] [27]Διοσκοροῦτος τέλη τῇ τρίτῃ μηνὸ[ς] [28]Φαμενὼθ τοῦ αὐτοῦ ἔτους, ἀκολού-[29]θως τῷ ἐκδεδομένῳ αὐτῷ συμβόλῳ, [30]τῆς βεβαιώσεως τῆς αὐτῆς δούλης [31]Διοσκοροῦτος πρὸς πᾶσαν βεβαίωσιν [32]ἐξακολουθούσης τῷ Ἀγαθῷ Δαίμον[ι] [33]τῷ καὶ Διονυσίῳ, ὡς καὶ ἡ ἰδιόγραφος [34]πρᾶσις περιέχει. ἣν ἐὰν συμβῇ παρα-[35]πεσῖν ἢ ἄλλως πως διαφθαρ[ῆ]ναι, μ[ὴ] [36]προσδεῖσθαι τὸν Ἰούλιον [Γερμανὸν - - -

7. *l*. Γαΐου.

the Thebaid. Agathodaemon also called Dionysius son of Dionysius son of Dionysius, his mother being Hermione, of Oxyrhynchus, acknowledges to Gaius Julius Germanus son of Gaius Julius Domitianus, in the street,[a] that he hereby confirms the autograph contract which the acknowledging party Agathodaemon also called Dionysius made with Julius Germanus on Tubi 25 of the current 13th year for the sale of a female slave called Dioscorous, aged about 25 years, without distinguishing marks, who became his property by purchase and formerly belonged to Heraclides also called Theon son of Machon, of the Sosicosmian tribe and the Althaean deme,[b] which slave Julius Germanus did then take over from him just as she was, not repudiable except for epilepsy or seizure by a claimant, for the price of 1200 drachmae of silver, which Agathodaemon also called Dionysius then received from Julius Germanus in full on the making of the autograph contract, out of which price Julius Germanus paid the tax on the sale of the said slave Dioscorous on Phamenoth 3 of the said year according to the receipt issued to him; and it is incumbent on Agathodaemon also called Dionysius to guarantee the sale of the said slave Dioscorous in every respect, as the autograph contract states. If the contract should happen to be lost or destroyed in some other way, Julius Germanus shall not require . . .

[a] See No. 7, note *b*.

[b] Theon being a citizen of Alexandria, which in the manner of a Greek city was organized in tribes and demes.

33. SALE OF AN ASS

P. Oxy. 1707. A.D. 204.

[1]{Ὁμολογεῖ} Ἀπολλώνιος Ἡφαιστίωνος [2]τ[ο]ῦ Ἀμμωνίου Σωσικόσμιος ὁ κ(αὶ) Ἀλθ<αι>εὺς [3]Ἀπολλωνίῳ Ἀπολλωνίου τοῦ Σαραπίω-[4]νος Εὐθηνοδίου τῷ καὶ Ἀλθεεῖ χαίρειν. [5]ὁμολογῶ πεπρακέναι σοι ὄνον θήλειαν [6]πρωτοβώλως μυόχρωμον ἀχάρα-[7]κτον τιμῆς τῆς συμπεφωνημέ-[8]νης πρὸς ἀλλήλους ἀργυρίου Σεβαστῶν [9]νομίσματος δραχμὰς ἑξακοσί-[10]ων, (γίνονται) (δρ.) χ, ἃς καὶ αὐτόθι ἀπέσχεν ὁ ὁ-[11]μολογῶν Ἀπολλώνιος παρὰ τοῦ [12]Ἀπολλωνίου, καὶ βε<βαι>ώσει πάσῃ βε-[13]βαιώσει ἀπ[ὸ] παντὸς τοῦ ἐπελευσο-[14]μένου, ταύτ[η]ν τοιαύτην ἀναπόρι-[15]φ[ο]ν. ἐὰν δὲ ἐπιλάβηταί τις αὐτῆς, [16]ἀποστήσει αὐτὸν ὁ Ἀπολλώνιος ταῖς [17]ἰδίαις αὐτοῦ δαπάναις. κυρία ἡ πρᾶσις. [18]ἔτους τρισκαιδεκάτου Αὐτοκρατόρων [19]Καισάρων Λουκίου Σεπτιμίου Σεουήρου [20]Εὐσεβοῦς Περτίνακος Ἀραβικοῦ [21]Ἀδιαβηνι[κ]οῦ Παρθικοῦ Μεγίστου [22]καὶ Μάρκου [Α]ὐρηλίου Ἀντωνίνου [23]Εὐσεβοῦς Σεβαστῶν καὶ Πουβλίου [24]Σεπτιμίου Γέτα Καίσαρος Σεβαστοῦ [25]Φαῶφι ε. (2nd hand in rude uncials) [26]Ἀπολλώνιος [27]ὁ προκίμενος [28]πέπρακα ὁ πρ-[29]όκιται.

4. *l.* Εὐθηνοδίῳ, Ἀλθαιεῖ. 6. *l.* πρωτοβόλον. 9. *l.* δραχμῶν. 28. *l.* ὡς.

33. SALE OF AN ASS

A.D. 204.

Apollonius son of Hephaestion son of Ammonius, of the Sosicosmian tribe and the Althaean deme. to Apollonius son of Apollonius son of Sarapion, of the Euthenodian tribe and the Althaean deme,[a] greeting. I acknowledge that I have sold to you a female ass, which has shed its first teeth, mouse-coloured, unbranded, at the price agreed upon between us of six hundred drachmae of Imperial silver coin, total dr. 600, which the acknowledging party Apollonius has received on the spot from Apollonius, and he will guarantee it with every guarantee against the proceedings of any person, just as it is, not repudiable.[b] If anyone lays claim to it, Apollonius will repel him at his own expense. This deed of sale is valid. The 13th year of the Emperors and Caesars Lucius Septimius Severus Pius Pertinax Arabicus Adiabenicus Parthicus Maximus and Marcus Aurelius Antoninus Pius, Augusti, and Publius Septimius Geta Caesar Augustus, Phaophi 5. (Signed) I, Apollonius the aforesaid, have sold as aforesaid.

[a] Both parties were Alexandrian citizens.

[b] That is, the purchaser had accepted the donkey as it stood, and could not afterwards return it and claim his money back.

34. SALE OF WHEAT

P. Hib. 84 (*a*), ll. 1-15. About 285 B.C.

[1][Βασιλεύοντος Πτολεμαίο]υ ἐφ' ἱερέως Μενελάου τοῦ Λάγου τῶι ε (ἔτει), μη-[2][νὸς Δίο]υ. ἀπέδοτ[ο] Ἐπιμένης Ἀθηναῖος Τιμοκλεῖ Χαλκιδεῖ πυ-[3][ρῶν ἀ]ρτάβας τριάκοντα, καὶ τὴν τιμὴν ἀπέχει Ἐπιμένης πα-[4][ρὰ Τι]μοκλέους ἅμα τῆι συγγραφῆι. ἀποδότω δὲ Ἐπιμένης τὸ[ν [5]σῖ]τον Τιμοκλεῖ ἐγ{γ} νέων τῶν ἐπιόντων ἀπ' ἅλω ἐν μηνὶ Πα-[6]νήμωι σῖτον καθαρὸν ἀπὸ πάντων μέτρωι τῶι χοι τῶι β[α]σιλικ[ῶι] [7]ἐν κώμηι Περόηι. ἐὰν δὲ μὴ ἀποδῶι, ἀποτεισάτω Ἐπι[μέ-][8]νης Τιμοκλεῖ τιμὴν τῆς ἀρτάβης ἑκάστης δραχμὰς [9][τέσ]σαρας, καὶ ἡ πρᾶξις ἔστω Τιμοκλεῖ ἐκ{κ} τῶν ὑπαρχόν-[10][των τῶν Ἐπιμένο]υς πράσσοντι τρόπωι ὧι ἂν βούληται. [11]ἡ δ[ὲ συγγραφὴ ἥδε κ]υρία ἔστω οὗ ἂν ἐπιφέρηι Τιμοκλῆς [12]ἢ [ἄλλος τις ὑπὲρ Τιμοκλ]έους πράσσων κατὰ ταὐτά. [13]μάρτυρες Ι[. . . . . Δ]ι[ο]νύσιος, [Ἀ]ριστόμαχος, Μελ[ι. -][14]νοις, Στάσιππος, Κ[. . . . . . .]ος. συγγραφοφύλαξ Διον[ύσιος [15]Ἱε]ροκλέους.

5. For ἀφ' ἅλω. 12. Or ταῦτα. 15. Ἱε]ροκλέους revised reading.

35. SALE OF ACACIA TREES

P. Oxy. 909. A.D. 225.

[1]Αὐρήλιος Πτολλίων Πτολλίωνος ἀπ' Ὀξυρύγχων [2]πόλεως ἐπίτροπος ἀφηλίκων τέκνων [3]Ἀπολλωνίου τοῦ καὶ Διδύμου Ὀνησᾶτος [4]καὶ ἡ τῶν

34. SALE OF WHEAT

About 285 B.C.

In the reign of Ptolemy,[a] the 5th year [b] of the priesthood of Menelaus [c] son of Lagus, in the month Dius. Epimenes, Athenian, has sold to Timocles, Chalcidian, thirty artabae of wheat, and Epimenes has received the price from Timocles on the date of this contract. Epimenes shall deliver the corn to Timocles out of the coming new crops from the threshing-floor in the month Panemus, free from all impurities, measured by the royal *choi* [d] standard, in the village of Peroe. If he fails to deliver it, Epimenes shall forfeit to Timocles as the value of each artaba four drachmae, and Timocles shall have the right of execution upon the property of Epimenes, making exaction in whatever way he chooses. This contract shall be valid wherever it is produced by Timocles or by any other person making exaction on behalf of Timocles in like manner. Witnesses: . . ., Dionysius, Aristomachus, Meli . . ., Stasippus, C . . . us. Keeper of the contract: Dionysius son of Hierocles.

[a] Ptolemy Soter.
[b] In view of other evidence this can scarcely mean the 5th year of the reign, *i.e.* 301–300 B.C.
[c] A brother of the king.
[d] The word has not yet been explained.

35. SALE OF ACACIA TREES

A.D. 225.

Aurelius Ptollion son of Ptollion, of Oxyrhynchus, guardian of the children of Apollonius also called Didymus son of Onesas, who are minors, and the

ἀφηλίκων μήτηρ καὶ ἐπακολου-[5]θήτρια Αὐρηλία Εὐδαιμονὶς Ἀντινόου [6]τοῦ καὶ Ἑρμοῦ Ἀντινοῒς χωρὶς κυρίου χρη-[7]ματίζουσα κατὰ Ῥωμαίων ἔθη τέκνων [8]δικαίῳ Αὐρηλίοις Σερήνῳ υἱῷ Αὐρηλίου [9]Ἀμμωνίου ἐξηγητεύσαντος τῆς Ὀξυρυγ-[10]χειτῶν πόλεως καὶ Σερήνῳ Σερήνου [11]καὶ Θεωνᾶτι χρηματίζοντι μητρὸς [12]Τααρμιύσιος καὶ Σωτηρίχῳ Διδύμου ἀπ[ὸ] [13]τῆς αὐτῆς πόλεως χαίρειν. ὁμολογοῦμεν [14]πεπρακέναι ὑμεῖν τοῖς τέσσαρσι ἐξ ἴσου [15]τὰς οὔσας ἐπὶ χώματος ἀμπελ[ι]κοῦ [16]κτήματος νεοφύτου τῶν ἀφηλίκων [17]περὶ κώμην Σενέπτα ἀκάνθας ἀριθμῷ [18]τελείας δεκατέσσαρας τειμῆς τῆς συμ-[19]πεφωνημένης πρὸς ἀλλήλους ἀργυ-[20]ρίου δραχμῶν χειλ[ί]ων διακοσίων, αἳ προσ-[21]εχώρησαν εἰς συνωνὴν πυροῦ χωρή-[22]σ[α]ντος ὑπὲρ μετρημάτων τῆς προκ[ει-][23]μένης ἀμπέλου χρόνων θεοῦ Κομόδο[υ] [24]ἐπὶ τῷ ὑμᾶς τὴν τῶν προκειμένων ἀκαν-[25]θῶν ἀναβολὴν ἐξ [ἐ]πιρίζων καὶ ἄρσιν [26]ταῖς ὑμῶν δαπάναις ποιήσασθαι ὁπόταν [27]αἱρῆσθαι, ἐπάναγκον δὲ μέχρι τοῦ Μεσορὴ [28]τοῦ ἐνεστῶτος δ (ἔτους), καὶ μετὰ τὴν τῶν ἀκανθῶν [29]ἀναβολὴν καὶ ἄρσιν τὸν [κ]όσμον τῶν τό-[30]πων τὸ ἴσον ποιήσασθαι ἡμᾶς τε κατὰ τὸ ἥ-[31]μι[σ]υ καὶ ὑμᾶς τοὺς πεπρακότας κατὰ τὸ ἕτερο[ν] [32]ἥμισυ καθὼς ἐπὶ τούτοις ἐστάθη, καὶ ἐπηρω-[33]τηθέντες ὡμολογήσαμεν. κυρία ἡ πρᾶσις [34]δισσὴ γραφεῖσα. (ἔτους) δ Αὐτοκράτορος Καίσαρ[ος] [35]Μάρκου Αὐρηλίου Σεουήρου Ἀλεξ[άνδρου Εὐσεβο]ῦς [36]Εὐτυχοῦς Σεβαστοῦ Τῦβι ιε. (2nd hand) [37]Αὐρήλιος Πτολλί[ων Πτολλίωνος μετ' ἐπα-][38]κολουθητρίας τῆ[ς μητρὸς - - -

mother of the minors, who gives her concurrence, Aurelia Eudaemonis daughter of Antinous also called Hermes, of Antinoopolis, acting without a guardian according to the Roman custom by the right of her children, to the Aurelii Serenus son of Aurelius Ammonius, formerly exegetes of Oxyrhynchus, and Serenus son of Serenus and Theonas styled as having Taarmiusis for mother and Soterichus son of Didymus, of the said city, greeting. We acknowledge that we have sold to you four in equal shares the 14 mature acacia trees growing upon the embankment of the minors' newly planted vineyard near the village of Senepta at the price agreed upon between us of 1200 silver drachmae, which sum has been applied to the purchase of wheat paid for the dues on the aforesaid vineyard which were owing from the reign of the deified Commodus, on condition that you dig up the aforesaid acacia trees from the roots and remove them at your own expense whenever you choose, though it must not be later than Mesore of the current 4th year, and after the digging up and removal of the acacia trees the ground shall be put in order by both parties equally, half by you and the other half by us the vendors, in accordance with our agreement to these terms, and in answer to the formal question we have given our consent. This deed of sale, written in duplicate, is valid. The 4th year of the Emperor Caesar Marcus Aurelius Severus Alexander Pius Felix Augustus, Tubi 15. (Signed) I, Aurelius Ptollion son of Ptollion, with the concurrence of the mother. . . .

---

27. *l.* αἱρῆσθε. 30. Transpose ἡμᾶς and ὑμᾶς. 32. *l.* ἐπερωτηθέντες.

36. SALE OF A LOOM

P. Oxy. 1705. A.D. 298.

[1]Οὐαλέριος Πετερμοῦθις στρατιώτης δι' ἐμοῦ Αὐρηλίου Σαραπίωνος Σαραπί-[2]ωνος ἀπὸ τῆς λαμπρᾶς καὶ λαμ(προτάτης) Ὀξυρυ[γ]χειτῶν πόλεως [τ]ῶν ἐξ ἐφηβίας [3]ἱερονικῶν Αὐρηλίᾳ Εὐδαιμονίδει τῇ καὶ Ἀπολλωνίᾳ ματρώνᾳ στ[ο]λάτᾳ [4]χαίρειν. ὁμολογῶ πεπρακέναι σοι ἐντεῦθεν ὃν κἀγὼ ἐώνημαι παρὰ Αὐρη-[5]λίου Σαραπάμμωνος Θώνιος ἀπὸ Ὀξυρύγχων πόλεως τῷ ἐνεστῶτι ἔτι, μηνὶ [6]Μεχεὶρ η, ἱστὸν ταρσικοϋφικὸν μήκους πηχῶν δέκα, πλάτους πη-[7]χῶν ἕξ, καὶ τὴν οὖσαν ἔν[θ]α ἀπόκειται ἐξαρτίαν πᾶσαν ὅση{ν} ἐὰν ᾖ, [8]τιμῆς τῆς συμπεφωνημ[έν]ης πρὸς ἀλλή[λ]ους ἀργυρίου Σεβαστῶν [9]νομίσματος ταλάντων δύο καὶ δραχμῶν χιλείων, ἅπερ αὐτόθι ἀπέσχον [10]παρὰ σοῦ ἐκ πλήρους διὰ [χ]ειρός, περὶ ἧς ἀριθμήσεως ἐπερωτηθεὶς [11]ὑπ[ὸ] σοῦ ὡμολόγησα, ὅνπερ ἱστὸν καὶ τὴν ἐξαρτίαν βαστάξεις [12]ἐντεῦθεν ἔνθα ἀπόκειται καὶ μετενεγκεῖς ὅπου ἐὰν θέλῃς ἀκωλύτως, [13]καὶ κρατεῖν σε καὶ κυριεύειν σὺν ἐκγόνοις καὶ τοῖς παρὰ σοῦ μεταλημψομέ-[14]νοις, καὶ ἐξουσίαν ἔχειν χρᾶσθαι καὶ ἐκμισθοῖν καὶ πωλεῖν ὡς ἐὰν αἱρῇ, [15]κα[ὶ] παρέξομαί σοι β[έ]βαιον διὰ παντὸς ἀπὸ πάντων [16]π[άσ]ῃ βεβαιώσι, καὶ τὸν ἐπελευσόμενόν σ[οι ἀ]ποστήσω παρα-[17]χ[ρῆ]μα ταῖς ἐμαυτοῦ δαπάναις, καθάπερ ἐκ δί[κης]. κυρία ἡ πρᾶσις [18]ἁπλῆ γραφεῖσα καὶ ἐπερωτ[η]θεὶς ὡμολόγη[σ]α. (ἔτους) ιδ [19]καὶ (ἔτους) ιγ τῶ[ν]

36. SALE OF A LOOM

A.D. 298.

Valerius Petermouthis, soldier, acting through me, Aurelius Sarapion son of Sarapion, of the illustrious and most illustrious city of Oxyrhynchus, victor in youth at the sacred games, to Aurelia Eudaemonis also called Apollonia, *matrona stolata*,[a] greeting. I acknowledge that I have sold to you herewith the loom for Tarsian[b] weaving which I bought myself from Aurelius Sarapammon son of Thonis, of Oxyrhynchus, in the current year on Mecheir 8, ten cubits long and six cubits broad, with all the fittings found in the place where it is kept whatever they amount to, at the price agreed upon between us of 2 talents and 1000 drachmae of Imperial silver coin, which I have herewith received from you in full by hand and of which I have formally acknowledged the payment; and this loom with its fittings you shall forthwith carry away from where it is kept and transfer it whither you wish without hindrance, and you with your descendants and successors shall possess and own it and have the right to use it or hire it out or sell it as you choose, and I will deliver it to you guaranteed for all time against all claims by every guarantee, and anyone who proceeds against you I will straightway repel at my own expense, as if on the strength of a legal decision. This deed of sale, made in a single copy, is valid, and in answer to the formal question I have given my assent. The 14th year and 13th year of our

[a] "Matron clad in the *stola*," *i.e.* a Roman wife and mother of honourable standing.

[b] Weaving of a special sort of cloth called after the city of Tarsus.

κυρίων ἡμῶν Διοκλη[τ]ιανοῦ κ[α]ὶ Μαξιμιανοῦ [20]Σεβαστῶν καὶ (ἔτους) ς τῶν κυρίων ἡμῶν Κωνσταντίου καὶ [21]Μαξιμιανοῦ τῶν ἐπιφανεστάτων Καισάρων Ἐπεὶφ ιβ, [22]ὑπατείας Ἀννικίου Φαύστου καὶ Οὐιρίου Γάλλου. (2nd hand) [23]Οὐαλέριος Παθερμοῦτις δι' ἐμοῦ Σαραπίωνος [24]πέπρακα τὸν ἱστὸν καὶ τὴν ἐξαρτίαν πᾶσαν, [25]καὶ ἀπέσχον τὰ τῆς τιμῆς ἀργυρίου τάλαντα δύο [26]καὶ δραχμὰς χιλίας πλήρη, καὶ βεβαιώσω ὡς [27]πρόκειται, καὶ ἐπερωτηθεὶς ὡμολόγησα.

37. SALE OF HOLY DAYS

P.S.I. 1016, ll. 16-37. 129 B.C.

Lines 1-15, which we omit, contain an abstract (as in No. 2), after which comes the contract proper.

[16]Βασιλεύοντος Πτολεμαίου θεοῦ Εὐεργέτου τοῦ Πτολεμαίου καὶ Κλεοπάτρας θεῶν Ἐπιφανῶν [17]καὶ βασιλίσσης Κλεοπάτρας τῆς γυναικὸς θεᾶς Εὐεργέτιδος (ἔτους) μβ, ἐφ' ἱερέως τοῦ ὄντος [18]Ἀλεξάνδρου καὶ θεῶν Σωτήρων καὶ θεῶν Ἀδελφῶν καὶ θεῶν Εὐεργετῶν καὶ θεῶν [19]Φιλοπατόρων καὶ θεῶν Ἐπιφανῶν καὶ θεοῦ Φιλομήτορος καὶ θεοῦ Εὐπάτορος καὶ θεῶν [20]Εὐεργετῶν, ἀθλοφόρου Βερενίκης Εὐεργέτιδος, κανηφόρου Ἀρσινόης Φιλαδέλφου, ἱερείας [21]Ἀρσινόης Φιλοπάτορος, ἐφ' ἱερείων καὶ ἱερειῶν τῶν ὄντων καὶ οὐσῶν ἐ[ν] Πτολεμαΐδι, [22]μηνὸς Ἀθὺρ κθ, ἐν Διὸς πόλει τῆι μεγάληι τῆς Θηβαΐδος ἐφ' Ἡρα-

21. l. ἱερέων.

lords Diocletianus and Maximianus Augusti and the 6th year of our lords Constantius and Maximianus the most noble Caesars, Epeiph 12, in the consulship of Annicius Faustus and Virius Gallus (Signed) I, Valerius Pathermouthis, acting through me, Sarapion, have sold the loom and all the fittings and have received the full price of 2 talents and 1000 drachmae of silver, and I will guarantee it as aforesaid, and in answer to the formal question I have given my assent.

37. SALE OF HOLY DAYS

129 B.C.

In the 42nd year of the reign of Ptolemy the god Euergetes, son of Ptolemy and Cleopatra, gods Epiphaneis, and of Queen Cleopatra his wife the goddess Euergetis, the priest of Alexander and the gods Soteres and the gods Adelphi and the gods Euergetae and the gods Philopatores and the gods Epiphaneis and the god Philometor and the god Eupator and the gods Euergetae, the athlophorus of Berenice Euergetis, the canephorus of Arsinoe Philadelphus, the priestess of Arsinoe Philopator,[a] likewise the priests and priestesses in Ptolemais, being those now in office, on the 29th of the month Hathur, at Diospolis Magna[b] in the Thebaid, before Heraclides, agoranomus of

[a] The foregoing are the eponymous priesthoods of Alexandria, the names of the priests and priestesses being, as usual, omitted; then come those of Ptolemais, treated still more summarily. Epiphaneis, Soteres, Adelphi, etc., are the titles under which the various kings aud queens were deified.

[b] Thebes, the modern Luxor.

κλεί[δ]ου ἀγορανόμου [23]τοῦ Περὶ Θήβας. [24]ἀπέδοτο Σεννοῦθις Ὥρου τῶν ἐκ τῶν Μεμνονείων τῆς Λιβύης τοῦ Παθυρίτου [25]ὡς (ἐτῶν) λ μέση μελίχ(ρους) στρογγυλοπρ(όσωπος) ἔνσιμος οὐλὴ παρὰ χαλινὸν δεξ(ιὸν) μῆλα μείζω μετὰ [26]κυρίου τοῦ ἑαυτῆς συγγενοῦς πρὸς γυναικογένειαν Ἁρσιήσιος τοῦ Πατήμιος μητρὸς [27]Λαβάιτος τῶν Πτολεμαίου τοῦ Πύρρου πεζῶν τακτομίσθου ὡς (ἐτῶν) λε μέσου μελιχροῦ [28]ὑποκλάστου πλατυπροσώπου εὐθύρ(ινος) ὦτα μεγάλα καὶ ἀφεστη(κότα) καὶ ἀρ(ιστερὸν) τετρη(μένον) [29]καὶ αὐτὸς Ἁρσιήσι{ο}ς τὸ ὑπάρχον αὐτοῖς γέρας ἡμερῶν ἁγνευτικῶν δέκα [30]καὶ τὰς τούτων καρπείας καὶ λειτουργίας καὶ τὰ συνκύροντα καὶ προσ-[31]εσόμενα πάντα κατ' ἐνιαυτὸν ἕκαστον καὶ τὸ ἐπιβάλλον αὐτοῖς μέρος [32]τῶν ἐπαγομένων καὶ τὰ προσκύροντα τούτοις πάντα ἐν ἱερῶι Ἀφροδισίωι [33]καλουμένωι Ἁθὺρ Νουεμοντεσεμα ἐν τοῖς κατὰ τοὺς τῶν Μεμνονείων [34]τάφοις. ἐπρίατο Ψενμῖνις Πετεμίνιος τῶν ἐκ τῶν Μεμνονείων [35]ὡς (ἐτῶν) μ μέσος μελίχρως τετα(νὸς) πλατυπρ(όσωπος) εὐθύριν οὐλὴ μετώ(πωι) ἐξ ἀμφοτέρων [36]χαλκοῦ νομίσματος ταλάντων τεσσάρων. βεβαιωταὶ τῶν κατὰ τὴν ὠνὴν [37]ταύτην πάντων οἱ ἀποδόμενοι, οὓς ἐδέξατο Ψενμῖνις ὁ πριάμενος.

24. l. ἀπέδοντο.

the nome of Peri Thebas. Sennouthis daughter of Horus from Memnonea[a] in the Libyan district of the Pathyrite nome, aged about 30, of medium height, fair-skinned, round-faced, snub-nosed, scar beside right corner of mouth, large cheeks, having with her as guardian her kinsman on the mother's side Harsiesis son of Patemis and Labais, *tactomisthus*[b] of the infantrymen of Ptolemaeus son of Pyrrhus, aged about 35, of medium height, fair-skinned, rather curly-haired, broad-faced, straight-nosed, ears large and prominent and the left one pierced, and Harsiesis himself have sold the privilege which they possess of ten holy days in each year with their proceeds and rights of office and everything that pertains to them or will accrue to them[c] and the portion falling to them of the intercalary days[d] and everything pertaining thereto in the temple of Aphrodite called Hathur Nouemontesema[e] among the tombs opposite those of Memnonea. Psenminis son of Peteminis, of Memnonea, aged about 40, of medium height, fair-skinned, smooth-haired, broad-faced, straight-nosed, scar on both sides of forehead, has bought them for four talents of copper money. Guarantors of all the terms of this sale: the vendors, whom Psenminis the purchaser has accepted.

[a] The village near the statues of Memnon on the west, or Libyan, side of the Nile.

[b] The word probably means "receiving fixed pay," but nothing is known about the status of the persons thus designated.

[c] The subject of the sale was a share in various priestly emoluments.

[d] *i.e.* a share in the proceeds of the intercalary days proportionate to the share in those of the 12 months.

[e] The well-known temple of Deir el Medina.

38. SALE IN THE FORM OF A LEASE

P. Lond. 1164 (*h*). A.D. 212.

[1]κ̄. Ἁρμιρυμίου τοῦ καὶ Μέλανος Ὥρου ἀργ(υρίου) (τάλαντον) α. [2]ἔτους εἰκοστοῦ Αὐτοκράτορος Καίσαρος Μάρκου Αὐρηλίου Ἀντωνίνου Παρθικοῦ Μεγίστου Βρεττανικοῦ Μεγίστου Εὐσεβοῦς [Σ]εβαστοῦ [3]μηνὸς Πανήμου Φαρμοῦθι κ̄,[a] διὰ τ[ῆς Ἀν]ου[β]ίωνος Ἀμμωνίου Ματιδίου τοῦ κ[αὶ] Καλλιτεκνείου ἐν Ἀντινόου πόλει χρη[μ]ατιστικῆς [4]τραπέζης. Ἁρμιρύμιος ὁ καὶ Μέλας Τήρου(ς) μητρὸς Σεναιῆτος ἀπὸ Τεντύρ[ε]ως τῆς μητροπόλεως Πβῆκι Πεβῶ[το]ς τοῦ [5]Βήκιος μητρὸς Σενθοτμήνιος ἀπὸ Πανὸς πόλεως μεμισθωκέναι τὸν Πβῆκιν τῷ Ἁρμιρυμίῳ τῷ καὶ Μέλανι κατὰ τήνδε τὴν [6]{κατα} μισθοπρασίαν ἐπὶ χρόνον ἔτη ἑξήκοντα ἀπὸ τῆς ἐνεστώσης καὶ ὑποκειμένης ἡμέρας τὸ ὑπάρχον αὐτῷ πλοῖον Ἑλλ[η]νικὸν [7]ἀγωγῆς (ἀρταβῶν) ῡ πλειόνων ἢ ἐλασσόνων κεχαλατριωμένον καὶ ἐστρωμένον καὶ σεσανιδ[ω]μένον διὰ νεὼς σὺν ἱστῷ καὶ κέρατι καὶ λιναρμένῳ [8]καὶ σχοινίοις καὶ κάδοις καὶ κρίκοις καὶ μαγγάνοις καὶ πηδαλίοις δυσὶ σὺν οἴαξι καὶ ὄκνοις καὶ κώπαις τέσσαρσι καὶ κοντοῖς πέ[ν]τε σὺν [9]θηλαῖς σιδηραῖς καὶ θυραβάθραις καὶ διαστῆρι κλιμακίῳ καὶ ἐργάτῃ καὶ ἀνκύραις σιδηραῖς δυσὶ σὺν σπάθαις σιδηραῖς καὶ μονοβόλῳ ἑνὶ [10]καὶ σχοινίο<ι>ς σεβενίνοις καὶ παρόλκῳ καὶ σχοινίοις ἀπογίοις καὶ

8. *l.* ὄνκοις.

---

[a] Day of the month. The text is taken from a roll which records a series of payments and of the contracts which gave

38. SALE IN THE FORM OF A LEASE

A.D. 212.

20th.[a] Payment of 1 talent by Harmirumius also called Melas son of Horus. The 20th year of the Emperor Caesar Marcus Aurelius Antoninus Parthicus Maximus Britannicus Maximus Pius Augustus, 20th day of Panemus or Pharmouthi, through the executory bank of Anubion son of Ammonius, of the Matidian tribe and the Callitecnean deme, in Antinoopolis.[b] Harmirumius also called Melas son of Teres, his mother being Senaies, of Tentyra the metropolis[c] (acknowledges) to Pbekis son of Pebos son of Bekis, his mother being Senthotmenis, of Panopolis, that Pbekis has leased to Harmirumius also called Melas by this deed of leasehold sale[d] for a period of 60 years from this present stated day the Greek boat belonging to him of 400 artabas' burden more or less, supplied with mats and furnished and decked throughout, with mast, yard, sail, ropes, jars, rings, pulleys, two rudders with handles and brackets, four oars and five punting-poles with iron tips, hatches, landing-plank, windlass, two iron anchors with iron flukes and one single-armed anchor, ropes of bast, towing-rope, and mooring-ropes, three

rise to them, the whole transaction being conducted through a bank.

[b] Founded by the Emperor Hadrian as a Greek city with tribes and demes.

[c] The capital of a nome was called a metropolis.

[d] The details show that the transaction was essentially a sale, though nominally a long lease. The only other contracts of the same type deal likewise with boats; hence it is supposed that the object of the vendors in calling the sale a form of lease was to retain certain privileges attaching to this class of property.

ἐμβόλια τρία καὶ μέτρῳ ἑν(ὶ) καὶ ζυγῷ καὶ Κιλικίῳ καὶ κατώτιον κατὰ γε[υ]στρίδα [11]συν κώπαις δυσὶ ἐξηρτισμένον πᾶσι τοῖς ἀνήκουσ‹ι› καὶ ὀβολίσκῳ σιδηρῷ φόρου τοῦ συ[μ]πεφωνημένου πρὸς ἀλλήλους τοῦ ἑξηκοντα-[12]ετοῦς χρόνου ἀργυρίου ταλάντου ἑνὸς καὶ δραχμῶν δισχειλίων, ἀφ᾽ ὧν αὐτόθι ἀνείρηται ὁ Πβῆκις παρὰ τοῦ Ἁρμιρυμίου τοῦ καὶ Μέ-[13]λανος ἀργυρίου τάλαντον ἕν, (γίνεται) τά(λ.) α, τὰς δὲ λοιπὰς τῶν φόρων δραχμὰς δισχειλίας ἀποκαταστήσει ὁ Ἁρμιρύμιος ὁ καὶ Μέλας [14]τῷ Πβήκι παραγινομένου αὐτοῦ εἰς τὸν Πανοπολείτην, λαμβάνων παρ᾽ αὐτοῦ τό τε να[υ]πηγικὸν τοῦ πλοίου καὶ ἄλλας προκτητικ[ὰς] ἀσ-[15]φαλείας τοῦ αὐτοῦ πλοίου πρὸς τὸ μένειν αὐτῷ καὶ τὰ ἀπ᾽ αὐτῶν δίκαια, ἐκδιδοῦντος [το]ῦ Πβήκιος τῷ αὐτῷ Ἁρμιρυμίῳ τῷ καὶ Μέλανι τὰ καθή-[16]κοντα γράμματα τῶν αὐτῶν δραχμῶν δισχειλίων. ἐντεῦθεν δὲ παρέλαβεν ὁ αὐτὸς παρὰ τοῦ Πβήκιος τὸ προκείμενον [π]λοῖον [17]σὺν τῇ καταρθίᾳ καὶ τῷ καταγευστρίῳ ἐφ᾽ ὅρμου Ἀντινόου πόλεως, καὶ ἀπὸ τοῦ νῦν εἰ[ς] τὸν ἀεὶ χρόνον κρατεῖν καὶ κυριεύειν τὸν Ἁρμιρύμιον [18]τὸν καὶ Μέλανα καὶ τοὺς παρ᾽ αὐτοῦ τοῦ μεμισθωμένου κατὰ μισθοπρασίαν αὐτῷ πλοίου καὶ διοικεῖν καὶ ἐπιτελεῖν περὶ αὐτοῦ ὡς ἐὰν αἱρῶν[ται] τρ[ό-][19]πον ἀνεμποδίστως, ἔτι δὲ καὶ μεταμισθοῖν καὶ ναυλολογῖν καὶ ἐκλεγέσθαι τὰ ἐξ αὐτοῦ περ[ι]γεινόμενα πάντα, ἔτι δὲ καὶ λύειν καὶ μετα[ρ]υθμ[ί-][20]ζειν, τῆς βεβαιώσεως διὰ παντὸς πρὸς πᾶσαν βεβαίωσιν ἐξακολουθούσης τῷ Πβήκει καὶ τοῖς παρ᾽ αὐτοῦ, οὓς καὶ μὴ ἐπελε[ύ]σεσ[θαι] [21]ἐπὶ τὸν μεμισθωμένον μηδὲ ἐπὶ τοὺς παρ᾽ αὐτοῦ τρόπῳ μηδενὶ παρευρέσει

shoots for corn, one measure, a balance, a Cilician cloth, a cup-shaped skiff[a] with two oars and provided with all the usual fittings and an iron spike, at the rent agreed upon between each other for the 60 years of one talent 2000 drachmae of silver. Of this sum Pbekis has received on the spot from Harmirumius also called Melas one talent of silver, total 1 tal., and the remaining 2000 drachmae of the rent Harmirumius also called Melas will deliver to Pbekis when he visits the Panopolite nome, receiving from him the boat-builder's receipt and other previously acquired securities for the said boat in order to preserve the rights derived from these, Pbekis issuing to the said Harmirumius also called Melas the proper receipt for the said 2000 drachmae. Herewith the said party has taken over from Pbekis the aforesaid boat with the fittings and the skiff at the port of Antinoopolis, and from now for all time Harmirumius also called Melas and his assigns shall possess and own the boat which has been leased to him by leasehold sale and shall administer it and deal with it in whatever way they choose without hindrance, and may moreover sublet it and charge for transport and appropriate all the proceeds derived from it, and may moreover break it up or remodel it; and it is incumbent on Pbekis and his assigns to guarantee it permanently in every way, nor shall they take proceedings against the lessee or his assigns in

[a] Apparently "in the shape of a tasting-cup" (*γευστρίς*).

10. *l.* *ἐμβολίοις τρισί*. 15. *l.* *ἐκδιδόντος*. 17. *l.* *καταρτίᾳ, κατὰ γευστρ<ίδα κατωτ>ίῳ* ? 18. *l.* *ὅν*. 19. *ναυλολογῖν* revised reading.

μηδεμιᾷ· ἐὰν δὲ ἐπέλθῃ τις καὶ μὴ βεβαιώ[σῃ, ἥ] τε 22 ἔφοδος ἄκυρος ἔστω καὶ προσαποτίσωσ[ι] τῷ μεμισθωμένῳ ἢ τοῖς παρ' αὐτοῦ διπλοῦς τοὺς φόρους <καὶ> εἰς τὸ δημόσιον τοὺς ἴσους καὶ τὰ β[λ]άβη 23 καὶ τὰ δαπανήματα χωρὶς τοῦ κυρίαν καὶ βεβαίαν μένειν τὴν μισθοπρασίαν. (2nd hand) Πβῆκις Πεβῶτος Πβήκιος μητρὸς Σενθοτμήνιος [ἀ]πὸ Πανὸς 24 πόλεως μεμίσθοκα κατὰ μισθοπρασίαν ἐπὶ χρόνον ἔτη ἑξήκοντα τὸ ὑπάρχον μοι τὸ προκείμενον πλοῖον Ἑλληνικὸν ἀγωγῆς (ἀρταβῶν) υ πλειόνων 25 ἢ ἐλασσόνων σὺν κατοθίῳ κατὰ γευστρίδα σὺν τῇ προκειμένῃ πάσῃ καταρθείᾳ φόρου ταλάντου ἑνὸς καὶ δραχμῶν δισχειλείων, ἀφ' ὧν 26 αὐτόθι ἀνείρημαι παρ' αὐτοῦ ἀργυρίου τάλαντον ἕν, τὰς δὲ λοιπὰς δραχμὰς δισχειλείας ἀπολήμψομαι παρ' αὐτοῦ ἐν τῷ Πανοπολείτῃ, 27 λαμβάνων παρ' ἐμοῦ τὰς προκτηθικὰς ἀσφαλείας, καὶ παρέδοκα αὐτῷ τὸ πλοῖον καὶ βεβαιόσω ὡς πρόκειται. Ἁρμιρύμιος ὁ καὶ Μέλα[ς] Τήρου(ς) 28 ἀπὸ Τεντύρης τῆς μητροπόλεως μεμίσθωμαι κα{ι}τὰ μισθωπρασίαν τὸ προκείμενον πλοῖον φόρου ἀργυρίου ταλάντου ἑνὸς καὶ δρα[χ]μῶν 29 δισχειλίων, ἀφ' ὧν αὐτόθι ἐκξωδίασεν ἀργυρίου τάλοντα ἕν, τὰς δὲ λυπὰς δραχμὰς δισχειλίας ἀποκαταστήσο αὐτῶι ὡς ἐπάνου δεδ[ή]λωται, 30 καὶ <ἐν>τεῦθεν ἔλαβον τὸ πλοῖον. Σαραπίων ἔγραψα ὑ(πὲρ) τοῦ πατρὸς γράμματα μὴ ἰδότος.

24. *l.* μεμίσθωκα. 25. *l.* κατωτίῳ, καταρτίᾳ. 27. *l.* λαμβάνοντος, προκτητικάς, παρέδωκα, βεβαιώσω. 28. *l.* μισθοπρασίαν. 29. *l.* ἐξωδίασα, τάλαντον, λοιπάς, ἀποκαταστήσω, ἐπάνω.

any manner on any pretext; and if anyone takes proceedings and fails to guarantee, the proceedings shall be invalid and in addition they shall forfeit to the lessee or his assigns twice the amount of the rent and to the treasury the same together with damages and expenses, the leasehold sale moreover remaining valid and guaranteed. (Signed) I, Pbekis son of Pebos son of Pbekis, my mother being Senthotmenis, of Panopolis, have leased by leasehold sale for a period of 60 years the aforesaid Greek boat belonging to me of 400 artabas' burden more or less together with the cup-shaped skiff with all the aforesaid fittings for a rent of one talent and 2000 drachmae, of which I have received from him on the spot one talent of silver and shall obtain from him the remaining 2000 drachmae in the Panopolite nome when he receives from me the previously acquired securities, and I have delivered to him the boat and will guarantee it as aforesaid. I, Harmirumius also called Melas son of Teres, of Tentyra the metropolis, have taken the aforesaid boat on lease by leasehold sale for a rent of one talent and 2000 drachmae of silver, of which sum I have paid on the spot one talent of silver, and the remaining 2000 drachmae I will deliver to him as explained above, and I have herewith received the boat. I, Sarapion, have written for my father, as he is illiterate.

39. LEASE OF LAND

P. Columbia 270, col. 1. 256 B.C.

[1]Βασιλεύοντος Πτολεμαίου τοῦ Πτολεμαίου Σωτῆρος (ἔτους) λ, ἐφ' ἱερέως [2]Ἀλεξάνδρου τοῦ Λεωνίδου Ἀλεξάνδρου καὶ θεῶν Ἀδελφῶν, κανηφόρου Ἀρσινόης [3]Φιλαδέλφου Πρεπούσης τῆς Δημητρίου, μηνὸς Πανήμου Αἰγυπτίων δὲ Ἐπεὶφ ῑ. [4]ἐξέλαβεν Ἡγήσαρχος Θεοπόμπου καὶ Θεόπομπος Ἡγησάρχου καὶ Νικόδημος Ἡγησάρχου, [5]οἱ τρεῖς Μακεδόνες τῆς ἐπιγονῆς, παρὰ Ζήνωνος τοῦ Ἀγρεοφῶντος Καυνίου τῶ[ν περὶ] [6]Ἀπολλώνιον τὸν διοικητήν, ἀπὸ τῶν δεδομένων παρὰ τοῦ βασιλέως ἐν τῶι Ἀρσινο[ί]τ[ηι] [7]νομῶι κατὰ Φιλαδέλφειαν Ἀπολλωνίωι τῶι διοικητῆι (ἀρουρῶν) (μυρίων), γῆς σπορίμου ἐν τῶι [8]γ̅ περι(χώματι) τῶι ἀπ<ὸ β>ορρᾶ πρὸς νότον (ἀρούρας) ρ εἰς ἐνιαυτόν, ἑκάστην (ἄρουραν) πρὸς πυρὸν ἀν(ὰ) (ἀρτάβας) ζ (ὄγδοον) ἀκίνδυνον [9]καὶ ἀνυπόλογον παντὸς ὑπολόγου. δοθήσεται δὲ εἰς μὲν τὴν πυροφόρον σπέρμα τῆι (ἀρούραι) (ἀρτάβης) (ἥμισυ), [10]εἰς δὲ τὴν κριθοφόρον κατὰ λόγον, καὶ εἰς ἀνήλωμα ἑκάστηι (ἀρούραι) κρ(ιθῆς) (ἀρτάβη) α καὶ εἰς βοτανισμὸν κρ(ιθῆς) (ἀρτάβης) (ἥμισυ) [11]καὶ εἰς ξυλοκοπίαν, ἐὰν ἐμπίπτηι κοπάς, ὅσον ἂν συγκριθῆι ἱκανὸν εἶναι δίδοσθαι εἰς ἑκάστην [12]ἀρουρῶν. ἀπομετρείτωσαν δὲ Ἡγήσαρχος καὶ Θεόπομπος καὶ Νικόδημος τὸν σῖτον εἰς τὸ [13]ἐκφόριον ἐν τῶι ἐμ Φιλαδελφείαι θησαυρῶι κατὰ τὸ σιτολογικὸν διάγραμμα ἐμ μηνὶ [14]Δαισίωι τῶι ἐν τῶι λα (ἔτει), ὡσαύτως δὲ καὶ ὃν

12. *l.* ἄρουραν.

[a] See No. 88, note *a*.

39. LEASE OF LAND

256 B.C.

In the 30th year of the reign of Ptolemy son of Ptolemy Soter, the priest of Alexander and the gods Adelphi being Alexander son of Leonidas, the canephorus of Arsinoe Philadelphus being Prepusa daughter of Demetrius, in the month Panemus, or in Egyptian style Epeiph 10. Hegesarchus son of Theopompus and Theopompus son of Hegesarchus and Nicodemus son of Hegesarchus, all three Macedonians of the Epigone, have taken on contract for a year from Zenon [a] son of Agreophon, Caunian, in the service of Apollonius the dioecetes, from the 10,000 arurae given by the king to Apollonius the dioecetes at Philadelphia in the Arsinoite nome, 100 arurae of arable land in the 3rd basin which stretches from north to south, at a rent in wheat of 7⅛ artabae for each arura, warranted against risk and not subject to deduction of any kind. There will be given as seed for the wheat-bearing land half an artaba to the arura and for the barley-bearing land a proportionate amount, and to meet expenses one artaba of barley for each arura and for weeding half an artaba of barley and for wood-cutting, if brushwood should be met with, as much as may be judged sufficient to be given for each arura. Hegesarchus and Theopompus and Nicodemus shall measure out the corn for rent at the granary in Philadelphia in accordance with the ordinance [b] concerning corn-collecting in the month Daesius of the 31st year and shall likewise repay whatever

[b] A royal ordinance, otherwise unknown, dealing with the collection of rents in corn.

ἂν λαμβάνωσιν σῖτον εἰς σπέρμα καὶ [15]βοτανισμὸν καὶ ἀνήλωμα καὶ ὅσον ἂν ἀργύριον εἰς τὴν κοπάδα δανείσωνται ἢ σῖτον [16]ἀντὶ τοῦ ἀργυρίου, τῶμ μὲν πυ(ρῶν) τὴν (ἀρτάβην) πρὸς χαλκὸν (δραχμῆς) (διωβόλου), τῆς δὲ κρ(ιθῆς) κατὰ λόγον. κατασπει-[17]ράτωσαν δὲ Ἡγήσαρχος καὶ Θεόπομπος καὶ Νικόδημος ἧς ἐξειλήφασι γῆς τὰ μὲν [18]δύο μέρη πυρῶι, τὸ δὲ τρίτον μέρος κριθῆι. ἐὰν δὲ μὴ ποιῶσι καθὰ συνεγράψαντο, [19]ἐξέστω Ζήνωνι ἑτέροις ἀπομισθοῦν τὴν γῆν· τὸ δὲ βλάβος ὃ ἂν καταβλά⟦β⟧ψωσι τὴν [20]Ἀπολλωνίου πρόσοδον ἢ πρὸς τὸ ἐκφόριον καὶ τὰ δάνεια ὃ ἂν προσοφειλήσωσι ἀποτεισά-[21]τωσαν Ζήνωνι παραχρῆμα ἡμιόλιον, ἡ δὲ πρᾶξις ἔστω Ζήνωνι ἢ ἄλλωι ὑπὲρ αὐτοῦ [22]πράσσοντι ἔκ τε αὐτῶν καὶ τῶν ἐγγύων καὶ τῶν ὑπαρχόντων αὐτοῖς πάντων [23]καὶ ἐξ ἑνὸς καὶ ἐκ πάντων ὡς πρὸς βασιλικά. ἔγγυοι τῶν κατὰ τὴν συγγραφὴν [24]εἰς ἔκτεισιν οἱ συγγεγραμμένοι ἀλλήλων καὶ Ἀμμώνιος Θέωνος Κυρηναῖος τῶν [ἐ]πέργων. [25]ἡ δὲ συγγραφὴ ἥδε κυρία ἔστω οὗ ἂν ἐπιφέρηται. μάρτυρες Δᾶμις Κλέωνος, Σώστρατος [26]Κλέωνος, οἱ δύο Ἑλένειοι, Θεόπομπος Ἀριστίωνος Θεσσαλὸς ἰατρός, Διόδωρος Ζωπύρου [27]Μάγνης τῶν περὶ Ἀπολλώνιον τὸν διοικητήν, Ἀγαθῖνος Πύρρου Κυρηναῖος τῶν ἐπέργων, [28]Ἄνοσις Τοτορχόιτος Σαΐτης κωμογραμματεὺς Φιλαδελφείας. [29]συγγ[ρα]φ[ο]φύλαξ Δᾶμις.

22. Corr. from του εγγυου, also αυτοις from αυτων.

corn they may receive for seed and for weeding and to meet expenses and whatever money they may borrow for the brushwood, or corn in place of the money, wheat at the rate of one artaba for 1 drachma 2 obols in copper and barley at a proportionate rate.[a] Hegesarchus and Theopompus and Nicodemus shall sow two-thirds of the land which they have taken on contract with wheat and the other third with barley. If they fail to do as they have agreed, Zenon shall be at liberty to let the land to others; and whatever loss they may cause to the revenue of Apollonius or whatever they may owe in respect of rent and loans, they shall forfeit to Zenon forthwith one and a half times that amount, and Zenon or his representative shall have the right of execution upon themselves and their sureties and all their property, both upon one and upon all, as in the case of debts to the Crown. Sureties for payment of the obligations of the contract: the contracting parties, each for the other, and Ammonius son of Theon, Cyrenaean, one of the employees.[b] This deed shall be valid wherever produced. Witnesses: Damis son of Cleon, Sostratus son of Cleon, both Heleneans; Theopompus son of Aristion, Thessalian, physician; Diodorus son of Zopyrus, Magnesian, in the service of Apollonius the dioecetes; Agathinus son of Pyrrhus, Cyrenaean, one of the employees; Anosis son of Totorchois, Saite, village scribe of Philadelphia. Keeper of the contract: Damis.

[a] The usual ratio of the value of barley to that of wheat was 3 : 5.

[b] The exact meaning is unknown.

40. LEASE OF CLERUCHIC LAND

P. Oxy. 1628. 73 B.C.

[1][Βασι]λευόντων Πτολεμαίου καὶ Κλεοπάτρας [τῆς καὶ [2]Τ]ρυφα[ί]νης θεῶν Φιλοπ[α]τό[ρ]ων [Φ]ιλαδέλφων ἔ[το]υ[ς θ], [3]τὰ [δ'] ἄλλα τῶν κοινῶν ὡς ἐν Ἀλεξανδρείαι γράφε[ται, μηνὸς] [4]Ἀπελλ[α]ίου καὶ Φαῶφι ιε, ἐν Ὀξυρύγχων πόλε[ι] τῆ[ς] [5]Θηβαΐδος. ἐμίσθωσεν Σαραπίων Ἀπολλωνίου Μακε[δὼν] [6]τῶν κατοίκων ἱππέων Ἀπολλωνίωι τῶι καὶ Παν[. . .] [7]Ἰσχυρίωνος τοῦ καὶ Νεχθενείβιος Πέρσηι τῆς ἐπιγονῆς, [8][οἱ] δύο ἀγυιᾶς Κλεοπάτρας Ἀφρ[οδί]της, ἀπὸ τοῦ κλήρου αὐ[τοῦ] [9]ἃς ἔχει περὶ Σεφὼ ἀρούρας δεκαπέντε εἰς τὸ ἔνατ[ο]ν ἔτ[ος], [10]ὥστε τὰς μὲν ἐν τῶι Διοκλέους κλήρωι ἀρούρ[α]ς τ[ρε]ῖς [11]πυροσπ[ο]ρῆσαι, τῶν δ' ἐν τῶι Φίλωνος ἀρουρῶν δεκ[α]δ[ύο] [12]τὸ μὲν ἥμ[ισ]υ κριθῆ, τὸ δ' ἄλλο ἥμισυ φακῶι, ἐκφορί[ο]υ [κ]α-[13][θ' ἑκά]στην ἄ[ρ]ουραν ἐκ γεωμετρίας τοῦ δοθέντος ε[ἰς] [14]σπορὰν σιτ[ικ]οῖς ἀρταβῶν τεσσάρων. καὶ ὁμολογεῖ [15]Ἀπολλώνιος ἔχειν παρὰ Σαραπίωνος εἰς σπέρματα [16]καὶ τὴν ἄλλην τῆς κατασπορᾶς δαπάνην ἀδιαφόρους [17][κριθῆ]ς μὲν ἀρτάβας ἑπτὰ ἥμισυ, φακοῦ δὲ ἀρτάβας [18][ἑπτὰ ἥ]μισυ, καὶ εἰς θρυοκοπίαν τῆς γῆς ἀναποδότους [19][χαλκοῦ δραχμὰς χι]λίας πεντακοσίας ἀκινδύνους [20][καὶ ἀνυπολόγους ἀπ]ὸ παντὸς κινδύνου. ἐπὶ δὲ τῶν ἐκφορίων [21]πλὴν τῶν τελῶ[ν, ἐάν τ]ι πραχθῇ Ἀπολλώνιος εἰς τὸ βασιλικὸν [22]ἢ εἰς ἕ[τερόν τι καθ' ὅν]τινοῦν τρόπον ὑπὲρ Σαραπίωνος [23]ἢ [τῆς γῆς, ὑπολογείτω ἀπὸ

[a] Ptolemy Auletes.

40. LEASE OF CLERUCHIC LAND

73 B.C.

The 9th year of the reign of Ptolemy [a] and Cleopatra also called Tryphaena, gods Philopatores and Philadelphi, and the rest of the formula as written in Alexandria,[b] the 15th of the month Apellaeus or Phaophi, at Oxyrhynchus in the Thebaid. Sarapion son of Apollonius, Macedonian, of the catoecic cavalry, has leased from his holding to Apollonius also called Pan . . . son of Ischyrion also called Nechthenibis, Persian of the Epigone, both parties domiciled in the street of Cleopatra Aphrodite, the 15 arurae which he owns near Sepho [c] for the 9th year, on condition that he sows the 3 arurae in the holding of Diocles [d] with wheat and half of the 12 arurae in the holding of Philon [d] with barley and the other half with lentils, at a rent of 4 artabae for each arura in accordance with the survey of the land assigned for sowing with corn. And Apollonius acknowledges that he has received from Sarapion for seed and for the other expenses of sowing 7½ artabae of barley and 7½ artabae of lentils, repayable at par, and for clearing the land from rushes 1500 drachmae of copper, not repayable, all free from risk of any sort and not subject to deduction. With regard to the rent, if apart from the taxes Apollonius is called upon to pay anything to the Treasury or meet any other claim whatsoever upon Sarapion or upon the land, he shall deduct the

[b] That is, the names of the eponymous priests and priestesses. *Cf.* No. 2, note *a*.

[c] A village in the Oxyrhynchite nome.

[d] Names of former cleruchs, after whom the land was permanently called.

τῶν ἐκ]φ[ορίων, τῶν] δὲ καρπῶν 24[κυριευέτω Σαραπίων ἕως ἂν τὰ ἐκφόρια κομίσητ]αι καὶ [
Verso: (2nd hand) 25(ἔτους?) θ μίσθω(σις) [

41. LEASE OF A PAPYRUS MARSH

B.G.U. 1121. 5 B.C.

1Πρωτάρ[χωι] 2παρὰ Διονυσίας [τ]ῆς Ἀχιλλέως ἀστῆς μετὰ κυρίου Εὐδήμου τοῦ (space left empty) 3καὶ παρὰ Ἱέρακος τοῦ Τιθοήους καὶ Πάπου τοῦ Ἀνδρονίκου ἀμφοτέρων Περσῶν τῆς ἐπ[ιγο(νῆς). 4π]ερὶ ὧν [διε]στάμεθα συγχωροῦμεν [π]ρὸς ἑατοὺς ἐπὶ το[ῖσδε] ὥστ' ἐπεὶ μεμίσθων5τ[αι] ὅ τε [Ἱέραξ καὶ Πά]πος παρὰ τῆς Διονυ[σίας] εἰς ἔ[τ]η [τρία ἀπὸ Θωὺθ τοῦ] ἐνεσ[τ]ῶτος 6ἕκ[το]υ καὶ εἰκοστοῦ ἔτους Καίσαρος τὸ ὑπάρχον αὐτῇ [τε καὶ τῷ ἀφήλικι αὐτῆς] υἱὸς 7Ἀχιλλεῖ Πτολεμαίου περὶ Ἀρσινοΐδα τὴν καὶ Εὐρυλόχου ἐν τῷ λεγο[μένωι] Κόλπω[ι, ὃ] 8προεῖχεν Ἱέραξ ὁ Ἱέρακος ἐπὶ τοῖς οὖσι ὁρίοις, ὃ προσκυρεῖ τῆι λε[γομ]ένῃ Βαθεί[αι] 9καὶ τοῖς ἐπικαλουμένοις Διοικητοῦ καὶ τῶι Πισὰτ καὶ Ἐμουεὶ καὶ [ἐπί τι μέ]ρος Τελκ[αρὼρ] 10ἕλος παπυρικὸν φόρου ἑσταμένου κατ' ἐνιαυτὸν ἕκαστον, ἀν[υ]πολόγου παντὸς ὑ[πολό-] 11γου καὶ ἀνηλώματος, ἀργυρίου Πτολεμαϊκοῦ δραχμῶν πεντακισχιλίων, ἐφ' ὧ[ι διορ-]12θώσονται ταύτας τῆι Διονυσίᾳ κατ' ἔτος, διδόντε[ς] ἀπὸ

4. *l.* ἑαυτούς. 6. *l.* υἱῷ.

---

[a] See No. 3, note *a*.

[b] The marshes in the north of the Delta were the chief home of the papyrus plant, which was used not only for the

amount from the rent; and Sarapion shall own the crops until he receives the rent . . . (Endorsed) Year 9. Lease . . .

41. LEASE OF A PAPYRUS MARSH

5 B.C.

To Protarchus [a] from Dionysia daughter of Achilleus, of civic rank, with her guardian Eudemus son of . . ., and from Hierax son of Tithoes and Papus son of Andronicus, both Persians of the Epigone. Concerning the matters that have been in debate we agree with each other on the following terms. Whereas Hierax and Papus have leased from Dionysia for three years from Thoth of the current 26th year of Caesar the papyrus marsh [b] belonging to her and her son, who is a minor, Achilleus son of Ptolemaeus, in the area of Arsinois also called Eurylochu [c] in the place called Colpus, which marsh was formerly owned by Hierax son of Hierax under its present boundaries, being bordered by the place called Batheia and that which bears the name of Dioecetu and by Pisat and Emoui and for a certain distance by Telkaror, at a fixed yearly rent of 5000 drachmae of Ptolemaic silver free from deduction of any kind and clear of expenses, on the understanding that they shall pay this sum to Dionysia every year in monthly instalments of 250 silver

fabrication of writing material, the precursor of our paper, but for various other purposes. It furnished sails for boats; it was woven into mats and sandals; and bundles of the long stems, skilfully knotted together, served as canoes.

[c] Probably in the neighbourhood of Alexandria, but nothing more is known about the places mentioned here.

Θω[ὺθ ἕ]ως Μεχε[ὶρ] [13]κατὰ μῆνα ἀργυρίου δρα[χ]-μὰ[ς] διακοσίας πεντήκοντα, ἀπὸ δὲ Φαμενὼθ ἕως Μεσ[ορὴ] [14]κατὰ μῆνα ἕκαστον [ἀ]ργυρίου δραχμὰς πεντακοσίας ὀγδοήκον[τα τρ]εῖς δύο ὀβ[ολούς], [15]ἐπὶ τούτοις ἀντέχεσθαι αὐτοὺς τῆς μισθώσεως ἐπὶ τὸν [χ]ρόνον, μὴ ἐξόντο[ς] [16]αὐτοῖς διδόναι τοῖς κατεργαζομένοις τὴν μίσθωσιν ἐ[ργάτ]αις [π]λεῖον τῶν [διδο-][17]μένων ἐν τῶι Κόλπωι [κατ]έργων, τελέσουσι δὲ καὶ ἐξαίρετα κατ' [ἐ]νιαυτὸν ἕ[καστον] [18]φορτία παπυρικὰ ἑξ[άγκαλ]α ἑκατόν, ἐργάζεσθαι δὲ τὰ μεμισθωμένα τὰ μὲ[ν] [19]ἐπιτήδεια σευουργοῦν[τας τ]ὰ δὲ λοιπὰ τῇ καθηκούσῃ εὐνοίᾳ καὶ μὴ δικολ[. . .-] [20]σειν . . . . απαρανθινολογήσειν μηδὲ βαριοτομήσειν μηδ' ἐπὶ μέ[ρει [21]ἐργάσεσθαι μηδὲ σχοινικὰ π]ωλεῖν μηδὲ ἑτέροις μεταμισθ[οῦν] μηδὲ καταν[έ-[22]μειν ἐν τῶι ἕλει κτήνη] μήτε ἴδια μήτ' ἀλλότρια, ἃ δ' ἐὰ[ν καταλα]μβάνω[σιν [23]ἐκστήσειν τοῖς ἰδίοις αὐτῶν δαπανήμασι . . . βαλεῖν δὲ τὸ ἕλος ἐν] τοῖς καθ[ή-[24]κουσι καιροῖς, ἔτι δὲ καὶ τοὺς καθ' ἑαυτοὺς ποταμοὺς καὶ τὰς πλαγίους δι]ώρυγας παρα[θά-[25]ψειν καὶ] ὀρύξειν [καὶ μεταβαλεῖν καὶ παρέξεσθαι πλωτὰς οἵας κα]ὶ παρείληφαν [τοῖς [26]ἰδίοις ἀνηλώμασιν, ἐὰν δὲ συμβῇ αὐτοῖς πρ . . . . ἔφοδον γενέσθαι ἢ [27]κατακλυσμὸν ἢ ξυλείας] ἐκκοπὴν ἢ κατὰ π[όλεως αἴτιον ἢ ἐγ δημοσίου [28]φόρων αφ . . . ς ἐποχὴ]ν ἢ πρὸς . . . . [. ἢ ἀπὸ θεοῦ γέν]ηταί τι περὶ τ[ὴν [29]μίσθωσιν αἴτιον, οὐδὲν τούτων] ἔσται πρὸς τὴν Διονυ[σίαν, καὶ] μὴ ἐξεῖναι τ[οῖς [30]μεμισθωμένοις ἐγλιπ]εῖν τὴν μίσθωσιν ἐν[τὸς τοῦ χρ]όνου, ἐὰν δέ τ[ι [31]τούτων παραβαίνωσιν], εἶναι αὐτοὺς παραχρῆμα ἀγωγίμους καὶ συνέχε-

drachmae from Thoth to Mecheir and of 583 drachmae 2 obols from Phamenoth to Mesore; they shall therefore take up the lease on these terms for that period. It shall not be lawful for them to pay the workmen employed under the lease more than the current wages at Colpus, and they shall make a special payment every year of 100 loads of papyrus with six bundles in each, and in working the property leased they shall . . . the suitable portions and treat the remainder with due consideration and not use pickaxes (?) nor gather immature . . . (?) nor cut from boats (?) nor work the property partially (?) nor sell articles made of rushes (?) nor sublet the land to others nor pasture either their own or others' cattle in the marsh, and whatever cattle they find there they shall remove at their own cost, and they shall . . . the marsh at the proper times, and the streams and the cross cuttings on their land they shall fill in and excavate and reshape and render navigable, just as they received them, at their own expense. And in the event of . . . aggression or inundation or destruction of wood, or if owing to civic causes or through government . . . there is a stoppage (?), or if any circumstance [natural (?)] or supernatural affects the lease, Dionysia shall have no responsibility and it shall not be lawful for the lessees to abandon the lease within the period. If they infringe any of these conditions, they shall straightway be liable to arrest and be imprisoned

19-20. Reading very doubtful. The last word in 19 possibly δικελλεύσειν. 27 and 28. πόλεως and αφ . . . ς ἐποχή]ν very doubtful.

σθα[ι [32]μέχρι τοῦ . . . .] καὶ ἐκτελέσαι καὶ ἐκτεῖσαι τῇ Δι[ονυ]σίᾳ ἃ [ἐ]ὰν ἐν[ο-[33]φιλήσωσι πρὸς τ]οὺς φόρους σὺν ἡμιολίᾳ καὶ ἑκάστου φορτίου οὗ ἐὰν μὴ ἀπ[ο-[34]δῶσιν τὴν ἐπὶ τοῦ κ]αιροῦ τιμὴν καὶ ἄλ[λα]ς ἐπίτιμον ἀργυ[ρ]ίου δραχμὰς χιλί[ας, [35]καὶ ἐξεῖναι] τῇι Διονυσίᾳ παρασυγγραφού[ντων αὐτ]ῶν ἐγ[βά]λλειν ἐ[ντὸς [36]τοῦ χρόνου καὶ ἑτέροις] μεταμισθοῦν καὶ πράσσ[ειν τ]ὸ ἐσόμενον ἀφεύρεμα [37][παρὰ τὴ]ν ἀναμίσθωσιν, τῆς πράξεως γινομένης τῇι Διονυσίᾳ ἔκ τῶ[ν [38]μεμισθω]μένων καὶ ἐξ ἑνὸς καὶ οὗ ἐὰν αὐτῶν αἱρῆται καὶ ἐκ τῶν ὑπαρχόντων [39][αὐτοῖς π]άντων καθάπερ ἐγ δίκης, ἀκ[ύ]ρων οὐσῶν ὧ[ν] ἐὰν ἐπενέγκ[ωσι [40]πίσ]τεων πασῶν καὶ σκέπης πάσης, ἐπιτελούντων δ' αὐτῶν κατὰ [τὰ [41]προγεγρα[μμένα καὶ τὴν Διονυσία[ν] παρέξεσθαι αὐτοῖς τὴν μίσθωσι[ν [42]ἀπερίλυτον ἐπὶ τ]ὸν χρόνον καὶ ἐάσε[ιν] αὐτοὺς τὰ ἐξ αὐτῆς ἀπ[ο]φέρεσθαι εἰς [τὸ [43]ἴδιον μηδ' ἐγ]βάλλειν αὐτοὺς ἐντὸς τοῦ χρόνου μ[ηδὲ π]λεῖον μηδὲν [44][πρᾶξαι ἢ] καὶ αὐτὴν ἐκτίνειν τά τε βλάβη καὶ δ[απανήμα]τα καὶ τὸ ἴσον [45][ἐπί-τι]μον καθάπερ ἐγ δίκης χωρὶς τοῦ κύρια εἶναι τὰ συν[κεχω(ρημένα)]. τὰ δὲ [46][ἑκατὸ]ν φορτία παραδώσουσιν [ο]ἱ μεμισθωμένοι ἐπὶ το[ῦ] Ἀνολ[μεθίου?] ὅρμου. ἀ[ξιοῦ(μεν)].

The text is restored in places from another imperfect copy of the same document.

42. LEASE OF LAND

P. Oxy. 499. A.D. 121.

[1]Ἐμίσθωσεν Τρύφων Ἀριστάνδρ[ο]υ [2]*καὶ* Σαραπίων Ἡρώδου *τῶν ἀπ'* Ὀ-[3]*ξυρύγχων πόλεως*

until they . . . have paid to Dionysia the amount which they owe for rent increased by one half and for every load which they fail to deliver the current price and in addition a penalty of 1000 silver drachmae; and it shall be lawful for Dionysia, if they break their contract, to evict them within the period and lease the land to others and exact the deficit as it stands at the date of re-letting, Dionysia having the right of execution upon the lessees or any one of them whom she chooses and upon all their property as if by legal decision, all assurances produced by them and all resort to protection being invalid. But if they fulfil the contract in accordance with the conditions above stated, Dionysia shall give them undisturbed possession of the lease for the period and allow them to appropriate the fruits of it and not evict them within the period nor exact any further payment, otherwise she shall herself forfeit the damages and costs and the like penalty as if by legal decision, in addition to the agreement remaining valid. The lessees shall deliver the 100 loads at the harbour of Anolmethius. We request (your sanction).

42. LEASE OF LAND

A.D. 121.

Tryphon son of Aristander and Sarapion son of Herodes, of Oxyrhynchus, have leased to Apollonius

Ἀπολλωνίῳ [4]Ὥρου τῶν ἀπὸ κώμης Σενέπ[τ]α [5]Πέρσης τῆς ἐπιγονῆς εἰς τὸ ἐν-[6]εστὸς ἕκτον ἔτος Ἁδριανοῦ [7]Καίσαρος τοῦ κυρίου ἀπὸ τῶν ὑ-[8]παρχόντων αὐτοῖς περὶ τὴν αὐ-[9]τὴν κώμην ἐκ τοῦ Δίωνος κλή-[10]ρου τὰς ἀπὸ ἐπικαλάμου ἀρούρας [11]δέκα ἥμισυ, ὧν γίτονες ἀπηλιώ-[12]του Διδύμου, <νότου> τῶν προγεγραμ-[13]μένων, βορρᾶ τῶν αὐτῶν, [14]λιβὸς Σεύθου Ποτάμωνος, [15]ὥστε ξυλαμῆσαι χόρτῳ εἰς κοπὴν [16]καὶ ἐπινομήν, φόρου ἑκάστης [17]ἀρούρης μηδεμιᾶς γεωμετρίας [18]γενομένης ἀνὰ ἀργυρίου δρα-[19]χμὰς τριάκοντα ἓξ ἀκίνδυνα [20]παντὸς κινδύνου, τῶν ὑπὲρ τῆς [21]γῆς δημοσίων ὄντων πρὸς τὸν [22][μ]εμισθωκότα, ὃν καὶ κυριεύειν [23]τῶν καρπῶν ἕως ἂν τὸν φόρον [24]κομίσηται. τῆς δὲ μισθώσεως [25]βεβαιουμένης ἀ[πο]δότω ὁ με-[26]μισθωμένος τ[ὸν φόρον] τῷ [27]Παῦνι μηνὶ τοῦ α[ὐτοῦ] ἔτους, [28]ὃ δ' ἂν προσοφειλ[ήσῃ] ἀπο-τει [29]σάτω μεθ' ἡμι[ολίας, κ]αὶ ἡ πρᾶ-[30]ξις ἔστω τῷ με[μισθω]κότι [31][ἔκ τε] τοῦ [αὐτοῦ Ἀπολ]λωνίου [32]καὶ ἐκ τῶν ὑπαρχόντων αὐτῷ [33]πάντων καθάπερ ἐγ δίκης. [34]κυρία ἡ μίσθωσις. (ἔτους) ἕκτου [35]Αὐτοκράτορος Καίσαρος Τραϊανοῦ [36]Ἁδριανοῦ Σεβαστοῦ Θὼθ κε. (2nd hand) [37]Σαραπίων Ἡρώδου συν-[38]μεμίσθωμαι τὰς προ-[39]κειμένας ἀρούρας [40]δέκα ἥμ[ι]συ μηδε-[41]μιᾶς γεωμετρίας [42]γενομένης ἀνὰ ἀργυ-[43]ρίου δρα[χ]μὰς τριά-[44]κοντα ἓξ κατ' ἄρουραν [45]ὡς πρόκειται. χρόνος [46]ὁ αὐτός.

Verso: [47]Ἀπολλωνίο(υ) [48]μί(σθωσις) ἰς τὸ ς [(ἔτος)].

5. *l.* Πέρσῃ. 37-38. *l.* συνμεμίσθωκα.

son of Horus, of the village of Senepta, Persian of the Epigone,[a] for the current 6th year of Hadrianus Caesar the lord, from their property at the said village in the holding of Dion, the 10½ arurae lately grown with corn, of which the boundaries are, on the east the land of Didymus, on the south that of the aforesaid lessors, on the north the same, on the west that of Seuthes son of Potamon, to be sown with grass for cutting and grazing, at a rent for each arura, without any remeasurement, of 36 drachmae clear of every risk, the taxes on the land being at the charge of the lessor, who shall also be the owner of the crop until he receives the rent. If this lease is guaranteed, the lessee shall pay the rent in the month Pauni of the said year, and if he is in arrears he shall forfeit the deficit increased by one half, and the lessor shall have the right of execution upon the said Apollonius and upon all his property as if by legal decision. This lease is valid. The 6th year of the Emperor Caesar Trajanus Hadrianus Augustus, Thoth 25. (Signed) I, Sarapion son of Herodes, am a party to the lease of the aforesaid 10½ arurae, without any remeasurement, at 36 drachmae the arura as aforesaid. Same date. (Endorsed) Lease of Apollonius for year 6.

[a] See Glossary.

43. OFFER TO LEASE A PALM-GROVE

P. Ryl. 172. A.D. 208.

[1]Φλαυίᾳ Πετρονίλλῃ τῇ [2]καὶ Τιτανιάδει μετὰ κυρίου [3]τοῦ ἀνδρὸς Γαΐου Οὐαλ{λ}ερίου [4]Πάνσα γυμνασιαρχήσαντος [5]παρὰ Καν[.]ερέως καὶ Ἑριήους [6]ἀδελφοῦ. βουλόμεθα μισθώσασ-[7]θαι παρὰ σοῦ τὸν ὑπάρχοντά [8]σοι φοινικῶνα περὶ κώμ(ην) [9]Ἡφ(αιστιάδα) ἐπικαλούμενον Ἑρεννίου [10]φόρου τοῦ παντὸς ἀργυρίου [11](δραχμῶν) χειλίων καὶ ἐξερέτων [12]φοίνικος μονοξύλου [13]ἀρτάβας δύο δρώμῳ φοι-[14]νιγηγῷ τῆς κώμης [15]καὶ σαλώτια δώδεκα, τὸν [16]δὲ φόρον ἀποδώσω σοι [17]ἅμα τῷ κατασπασμῷ ἀν-[18]υπερθέτως, τῶν δὲ ἔργων [19]πάντων ὄντων πρὸς ἐμὲ [20]τὸν μεμισθωμένον κα-[21]τασπασμὸν ὠχείας πο-[22]τισμοῦ περιχωμα-τ[ι]σμοῦ [23]ἀναβολῆς διορύγων τρίτον [24]μέρος καὶ τὸ ὕμισου τῆς κα-[25]θάρσεως· καὶ σαβαυτίων [26]ἀρτάβας δύο. (2nd hand) [27]Γάιος Οὐαλέριος Πάν-[28]σας μεμίσθωκα ὡς [29]πρόκειται, ἐπὰν δὲ [30]μή τις προσθῇ [31]σοι, μενεῖς ἐπὶ [32]τῇ προγεγραμμένῃ [33]μισθώσι. (1st hand) [34]ἔτους ιζ Λουκίου Σεπτιμίου [35]Σευήρου Εὐσεβοῦς Περτίνακος [36]Ἀραβικοῦ Ἀδιαβηνικοῦ [37]καὶ Μάρκου Αὐρηλίου Ἀντωνίνου [38]Εὐσεβῶν Σεβαστῶν καὶ Πουπλίου [39]Σεπτιμίου Γέτα Καίσαρος Σεβαστοῦ [40]Θὼθ ιζ.

11. *l.* ἐξαιρέτων.
13. *l.* ἀρταβῶν, δρόμῳ φοινικηγῷ. 15. *l.* σαλωτίων.
20-21. *l.* κατασπασμοῦ. 23. *l.* διωρύγων.
23-24. *l.* τρίτου μέρους, τοῦ ἡμίσους. 38. *l.* Εὐσεβοῦς.

43. OFFER TO LEASE A PALM-GROVE

A.D. 208.

To Flavia Petronilla also called Titanias with her guardian her husband Gaius Valerius Pansa, ex-gymnasiarch, from Kan[.]ereus and Heries his brother. We desire to lease from you the palm-grove called that of Herennius belonging to you in the area of the village of Hephaestias at a total rental of 1000 silver drachmae and a special payment of 2 artabae of dates on single stems,[a] measured by the dromos date-measure[b] of the village, and of 12 *salotia*.[c] And I will pay you the rent at the time of the plucking without delay. I, the lessee, shall be responsible for all the works, plucking, fertilization, irrigation, formation of basins, a third share of embanking canals and a half share of cleansing them. I will pay also 2 artabae of *sabautia*.[c] (Signed) I, Gaius Valerius Pansa, have let it on the above terms, and so long as no one makes a higher bid, you shall retain possession of the aforesaid lease. (Dated) The 17th year of Lucius Septimius Severus Pius Pertinax Arabicus Adiabenicus and Marcus Aurelius Antoninus Pius, Augusti, and Publius Septimius Geta Caesar Augustus, Thoth 17.

[a] That is, with one date on each stem.

[b] A "dromos" standard of measure was probably a temple standard, being used in transactions in the dromos (*i.e.* avenue) of a particular temple.

[c] Meaning unknown.

44. LEASE OF A PERFUMERY BUSINESS

P. Fay. 93. A.D. 161.

1Κάστορι Ἀντιφίλου Σωσικοσμίῳ τῷ 2καὶ Ἀλθαιεῖ 3παρὰ Σαραπίωνος Ἀρτεμιδώρου 4τοῦ Πτολεμαίου ἀπὸ ἀμφόδου 5Χηνοβοσκίων Ἑτέρων. βούλομαι 6μισθώσασθαι παρὰ σοῦ τὴν μυρο-7πωλαϊκὴν καὶ ἀροματικὴν ἐργασίαν 8θ[έ]λων ἀπὸ τοῦ ἐπιβάλλοντός σοι 9[ἡμί]σους μέρους τέταρτον μέρος 10Θεμίστου μερίδος (2nd hand) χωρὶς ἀγο-11ρῶν σὺν πανηγύρεσιν 12πρὸς μόνον τὸ ἐνεστὸς 13β (ἔτος) φόρου τοῦ παντὸς ἀρ-14γ(υρίου) (δραχμῶν) τεσσεράκοντα πέν-15τε, ὧν καὶ τὴν διαγρα-16φὴν ποιήσ[ο]μαι κατὰ 17μῆνα τὸ αἱροῦν ἐξ ἴσου 18ἐὰν φαίνηται μισθῶ-19σαι. (3rd hand) Κάστωρ Ἀντιφίλου μεμί-20σθωκα κατὼς πρόκιται. 21ἔτους ⟦β⟧ Ἀντωνίνου καὶ <Οὐ>ήρου 22τῶν κυρίων Σεβαστῶν Θὼθ ε.

6. *l*. μυροπωλικήν. 20. *l*. καθώς.

45. LEASE OF GEESE

P.S.I. 961, ll. 1-39. A.D. 176.

1Ἔτους ἑπτακαιδεκάτου Αὐτοκράτορος Καίσαρος 2Μάρκου Αὐρηλίου Ἀντωνείνου Σεβαστοῦ 3Ἀρμενιακοῦ Μηδικοῦ Παρθικοῦ Γερμανικοῦ 4Σαρματικοῦ Μεγίστου, μηνὸς Σεβαστοῦ Θὼθ κδ, 5ἐν Πτολεμαΐδι Εὐεργέτιδι τοῦ Ἀρσινοείτου νομοῦ. 6ἐμ[ίσ]θωσεν Ἀμάτιος ὁ καὶ Παυλεῖνος κεκοσμη-7τευκὼς υἱὸς Πάτρωνος γεγυμνασιαρχηκότος ὡς 8ἐτῶν τεσσεράκοντα τεσσάρων ἄσημος Νειλάμ-

44. LEASE OF A PERFUMERY BUSINESS

A.D. 161.

To Castor son of Antiphilus, of the Sosicosmian tribe and the Althaean deme,[a] from Sarapion son of Artemidorus son of Ptolemaeus, of the Second Goosefarm quarter. I wish to lease from you the retailing of perfumes and spices, desiring a fourth part of the half share allotted to you in the division of Themistes,[b] exclusive of markets and festivals, for the present second year only at a total rent of forty-five drachmae of silver, which I will pay monthly in equal instalments if you agree to give the lease. (Signed) I, Castor son of Antiphilus, have given the lease on the aforesaid terms. The (second) year of Antoninus and Verus the lords Augusti, Thoth 5.

[a] *Cf.* No. 32, note *b*.
[b] Theadelphia, where the papyrus was found, lay in this section of the Arsinoite nome. The wording indicates that the business was a government monopoly.

45. LEASE OF GEESE

A.D. 176.

The 17th year of the Emperor and Caesar Marcus Aurelius Antoninus Augustus Armenicus Parthicus Germanicus Sarmaticus Maximus, 24th of the month Sebastus or Thoth, at Ptolemais Euergetis[a] in the Arsinoite nome. Amatius also called Paulinus, ex-cosmetes, son of Patron ex-gymnasiarch, aged about 44 years, with no distinctive mark, has leased

[a] Capital of the nome, formerly called Crocodilopolis.

[9]μωνι Νείλου ἀπελευθέρου Λουρίου τοῦ καὶ Ἀπολλω-[10]νίου ὡς ἐτῶν εἴκοσι οὐλὴ ἀντικνημείῳ ἀριστερῷ [11]καὶ Πόννιτι Ἡρακλήου τοῦ Ἡρακλήου ἀπὸ κώμης [12]Κερκήσεως ὡς ἐτῶν τεσσεράκοντα ὀκτὼ οὐλὴ [13]ἀντικνημείῳ δεξιῷ καὶ Ὀρσενούφει Πάσειτος τοῦ Ὀρ-[14]σενούφεως ὡς ἐτῶν εἴκοσι ἐννέα οὐλὴ ὑπὲρ [15]ἀστράγαλον ἐντὸς ποδὸς δεξιοῦ, τοῖς τρισὶ ἐξ ἀλληλεν-[16]γύης, χῆνες τοκάδες εἴκοσι τρεῖς, οὓς καὶ παρέλαβαν [17]τῇ ἐνεστώσῃ ἡμέρᾳ, συντετειμημένους ἀργυρίου δρα-[18]χμῶν ἐνακοσίων εἴκοσι, εἰς ἐνιαυτὸν ἕνα, φόρου [19]πάντων τοῦ ὅλου ἔτους χηνῶν τελείων εἴκοσι τριῶν [20]ἀνυπολόγων καὶ ἀκινδύνων, καὶ μετὰ τὸν χρόνον [21]ἐπάναγκον τοὺς περὶ Νειλάμμωνα παραδώσειν [22]ὁμοίως ἐξ ἀλληλενγύης τῷ Ἀματίῳ τῷ καὶ Παυλεί-[23]νῳ τοὺς προ[κει]μένους χῆνες τοκάδες εἴκοσι τρεῖς [24][ἢ ἀ]ποδότωσαν αὐτῷ τ[ὰς τ]ῆς συντειμήσεως ἀργυρίο(υ) [25]δ[ραχ]μὰς ἐνακοσίας εἴκ[οσ]ι [ἀ]νυπερθέτως, ἐὰν δὲ [26]μ[ὴ] ἀποδῶσειν, χορηγήσειν αὐτοὺς ὁμοίως .[. .] [27] .[. .]ς τοὺς τοῦ φόρου χῆ[ν]ες τελείους εἴκοσι τρ[εῖς], [28]τ[ῆς] περὶ ἁπάντων πράξεως γεινομένης τῷ Ἀμα[τίῳ] [29]τ[ῷ] καὶ Παυλείνῳ ἐκ τῶν περὶ τὸν Νειλάμμωνα [30]κ[αὶ] οὗ ἐὰν αὐτῶν αἱρῆται [κ]αὶ ἐκ τῶν ὑπαρχόντων α[ὐ-][31]τοῖ[ς] πάντων καθάπερ ἐκ [δί]κης. (2nd hand) Νιλάμω<ν> Νείλου καὶ [32]Πόνις Ἡρακλήου καὶ Ὀρσενοῦφις Πάσιτος οἱ τρῖς μεμι[σ-][33]θώμεθα ἐξ ἀλλυλυνγύοι[ς] παρὰ τοῦ Ἀματίου τοῦ καὶ [34]Παυλ[ί]νου χῆνες τοκάτες ε[ἴκ]οσι τρῖς οὓς καὶ παρε[λά-][35]βα[με]ν συντετιμη<μέ>νους ἀ[ργυρ]ίου δραχμῶν

16. *l.* χῆνας τοκάδας; so in ll. 23, 34. 26-27. κ[ατὰ] ἔ[το]ς? 27. *l.* χῆνας. 33. *l.* ἀλληλενγύης.

to Nilammon son of Nilus, freedman of Lurius also called Apollonius, aged about 20 years, with a scar on the left shin, and to Ponnis son of Heraclius son of Heraclius, of the village of Kerkesis, aged about 48 years, with a scar on the right shin, and to Orsenouphis son of Pasis son of Orsenouphis, aged about 29 years, with a scar above the ankle of the right foot on the inside, to all three on mutual security, 23 brood geese, which they have received on the present day, valued at 920 silver drachmae, for one year, at a general rent for the whole year of 23 full-grown geese[a] not subject to deduction and warranted against risk; and at the end of the term Nilammon and his partners shall be bound to surrender, likewise on mutual security, to Amatius also called Paulinus the aforesaid 23 brood geese, on pain of paying him the 920 silver drachmae of the valuation without delay; and if they fail to pay, they shall still deliver in like manner yearly (?) the 23 full-grown geese of the rent; and Amatius also called Paulinus shall have for all claims the right of execution upon Nilammon and his partners and upon whichever of them he chooses and upon all their property as if by legal decision. (Signed) We, Nilammon son of Nilus and Ponnis son of Heraclius and Orsenouphis son of Pasis, have all three leased on mutual security from Amatius also called Paulinus 23 brood geese, which we have received, valued at 920 silver drachmae, for one year

[a] That is, young geese of about a year old from the offspring of the 23 leased geese. The rest of the brood would of course become the property of the lessees.

ἐνακοσ[ί-][36]ων [εἴ]κοσι εἰς ἐνιαυτὸν ἕ[να] φόρου χηνῶν τελεί[ων εἴ-][37]κοσ[ι τ]ριῶν καὶ ἐπεὶ ταῖς ἄλλ[αι]ς διαστολὲς καθὼς π[ρό-][38]κε[ιται]. Διονύσιος Σαραπίων<ος> ἔγ[ρα]ψα ὑπὲρ αὐτῶν ἀγραμμάτ[ων]. [39](3rd hand) κατεχω(ρίσθη) Θὼ[θ] κδ.

37. *l.* διαστολαῖς.

46. LEASE OF DINING-ROOMS

P. Oxy. 1129. A.D. 449.

[1]Μετὰ τὴν ὑπατίαν Φλαουίων Ζήνωνος καὶ Ποστουμιανοῦ [2]τῶν λαμπροτάτων Τῦβι κδ. [3]Αὐρηλίᾳ Μίκι θυγατρὶ Θεοδώρου ἀπὸ τῆς λαμπρᾶς [4]καὶ λαμπροτάτης Ὀξυρυγχιτῶν πόλεως παρὰ Αὐρηλίου [5]Φοιβάμμωνος υἱοῦ Ἀρτεμιδώρου ἀπὸ τῆς αὐτῆς πόλεως. [6]ἑκουσίως ἐπιδέχομαι μισθώσασθαι ἀπὸ νευμηνίας [7]τοῦ ἑξῆς μηνὸς Μεχεὶρ τοῦ ἐνεστῶτος ἔτους ρκε ϟδ [8]τῆς παρούσης δευτέρας ἰνδικτίονος τοὺς διαφέρον-[9]τάς σοι ἀπὸ οἰκίας οὔσης ἐν τῇ αὐτῇ πόλει ἐπ' ἀμφόδου [10]Μικρῆς Τευμε[ν]ούθεως δύο τόπους ἤτοι συμπόσια [11]σὺν χρηστηρίοις πᾶσι, καὶ τελέσω ὑπὲρ ἐνοικίου ἐνιαυ-[12]σίως ἀργυρίου μυριάδας χιλίας διακοσίας, ἅσπερ ἀπο-[13]δώσω κατ' ἔτος δι' ἑξαμήνου τὸ ἥμισυ, καὶ ὁπόταν [14]βουληθῇς παραδώσω τοὺς αὐτοὺς ἀνυπερθέτως. [15]κυρία ἡ μίσθωσις καὶ ἐπερωτηθεὶς ὡμολόγησα. (2nd hand) [16]Αὐρήλιος Φοιβάμμων Ἀρτεμιδώρου ὁ προκείμενος μεμίσ-[17]θωμαι [τοὺ]ς τόπου[ς] κα[ὶ ἀ]π[ο]δώσω τὸ ἐνοίκιον [ὡς] πρόκειται. [18][. . . . .] . . [. . . . . ἔγρα]ψα ὑπὲρ α[ὐτοῦ γράμματα] [19]μὴ εἰδ[ότος]. [20]+ *di emu No . . . osios* . .

at a rent of 23 full-grown geese and on the other conditions as stated above. I, Dionysius son of Sarapion, have written for them, as they are illiterate. (Subscribed) Registered Thoth 24.

46. LEASE OF DINING-ROOMS

A.D. 449

The year after the consulship of Flavius Zenon and Flavius Postumianus the most illustrious, Tubi 24. To Aurelia Mikis daughter of Theodorus, of the illustrious and most illustrious city of Oxyrhynchus, from Aurelius Phoebammon son of Artemidorus, of the said city. I voluntarily undertake to lease from the 1st of the next month Mecheir of the current 125th = 94th year [a] and of the present 2nd indiction two rooms or dining-rooms belonging to you in a house in the said city in the quarter Small Teumenouthis with all appurtenances, and I will pay as rent annually 1200 myriads [b] of silver, which I will deliver every year, one half every six months, and whenever you wish I will surrender the said rooms without delay. This lease is valid, and in answer to the formal question I have given my consent. (Signed) I, Aurelius Phoebammon son of Artemidorus, the aforesaid, have leased the rooms and will pay the rent as stated above. I, . . ., have written for him, as he is illiterate. (Subscribed) Executed by me, No . . . osis.

[a] See No. 24, p. 71, note *a*.
[b] *i.e.*, myriads of denarii or tetradrachms.

47. LEASE OF PART OF A HOUSE

P. Oxy. 1038. A.D. 568.

[1]+ Βασιλείας καὶ ὑπατίας [2]τοῦ θειοτάτου καὶ εὐσεβεστάτου [3]ἡμῶν δεσπότου Φλαουίου [4]Ἰουστίνου τοῦ αἰωνίου Αὐγούστου [5]καὶ Αὐτοκράτορος ἔτους γ [6]Μεσορὴ β ἰνδ(ικτίονος) α. [7]Φλ(αουίᾳ) Εὐφημίᾳ τῇ ἐνδόξ(ῳ) θυγατρὶ [8]τοῦ τῆς ἐνδόξ(ου) μνήμης [9]Μουσαίου γεουχούσ<ῃ> καὶ ἐνταῦθα τῇ [10]λαμπρᾷ Ὀξυρυγχίτων πόλει [11]διὰ σοῦ Φλ(αουίου) Ἀναστασίου τοῦ περιβλ(έπτου) [12]αὐτῆς διοικ(ητοῦ) καὶ σοῦ Ἱερημίου τοῦ [13]θαυμ(ασίου) ἐνοικολόγου Αὐρήλιος [14]Στέφανος ἀρτοκ(όπος) υἱὸς Ἡρακλάμμωνο(ς) [15]μητρ(ὸς) Νόννας ἀπὸ τῆς αὐτῆς [16]πόλεως χαίρειν. ἑκουσίως ἐπιδέχομαι [17]μισθώσασθαι ἀπὸ νεομηνίας [18]τοῦ Θὼθ μηνὸς τῆς σὺν θεῷ [19]δευτέρας ἰνδ(ικτίονος) ἀπὸ τῶν ὑπαρχ(όντων) τῇ [20]ὑμῶν ἐνδοξ(ότητι) ἀπὸ οἰκίας νευούσης [21]ἐπὶ νότον διακειμ(ένης) ἐπὶ ταύτης [22]τῆς πόλεως ἐπ' ἀμφόδου [23]τῆς ἁγίας Εὐφημίας ὁλόκληρ(ον) [24]ἐπίπεδον τόπον νεύοντα καὶ [25]αὐτὸν ἐπὶ νότον σὺν χρηστηρίοις [26]πᾶσιν καὶ δικαίοις ἐξ ὅλης τῆς οἰκί[ας], [27]καὶ τελέσω ὑπὲρ ἐνοικ(ίου) τούτου [28]ἐνιαυσίως κεράτια δέκα νομιτ(ευόμενα), [29]γί(νεται) κερ(άτ.) ι νομ(ιτευόμ.), ὅπερ ἐνοίκιον ἀπο-[30]δώσω κατ' ἔτος δι' ἑξαμήνου τὸ ἥμισυ, καὶ [31]ὁπόταν βουληθείης ἀντιπαραδώσω [32]τὴν {ομη} νομὴν τοῦ τόπου ὡς καὶ παρείληφ(α). [33]κυρ(ία) ἡ μίσθ(ωσις) ἁπλ(ῆ) γραφ(εῖσα) καὶ ἐπερ(ωτηθεὶς) ὡμολ(όγησα). [34]Στέφανος υἱὸς Ἡρακλάμμωνος [35]στοιχεῖ ἡμῖν ἡ παροῦσα μίσθ(ωσις) ὡ[ς] πρόκ(ειται). [36]Ἰωάννης

47. LEASE OF PART OF A HOUSE

A.D. 568.

The 3rd year of the reign and consulship of our most godlike and pious master Flavius Justinus the eternal Augustus and Imperator, Mesore 2, 1st indiction. To Flavia Euphemia, the honourable daughter of Musaeus of honoured memory, landowner at this illustrious city of Oxyrhynchus, through you, Flavius Anastasius, her respected steward, and you, Jeremiah, her admirable rent-collector, from Aurelius Stephen, baker, son of Heraclammon and Nonna, of the said city, greeting. I voluntarily undertake to lease from the 1st of the month Thoth of the (D.V.) 2nd indiction, from a house in your honour's property, facing south, situated in this city in the quarter of St. Euphemia, a complete room on the ground floor, also facing south, with all appurtenances and rights attaching to all the house, and I will pay for it an annual rent of ten carats [a] current coin, total 10 car. current, which rent I will deliver every year, one half every six months, and whenever you wish I will surrender the possession of the room just as I received it. This lease, written in one copy only, is valid, and in answer to the formal question I have given my consent. (Signed) I, Stephen son of Heraclammon, agree to the present lease as stated above. I, John,

[a] See No. 23, p. 69, note *a*.

ἀξ(ιωθεὶς) ἔ[γρ(αψα)] ὑ(πὲρ) <αὐτοῦ> ἀγρ(αμμάτου) ὄ[ν]τ(ος). 37 [+*di emu Ioannu* . .] . . . . .+

Verso: +μίσθ(ωσις) Στεφάνου υἱοῦ Ἡρακλάμμωνος ἀπὸ τῆς Ὀξυρυγχ(ιτῶν) λόγ(ῳ) ἐνοικ(ίου) κερ(ατίων) ι νομιτ(ευομένων).

48. LEASE OF A MILLING-BAKERY

P. Oxy. 1890. A.D. 508.

1 +Μετὰ τὴν ὑπατίαν τοῦ δεσπότου ἡμῶν Φλα-
(ουίου) Ἀναστασίου τοῦ αἰ[ω]νίου Αὐγούστου τὸ
γ′ καὶ Βηναντίου τοῦ λαμπρο(τάτου) Χοίακ α′
ἰνδικ(τίονος) β, ἐν Ὀξυρύγχων πόλει. 2 Αὐρήλιοι
Ἀπφουᾶς ὁ καὶ Καταμίνας υἱὸς Πιηοῦτος μη[τ]ρὸς
Ὀλυμπιανῆς καὶ ὁ τούτου υἱὸς Ἀβραὰμ ἐκ μη-
τρὸς Ἡραείδος ἀμφότεροι ὁρμώμενοι 3 ἀπὸ ταύτης
τῆς λαμπρᾶς Ὀξυρυγχιτῶν πόλεως, κριβανεῖς καὶ
μυλόναρχοι, τῇ εὐγενεστάτῃ Σερήνᾳ θυγατρὶ τοῦ
τῆς μακαρίας μνήμης Πέτρου 4 ἀπὸ τῆς αὐτῆς
πόλεως χαίρειν. ὁμολογοῦμεν ἐξ ἀλληλεγγύης ἑκου-
σίως καὶ αὐθαιρέτως μεμισθῶσθαι παρὰ τῆς σῆς
εὐγενείας ἀπὸ τῆς σήμερον 5 ἡμέρας ἥτις ἐστὶν
Χοίακ νεομηνία τοῦ ἐνεστῶτος ἔτους ρπε ρνδ τῆς
παρούσης δευτέρας ἰνδικτίονος ἕως Ἁθὺρ νεομηνίας
τῆς σὺν θεῷ 6 τρίτης ἐπινεμήσεως, ἀρτοποιείας τῆς
αὐτῆς τρίτης, τὸ δ[ι]αφέρον αὐτῇ μυλοκριβάνιον
διακείμενον ἐν τῷ λιβικῷ ὄρει ταύτης τῆς πόλεως
7 ἐν τῷ μ[ο]ναστηρίῳ τῷ καλουμένῳ ἀββᾶ Κο-
πρεοῦτ[ο]ς τῷ διαφέροντι τῇ σῇ εὐγενείᾳ καὶ περι-
ελθόντι εἰς αὐτὴν ἐκ παραχωρήσεως 8 Κοπρεοῦτος
τοῦ εὐλαβεστάτου μονάζοντος, ἐν ᾧ ἐστιν κλίβανοι

have written for him at his request, as he is illiterate. (Subscribed) Executed by me, John. (Endorsed) Lease of Stephen son of Heraclammon, of Oxyrhynchus, at a rent of 10 carats current coin.

48. LEASE OF A MILLING-BAKERY

A.D. 508.

The year after the consulship of our master Flavius Anastasius the eternal Augustus, for the third time, and Venantius the most illustrious, Choiak 1, 2nd indiction, at Oxyrhynchus. Aurelius Apphouas also called Cataminas, son of Pieous and Olympiane, and his son Abraham, whose mother is Herais, both inhabitants of this illustrious city of Oxyrhynchus, bakers and master-millers, to the most noble Serena daughter of Peter of blessed memory, of the said city, greeting. We acknowledge on our mutual security that we have voluntarily and of our own choice leased from your nobility from the present day, which is Choiak 1 of the current 185th = 154th year in the present 2nd indiction, up to Hathur 1 of the (D.V.) 3rd indiction, for the bread-making of the said 3rd indiction, the milling-bakery which belongs to you, situated in the western desert of this city in the monastery called that of Abbot Copreous, which belongs to your nobility and came to you by cession from Copreous the most discreet monk, containing 3

τρεῖς καὶ μυλῶνες δύο καὶ λίθος σιτοκοπικὸς σὺν θυείῃ καὶ λίθος στεγικὸς [9]σὺν θυείῃ καὶ [τ]ὰ ἄλλα πάντα χωρή[μ]ατα καὶ χρηστήρι[α] ἤτοι δικαιώματα τὰ ἀνήκοντα τῷ αὐτῷ κλιβανίῳ, ἐπὶ τῷ ἡμᾶς ἐξ ἀλληλεγγύης [10]ἔχεσθαι τῆς το[ύ]του μισθώσεως καὶ τὴν ἐργασ[ί]αν τοῦ [τ]ε κλιβανέος καὶ μυλονάρχου ἐν αὐτοῖς ἀποπληρῶσαι ἐπὶ τὸν εἰρημένον χρόνον [11]καὶ διδόναι ἡμᾶς τῇ σῇ εὐγενείᾳ λόγῳ ἐνοικίου ἤτοι φόρου τοῦ εἰρημένου χρόνου ὑπὲρ κλιβάνων τεσσάρων ἄρτον ἕνα θυρουρικὸν [12]καὶ ὑπὲρ τῶν μυλαίων καὶ τῆς πίλας χρυσοῦ νο[μι]σμάτια {δύο ἥμισυ} τρία, καὶ ὑπὲρ ἑορτικῶν ὄρνεα τρία καὶ ᾠὰ τρ[ι]άκοντα, δηλαδὴ τῆς σῆς [13]εὐγενείας παρεχούσης ἡμῖν λόγῳ προχρεί[ας] χρυ[σ]οῦ νομίσματα δώδεκα. καὶ τοῦτο δὲ προσομολογοῦμεν ἐξ ἀλληλεγγύης τὴν [14]νομὴν τῶν εἰρημένων πραγμάτων καὶ τὴν δεσποτίαν φυλάττιν σοι ἀκέραιον καὶ ἄτρωτον καὶ ἅπαντα τὰ τούτων δίκαια καὶ ἀποκαταστῆσαι [15]τῇ σῇ εὐγενείᾳ μετὰ τὴν συμπλήρωσιν τοῦ εἰρημένου χρόνου ἄνευ τινὸς ἀντιλογίας καὶ ὑπερθέσεως, καὶ ἐπὶ τούτοις παρὰ τῆς σῆς εὐγενείας [16]ἐπερωτηθέντες κατὰ πρόσωπον ὡμολογήσαμεν, ὑποθέμενοι εἰς τὸ δίκαιον ταύτης τῆς μισθώσεως ἅπαντα ἡμῶν τὰ ὑπάρχοντα [17]καὶ ὑπάρξοντα ἐνεχύρου λόγῳ καὶ ὑποθήκης δικαίῳ. κυρία ἡ μίσθωσις ἁπλ(ῆ) γραφ(εῖσα) καὶ ἐπερ(ωτηθέντες) ὡμολ(ογήσαμεν). + (2nd hand) + Ἀβράμ. (3rd hand) [18]Αὐρήλιοι Ἀπφου[ᾶ]ς ὁ καὶ Καταμίνας υἱὸς Πι⟨η⟩οῦτος μητρὸς Ὀλυμπιανῆς καὶ ὁ τούτου υἱὸς Ἀβραὰμ ἐκ μητρὸς Ἡραείδος οἱ προγεγραμμένοι [19]κριβανῖς καὶ μ[υ]λόναρχῃ πεποιήμεθα ἐξ ἀλ⟨λ⟩ηλε[γ]γύης τήνδε τὴν μίσθωσιν τοῦ εἰρημέν[ο]υ μυλοκριβανίου καὶ

baking-ovens, 2 mills, a stone for crushing corn with a mortar, a covering stone[a] with a mortar, and all the other receptacles and utensils or properties pertaining to the said bakery, on condition that we take up the lease of it on mutual security and will perform the baking and milling work there for the said period and pay to your nobility by way of rent or charge for the said period for 4 baking-ovens one doorkeeper's loaf, and for the mills and mortar 3 solidi of gold, and for festivities 3 chickens and 30 eggs, with the understanding that your nobility provides us with 12 solidi of gold by way of advance. Moreover we acknowledge that we will on our mutual security keep for you the possession and ownership of the said objects unimpaired and uninjured, with all the rights appertaining to them, and will restore them to your nobility after the termination of the said period without any objection or delay, and on these terms, having been personally questioned by your nobility, we gave our consent, pledging for the observance of this lease all our property present or future as security and by right of pledge. This lease, made in one copy, is valid, and in answer to the formal question we have given our consent. (1st signature) Abraham. (2nd signature) We, Aurelius Apphouas called also Cataminas, son of Pieous and Olympiane, and his son Abraham, whose mother is Herais, the aforesaid bakers and master-millers, have on our mutual security taken this lease of the said milling-

[a] It is not clear what this implement was.

10. *l.* κλιβανέως. 19. *l.* μυλωνάρχαι.

τῶν προγεγραμ-[20]μένων ἐν αὐτῷ πάντων πραγμάτων κ[α]ὶ δικαιωμάτων, καὶ ἀποδώσομεν ἐξ ἀλληλεγγύης τὸ[ν] προκείμενον τρόπον, καὶ συνφωνῖ ἡμῖν [21]πάντα τὰ ἐγγεγραμμένα ὡς πρόκειται, καὶ ἐπερωτηθέντες ὡμολογήσαμεν. Αὐρήλιος Σερῆνος υἱὸς Ἰωάννου ἀξιωθεὶς ἔγραψα ὑπὲρ [22]αὐτ[ῶν] Ἄπφιου μὲν γράμ{α}ματα μὴ εἰδόστως, Ἀβρααμίου πρὸ ἐμοῦ τὸ ὄνομα αὐτοῦ βαλό‹ν›τος. (1st hand?) [23]*di emu Ninousu etelioth*(*e*). On the verso an endorsement, beginning [24]+μίσθ(ωσις) Ἀπφ(ουᾶ) τοῦ[καὶ Καταμίν]ας καὶ τοῦ τούτου υἱοῦ Ἀβ[ραάμ - - -

22. *l.* Ἀπφουᾶ, εἰδότος.

49. CESSION OF LAND

P. Oxy. 1636. A.D. 249.

[1][Αὐρήλιος] Σερῆνος ὁ καὶ Σαραπίων Ἀγαθείνου [2][μητρὸς Τ]αποσειριάδος ἀπ' Ὀξυρύγχων πόλεως [3][Αὐρηλί]ῳ Πανεσνεῖ Πτόλ[λι]δος μητρὸς Ἀν-[4][. . . . . .]ς ἀπὸ κώμης Σερύφεως χαίρειν. [5][ὁμολογῶ] παρακεχωρηκέναι ἀπὸ τοῦ νῦν [6][εἰς τὸν ἀεὶ] χρόνον ἀπὸ τοῦ ὑπάρξαντός μοι ἀγορα-[7][στικῷ δικ]αίῳ περὶ [τ]ὴν αὐτὴν Σερῦφιν ἐκ τοῦ [8][. . . . . . .]ς κλήρου διμοίρου μέρους σειτικῆς [9][ἀρούρης μ]ιᾶς ἐ[ν θ]ρύοις μεθ' ὃ ἀ[πε]δόμην υἱοῖς [10][Αὐρηλ(ίου) Σ]ωτίω[νο]ς γυμνασιαρχ(ήσαντος) τ[ῆ]ς αὐτῆς πόλεως [11][καὶ . . . . .] . ημι Στε-[φά]νου γυμνασιαρ[χ(ήσαντος)] τῆς αὐτῆς πό(λεως) [12][τρίτον μ]έρος τὸ λ[ο]ιπ[ὸ]ν τρίτον μέρος πρότερον [13][Κατιλλιανο]ῦ τοῦ καὶ Οὐάρου, ἧς ὅλης γείτονες νότου [14][. . . . . .], βορρᾶ γύης, ἀπηλιώτου

bakery and all the aforesaid objects and properties in it, and we will return them on our mutual security in the manner before stated, and we agree to all the terms of the deed as stated above, and in answer to the formal question we have given our consent. I, Aurelius Serenus son of John, have written for them by request, Apphouas being illiterate and Abraham signing his name before me. (Signed by notary) Executed by me, Ninousus. (Endorsed) Lease of Apphouas also called Cataminas and his son Abraham . . .

49. CESSION OF LAND

A.D. 249.

Aurelius Serenus also called Sarapion, son of Agathinus and Taposirias, of Oxyrhynchus, to Aurelius Panesneus son of Ptollis and An . . ., of the village of Seruphis, greeting. I acknowledge that I have ceded to you from now for all time from my property by right of purchase in the area of the said Seruphis in the holding of . . ., consisting of the $\frac{2}{3}$ part of 1 arura of corn land full of rushes, after deducting the $\frac{1}{3}$ part which I sold to the sons of Aurelius Sotion, ex-gymnasiarch of the said city, and to . . . son of Stephanus, ex-gymnasiarch of the said city, the remaining $\frac{1}{3}$ part formerly owned by Catillianus also called Varus, of all of which the adjacent areas are, on the south . . ., on the north

ἑτέρων ἰδιωτική, [15][λι]β[ὸ]ς [σοῦ το]ῦ παραχωρουμένου, τὰς δὲ συμπεφω-[16][ν]ημένα[ς πρ]ὸς ἀλλήλους ὑπὲρ παρα[χ]ωρητικοῦ [17]τοῦ αὐτ[οῦ μ]έ[ρο]υς τρίτου ἀ[ργ]υρίο[υ Σ]εβαστοῦ νομίσ-[18][μ]ατος δ[ραχ]μὰς τετρακο[σ]ία[ς] αὐ[τό]θι ἀπέσχον [19][π]αρὰ σοῦ παραχρῆμα διὰ χ[ειρ]ός, καὶ ἐπά‹να›γκες [20]παρέξο[μαί σο]ι κ[αὶ ἐ]κγόνοις [κ]αὶ τοῖς παρὰ σοῦ μετα-[21][λ]ημψομένοις τ[ὸ τ]ῆς ἀρούρης τρίτον β[έ]βαιον [22][ἀ]πὸ τοῦ ἐμοῦ ὀνό[μα]τος καὶ ἀπὸ παντὸς τοῦ ἐξ ὀ-[23][ν]όματός μου ἐπελε[υσο]μένο[υ] σοι, ἀρκουμένου σοι [24]τῇ εἴς με ἀπὸ τ[οῦ] προτεταγμένο[υ] μου προκτήτο-[25][ρ]ος {μου} Κατιλλια[νο]ῦ τοῦ καὶ Οὐάρου τ[ο]ῦ αὐτοῦ ἀρού-[26][ρ]ης τρίτου βεβ[αι]ώσει, ὅπερ καὶ παρέξομαί σοι [27][ἀ]πὸ τῶν ὑπὲρ αὐτ[ο]ῦ τελουμένων δημοσίων [28]καὶ ἐπιμε[ρ]ισμῶν παντοίων τῶν μέχρι τοῦ [29]διελθ[όντος] ϛ (ἔτους) καὶ α[ὐτ]οῦ τοῦ διελθόντος ϛ (ἔτους) διὰ τὸ [30]τὰ ἀπὸ το[ῦ ἐ]νεστῶ[τ]ος α (ἔτους) τούτου πρόσφορα εἶναι [31]σοῦ τοῦ παραχω[ρ]ουμένου, πρὸς ὃν καὶ ε[ἶ]να[ι] [32]τὰ ἀπὸ τοῦ αὐτοῦ α (ἔτους) δημόσια παντοῖα. κυρία [33][ἡ π]αραχώρησις [δ]ισσὴ γραφεῖσα, ἣν ὁπηνίκα [34]ἐὰν αἱρῇ δημοσιώσεις δι[ὰ] τοῦ καταλογείου, οὐ [35]προσδεόμενος μεταλήμψεως μου διὰ τὸ ἐν-[36]τεῦθεν ε[ὐ]δοκεῖν με τῇ ἐσομένῃ ὑπὸ σοῦ [37]δημοσιώσει, περὶ δὲ τοῦ ταῦτα οὕτως ὀρθῶς [38]καλῶς γενέσθαι ἐπερωτηθεὶς ὑπὸ σοῦ ὡμολόγησα. [39](ἔτους) α Αὐτοκράτορος Καίσαρος Γαΐ[ο]υ Μεσσίου [40]Κυίντο[υ] Δεκίου Τραϊανοῦ Εὐσεβοῦς Εὐτυχοῦς [41]Σεβαστοῦ Χοίακ α. (2nd hand) [42][Αὐρ]ήλιος Πανεσνεὺς Πτόλλιδος ἔσχον τὴν κα-[43][ταγραφὴ]ν ὡς πρόκειται, καὶ ἐπερωτηθεὶς [44][ὡμολόγησ]α.

23. *l.* σου for σοι after ἀρκουμένου.

a field, on the east private land of other persons, on the west land of you, to whom the cession is made, and I have received on the spot from you straightway from hand to hand the sum agreed upon between us for the cession of the said $\frac{1}{3}$ part, 400 drachmae of Imperial silver coin, and I am bound to deliver the $\frac{1}{3}$ arura to you and your descendants and successors guaranteed from claims made against you in my name or by any other person in my name, you being satisfied with the guarantee of the said $\frac{1}{3}$ arura which I received from my above-mentioned predecessor Catillianus also called Varus, which land I am also to deliver to you free from the taxes paid upon it and imposts of all kinds up to the past 6th year [a] and including the past 6th year, because the profits of it from the present 1st year onwards belong to you, to whom the cession is made, who are also responsible for the taxes of all kinds from the said 1st year onwards. This deed of cession, written in duplicate, is valid; and whenever you choose you shall publish it through the bureau [b] without requiring my concurrence, because I hereby agree to the future publication of it by you; and having been asked by you the formal question whether this is done rightly and fairly I have given my consent. The 1st year of the Emperor Caesar Gaius Messius Quintus Decius Trajanus Pius Felix Augustus, Choiak 1. (Signed) I, Aurelius Panesneus son of Ptollis, have received the conveyance as stated above, and in answer to the formal question I have

[a] Of the Philippi.

[b] The bureau of the archidicastes in Alexandria, by which private agreements were proved and publicly recorded.

Αὐρήλιος Θέων ὁ καὶ Ἀσκληπιά-[45][δης ἐπικαλ]ούμενος Ζωίλος ἔγραψα ὑπὲρ αὐτοῦ [46][μὴ εἰδότος γ]ράμματα.

50. DEED OF GIFT

P. Grenf. ii. 68. A.D. 247.

[1]Αὐρήλιος Πετοσῖρις Πετοσίριο[ς] νεκροτάφος ἀπὸ [2]Ἰβειτῶν πόλεως Αὐρηλίῳ Πετεχῶντι υἱῷ Τμάρσιος [3]ἀπὸ κώμης Κύσεως χαίρειν. ὁμολογῶ χαρίζεσθ[αί] σοι [4]χάριτι ἀναφαιρέτῳ καὶ ἀμετανοήτῳ, εὐνοίας ἕν[εκ]εν [5]{καὶ ἀμετανοή[τῳ]} ἣν ἔδειξας εἰς ἐμέ, ἀπὸ τῆς ὑπαρ-[6]χούσης μοι κηδείας νεκροταφικῆς ἐν Κύσει με[τὰ] καὶ [7]τῶν κωμῶν [τ]ῆς Κύσεως μέρος τέταρτον ἀπὸ [8]τοῦ νῦν μέχρ[ι] παντός· καὶ οὐκ ἐξέσται μοι οὔ[τε ἄλ]λῳ [9]τινὶ τῶν ἐμῶ[ν] μετελθεῖν σε περὶ τῆσδε τῆ[ς] δό-[10]σεως διὰ τὸ οὕτως μοι δεδόχθαι. ἡ δὲ χάρις α[ὕ]τη [11]ἁπλῆ [γρ]αφεῖσα [κυ]ρία ἔστω καὶ βεβαία ὡς ἐν δημοσίῳ [12]κατακειμέν[η, κ]αὶ ἐπερωτηθε[ὶς] ὡμολόγησα. [13](ἔτους) ε Αὐτοκρατόρων Καισάρων Μάρκων Ἰουλίων [14]Φιλίππων Εὐσεβῶν Εὐτυχῶν Σεβαστῶν [15]Χοίακ κε. (2nd hand) [16]Αὐρήλιος Κλαύδιος Ψεναμούνιος παρανέγνων. (1st hand) [17]Αὐρήλιος Πετοσῖρις ὁ προκείμενος ἐχαρισάμην ὡ[ς] [18]πρόκειται, καὶ ἐπε[ρ]ωτηθεὶς ὡμολ[όγ]ησα. ἔγραψ[α] [19]ὑπὲρ αὐτοῦ Αὐρή[λι]ος Φιλεῖνος ὁ καὶ Θεόγνωστος [20]ἐρωτηθείς. (3rd hand) [21]Αὐρήλιος Φιλοσάραπις Ἀπολλωνίου μαρτ[υρ]ῶ. (4th hand) [22]Αὐρήλιος Ἀμμώνιος Ψά[ι]τος μαρτυρῶ.

5. καὶ ἀμετανοήτῳ perhaps miswritten for καὶ φιλοστοργίας (Wilcken).

given my consent. I, Aurelius Theon also called Asclepiades, surnamed Zoilus, have written for him, as he is illiterate.

50. DEED OF GIFT

A.D. 247.

Aurelius Petosiris son of Petosiris, grave-digger, of the city of Hibis,[a] to Aurelius Petechon son of Tmarsis, of the village of Kusis, greeting. I acknowledge that I give to you by gift inalienable and irrevocable, for the goodwill which you have shown me, a fourth share in the grave-digging business belonging to me in Kusis together with the villages of Kusis from now for all time; and it shall not be lawful for me or any other of my family to take action against you regarding this gift, because I have so resolved. This deed of gift, made in one copy, shall be valid and guaranteed as though deposited in a public registry, and in answer to the formal question I have given my assent. The 5th year of the Emperors and Caesars Marci Julii Philippi Pii Felices Augusti, Choiak 25. (Signed) I, Aurelius Claudius son of Psenamounis have read it over. I, Aurelius Petosiris the aforesaid, have made the gift as aforesaid and in answer to the formal question I have given my assent. I, Aurelius Philinus, called also Theognostus, wrote for him at his request. I, Aurelius Philosarapis son of Apollonius, witness. I, Aurelius Ammonius son of Psais, witness.

[a] Capital of the Ἰβίτης νομός, as the Great Oasis was called.

51. DIVISION OF PROPERTY IN SLAVES

P.S.I. 903. A.D. 47.

[1]Ἔτους ἑβδόμου Τιβερίου Κλαυδίου Καίσαρος Σεβαστοῦ Γερμανικοῦ Αὐτοκράτορος [2]μηνὸς Ξανθικοῦ ἐνάτῃ καὶ εἰκάδι, ἐν Τεβτύνει τῆς Πολέ-[3]μωνος μερίδος τοῦ Ἀρσινοείτου νομοῦ. ὁμολογοῦσιν ἀλλήλοις Ἁρυώτης ὡς ἐτῶν [4]τριάκοντα πέντε οὐλὴ ὑπὸ σεαγόναν ἀριστερὰν καὶ Κρονίων ὡς ἐτῶν τριάκοντα οὐλὴ [5]πήχι ἀριστερῷ καὶ Ἁρυώτης νεώτερος ὁ καὶ Ἀραβάρχης ὡς ἐτῶν εἴκοσι ἑπτὰ οὐλὴ [6]ὑπὲρ ὀφρὺν ἀρ<ισ>τεράν, οἱ τρῖς Ἡρωδίωνος, διειρῆσθαι πρὸς ἑαυτοὺς ἐξ εὐδοκού<ν>των ἐπὶ τοῦ [7]παρόντος διαιρέσι ἀπὸ τῆς ἐνεστώσης ἡμέρας ἐπὶ τὸν ἅπαντα χρόνον τὰ ὑπάρ-[8]χοντα αὐτοῖς πατρικὰ δουλικὰ σώματα τέσσαρα, Θερμουθάριον καὶ Σαμβοῦν [9]καὶ Ἡρακλᾶν καὶ Ἡρακλοῦν χωλήν, <ἐφ' ᾧ> τὸν μὲν Ἁρυώτην πρεσβύτερον λελονχέναι εἰς [10]τὸ ἐπιβάλλον ἑαυτῷ μέρος Σαμβοῦν σὺν τοῖς ἐσομένοις ἐξ αὐτῆς δουλικοῖς [11]ἐνγόνοις, τὸν δὲ Κρονίωνα καὶ αὐτὸν λελονχέναι εἰς τὸ καὶ αὐτῷ ἐπιβάλλον μέρος [12]τὸν προγεγραμμένον Ἡρακλᾶν, τὸν δὲ Ἁρυώτην νεώτερον τὸν καὶ Ἀραβάρχην καὶ [13]αὐτὸν λελονχέναι εἰς τὸ καὶ αὐτῷ ἐπιβάλλον τὰς προγεγραμμένας δούλας Θερμου-[14]θάριον καὶ Ἡρακλοῦν χωλὴν σὺν τοῖς ἐσομένοις ἐξ αὐτῶν δουλικοῖς ἐνγόνοις· [15]μένιν δὲ τῇ τῶν ὁμολογού<ν>των μητρὶ Ταορσεῦτι Ἁρυώτου τὴν διατεταγμένην αὐ-[16]τῇ ὑπὸ τοῦ τῶν ὁμολογού<ν>των πατρὸς δουλίαν, ἐφ' ὃν χρόνον περίεστιν ἡ Τα-[17]ορσεῦς, τῆς προγεγραμμένης [δού]λης Θερμουθαρίου. κρατεῖν οὖν

51. DIVISION OF PROPERTY IN SLAVES

A.D. 47.

The 7th year of Tiberius Claudius Caesar Augustus Germanicus Imperator, the 29th of the month Xandicus, at Tebtunis in the division of Polemon in the Arsinoite nome. Haruotes, aged about 35 years, with a scar below the left jaw, and Cronion, aged about 30 years, with a scar on the left forearm, and Haruotes the younger also called Arabarches, aged about 27 years, with a scar above the left eyebrow, all three sons of Herodion, mutually acknowledge that they have divided between themselves, as consenting parties here and now to the division, from the present day for all time the four slaves belonging to them by inheritance from their father, Thermoutharion and Sambous and Heraclas and limping Heraclous, on the basis that Haruotes the elder has obtained for the portion falling to him Sambous with the future slave children who may be born of her, and Cronion likewise has obtained for the portion falling to him the aforesaid Heraclas, and Haruotes the younger also called Arabarches has likewise obtained for the portion falling to him Thermoutharion and limping Heraclous with the future slave children who may be born of them, but that the mother of the acknowledging parties, Taorseus daughter of Haruotes, shall retain the service of the aforesaid slave Thermoutharion, devised to her by the acknowledging parties' father, for as long as Taorseus survives. Each of the ac-

4. *l.* σιαγόνα.

καὶ δεσ-[18]πόζιν ἕκαστον τῶν ὁμολογούντων καὶ τοὺς παρ᾽ αὐτῶν καὶ τοὺς μεταλημψομέ-[19]νους ὧν λελόνχασι μερῶν ἀπὸ τῆς ἐνεστῶτος ἡμέρας ἐπὶ τὸν ἅπαν-[20]τα χρόνον ἀναμφιλέκτως, καὶ μὴ ἐπιπορεύεσθαι ἕκαστον τῶν ὁμολο-[21]γού<ν>των ἐφ᾽ ἃ ὁ ἕτερος αὐτῶν κεκλήρωται τρόπῳ μηθενί. ὅ τι δ᾽ ἂν τῶν προγεγραμμέ(νων) [22]παρασυνγραφῇ τις τῶν ὁμολογού<ν>των, ἀποτισάτω ὁ μὴ ἐνμένων τῷ ἐνμένοντι τά τε βλάβη [23]καὶ δαπανήματα διπλᾶ καὶ ἐπίτιμον ἀργυρίου δραχμὰς χιλίας πεντα-[24]κοσίας καὶ εἰς τὸ δημόσιον τὰς ἴσας, καὶ μηθὲν ἧσσον χωρὶς τοῦ [25]μένιν τὰ διωμολογημένα περὶ αὐτῶν, καθώτι καὶ εἰσὶν ἑκόντες [26]περὶ ἁπάντων συνκεχωρηκότες. ὑπογραφὴ ἰδία τῶν τριῶ(ν) γεγραμ(μένων)· (2nd hand) [27]Ἁρυώτης Ἡρωδίωνος συνδιίρημε ἐπὶ τοῦ παρώντος καὶ λέλωνχα εἰς τὸ ⟦αὐτὸ⟧ ἐπιβάλλων [28]μοι μέρος τὴν προγεγραμ-<μ>ένην δούλην Σαμβοῦν καὶ ἕκαστα ποήσωι καθὼς πρόκιται. (3rd hand) [29]Κρονίων Ἡρωδίωνος συνδιείρημαι ἐπὶ τοῦ παρώντος καὶ λέλωνχα εἰς τὸ ἐπιβάλλων μο<ι> μέ-[30]ρος τὸν πρωγεγραμμένον δοῦλων Ἡρακλᾶν καὶ ἕκαστα ποήσω καθὼς πρώκιται. (4th hand) [31]Ἁρυώτης νεότερος ὃς κὲ Ἀραβάρχης Ἡροδίωνος συνδιείρημαι ἐπὶ τοῦ παρόντος καὶ [32]λέλωγχα εἰς τὼ ἐπιβάλον μοι μέρος τὰς προγεγραμ<μ>ένας δούλας δύας Θερμου-[33]θάριον καὶ Ἡρακλοῦ<ν> χωλὴν καὶ ἕκαστα ποήσω καθὼς πρώκειται.

19. *l.* ἐνεστώσης. 25. *l.* καθότι.
27. *l.* συνδιείρημαι, παρόντος, λέλογχα, ἐπιβάλλον, and similarly in ll. 29–33. 31. κέ for καί.

knowledging parties therefore and their assigns and successors shall possess and be masters of the portions which they have obtained from the present day for all time without dispute, and none of the acknowledging parties shall lay claim in any manner to what has been allotted to another. If any of the acknowledging parties violates any of the above provisions, the one who infringes them shall forfeit to the one who observes them both the damages and the expenses doubled and a penalty of 1500 silver drachmae and to the Treasury the like sum, and the agreement about the property shall none the less hold good, as made with their voluntary concurrence on every point. Autograph subscription of the three persons mentioned: (Signed) I, Haruotes son of Herodion, am a party to the division made at this present time and have obtained for the portion falling to me the aforesaid slave Sambous and I will do everything as stated above. I, Cronion son of Herodion, am a party to the division made at this present time and have obtained for the portion falling to me the aforesaid slave Heraclas and I will do everything as stated above. I, Haruotes the younger also called Arabarches son of Herodion, am a party to the division made at this present time and have obtained for the portion falling to me the aforesaid two slaves Thermoutharion and limping Heraclous and I will do everything as stated above.

52. DIVISION OF PROPERTY HELD ON LEASE

P. Ryl. 157. A.D. 135.

1[Εὐδαιμονὶς] ἡ καὶ Τετῆς καὶ Σοῆρις ἡ καὶ Σουεροῦς ἀμφότεραι Ἡρώδου τοῦ καὶ Τιβερίου Ἥρωνος, ἡ μὲν 2[Τετῆς δ]ιὰ Διονυσίου τοῦ καὶ Πλάντα ἐπικαλουμένου Λούπου Διονυσίου ἀνδρός, ἡ δὲ Σουεροῦς διὰ Διοσκουρίδου 3[τοῦ καὶ . . . . .] Πλούτωνος ἀνδρός, ἀλλήλαις χα[ί]ρειν. ὁμολογοῦμεν διῃρῆσθαι πρὸς ἀλλήλας ἐπὶ τοῦ παρόντος 4[ὃ ἔχομεν ἐ]ν μισθώσει οὐσιακ[ὸ]ν ἀμπελικὸν κτῆμα ἐν κώμῃ Θραγὴ τοῦ Περὶ Πόλιν Ἄνω ἐκ τοῦ Ξένωνος κλήρου 5[. . . . . . ὅσου] ἐστὶν ἀρουρηδοῦ ἐν ὧι πωμάριον καὶ κεκληρῶσθαι τὴν μὲν Σοῆριν τὴν καὶ Σουεροῦν τὴν νοτίνην 6[μερίδα δοῦσ]α<ν> [ὑ]πὲρ ἐκλογῆς τῇ Εὐδαιμονίδι παραχρῆμα ἀργυρίου δραχμὰς διακοσίας δέκα, ἧς ἐστιν σχοινισμὸς 7[. . . . . ἀ]ρχομένου νότου ε[ἰ]ς β[ο]ρρᾶ ἐντὸς τείχους τοῦ κτήματος ἐν [σ]ταδίωι δευτέρωι μετὰ λιβικὸν τεῖχος 8[σχοινίον ἕν], ἀπὸ τείχους λιβικο[ῦ] εἰς ἀπηλιώτην ἐπί τι σχοινίον ἓν ἥ[μισ]υ τέταρτον ἑκκαιδέκατον δυοτριακοστὸν 9[τετρακαιεξηκ]οστόν, ἀπὸ δὲ τοῦ αὐτοῦ ὁρίου ἐκβά[σ]εως εἰς βορρᾶ σχοινίου ἥμισυ ὄγδο[ο]ν [ἑ]κκαιδέκατον δυοτρια-10[κοστὸν καὶ ἀπ]ὸ τούτου τοῦ ὁρί[ο]υ εἰς ἀπηλιώτη[ν μ]έχρι τε[ί]χους ἀπηλιωτικοῦ ὅ ἐστιν ὅρι[ο]ν τοῦ κτήματος 11[τοῦ παντὸς ἐ]κβάσεως σχ[ο]ινίου τέταρτον ὄγδοον δυοτριακοστόν, τὴν δὲ Εὐδαιμον[ί]δα τὴν καὶ Τετῆν κε-12[κληρῶσθαι] τὴν βορίνην μερίδα, λαβ[ο]ῦσα<ν> παρὰ τῆς Σουεροῦτος ὡς πρόκειται τὰς τοῦ ἀργυρί[ο]υ δραχ(μὰς) διακοσίας δέκα, 13[κατὰ τοὺς πρ]οκει-

52. DIVISION OF PROPERTY HELD ON LEASE

A.D. 135.

Eudaemonis also called Tetes and Soeris also called Souerous, both daughters of Herodes also called Tiberius son of Heron, Tetes acting through her husband Dionysius also called Plantas surnamed Lupus, son of Dionysius, and Souerous through her husband Dioscurides also called . . . son of Pluton, mutual greetings. We acknowledge that we have divided between each other at this present time the domain-land[a] vineyard which we hold on lease in the village Thrage in the toparchy of the Upper Suburb,[b] being part of the holding of Xenon . . . whatever the extent of its acreage is, containing an orchard, and that Soeris also called Souerous has been allotted the southern portion, having forthwith paid to Eudaemonis for the choice 210 silver drachmae. Its measurements are . . . beginning from south to north inside the wall of the plot in the second stade[c] following the western wall 1 schoenion,[d] from the western wall eastward for a certain distance $1\frac{5}{8}\frac{5}{4}$ schoenia, and from this latter boundary turning off to the north $\frac{2}{3}\frac{3}{2}$ of a schoenion, and from this boundary eastward up to the eastern wall which is the boundary of the whole plot $\frac{1}{3}\frac{3}{2}$ of a schoenion. And we acknowledge that Eudaemonis also called Tetes has been allotted the northern portion, having received from Souerous as aforesaid the 210 drachmae of silver, in accordance

[a] Hereditary property of the Emperor, augmented from time to time by bequests and confiscations.

[b] In the Hermopolite nome.

[c] Meaning obscure.

[d] 1 schoenion = 100 cubits or nearly 50 yards.

μένους σχοινισμοὺς τ[ῆ]ς νοτίνης μερίδος ὅσου ἐστὶν ἀρουρηδοῦ. ἔσται δὲ ἡ ἀνόρθωσις τῶν [14][νῦν ἀποκαθι]σ̣τ̣ανομένων κοινῶν [τ]ειχῶ[ν] ἀ[πὸ κ]οινῶν λ[η]μμάτων. ποτιεῖ [δέ] ἑκάστη ἡμῶν τὴν ἰδίαν μερίδα [15][. . . . .]σι καὶ κυκλευταῖς καὶ ἀ[ν]τηρευτα[ῖ]ς [ἀπὸ το]ῦ κοινοῦ ἡμῶν λάκκου ὄντος ἐν κτήματι ἰδί[ω]ι ἡμῶν ἀπὸ λιβι-[16][κοῦ τείχους τοῦ ο]ὐσιακοῦ κτήματος [.] . σ . παρ[. . . .] ἡμέραν, τῆς δαπάνης τῆς τε ἐπισκευῆς καὶ κατασκευῆς τοῦ ξυλικοῦ [17][ὀργάνου καὶ ὁμ]οίως λάκκου καὶ ἀναψη[σμοῦ οὔσης π]ρ[ὸ]ς ἀμφοτέρους. παρέξει δὲ ἡ λαχοῦσα τὴν ν[ο]τίνην μερίδα τῇ λαχούσῃ [18][τὴν βορρίνη]ν πρ[ὸ]ς μόνας τὰς ἡμ[έ]ρας τῆς τρύγης εἴσ[ο]δον καὶ ἔξοδον διὰ ἀπηλιωτικ[ο]ῦ τείχους π[ρὸ]ς βορρίνωι ὁρίωι αὐτῆς, [19][καὶ ὁμοίως] ἡ [λ]αχοῦσα τὴν βορρίνην π[αρ]έξει τῇ λαχούσῃ τὴν νοτίνην τὸ ὑδραγωγεῖσθαι τὸ ὕδωρ διὰ τοῦ προόντος ὑδρα-[20][γωγοῦ το]ῦ πρὸς τῷ λιβικῶι τείχε[ι] τοῦ κτήματος πρ[ὸ]ς τὸ ποτίζεσθαι ὅλην τὴν νοτίνην μερίδα, καὶ ὁμοίως, εἰ χρεία γείνοιτο [21][ποτίσαι ἐ]ν ἀναβάσει ἀπὸ ποδὸς τὴν αὐτὴν νοτίνην μερίδα, παρέξει ἡ λαβοῦσα τὴν βορρίνην μερίδα τὸ ὑδραγωγεῖσθαι δι' αὐ-[22][τῆς, τῶν] δημοσίων πάντων τοῦ κτήματος σιτικῶν τε καὶ ἀργυρικῶν τῶν ἔμπροσθεν καὶ τῶν ἐπεσομένων χρόνων καὶ [23][τῶν ἀνη]κόντων τῷ φίσκωι ὄντων πρὸς ἀμφοτέρας διὰ τὸ ἐπὶ τούτοις συμπεφωνηκέναι. ἡ διαίρεσις κυρίαι μέν[ο]ντος [24][ἡμῖν τοῦ λόγ]ου περὶ ὧν ἔχομεν πρὸς ἀλλήλας. (ἔτους) ιθ

23. *l.* κυρία.

with the aforesaid measurements of the southern portion, whatever the extent of its acreage is. The restoration of the common walls now being reconstructed shall be paid for out of our common revenues. Each of us shall irrigate her own portion, by means of . . . and men working the water-wheel and banking the channels, from our common reservoir which is in our private plot beyond the western wall of the domain-land plot . . ., the cost of maintaining and repairing the wooden water-wheel and likewise the reservoir and of cleansing it being borne by us both. The recipient of the southern portion shall permit the recipient of the northern portion, for the time of the vintage only, entrance and exit through the eastern wall near her northern boundary, and likewise the recipient of the northern portion shall permit the recipient of the southern portion to conduct water by means of the existing channel at the western wall of the plot for the irrigation of all the southern portion, and likewise, if it should become necessary at the inundation to irrigate the said southern portion by foot,[a] the recipient of the northern portion shall permit water to be conducted through it. All public imposts on the plot both in corn and in money for the past and the future and the dues to the Treasury shall be borne by us both; for we have agreed to these terms. This division is valid, without prejudice to matters pending between us. The 19th

[a] *Cf.* Deuteronomy xi. 10, "the land of Egypt . . . where thou sowedst thy seed and wateredst it with thy foot." Perhaps by opening and closing with the foot the mud embankments of the small runnels. Or the phrase in the present document may refer to a machine, such as the Archimedean screw which in Egypt was worked like a treadmill.

Αὐτοκράτορος Καίσαρος Τραϊανοῦ Ἁδριανοῦ Σεβα[σ]τοῦ Ἐπεὶφ τετρὰς καὶ εἰκάς. (2nd hand) 25[Εὐδαιμον]ὶς ἡ καὶ Τετῆς Ἡρώδ[ου τ]οῦ καὶ Τιβερίου Ἥρωνος διὰ Διονυσίου τοῦ καὶ Πλάντα ἐπικαλουμένου 26[Λούπου Διον]υσί[ο]υ ἀνδρὸς [διῃρημα]ι [κ]αθὼς πρόκειται.

53. DIVISION OF AN INHERITANCE

P. Tebt. 319. A.D. 248.

1Αὐρηλίῳ Μαξίμῳ τῷ καὶ Ἑρμαΐσκῳ ἱερεῖ ἀρχιδικαστῇ 2καὶ πρὸς τῇ ἐπιμελείᾳ τῶν χρηματιστῶν καὶ τῶν ἄλλων κριτηρίων 3παρὰ Μάρκου Αὐρηλίου Ἡρώδου <τοῦ> καὶ Λουρίου Ἀντινοέως καὶ παρὰ Μάρκου 4Αὐρηλίου Σαραπάμμωνος καὶ ὡς χρηματίζει. ἐπεὶ κατήντησεν εἴς τε τὸν 5Αὐρήλιον Σαραπάμμωνα καὶ Λούριον κατὰ διαδοχὴν κληρονομίας 6σιτικὰ ἐδάφη περὶ κώμην Κερκευσεῖριν τοῦ Ἀρσινοΐτου νομοῦ τῆς 7Πολέμωνος μερίδος ἐν δυσὶ σφραγεῖσι ἄρουραι ἑπτά, περὶ δὲ κώ-8μην Τεπτῦνιν τῆς αὐτῆς μερίδος ἐν τόπῳ ἐπικαλουμένῳ Καρίω-9νι ὁμοίως (ἄρουραι) ζ, περὶ δὲ κώμην Κερκῆσιν (ἄρουρα) α, ἐπὶ τὸ αὐτὸ 10(ἄρουραι) ιε, αἵ γε μέχρι νῦν ἦσαν ἀδιαίρετοι, ἔδοξεν δὲ νῦν αὐτοῖς 11ταύτας δι[αιρή]σασθαι ἐπὶ τῷ ἕκαστον αὐτῶν ἐπιγεινώσκειν 12τ[ὸ] ἴδιον μ[έρος, τ]ὰ νῦν συνχωροῦσιν ὅ τε Αὐρήλιος Ἰούλιος 13κ[α]ὶ Αὐρήλι[ος Σα]ραπάμμων διῃρῆσθαι τὰς προκειμένας 14ἀρούρας καὶ ἀπὸ μὲν τῶν περὶ κώμην

12 and 31. *l.* Λούριος instead of Ἰούλιος.

year of the Emperor Caesar Trajanus Hadrianus Augustus, Epeiph 24. (Signed) I, Eudaemonis also called Tetes, daughter of Herodes also called Tiberius son of Heron, acting through my husband Dionysius also called Plantas surnamed Lupus, son of Dionysius, have made the division as aforesaid.

53. DIVISION OF AN INHERITANCE

A.D. 248.

To Aurelius Maximus also called Hermaiscus, priest, archidicastes,[a] and superintendent of the chrematistae [b] and the other courts, from Marcus Aurelius Herodes also called Lurius, of Antinoe, and from Marcus Aurelius Sarapammon, however else he is styled. Whereas Aurelius Sarapammon and Lurius as successors to an inheritance have come into possession of certain corn lands comprising in the area of the village of Kerkeosiris in the division of Polemon in the Arsinoite nome 7 arurae in two plots, in the area of the village of Tebtunis in the same division in the place called Karion 7 arurae likewise, in the area of the village of Kerkesis 1 arura, making a total of 15 arurae, which have hitherto been undivided, and as they have now decided to divide these on the understanding that each of them acknowledges his own portion, Aurelius Lurius and Aurelius Sarapammon now agree that they have divided the aforesaid arurae and that of the 7 arurae in the area of the village of Kerkeosiris

[a] A judicial officer in Alexandria, one of whose functions was to legalize agreements such as the present one.

[b] Originally circuit judges, but in Roman times an Alexandrian court.

Κερκευσεῖριν (ἀρουρῶν) ζ ἐσχη-[15]κέναι ἕκαστον αὐτῶν (ἀρούρας) γ (ἥμισυ), ἀπὸ μὲν τῶν περὶ κώμην Τεπτῦ-[16]νιν (ἀρουρῶν) ζ ἕκαστον αὐτῶν ἐσχηκέναι (ἀρούρας) γ (ἥμισυ), καὶ ἀπὸ μὲν [17]τῶν περὶ κώμην Κερκῆσιν ἐσχηκέναι ἕκαστον αὐτῶν ταύτης [18]τὸ ἥμισυ μέρος, πρὸς τὸ ἀπὸ τοῦ νῦν ἕκαστον αὐτῶν [19]κρατεῖν καὶ κυριεύειν τοῦ ἐπιβεβληκότος αὐτῷ μέρους (ἀρουρῶν) ζ (ἡμίσους) [20]καὶ διοικεῖ[ν] καὶ ἐπιτελεῖν περὶ {ε} αὐτῶν ἕκαστον ὃ ἐὰν αἱρῆται· τὸν [21]δὲ Α[ὐ]ρήλιον Σαραπάμμωνα ἐξουσίαν ἔχειν τῶν ἑαυτοῦ ὑπαρχόν-[22]των ὄντων περὶ Θεογονίδα κώμην ἀπὸ (ἀρουρῶν) ϛ (ἀρουρῶν) γ [23]διὰ τὸ τὸν Λούριον πεπρακέναι τὸ κατ' αὐτὸν μέρος [24]ἥμισυ, εἰακέναι δὲ αὐτοὺς κοινὰς τὰς [25]ὑπαρχούσας (ἀρούρας) β οὔσας περὶ κώμην Τε-[26]πτῦνιν ἐν τόπῳ καλουμένῳ Παγαγόρῳ [27]ἄχρις ἂν περὶ τούτων τι αὐτοῖς δόξῃ, [28]μένοντος δὲ αὐτοῖς λόγου περὶ ὧν ἂν ἑτέ-[29]ρων εὑρίσκωσιν τῆς κλ[η]ρονομίας [30]ὑπαρχόντων. οὐκ ἐπελεύσεται δὲ ὁ Αὐ-[31]ρήλιος Ἰούλιος πρὸς τὸν Αὐρήλιον Σαραπάμ-[32]μωνα χάριν τοῦ ἐν τῇ μητροπ‹ό›λει οἰκήμα-[33]τος διὰ τὸ πεπρακέναι αὐτὸν τὸ κα-[34]τ' αὐτὸν μέρος ἥμισυ. καὶ τὰ ἑξῆς. [35](ἔτους) ε Φιλίππων Μεχεὶρ θ.

54. RESIGNATION OF CLAIMS TO AN ESTATE

P. Tebt. 380. A.D. 67.

[1]Ἔτους τρισκ[α]ιδεκάτου Νέρωνος [2]Κλαυδίου Καίσαρος Σεβαστοῦ [3]Γερμανικοῦ Αὐτοκράτορος μηνὸ[ς] [4]Ξαντικοῦ κα Μεχεὶρ μιᾷ καὶ εἰ-[5]κάδει ἐν

each of them has received 3½ arurae, of the 7 arurae in the area of the village of Tebtunis each of them has received 3½ arurae, and of the arura in the area of the village of Kerkesis each of them has received one half, so that each of them may henceforth possess and own the portion of 7½ arurae which has fallen to him and may each administer and dispose of them in whatever way he chooses; and that Aurelius Sarapammon shall have entire control of his property in the area of the village of Theogonis consisting of 3 arurae out of 6, because Lurius has sold his half share, and that they have left under joint ownership the 2 arurae belonging to them in the area of the village of Tebtunis in the place called Pagagorus until they come to some decision concerning them, while reserving their rights concerning any other property which they may find to form part of the estate. And Aurelius Lurius shall not proceed against Aurelius Sarapammon on account of the building in the metropolis, because he has sold his own half share. And the rest of it.[a] The 5th year of the Philippi, Mecheir 9.

[a] That is, the concluding formulae, the papyrus being only a partial copy of the original deed.

54. RESIGNATION OF CLAIMS TO AN ESTATE

A.D. 67.

The 13th year of Nero Claudius Caesar Augustus Germanicus Imperator, the 21st of the month Xandicus or Mecheir, at Tebtunis in the division

4. *l.* Ξανδικοῦ.

Τεβτύνι τῆς Πολέμωνος [6]μερίδος τοῦ Ἀρσινοείτου νομοῦ. [7]ὁμολογεῖ Θ[ο]μμοῦς ἡ καὶ Πρωτοῦς [8]Πετεσούχου ὡς ἐτῶν τριάκοντα [9]τεσσάρων οὐλὴ χιρεὶ δεξιᾷ ἐκτό(ς), [10]μετὰ κυρί[ο]υ τοῦ ἑαυτῆς προσγε-[11]νοῦς Ὀρσεῦτος τοῦ Πακήβκιος [12]ὡς ἐτῶν τριάκοντα δύο οὐλὴ [13]χειρεὶ ἀρι[στ]ερᾷ ὑπ' ἀντίχιρι, τῶι [14]ἑαυτῆς ὁμοπατρίῳ καὶ ὁμο-[15]μητρίῳ [ἀ]δελφῶι Σαμβᾶτει [16]ὡς ἐτῶν τ[ρι]άκοντα ἑπτὰ οὐλὴ [17]ὀφρύει δεξιᾷ ἄκρᾳ, τὴν ὁμο-[18]λογοῦσαν Θομμοῦν τὴν καὶ Πρω-[19]τ{αρ}οῦν ἐκσίστασθαι τῶι Σαμ-[20]βᾷ πάντων τῶν ὑπὸ τοῦ ἀμ-[21]φοτέρων αὐτῶν πατρὸς Πετε-[22]σούχου το[ῦ] Ἀπολλωνίου κατα-[23]λιφθησωμένων ὑπαρχόν-[24]των ἁπάντων καὶ μὴ ἐπελεύ-[25]σεσθαι αὐτὴν τὴν ὁμολογοῦ-[26]σαν μηδὲ τοὺς παρ' αὐτῆς ἐπὶ [27]τὸν Σαμβᾶν περὶ μηδενὸς [28]τῶν ὑπὸ τοῦ προγεγραμμέ-[29]νου πατρὸς Πετεσούχου [30]καταλιφθησωμένων. ὑπο-[31]γραφεῖς τῆς ὁμο(λογούσης) καὶ το(ῦ) ἐπιγραψ⟨αμ⟩έ-[32]νου αὐτῆς κυρίου Λυσᾶς Διδύ-[33]μου ὡς (ἐτῶν) μζ οὐλὴ ποδεὶ ἀριστερῶι {και} [34]καὶ Θέων Ἥρωνος (ἐτῶν) νθ ο(ὐλὴ) γόνα(τι) δεξ[ιῷ]. (2nd hand) [35]Θομμοῦς ἡ κα[ὶ] Πρωτοῦς Πετεσούχου μετὰ [36]κυρίου τοῦ πρ[οσ]γενοῦς Ὀρσεῦτος τοῦ Π[α]κήβκι-[37]ος ὁμολογῶ [ἐξί]σθασθε τῷ ἀδελφῷ μ[ου] [38]Σαμβᾶτι πάντων τῶν ὑπὸ τοῦ ἀμφοτέ-[39]ρων πατρὸς [Π]ετ[ε]σ[ούχο]υ τ[οῦ] Ἀπολλ[ω-][40]νίου καταλ[ι]φθησωμένων ὑπαρχώ-[41][τ]ων πάντω[ν κ]αὶ μὴ ἐπελεύσεσθαι πε-[42]ρὶ μηδενὸς τρώπῳ μηδενὶ καθὼς [43][πρ]όκιτε. ἔγραψεν ὑπὲρ [α]ὐτῶν Λυσᾶς Διδύ-[44][μου] διὰ τὸ μὴ εἰδ[έ]νε αὐτοὺς γράμματα. (3rd hand) [45][Σαμ]βᾶ[ς Π]ετεσούχου γέ-[46][γονεν εἴς με ἡ ὁμολογία. - - -

of Polemon in the Arsinoite nome. Thommous also called Protous, daughter of Petesouchus, aged about 34 years, with a scar on the outside of her right hand, having with her as guardian her kinsman Orseus son of Pakebkis, aged about 32 years, with a scar on the left hand under the thumb, acknowledges to her brother Sambas, son of the same father and mother, aged about 37 years, with a scar at the tip of the right eyebrow, that she, Thommous also called Protous, resigns to Sambas all the property that shall be left by their father Petesouchus son of Apollonius, and that neither she herself, the acknowledging party, nor her assigns will take proceedings against Sambas concerning any of the property that shall be left by their aforesaid father Petesouchus. Signatories: for the acknowledging party and her professed guardian, Lysas son of Didymus, aged about 47 years, with a scar on the left foot; and (for Sambas), Theon son of Heron, aged 59, with a scar on the right knee. (Signed) I, Thommous also called Protous, daughter of Petesouchus, having with me as guardian my kinsman Orseus son of Pakebkis, acknowledge that I resign to my brother Sambas all the property that shall be left by our father Petesouchus son of Apollonius and that I will not take proceedings against him concerning any of it in any manner as aforesaid. Lysas son of Didymus wrote for them, as they are illiterate. (Signed) I, Sambas son of Petesouchus, have had the acknowledgement made to me . . .

19 and 37. *l.* ἐξίστασθαι. 22 and 30. *l.* καταλειφθησομένων. 31. Revised reading. 40. *l.* καταλειφθησομένων ὑπαρχόντων. 42. *l.* τρόπῳ. 43. *l.* πρόκειται. 44. *l.* εἰδέναι.

55. SETTLEMENT OF CLAIMS

P.Oxy. 1644. 63–62 B.C.

1Βασι[λεύοντο]ς Πτολεμαίου θεοῦ Νέου Διονύσ[ο]υ Φιλ[οπά]τορος Φιλαδέλφου 2ἔτου[ς ἐνν]εακαιδεκάτου, τὰ δ' ἄλλα τῶν κοινῶ[ν] ὡς ἐν Ἀλ[εξ]ανδρείᾳ 3γράφετ[αι, μ]ηνὸς Περιτίου καὶ Χοίαχ ἐν Ὀξυρύγχων πόλει 4τῆ[ς Θη]βαΐδος. ὁμολογοῦσιν Πασίων καὶ Πτολεμαῖος καὶ 5Ἀπ[ο]λλ[ώ]νιος, οἱ τρεῖς Διονυσίου Μακεδόνες τῶν ἐν τοῖς κατοίκοις 6ἱππεῦ[σιν], τῶι τῆς γ[ε]νομένης αὐτῶ[ν] ἀδελφῆς Βερενίκης 7τετε[λε]υ[τ]ηκυίας υἱῶι Μοσχίωνι .[. . .] . [. .]ος Μακε-8δόν[ι τῶν κα]τοίκων ἱππέων, πάντες ἀγυιᾶς Κλεοπάτρας 9Ἀφροδί[τ]ης, μηθὲν ἐγκαλεῖν αὐτοὺς μηδ' ἄλλον ὑπὲρ αὐτῶν 10μηδ' ἐγκαλέσειν μηδ' ἐπελεύσεσθαι τῶι Μοσχίωνι μηδὲ τοῖς 11παρ' αὐ[το]ῦ περὶ οὗ ἔθετο ὁ Μοσχίων τῆι τῶν ὁμολογούντων 12μητρί, αὐτοῦ δὲ Μοσχίωνος κατὰ μητέρα μάμμηι, Ἀρσινόηι 13Π[τολ]εμαίου, καὶ ταύτης μετηλλαχυίας τὸν βίον, 14δ[α]νείου ἐντόκου ἀργυρικοῦ κεφαλαίου ἄλλως χρηματί-15σθ[έντος] κατὰ συγγραφὴν διὰ τοῦ ἐν τῆι προειρημένηι πόλει 16μνημονείου ἐν τοῖς ἔμπροσθεν χρόνοις, μηδὲ περὶ ἄλλου 17μηδενὸς ἁπλῶς τῶν κατὰ τὴν δηλουμένην τοῦ δανείου 18συγγραφήν, ἕνεκα τοῦ τὸν Μοσχίωνα διά τινας αἰτίας τὸν 19καινοχωρισμὸν τῆς προειρημένης ἀργ[υ]ρικῆς συναλλάξεως 20εἰς τὴν Ἀρσινόην ἐν πίσ[τει] διὰ τὴν προγεγραμμένην 21ἰδιότη[τ]α πεποιῆσθαι. [ἐ]ὰν δέ τις ἡμῶν παρὰ τὰ προγε-22γραμ[μ]ένα παρασυγγραφ[ῇ] ἢ ἐπέλθῃ τ[ῶι] Μοσχίωνι, χωρὶς 23τοῦ τὴν ἔφοδον ἄκυρο[ν]

55. SETTLEMENT OF CLAIMS

63–62 B.C.

The 19th year of the reign of Ptolemy, the god Neus Dionysus[a] Philopator Philadelphus, and the rest of the formula as written in Alexandria,[b] the[c] of the month Peritius or Choiak, at Oxyrhynchus in the Thebaid. Pasion and Ptolemaeus and Apollonius, all three sons of Dionysius, Macedonians of the catoecic cavalry, acknowledge to the son of their deceased sister Berenice, Moschion son of . . ., Macedonian of the catoecic cavalry, all the parties being domiciled in the street of Cleopatra Aphrodite, that neither they nor other person acting for them make or will make any claim or take any proceedings against Moschion or his assigns concerning the loan of money at interest which Moschion obtained from the mother of the acknowledging parties and his own maternal grandmother, Arsinoe daughter of Ptolemaeus, who has also died, and which moreover has been embodied in a contract executed through the record-office in the aforesaid city in former times, or concerning any other provision whatever of the said contract of loan, because Moschion for certain reasons has effected a renewal of the aforesaid money-agreement with Arsinoe under a pledge on account of the above-mentioned kinship. If any of us violates the above agreement or takes proceedings against Moschion, not only shall the proceedings be invalid

[a] "The new Dionysus" was one of the titles assumed by this Ptolemy, who is known to history by the nickname of Auletes, "the flute-player." [b] See No. 2, note *a*.

[c] The date has not been filled in.

εἶναι καὶ π[ρο]σαποτεισάτω [24]ὁ ἐπ[ελ]θὼν ἢ ὁ ὑπὲ[ρ αὐτ]οῦ ἐπελευσ[όμ]εν[ο]ς Μοσχίωνι [25]ἢ [ᾧ]ι ἐ[ὰ]ν ἐπέλθῃ τῶ[ν π]αρ' αὐτοῦ ἐπί[τιμ]ον ἀργυρίου [26]δραχμὰς πε[ντ]ακοσί[ας] καὶ εἰς τὸ βασιλι-κ[ὸ]ν τὰς ἴσας, καὶ μηθὲν [27]ἧττον. ἐπ[ὶ δ]ὲ πᾶσ[ι τ]οῖς προγεγραμμένοις συν-[28]ευδοκοῦσιν [οἱ τ]ῶν ὁμ[ολο]γούντων μ[άρτυ]ρες, τοῦ μὲν [29][Πασίωνος Διον]ύσιος - - -

Verso: [33]ἔτους ιθ Χοίαχ. [ὁμολο]γία [34]Πασίωνος καὶ τῶν ἀδελφῶν [35]π[ρὸς] Μοσχίωνα.

56. SETTLEMENT OF CLAIMS

B.G.U. 405. A.D. 348.

[1]Ὑπατείας Φλαουίου Φιλίππου τοῦ λαμπροτάτου [2]ἐπάρχου τοῦ ἱεροῦ πραιτωρίου καὶ Φλαουίου Σαλιᾶ [3]τοῦ λαμτροτάτου μαγίστρου τῶν ἱππέων Φαμενὼθ ι. [4]Αὐρηλία Οὐαλερία θυγάτηρ Ἀλυπίου Αὐρηλίᾳ [5]Νεμεσίλλᾳ ὁμογαστρίῳ μου ἀδελφῇ ἀπὸ κώ-[6]μης Φιλαδελφίας τοῦ Ἀρσινοείτου νομοῦ χα(ίρειν). [7]ἐπιδὴ λίθον σιτοκόπτην καὶ σιταλετικὴν μη-[8]χανὴν πατρῷα ἡμῶν ὄντα ἐκληρώθη-[9]μεν κἀγὼ μονὴ τὸν λίθον ἦρκα καὶ πέπρα-[10]κα εἰς τὸ ἑροῦν μοι μέρος, κατὰ τοῦτο ὁμολογῶ [11]μὴ ἔχειν μέρος εἰς τὴν προλεχθεῖσαν σιτα-[12]λετικὴν μηχανήν, ἀλλὰ ξένον με εἶναι [13]καὶ ἀλλότριον αὐτῆς, καὶ οὐδείς σοι ἐπελεύ-[14]σεται περὶ αὐτῆς, οὔτε ἐγὼ ἡ Οὐαλερία οὔτε τέ-[15]κνα μου οὔτε κληρονόμοι οὔτε ἕτερος οὐδίς· [16]καὶ ἐξεδόμην σοι τὴν χῖρά μου ταύτην πρὸς [17]ἀσφάλιαν. ἡ ὁμολογία κυρία καὶ

10. *l.* αἱροῦν.

but the aggressor or his representative shall further forfeit to Moschion or the assign of Moschion whom he sues a penalty of 500 drachmae of silver and to the State the like amount, and none the less (the agreement shall be valid). The witnesses of the acknowledging parties consent with them to all the above provisions: for Pasion, Dionysius . . . (Endorsed) Year 19, Choiak. Agreement of Pasion and his brothers with Moschion.

56. SETTLEMENT OF CLAIMS

A.D. 348.

In the consulship of Flavius Philippus the most illustrious praefect of the sacred praetorium [a] and Flavius Salias the most illustrious master of the horse, Phamenoth 10. Aurelia Valeria daughter of Alypius to Aurelia Nemesilla her sister born of the same mother, of the village of Philadelphia in the Arsinoite nome, greeting. Whereas we were allotted a stone for crushing corn and an instrument for grinding corn from our father's estate, and I singly have taken the stone and sold it for the portion falling to me, I accordingly acknowledge that I have no share in the aforesaid instrument for grinding corn but am estranged and alienated from it, and no one shall take proceedings against you concerning it, neither I, Valeria, nor my children nor heirs nor any other person; and I have issued to you this my bond for assurance. This acknowledgement is valid, and in answer to the formal

[a] Originally commander of the Emperor's bodyguard, but in Byzantine times a very high civil magistrate.

ἐπερω-[18]τηθεῖσα ὡ[μ]ολόγησα. Αὐρηλία Οὐαλερία [19]ἡ προκιμέ[ν]η ἐξεδόμην τὴν ἀσφάλιαν [20]τοῦ μὴ ἔχειν μέρος εἰς τὴν μηχανὴν καὶ [21]συνευδοκῶ τοῖς ἐνγεγραμμένοις ὡς πρόκιται. [22]Αὐρήλιος Σαραπίων Ἰουλιανοῦ ἀπὸ τῆς Ἀλεξαν-[23]δρείας κατοικῶν ἐν τῇ αὐτῇ κώμῃ ἔγραψα [24]ὑπὲρ αὐτῆς γράμματα μὴ εἰδυείης.

57. INDEMNIFICATION OF A SURETY

P. Oxy. 270. A.D. 94.

[1]Ἔτους τρισκαιδεκάτου Αὐτοκράτορος Καίσαρος Δομιτιανοῦ Σεβαστοῦ [2]Γερμανικοῦ Μεχεὶρ , ἐν Ὀξυρύγχων πόλει τῆς Θηβαΐδος. [3]ὁμολογεῖ Λουκία ἡ καὶ Θαϊσᾶς Λουκίου μητρὸς Σινθώνιος τῆς Θέωνος Περ-[4]σείνη μετὰ κυρίου τοῦ ἐξανεψίου Ἡρᾶτος τοῦ Ἡρακλείδου τοῦ Ἡρακλείδου [5]μητρὸς Πλουτάρχης Σαραπίωνος Σαραπίωνι τῷ καὶ Κλάρῳ {Σαραπίωνι [6]τῷ καὶ Κλάρῳ} Σαραπίωνος τοῦ Ἡρακλείδου μητρὸς Κλάρας τῆς [7]Ναρκίσσου, πάντες τῶν ἀπὸ Ὀξυρύγχων πόλεως, ἐν ἀγυιᾷ, ἀπαρε-[8]νόχλητον καὶ ἀνείσπρακτον παρέξασθαι τὸν Σαραπίωνα τὸν καὶ [9]Κλάρον καὶ τοὺς παρ' αὐτοῦ κατὰ πάντα τρόπον ὑπὲρ ἧς πεποίηται [10]ὁ αὐτὸς Σαραπίων ὁ καὶ Κλάρος ἐγγύης Ἡρακλείδῃ Ἀπολλωνίου [11]τοῦ Χαιρήμονος μητρὸς Ἡραΐδος Διδύμου ἀπὸ τῆς αὐτῆς πόλεως [12]καθ' ὁμολογίαν διὰ τοῦ αὐτοῦ μνημονείου τῷ ἐνεστῶτι μηνὶ Με-[13]χείρ, ὧν ἡ ὁμολογοῦσα δεδάνεισται παρ' αὐτοῦ κατὰ δανείου συν-[14]γραφὴν διὰ τοῦ αὐτοῦ μνη-

question I have given my assent. (Signed) I, Aurelia Valeria the aforesaid, have issued the assurance that I have no share in the instrument and I agree to the terms of the deed as above. I, Aurelius Sarapion son of Julianus, of Alexandria, dwelling in the said village, have written for her, as she is illiterate.

57. INDEMNIFICATION OF A SURETY

A.D. 94.

The 13th year of the Emperor Caesar Domitianus Augustus Germanicus, Mecheir[a] , at Oxyrhynchus in the Thebaid. Lucia also called Thaisas daughter of Lucius and of Sinthonis daughter of Theon, Persian, with her guardian her second cousin Heras son of Heraclides son of Heraclides, his mother being Plutarcha daughter of Sarapion, acknowledges to Sarapion also called Clarus son of Sarapion son of Heraclides, his mother being Clara daughter of Narcissus, all parties being of Oxyrhynchus, by deed executed in the street,[b] that she shall safeguard Sarapion also called Clarus and his assigns in every way against molestation and exaction on account of the security which the said Sarapion also called Clarus has given to Heraclides son of Apollonius son of Chaeremon, his mother being Herais daughter of Didymus, of the said city, according to an agreement made through the same record-office in the present month Mecheir, for the sum which the acknowledging party has borrowed from him according to a contract of loan made through the same record-

[a] The date is not filled in.

[b] See No. 7, note *b*.

μονείου τῷ αὐτῷ μηνὶ Μεχεὶρ ἀργυρίου [15]δραχμῶν τρισχιλίων πεντακοσίων κεφαλαίου τόκου δραχμιαίου [16]ἑκάστης μνᾶς κατὰ μῆνα ἀπὸ τοῦ αὐτοῦ μηνὸς ἐπὶ ὑποθήκῃ ταῖς [17]σημανθείσαις αὐτῆς περὶ Σερῦφιν ἐκ τοῦ Δημητρίου Μιλησίου κλή-[18]ρου κατοικικῆς καὶ ὠνημένης ἀρούραις τρισὶ ἡμίσει, καὶ ἐκ τοῦ αὐτοῦ [19]κλήρου ἀπὸ κατοικικῆς καὶ ὠνημένης ἀρουρῶν δέκα δύο μεθ' ἃς [20]ὑπέθετο Ταaφύγχει Θωνίωνος ἀρούρας ἑπτὰ ταῖς λοιπαῖς ἀρουραῖς [21]πέντε, καὶ ἐκ τοῦ Καλλίου τρίτῳ μέρει κατοικικῆς καὶ ὠνημένης [22]ἀρουρῶν ὀκτώ, ὅ ἐστιν ἄρουραι δύο δίμοιρον, καὶ περὶ Σύρων [23]Κώμην ἐκ τοῦ Ἡρακλείδου σὺν τῷ Ἀλεξάνδρου κατοικικῆς ἀρού-[24]ραις ἓξ ἡμίσει τετάρτῳ, καὶ ἐκ τοῦ Ἀλεξάνδρου καὶ ἄλλων κα-[25]τοικικῆς καὶ ὠνημένης ἀρούραις ἓξ ἡμίσει, ταῖς ἐπὶ τὸ αὐτὸ κατοι-[26]κικῆς καὶ ὠνημένης εἰς κατοικίαν ἀρούραις εἴκοσι τέσσαρσι τρί-[27]τῳ δωδεκάτῳ, εἰς προθεσμίαν τριακάδα Τῦβι τοῦ πεντεκαι-[28]δεκάτου ἔτους Αὐτοκράτορος Καίσαρος Δομιτιανοῦ Σεβαστοῦ [29]Γερμανικοῦ. ἐὰν δὲ τῆς προθεσμίας ἐνστάσης μὴ ἀποδῷ ἡ ὁ-[30]μολογοῦσα τῷ Ἡρακλείδῃ τὸ κεφά[λ]αιον καὶ τοὺς τόκους, ἀπαι-[31]τηθῇ δὲ ὑπὲρ αὐτῆ[ς ὁ Σαρ]απίων ὁ καὶ Κλάρος, κυριε[ύ]ειν αὐ-[32]τὸν Σαραπίων[α] τὸν [καὶ Κ]λάρον τῶν προκειμένω[ν] ἀρουρῶν [33]εἴκοσι τεσσάρω[ν τρίτου δ]ωδεκάτου εἰς τὸν ἅπαντα χ[ρ]όν[ον ὡ-[34]ς ἂν πράσεως [αὐτῷ γενο]μένης καὶ [ἀ]ποφέρεσθαι τὰ ἐξ αὐτῶν [35]καὶ ἑτέροις αὐ[τὰς πωλ]εῖν καὶ χρᾶσ[θαι ὡς] ἐὰν αἱρῆται, μηδε-[36]μιᾶς τῇ ὁμολογούσῃ ἢ ταῖς [παρ' αὐτῆς ἐ]φ[όδ]ου κ[α]ταλειπο-[37]μένης ἐπὶ τὸν Σαραπίωνα τὸν καὶ Κλάρον μηδὲ ἐ[πὶ] τοὺς πα-[38]ρ' αὐτοῦ

office in the same month Mecheir, namely 3500 drachmae capital, bearing interest at 1 drachma a month on each mina beginning from the said month, on mortgage of the following specified property of hers: in the area of Seruphis from the holding of Demetrius the Milesian $3\frac{1}{2}$ arurae of catoecic and purchased land, and from the same holding out of 12 arurae of catoecic and purchased land the 5 arurae remaining after the 7 which she mortgaged to Taaphunchis daughter of Thonion, and from the holding of Callias a third share of 8 arurae of catoecic and purchased land, making $2\frac{2}{3}$ arurae, and in the area of Syron Kome from the holding of Heraclides together with that of Alexander $6\frac{3}{4}$ arurae of catoecic land, and from the holding of Alexander and others $6\frac{1}{2}$ arurae of catoecic and purchased land, making a total of $24\frac{5}{12}$ arurae of catoecic land and land purchased for conversion into catoecic, the date for repayment being 30th Tubi of the 15th year of the Emperor Caesar Domitianus Augustus Germanicus. If on the advent of the appointed date the acknowledging party does not repay to Heraclides the capital and interest and Sarapion also called Clarus is called upon to pay for her, he, Sarapion also called Clarus, shall become owner of the aforesaid $24\frac{5}{12}$ arurae for all time as if he had purchased them and shall appropriate the produce of them and sell them to others and use them as he chooses, no claim being left to the acknowledging party or her assigns against Sarapion also called Clarus or against his

36. *l.* τοῖς.

μηδὲ ἐπὶ τὰς προκειμένας ἀρούρας μηδὲ ἐπὶ μέρος [39]μηδὲ ἐπὶ τὰ ἐξ αὐτῶν κατὰ μηδένα τρόπον, ἐπάν[α]νκον [40]δ' αὐτὴν παρέξασθαι αὐτῷ καὶ τοῖς παρ' αὐτοῦ ταύτας διὰ παν-[41]τὸς μὲν βεβαίας ἀπὸ πάντων πάσῃ βεβαιώσει καὶ καθαρὰς [42]ἀπὸ δημοσίων καὶ τελεσμάτων πάντων τῶν ἕως τῆς προθεσ-[43]μίας καὶ αὐτῆς τῆς προθεσμίας. ἐὰν δέ τι τούτων ἡ ὁμολογοῦσα [44]παρασυνγραφῇ, ἄκυρον [ἔ]στω καὶ προσαποτισάτω τῷ [Σ]αραπίω-[45]νι τῷ καὶ Κλάρῳ ἢ τοῖς παρ' αὐτοῦ καθ' ὃ ἐὰν παρα-[σ]υνγραφῇ εἶδος [46]τό τε βλάβος καὶ ἐπίτιμον ἀργυρίου δραχμὰς χιλίας καὶ εἰς τὸ δημό-[47]σιον τὰς ἴσας, καὶ μηδὲν ἧσσον τὰ διωμολογημένα κύρια ἔστω, [48]τῆς πράξεως γινομένης τῷ Σαραπίωνι τῷ καὶ Κλάρῳ ἔκ τε τῆς [49]ὁμολογούσης καὶ ἐκ τῶν προκιμένων ἀρουρῶν καὶ ἐκ τῶν ἄλλων ὑπαρχ(όν)-[50]των αὐτῇ πάντων. κυρία ἡ ὁμολογία.

58. AGREEMENT OF INDEMNITY

P. Tebt. 392. A.D. 134–135.

[1][Ἔτους ἐνν]εακαιδεκάτου Αὐτοκράτορος [2][Καίσαρος Τ]ραϊανοῦ Ἁδριανοῦ Σεβαστοῦ [3][. . . . . . ἐν Τ]εβτύνι τῆς Πολέμωνος μερίδος [4][τοῦ Ἀρσινοΐ]του νομ[ο]ῦ. ὁμ[ο]λογεῖ Κρονίων [5][Κρονίωνος] τοῦ Ἥρ[ω]νος ὡς [ἐ]τῶν εἴκοσι [6][. . . . . . οὐλ]ὴ ἀντικνημίωι δεξιῶι [7][τῇ ἑαυτοῦ] ὁμοπ[α]τρείωι καὶ ὁμομητ[ρεί]ῳ [8][ἀδελφῇ Εὐδ]αιμο[νίδι] τῇ καὶ Πολίττῃ ὡ[ς [9]ἐτῶν τεσσαρ]άκοντα ἓξ οὐλὴ γόνατι δεξι[ῶ]ι, [10][μετὰ κυρίο]υ τοῦ ἑαυτῆς υἱοῦ Εὐ[τ]ύχου [11][. . . . .] ὡς ἐτῶν εἴκοσι οὐλὴι χειρὶ

assigns or upon the aforesaid arurae or part of them or upon the produce of them in any way, and she shall be bound to deliver them to him and his assigns guaranteed for ever against every risk by every kind of guarantee and free from all public dues and charges up to, and inclusive of, the appointed date. If the acknowledging party violates any of these provisions, her action shall be invalid and she shall further forfeit to Sarapion or his assigns on any instance of violation both the damages and a penalty of 1000 silver drachmae and to the Treasury the like sum, and the terms of the agreement shall be none the less valid, Sarapion also called Clarus having the right of execution upon the acknowledging party and upon the aforesaid arurae and all her other property. This agreement is valid.

58. AGREEMENT OF INDEMNITY

A.D. 134–135.

The 19th year of the Emperor Caesar Trajanus Hadrianus Augustus . . . at Tebtunis in the division of Polemon in the Arsinoite nome. Cronion, son of Cronion son of Heron, aged about 2[.] years, with a scar on the right shin, acknowledges to his sister Eudaemonis also called Politta, daughter of the same father and mother, aged about 46 years, with a scar on the right knee, having with her as guardian her son Eutychus . . . aged about 20 years, with

[12][ἀριστερᾷ, ἐ]πάνανκον τὸν Κρ[ο]νίωνα [13][παρέξεσθαι] τὴν ἀδελφὴν Εὐδαιμωνίδ(α) [14][τὴν καὶ Πόλι]τταν ἀπαρανόχλητον καὶ [15][ἀνείσπρ]ακτον κ[αὶ] ἀπερίσπαστον [16][κα]τὰ πά[ντα] τρόπ[ον ὑπὲρ] ὧν [γ]ράφεται [17][ὁ ἀ]νὴρ αὐτῆς ὧν δὲ κ[αὶ ἀδ]ελφὸς Ὡρίων, [18][ὃς] τετελεύτηκεν, Τα[ω]τίωι Ἡρακ[λ]είδ[ου [19]καθ' ὁ]μολογείαν παρα[θή]κης ἐπὶ τοῦ [20][τρί]του ἔτους Ἁδριαν[οῦ Κα]ίσαρος τοῦ κυρίου [21]Μ[ε]σορὴ νουμηνίᾳ διὰ τοῦ ἐνταῦθα γ[ρα]φείου [22]χρυσίου [δ]οκιμίου τεταρτῶν πέντε καὶ ἀ[ργυρίο]υ [23][ἐ]πισήμου καὶ ἕτερα ἐφ' οἷς ἡ ὁμολογεί[α] [24]περιέχει, διὰ τὸ τὸν Κρονίωνα ἐσχη-[25]κέναι ταύτας εἰς τὸ ἴδιον, τὸν δὲ Ὡρίωνα [26]μηδὲν ἁπλῶς λαβόντα κα[τ]ὰ παρά-[27]κλησιν γεγράπται αὐτῶν. (2nd hand) Κρονίων Κρονί-[28]ωνος ὁμολογῶ παρέξεσθαι τὴν ἀδελ-[29]φήν μου Εὐδεμονίδαν τὴ⟨ν⟩ καὶ Πόλιττα⟨ν⟩ [30]ἀπαρανώχλητον καὶ ἀλίσπαρτον καὶ ἀ-[31]περίσπαστον κατὰ π[ά]ντα τρόπον ὑπὲρ [32]ὧν γράφετε ὁ ἀδελφὸς ἡμῶν Ὡρίων Τα-[33]ωτίῳ Ἡρακλείδου κατὰ παραθήκην ἐφ' ο[ἷς] [34]περιέχι{ν} διὰ τὸ ἐμὲ ἐσχηκέναι εἰ[ς] τὸ εἴ-[35]διον, τὸν δὲ Ὡρίωνα μηδὲν ἁπλῶς λαβ-[36]όντα κατὰ παράκλησι⟨ν⟩ γεγράπετε αὐ-[37]τῶν καθὼς πρόκιται. ἔγραψεν ὑπὲ[ρ αὐ]τοῦ [38]Ἀγαθῆς Ἀρείου μὴ εἰδότος γράμμα[τα (3rd hand) [39]ἐν]τ[έτακται δι]ὰ τοῦ ἐν Τεβτύνι γραφ[είο]υ.

13. *l.* Εὐδαιμονίδα; so in 29. 14. *l.* ἀπαρενόχλητον; so in 30. 23. *l.* ἑτέρων. 27. *l.* γεγράφθαι. 30. *l.* ἀνείσπρακτον. 32. *l.* γράφεται. 36. *l.* γεγράφθαι.

a scar on the left hand, that he is bound to guarantee his sister Eudaemonis also called Politta against molestation or exaction or annoyance of any kind on account of the liabilities of her deceased husband Horion, who was also her brother, to Taotion daughter of Heraclides in virtue of a contract of deposit made in the 3rd year of Hadrianus Caesar the lord, Mesore 1, through the record-office here, namely 5 quarters of standard gold with silver coin and other items, on the terms stated in the contract, because Cronion has received these sums for his own use, whereas Horion has had nothing at all and was only entered in the deed on their instance. (Signed) I, Cronion son of Cronion, agree to guarantee my sister Eudaemonis also called Politta against molestation, exaction or annoyance of any kind on account of the liabilities of our brother Horion to Taotion daughter of Heraclides in virtue of a contract of deposit on the terms therein stated, because I have received the sums for my own use and Horion has had nothing at all, having been entered in the deed on our instance as aforesaid. Agathes son of Arius wrote for him, as he is illiterate. (Subscribed) Registered by the record-office at Tebtunis.

59. ACKNOWLEDGEMENT OF RESPONSIBILITY TO A CO-GUARDIAN

P. Hamb. i. 70. Middle of 2nd cent. A.D.

[1][Τίτος Φ]λαούιος Καπίτων Τίτῳ [2][Φλαουίῳ Σ]αραπίωνι συνεπιτρόπῳ [3][. . . . . Λ]ονγίνου Οὐάλεντος ἀφή-[4]λ[ικος <κληρονόμου> γεγο]νότος κατὰ διαθήκην [5]Φ[λαουίας] Πτολέμας μετηλλαχυείης [6][τῷ . . . . μηνὶ] τοῦ ὀγδόου ἔτους Ἀντωνίνου [7][Καίσαρος τ]οῦ κυρίου, μάμμης οὔσης τοῦ προγε-[8][γ]ρα[μ]μέ[νο]υ ἀφήλικος, χαίρειν. [9]ἐπεὶ δια[κ]ατέλειψέ μοι ἡ Φλαουία Πτο-[10]λέμα κ[α]τὰ <τ>ὴν ἐπὶ σαὶ διαθήκην [11]κλήρου κ[α]τοικικοῦ ἀρούρας τρεῖς, ἃς [12]καὶ μετὰ τελευτὰν αὐτῆς καρπίζο-[13]μαι καὶ τὰ περιγινόμενα ἐξ αὐτῶν [14]εἰς τὸ εἴδιον ἀποφέρω, τελοῦντός [15]μου τὰ περὶ αὐτῶν πάντα δημόσια [16]εἰς ὄνομα τῆς Φλαουίας Πτολέμας, [17]ὁμολογῶ, ἐάν τις ζήτησις γένηται [18]περὶ τῶν περιγεινομένων αὐτῶν [19]ἢ ἑτέρου τινὸς αὐτῶν ὅταν τὸν λόγον [20]δίδομεν τῷ ἀφήλικι, ἐγὼ αὐτὸς τὰ [21]περὶ τούτων ἐγβιβάσω ἰδίαις δαπά-[22]ναις καὶ τὸ περὶ τούτου κριθησόμενον [23]ἐάνπερ κρίσις γένηται ἀπαρτειῶ. [24]τὸ δὲ χει[ρ]όγραφον τοῦτώ εἰστιν [25]ἐμὸν ἰδι[ό]γραφον γεγραμμένον [26]δισσὸν χωρὶς ἀλύφαδος καὶ ἐπιγραφῆς, [27]ὃ καὶ κύριον [ἔ]στω πανταχοῦ καὶ παντὶ [28]τῷ ἐπιφέροντι ὡς ἐν δημοσίῳ κα-[29]τακεχωρισμένον. ἐὰν δέ τις ἀνάνκη [30]γέ[ν]ηται, προσφωνήσω τὸ ἴσον {δι} ὥστε γενέσ-[31]θαι διὰ δημοσίου χρηματισμοῦ ἀνυπερ-[32]θέτως.

10. *l.* ἐπὶ σέ. 24. *l.* τοῦτό ἐστιν. 26. *l.* ἀλείφατος.

59. ACKNOWLEDGEMENT OF RESPONSIBILITY TO A CO-GUARDIAN

Middle of 2nd cent. A.D.

Titus Flavius Capito to Titus Flavius Sarapion, co-guardian of . . . Longinus Valens, minor, made heir by will of Flavia Ptolema, who died in the month . . . of the 8th year of Antoninus Caesar the lord and was the grandmother of the aforesaid minor, greeting. Whereas Flavia Ptolema by the will under your trust bequeathed to me three arurae of a catoecic holding, of which after her death I am enjoying the use and appropriating the income, while paying all the public dues on them in the name of Flavia Ptolema, I acknowledge that, if any inquiry is made about the income or about any other point when we render our account to the minor, I will myself see the proceedings through at my own expense and if a trial is held will carry out the judgement concerning this matter. This bond is in my own hand, written in duplicate, without erasure or insertion, and it shall be valid wherever produced and whosoever produces it, as if registered in a public record-office. And if any necessity arises, I will make a declaration to the same effect to be embodied in an official deed without delay.

Verso: [1][χειρόγραφον ὃ ἔ]γραψα Σαραπίωνι περὶ τῶν ἐγ Πτολέμας τόπων [2][ἀρ(ουρῶν) γ ἤ]τοι τοῦ ληγάτου.

60. APPOINTMENT OF A REPRESENTATIVE

P. Oxy. 261. A.D. 55.

[1]Ἔτους δευτέρου Νέρωνος Κλαυδίου [Κ]αίσα[ρ]ος [2]Σεβαστοῦ Γερμανικοῦ Αὐτοκράτορος μ[η]νὸς Νέου [3][Σ]εβαστοῦ ἐν Ὀξυρύγχων πόλ[ει] τῆς Θηβαΐδος. [4][ὁμολο]γεῖ Δημητρία Χαιρήμονος ἀστήι, μετὰ κυρίου [5][τοῦ τῆς] ὑ[ι]δῆς αὐτῆς Δημητρίας ἀστῆς ἀνδρὸς Θέω-[6]νο[ς τ]οῦ Ἀντιόχου Αὐξιμητορείου τοῦ καὶ Ληνείου, [7]τῷ ἑαυτῆς [μ]ὲν υἱωνῷ, τῆς δὲ ὑιδῆς Δημητρίας [8]ἀδελφῷ, Χαιρήμονι Χαιρήμονος Μαρωνεῖ ἐν ἀ-[9]γυιᾷ, περὶ ὧν προφέρεται ἡ ὁμολογοῦσα Δημητρία [10]ἔχειν πρὸς Ἐπίμαχον Πολυδεύκους ἢ καὶ αὐτὸς [11]ὁ Ἐπίμαχος προφέρεται ἔχειν πρὸς αὐτήν, οὐ δυ-[12]ναμένη προσκαρτερῆσαι τῷ κριτηρίῳ διὰ γυναι-[13]κείαν ἀσθένειαν, συνεστακέναι αὐτὴν τὸν προ-[14]γεγραμμένον υἱωνὸν Χα[ιρ]ήμονα ἔγδικον [15]ἐπί τε πάσης ἐξουσίας καὶ παντὸς κριτηρίου κα-[16]θὰ καὶ αὐτῇ τῇ συνεστακυίᾳ Δημητρίᾳ παρούσῃ [17]ἐξῆν· εὐδοκεῖ γὰρ τῇδε τῇ συστάσει. κυρία [18]ἡ συγγραφή.

4. *l.* ἀστή.

(Endorsed) Bond which I wrote[a] for Sarapion about the 3 arurae from the estate of Ptolema forming the bequest.

[a] The present text is merely a draft, undated and corrected and written on a sheet already used.

60. APPOINTMENT OF A REPRESENTATIVE

A.D. 55.

The 2nd year of Nero Claudius Caesar Augustus Germanicus Imperator, on the of the month Neus Sebastus,[a] at Oxyrhynchus in the Thebaid. Demetria daughter of Chaeremon, of civic rank,[b] with her guardian the husband of her grand-daughter Demetria, of civic rank, namely Theon son of Antiochus, of the Auximetorean tribe and the Lenean deme, acknowledges to her grandson, the brother of her grand-daughter Demetria, Chaeremon son of Chaeremon, of the Maronean deme, in the street,[c] that touching the claims which the acknowledging party Demetria advances against Epimachus son of Polydeuces or which Epimachus himself advances against her, being unable to attend the court by reason of womanly weakness she has appointed her aforesaid grandson Chaeremon to represent her before every authority and every court, with the same powers as Demetria who has appointed him would herself have had if present; for she consents to this appointment. The contract is valid.

[a] =Hathur; the date is not filled in.

[b] The whole family possessed the Alexandrian citizenship. *Cf.* No. 32, note *b*.

[c] See No. 7, note *b*.

61. COMPROMISSUM

P. Lond. 992. A.D. 507.

1[+ Ὑπατ]εί[ας] τοῦ δεσ[πό]του ἡμῶν Φλα(ουίου) [Ἀν]αστασίου τοῦ αἰωνί[ου] Αὐγούστου Αὐτοκράτορος 2τὸ γ̄ Ἐπεὶφ [.] πρώτης ἰνδικ(τίονος). 3[ἑκόντες] ποιοῦντ[αι] πρὸς ἑαυτοὺς τὴν ὁμολογίαν τοῦ κομπρομίσσου 4[ἐκ μὲν τοῦ] ἑνὸς μ[έ]ρους Φλ(αούιοι) Σιλβανὸς καὶ Σαραπίων στρατιῶται ἀριθμοῦ 5Ἑρμοῦ πόλεως καὶ Αὐρήλιος Ἴσακος ὁμογνήσιοι ἀδελφοὶ ἐκ πατρὸς 6Φοιβ[άμ]μωνος ἀπὸ τῆς αὐτῆς πόλεως, Ἴσακος τὸν λόγον ποιούμενος ὑπέρ τε ἑαυτοῦ 7καὶ ὑπὲρ [τῶν κληρο]νόμων Τυράννου τοῦ ἀπογενομένου ἡμῶν ἀδελφοῦ, 8ἐκ δὲ [τοῦ] ἑτέρου μέρους Φλ(αούιος) Βῆς Νικῶν στρατιώτης τοῦ αὐτοῦ ἀριθμοῦ καὶ 9ἡ τούτου γαμετὴ Ἀρχοντία ἀδελφὴ τῶν προγεγραμμένων ἐκ τῶν αὐτῶν 10γονέων ἀπὸ τῆς αὐτῆς πόλεως ἀλλήλοις χαίρ(ειν). ἐπειδὴ ἠμφισβητήσαμεν 11πρὸς ἑαυτοὺς περὶ φανερῶν κεφαλαίων καὶ πρὸ δίκης καὶ φιλονικείας 12ἔδοξεν ἡμῖν κοινῇ γνώμῃ ἀπαντῆσαι εἰς δίαιταν πρὸς Καρδημέου καὶ 13Ζηνόδωτος τοὺς ἐλλογιμωτάτους σχολαστικοὺς φόρου Θηβαΐδος καὶ στοιχεῖ[ν] 14καὶ πείθεσθαι τοῖς ὁρισθησομένοις παρὰ τῆς αὐτῶν παιδεύσεως, κατὰ τοῦτο ὁμολογ[οῦμεν] 15ὀμνύν[τ]ες τόν τε παντοκράτορα Θεὸν καὶ τὴν θείαν καὶ οὐρανίαν τύχην τοῦ τὰ πάντα 16νικῶντος δεσπότου ἡμῶν Φλα(ουίου) Ἀναστασίου τοῦ αἰωνίου Αὐγούστου Αὐτοκράτορος 17ἀπαντᾶν ἡμᾶς πρὸς τοὺς προειρημένους διαιτητὰς καὶ διαιτᾶσθαι ἐπ' αὐτοὺς 18ἕως ὀγδόη[ς τοῦ παρόντ]ος μηνὸς Ἐπεὶφ τῆς παρ[ο]ύσης πρώτης ἰνδικτίονος 19[καὶ πείθεσθαι

61. COMPROMISSUM[a]

A.D. 507.

In the 3rd consulship of our master Flavius Anastasius the eternal Augustus and Imperator, Epeiph . . ., 1st indiction. The following parties make a voluntary agreement with each other to accept arbitration: on the one side the Flavii Silvanus and Sarapion, soldiers of the *numerus*[b] of Hermopolis, and Aurelius Isaac, full brothers, their father being Phoebammon, of the said city, Isaac speaking for himself and for the heirs of Tyrannus our deceased brother, and on the other side Flavius Bes Nikon, soldier of the said *numerus*, and his wife Archontia, sister of those aforesaid by the same parents, of the said city; with mutual greetings. Seeing that we had a dispute with each other about certain capital sums and in preference to litigation and strife resolved unanimously to meet for arbitration before Cardemeas and Zenodotus, those most distinguished advocates of the forum of the Thebaid, and assent and submit to the rulings given by their erudition, we accordingly agree, swearing by Almighty God and the divine and heavenly fortune of our all-conquering master Flavius Anastasius the eternal Augustus and Imperator, that we will appear before the aforesaid arbitrators and let them arbitrate between us not later than the 8th of the present month Epeiph of the present 1st indiction

[a] A mutual agreement to submit to arbitration.
[b] A military force.

12-13. *l.* Καρδημέαν καὶ Ζηνόδοτον.

ἡμᾶς τοῖς] ὁρισθησ[ο]μένοις παρ' αὐτῶν, τὸν δὲ μὴ ἀπαντῶντα [20][πρὸς αὐτοὺς ἢ καὶ μὴ πειθ]όμενον τοῖς ὁρισθησομένοις παρ' αὐτῶν παρέξει[ν [21]. . . . . τ]ῷ ἐμμένοντι λόγῳ προστίμου χρυσοῦ νομισμάτια [22][. . . . .]ος οὗτος κύριος καὶ βέβαιος καὶ ἐπερ(ωτηθέντες) ὡμολ(ογήσαμεν). (2nd hand) [23][. . . . . ὁ πρ]οκ(είμενος) στηχῖ μοι ὡς πρόκ(ειται). (3rd hand) Αὐρ(ηλία) Ἀρχοντία Φοιβάμμωνος [24][πεποίημαι τοῦτο τὸ κομπρό]μισσον ὡς πρόκ(ειται). Ἀστέριος Κολλούθου ἀπὸ Ἀντι(νόου πόλεως) ἔγραψα ὑπὲρ αὐτῆς [25][γράμματα μὴ εἰδυίας]. (1st hand) [26][δι' ἐμο]ῦ Ὥρου ἐγράφη ο . . . . . .

23. l. στοιχεῖ.

62. LOAN ON MORTGAGE (ὑποθήκη)

P. Oxy. 507. A.D. 169.

[1]Ἁρμιῦσ[ις - - -] [2]ἀπὸ τοῦ α[- - -] [3]Διογένει Σαραπ[ίωνος . . . .] [4]ἠγορανομηκό[τι ἐνάρχῳ γυμνα-][5]σιάρχῳ τῆς Ὀξυ[ρύγχων πόλεως νε-][6]ωκόρῳ Τύχη[ς χαίρειν. ὁ-][7]μολογῶ παρειλ[ηφέναι παρὰ σοῦ ἀρ-][8]γυρίου δραχμ[ὰς διακοσίας ἑξήκοντα] [9]κεφαλαίου, αἷς [οὐδὲν προσῆκται, τόκου] [10]δραχμιαίου ἑκάστη[ς μνᾶς τοῦ μη-][11]νὸς ἑκάστου ἀπὸ τοῦ [ὄντος μηνὸς] [12]Φαρμοῦθι. ἀποδώσ[ω δὲ τὸ κεφά-][13]λαιον σὺν τοῖς τόκ[οις τῇ τριακάδι] [14]τοῦ Φαμεν[ὼθ τοῦ εἰσ]ιόντος [15]δεκάτου ἔτου[ς Αὐρηλί]ου Ἀντωνίνου [16]Καίσαρος τοῦ κυ[ρίου χωρὶ]ς ὑπερθέ-[17]σεως, εἰ δὲ μή, [ἐκτε]ίσω σοι

and submit to their rulings and that the party who fails to appear before them or fails to obey their rulings shall pay . . . to the party who conforms to them by way of penalty . . . gold solidi . . . This agreement is valid and guaranteed, and in answer to the formal question we have given our consent. (Signed) I, . . . the aforesaid, consent to . . . as stated above. I, Aurelia Archontia daughter of Phoebammon, have made this acceptance of arbitration as stated above. I, Asterius son of Colluthus, of Antinoopolis, have written for her, as she is illiterate. (Docket) . . . was written by me, Horus . . .

62. LOAN ON MORTGAGE (ὑποθήκη)

A.D. 169.

Harmiusis . . . to Diogenes son of Sarapion . . . , ex-agoranomus, gymnasiarch in office at Oxyryhnchus, priest of Fortune, greeting. I acknowledge that I have received from you the sum of 260 drachmae of silver, to which nothing has been added, at the interest of one drachma the mina for each month from the current month of Pharmouthi. And I will repay the principal with the interest on Phamenoth 30 of the coming 10th year of Aurelius Antoninus Caesar the lord without delay, otherwise I shall forfeit to you the amount increased by one

μεθ’ ἡ-[18]μιολίας σὺν τοῖς καὶ τῆς ὑπερχρονεί-[19]ας ἴσοις δρα[χ]μιαίοις τόκοις ἑκάσ-[20]της μνᾶς κατὰ μῆνα, τῆς πράξεως [21]σοι οὔσης ἔκ τε ἐμοῦ καὶ ἐκ τῶν ὑπαρ-[22]χόντων μοι π[ά]ντων. τὰς δὲ [23]προκειμένας δραχμὰς διακοσίας [24]ἑξήκοντα κατατέθειμαι εἰς συν-[25]ωνὴν χόρτου ἀποτ[ε]θησομένου [26]ἐν ᾧ ἔχω ἐν μισθώσει καμηλῶ-[27]νι Σιμίλεως ἐν τῇ Ὀξυρύγχω[ν] πό-[28]λει, ὅνπερ χόρτον οὐκ ἐξέσται μοι [29]βαστάξαι οὐδὲ πωλεῖν οὐδὲ ὑποτί-[30]θεσθαι ἄχρι οὗ ἀποδῶ σοι τὸ κεφά-[31]λαιον καὶ τοὺς τόκους διὰ τὸ ὑπένγυ-[32]όν σοι εἶναι. ἐὰν δέ τις κίνδυνος [33]συμβῇ τοῦ αὐτοῦ χόρτου, οὐδὲν [34]βλάβος ἐξακολουθήσι σοι διὰ τὸ [35]εἶναι τὸ ἀργύριον σὺν τοῖς τόκοις [36]ἀκίνδυνον παντὸς κινδύνου. κύρι-[37]ον τὸ χειρό[γ]ραφον δισσὸν γραφὲν [38]πανταχῇ ἐ[πιφ]ερόμενον. [39](ἔτους) θ Αὐτοκράτορος Καίσαρος [40]Μάρκου Αὐρη[λί]ου Ἀντωνίνου Σεβαστοῦ [41]Ἀρμενιακο[ῦ Μ]ηδικοῦ Παρθικοῦ Μεγίστου [42][Φαρμοῦθι .].

63. LOAN ON MORTGAGE (ὑπάλλαγμα)

P. Ryl. 177. A.D. 246.

[1]Χρῆσις (δραχμῶν) Ἀϡκ. [2][Αὐρήλ(ιοι) Μέλας . . . . μητρὸς] Τεεῦτος ὡς (ἐτῶν) ξ οὐλ(ὴ) δακτύλ(ῳ) μέσῳ ἀριστ(ερᾶς) χειρὸς καὶ Σίλβανος Χαῶτος μητρὸς Τανεχώτιδος [3][ὡς (ἐτῶν) . . οὐλ(ὴ) δακτύλ(ῳ) . . . . ἀρ]ιστ(ερᾶς) χειρὸς ἀμφ[ό]τεροι ἀπὸ κώμης Μαγδώλω[ν] Μιρῆ τοῦ Περὶ Πόλιν Κάτω Αὐρηλίῳ Σόιτι Χαῦτος [4][μητρὸς . . . . . . Ἑρμοπολίτ]ῃ χαίρειν. ὁμολογοῦμεν ἐσχη[κ]έ[ν]αι

half together with the same interest for the overtime at one drachma the month on each mina, and you shall have the right of execution upon myself and upon all my property. The aforesaid 260 drachmae I have invested in purchases of hay to be stored in the camel-yard of Similis at Oxyrhynchus which I have on lease, which hay it shall not be lawful for me to remove or sell or pledge until I repay to you the principal and interest, because it is mortgaged to you. And if any accident happens to the said hay, no damage shall accrue to you, because the money, including the interest, is guaranteed against all risks. This bond, which is written in duplicate, is valid wherever produced. The 9th year of the Emperor Caesar Marcus Aurelius Antoninus Augustus Armeniacus Medicus Parthicus Maximus, Pharmouthi . . .

63. LOAN ON MORTGAGE (ὑπάλλαγμα)

A.D. 246.

Loan of 1920 drachmae. Aurelius Melas son of . . . and of Teeus, aged about 60 years, with a scar on the middle finger of his left hand, and Aurelius Silvanus son of Chaos and Tanechotis, aged about . . years, with a scar on the . . . finger of his left hand, both of the village of Magdola Mire in the district of the Lower Suburb,[a] to Aurelius Sois son of Chaus and . . . , of Hermopolis, greeting. We acknowledge

[a] See No. 52, note *b*.

παρὰ σοῦ διὰ χειρὸς ἐξ οἴκου χρῆσιν ἔντοκον 5[. . . . .] . *ἀργυρίου δραχμὰς χειλίας ἐννακοσίας εἴκοσι, γ(ίνονται) ἀργ(υρίου) (δραχμαὶ)* ͵Α⳨κ, *ἃς καὶ ἀποδώσομέν σοι ἐξ ἀλ-*6[*ληλεγγύης* . . . . *τοῦ*] *ἐνεστῶτος* δ (*ἔτους*) Μάρκων Ἰουλίων Φιλ[ί]ππων Καισάρων *τῶν κυρίων* Σεβαστῶν *ἀνυπερθέ-*7[*τως, ὧν πρὸς ἀσφάλειαν καὶ*] *ἔκτεισιν ἐντεῦθεν ὑπαλλάσσομέ*[*ν*] *σοι κατὰ τ*[*ό*]*δε τὸ γράμμα τὸ ὑπάρχον ἡμῖν κοινῶς* 8[*ἐξ ἴσου ἐν τῇ αὐτῇ κώμῃ ἥ*]*μισυ μέρος οἰκίας καινῆς καὶ αὐλῆς κ*[*αὶ χρη*]*στηρίων καὶ ἀνηκόντων πάντων καὶ εἰσόδων* 9[*καὶ ἐξόδων τὸ πρότερον*] Πεκύσιος *τῆς αὐτῆς κώμης, γείτονες* [*τῶ*]*ν ὅλων νότ(ου) οἰκία* Τερῆτος Μεγχήους, *βορρᾶ* 10[. . . . . , *ἀπηλιώτου ῥύ*]*μη δι' ἧς εἴσοδος καὶ ἔξοδος, λιβὸς ἔπαυλ*[*ις* Φοι]*βάμμωνος* Τρύφωνος· *τὸ δὲ ὑπηλλαγμένον* 11[*ἥμισυ μέρος οἰκίας φυ*]*λάξομ(εν) ἀνεξαλλοτρίωτον καὶ ἀκαταχρημάτι*[*στ*]*ον ἄχρι οὗ ἀποδῶμεν ἢ πραχθῶμεν ὡς πρόκ(ειται),* 12[*γεινομένης σοι τῆς πράξεως ἔκ τε ἡμῶν*] *κ*[*αὶ ἐ*]*ξ* [*οὗ*] *ἐὰν* [*α*]*ἱρῇ ἡμῶν ἀλλη-*[*λεγγ*]*ύων ὄντων εἰς ἔκτεισιν καὶ ἐκ τῶν ὑπαρ-*13[*χόντων ἡμῖν πάντων καὶ ἐξ αὐτοῦ τοῦ ὑπαλλάγμ*]*ατος καθάπερ ἐκ δίκης, καὶ βεβαιώσομεν πάσῃ βεβαιώσει ἀπό τε δημοσίων* 14[*καὶ ἰδιωτικῶν καὶ πάντων ἁπλῶς, κυρίων μενόν*]*των ὧν σοι ὀφείλει ὁ ἕτερος* [*ἡμ*]*ῶν* Αὐρήλιος Μέλας· *περὶ δὲ τοῦ ὀρθῶς καλῶς* 15[*γεγενῆσθαι ἐπερωτηθέντες ὑπὸ σοῦ ὡμολογήσαμεν*]. (*ἔτους*) δ Αὐτοκράτορος Κ[αί]σαρος Μάρκου Ἰουλίου Φιλίππου Εὐσεβοῦς 16[*καὶ* Μάρκου Ἰουλίου Φιλίππου *τοῦ γενναιοτάτο*]*υ καὶ ἐπιφανεστάτου* Κ[αίσα]ρος Σεβαστῶν Θὼθ δ.

that we have received from you by hand out of your house a loan at interest . . . of one thousand nine hundred and twenty silver drachmae, total 1920 silver dr., which we will repay to you on our mutual responsibility on . . . of the current 4th year of the Marci Julii Philippi Caesars and lords Augusti with no delay. For the security and repayment of this sum we herewith mortgage to you in accordance with this deed the half share which we own jointly and equally of a new house and courtyard in the said village and of all its furniture and appurtenances and entrances and exits, formerly the property of Pekusis of the said village, the boundaries of its whole area being on the south the house of Teres son of Menches, on the north . . ., on the east a street by which is the entrance and exit, on the west the homestead of Phoebammon son of Tryphon. The mortgaged half share of the house we will keep unalienated and uninvolved until we make repayment or distraint is made on us, as aforesaid, you having the right of execution upon us or upon whichever of us you choose, since we are mutually responsible for repayment, and upon all our property and upon the mortgage itself, as if by legal decision; and we will guarantee it with every guarantee against both public and private claims and all claims whatsoever, the debts which one of us, Aurelius Melas, owes to you remaining valid; and in answer to your question whether this has been rightly and fairly done we have given our consent. The 4th year of the Emperor and Caesar Marcus Julius Philippus Pius and of Marcus Julius Philippus the most noble and eminent Caesar,

Αὐρήλ(ιος) Κοπρέας ὁ καὶ Εὐδέμων 17[ἔγραψα ὑπὲρ αὐτῶν μὴ εἰδότων γράμματα].

16. *l.* Εὐδαίμων.

64. LOAN ON SECURITY OF LAND

P. Oxy. 1892. A.D. 581.

1+ Β[α]σιλείας τοῦ θειοτάτου κ[α]ὶ ε[ὐσεβ(εστάτου) ἡμῶν] 2δεσπ(ότου) μ[εγί]στου εὐεργέτου Φλ[(αουίου) Τιβερίου Νέου] 3Κωνσ[τα]ντίνου τοῦ αἰωνίου Α[ὐγούστου] 4καὶ [Αὐ]τοκρ(άτορος) ἔτο[υ]ς ζ, ὑ[π]ατίας το[ῦ αὐτοῦ] 5εὐσ[ε]β(εστάτου) ἡμῶν δεσπ(ότου) ἔτο[υ]ς γ, Θὼ[θ . ἰνδικ(τίονος) ιε]. 6τῷ [α]ἰδεσίμῳ Ἐπιμάχῳ ἐπικειμ[ένῳ τοῦ] 7θείου οἴκου υἱῷ τοῦ τῆς μακαρία[ς μνήμης] 8Ἰούστου ἀπὸ τα[ύ]της τῆς λαμπρᾶς Ὀξυ[ρυγχ(ιτῶν) πόλεως], 9Ἁρεώτης πρεσβύτερος τῆς ἁγίας ἐκ[κλησίας] 10υἱὸς Φὶβ μητρὸς Ἐρεβέκκας ὁρμώ[μενος] 11ἀπὸ κτήματος Ἀπὲλ τοῦ Ὀξυρυγχίτο[υ νομοῦ] 12χαίρειν. ὁμολογῶ ἐσχηκέναι παρὰ τ[ῆς σῆς] 13αἰδεσιμότητος ἐν χρήσε[ι δι]ὰ χειρὸ[ς ἐξ οἴκου] 14εἰς ἀναγκαίας μου χρείας χρυσοῦ νομισμάτ[ια] 15τρία ἰδιωτικῷ ξυγῷ νομιτευόμεν[α], 16γί(νεται) χρ(υσ.) νο(μ.) γ ἰδ(ι.) ζ[υγ(ῷ)], καὶ ταῦτα ὁμολ[ογῶ] 17παρασχεῖν τῇ σῇ αἰδεσιμότητι ἐν [τρισὶ] 18καταβολαῖς οὕτως, τῷ μὲν Ἁ[θὺ]ρ μη[νὶ] 19τοῦ ἐνεστῶτος (ἔτους) σνη σκζ τῆ[ς παρούσης] 20πεντεκαιδεκάτης ἰνδ(ικτίονος) χρυσοῦ νομισμάτιον 21ἕν, τῷ δὲ Ἁθὺρ μηνὶ τῆς εἰσιο[ύση]ς πρώτης 22ἐπινεμήσεως ἕτερον χρυσ[οῦ νο]μισμάτιον ἕν, 23καὶ ἐν τ[ῷ] Ἁθὺρ μηνὶ τῆ[ς μελλού]σης δευτέρας 24ἐπινεμήσεως τὸ ὑπό[λοιπον

Augusti, Thoth 4. (Signed) I, Aurelius Copreas also called Eudaemon, have written for them, as they are illiterate.

64. LOAN ON SECURITY OF LAND

A.D. 581.

In the 7th year of the reign of our most godlike and pious master and greatest benefactor Flavius Tiberius Novus Constantinus the eternal Augustus and Imperator, the 3rd year of the consulship of our said most pious master, Thoth [.], 15th indiction. To the worshipful Epimachus, overseer of the Imperial estate, son of Justus of blessed memory, of this illustrious city of Oxyrhynchus, from Hareotes, presbyter of the holy church, son of Phib and Rebecca, native of the estate of Apel in the Oxyrhynchite nome, greeting. I acknowledge that I have received from your worship on loan from hand to hand out of your house for my pressing needs three gold solidi current coin on the private standard,[a] total 3 gold solidi private standard, and these I agree to deliver to your reverence in three instalments as follows: in the month Hathur of the current 258th = 227th year[b] in the present fifteenth indiction one gold solidus, in the month Hathur of the coming first indiction another gold solidus, and in the month Hathur of the succeeding second indiction the remain-

[a] Solidi were reckoned by different standards of weight, so that 3 solidi according to one standard might be equal to 3 and a fraction according to another standard.

[b] See No. 24, p. 71, note *a*.

ἓν νο]μισμά[τιον], [25]ἀνυπολόγως, εἰ δ[ὲ ἀγνώμονα? ποιή]σω περ[ὶ τὴν] [26]ἀπόδοσιν τῆς πρώ[της ἢ δευτέρας] ἢ τρίτη‹ς› κατ[α]βολ[ῆ‹ς›], [27]ἐπὶ τῷ τὴν σὴ[ν α]ἰδ[εσιμότητα κ]ατασχεῖν [28]καὶ νέμεσθαι τὸ διαφέρο[ν] μοι ἰ[δ]ιόκτητ[ον] [29]γονικόν μο[υ] ἡμιαρούριον τυγχάν[ον] [30]ἐν μηχ[α]νῇ καλουμένῃ κυλλῆς διω . . . σι [31]ἐν τῷ αὐτῷ μου κτήματι ἐκ βορρᾶ τοῦ λά[κκου] [32]μετὰ τῆς ἀν[τ]ιλογίας τοῦ αὐτοῦ λάκκου [33]κ[αὶ] παντὸς δικαίου κα[ὶ] ἐξ αὐ[τ]οῦ τὸ ἱκανὸν [34][το]ῦ αὐτοῦ χρέους περιπ[οιῆ]σαι κινδ[ύν]ῳ [35]τῶν ἐμοὶ ὑπαρχόντ[ων ὑπ]οκειμέ[ν]ων [36]εἰ[ς το]ῦτο. κύριον τὸ γραμμά[τιον ἁπ]λοῦν γραφὲν [37]καὶ ἐπερωτηθεὶς ὡμολό[γ]ησα. (2nd hand) [38][Ἁ]ρεώτης πρεσβ[ύ]τερος [υἱ]ὸς [39]Φὶβ ὁ προγεγραμμένος πεποίημ[α]ι [40]τοῦτο τὸ γραμ[μ]άτιον τῶν τριῶ[ν] [41][νομ]ισμάτων κατὰ τὴν ἀνωτέρ[αν [42]ὁμολ]όγησιν, καὶ [συ]μφ(ωνεῖ) μοι πάντα [τὰ ἐγγε-[43]γρ(αμμένα) ὡ]ς πρόκ(ειται). Δ . . . . . [. . . . . [44]ἔγ]ραψα ὑπὲρ αὐτοῦ [ἀγ]ρ[αμμάτου ὄντος]. [45]⳩ di emu [

Verso: [46]+ γρ(αμμάτιον) Ἀρεώτου πρεσβυτέρου υἱοῦ [Φὶβ] ἀπὸ κτήμ(ατος) Ἀπὲλ χρ(υσοῦ) νο(μισματίων) γ ἰδ(ιωτικῷ) ζυγ(ῷ).

65. LOAN WITH PARTIAL ANTICHRESIS

B.G.U. 1273, ll. 1-40. 221–220 B.C.

Inner text of a contract in duplicate, restored from outer text and from another copy.

[1]Βασιλε[ύο]ντος Πτολεμαίου [το]ῦ Πτολ[ε]μαίου καὶ Βερενίκης [2]θεῶ[ν Ε]ὐερ[γε]τῶν ἔ[τους π]ρ[ώτ]ου,

ing solidus, without deduction, under the stipulation that, if I make default in the payment of the first or second or third instalment, your worship may occupy and use the half arura belonging to me by right of descent and situated in the field called that of the crooked . . . in my said estate to the north of the cistern, with my claim to a share in the said cistern and all rights, and thereby amass the equivalent of the said debt, on the security of my property, which is pledged to this end. This deed, written in one copy only, is valid, and in answer to the formal question I have given my consent. (Signed) I, Hareotes, presbyter, son of Phib, the above-mentioned, have made this deed concerning the three solidi as acknowledged above, and I agree to all that is therein written as aforesaid. I, . . ., have written for him, as he is illiterate. (Subscribed) Executed by me, . . . (Endorsed) Deed of Hareotes, presbyter, son of Phib, of the estate of Apel, concerning 3 gold solidi on the private standard.

65. LOAN WITH PARTIAL ANTICHRESIS

221–220 B.C.

In the 1st year of the reign of Ptolemy [a] son of Ptolemy and Berenice, gods Euergetae, the priest

[a] Ptolemy Philopator, whose father and mother were deified with the title of Euergetae.

---

1. βασιλε[υό]ντων Edd. (an oversight).

ἐφ' [ἱ]ε[ρέως Ν]ικάνορος τοῦ Βακχίου 3Ἀλεξάν[δ]ρου καὶ θεῶν [Ἀδελ]φῶν [καὶ θεῶν Εὐεργετῶν, κανηφό]ρου Ἀρσινόης 4Φιλα[δέλφ]ου Ἀριστομ[άχης τῆς Πτολεμαίου, μηνὸς Γορ]πιείου ὀκτωκαι-5δεκάτηι, ἐγ κώμηι Τ[ακόναι τοῦ Ὀξυρυγχίτου ν]ομοῦ. ἐδάνει[σ]εν 6Δημητρία Ἀπολλο[δότου Κυρηναία μετὰ κυρίου Ἀπολλ]οφάνους 7τοῦ Ἀπολλοδότο[υ Κυρηναίου τῆς ἐ]π[ι]γον[ῆς Ἀπολλω]νίωι Πάτρωνος Κυρηναίωι τῆς ἐπιγον[ῆς χαλκο]ῦ 8νομίσματος ὀφθα[λμο]φανοῦς δρα[χ]μὰς [τετ]ρακοσίας τόκου ὡς ἐγ 9δύο δραχμῶν τὴν μνᾶν τὸν μῆνα ἕκαστον, [ἀ]ντὶ δὲ τοῦ τόκου [το]ῦ 10δανείου τούτου ἐ[μ]ίσθωσεν Ἀπολλώνιος Δημη[τ]ρίαι τὸν αὐτοῦ πατρικὸν 11πύργον τὸν ὄντα ἐγ κώμηι Τακόναι τοῦ Ὀξυρυγχίτου [νομ]οῦ αὐτὸν καὶ τὰς θύ[ρας] εἰς ἐνιαυτὸν α ἀπὸ 12μηνὸς Ὑπερβερεταίου τοῦ ἐν τῶι πρ[ώτωι ἔτει, ἐφ' ὧι] ἐνοικήσει Δημητ[ρ]ί[α κ]αὶ 13οἱ παρ' αὐτῆς ἐν τῶι πύργωι τούτωι [τὸν συγγεγραμμέ]νον χρόνον [χ]ρώ[με]ν[ο]ι 14τρόπωι ὧι ἂν βούλωνται καὶ διοδ[ευόμενοι διὰ τῆς προ]υπαρχού[σης] ἐκ τοῦ 15πύργου εἰς τὴν ῥύμην διόδου· γε[ίτον]ες [τοῦ πύργου ἀ]πὸ νότου Σωσιβίου ο[ἰ]κία, 16[ἀπὸ δὲ ἀπηλιώτου τῶν Ἀπολλωνίου ἀδελφῶν μέρος, ἀπὸ δὲ βορρᾶ ῥύμη δημοσία, 17καὶ ἀπὸ λιβὸς ῥύμη δημοσία. τὸ δὲ δάνειον τοῦτο ἀποδότω Ἀπολλώνιος Δημητρίαι 18ἐμ μηνὶ Γορπιείωι τῶι ἐν τῶι δευτέρωι ἔτει σὺν τῶι τόκωι. ἐὰν δὲ μὴ ἀποδῶι 19κατὰ τὰ γεγραμμένα, τῶν μὲν τριακοσίων τόκον διδότω Ἀπολλώνιος Δημητρίαι 20ἐπὶ τὸν ἐσόμενον χρόνον ὡς ἐγ δύο δραχμῶν τὴν μνᾶν τὸμ μῆνα ἕκαστον, ἀντὶ δὲ 21τοῦ τόκου τῶν λοιπῶν ἑκατὸν δραχμῶν ἐνοικείτω Δημητρία καὶ οἱ

of Alexander and the gods Adelphi and the gods Euergetae being Nicanor son of Bacchias, the canephorus of Arsinoe Philadelphus being Aristomache daughter of Ptolemaeus, the 18th of the month Gorpiaeus, at the village of Takona in the Oxyrhynchite nome. Demetria daughter of Apollodotus, Cyrenaean, with her guardian Apollophanes son of Apollodotus, Cyrenaean of the Epigone, has lent to Apollonius son of Patron, Cyrenaean of the Epigone, 400 drachmae in copper money produced to view,[a] bearing interest at the rate of 2 drachmae the mina each month, but in place of the interest on this loan Apollonius has leased to Demetria his tower inherited from his father in the village of Takona in the Oxyrhynchite nome, doors and all, for 1 year from the month Hyperberetaeus of the 1st year, on the understanding that Demetria and her assigns shall inhabit this tower for the term of the contract, using it in whatever manner they wish and having a right of way through the existing passage from the tower to the street, the boundaries of the tower being, on the south the house of Sosibius, on the east the portion of Apollonius's brothers, on the north a public street, and on the west a public street. This loan Apollonius shall repay to Demetria in the month Gorpiaeus of the 2nd year with the interest.[b] If he fails to repay it as stated, Apollonius shall continue to pay to Demetria interest on 300 drachmae for the subsequent time at the rate of 2 drachmae the mina each month, but in place of the interest on the remaining 100 drachmae Demetria and her assigns

[a] That is, submitted to the inspection of the witnesses.

[b] The interest for the year, being equivalent to the rent of the tower, would not actually be handed over.

παρ' αὐτῆς [22]ἐν τῶι πύργωι τούτωι] ἐν[οι]κοῦντες καὶ χρώμενοι τ[ρό-[23]πωι ὧι ἂν βούλωνται καὶ διοδευόμενοι] καθότι γέγραπται, ἕως ἂν [24][ἀποδῶι Ἀπολλώνιος Δημητρία]ι τὰς τετρακοσίας δραχμὰς τὸ δάνειον τοῦτο [25][καὶ τὸν τόκον τῶν τριακοσίων δ]ραχμῶν τοῦ ὑπερπεσόντος ὑπὲρ τὸν ἐνιαυτὸν [26][χρόνου, καὶ βεβαιούτω Ἀπολλώνι]ος Δημητρίαι κ[αὶ] τοῖς παρ' αὐτῆς τὸν πύργον το[ῦ-[27]τον καὶ τὴν δίοδον καὶ τὰς θύρας κατὰ τ]ὸν προγεγραμμένον ἐνιαυτὸν καὶ ἐπὶ τὸν ἐχόμεν[ον [28]χρόνον, ἕως ἂν ἀποδῶι αὐτῆι Ἀπολ]λώνιος τὸ δάνειον τοῦτο τὰς τετρακοσίας δραχμὰς [29][καὶ τὸν τόκον τῶν τριακο]σίων δραχμῶν καθότι προγέγραπται. ἐὰν δὲ μὴ βεβαι-[30][οῖ κατὰ τὰ γεγραμμένα], ἀποτεισάτω Ἀπολλώνιος Δημητρίαι τὸ μὲν δάνειον [31][τοῦτο τὰς τετρακοσί]ας δραχμὰς ἡμιολίους, τὸν δὲ τόκον τῶν τριακοσίων [32]δ[ραχμῶν] ἁπλ[οῦν, καὶ] ἡ [π]ρᾶξις ἔστω Δημητρίαι κατὰ τὸ διάγραμμα καὶ μηδὲν ἧσ-[33]σον κυρία {[δ]ὲ} ἔστω ἡ μίσθωσ[ι]ς τὸν συγγεγραμμένον χρόν<ον>, καὶ ἐξέστω Δημητρίαι [34]κ[αὶ τοῖ]ς π[αρ'] αὐτῆς ἀντιεξάγειν τὸν ἐξάγοντα αὐτοὺς ἐκ τοῦ πύργου το[ύ-][35]του καὶ τῆς διόδου ἀν[υ]πευθύνοις οὖσι πάσης ζημίας καὶ ἀνυποδίκοις. ἡ δὲ [36]συγγραφὴ ἥδε κυρία ἔστω οὗ ἂν ἐπιφέρηται. μάρτυρες Τιμόλαος Θεσσαλὸς [37]δεκανικός, Παρμενίων Πέρσης ἰδι[ώ]της, ἀμφότεροι τῶν Φίλωνος [38]⟦ανγαρημοι⟧, Περδίκκας Πολυάρχου Πέρσης, Φιλωνάδης [39]Λυσανίου Κυρηναῖος, Δημήτριος Θεμίσωνος Κυρηναῖος, Νουμή-[40]νιος Καλλιξένου Χαλκιδεύς, οἱ τέσσαρες τῆς ἐπιγονῆς.

38. ανγαρημοι doubtful and obscure.

shall inhabit the said tower, occupying and using it in whatever manner they wish and having a right of way as stated, until Apollonius repays to Demetria the 400 drachmae forming this loan and the interest on the 300 drachmae for the overtime in excess of the year, and Apollonius shall guarantee to Demetria and her assigns the use of the said tower and passage and doors during the aforesaid year and for the ensuing time until Apollonius repays to her this loan of 400 drachmae and the interest on the 300 drachmae as stated above. If he fails to guarantee as stated, Apollonius shall forfeit to Demetria this loan of 400 drachmae increased by one half and the interest on the 300 drachmae pure and simple, and Demetria shall have the right of execution in accordance with the ordinance [a] and the lease shall be no less valid for the term of the contract, and it shall be lawful for Demetria and her assigns to counter-eject anyone who tries to eject them from the said tower and passage without being liable to any penalty or legal action. This contract shall be valid wherever it is produced. Witnesses: Timolaus, Thessalian, decurion, Parmenion, Persian, private, both of the troop of Philon; Perdiccas son of Polyarchus, Persian, Philonades son of Lysanias, Cyrenaean, Demetrius son of Themison, Cyrenaean, Numenius son of Callixenus, Chalcidian, all four of the Epigone.

[a] A royal ordinance dealing with questions of legal procedure.

66. LOAN OF MONEY

P. Cairo Zen. 59001, ll. 26-56. 273 B.C.

Outer text of a contract written in duplicate. Restored from the inner text.

[26][Βασιλεύοντος Πτολεμαίο]υ τοῦ Πτολεμαίου [27][ἔτους δωδεκάτου, ἐφ' ἱερέως Λ]εοντ[ί]σκου τοῦ Καλ-[28][λιμήδους, μηνὸς Περιτίου, ἐ]μ Πίτωι τοῦ Μεμφί-[29][του νομοῦ. ἐδάνεισεν Δι]ονύσιος Ἀπολλωνίο[υ [30]Γαζαῖος τῶν περὶ Δείν]ωνα Ἰσιδώρωι Θραικ[ὶ [31]τῶν Λυκόφρονος τεσσα]ρακονταρούρωι ἀργυ-[32][ρίου δραχμὰς τριάκοντ]α τέσσαρας, τοῦτο [33][δ' ἐστὶν ἡ τιμὴ τοῦ βασιλικο]ῦ σίτου, τόκου ὡς [34][δύο δραχμῶν τῆι μνᾶι ἑ]κάστηι τὸμ μῆνα [35][ἕκαστον. ἀποδότω δ]ὲ Ἰσίδωρος Διονυσίωι [36][τὸ δάνειον ἐμ μηνὶ Ἀ]ρτεμισίωι τῶι ἐν τῶ[ι [37]τρεισκαιδεκάτωι ἔτε]ι καὶ [τὸ]ν τ[όκον. ἐὰν [38]δὲ μὴ ἀποδῶι ἐν τῶι γεγραμμένωι χρόνωι, [39]ἀποτεισάτω τὸ δάν]ειον ἡμιόλιον, καὶ ἡ πρᾶ-[40][ξις ἔστω Διονυσίωι ἐκ] τῶν ὑπαρχόντων τῶν [41][Ἰσιδώρου καὶ τῶν τοῦ] ἐγγύου πράσσοντι [42][τρόπον ὃν ἂν βούληται] Διονύσιος πρὸς βασι-[43][λικά. ἔγγυος τοῦ δα]νείου Ἰσιδώρου καὶ τῶν [44][κατὰ τὴν συγγραφὴ]ν πάντων εἰς ἔκτεισ[ιν [45]Διονυσίωι Δημήτ]ριος Δάμωνος Θρᾶιξ τῶν Λυκόφρον[ος] σύγκλη-[46][ρος μετὰ Δάμωνος(?) ἀρουρῶν τεσσ]αράκοντα. [ἡ δὲ συγγραφὴ ἥδε] κυρία ἔστω οὗ ἂν ἐπιφέρηι [47][Διονύσιος ἢ ὧι ἂν Διον]ύσιος παραδῶι. μάρτυρες [48][Βίθυς Θρᾶιξ ἑκατονδεκ]άρουρος, Τηρηϊτὴς Θρᾶιξ [49][τεσσαρακοντάρουρος, Ἑ]βρύζελμις Θρᾶιξ τεσσαρακον-[50][τάρουρος, Ποσειδώ-

48. Τηρήπης Ed.

66. LOAN OF MONEY

273 B.C.

In the 12th year of the reign of Ptolemy [a] son of Ptolemy, in the priesthood of Leontiscus son of Callimedes, in the month Peritius, at Pitos in the Memphite nome. Dionysius son of Apollonius, Gazaean, in the service of Dinon, has lent to Isidorus, Thracian, of the troop of Lycophron, holder of 40 arurae, 34 drachmae of silver, this being the price of the Crown corn,[b] on interest at the rate of 2 drachmae each month on each mina. Isidorus shall repay the loan to Dionysius in the month Artemisius [c] of the 13th year with the interest. If he fails to repay in the stated time, he shall forfeit one and a half times the amount of the loan, and Dionysius shall have the right of execution upon the property of Isidorus and that of his surety, making exaction in whatever way he chooses as in respect of debts to the Crown. Surety of Isidorus for payment to Dionysius of the loan and all the liabilities of the contract: Demetrius son of Damon, Thracian, of the troop of Lycophron, part-holder with Damon (?) of forty arurae. This contract shall be valid wherever produced by Dionysius or by the person to whom Dionysius transmits it. Witnesses: Bithys, Thracian, holder of 110 arurae, Tereites, Thracian, holder of 40 arurae, Hebryzelmis, Thracian, holder of 40 arurae, Posi-

[a] Ptolemy Philadelphus.

[b] Probably corn which cleruchs were obliged to sell to the Crown at a fixed price. Isidorus may have borrowed the amount which he counted on receiving from the Crown after the harvest.

[c] That is, three months after the date of the contract.

νιος] Θρᾶιξ ἑβδομηκοντάρουρος, 51[Ζίπυρος Θρᾶιξ σύγκληρος μετ]ὰ Βίθυος ἀρουρῶν ἑξήκοντα, Διονύσιος Θρᾶιξ ἑξηκον-52[τάρουρος, οὗτοι τῶν Λυκόφ]ρονος. 53[συγγρ]αφοφύλαξ Βίθυς. 54(In large hand) [ἔχω] κυρίαν.

Verso: 55πρὸς Ἰσίδωρον 56(δραχμῶν) λδ. Below, names of witnesses and principals.

67. LOAN OF MONEY

P. Amh. 50. 106 B.C.

1[a]Ἔτους ια τοῦ καὶ η Μεσορὴ ιδ, ἐν Κροκο-2δίλων πόλει ἐπὶ Πανίσκου ἀγοραν[όμου] 3τῆς ἄνω τοπαρχίας τοῦ Παθυρίτου. 4ἐδάνεισεν Ἑριενοῦφις Ψεμμίνιος 5τῶν ἐπανηκότων ἐκ τοῦ παραγγέλ(ματος) 6Εὐνόωι Πατσεοῦτος καὶ Πατ-7σεοῦτι Ὀρσέους, τοῖς δυσὶ Πέρσαι[ς] 8τῆς ἐπιγονῆς τῶν ἐκ Παθύρεως, 9χαλκοῦ νο(μίσματος) (τάλαντα) πέντε δραχμὰς 10δισχιλίας ἄτοκα εἰς ἡμέρας τριά-11κοντα ἀπὸ ια τοῦ Μεσορὴ τοῦ προκ(ειμένου) (ἔτους). 12τὸ δὲ δά(νειον) τοῦτο ἀποδότωσαν οἱ δεδα(νεισμένοι) 13Ἑριενούφει ἐμ μηνὶ Θωὺθ ε τοῦ ιβ 14τοῦ καὶ θ (ἔτους). ἐὰν δὲ μὴ ἀποδῶσι 15ἐν τῶι ὡρισμένωι χρόνωι καθότι 16προγέγραπται, ἀποτεισάτωσαν 17ἐν τῆι ἐχομένηι ἡμέραι παρα-18χρῆμα τὰ τοῦ χα(λκοῦ) (τάλαντα) ε Ἀ ἡμιόλιον 19καὶ τοῦ ὑπερπεσόντος χρόνου τόκους 20διδράχμους τῆς μνᾶς τὸν μῆνα 21ἕκαστον. ἔγγυοι ἀλλήλων εἰς ἔκτεισιν 22τῶν διὰ τοῦ δανείου τούτου πάντων 23αὐτοὶ οἱ δεδα(νεισμένοι), ἡ δὲ πρᾶξις ἔστω 24Ἑριενούφει ἔκ τε

[a] See No. 27, note *a*.

donius, Thracian, holder of 70 arurae, Zipyrus, Thracian, part-holder with Bithys of 60 arurae, Dionysius, Thracian, holder of 60 arurae, all belonging to the troop of Lycophron. Keeper of the contract: Bithys. (Acknowledgement by Bithys) I have received the contract, being valid. (Endorsed) Contract with Isidorus concerning 34 drachmae.

67. LOAN OF MONEY

106 B.C.

The 11th which is also the 8th year,[a] Mesore 14, in Crocodilopolis, before Paniscus, agoranomus of the upper toparchy of the Pathyrite nome. Herienouphis son of Psemminis, one of those who have returned in consequence of the order,[b] has lent to Eunous son of Patseous and to Patseous son of Orses, both of them Persians of the Epigone from Pathyris, five talents two thousand drachmae of copper money without interest for thirty days from the 11th of Mesore of the aforesaid year. This loan the borrowers shall repay to Herienouphis on the 5th of the month Thoth of the 12th which is also the 9th year. If they do not repay in the specified time as written above, they shall forthwith forfeit on the following day the 5 talents 2000 dr. increased by one half and interest for the overtime at the rate of two drachmae on the mina each month. The borrowers themselves are sureties for each other for the payment of all the liabilities of this loan, and Herienouphis shall have the right of execution upon

[b] Perhaps a reference to a royal proclamation ordering natives to return to their own villages.

αὐτῶ[ν καὶ ἐξ ἑνὸς] [25]καὶ ὁποτέρου οὗ ἂν βού[ληται καὶ] [26]ἐκ τῶν τούτοις ὑπ(αρχόντων) πάντω[ν καθάπερ [27]ἐγ δίκης.

68. LOAN OF WHEAT

P. Tebt. 110. 92 or 59 B.C.

[1]Πε[τ]εσοῦχος ὁ καὶ Πετεῦρι{ο}ς Σελεβοῦτος [2]Πέρσης τῆς ἐπιγονῆς Ἑρμίᾳ τῷ καὶ Ἑρ-[3]γεῖ Πετεσούχου χαίρειν. ὁμολογῶ ἔχειν [4]παρὰ σοῦ πυρῶν ἀρτάβας εἴκοσι τέσσαρες [5]ἥμισυ σὺν ἡμιολίᾳ, ἃς καὶ ἀποδώσω σοι ἐμ μ-[6]ην[ὶ] Παῦνι τοῦ δευτέρου καὶ εἰκοστοῦ ἔτους [7]κα[θ]εσ<τα>μένας εἰς Κ<ερκ>ευσῖριν μέτρῳ δρόμου. [8]ἂν δ[ὲ] μὴ ἀποδῶ σοι, ἐκτίσω σοι{ι} παραχρῆμα [9]τιμὴν ἑκάστης ἀρτάβη{α}ς χαλκοῦ δραχμὰς [10]τρισκιλίας ἢ τὴν ἐσομένην πλίσ<την> τιμὴν κ-[11]αὶ [ἐ]πίτιμον ἀργυρίου ἐπισήμου δραχμὰς [12]ἑξ[ή]κοντα καὶ τὸ βλάβος καὶ εἰς τὸ βασιλικὸν τ-[13]ὸ ἴσον. ἡ χεὶρ ἥδε κυρία ἔστω πανταχῇ ἐπιφερο-[14]μένη. [15]ἔρρωσο. ἔτους κβ Μεχεὶρ κγ.

4. *l.* τέσσαρας. 10. *l.* τρισχιλίας.

69. LOAN OF MONEY

P. Oxy. 269. A.D. 57.

(Col. 1) [1]Ἀντίγρα(φον). Διό[σκο]ρος Ζηνοδ[ώρου Πέρ]σαι τῆς ἐπιγονῆς Τρύφων[ι] [2]Διονυσίο[υ χα]ίρειν. ὁ[μ]ολογ[ῶ ἔχει]ν παρὰ σοῦ ἐπὶ τοῦ πρὸς Ὀξυρύγχων [3]πόλει [Σαραπ]είου διὰ τῆς

their persons together or singly or upon whichever he chooses and upon all their property as if by legal decision.

68. LOAN OF WHEAT

92 or 59 B.C.

Petesouchus also called Peteuris son of Selebous, Persian of the Epigone, to Hermias also called Hergeus son of Petesouchus, greeting. I acknowledge that I have received from you $24\frac{1}{2}$ artabae of wheat with an additional one half,[a] which I will repay to you in the month Pauni of the 22nd year conveyed to Kerkeosiris and measured by the dromos measure.[b] If I fail to repay you, I will forfeit to you forthwith as the value of each artaba 3000 drachmae of copper or the highest price then current, and a fine of 60 drachmae of coined silver and the damage, and to the Treasury the like amount. This bond shall be valid wherever produced. Goodbye. The 22nd year, Mecheir 23.

[a] The meaning is that the loan was to be repaid at 150 per cent., *i.e.* the borrower received $24\frac{1}{2}$ artabae and gave $36\frac{3}{4}$ in return.

[b] See No. 43, note *b*.

69. LOAN OF MONEY

A.D. 57.

Copy. Dioscorus son of Zenodorus, Persians of the Epigone, to Tryphon son of Dionysius greeting. I acknowledge that I have received from you at the Serapeum by Oxyrhynchus through the bank of

Ἀ[ρχιβίου] τοῦ Ἀρχιβίου τραπέζης ἀργ[υ]ρίου [4]Σεβαστ[οῦ νο]μίσματος δρ[αχ]μὰς πεντήκοντα δύο κεφαλαίου [5]αἷς οὐδ[ὲν τ]ῶι καθόλου π[ροσ]ῆκτ[α]ι, ἃς καὶ ἀποδώσω σοι τῇ τριακάδι [6]τοῦ Κα[ισαρεί]ου μηνὸς τοῦ [ἐ]νεστῶτος γ (ἔτους) Νέρωνος Κλαυδ[ί]ου [7]Καίσαρ[ος Σεβ]αστοῦ Γερμ[ανι]κοῦ Αὐτοκράτορος χωρὶς πάσης [8]ὑπερ[θέσ]εως. ἐὰν δὲ μ[ὴ ἀπ]οδ[ῶ]ι καθὰ γέγραπται, ἐκτείσω σοι [9]τ[ὸ π]ρο[κ]είμενον κεφ[άλ]αιον μεθ' ἡμιολίας καὶ τοῦ ὑπερπεσόν-[10]τος χρ[όν]ου τοὺς καθήκοντας τόκους, τῆς πράξεώς σου [11]οὔσης ἔ[κ τ]ε ἐμοῦ καὶ ἐ[κ] τῶν ὑπαρχόντων αὐτῶι πάντων [12]καθάπερ ἐγ δίκης. κυρί[α] ἡ χε[ὶ]ρ πανταχῇ ἐπιφερομέν[η] [13]καὶ παντὶ τῶι ἐπιφέροντι. (ἔτους) γ Νέρω[ν]ος Κλαυδίου Καίσαρος [14]Σεβαστοῦ Γερμανικοῦ [Α]ὐτοκράτορ[ος μ]ηνὸς Γερμανικείου ιη Σεβα(στῇ). [15]ὑπογρα(φῆς) ἀντίγρα(φον). Διόσκορος Ζηνοδώρου [ἔ]χωι τὰς τοῦ ἀργυρίου [16]δραχμὰς πεντήκ[ο]ντα δύο κεφαλαίου καὶ ἀποδώσωι [17]καθότι πρόκειται. Ζωίλος Ὥρου ἔγραψα ὑπὲρ αὐτοῦ μὴ ε[ἰ]δότος [18]γράμματα. (ἔτους) γ Νέρωνος Κλαυδίου Καίσαρος Σεβαστοῦ Γερμανικοῦ [19]Αὐτοκράτορος μηνὸς Γερμανικείου ιη Σεβαστῇ. [20]σημε<ι>ώσεω(ς) ἀντίγρα(φον). ἔτους γ Νέρωνος Κλαυδίου Καίσαρος Σεβαστοῦ [21]Γερμα[νι]κοῦ Αὐτοκρά[τ]ορος μηνὸς Γερμανικείου ιη Σεβασ<τ>ῇ. [22]διὰ Θέωνος τοῦ Σύρου τοῦ συνεσταμένου ὑπὸ Ἀρχιβίου τραπεζείτο(υ) γέγο(νεν) ἡ διαγρα(φή).

(Col. 2) (2nd hand) [1]Τρύφων Ἀμμωνᾶτι [2]τῷ [μ]ακρῷ τῷ φιλτά-[3]τῳ χαίρειν. ἐὰν δύ-[4]νῃ, ἐρωτηθεὶς ὄχλη-[5]σον Διόσκορον καὶ ἔκ-[6]πραξον αὐτὸν

(Col. 1) 10. *l.* σοι. 11. *l.* μοι for αυτωι.

Archibius son of Archibius the sum of 52 silver drachmae of the Imperial coinage, to which no addition at all has been made, and I will repay you on the 30th of the month Caesareus[a] of the current 3rd year of Nero Claudius Caesar Augustus Germanicus Imperator without any delay. If I fail to repay you as stated, I will forfeit to you the aforesaid capital increased by one half, with proper interest for the overtime, you having the right of execution upon me and upon all my property as if by legal decision. This note of hand is valid wheresoever and by whomsoever presented. The 3rd year of Nero Claudius Caesar Augustus Germanicus Imperator, the 18th of the month Germaniceus,[b] *dies augustus*.[c] Copy of signature. I, Dioscorus son of Zenodorus, have received the sum of 52 silver drachmae and will repay it as aforesaid. I, Zoilus son of Horus, have written for him, as he is illiterate. The 3rd year of Nero Claudius Caesar Augustus Germanicus Imperator, the 18th of the month Germaniceus, *dies augustus*. Copy of docket. The 3rd year of Nero Claudius Caesar Augustus Germanicus Imperator, the 18th of the month Germaniceus, *dies augustus*. The payment has been made through Theon son of Syrus, designated by Archibius, banker. (The enclosing letter) Tryphon to his dearest friend, the tall Ammonas, greeting. If you can, please importune Dioscorus and exact from him the fulfilment of

[a] =the Egyptian Mesore.

[b] =Pachon.

[c] Being the anniversary of a birthday or other notable event in the life of the Imperial family.

τὸ [7]χειρόγραφον, καὶ [8]ἐάν σοι δῦ τὸ ἀργύριον, [9]δὺς αὐτῷ ἀποχήν, [10]καὶ ἐὰν εὕ[ρ]ῃς ἀσφα-[11]λήν, δὺς αὐτῷ τὸ ἀρ-[12]γύριον ἐνένκαι μοι. [13]ἄσπασαι τοὺς <σ>οὺς [14]πάντας. ἔρρωσ[ο].

(Col. 2) 8. *l.* δοῖ (= δῷ). 9. *l.* δός (so in l. 11) or perhaps δοῖς (subj. instead of imper.).

70. LOAN THROUGH A BANK

P. Tebt. 389. A.D. 141.

[1]Ἔτους τετάρτου Αὐτοκράτορο[ς] Καίσαρος Τίτου [2]Αἰλίου Ἁδριανοῦ Ἀντωνείνου Σεβαστοῦ [3]Εὐσεβοῦς Φαρμοῦθι κζ, κατὰ διεγβολὴν [4]τῆς Σα[β]είνου τραπ(έζης) Ταμείων. Ἰσιδώρα [5]Ἡρακλείδου τ[ο]ῦ Μελεδήμου μετὰ κυρίου [6]τ[ο]ῦ συγγενοῦς Ἀπίωνος τοῦ Ἀπίωνος Τα-[7]μύσθα̣ Ὠρι[γέ]νους τοῦ Ὠριγέν[ο]υς μετὰ κυρίου [8]τοῦ υἱοῦ Πτολεμαίου τοῦ Πτολεμαίου χρῆσιν [9]ἀργυρίου κεφαλαίου δραχμὰς τρισχειλίας [10]πεν[τακοσίας, (γίνονται) (δραχμαὶ) Ἁ]φ, εἰς ἐνιαυτὸν [ἕ]να [11][ἀπ]ὸ τοῦ ἐνεσ[τ]ῶτος μηνὸς Παχὼν τόκων [12][δ]ρα[χ]μιαί[ων ἑ]κάστῃ μνᾷ κατὰ μῆνα, [13]ἃς καὶ ἀπ[οδώσειν ἐ]ν μηνὶ Φαρμοῦθι [14]τοῦ εἰσι[όντος ε ἔτου]ς [Ἀ]ντωνίν[ου] Καίσαρος τοῦ [κυ]ρίου [15][σ]ὺν ταῖς συναγομέναις τόκου αὐτῶν δραχμαῖς [16]τετρακ[ο]σίαις εἴκοσι, ἀκολούθως ᾗ [π]ε-[17]ποίητ[α]ι Ταμύσ[θα] κεφαλαίου δικαίου γραφείσ-[⟦αις⟧]ῃ [18]ὑπαλλαγῇ δι[ὰ] τῆς βιβλιοθήκης.

16. η corr. from αι[ς.

his bond. If he pays you the money, give him a receipt; and if you find a safe person, give him the money to bring to me. Salute from me all your family. Goodbye.

70. LOAN THROUGH A BANK

A.D. 141.

The 4th year of the Emperor Caesar Titus Aelius Hadrianus Antoninus Augustus Pius, Pharmouthi 27, by a draft of the bank of Sabinus in the Treasuries' quarter. Isidora daughter of Heraclides son of Meledemus, with her guardian her kinsman Apion son of Apion, notifies Tamystha daughter of Origenes son of Origenes, with her guardian her son Ptolemaeus son of Ptolemaeus, that she, Tamystha, has received the loan of the capital sum of three thousand five hundred drachmae of silver, total 3500 dr., for one year from the present month Pachon, at the monthly interest of 1 drachma on each mina, which sum she will repay in the month Pharmouthi of the coming 5th year of Antoninus Caesar the lord with the interest accruing on it to the amount of 420 drachmae, in accordance with a contract of mortgage which Tamystha has made on her rights over a sum of money, and which was drawn up through the record-office.

71. ACKNOWLEDGEMENT OF A DEPOSIT

P. Oxy. 1039. A.D. 210.

[1][᾿Απο]λλώνιος Σαραπίωνος [τοῦ Σαρα-][2]πίωνος μητρὸς Σινθεῦτ[ος ἀπ᾿ ᾿Οξυ-][3]ρύγχων πόλεως Θέωνι Κ . [. . . . . .] [4]τοῦ καὶ Χαιρήμονος μητρὸς ᾿Απί[ας ἀπὸ] [5]τῆς αὐτῆς πόλεως χαίρειν. [ὁμολο-][6]γῶ ἐσχηκέναι παρὰ σοῦ διὰ χ[ειρὸς] [7]ἐν παραθέσει ἀργυρίου Σεβασ[τοῦ] [8]νομίσματος δραχμὰς ἑξακ[οσίας], [9]ἅσπερ ὁπηνίκα ἐὰν αἱρῇ ἀπ[οκα-][10]ταστήσω σοι ἄνευ πάσης ὑπε[ρθέ-][11]σεως [καὶ] εὑρησολογ[ία]ς, εἰ δ[ὲ μή], [12]ἐκτείσ[ω σοι] κατὰ τὸν τῶν παρ[α-][13]θηκῶ[ν νόμον], γεινομένης [σοι] [14]τῆς πρ[ά]ξε[ως] ἔκ τε ἐμοῦ καὶ [ἐκ] [15]τῶν ὑπαρχόντων μοι πάντω[ν]. [16]κύρια τὴ τῆς παραθήκης γρά[μ-][17]ματα δισσὰ γραφέντα ὑπ᾿ ἐμ[οῦ] [18]τοῦ ᾿Απολλωνίου πανταχῇ ἐπιφ[ε-][19]ρόμενα καὶ παντὶ τῷ ὑπὲρ σο[ῦ] [20]ἐπιφέροντι. (ἔτους) ιθ Αὐτοκρατό[ρων] [21]Καισάρων Λουκίου Σεπτιμίου Σεουή[ρου] [22]Περτίνακος ᾿Αραβ[ι]κοῦ ᾿Αδιαβην[ικοῦ] [23]Παρθικοῦ Βρεταννικοῦ Μεγίστο[υ] [24]καὶ Μάρκου Αὐρηλίου ᾿Αντωνίνου [25]⟦καὶ Πουβλίου Σεπτιμίου Γέτα⟧ [26]Βρεταννικῶν Μεγίστων Εὐσεβῶ[ν] [27]Σεβαστῶν Φαῶφι ιγ.

11. *l.* εὑρησιλογίας. 16. *l.* τά.

71. ACKNOWLEDGEMENT OF A DEPOSIT

A.D. 210.

Apollonius son of Sarapion son of Sarapion, his mother being Sintheus, of Oxyrhynchus, to Theon son of C . . . also called Chaeremon, his mother being Apia, of the said city, greeting. I acknowledge that I have received from you by hand on deposit 600 silver drachmae of the Imperial coinage, which I will restore to you whenever you choose without any delay or equivocation, otherwise I will forfeit them to you in accordance with the law concerning deposits, and you shall have the right of execution upon me and upon all my property. This deed of deposit written in duplicate by me, Apollonius, is valid wherever produced and whosoever produces it on your behalf. The 19th year of the Emperors and Caesars Lucius Septimius Severus Pertinax Arabicus Adiabenicus Parthicus Britannicus Maximus and Marcus Aurelius Antoninus and Publius Septimius Geta,[a] Britannici Maximi Pii Augusti, Phaophi 13.

[a] The name of Geta, who was murdered by Caracalla, has been deleted.

II. RECEIPTS

72. RECEIPT FOR RENT OF SOWS

P.S.I. 379. 248 B.C.

(Inner text) [1](Ἔτους) λζ Χοίαχ κβ̄. ὁμολο-[2]γεῖ Ἡρακλείδης ἔχειν [3]παρὰ Πετοσίριος τοῦ [4]Πετενούριος ⟦ἔχειν⟧ [5]εἰς τὸν φόρον τοῦ λζ (ἔτους) [6]δέλφακας δεκαέξ. (Outer text) [7]Ἔτους ἑβδόμου [8]καὶ τριακοστοῦ [9]Χοίαχ δευτέραι [10]καὶ ἰκάδι. ὁμολογεῖ [11]Ἡρακλείδης ὁ πα-[12]ρὰ Ζήνωνος ἔχειν [13]παρὰ Πετοσίριος [14]τοῦ Πετενού-[15]ριος τοῦ ἐν τῆι [16]Δικαίου νήσωι [17]ὑοφορβοῦ εἰς τὸν [18]φόρον τοῦ ἑβδόμου [19]καὶ τριακοστοῦ [20]ἔτους ὧν ἔχ[ει] [21]τοκάδων δέκα [22]δέλφακας δεκα-[23]επτά.

73. RECEIPT FOR RENT OF LAND

P. Amh. 104. A.D. 125.

[1]Δημητρία ἡ καὶ Τασεῦς Ἀπολλω-[2]νίδου μετὰ κυρίου τοῦ ἐμαυτῆς υἱ-[3]οῦ Ἀρείου Νεάρχου τοῦ καὶ Μεγχήους [4]Ἀνουβίωνι Σεραπίωνος γεοργῶι

4. *l.* γεωργῶι.

II. RECEIPTS

72. RECEIPT FOR RENT OF SOWS

248 B.C.

(Inner text)[a] Year 37, Choiach 22. Heraclides acknowledges that he has received from Petosiris son of Petenouris for the 37th year's rent sixteen young pigs. (Outer text) The thirty-seventh year, twenty-second day of Choiach. Heraclides, employee of Zenon, acknowledges that he has received from Petosiris son of Petenouris, the swineherd in Dicaei Nesus,[b] for the thirty-seventh year's rent of the ten sows which he has leased, seventeen[c] young pigs.

[a] The receipt was written in duplicate, the inner text being sealed up.

[b] A village in the Fayum.

[c] The inner text says "sixteen."

73. RECEIPT FOR RENT OF LAND

A.D. 125.

Demetria also called Taseus daughter of Apollonides, having with me as guardian my son Arius son of Nearchus also called Menches, to Anubion son of Serapion, cultivator, greeting. I

[5]χαίρειν. μεμέτρημαι παρὰ σοῦ πάν-[6]τα τὰ ἐκφόρια ὧν ἐγεώργησάς μου [7]ἀρουρῶν γενήματος τοῦ διε-[8]ληλυθότος ἐνάτου ἔτους Ἁδριανοῦ [9]Καίσαρος τοῦ κυρίου, καὶ οὐδέν σοι [10]ἐνκαλῶ περὶ οὐδενὸς ἁπλῶς, τῶν [11]δημοσίων [ὄ]ντων πρὸς ἐμὲ τὴν [12]κάτοικον. ἔτους δεκάτου Αὐτοκράτορος [13]Καίσαρος Τραϊανοῦ Ἁδριανοῦ Σεβαστοῦ [14]Θὼτ ιγ. Ἄρειος Νεάρχου ἐπιγέγραμ-[15]μαι τῆς μητρός μου κύριος καὶ ἔγρα-[16]ψα ὑπὲρ αὐτῆς μὴ εἰδυίης γράμμα-[17]τα.

74. RECEIPT FOR REPAYMENT OF A LOAN

P. Ryl. 174. A.D. 112.

[1][Ἔτου]ς ἑκκαιδεκάτου Αὐτοκράτορος Καίσαρος Νερούα Τραϊανοῦ [2][Σεβασ]τοῦ Γερμανικοῦ Δακικοῦ μηνὸς Ἀπελλαίου Φαῶφι κς, ἐν Πτο-[3][λεμαΐδι Ε]ὐεργέτιδι Ἀρσινοείτου νομοῦ. ὁμολογεῖ Ἡρακλοῦς Ἀμμωνί[ο]υ [4][ὡς ἐτῶν ἑ]ξήκοντα ἓξ οὐλὴ μετώπῳ μέσῳ μετὰ κυρίου τοῦ υἱοῦ Σαβεί-[5][νου Διδᾶ] ὡς ἐτῶν τεσσαράκοντα τριῶν οὐλὴ μετώπῳ μέσῳ [6][Τασου]χαρίῳ Πετερμούθεως τοῦ Ποσειδωνίου ὡς ἐτῶν ἑξήκοντα [7][οὐλὴ] γενείῳ μέσ[ῳ] καὶ φακὸς παρὰ ῥινὶ ἐξ ἀριστερῶν μετὰ κυρίου [8][τοῦ υἱοῦ] Ἰσιδώρου τοῦ Ἀσκληπιάδου ὡς ἐτῶν εἴκοσι ὀκτὼ οὐλὴι [9][. . . . .] ἐξ ἀριστερῶν ἀπέχειν τὴν Ἡρακλοῦν παρὰ τῆς Τασουχαρίου [10][διὰ τῆς Ἀρ]ποχρατίωνος τραπέζης Ταμείων ἀργυρίου δραχμὰς χειλίας [11][ἑξακοσί]ας δεκαδύο ἃς ὤφειλεν αὐτῇ ἡ Τασουχάριον κατὰ δάνειον [12][τελειω]θὲν διὰ τοῦ

10. *l.* Ἀρ]ποκρατίωνος: so also in 27.

have received from you all the rent of the land of mine which you cultivated, measured out from the produce of the past ninth year of Hadrianus Caesar the lord, and I have no claim against you concerning anything whatever, the public charges being borne by me the holder. The tenth year of the Emperor Caesar Trajanus Hadrianus Augustus, Thoth 13. I, Arius son of Nearchus, have professed myself guardian of my mother and wrote for her, as she is illiterate.

74. RECEIPT FOR REPAYMENT OF A LOAN

A.D. 112.

The 16th year of the Emperor Caesar Nerva Trajanus Augustus Germanicus Dacicus, the 26th of the month Apellaeus or Phaophi, at Ptolemais Euergetis[a] in the Arsinoite nome. Heraclous daughter of Ammonius, aged about 66 years, with a scar in the middle of her forehead, having with her as guardian her son Sabinus son of Didas, aged about 43 years, with a scar in the middle of his forehead, acknowledges to Tasoucharion daughter of Petermouthis son of Posidonius, aged about 60 years, with a scar in the middle of her chin and a mole at the left side of her nose, having with her as guardian her son Isidorus son of Asclepiades, aged about 28 years, with a scar on the left side of . . . , that she, Heraclous, has received from Tasoucharion through the bank of Harpocration in the Treasuries quarter 1612 silver drachmae which Tasoucharion owed to her on the evidence of a deed

[a] See No. 45, p. 135, note *a*.

αὐτ[ο]ῦ γραφείου καὶ διεγβολὴν τῆς Σαραπίωνος τραπέζ(ης) [13][τῷ δεκ]άτῳ πρώ[τ]ῳ ἔτει Τραϊανοῦ Καίσαρος τοῦ κυρίου μηνὶ Καισαρείῳ [14][. . . . κ]αὶ εἰκάδι, [ἃ] καὶ ἀναδεδόσθαι αὐτῇ εἰς ἀθέτησιν καὶ ἀκύρωσιν. [15][καὶ μὴ] ἐπελεύσ[εσθ]αι μήτε αὐτὴν Ἡρακλοῦν μηδὲ τοὺς παρ' αὐτῆς [16][ἐπὶ τὴν] Τασουχάρ[ιον] μηδὲ ἐπὶ τοὺς παρ' αὐτῆς μήτε περὶ ὧν ἀπέχει [17][ὡς π]ρόκειται [ἀρ]γυρίου δραχμῶν χειλίων ἑξακοσίων δεκαδύο [18][μηδὲ] περὶ τόκων αὐτῶν διὰ τὸ καὶ τούτους αὐτὴν ἀπεσχηκέναι [19][μηδὲ π]ερὶ ἄλλου μηδενὸς ἁπλῶς πράγματος μηδὲ ὀφειλήματος μηδὲ [20][μηδενὸ]ς τῷ καθόλου ἐνγράπτου μηδὲ ἀγράφου ἀπὸ τῶν ἔμπροσθεν χρόνω(ν) [21][μέχρι] τῆς ἐνεστώσης ἡμέρας τρόπῳ μηδενί· καὶ συνχωρεῖ ἡ Ἡρακλοῦς [22][ἄκυρο]ν εἶναι κατὰ πάντα τρόπον ἣν πεποίηται ἡ Τασουχάρι[ο]ν διὰ τῆς [23][τῶν ἐ]νκτήσ[ε]ων [β]ιβλι[ο]θήκης ἑκ[ο]ύσιον κατ[ο]χὴν τοῦ ὀνόματος [24][αὐτῆς] εἰς τὸν [τ]ῆ[ς Ἡ]ρακλοῦτος λόγον, ὅπερ καὶ τῆς κατοχῆς ὑπόμνημα [25][ἀναδε]δόσθαι αὐτῇ ὁμοίως εἰς ἀκύρωσιν. τὰ προγεγραμμένα κύρια. (2nd hand) Ἡρακλοῦς [26][Ἀμμ]ωνίου μετὰ κυρίου τοῦ υἱοῦ Σαβίνου τοῦ Διδᾶ ἀπέχω παρὰ [27][τῆς] Τασουχαρίου διὰ τῆς Ἁρποχρατίωνος τραπέζης Ταμίων [28][τὰς] τοῦ ἀργυρίου δραχμὰς χιλίας ἑξακοσίας δεκαδύο [29][ἃς ὤφ]ιλέ μοι κατὰ τὸ δηλούμενον δάνιον καὶ διεκ-[30][βολήν], ἃ καὶ ἀναδέδωκα εἰς ἀκύροσιν καὶ οὐκ ἐπελεύσομαι [31][οὔτε π]ερὶ ὧν ἀπέχω οὔτε περὶ τόκων αὐτῶν οὔτε περὶ ἄλ-[32][λου οὐ]δενὸς ἁπλῶς ἐνγράπτου ο<ὐ>δὲ ἀγράφου μέχρι τῆς ἐνεσ-[33][τώση]ς ἡμέρας τρόπο̣ μηδενί, καὶ συνχορô

30. *l.* ἀκύρωσιν. 33. *l.* τρόπῳ, συνχωρῶ.

of loan executed through this same record-office and of a draft of the bank of Sarapion in the 11th year of Trajanus Caesar the lord, the 2[.] of the month Caesareus,[a] which documents have been surrendered to her to be annulled and cancelled, and that neither Heraclous herself nor her assigns will take proceedings against Tasoucharion or her assigns with regard to the 1612 silver drachmae which she has received as aforesaid or to the interest on them, seeing that this too she has received, or about any other matter at all or debt or claim of any kind, written or unwritten, from times past up to the present day, in any manner; and Heraclous admits that the voluntary notification of personal liability which Tasoucharion has made in favour of Heraclous through the property registration-office is in every respect invalid, which deed of lien has been likewise surrendered to her to be cancelled. The above agreement is valid. (Subscribed and signed) I, Heraclous daughter of Ammonius, having with me as guardian my son Sabinus son of Didas, have received from Tasoucharion through the bank of Harpocration in the Treasuries quarter the 1612 silver drachmae which she owed me on the evidence of the specified deed of loan and of the draft, which documents I have surrendered to her to be cancelled and I will not take proceedings against her about the sum which I have received or the interest on it or any other matter at all, written or unwritten, up to the present day in any manner, and I admit that the

[a] = the Egyptian Pachon.

ἄκυρον εἶναι ἣν [34][πεποί]ηται ἡ Τασουχάριον κατοχὴν τοῦ ὀνόματος αὐτῆς [35][καθὼ]ς πρόκιται. Σαβῖνος ‹ἔγραψα› καὶ ὑπὲρ τῆς μητρός μου μὴ εἰδυ‹ί›ης [36][γράμ]μα‹τα›. (3rd hand) Τασουχάριον Πετερμούθεω(ς) μετὰ κυρίου τοῦ υἱοῦ Ἰσιδώρου το(ῦ) Ἀσκληπ(ιάδου) [37][γέγο(νεν) εἴς] με ἡ ἀποχὴ καθὼς πρόκιται. Ἰσίδωρος ἔγραψα καὶ ὑπὲρ τῆς μητρός μο(υ) μὴ εἰδυίη(ς) γράμματ(α). [38][(ἔτους) ιϛ] μη(νὸς) Φαῶφι κϛ.

On the verso a red stamp showing head and shoulders of the Emperor surrounded by a legend in two circles: (ἔτους) ιϛ Αὐτοκράτορος Καίσαρος Νερούα Τραϊανοῦ Σεβαστοῦ Γερμανικοῦ Δακικοῦ.

75. RECEIPT FOR SETTLEMENT OF A LOAN

P. Lond. 332. A.D. 166.

[1]Ἔτους ἑβδόμου Αὐτοκράτορος [2]Καίσαρος Μάρκου Αὐρηλίου [3]Ἀντωνίνου [4]Σεβαστοῦ καὶ Αὐτοκράτορος [5]Καίσαρος Λουκίου Αὐρηλίου [6]Οὐήρου Σεβαστοῦ Θὼθ ιγ, διὰ [7]τῆς Σαραπίωνος τραπ(έζης) Ταμείων. [8]Δίδυμος Διδύμου τοῦ καὶ Δη-[9]μητρίου Σωσικόσμιος ὁ καὶ [10]Ἀλθαιεὺς καὶ Τεσενοῦφις [11]Τεσενούφεως καὶ Τεσε-[12]νοῦφις ἕτερος Τεσενού-[13]φεως καὶ Πανεφρῆμις Στο-[14]τοήτιος καὶ Παβοῦς Σαταβοῦ-[15]τος Κλαυδιανῷ τῷ καὶ Σε-[16]ρήνῳ υἱῷ Μύσθου κε-[17]κοσμητ(ευκότι), ἀπέχειν αὐτὸν [18]παρὰ τῶν προγεγρ(αμμένων) ἴσας ὧν [19]ὤφειλαν αὐτῷ κατὰ διαγρ(αφὴν) [20]τῆς αὐτῆς τραπ(έζης), ἣν καὶ ἀναδέ-[21]δωκεν αὐτοῖς εἰς ἀθέτη-[22]σιν καὶ ἀκύρωσιν, ἀργυρίου [23]δραχμὰς χειλίας ἑκατὸν

notification of personal liability which Tasoucharion has made is invalid as aforesaid. I, Sabinus, have written for my mother also, as she is illiterate. I, Tasoucharion daughter of Petermouthis, having with me as guardian my son Isidorus son of Asclepiades, have had the receipt made to me as aforesaid. I, Isidorus, have written for my mother also, as she is illiterate. Year 16, Phaophi 26. (Legend round the stamp) Year 16 of the Emperor Caesar Nerva Trajanus Augustus Germanicus Dacicus.

75. RECEIPT FOR SETTLEMENT OF A LOAN

A.D. 166.

The 7th year of the Emperor Caesar Marcus Aurelius Antoninus Augustus and the Emperor Caesar Lucius Aurelius Verus Augustus, Thoth 13, through the bank of Sarapion in the Treasuries quarter.[a] Didymus son of Didymus also called Demetrius, of the Sosicosmian tribe and the Althaean deme,[b] and Tesenouphis son of Tesenouphis and another Tesenouphis son of Tesenouphis and Panephremis son of Stotoetis and Pabous son of Satabous notify Claudianus also called Serenus son of Musthes, ex-cosmetes, that he has received from the aforesaid persons the amount which they owed him according to a note of payment of the said bank, which note he has given up to them to be annulled and cancelled, namely one thousand

[a] In Arsinoe (=Ptolemais Euergetis); compare No. 74.
[b] See No. 32, note *b*.

[24]εἴκοσι τέσσαρες, γ(ίνονται) (δραχμαὶ) Ἀρκδ, [25]καὶ μηδὲν αὐτοῖς ἐνκαλεῖν [26]μέχρι τῆς ἐνεστ(ώσης) ἡμέρας. (2nd hand) [27]Σερῆνος ὁ καὶ Κλαυδιανὸς [28]ἀπέχω καθὼς πρόκειται.

76. RECEIPT FOR EARNEST-MONEY

P. Lond. 334. A.D. 166.

[1]Ἔτους ἑβδόμου Αὐτοκράτορος Καίσαρος Μάρκου Αὐρηλίου [2]Ἀντων[ίνου] Σεβαστοῦ καὶ Αὐτοκράτορος Καίσαρος Λουκίου [3]Αὐρηλίου Οὐήρου Σεβαστοῦ Φαῶφι κβ, δι[ὰ γρα]φείου Νείλου πόλε-[4]ως τῆς Ἡρακλείδου μερίδος τοῦ Ἀρσινο[ί]του νομοῦ. ὁμολογοῦσι [5]Θασῆς Στοτοήτεως τοῦ Ὥρου ἀπὸ κώμης Σοκνοπαίου Νήσου ἱέρεια [6]ὡς (ἐτῶν) ν οὐλ(ὴ) ὑπ[ὲρ ἀγκ]ῶνα ἀριστερὸν μετὰ κυρίου τοῦ υἱοῦ Στοτοήτεω[ς] [7]Στοτοήτεως [τοῦ] Στοτοήτεως ἱερέως πρώτης φυλῆς[a] Σοκνοπαίου θεοῦ [8]μεγάλου μεγά[λου ὡ]ς (ἐτῶν) λ οὐλ(ὴ) μετώπῳ ἐκ δεξιῶν καὶ Θασῆς Ὥρου τοῦ Πα-[9]νεφρύμεω[ς ὡς (ἐτῶν)] λ οὐλ(ὴ) γεννίῳ μέσῳ μετὰ κυρίου τοῦ ἑαυτῆς ἀνδρὸ[ς] [10]Πανούφεως [Ἀγχώ]φεως τοῦ Ἀγχώφεως [ἱ]ερεῖ τῆς αὐτῆς φυλῆς τοῦ αὐ-[11]τοῦ θεοῦ ὡς (ἐτῶν) λα [οὐλ(ὴ)] μετώπ(ῳ) ἐξ ἀριστερῶν Τα[ουῆ]τι Στοτοήτεως τοῦ Στοτοήτεως ὡς (ἐτῶν) μη ἀσήμῳ μετὰ [12]κυρίου τοῦ ἑαυ[τῆς ἀν]δρὸς Παβοῦτος Σαταβοῦτος τοῦ Ἁρπαγάθου ὡς (ἐτῶν) [13]{(ἐτῶν)} ξ ἀσήμῳ [ἔχειν] παρ' αὐτῆς τὰς ὁμολογούσας παρα-

9. *l.* γενείῳ. 10. *l.* ἱερέως. 13. *l.* ἀσήμου.

[a] The priests in Egyptian temples were divided into five "tribes."

one hundred and twenty-four drachmae, total 1124 dr., and that he has no claim against them up to the present day. (Signed) I, Serenus also called Claudianus, have received the sum as aforesaid.

76. RECEIPT FOR EARNEST-MONEY

A.D. 166.

The 7th year of the Emperor Caesar Marcus Aurelius Antoninus Augustus and the Emperor Caesar Lucius Aurelius Verus Augustus, Phaophi 22, through the record-office of Nilopolis in the division of Heraclides in the Arsinoite nome. Thases daughter of Stotoetis son of Horus, of the village of Socnopaei Nesus, priestess, aged about 50 years, with a scar above the left elbow, with her guardian her son Stotoetis son of Stotoetis son of Stotoetis, priest of the first tribe[a] of the twice great god Socnopaeus,[b] aged about 30 years, with a scar on the right side of the forehead, and Thases daughter of Horus son of Panephrumis, aged about 30 years, with a scar on the middle of the chin, with her guardian her husband Panouphis son of Anchophis son of Anchophis, priest of the same tribe of the same god, aged about 31 years, with a scar on the left side of the forehead, acknowledge to Taoues daughter of Stotoetis son of Stotoetis, aged about 48 years, without distinctive mark, with her guardian her husband Pabous son of Satabous son of Harpagathes, aged about 60 years, without distinctive mark, that they,

[b] A form of the crocodile-headed god Sobek. The village of Socnopaei Nesus, which was called after him, lay on the farther side of Lake Moeris in the Fayum.

χρῆμα διὰ χειρὸς ἀργυ-14ρίου κεφαλαί[ου δρα]χμὰς δεκατέσσαρες ἀρραβῶνα ἀναπόρειφον ἀπὸ τῆς 15συμπεφωνη[μένης τει]μῆς ἀργυρίου δραχμῶν εἴκοσι μιᾶς τοῦ ὑπάρχ[ον-]16τος τῆς Θασῆτος Στ[οτοήτ]εως ἕκτου μέρους ἑβδόμου μέρους οἰκίας 17οὖσα ἐν κώμ[ῃ Σοκνο]παίου Νήσου καὶ τοῦ ἐπιβάλλοντος μέρους τῆς Θα[σῆ-]18τος Ὥρου ὅσου [ἂν ᾖ] τῆς αὐτῆς οἰκίας, ἧς γίτονες τῆς ὅλης οἰκία[ς, κ]αθὼς 19ἐξυμφώνου ὑπηγ[ό]ρ[ευ]σαν, νότου εἴσοδος καὶ ἔξοδος, βορρᾶ οἰκία 20Σ[ατα]βοῦτος, λιβὸς ἑτέρων οἰκόπεδα, ἀπηλιώτου Ἀγχώφεως 21οἰκία, ὧν καὶ τὴν καταγραφὴν ποιήσωνται αἱ {ο} ὁμολογοῦσαι τῇ 22Ταουῆτι ὁπότε [ἂν] αἱρῆται, αὐτῶν λαμβανόντων παρ' αὐτῆς τὰς λοι-23πὰ[ς] τῆς τειμῆς [δρα]χμὰς ἑπτά, ἐὰν δὲ μὴι καταγράψωσι, ἐκτίσιν αὐ-24τὰς τὸν ἀρραβ[ῶν]α διπλοῦν μεθ' ἡμιολίας καὶ τόκων, γινομένης 25[τῆς] πράξεως τῇ Ταουῆτι ἔκ τε τῶν ὁμολογουσῶν καὶ ἐκ τῶν ὑπαρχόν-26των αὐταῖς π[άντω]ν καθάπερ ἐκ δίκης. ὑπογρ(αφεὺς) Στοτοῆτις Τεσενούφεως 27ὡς (ἐτῶν) [.]ε οὐλ(ὴ) ὀφρύσιν ἀμφοτέραις. (2nd hand) Θασῆς Στοτοήτεως μετὰ κυ-28ρίου τοῦ υἱοῦ Στοτοήτεως τοῦ Στοτοήτεως καὶ Θ[ασ]ῆς Ὥρου 29[μετὰ] κυρίου τοῦ ἀνδρὸς Πανούφεως Ἀγχώφεως ὁμο-30λ[ογοῦ]μεν ἔχιν παρὰ τῆς Ταουήτ[ιος] τὰς τοῦ ἀργυρίου 31δ[ρα]χμὰς δεκατέσσαρες ἀραβῶνα ἀναπόριφον τοῦ 32ἐ[πιβ]άλ[λοντο]ς Θασῆτ[ος] Ὥρου μέρος καὶ ἕκτον μέρος 33ἑβ[δ]όμου μέρους τῆς Θασῆτος Στοτοή(τεως) οὐσῶν ἐν τῇ 34πρ[ο]κειμένῃ οἰκίᾳ ὧν αἱ γιτνίαι πρόκινται καὶ κα-35τα[γρά]ψω

14. *l.* δεκατέσσαρας, so also in l. 31. 17. *l.* οὔσης, Νήσῳ. 19. *l.* ἐκ συμφώνου. 21. *l.* ποιήσονται. 32. *l.* μέρους,

the acknowledging parties, have forthwith received from her by hand the sum of 14 silver drachmae as irrepudiable earnest-money out of the 21 silver drachmae agreed upon as the price of the 6th share owned by Thases daughter of Stotoetis in the 7th share of a house standing in the village of Socnopaei Nesus and of the share, whatever it may be, falling to Thases daughter of Horus in the same house, the boundaries of the whole house being, as they have stated in agreement, on the south the entrance and exit, on the north the house of Satabous, on the west sites of other persons, on the east the house of Anchophis. The acknowledging parties will make the conveyance of their shares to Taoues whenever she chooses, they receiving from her the remaining 7 drachmae of the price ; and if they fail to make the conveyance, they shall forfeit double the earnest-money with an additional one half and interest, Taoues having the right of execution upon the acknowledging parties and all their property as if by legal decision. Signatory : Stotoetis son of Tesenouphis, aged about [.]5 years, with a scar on both eyebrows. (Signed) We, Thases daughter of Stotoetis, with my son Stotoetis son of Stotoetis as guardian, and Thases daughter of Horus, with my husband Panouphis son of Anchophis as guardian, acknowledge that we have received from Taoues the 14 drachmae of silver as irrepudiable earnest-money for the share falling to Thases daughter of Horus and the 6th part of a 7th share belonging to Thases daughter of Stotoetis in the aforesaid house, whose boundaries are stated above, and we will make the

---

ἕκτου μέρους. **33.** *l.* ὄντων. **34.** *l.* ἧς, καταγράψομεν.

ὁπότε ἐὰν αἱρῆται καθὼς πρόκειται. Στοτο-[36]ῆτ[ις] ἔγραψα ὑπὲρ αὐτῶν ἀγραμμάτ[ω]ν.

77. RECEIPT FOR SALE OF CONFISCATED PROPERTY

P. Oxy. 513. A.D. 184.

[1][Διογένης ὁ καὶ Διονύσιος Σ]αραπίωνος τοῦ Ἑρμίου [Φυλα-][2]ξιθ[α]λ[άσσειος ὁ κα]ὶ [Ἀλθα]ιεὺς Σερήνῳ Φιλίσκου τοῦ Σ[αρα-][3]πίωνος μητρὸς Ἑλένης ἀπ' Ὀξυρύγχων πόλεως χ[αίρειν]. [4]ἐπεὶ ἐκυρώθην ὑπὸ Νεμεσιανοῦ τοῦ στρατηγή-[5]σαντος τοῦ νομοῦ τῷ δευτέρῳ καὶ εἰκοστῷ [6]ἔτι Αὐρηλίου Κομμόδ[ο]υ Ἀντωνίνου [7]Καίσαρος τοῦ κυρίου μην[ὶ Ἁ]δριανοῦ ἀπὸ ἀπρά-[8]των τῆς διοικήσεως οἰκ[ίαν] καὶ αἴθριον καὶ αὐ-[9]λὴν σὺν χρηστηρίοις ὄ[ντα ἐπ'] ἀμφόδου Λυκίων [10]Παρεμβολῆς πρό-τερ[ον Σαρα]πίωνος γενομένου [11][.] . ιγ . [.]γου τεταρτ[. . . . .] τῶν τῆς συντειμή-[12][σε]ως δραχμῶν ἑξακ[οσίων κ]αὶ τῶν ἑπομένων, κ[αὶ [13]ταύ]τας παρεγράφην ὑπὸ τ[οῦ τοῦ] νομοῦ βασιλι-κοῦ [14][γραμ]ματέως Περικλέους σ[ὺ]ν προσδια-γραφομέν[οις [15]ἐν] δραχμαῖς ἑξακοσίαις τριάκοντα ἑπτὰ τριωβόλῳ [16][ὁ]μοίως καὶ ὑπὲρ τόκου δευτέρου καὶ εἰκοστοῦ ἔτους [17][δρ]αχ(μὰς) τριάκοντα ἐννέα τριώβολον ἡμιωβέλ(ιον) χαλ(κοῦς) τ[ρῖς] καὶ τρίτου καὶ εἰκ[ο-[18]στο]ῦ ἔτους δραχμὰς εἴκοσι ὀκτὼ ὀβολ(οὺς) δύο [ἡ]μιωβέλ(ιον), γίνονται τό-[19][κου] δραχμαὶ ἑξήκο[ν]τα ὀκτὼ χαλκοῖ τρῖς, διέγραψα δὲ εἰς τὸ [20][δημ]όσιον τὰς τῆς τειμῆς τῆς οἰκίας σύνπαντι [21][δρ]αχμὰς ἑξακοσίας τριάκοντα ἑπτὰ

conveyance whenever she chooses as aforesaid. I, Stotoetis, have written for them, as they are illiterate.

77. RECEIPT FOR SALE OF CONFISCATED PROPERTY

A.D. 184.

Diogenes also called Dionysius son of Sarapion son of Hermias, of the Phylaxithalassian tribe and the Althaean deme,[a] to Serenus son of Philiscus son of Sarapion and of Helena, of Oxyrhynchus, greeting. Whereas in the 22nd year of Aurelius Commodus Antoninus Caesar the lord, in the month Hadrianus,[b] I was assigned by Nemesianus, then strategus of the nome, from the unsold property of the Treasury a house with central court and yard, with the fixtures, in the quarter of the Lycians' Camp, previously owned by Sarapion, late . . ., at the assessment price of 600 drachmae and the extra charges, and whereas I was registered by the royal scribe of the nome, Pericles, as owing this sum together with the additional charges, making 637 drachmae 3 obols, and likewise for interest for the 22nd year 39 drachmae 3½ obols 3 chalci,[c] and as interest for the 23rd year 28 drachmae 2½ obols, making a total of 68 drachmae 3 chalci for interest, and whereas I paid to the account of the State as the price of the house in all 637

[a] See No. 32, note *b*. [b] = the Egyptian Choiak.
[c] 1 obol = 8 chalci.

7. *l.* 'Α]δριανῷ.

τριώβολον 22[ὁμο]ίως καὶ τὸν τόκον τὸν [ὀ]ν[ό]ματί μου παραγρα-23[φέ]ντα ὄν‹τα› ἐν δραχμαῖς ἑξή-κ[ο]ντα ὀκτὼ χαλκοῖς τρισί, ὧν 24[κα]ὶ τὰ σύμβολα ἐπὶ ὑπογραφῆς μου τοῦ Διογένους τοῦ 25[κ]αὶ Διονυσίου ἀνέδωκα σ[οὶ τῷ Σ]ερήνῳ ἕνεκα τοῦ ὑ-26[π]ερβεβλῆσθαι τὴν προκειμένην οἰκίαν ὑπὸ σοῦ 27[το]ῦ Σερήνου καὶ ἀναβεβι‹βά›σθαι εἰς δραχμὰς χειλίας 28[ὀκ]τακοσίας καὶ παραδεδόσθαι σοι ταύτην ἐξ ἐπιστο-29[λῆς τ]οῦ κρατίστου διοικητοῦ Οὐεστι-δίου Ῥ[ο]υφείν[ο]υ 30[. . . . .] . [.]ς τοῦ σ[τ]ρατη-γήσαντος τῷ ἐνεστῶτι τετ[ά]ρ-31[τ]ῳ καὶ εἰκοστῷ ἔτει Μεχεὶρ τριακάδι τῶν δραχμῶν 32[χ]ειλίων ὀκτακοσίων καὶ τῶν ἑπο[μ]ένων καὶ τὸν 33βασι[λι]-κὸν παρα[γ]εγραφέναι σε ἀκολούθως ᾧ με-34τέδω-κεν προσγράφῳ μετὰ τὰς διαγραφείσας ὑπ' ἐμοῦ 35[δ]ραχμὰς ἑξακοσίας τὰς λοιπὰς δραχμὰς χειλίας δια-36κοσίας καὶ τὰ τούτων προσδιαγραφόμενα, ὁμολογῶ 37[κ]ατὰ προσφώνησιν Ἐπιμάχου ἀσχο-λουμένου ὠνὴν τῆς 38[ἐπ]ὶ τοῦ πρὸς Ὀξυρύγχων πόλει Σαραπείου τραπέζης ἀπεσ-39[χηκ]έναι με παρὰ σοῦ ἃς διέγραψα ὡς πρόκειται ὑπὲρ μὲν 40[τιμῆ]ς καὶ προσδιαγραφομένων δραχμὰς ἑξα-κοσίας τριά-41[κον]τα ἑπτὰ ‹τριώβολον› ὑπὲρ δὲ τόκου δραχμὰς ἑξήκοντα ὀκτὼ 42[χαλ(κοῦς) τρῖς], τὰς ἐπὶ τὸ αὐτὸ δραχμὰς ἑπτακοσίας πέντε τριώ-βολον χαλκοῦς 43[τρῖς, καὶ μη]δέν σοι ἐνκαλεῖν μηδὲ ἐνκαλέσειν μήτε 44[περὶ το]ύτων μηδὲ περὶ ἄλλου μηδενὸς ἁπλῶς μεχρὶ 45[τῆς ἐν]εστώσης, καὶ ἐάν τις ζήτησις περὶ τούτου πρὸς σὲ γέ-46[νηται] ἢ τοὺς παρὰ σοῦ μεταλημψομένους ἐγὼ αὐτὸς τοῦ-47[το ἀν]αδέξομαι. παρὼν δὲ ὁ πατήρ μου Σαρα-πίων Ἑρμίου τ[οῦ 48Ἑ]ρμίου Σ]ωσικόσμιος ὁ καὶ

drachmae 3 obols and likewise the interest entered against me to the amount of 68 drachmae 3 chalci, the receipts for which payments with the signature of me, Diogenes also called Dionysius, I have delivered to you, Serenus, because you have made a higher bid for the aforesaid house, raising the price to 1800 drachmae, and it has been made over to you by a letter of his excellency the dioecetes, Ventidius Rufinus . . ., ex-strategus, in the present 24th year on Mecheir 30 for the 1800 drachmae and the extra charges, and the royal scribe has debited you in accordance with the supplementary note which he issued, after deducting the 600 drachmae paid by me, with the remaining 1200 drachmae and the additional charges, I acknowledge that according to a communication from Epimachus who farms the bank[a] at the Serapeum by Oxyrhynchus I have received from you the sums which I paid as aforesaid, for the price and the additional charges 637 drachmae 3 obols and for interest 68 drachmae 3 chalci, making a total of 705 drachmae 3 obols 3 chalci, and that I neither make nor will make any claim against you with regard to this or any other matter whatever up to the present day, and if any action is brought against you or your assigns with regard to this, I will take the responsibility upon myself. My father, Sarapion son of Hermias son of Hermias, of the

[a] The bank was government property farmed out to the highest bidder.

29. *l.* Οὐεντιδίου.

Ἀλθαιεὺς ⟦ὁ⟧ εὐδο[κ]εῖ το[ῖ]ς [49][προκ]ειμένοις. κυρία ἡ ἀποχή. (ἔτους) κδ Αὐτοκράτορος Καίσαρος [50][Μάρκο]υ Α[ὐρ]ηλίου Κομμόδου Ἀντωνίνου Σεβαστοῦ Εὐσεβοῦς [51][Ἀρμενι]ακοῦ Μηδικοῦ Παρθικοῦ Σαρματικοῦ Γερμανικοῦ Μεγίστου [52][Ἐπεὶφ δ̅] (2nd hand) Διογένης ὁ καὶ Διονύσιος Σαραπίωνος Φυλαξιθα-[53][λάσσε]ιος ὁ καὶ Ἀλθαιεὺς ἀπέσχον παρὰ τοῦ Σερήνου τὰς [54][προκειμένας] ἐπὶ τὸ αὐτὸ δραχμὰς ἑπτακοσίας [55][πέντε τρι]ώβολον χαλκοῦς τρεῖς πλήρης καὶ οὐ-[56][δὲν αὐτ]ῷ ἐνκαλῶ οὔτε περὶ τούτου οὔτε περὶ ἄλλου [57][οὐδε]νὸς ἁπλῶς ὡς πρόκειται, καὶ ἐάν τις ζήτη-[58][σις] περὶ τούτου γένηται πρὸς αὐτὸν ἢ τοὺς αὐτοῦ [59][ἐγὼ] αὐτὸς τοῦτ[ο] ἀναδέξομαι. (3rd hand) Σερῆνος Φιλίσκου τοῦ Σαρα-[60][πίωνος] μητρὸς Ἑλένη[ς ε]ὐδοκῶ τοῖς προκειμένοις κ[αὶ] ἔσχον τὰ [61][σύμβ]ολα ἐφ' ὑπο[γραφῆς] σου [ὡς πρό]κειται. (4th hand) Σαραπίων [62][Ἑρ]μίου τοῦ Ἑρ[μίου Σωσικόσ]μιος ὁ καὶ [Ἀλ-[63]θ]αιεὺς εὐδο[κῶ πᾶσι τοῖς προ]κειμέ[νοις. (5th hand) [64]Ἐ]πεὶφ δ . [. . . . .] . ι κολλ . [. . . .] [65]κεχρη(μάτισται ?) [

78. RECEIPT FOR A MUMMY

P. Hamb. 74. A.D. 173 or 174.

[1][Ὁ δεῖνα] τῶν ἀπὸ Ἀχω-[2][. . . . .]είτου νομοῦ [3][κυβερνήτης πλο]ίου νεκρηγοῦ [4][τῷ δεῖνι χ]αίριν. ὁμολογῶ παρει-[5][ληφέναι παρ]ὰ σοῦ σῶμα εἱλισμένον [6][. . . . ., ὃ]ν καὶ ἀποκαταστήσω [7][εἰς ὅρμον] Κερκὴ τοῦ

Sosicosmian tribe and the Althaean deme, being present consents to the above statement. This receipt is valid. The 24th year of the Emperor Caesar Marcus Aurelius Commodus Antoninus Augustus Pius Armeniacus Medicus Parthicus Sarmaticus Germanicus Maximus, Epeiph 4. (Signed) I, Diogenes also called Dionysius son of Sarapion, of the Phylaxithalassian tribe and the Althaean deme, have received from Serenus the aforesaid total of 705 drachmae 3 obols 3 chalci in full, and I neither make nor will make any claim against him with regard to this or any other matter whatever as aforesaid, and if any action is brought against him or his with regard to this, I will take the responsibility upon myself. I, Serenus son of Philiscus son of Sarapion and of Helena, consent to the above statement and have received the receipts with your signature as aforesaid. I, Sarapion son of Hermias son of Hermias, of the Sosicosmian tribe and the Althaean deme, consent to all the above. (Subscribed) Epeiph 4, registered . . .

78. RECEIPT FOR A MUMMY

A.D. 173 or 174.

. . ., inhabitant of Acho . . . in the . . . nome, pilot of a boat for carrying corpses, to . . . greeting. I acknowledge that I have received from you the bandaged mummy of . . ., whom I will transport to the harbour of Kerke in the Memphite nome

Μεμφείτου νομοῦ 8[καὶ παρα]δώσω Θακάρις ἐνταφια-9[στῇ, καὶ ν]αύλου καὶ τέλους καὶ πάσης 10[δαπάνης] τοῦ πλοίου τὸ συμπεφω-11[νημένο]ν ναῦλον, ὃ καὶ ἀπέσχον. 12[(ἔτους) ιγ (or ιδ) Α]ὐτοκράτορος Καίσαρος Μάρκου 13[Αὐρηλί]ου Ἀντωνείνου Σεβαστοῦ Ἀρμε-14[νιακοῦ Μη]δικοῦ Παρθικοῦ Γερμανικοῦ 15[Μεγίστο]υ Φ[α]ρμοῦθ[ι . .].

8. *l*. Θακάρει.

79. RECEIPT FOR WAGES FOR NURSING

P. Oxy. 91. A.D. 187.

1Χωσίων Σαραπίωνος τοῦ Ἁρποκρα-2τίωνος μητρὸς Σαραπιάδος ἀπ' Ὀξυρύγ-3χων πόλεως Ταναντήρει Θώνιος τοῦ 4Θώνιος μητρὸς Ζωΐλοῦτος ἀπὸ τῆς αὐ-5τῆς πόλεως, μετὰ κυρίου Δημητρίου Ὡρί-6ωνος μητρὸς Ἀρσινόης ἀπὸ τῆς αὐτῆς 7πόλεως, χαίρειν. ὁμολογῶ ἀπεσχηκέναι 8παρὰ σοῦ διὰ Ἡλιοδώρου καὶ τῶν σὺν αὐ-9τῷ ἐπιτηρητῶν τῆς ἐπὶ τοῦ πρὸς Ὀξυ-10ρύγχων πόλει Σαραπείου τραπέζης, 11ἧς ὑπόσχεσις ἐδόθη ὑπὸ Ἐπιμάχου, 12ἀργυρίου Σεβαστοῦ νομίσματος δρα-13χμὰς τετρακοσίας, οὔσας ὑπὲρ τρο-14φείων καὶ ἐλαίου καὶ ἱματισμοῦ καὶ 15τῆς ἄλλης δαπάνης πάσης ἐτῶν δύο 16ὧν ἐτρόφευσεν ἡ δούλη μου Σαραπιὰς 17τὴν θυγατέρα σου Ἑλένην χρηματί-18ζουσαν ἐξ οὗ, ἣν καὶ παρείληφας ἀπο-19γεγαλακτισμένην καὶ τετευχυῖαν 20πάσης ἐπιμελείας, καὶ μηδέν σοι 21ἐνκαλεῖν μηδὲ ἐνκαλέσειν μηδὲ 22ἐπελεύσεσθαι μήτε περὶ τούτων 23μηδὲ περὶ ἄλλου μηδενὸς ἁπλῶς 24μέχρι τῆς ἐνεστώσης ἡμ[έ]ρας. 25κυρία ἡ ἀποχή. (ἔτους)

and deliver to Thakaris, funeral undertaker, and for freight and toll and all expenses of the boat the fee agreed upon, which I have received. The 13th[a] year of the Emperor Caesar Marcus Aurelius Antoninus Augustus Armeniacus Medicus Parthicus Germanicus Maximus, Pharmouthi . . .

[a] Or 14th.

79. RECEIPT FOR WAGES FOR NURSING

A.D. 187.

Chosion son of Sarapion son of Harpocration, his mother being Sarapias, of Oxyrhynchus, to Tanenteris daughter of Thonis son of Thonis, her mother being Zoilous, of the said city, with her guardian Demetrius son of Horion and Arsinoe, of the said city, greeting. I acknowledge that I have received from you through Heliodorus and his fellow supervisors of the bank at the Serapeum by Oxyrhynchus, for which Epimachus issued the promise of payment, 400 silver drachmae of Imperial coin for nurse's wages, oil, clothing, and all other expenses of the two years for which my slave Sarapias nursed your daughter Helena, styled as daughter of her male parent,[a] whom you have received back after having been weaned and treated with every attention, and that I neither make nor will make any claim upon you nor will take any proceedings about this or about any other matter whatsoever up to the present day. This receipt is valid. The 28th year of the Emperor

[a] The scribe had not troubled to find out the father's name.

κη ^{26}Αὐτοκράτορος Κα[ί]σαρος Μάρκου ^{27}Αὐρηλίου Κομ[μ]όδου Ἀντωνίνο[υ] ^{28}Εὐσεβοῦς Εὐτυχοῦς Σεβαστοῦ ^{29}Ἀρμενιακοῦ Μηδι[κ]οῦ Παρθικοῦ ^{30}Σαρματικοῦ Γερμανικοῦ Μεγίστου ^{31}Βρεταννικοῦ Φαῶφι ιε. (2nd hand) Χωσίων ^{32}Σαραπίωνος ἀπέσχον τὰς ^{33}τῶν τροφείων δραχμὰς ^{34}τετρακοσίας καὶ οὐδὲν ἐνκα-^{35}λῶ ὡς πρόκειται. [Τ]ανεντῆρις ^{36}Θώνιος μετὰ κ[υ]ρίου Δημη-^{37}τρίου Ὡρίωνος εὐδοκῶ κ[αὶ] ^{38}παρείληφα τὴν θυγατέρ[α] ^{39}ὡς πρόκιται. Πλουτίων Ἑρμ[οῦ] ^{40}ἔγραψα ὑ[πὲρ αὐ]τῶ[ν] μὴ ε[ἰδότων γράμματα].

80. RECEIPT FOR PART OF A WATER-WHEEL

P. Oxy. 1900. A.D. 528.

^{1} ☧ Ὑπατίᾳ τοῦ δεσπότου ἡμῶν Φλαουίο[υ Ἰουστινιανοῦ] ^{2}τοῦ αἰωνίου Αὐγούστου ‹τὸ β´› Φαῶφι κζ ἰνδ(ικτίονος) ζ ἐν Ὀξυ[ρ(υγχιτῶν)]. ^{3}τῇ ἁγίᾳ τοῦ θεοῦ καθολικῇ ἐκκ[λ]ησίᾳ τῇ [ὑ]π[ὸ] ^{4}τὸν ἁγιώτατον καὶ θεοφιλέστατον πατέρα ἡμ[ῶν] ^{5}ἀββᾶ Πέτρον ἐπίσκοπον ταύτης τῆς λαμπρᾶς Ὀ[ξυρ-]^{6}υγχιτῶν πόλεως δ[ι]ὰ σοῦ τοῦ εὐλαβεστάτου Φὶβ ^{7}πρεσβυτέρου καὶ καθολικοῦ οἰκονό‹μο›υ Αὐρήλιος ^{8}Ψεεῖς υἱὸς Φοιβάμμωνος μητρὸς Θέκλας ἀπὸ ^{9}ἐποικίου Κωλώτου κτήματος τῆς αὐτῆς καθ[ο-]^{10}λικῆς ἐκκλησίας τοῦ Ὀξυρυγχίτου νομοῦ ἐναπόγρα-^{11}φως γεωργὸς χαίρειν. χρείας καὶ νῦν γεναμένης ^{12}εἰς τὴν ὑφ᾽ ἐμὲ ἐκκλησιαστικὴν μηχανὴν καλουμέ-^{13}νην Ἀγροικικοῖς ἀντλοῦσαν εἰς ἄμπελον καὶ εἰς ^{14}ἀρώσιμον γῆν ἄξονος ἑνός, ἀνελθὼν ἐπὶ τῆς ^{15}[πό]λεως ἠξίωσα τὴν ὑμῶν

10. *l.* ἐναπόγραφος. 12. = ὑπ᾽ ἐμέ.

Caesar Marcus Aurelius Commodus Antoninus Pius Felix Augustus Armeniacus Medicus Parthicus Sarmaticus Germanicus Maximus Britannicus, Phaophi 15. (Signed) I, Chosion son of Sarapion, have received the 400 drachmae forming the nurse's wages, and I make no claim as stated above. I, Tanenteris daughter of Thonis, with my guardian Demetrius son of Horion, assent, and I have received back my daughter as stated above. I, Plution son of Hermes, have written for them, as they are illiterate.

80. RECEIPT FOR PART OF A WATER-WHEEL

A.D. 528.

In the 2nd year of the consulship of our master Flavius Justinianus the eternal Augustus, Phaophi 27, 7th indiction, at Oxyrhynchus. To the holy principal church of God under our most holy and pious father Abbot Peter, bishop of this illustrious city of Oxyrhynchus, through you the most discreet Phib, presbyter and principal steward, Aurelius Pseeis son of Phoebammon and Thecla, of the hamlet of Colotes, a holding of the said principal church in the Oxyrhynchite nome, enrolled as cultivator,[a] greeting. There being need just now of one axle for the church's machine under my charge, which is called "In the Rustics"[b] and draws water for vine-land and arable land, I went up to the city and asked your piety

[a] These enrolled cultivators were bondsmen attached to the soil. See No. 26.

[b] The water-wheels are sometimes distinguished by special names.

θεοφιλείαν ὥστ[ε 16κε]λεῦσαί μοι παρασχεθῆναι τὸν αὐτὸν ἄξονα, 17[καὶ] εὐθέως ἡ ὑμῶν θεοφιλεία πρόνοιαν 18[ποιου]μένη τῆς συστάσεως τῶν ἐκκλησίας 19[πραγ]μάτων τοῦτον παρέσχετό μοι διὰ τ[οῦ εὐλαβε-20στάτο]υ Λουκᾶ μονάζοντος καινὸν [ἐπιτήδειον 21ἀντλη]τικὸν εὐάρεστον. ἐδεξάμ{εν}ην ε[ἰς ἀνα-22πλήρω]σιν πάντων τῶν μηχανικῶν ὀρ[γάνων 23ἐν τῇ σή]μερον ἡμέρᾳ ἥτις ἐστὶν Φαῶφι [εἰκὰς ἑβ-24δόμη τ]οῦ ἐνεστῶτος ἔτους σε ροδ τῆς πα[ρούσης 25ἑβδόμ]ης ἰνδ(ικτίονος) ὑδροπαροχείας δὲ καρπῶν τ[ῆς ὀγδόης 26ἐπινεμή]σεως, καὶ πρὸς ἀπόδειξιν τῆς ὑ[ποδοχῆς 27ταύτη]ν πεποίημαι τὴν χειρογραφείαν ἥτ[ις κυρία 28ἐστὶ ἁπ]λ(ῆ) γραφ(εῖσα) καὶ ἐπ[ε]ρ(ωτηθεὶς) ὡμολόγησα. ☧ [Αὐρήλιος 29Ψεεῖς υἱὸ]ς Φοιβάμμωνος ὁ προγεγραμ[μένος 30πεποίημ]αι τὴν χειρογραφείαν ὑποδεξά[μενος τὸν 31εἰρημέν]ον ἄξονα καὶ συμφωνῖ μοι πάντα [τὰ ἐγγεγραμμ(ένα) 32ὡς πρόκει]ται. Αὐρήλιος Φιλόξενος υἱὸς τοῦ μα[καρίου 33 . . . ἔγρ]αψα ὑπὲρ αὐτοῦ ἀγραμμ(άτου) ὄντος. 34 ⳩ *di emu Philoxenu etelioth(e)* . . [

Verso 35+χειρογραφ(ία) Ψεε(ῖς) υἱοῦ Φοιβάμμωνος ἀπὸ ἐποικ(ίου) Κ[ω]λ[ώτου ὑποδοχ(ῆς) ἄξονος ἑνός].

81. RECEIPT FOR ANNUAL OFFERING TO A MONASTERY

P.S.I. 786. A.D. 581.

1+Βασιλ[είας τοῦ θειο]τάτου [κα]ὶ εὐσε-2βεστάτου ‹ἡμῶν δεσπότου› με[γίστου εὐερ]γέτου

to order the said axle to be supplied to me; and straightway your piety, taking thought for the state of the church's property, supplied this to me through the most discreet monk Luke, a new, serviceable one, suitable for irrigation and satisfactory; and I have received it in completion of all the mechanical implements[a] on this 27th day of Phaophi of the current 205th, which is the 174th year, in the present seventh indiction for the irrigation of the crops of the eighth indiction, and in declaration of the receipt I have made this deed, which is valid and which is written in one copy only, and in answer to the formal question I have given my assent. (Signed) I, Aurelius Pseeis son of Phoebammon, the above-mentioned, have made the deed after receiving the said axle, and I agree to all that is written therein, as aforesaid. I, Aurelius Philoxenus son of the late . . . have written for him, as he is illiterate. (Subscribed) Executed by me, Philoxenus . . . (Endorsed) Deed of Pseeis son of Phoebammon, of the hamlet of Colotes, concerning receipt of one axle.

[a] The writer probably means that all the parts of the water-wheel were now complete.

81. RECEIPT FOR ANNUAL OFFERING TO A MONASTERY

A.D. 581.

The 6th year of the reign of our most godlike and pious master and greatest benefactor Flavius

Φλα(ουίου) Τιβερίου [3]Κωνσταντίν[ου τοῦ] αἰωνίου Αὐγούστου καὶ Αὐτοκρ(άτορος) [4]ἔτους ς̄, ὑπατίας τοῦ αὐτοῦ εὐσεβ(εστάτου) ἡμῶν [5]δεσπότου ἔτους β̄, Τῦβι ζ̄, ἰνδ(ικτίονος) ιδ. [6]κληρονόμοις τ[οῦ τ]ῆ[ς λ]ογίας μνήμης [7]Γεροντίου γενομένο[υ σ]χολαστικοῦ διὰ [8]'Ανοὺπ τοῦ θα[υ]μασιωτάτου αὐτῶν {δι} οἰκ(ονόμου) [9]Κόλλουθος μονάζ(ων) τοῦ ὄρους κώμ(ης) [10]Βερκὺ υἱὸς Γεωργίου. ἔσχον καὶ ἐπληρ(ώθην) [11]παρὰ τῆς ὑμῶν θαυμα(σιότητος) τὴν ἐξ ἔθους [12]ἁγίαν προσφορὰν διδομένην εἰς τὸ αὐτὸ [13]ὄρος ἐπὶ τῆς παρελθούσης [14]τρεισκαιδεκάτης ἰνδ(ικτίονος) τὰ αἱροῦντά μοι [15]πλήρης, ὅ ἐστιν χρυσοῦ νομίσματα [16]ἓξ ἰδιωτικ(ῷ) ζυγῷ, γί(νεται) χρ(υσ.) νο(μ.) ς ἰδ(ι.) [17]ζυγ(ῷ), καὶ πρὸς ἀπόδειξιν τῆς [18]προσφορᾶς ταύτην πεποίημαι [19]τὴν ἀπόδειξ(ιν), ἥτις κυρ(ία) οὖσα ἁπλ(ῆ) [20]γραφ(εῖσα), καὶ ἐπερ(ωτηθεὶς) ὡμολ(όγησα). + Κόλλουθος [21]μονάζ(ων) υἱὸς Γεωργίου στοιχεῖ μοι [22]αὕτη ἡ ἀπόδειξ(ις) ὡς πρόκ(ειται). Παπνούτιο(ς) [23]ἀξ(ιωθεὶς) ἔγραψα ὑπὲρ αὐτοῦ ἀγραμμάτ(ου) ὄντος. (2nd hand) [24]Κολλούθου στηχῖ μα. (1st hand) [25]+ δι' ἐμοῦ ἐγράφη +

Verso: [26]+ ἀπόδειξ(ις) Κολλούθου μονά[ζοντος] το[ῦ ὄρους] [27]κώμ(ης) Βερκὺ χρ(υσοῦ) νο(μισμάτων) ς ἰδ(ιωτικῷ).

19. οὖσα for ἐστίν. 24. *l.* Κόλλουθος στοιχεῖ μοι.

Tiberius Constantinus the eternal Augustus and Imperator, the 2nd year of the consulship of our said most pious master, Tubi 7, 14th indiction. To the heirs of Gerontius of learned memory, the late advocate, through Anoup, their most admirable steward, from Colluthus, monk of the desert monastery of the village Berku, son of George. I have received in full satisfaction from your excellencies the customary holy offering[a] given for the said monastery, being the instalments due to me in the past 13th indiction fully paid, namely six gold solidi on the private standard, total 6 gold sol. on the private standard, and in acknowledgement of the offering I have made this acknowledgement, which is valid, written in a single copy, and in answer to the formal question I have given my assent. (Signed) I, Colluthus, monk, son of George, agree to this acknowledgement, as stated above. I, Papnoutius, wrote for him at his request, as he is illiterate. (In Colluthus's hand) I, Colluthus, agree. Written by me. (Endorsed) Acknowledgement of Colluthus, monk of the desert monastery of the village Berku, for 6 gold solidi on the private standard.

[a] Probably a pious bequest made by Gerontius.

III. WILLS

82. AN EARLY PTOLEMAIC WILL

P. Eleph. 2, ll. 1-18. 284 B.C.

[1]Βασιλεύοντος Πτολεμαίου (ἔτους) μ μηνὸς Γορπιαίου, ἐφ' ἱερέως Μενελάου τοῦ Λαάγου. συγγρα-[2]φὴ καὶ ὁμολογία. τάδε διέθετο Διονύσιος Τημνίτης Καλλίσται Τημνίτει τῆι αὑτοῦ γυναι-[3]κί. ἐὰν δέ τι πάσχηι Διονύσιος, καταλείπειν τὰ ὑπάρχοντα αὑτοῦ πάντα Καλλίσται καὶ κυρίαν [4]εἶναι τῶν ὑπαρχόντων πάντων μέχρι ἂν ζῆι. ἐὰν δέ τι πάσχηι Καλλίστα Διονυσίου ζῶντος, [5]κύριον εἶναι Διονύσιον τῶν ὑπαρχόντων· ἐὰν δέ τι πάσχηι Διονύσιος, καταλειπέτω τὰ ὑπάρχοντα [6]πᾶσιν τοῖς υἱοῖς τοῖς αὑτοῦ. κατὰ ταὐτὰ δὲ καὶ Καλλίστα, ἐάν τι πάσχηι, καταλειπέτω τὰ ὑ-[7]πάρχοντα πᾶσι τοῖς υἱοῖς πλὴν τῶν μερῶν ὧν ἂν λαμβάνωσι παρὰ Διονυσίου καὶ Καλλίστας ἐργαζό-[8]μενοι Βάκχιος, Ἡρακλείδης, Μητρόδωρος, τοῦ πατρὸς ζῶντος καὶ τῆς μητρός· γημάντων δὲ καὶ κα-[9]ταχωρισθέντων Βακχίου, Ἡρακλείδου, Μητροδώρου, ἔστω τὰ ὑπάρχοντα τὰ Διονυσίου καὶ Καλλίσ-[10]τας κοινὰ πάντων τῶν υἱῶν. ἐὰν

---

[a] This includes the 20 years during which Ptolemy I. was content with the title of satrap.

III. WILLS

82. AN EARLY PTOLEMAIC WILL

284 B.C.

In the 40th year[a] of the reign of Ptolemy, the month Gorpiaeus, Menelaus[b] son of Lagus being priest. Contract and agreement. Dionysius, Temnian, has made this testamentary pact with his wife Callista, Temnian. Should aught happen to Dionysius, he shall leave all his property to Callista and she shall be owner of all the property so long as she lives. Should aught happen to Callista while Dionysius is alive, Dionysius shall be owner of the property; and should aught happen to Dionysius, he shall leave the property to all his sons. In like manner Callista, should aught happen to her, shall leave the property to all the sons, except[c] the portions which Bacchius, Heraclides and Metrodorus may receive from Dionysius and Callista for their labours in the lifetime of their father and mother; but if Bacchius, Heraclides and Metrodorus are married and settled, the property of Dionysius and Callista shall be shared in common by all the sons. If in

[b] See No. 34, note c.

[c] This exception is to be understood as qualifying the preceding sentence also.

δέ τι ἐξαπορῶνται ἢ χρέος ὀφείλωσιν Διονύσιος ἢ Καλλίστα ζῶντες, [11]τρεφέτωσαν αὐτοὺς οἱ υἱεῖς πάντες κοινῆι καὶ συναποτινέτωσαν τὰ χρέα πάντες. ἐὰν δέ τις αὐτῶν [12]μὴ θέληι ἢ τράφειν ἢ συναποτίνειν ἢ μὴ συνθάπτωσιν, ἀποτεισάτω ἀργυρίου δραχμὰς χιλίας, [13]καὶ ἡ πρᾶξις ἔστω ἐκ τοῦ ἀτακτοῦντος καὶ μὴ ποιοῦντος κατὰ τὰ γεγραμμένα. ἐὰν δὲ [14]καταλείπωσιν Διονύσιος ἢ Καλλίστα χρέος τι, ἐξέστω τοῖς υἱοῖς μὴ ἐμβατεύειν ἐὰμ μὴ βούλων-[15]ται τελευτήσαντος Διονυσίου καὶ Καλλίστας. ἡ δὲ συγγραφὴ ἥδε κυρία ἔστω πάντηι πάντως [16]ὅπου ἂν ἐπιφέρηται, ὡς ἐκεῖ τοῦ συναλλάγματος γεγενημένου. τὴν δὲ συγγραφὴν ἑκόντες ἔθεν-[17]το παρὰ συγγραφοφύλακα Ἡράκλειτον. μάρτυρες Πολυκράτης Ἀρκάς, Ἀνδροσθένης Κῶιος, [18]Νουμήνιος Κρής, Σιμωνίδης Μαρωνίτης, Λύσις, Ἡράκλειτος Τημνῖται. Below, the duplicate or outer text. On the verso, names and seals of the five principals and the six witnesses.

83. WILL OF A SOLDIER

P. Grenf. i. 21. 126 B.C.

[1][Ἔτους μδ Παῦνι θ̄, ἐν Παθύρει ἐπ'] Ἀσκληπιάδου ἀγορανόμου. τάδε διέθετο ὑγιαίνων νοῶν φρονῶν Δρύτων Παμφίλου Κρὴς τῶν διαδόχων καὶ [2][τοῦ ἐπιτάγματος ἱππάρχη]ς ἐπ' ἀνδρῶν. ε[ἴ]η μέμ μοι ὑγιαίνοντι τῶν ἐμαυτοῦ κύριον εἶναι, ἐὰν δέ τι ἀνθρώπινον πάθω, καταλείπω καὶ [3][δίδωμι τὰ ὑπάρχοντά μοι ἔγγαι]ά τε καὶ ἔπιπλα καὶ κτήνη καὶ ὅσα ἂν προσεπικτήσωμαι, τὸν μὲν

their lifetime Dionysius or Callista is in need or in debt, all the sons in common shall support them and contribute to pay their debts. If any one of them refuses to support them or contribute or does not help to bury them, he shall forfeit 1000 drachmae of silver and there shall be right of execution on him who is insubordinate and does not act in the manner stated. If Dionysius or Callista leaves any debt, it shall be permissible for their sons not to take up the inheritance if they do not wish to after the death of Dionysius and Callista. This contract shall be valid in every respect wherever it is produced, as if the compact had been made there. They have of their own free will placed the contract in the keeping of Heraclitus. Witnesses: Polycrates, Arcadian; Androsthenes, Coan; Numenius, Cretan; Simonides, Maronean; Lysis and Heraclitus, Temnians.

83. WILL OF A SOLDIER

126 B.C.

The 44th year, Pauni 9, at Pathyris, before Asclepiades the agoranomus. Dryton son of Pamphilus, Cretan, one of the *diadochi* [a] and belonging to the reserve,[b] hipparch over men,[b] being sound of body, sane and sensible, has made the following will. May it be mine to own my property in good health, but if I should suffer the lot of man, I bequeath and give my property in land and movable objects and cattle and whatever else I may have acquired,

[a] An honorific title.

[b] Makeshift translations; the exact meaning of the phrases is unknown.

ἵππον ἐφ' οὗ στρατεύομαι καὶ τὰ ὅπλα [4][πάντα Ἐσθλάδηι, τῶι ἐξ ἐμ]οῦ καὶ ἐξ Σαραπιάδος τῆς Ἐσθλάδου τοῦ Θέωνος ἀστῆς ἧι συνήμην γυναικί, κατὰ νόμους καὶ κατὰ διαθήκην [5][τὴν κεχρηματισμένην] διὰ τοῦ ἐν Διὸς πό(λει) τῆι μι(κρᾶι) ἀρχείου ἐπὶ Διονυσίου ἀγορανόμου ἐν τῶι ϛ (ἔτει) ἐπὶ τοῦ Φιλομήτορος, ἧ διασαφεῖ τά τε ἄλλα [6][καὶ ἐπίτροπον . . . .]ν ὄντα συγγενῆι κατέστησεν, καὶ ἀπὸ τῶν οἰκετικῶν σωμάτων δ̄, ὧν ὀνόματα Μυρσίνην καὶ ταύτης [7][τὰ γ̄ παιδία, τὰ δὲ] λοιπὰ θ[ηλ]υκὰ β αἷς ὀνόματα Εἰρήνην καὶ Ἀμπέλιον Ἀπολλωνίαι καὶ ταῖς ἀδ(ελφαῖς) οὔσι ε̄, καὶ τὸν ὑπάρχοντά μοι ἐπὶ τοῦ [8][. . . . .] τοῦ Πα[θυ]ρ(ίτου) ἔδα(φος) ἀμπελῶ(νος) καὶ τὰ ἐν τούτωι φρέατα ἐξ ὀπτῆς πλί(νθου) καὶ τἆλλα συνκύροντα καὶ τὴν ἅμαξαν σὺν τῆι [9][ἐπισκευῆι καὶ τὸν περιστ]ερῶνα κ[αὶ] τὸν ἄλλον ἡμιτέλεστον καὶ αὐλήν, ὧν γείτονες νό(του) ψιλοὶ <τόποι> τοῦ αὐ(τοῦ) Ἐσθλάδου, βο(ρρᾶ) οἶκος κεκαμαρωμένος Ἀπολλω(νίας) τῆς νεω(τέρας), [10][ἀπη]λι(ώτου) τόπ[ος ψιλὸ]ς Πετρασ[. .]ι τοῦ Ἐσθλά[δο]υ, λι(βὸς) ψιλὸς τόπος Ἐσθλάδου ἕως τῆ[ς] ἀνεῳγμένης θύ(ρας) ἐπὶ λίβα. τοὺς δὲ λο(ιποὺς) οἴκους καὶ χρητῆρας [11][. . . .] . λλιαν[. . . . .] καὶ ψιλὸν τόπον εἰς [π]εριστερῶνα ἀποδεδειγμένον ὑποκάτω τῆς Ἐσθλά(δου) θύ(ρας) καὶ ἀπὸ λι(βὸς) τῆς καμάρας δίδωμι [12][Ἀπολ]λωνίαι καὶ Ἀριστοῖ καὶ Ἀφροδισίαι καὶ Νι[κα]ρίωι καὶ Ἀπολλωνίαι νεωτέραι οὔσι ε̄ ταῖς ἐξ ἐμοῦ καὶ ἐξ Ἀπολλωνίας τῆς καὶ Σεμμώνθιος [13][ἧι σύ]νειμι γυ(ναικί), κατὰ

5. Revised and restored by E.-H.: π]αρά Ed. 6 and 7. Restored by E.-H. 7. *l.* οὔσαις (so in l. 12), τὸ ὑπάρχον.

first my war-horse and all my armour to Esthladas my son by my former wife Sarapias daughter of Esthladas son of Theon, of civic rank,[a] in accordance with the laws and with the will which has been made through the record-office at Diospolis Parva before Dionysius the agoranomus in the 6th year of the reign of Philometor, which will besides the other matters which it sets forth appointed as his guardian (?) . . . being a kinsman, and of the household slaves I give him 4, whose names are Myrsine and her 3 children (?)—but the remaining two females, whose names are Irene and Ampelion, I give to Apollonia and her sisters, being 5 in all—also the vineyard site belonging to me at . . . in the Pathyrite nome and the wells therein of baked brick and the other appurtenances and the cart with the harness and the dove-cote and the other half-finished one and a yard of which the boundaries are, on the south waste grounds of the said Esthladas, on the north a vaulted room of Apollonia the younger, on the east waste ground of Petras . . . son of Esthladas, on the west waste ground of Esthladas up to the door opening to the west. The remaining rooms and fixtures and . . . and the waste ground assigned for a dovecote down beyond the door of Esthladas and to the west of the vaulted chamber I give to Apollonia and Aristo and Aphrodisia and Nicarion and Apollonia the younger, being 5 in all, my daughters by my present wife Apollonia also called Semmonthis, in

[a] That is, belonging to a family which possessed the citizenship in one of the Greek cities in Egypt.

---

10. Or Πετρασ[. .]υ. First η of χρητηρας above the line.
11. . λλιαν Wilcken: [καὶ π]αλαιὰν [οἰκίαν]?

νό(μους), καὶ τὰ θη[λ]υκὰ β σώμα[τ]α καὶ τὴν βοῦν ἐξ ἴσου κυριευέτωσαν ταῖς οἰκίαις καθ' ὃν πεποίημαι μερισμόν. [14]*[δότ]ω δὲ Ἐσθλάδας ἀπὸ τοῦ δεδομένου αὐ(τῶι) ψιλο[ῦ τ]όπου ἀπέναντι τῆς θύ(ρας) αὐ(τοῦ) ἐπὶ λί[β]α πή(χεις) ἐμβαδοὺς δ εἰς κλιβάνου τόπον. τὰ δὲ λο(ιπὰ) οἰκόπεδα* [15]*[καὶ ψι]λοὶ τόποι ἐν Διὸς πό(λει) τῆι μεγά(λῃι) ἐν τῶι Ἀμμω(νείωι) [κ]αὶ ἐν τοῖς κεραμείοις ἐχέτω Ἐσθλάδας κατὰ τὸ (ἥμισυ), Ἀπολλω(νία) δὲ καὶ ἀδελφαὶ κατὰ τὸ (ἥμισυ), καὶ* [16]*[τἆλλα ὑ]πάρχοντά μοι πάντα σύμβο(λά) τε σιτικὰ [κα]ὶ ἀργυ(ρικὰ) καὶ ἔπιπλα πάντα κατὰ τὸ (ἥμισυ). δότω δὲ Ἐσθλά(δας) καὶ αἱ περὶ Ἀπολλωνίαν κατὰ κοινὸν* [17]*[εἰς οἰκ]οδομὴν περιστερῶνος ἀνηλώματα ε[ἰς] τὸν ἀποδεδειγμένον περιστερῶνα ἕως ἂν ἐπιτελέσωσι, καὶ Ἀπολλωνίαι τῆι καὶ Σεμμώνθει* [18]*[τῆι ἐ]μῆι γυ(ναικὶ) ἐτῶν δ, ἐὰν παραμείνηι ἐ[ν τῶι] οἴκωι ἀνέγκλητος οὖσα, εἰς τροφὴν αὐ(τῆς) καὶ ταῖς β θυγατράσιν ἑκάσ(του) μη(νὸς) (πυροῦ) β ἥμισυ, κρότω(νος) (δωδέκατον), χα(λκοῦ) σ,* [19]*[καὶ] μετὰ δ ἔτη τὰ αὐτὰ μετρήματα [δότ]ωσαν ταῖς β νεωτέραι<ς> ἐκ κοινοῦ ἕως ἐτῶν ια. δότωσαν δὲ Ταχράτει εἰς φερνὴν* [20]*[χαλκο]ῦ τά(λαντα) ιβ ἐκ τῶν κοινῶν. ὅσα δ' ἂν φαίνητ[αι ἐπ]ίκτη(τα) ἔχουσα ἡ Σεμμῶνθις ὄντα αὐτῆι συνοῦσα Δρύτωνι, κυριευέτω αὐτῶν,* [21]*[οἱ δ' ἐπ]ελεύσοντες ἐπ' αὐτὴν περὶ τούτ[ων . . . . .]*
[22]*(ἔτους) μδ Παῦνι θ.*

19. [καὶ] μετά E.-H.: [ἐπὶ] δὲ τά Ed., but the δ is very doubtful. 21. *l.* ἐπελευσόμενοι.

accordance with the laws, and they shall own the 2 female slaves and the cow in equal shares for their households, according to the division which I have made. Esthladas shall give up from the waste ground given to him opposite his door which opens to the west 4 square cubits for the site of an oven. Of the remaining buildings and waste grounds at Diospolis Magna in the Ammonium[a] and in the potters' quarter Esthladas shall receive half and Apollonia and her sisters half, and of all my other property in corn and money contracts and all movable objects each party shall take half. Esthladas and Apollonia with her sisters shall provide funds in common for the building of a dove-cote on the site assigned until they finish it; and to my wife Apollonia also called Semmonthis, if she stays at home living irreproachably, they shall give every month for 4 years, for the maintenance of herself and for her 2 daughters,[b] $2\frac{1}{2}$ artabae of wheat, $\frac{1}{12}$ of croton, and 200 copper drachmae; and after 4 years they shall give the same amounts in common to the two younger daughters for 11 years. They shall give to Tachratis[c] for a dowry 12 copper talents out of the common funds. Whatever property Semmonthis may have manifestly acquired for herself while living with Dryton, she shall continue to own, and anyone who takes proceedings against her about this . . . Year 44, Pauni 9.

[a] At Thebes in the quarter of the temple of Ammon.

[b] Perhaps the second and third daughters, but the meaning is rather obscure.

[c] The Egyptian name of Aphrodisia the second daughter.

84. A WILL OF THE ROMAN PERIOD

P. Oxy. 494. A.D. 156–165.

[1] Ἀντίγραφον. ἔτους ἐννεακαιδεκάτου Αὐτοκράτορος Καίσαρος Τίτου Αἰλίο[υ] Ἁδριανοῦ Ἀντωνίνου Σεβαστοῦ Εὐσεβοῦς [2] μηνὸς Γερμανικείου λ ἐν Ὀξυρύγχων πόλει τῆς Θηβαΐδος, ἀγαθῇ τύχῃ. τάδε διεθέμην νοῶν καὶ φρονῶν [3] Ἀκουσίλαος Δείου τοῦ Διονυσίου τοῦ καὶ Ἀκουσιλάου μητρὸς Διονυσίας Θέωνος ἀπ' Ὀξυρύγχων πόλεως ἐν ἀγυιᾷ. ἐφ' ὃν μὲν πε-[4]ρίειμι χρόνον ἔχειν με τὴν τῶν ἰδίων ἐξουσίαν ὃ ἐὰν βούλωμαι ἐπιτελεῖν καὶ μεταδιατίθεσθαι καὶ ἀκυροῦν τὴν δια-[5]θήκην ταύτην, ὃ δ' ἂν ἐπιτελέσω κύριον ὑπάρχειν. ἐὰν δὲ ἐπὶ ταύτῃ τῇ διαθήκῃ τελευτήσω, ἐλεύθερα ἀφίημι ὑπὸ [6] Δία Γῆν Ἥλιον κατ' εὔνοιαν καὶ φιλοστοργίαν δοῦλά μου σώματα Ψεναμοῦνιν τὸν καὶ Ἀμμώνιον καὶ Ἑρμᾶν καὶ Ἀπολλω-[7]νοῦν τὴν καὶ Δημητρίαν καὶ θυγατέρα αὐτῆς Διογενίδα καὶ ἄλλην μου δούλην Δ[ι]ογενί[δ]α, καταλείπω δὲ τῇ γυναικί [8] μου οὔσῃ μου καὶ ἀνεψιᾷ Ἀριστοῦτι τῇ καὶ Ἀπολλωναρίῳ Ἡρακλείδου τοῦ Διονυσίου τοῦ καὶ Ἀκουσιλάου μητρὸς Ἡραΐδος Ἀ-[9]λεξάνδρου εὐνοούσῃ μοι καὶ πᾶσαν πίστιν μοι ἐνδεικνυμένῃ ἃ ἐὰν ἀπολίπω ἔπιπλα καὶ σκεύη καὶ χρυσία καὶ ἱμάτια [10] καὶ κόσμα καὶ πυρὸν καὶ ὄσπρεα καὶ γενήματα καὶ ἐνδομενείαν πᾶσαν καὶ ὀφειλήματα ἔνγραφα καὶ ἄγραφα, [11] κληρονόμον δὲ ἀπολείπω τὸν γεγονότα μοι ἐκ τῆς προγεγραμμένης μου γυν[α]ικὸς Ἀριστοῦτος τῆς καὶ Ἀπολ[λω-][12]ναρίου

[a] The original will was written in A.D. 156 and opened in 165, perhaps on the death of the testator. The present docu-

84. A WILL OF THE ROMAN PERIOD

A.D. 156–165

Copy.[a] The 19th year of the Emperor Caesar Titus Aelius Hadrianus Antoninus Augustus Pius, the 30th of the month Germaniceus,[b] at Oxyrhynchus in the Thebaid; for good fortune. This is the will made in the street[c] by me Acusilaus son of Dius son of Dionysius also called Acusilaus and of Dionysia daughter of Theon, of the city of Oxyrhynchus, being sensible and in my right mind. So long as I survive I am to have power over my property, to make whatever disposition I choose and to alter and revoke the present will, and whatever disposition I make shall be valid. But if I die leaving the present will, I set free under the sanction of Zeus, Earth and Sun, for their goodwill and affection, my slaves Psenamounis also called Ammonius and Hermas and Apollonous also called Demetria and her daughter Diogenis and another slave of mine called Diogenis. I bequeath to my wife and cousin Aristous also called Apollonarion daughter of Heraclides son of Dionysius also called Acusilaus and of Herais daughter of Alexander, being well disposed and showing all faithfulness towards me, whatever I may leave in the way of furniture, utensils, objects of gold, clothing, ornaments, wheat, pulse, crops, all my household stock, and debts owed to me, recorded and unrecorded. I leave my son Dius by my aforesaid wife Aristous also called Apollonarion, if he

ment contains (1) a copy of the body of the will, and (2) statements by four of the original witnesses that they acknowledge the seals to be theirs.

[b] Germaniceus = the Egyptian Pachon.

[c] See No. 7, note *b*.

υἱὸν Δεῖον ἐὰν ζῇ, εἰ δὲ μή, τὰ τούτου τέκνα, ὧν ἐὰν ἀπολίπω ὑπαρχόντων καὶ ἑτέρων δούλων σ[ωμ]ά-[13]των καὶ τῶν ἀπὸ τοῦ νῦν ἐσομένων ἐκ τῶν προγεγραμμένων θηλειῶν δούλων ἐκγόνων, ὧν πάν-[14]των τὴν χρῆσιν καὶ προσόδους πάσας μετὰ τὰ δημόσια ἕξει ἡ αὐτὴ γυνή μου Ἀριστοῦς ἡ καὶ Ἀπολλω-[15]νάριον ἐπὶ τὸν τῆς ζωῆς αὐτῆς χρόνον καὶ τὴν δουλείαν καὶ ἀποφορὰς τῶν μετὰ ⟦. . .⟧ τελευτήν μο[υ] [16]ἐλευθερουμένων δούλων σωμάτων. ἡ δ' αὐτὴ γυνή μου χορηγήσει τῷ υἱῷ μου Δείῳ εἰς δ[ι]α[τρο-][17]φὴν αὐτοῦ καὶ τὴν ἄλλην δαπάνην κατὰ μῆν[α] ἐν Ὀξυρύγχων πόλει πυροῦ μέτρῳ ἐξωδιαστικῷ . . . . [18]ἀρτάβας δύο καὶ δραχμὰς ἑξήκοντα καὶ ὑπὲρ ἱματισμοῦ κατ' ἔτος δραχμὰς διακοσίας. τῇ δ' αὐτῇ [19]γυναικὶ Ἀριστοῦτι τῇ καὶ Ἀπολλωναρίῳ ἐξέστω δι' αὐτῆς πωλεῖν καὶ ὑποτίθεσθαι ἃ ἐὰν αἱρῆται [20]ἀφ' ὧν ἐὰν ἀπολίπω τῷ υἱῷ μου Δείῳ ὑπαρχόν[των] καὶ σωμάτων καὶ καταχρᾶσθαι εἰς τὸ [21]ἴδιον χρ[έ]ος τοῖς ἐμπεσουμένοις ἤτοι ἐκ πράσεως καὶ ἐξ ὑποθήκης ἀργυρίοις. ἡ δ' αὐτὴ γυ-[22]νή μου Ἀρι[σ]τοῦς ἡ καὶ Ἀπολλωνάριον ἀποδώσει πάντα ἃ ἐὰν φανῶ ὀφείλων. δώσει δὲ ἡ [23]γυνή μου καὶ μετὰ τελευτὴν αὐτῆς ὁ υἱός μου Δεῖος τοῖς δούλοις μου καὶ ἀπελευθέρ[οι]ς εἰς [24]εὐωχίαν αὐτῶν ἣν ποιήσονται πλησίον τοῦ τάφου μου κατ' ἔτος τῇ γενεθλίᾳ μου ἐφ' ᾧ δι-[25]έπειν ἀργυρίου δραχμὰς ἑκατόν. ὅσα δ' ἂν ὑπὸ τὸ ἐκδόσιμον τῆς διαθήκης γράψω ἤτοι ἀφαιρού-[26]μενός τι ἢ προσδιατάσσων ἢ ἑτέροις χαριζόμενος ἢ καὶ ἄλλο τι βουλόμενος καὶ αὐτὰ ἔστω κύρια [27]ὡς δ' εἶν[α]ι τῇ διαθήκῃ ἐνγεγραμμένα, παρὰ δὲ ταῦτα μὴ οὔσης μηδενὶ τῷ καθόλου ἐξου-[28]σίας παρα-

lives, and if not, his children, heir to all the property that I leave and to my other slaves and the future offspring of the aforesaid female slaves, of all which things my said wife Aristous also called Apollonarion shall have the use and entire income, after payment of the taxes, for the term of her life, together with the service and the earnings of the slaves who are to be freed after my death.[a] My said wife shall supply to my son Dius every month at Oxyrhynchus for his sustenance and other expenses two artabae of wheat by the measure used for payment . . . and 60 drachmae, and for clothing 200 drachmae yearly. My said wife Aristous also called Apollonarion shall have the right to sell and mortgage on her own authority anything she chooses out of the property and slaves bequeathed to my son Dius and to use for her personal requirements the money accruing from the sale or mortgage. My said wife Aristous also called Apollonarion shall pay all the debts which I shall be found to owe. My wife, and after her death my son Dius, shall give to my slaves and freedmen for a feast which they shall hold beside my tomb every year on my birthday 100 silver drachmae wherewith to furnish it. Anything that I append to the officially returned copy[b] of the will, whether cancelling or supplementing or making bequests to other persons or with any other purpose, shall also be valid as if contained in the actual will; beyond this no one shall have any power at all to

[a] Assuming that they would not leave the household.
[b] The copy presented to the record-office for authentication and then returned to the testator.

βαίνει[ν, τὸν] δὲ παραβησόμενον ἐκτίνειν τῷ ἐμμένοντι τό τε βλάβος καὶ ἐπίτειμον [29]ἀργυρίου τάλαντα δύο καὶ εἰς τὸ δημόσιον τὰ ἴσα καὶ μηδὲν [ἧ]σσον μένειν κύρια τὰ προκείμενα. [30]ἡ διαθήκη κυρία. Ἀκουσίλαος Δείου ὁ προγεγραμμένος πεποίημαι τὴν διαθήκην, ἧς ὅλον τὸ σῶμά [31]ἐστίν μου ἰδι[ό-γ]ραφ[ο]ν, ἐπὶ πᾶσι τοῖς προκειμένο[ις], καὶ εἰμὶ (ἐτῶν) μη οὐ(λὴ) ποδ(ὶ) δεξ(ιῷ) κα[ὶ] ἔστ[ι]ν μου ἡ σφραγὶς Θώνιος. (2nd hand) [32]Δίδυμος Ὀννώφριος τοῦ καὶ Χαιρήμονος Ἡρώδου ἀπ' Ὀξυρύγ[χω]ν πόλεως ἶς τῶν [33]μαρτυρησάντων τῇ προκιμέ[νῃ δ]ιαθήκῃ ἐγνώρισα τὴν ἰδίαν μοῦ σφραγῖ-[34]δα οὖσαν γλύμματος Ἑρμοῦ καὶ ἐσφράγισα τῇ αὐτῇ σφραγῖδι. (3rd hand) Ἀσκληπιάδης [35]Εὐδαίμονος τοῦ Ἀσκληπιάδου ἀπ' Ὀξυρύγχων π[ό]λεως ἕτ[ε]ρ[ο]ς τῶν μαρτυρησάν-[36]των τῇ προκειμένῃ διαθήκῃ ἐγνώρισα τὴν ἰδίαν μου σφρ[αγε]ῖδα οὖσαν [37]γλύμματος Σαράπιδο[ς] καὶ ἐσφράγισα τῇ αὐτῇ σφραγεῖδι. (4th hand) Δίδυμος Διδύμου [38]τοῦ Ἐνθέσμο[υ] ἀγορανόμ[ο]ς τῆς Ὀξυρυγχιτῶν πόλεως ἕτερος τῶν [39]μαρτυρησάντων τῇ αὐτῇ διαθήκῃ ἐγνώρ[ι]σα τὴν ἰδίαν μου σ{σ}φραγῖδα [40]οὖσαν γλύμματος Ἀπόλλωνος καὶ ἐσφράγισα τῇ αὐτῇ σφραγῖδι. (5th hand) Ἀσκλη-[41]πιάδης Ἀσκληπ[ι]άδου τοῦ Παϋσιρ[ί]ωνος ἀπὸ τῆς αὐτῆς πόλεως ἕτερος τῶν [42][μαρτυρησάντω]ν τῇ αὐτῇ διαθήκῃ ἐγνώρισα τὴν ἰδίαν μ[ο]υ σφ[ρ]αγεῖδα [43][οὖσαν γλύμμα]τος Ἡρακλέους καὶ ἐσφράγισα τῇ αὐτῇ σφραγῖδα. (6th hand) [44][παρ]ετέθη ς (ἔτους) Ἁθύρ.

43. *l.* σφραγῖδι.

infringe it, and the party who infringes it shall forfeit to the party who abides by it the damages and a penalty of 2 silver talents and to the Treasury the like sum, the above provisions remaining none the less valid. This will is valid. I, the aforesaid Acusilaus son of Dius, have made this will, the whole body of which is in my own writing, with all the above provisions. I am 48 years of age, with a scar on the right foot, and my seal is an image of Thonis.[a] (Certified) I, Didymus son of Onnophis also called Chaeremon son of Herodes, of Oxyrhynchus, one of the witnesses to the above will, have recognized my seal being an imprint of a Hermes, and I sealed with the said seal. I, Asclepiades son of Eudaemon son of Asclepiades, of Oxyrhynchus, another of the witnesses to the above will, have recognized my seal being an imprint of a Sarapis, and I sealed with the said seal. I, Didymus son of Didymus son of Enthesmos, agoranomus of Oxyrhynchus, another of the witnesses to the said will, have recognized my seal being an imprint of an Apollo, and I sealed with the said seal. I, Asclepiades son of Asclepiades son of Pausirion of the said city, have recognized my seal being an imprint of a Heracles, and I sealed with the said seal. (Endorsed) Deposited[b] in the 6th year, Hathur.

[a] Mythical guard of the Canopic mouth of the Nile (Herod. ii. 113).

[b] In the property registration-office, with the rest of the file.

85. GREEK VERSION OF A ROMAN WILL

B.G.U. 326. A.D. 189–194.

(Col. 1) 1[Ἑρμηνί]α διαθ(ήκης). 2[Γάιος Λογγῖνος Κάστωρ οὐε]τρανὸς ἐντίμως ἀπολυθε[ὶ]ς 3[ἐκ κλάσσης πραιτωρί]ας Μισηνῶν [δια]θήκην ἐποί[ησ]εν. 4[ἐλευθέρας εἶναι κελεύω] Μαρκέλλαν δού[λη]ν μ[ο]υ μίζονα ἐ[τ]ῶν 5[τριάκοντα καὶ Κλεοπάτραν] δούλην μου μ[ίζονα] ἐτῶν τριάκ[οντ]α 6[καὶ ἑκάστη ἔστω κληρο]νόμος ἐξ ἴσου μ[έρους] ἐμοῦ. {κληρον[ομ .].}. 7[οἱ δὲ λοιποὶ πά]ν[τε]ς ἀποκληρόνομοί [μου] ἔστωσαν. προσε[ρ]χέσ-8[θωσάν τε τῇ κληρονομίᾳ] μου ἑκάστη ὑπὲρ τοῦ ἰδίου μέρους ὁπότ[α]ν 9[φαίνηται ἑκάστῃ μα]ρ[τύ]ρασθαι ἑαυτὴν ἐμοῦ κλ[η]ρονόμον εἶναι, μὴ ἐξῖ-10[ναι δὲ] π[ι]π[ρά]σκειν μηδὲ ὑποτίθεσθαι. ἀλλ' εἴ τι ἐὰν ἀν[θ]ρώπιν[ο]ν πά-11θῃ Μαρκέλλ[α] ἡ προγεγραμμένη, τότε τὸ μέρος τῆς κληρονομίας ἑαυτῆς 12[πρ]ὸς Σαραπίωνα καὶ Σωκράτην καὶ Λόγγον καταντῆσαι θέλω. ὁμοίως 13[Κλε]οπάτραν τὸ μέρος αὐτῆς πρὸς Νεῖλον καταντῆσαι θέλω. ὃς ἐάν μου κλη-14[ρον]όμος γέ[νητ]αι ὑπεύθυνος ἔστω δῶναι ποιῆσαι παρασχέσθαι ταῦ-15[τα] πάντα [ἃ ἐ]ν ταύτῃ τῇ διαθήκῃ μου γεγραμμένα εἴη τῇ τε πίστι 16[α]ὐτῆς παρακατατίθομαι. 17[Σαρ]απιὰς δούλη μου, θυγάτηρ Κλεοπάτρας ἀπελευθέρας μου, ἐλευθέρα ἔστω, 18[ᾗ κ]αὶ δίδωμι καταλίπω ἀρούρας σιτικὰς πέντε ἃς ἔχω περὶ κώμην Κα-19[ρα]νίδα ἐν τόπῳ λεγομένῳ Στρουθῷ, ὁμοίως ἄρουραν μίαν τέταρτον 20[κο]ιλάδος, ὁμοίως τρίτον μέρος οἰκίας μου καὶ τρίτον μέρος ἐκ τῆς αὐ-21[τ]ῆς οἰκίας ὃ ἠγόρασα πρότερον παρὰ Πραπεθεῦτος μητρὸς Θασεῦτος, 22[ὁ]μοίως τρίτον μέρος

85. GREEK VERSION OF A ROMAN WILL

A.D. 189–194.

Translation of will. Gaius Longinus Castor, veteran honourably discharged from the praetorian fleet of Misenum, has made a will. I direct that my slave Marcella aged over thirty years and my slave Cleopatra aged over thirty years shall be freed, and they shall each in equal portion be my heirs. All the others shall be disinherited. They shall enter on the inheritance, each on her own portion, as soon as they each think proper to attest that they are my heirs, and it shall not be lawful to sell or mortgage it. But if the aforesaid Marcella suffers the lot of human kind, then I wish her portion of the inheritance to go to Sarapion and Socrates and Longus. Likewise for Cleopatra, I wish her portion to go to Nilus. Whoever becomes my heir shall be obliged to give, perform, and provide all things that are written in this my will, and I commit them to its trust. My slave Sarapias daughter of my freedwoman Cleopatra shall be freed, and I give and bequeath to her five arurae of corn land which I own in the area of the village of Karanis in a place called Ostrich, likewise one and a quarter arurae of a ravine, likewise a third portion of my house and the third portion of the same which I bought formerly from Prapetheus mother of Thaseus, likewise a third portion of a palm-grove

(Col. 1) 6. Or perhaps [αἳ καὶ ἔστωσαν κατὰ] ν.μο[υ]ς . . . ἐμοῦ κληρον[όμο]ι (E.-H.). 11. *l.* αὐτῆς. 14. *l.* δοῦναι. 15. *l.* παρακατατίθεμαι.

φοινικῶνος ὃν ἔχω ἔγγιστα τῆς διώρυγος ὃ καλεῖται (Col. 2) [1]Παλαι[ὰ] Διῶρυξ. ἐκκο[μι]σθῆναι περιστ[αλ]ῆναί τε ἐμαυτὸ[ν] θέλω τῇ φροντίδι καὶ εὐσεβείᾳ [2]τῶν [κ]ληρονόμων μου. εἴ τι ἐὰν ἐγὼ μετὰ ταῦτα γεγραμμένον καταλίπω τῇ ἐμῇ χειρὶ γεγραμμένον [3]οἵῳ δή[π]οτε τρόπῳ, βέβα[ιό]ν μοι εἶναι θέλω. ταύτῃ τῇ διαθήκῃ δόλος πονηρὸς ἀπέστη. οἰκετίαν χρή-[4]ματα τ[αύ]της διαθήκης γενομένης ἐπρίατο Ἰούλιος Πετρωνιανὸς σηστερτίου νούμμου ἑνός, ζυ-[5]γοστα[τοῦ]ντος Γαΐου Λουκρητίου Σατορνείλου, ἐπέγνοι. ἀντεμαρτύρατο Μάρκον Σεμπρώνιον Ἡρα-[6]κλια[νόν], ἐπέγνοι. ἡ δια[θή]κη ἐγένετο ἐν κ[ώ]μῃ Καρανίδι νομῷ Ἀρσινοείτῃ πρὸ ιε̅ Καλανδῶν Νο-[7]εμβρ[ί]ων δυσὶ Σιλάνοις ὑ[πά]τοις, (ἔτους) λʹ Αὐτοκράτορος Καίσαρος Μάρ[κο]υ Αὐρηλίου Κο[μ]όδου Ἀντω[ν]είνου [8]Εὐσεβοῦς Εὐτυχοῦς Σεβαστοῦ Ἀρμενιακοῦ Μηδικοῦ Παρθικοῦ Σαρματικοῦ Γερμανικοῦ Ἁθὺρ κα̅. εἰ δέ [9]τι πε[ρ]ισσὰ γράμματα τῇ χειρί μου γεγραμμένα καταλίπω, βέβαια εἶναι θέλω. [10]ἠνύγη [κ]αὶ ἀνεγνώσθη Ἀρσινοείτῃ μητροπόλει ἐν τῇ Σεβαστῇ ἀγορᾷ ἐν τῇ στατιῶνι τῆς εἰκοσ-[11]τῆς τῶν κληρονομιῶν καὶ ἐλευθεριῶν πρὸ θ̅ Καλανδῶν Μαρτίων ὑπάτοις τοῖς οὖσι, (ἔτους) β̅ [12]Αὐτοκράτορος Καίσαρος Λουκίο[υ] Σεπτιμίου Σεουήρου Περτίνακος Σεβαστοῦ Μεχεὶρ κζ̅. οἱ λοιποὶ σφρα(γισταὶ) [13]Γάιος Λογγῖνος Ἀκύλας, ἐπέγνοι, Ἰούλιος Βολύσσιος, Μάρκος Ἀντίστιος Πετρωνιανός, Ἰούλιος [14]Γέμελλος οὐετρ[α]νός.

[15]Ἑρμηνία κωδικίλλων διπτύχων. Γάιος Λογ-

(Col. 1) 22. *l.* ἧ. (Col. 2) 3. *l.* ἀπέστω. 5. ἐπέγνοι = ἐπέγνω (so in 6, etc.). 6. *l.* Δεκεμβρίων (to correspond with the Egyptian date). 10. *l.* ἠνοίγη.

which I own close to the canal called Old Canal. I wish my body to be carried out and dressed for burial through the care and piety of my heirs. If I leave any later provision written by my hand in any manner whatsoever, I wish it to hold good. May evil guile be absent from this will. On the making of this will Julius Petronianus bought[a] the household and chattels for one sestertius, Gaius Lucretius Saturnilus being the scale-holder (acknowledged)[b] and Marcus Sempronius Heraclianus being called to witness (acknowledged). The will was made in the village of Karanis in the Arsinoite nome on November 17 in the consulship of the two Silani, in the 30th year of the Emperor Caesar Marcus Aurelius Commodus Antoninus Pius Felix Augustus Armeniacus Medicus Parthicus Sarmaticus Germanicus, Hathur 21. If I leave any further document written by my hand, I wish it to hold good. Opened and read in the Arsinoite metropolis in the Forum Augustum in the office of the five per cent tax on inheritances and manumissions on February 21 in the consulship of the present consuls, in the 2nd year of the Emperor Caesar Lucius Septimius Severus Pertinax Augustus, Mecheir 27. The remaining sealers: Gaius Longinus Acylas (acknowledged), Julius Bolyssius, Marcus Antistius Petronianus, Julius Gemellus, veteran. Translation of the codicillary tablets.[c] I, Gaius

[a] According to Roman procedure, the estate was emancipated by this fictitious sale, so that after the death of the testator it could be distributed in accordance with his wishes by the nominal purchaser instead of descending to the nearest relatives.

[b] The persons whose names are thus distinguished were present at the opening of the will and acknowledged their seals.

[c] Added to the will at a date not specified.

γῖνος Κάστωρ οὐετρανὸς ἀπολυθεὶς ἐν-[16]*τίμως ἐκ κλάσσης πραιτωρίας Μισηνῶν κωδικίλλους ἐποίησα. Μάρκον Σεμπρώνιον Ἡρα-*[17]*κλιανὸν φίλον καὶ ἀξιόλο[γ]ον ἐποίησα ἐπίτροπον τῇ ἰδίᾳ πίστι. συνγενεῖ Ἰουλίῳ Σερήνῳ δίδωμι* [18]*καταλίπω σηστερτίους νούμμους Ἀ. πρὸ ζ̄ Εἰδῶν Φεβραρίων τῇ ἰδίᾳ μου χειρὶ ἔγραψα. ἐσφρά-*[19]*γισαν Λογγῖνος Ἀκύλας καὶ Οὐαλέριος Πρίσκος. σφραγισταὶ Γάιος Λογγῖνος Ἀκύλας, ἐπέγνοι, Ἰού-*[20]*λιος Φιλόξενος, Γάιος Λουκρήτιος Σατορνεῖλος, ἐπέγνοι, Γάιος Λογγῖνος Κάστωρ, Ἰούλιος Γέμελλος οὐε-*[21]*τρανός. ἠνύγησαν καὶ ἀνεγνώσθησαν τῇ αὐτῇ ἡμέρᾳ ἐν ᾗ καὶ ἡ διαθήκη ἐλύθη.*

(2nd hand) [22]*Γάιος Λούκ{κ}ιος Γεμινι[ανὸ]ς νομικὸς Ῥωμαϊκὸς ἡρμήνευσα τὸ προκείμενον ἀντίγραφον καὶ ἔστιν σύμφω-*[23]*νον τῇ αὐθεντικῇ διαθήκῃ.*

Verso: *[Γ]αΐ[ου Λογγείνου] Κ[άσ]τορος.*

21. *l.* *ἠνοίγησαν.*

86. A BYZANTINE WILL

P. Lond. 1727. A.D. 583–584.

[1]*[+ Βασ]ιλείας τοῦ θειοτ[άτου ἡμῶν δεσ]πότου Φλαυίου [Τι]βερίου Μαυρικίου* [2]*τοῦ αἰωνίου Α[ὐ]γούστου καὶ] Αὐτοκράτορος ἔτους δευ[τέρου* [3]*- - - ἐν Συήνῃ].* [4]*Αὐρήλιοι Πατερμοῦθις υἱὸς Μηνᾶ μητρὸς Τσίας ν[αύτης ἀπὸ Συήνης καὶ]* [5]*Τκακὼ ἡ τούτου σύμβιος θυ[γάτ]ηρ Ἰακώβο[υ] μητρὸς Ταπί[ας* [6]*ὁρμωμένη ἀπὸ Συήνης οἱ κα]ὶ ἑξῆς ὑπογραφέα παρέχοντες* [7]*[τὸν ὑπὲρ αὐ]τῶν ὑπογράφοντα καὶ μάρτυρας τοὺς ἑξῆς κατ' ἐπιτρο-*

Longinus Castor, veteran honourably discharged from the praetorian fleet of Misenum, have made a codicil. I have appointed Marcus Sempronius Heraclianus, my respected friend, trustee to act on his own good faith. To my kinsman Julius Serenus I give and bequeath 4000 sestertii. Written in my own hand on February 7. Sealed by Longinus Acylas and Valerius Priscus.[a] Sealers: Gaius Longinus Acylas (acknowledged), Julius Philoxenus, Gaius Lucretius Saturnilus (acknowledged), Gaius Longinus Castor, Julius Gemellus, veteran. Opened and read on the same day on which the will was unsealed. (Subscribed) I, Gaius Lucius Geminianus, expert in Roman law, translated the foregoing copy and it agrees with the original will. (Endorsed) Of Gaius Longinus Castor.

[a] Perhaps this sentence should have been deleted and the name of Valerius Priscus added to the following list.

86. A BYZANTINE WILL

A.D. 583–584.

In the 2nd year of the reign of our most godlike master Flavius Tiberius Mauricius the eternal Augustus and Imperator, . . ., at Syene. Aurelius Patermouthis son of Menas and Tsia, sailor, of Syene, and Aurelia Tkako his wife, daughter of Jacob and Tapia, of Syene, bringing also a signatory who signs for them below and witnesses who witness

8[πὴν κα]ὶ [α]ἴτησιν καὶ ἀξίωσιν μαρτυροῦντας τῇδε τῇ ὁμολογίᾳ 9χαίρειν. ἐπειδήπερ συνζεύχθημεν ἀλλήλοις εἰς γάμον κοινωνίαν, 10οὐ τὴν τυχοῦσαν ἀνάπαυσιν καὶ θάλψιν ἐνδεικνύμενοι 11ἀλλήλοις, ἀναπαύοντες καὶ θάλποντες καὶ δουλεύοντες 12καὶ ὑπακούοντες καὶ ὑποτάττοντες, ἁπλῶς ἐν μηδενὶ 13παρεπικρίνοντες ἀλλὰ ἐν ὑποταγῇ πάσῃ, τοίνυν εὐλαβού-14μενοι μήποτε παρὰ προσδοκίαν ἡμῶν τινα ἐξ ἡμῶν 15τέλει τοῦ βίου χρησάμενον καὶ τῶν ἐνταῦθα τοῦ κόσμου 16ἐπαναχωρῆσαι πραγμάτων καὶ εὑρεθείῃ τὸν ζῶντα ὑστερού-17μενον παρὰ τῶν ἀμφοῖν ἡμῶν τέκνων, ὅθεν νοο<ῦ>ντες 18φρονοῦντες λογισμούς, ἔχοντες ἐρρωμένας τὰς διανοίας, 19τὰς φρένας ἀπαθεῖς, τὰς αἰσθήσεις ὑγιεῖς, ἐπὶ ποδῶν 20βαδίζοντες ἐπ᾽ ἀγορᾶ{ι}ς, παρερχόμενοι εἰς ταύτην τὴν 21ἔγγραφον ὁμολογίαν δι᾽ ἧς ὁμολογοῦμεν ἡμεῖς οἱ προ-22γεγραμμένοι ἑκόντες καὶ πεπει<σ>μένοι, δίχα παντὸς 23δόλου καὶ φόβου καὶ βίας καὶ ἀπάτης καὶ ἀνάγκης καὶ συναρπαγῆς 24καὶ κολακίας καὶ μηχανῆς καὶ κακοηθείας καὶ ἐλαττώ-25ματος παντός, δὶς τρὶς βουλευσάμενοι, ὡς εἴη μὲν ἡμᾶς ζῶντας 26καὶ ὑγιαίνοντας ἐναπολαύειν χρησόμεθα πάντων τῶν 27πραγμάτων ἡμῶν καθ᾽ ἣν ἂν βουλόμεθα διοίκησιν, 28ἐπὰν δὲ παρασταίῃ τῷ τῶν ὅλων δεσπότῃ Χριστῷ, ὅπερ 29ἀπείη, τινὰ ἐξ ἡμῶν τέλει τοῦ βίου χρήσασθαι, ἐφ᾽ ᾧ τὸν ζῶντα 30ἔχειν καὶ κατέχειν πάντων τῶν καταλειφθησομένων 31πραγμάτων ὑπὸ τοῦ τετελευτηκότος τὰ περιελθόντα εἰς αὐτὸν 32ἀπὸ γονέων διαδοχῆς καὶ ἀπὸ ἀγορασιαστικοῦ δικαίου καὶ ἀπὸ ἱδρώτων <καὶ> 33καμάτων ἔν τε οἰκίαις καὶ χρυσοῖς καὶ ἀργυροῖς

this agreement below as authorized, requested, and required, greeting. Whereas we have been joined together in wedlock, affording each other no ordinary peace and comfort, soothing and comforting and serving and obeying and submitting, in no single matter disagreeing but living in all submissiveness, therefore we, providing against the chance that contrary to our expectation one of us should depart this life and the things of this world and the survivor should find himself reduced to want by our common children, being sane and of clear judgement, having our understanding vigorous, our minds unimpaired, our senses sound, walking on our feet at market, come forward to make this written agreement. Hereby we the aforesaid agree, of our own free will and consent, without any guile or fear or violence or deceit or compulsion or robbery or flattery or intrigue or malice or subjection of any sort, after deliberating twice and thrice, that—though we pray it may be granted us to enjoy, alive and well, all our possessions and deal with them as we choose, yet if (which Heaven avert) it should please Christ the Master of all that one of us should die—the survivor shall receive and keep, of all the possessions left by the deceased, those which were acquired by inheritance from parents and by right of purchase and by sweat and labour, comprising houses and objects of gold and silver and copper and mountain-

9. *l.* *συνεζεύχθημεν, γάμων.* 16. *l.* *εὑρεθῆναι.* 20. *l.* *παρερχόμεθα.* 26. *l.* *καὶ χρήσασθαι* (?). 31. *l.* *τῶν περιελθόντων.*

καὶ χαλκοῖς καὶ [34]ὀριχαλκοῖς καὶ ἐσθήμασι καὶ ὑφάσμασι καὶ παντοί<οι>ς λεπτοῖς [35]εἴδεσι ἀπὸ μεγάλου εἴδους μέχρι ἐλαχίστου τινὸς καὶ τούτων [36]κατακυριεύειν καὶ δεσπόζειν καὶ διοικεῖν καὶ οἰκεῖν καὶ φιλοκαλεῖν [37]καὶ ἐξ αὐτῶν τρέφεσθαι καὶ ἱματίζ<εσθ>αι καὶ κηδεῦσαι καὶ ἐκτελέσαι [38]τὰς προσφορὰς τοῦ ἀποθανόντος, μηδενὸς τῶν τέκνων [39]ἡμῶν δυνομένου μήτε δυνησομένου ἐπελεύσασθαι τῷ ζῶντι [40]ἢ ἐγκαλεῖν ἢ λογοθετῆσαι ἢ κωλυομένου ἄχρι τελευτῆς αὐτοῦ, καὶ [41]μετὰ τὴν τελευτὴν ἐφ' ᾧ ἅπαντα τὰ ὑφ' ἡμῶν καταλειφθησό-[42]μενα πράγματα σταλήσεται εἰς τὰ κοινὰ ἡμῶν τέκνα ἐξ ἰσομοιρίας [43]καὶ μὴ διαφορὰν τέκνῳ παρὰ τέκνον ποιήσασθαι, καὶ εἰ ὀφθείη{ν} [44]χρεωστῶν ὁ τετελευτηκὼς ἢ καὶ χρεωστούμενος ἐφ' ᾧ τὴν [45]πᾶσαν δοσοληµψίαν ποιήσασθαι ὑπὲρ αὐτοῦ ἄχρι τελευτῆς αὐτοῦ καὶ [46]μετὰ τὴν τελευτὴν πᾶν τὸ πάκτον ἐπαναδραμεῖν εἰς τὰ αὐτὰ [47]κοινὰ ἡμῶν τέκνα, εἰ δέ τις ἐθελήσειεν ἐκ τῶν τέκνων [48]ἡμῶν ἢ ἄλλος ἐπελεύσασθαι τῷ ζῶντι ἢ ἀθετῆσαι ἢ παραβῆναι [49]ἢ παρασαλεῦσαι ταύτην ἡμῶν τὴν ἀλληλομολογίαν [50]ἢ δίαιταν κινεῖν, ἐφ' ᾧ τὸν ἐπελευσόμενον πρῶτον μὲν ἀλλό-[51]τριον καὶ ἄκληρον ἔσεσθαι τῆς παντοίας ὑποστάσεως τοῦ [52]ἐπιχειροῦντος παραβαίνειν, ἔπειτα ἐπιγινώσκει<ν> λόγῳ προστίμου [53]χρυσοῦ νομίσματα δώδεκα ἔργῳ καὶ δυνάμει ἀπαιτούμενα ἐκ τῆς [54]ὑποστάσεως τοῦ παραβαίνοντος μετὰ καὶ τοῦ μ<ὴ> {εν} ἰσχύειν κατὰ [55]τῶν ἐγγεγραμμένων ἀλλὰ ἐρρῶσθαι αὐτὰ ἐπὶ τὸ παντεί. [56]καὶ προσεπὶ τούτοις πᾶσι ἐπωμοσάμεθα τὸν θεῖον καὶ σεβάσμιον [57]ὅρκον τοῦ παντοκράτορος Θεοῦ καὶ τῆς νίκης καὶ διαμονῆς τῶν

copper[a] and clothes and woven materials and minor objects of all kinds, large or little, and shall be owner and master of these and administer and manage and keep them in repair and out of them shall feed and clothe himself and bury the deceased and execute his bequests, none of our children being able now or in future to proceed against the survivor or bring a claim or call him to account or obstruct him until his death, and that after his death all the possessions left by us shall go to our common children in equal portions, no difference being made between one child and another, and that if the deceased be found to be in debt or to have a debt owing to him, the survivor shall have sole power to pay and receive on his behalf until his own death, and after his death all the contract shall devolve upon our said common children, and that if one of our children or other person should seek to proceed against the survivor or to set aside or transgress or disturb this mutual agreement of ours or start arbitration, the assailant shall in the first place have no interest or portion in any of the property inheritable by the intending transgressor, and secondly shall pay as penalty twelve gold solidi, to be really and truly exacted from the property of the transgressor, while so far from his upsetting this deed it shall hold good in every point. And to all this we have sworn the divine and imperial oath by Almighty God and by the supremacy and permanence of our most gracious

[a] Probably brass, *i.e.* an alloy of copper and zinc.

40. *l.* κωλύειν. 54. μεν miswritten for μη. 55. εγ corr. from προ: *l.* ἐπὶ τῷ παντί.

γαληνοτάτων [58]ἡμῶν δεσποτῶν μὴ παραβαίνειν τὰ προδεδηλουμένα διάστολα [59]καὶ πρὸς ἡμῶν ἀσφάλειαν ταύτην ἐξεδόμεθα τὴν ἀλληλομολογίαν [60]κυρίαν οὖσαν καὶ βεβαίαν καὶ ἔννομον ἁπανταχοῦ προφερομένην μεθ' [61]ὑπογραφῆς τοῦ ὑπὲρ ἡμῶν ὑπογράφ(οντος) καὶ τῶν ἑξῆς μαρτυρούντων καὶ [62]ἐπερωτ(ηθέντες) ὡμολογήσαμεν. + (2nd hand) ☧ Αὐρήλιος Πατερμοῦθις υἱὸς Μηνᾶ μητρὸς Τσίας [63]ναύτης ἀπὸ Συήνης καὶ ἡ τούτου σύμβιος Αὐρηλία Τκακὼ θυγάτηρ Ἰακώβου [64]μητρὸς Ταπίας ὁρμώμενοι ἐν Συήνῃ οἱ προκ(είμενοι) ἐθέμην τὴν παροῦσαν ἀλληλομολογίαν [65]καὶ στοιχεῖ ἡμῖν πάντα τὰ ἐγγεγραμμένα ὡς πρόκ(ειται). Φλ(αύιος) Μάρκος Ἄπα Δίου στρ(ατιώτης) ἀριθμοῦ [66]Συήνης ἀξιωθεὶς ἔγραψα ὑπὲρ αὐτῶν παρόντων καὶ εἰπόντων μοι γράμματα [67]μὴ εἰδότων. ☧ (3rd hand) {Φ} [68]Φλαύιος Κῦρος Ἰωάνου κεντυρίων ἀριθμ(οῦ) Συήνης μαρτυρῶ. ☧ (4th hand) [69]☧ Φλ(αύιος) Ἰωάννης Πατερμουθίου ἀπὸ βικαρ(ιανῶν) ἀριθμοῦ Σηύνης μαρτυρῶ. ☧ (5th hand) [70]+ Θεόφιλος ἐλ(άχιστ)ο(ς) διάκο(νος) μαρτυρῶ τῇ ὁμολογίᾳ αἰτηθεὶς παρὰ τῶν θεμένων. (6th hand) ☧ Φλ(αύιος) Ἀτρῆς Βίκτωρ στρα(τιώτης) ἀριθμοῦ Συήνης μαρτυρῶ. (7th hand) [72]Φλ(αύιος) Ἰωάννης Κόλουθος κεντηρίων ἀριθμοῦ Συήνης μαρτυρῶ. (1st hand) [73]+ δι' ἐμοῦ Ἀλλάμονος Πέτρου ἀπὸ βικ(αριανῶν) ἐγράφη. +

Verso (8th hand) [74]ἀλληλομολογί(α) . [. . . .]τι Πατερμο(υ)θίο(υ) [καὶ Τκακώ +] + +

sovereigns not to transgress the aforesaid terms, and for our security we have issued this mutual agreement, which is valid and guaranteed and legal wherever produced, with the subscription of him who signs for us and of those who witness below, and in answer to the formal question we have given our assent. (Signed) We the aforesaid, Aurelius Patermouthis son of Menas and Tsia, sailor, of Syene, and his wife Aurelia Tkako daughter of Jacob and Tapia, also of Syene, have made the present mutual agreement and we assent to all its contents as aforesaid. I, Flavius Marcus son of Apa Dius, soldier of the *numerus* of Syene, have written for them as requested, they being present and dictating to me, as they are illiterate. I, Flavius Cyrus son of John, centurion of the *numerus* of Syene, witness. I, Flavius John son of Patermouthius, *vicarianus* of the *numerus* of Syene, witness. I, Theophilus, most humble deacon, witness the agreement at the request of the principals. I, Flavius Atres Victor, soldier of the *numerus* of Syene, witness. I, Flavius John son of Colluthus, centurion of the *numerus* of Syene, witness. Executed by me, Allamon son of Peter, *vicarianus*. (Endorsed) Mutual agreement of Patermouthius and Tkako.

58. *l.* προδεδηλωμένα. 64. *l.* ἐθέμεθα. 69. *l.* Συήνης. 72. *l.* Κολλούθου, κεντυρίων.

IV. DISOWNMENT

87. DEED OF DISOWNMENT

P. Cairo Masp. 67353. A.D. 569.

[1] ⳨ Βασιλείας καὶ ὑπατείας τοῦ θει[οτάτου] ἡμ[ῶ]ν δεσπότου Φλαυίου Ἰουστίν[ου] [2]τοῦ αἰωνίου Αὐγού[στ]ου Αὐτοκ[ρ]άτορος ἔτους πέμπτου Ἁθὺρ ἑκκ[αι-][3]δεκάτῃ τρίτης ἰνδικ(τίονος), ἐν [Ἀντιν]όου πόλει τῇ λαμπροτάτῃ. (Fragment 2) [4]. . . . . πρόγραμμα ἀποκηρύξεώς τε καὶ ἀπαγορεύσεως, ἀπαθεῖς ἔχων τὰς φρέ[νας] [5]καὶ διανοί[α]ς, ὀρθῷ καὶ ἀκριβεῖ λογισμῷ, δίχα παντὸς δόλου καὶ φόβου καὶ βία[ς] [6]καὶ ἀνάγκης καὶ ἀπάτης, ἐν δημοσίῳ καὶ πρακτικῷ τόπῳ. καὶ τοῦτο διαπέμ[πο]μ[αι] [7]τοῖς πατρολῴοις μου υἱοῖς ἕως ὀνόμ[α]τος καὶ μόνου, φημὶ δὴ Διονυσίᾳ καὶ [8]Ἰωάννῃ καὶ Παυλίνῃ καὶ Ἀνδρέᾳ τοῖς [ἀποβ]ολιμαίοις - - - (Frag. 3) [9]οἰόμενοι εὑρεῖν ὑμᾶς βοηθοὺς ἐν ἅπασι καὶ γηροκόμους καὶ ὑποτακτ[ικοὺς [10]κ]αὶ ὑπηκόους, ἔκ τε τῶν ἐναντί[ων] ἐν ἡληκίᾳ γεγένησθε ἀντίπαλοί μοι ὡς [11]καὶ μέγαιροι ὡς ἐκ πείρας ἔσχον τὴν ἄσπλ[αγ]χνον ὑμῶν πατροκτασίαν καὶ [12]ἀθε[τ]ητικ[ὴν] γνώμην, ἐφ' ὅ τι νοσοβαρὴς ἐγενάμην παρ' ὑμῶν - - - (Frag. 4) [13]- - - ποιότ]ητι καὶ ποσό[τ]ητι ἀπὸ πολυτελοῦς

IV. DISOWNMENT

87. DEED OF DISOWNMENT

A.D. 569.

In the 5th year of the reign and consulship of our most godlike master Flavius Justinus the eternal Augustus and Imperator, Hathur 16, 3rd indiction, in the most illustrious Antinoopolis.

(Fragment 2) . . . proclamation of disownment and rejection, having my mind and understanding unaffected, with true and unerring judgement, without any guile or fear or violence or compulsion or deceit, in a public place of business. And this I transmit to my parricidal children, though children in name only, that is, to Dionysia and John and Paulina and Andrew the outcast ones . . .

(Frag. 3) . . . thinking to find you helpful in all things, a comfort to my old age, submissive and obedient, and on the contrary you in your prime have set yourselves against me like rancorous things, as I learned through experience of your heartless parricidal conduct and lawless disposition, seeing that I fell grievously ill through you . . .

(Frag. 4) . . . in every quality and quantity, from

---

10. *l.* ἡλικίᾳ.

μέχρι ἀσσαρ[ίου ἑνὸς] [14]καὶ ἑνὸς ὀβολοῦ, εἰ μὴ τὸ ἀπὸ νόμων τυπωθὲν μόνον Φαλκίδιον ἤτοι δω[δεκάτην] [15]μοῖραν τοῦ ὑμῶν ἀκλήρου, καὶ οὐκ ἐξὼν ἔτι ὑμῖν τοῦ λοιποῦ ὀνομάσ[αι με] [16]ὡς πατέρα, ὅσον κἀγὼ ὑμᾶς ἀπεταξάμην καὶ ἐβδελαξάμην ἀπὸ το[ῦ νῦν] [17]καὶ ἐπὶ τὸν ἀεὶ ἑξῆς ἅπαντ[α πα]ν[τ]ελῆ χρόνον ὡς ἀποβολιμαίους κ[αὶ νόθους] [18]καὶ δουλοχείρονας - - - (Frag. 5) [19]- - - κορακοβροσίαν γεν[έσθ]αι καὶ ὀμματωρυξίαν, τούτου [τοῦ [20]τ]ρόπου ὑμᾶς παραχαράττω μηδὲν λήμψασθαι μήτε μὴν δοῦναι [ὑπὲρ [21]ἐ]μοῦ περιόντος τε ἢ καὶ θνήσκοντος διὰ τὸ ἐμοὶ ὀρθῶς καὶ δικα[ίως] [22]δεδόχθαι. καὶ ἐξορκίζω πάντα κριτὴν καὶ δικαστὴν καὶ πάντα [θρόνον] [23]καὶ ἀρχὴν καὶ ἐξουσίαν ἀεὶ φυλάξαι τὰ ἐπὶ τοῖς τοιούτοις ἀπαιδεύτ[οις] [24]υἱοῖς . . . . [ὑ]πὲρ ἐμοῦ ἀπαγορεύσεως καὶ ἀποκηρύξεως γρ[α - - -] (Frag. 6) [25]- - - τόπον. ἐξορκίζω δὲ ἅμα καὶ τ[ὸ]ν δημόσιον [σ]κρίβα καὶ [τ]αβουλ[άριον [26]κ]αὶ δημέκδικον τῆστε τῆς λαμπρᾶς [Ἀ]ντινοέων πό[λεως] [27]κατὰ τοῦ θεοῦ πρὸ πάντων καὶ τῆ[ς θείας καὶ οὐρανίας τύχης τῶν [28]οἰ]κουμενικῶν ἡμῶν δεσποτῶν καὶ βασιλέων Φλαυίων Ἰου[στίνου [29]κ]αὶ Αἰλίας Σοφίας τῶν αἰωνίων [Α]ὐτοκρα[τόρω]ν τὴν συνήθη [30][ἀ]ποδημίωσιν προσθέσθαι τοῖς διατυπωθῖσι παρ' ἐμοῦ ὁρισμοῖς κ[αὶ [31]ἀ]εὶ βραβεύειν καὶ ἐκφωνῆσαι πάντη ἀηττήτως εἰς ἔκπληξιν μάλιστ[α [32]τ]ῶν μελλόντων τὰ ἴσα τούτοις τοῖς ἀσεβέσι διαπράξασθαι. ἐχρῆν γὰρ [κα-[33]τ]ὰ τὸν θεῖον νόμον τοὺς ἑαυτῶν γονεῖς ἄκρως τιμᾶν, τοὐναντίων δὲ [34][οἱ] τοιοῦτοι κάκιστοι ἐλοιδώ[ρησα]ν

things costly down to one as or one obol, excepting only the Falcidian portion [a] prescribed by law or the twelfth part of your lost inheritance, and it is no longer lawful for you in future to call me father, inasmuch as I reject and abhor you from now to the utter end of all succeeding time as outcasts and bastards and lower than slaves . . .

(Frag. 5) . . . for ravens to devour the flesh and peck out the eyes, in this manner I debar you from receiving or giving anything on my behalf, whether I be alive or dead, because I have rightly and justly thus resolved. And I adjure every judge and dicast and every tribunal and magistracy and authority to uphold always this deed of rejection and disownment executed on my behalf against these so ill-conducted children . . .

(Frag. 6) . . . place. I also adjure the public scribe and the *tabularius* and the public *defensor* of this illustrious Antinoopolis, by God before all and by the divine and heavenly fortune of our universal rulers and sovereigns Flavius Justinus and Flavia Aelia Sophia the eternal Imperators, to give the customary publicity to the decisions formulated by me and always to arbitrate and give judgement quite inflexibly, to the terror especially of such as are disposed to imitate the deeds of these impious ones. For whereas according to the divine law they ought to have most highly honoured their own parents, these most wicked ones have contrariwise reviled

[a] The portion of the inheritance to which children were entitled by the Falcidian law.

15. *l.* ἐξόν. 16. *l.* ἐβδελυξάμην. 19. *l.* κορακοβρωσίαν. 25. *l.* σκρίβαν. 26. *l.* τῆσδε. 33. *l.* τοὐναντίον.

κ[α]ὶ [κατε]φρόνησαν τὸν πατ[ρι]κ[ὸν?] [35]*θεσμόν. καὶ τοῦτο ἐξέταξα μετὰ τοῦ προκειμένου Φαλκ[ιδίο]υ τῇ ἐμῇ* [36]*[δ]ιαθήκῃ καὶ εἰς εἴδησιν πάντων κυρίαν οὖσαν καὶ βεβαί[α]ν [π]ανταχο[ῦ* [37]*προφερομένην [τὴν παροῦσαν ἀποκήρυξιν ἀνέθηκα* (?).

37. Restored from P. Cairo Masp. 67097.

and contemned the parental ordinance. And this, along with the aforesaid Falcidian provision, I have set forth in my will, and I have put up this proclamation of disownment so that all men may know, being valid and guaranteed wherever produced.

V. LETTERS

88. FROM HIEROCLES TO ZENON

P. Cairo Zen. 59060. 257 B.C.

[1]Ἱεροκλῆς Ζήνων[ι χ]αίρειν. [εἰ ἔ]ρρωσαι, ἔχοι ἂν καλῶς· ὑγιαίνομεν δὲ καὶ ἡμεῖς. ἔ[γραψάς] [2]μοι περὶ Πύρρου, εἰ [μὲ]ν ἀκρει[βῶ]ς ἐπιστάμεθα, ἀλείφειν αὐτόν, εἰ δὲ μέ, μὴ συνβῆ[ι ἀνήλω-][3]μά τε μάταιον προσπεσεῖν καὶ [ἀ]πὸ τῶν γραμμάτων ἀποσ{σ}παθῆναι. π[ερ]ὶ μὲν οὖ[ν τοῦ με] [4]ἐπίσ{σ}τασθαι οἱ θεοὶ μάλιστ᾿ ἂν εἰδέησαν, Πτολεμαίωι δὲ φαίνεται, ὅσα κατ᾿ ἄ[νθρωπον], [5]ὅτι τῶν νῦν ἀλιφομένων, οἳ προειλήφασιν χρόνον πολύν, πολὺ κρείττων Πύ[ρρος ?] [6]καὶ σφόδρα ὀλίγου χρόνου πολὺ ὑπερέξει αὐτῶν· προσπορεύεται δὲ καὶ πρὸς [ταῦτα] [7]καὶ πρὸς τὰ λοιπὰ μαθήματα· σὺν δὲ θεοῖς εἰπεῖν, ἐλπίζω σε στεφανωθήσεσθαι. ἀπ[όστειλον] [8]δὲ αὐτῶι ἐγλουστρίδα ὅ τι τάχος, καὶ μάλιστα μὲν ἔστω τὸ δέρμα αἴγειον, εἰ δὲ μέ, [μόσχειον] [9]λεπτόν, καὶ χιτῶνα καὶ ἱμάτιον καὶ τὸ στρωμάτιον καὶ περίστρωμα καὶ προσ[κεφάλαια] [10]καὶ τὸ μέλι. ἔγραψας δέ μοι θαυμάζεις εἰ μὴ

2. *l.* μή. 3. *l.* ἀποσπασθῆναι. 5. π. [. . . . . .] Ed. 8. *l.* μή.

V. LETTERS

88. FROM HIEROCLES TO ZENON

257 B.C.

Hierocles to Zenon[a] greeting. If you are well, it would be excellent. I too am in good health. You wrote to me about Pyrrhus, telling me to train[b] him if I am quite certain of his success,[c] but if not, to avoid incurring useless expense and distracting him from his studies. Now as for my being certain, the gods should know best, but it seems to Ptolemaeus, as far as a man can tell, that Pyrrhus is much better than those now being trained, though they started long before him, and that in a very short time he will be far ahead of them; moreover he is pursuing his other studies as well; and to speak with the gods' leave, I hope to see you crowned. Make haste to send him a bathing-apron, and if possible let it be of goatskin or, if not, of thin sheepskin, and a tunic and cloak, and the mattress, coverlet and pillows, and the honey. You wrote to me that you were

[a] The person to whom this and the following letters were addressed was the private agent of Apollonius the dioecetes. financial minister of Ptolemy II.

[b] For competition in the public games.

[c] A fuller version of the same letter, in the British Museum, has ὅτι νικήσει after ἐπιστάμεθα.

κατέχω ὅτι τούτοις πᾶσι τέλος ἀκ[ολουθεῖ]. [11]ἐπίσταμαι, ἀλλὰ σὺ εἱκανὸς εἶ διοικῶν ἵνα ἀποσταλῆι ὡς ἀσφαλέστατα.

Verso : [12]Ζήνωνι. (To left, in small hand) Ἱεροκλῆς περὶ Πύρρου. [13](ἔτους) κθ Ξανδικοῦ γ̅, ἐμ Μέμφει.

89. FROM PROMETHION TO ZENON

P.S.I. 333. 256 B.C.

[1]Προμηθίων Ζήνωνι χαίρειν. [σ]υνέβη ἡμῖν ἀγωνιᾶσαι ἀκούσαν-[2]τας ἐπὶ πλείονα ⟦σε⟧ χρόνον ἑλκ[υσ]θῆναί σε ἐν ἀρρωστίαι, νυνὶ δὲ ἀκού-[3]σαντές σε ὑγιαίνειν καὶ εἶναι ἤδη πρὸς τῶι ἀναλαμβάνειν ἥσθημεν· [4]ὑγιαίνομεν δὲ καὶ αὐτ[οί]. ἐδώκαμεν πρότερον Ἡρακλείδει τῶι [5]παρ' ὑμῶν ἐκ τοῦ σοῦ λόγ[ο]υ, [καθάπερ ἡμ]ῖν ἔγραψας, ἀργυρίου (δραχμὰς) ρ̅ν̅, [6]κομίζει δὲ νυνὶ μύρου ἵνια ι̅ ἐν [ἀλ]αβάστροις κ̅α̅, οἵ εἰσιν ἐσφραγισμένοι [7]τῶι ἐμῶι δακτυλίωι. ἐπέστειλ[ε] γάρ μοι Ἀπολλώνιος πριάμενον [8]δοῦναι τούτωι καὶ στεφάνους βαλαυστίνων τ. οὐκ ἔφθημεν [9]οὖν αὐτῶι τούτους συν[δο]ῦν[αι διὰ] τὸ μὴ εἶναι ἑτοίμους, εἰς δὲ [10]Ναύκρατιν αὐτῶι παροίσει Πα . .[. . .].· πρὸ γὰρ τῆς λ συντελεσθήσονται. [11]τὴν δὲ τιμὴν τούτων τε καὶ τοῦ μύρου ἐκ τοῦ λόγου ὑμῶν [12]διαγεγράφαμεν, καθάπερ Ἀπολλώνιος ἔγραψεν. δεδώκαμεν δὲ [13]καὶ τοῦ πλοιαρίου ἐν ὧι ἀναπλεῖ [να]ῦ[λ]ο[ν] χαλκοῦ (δραχμὰς) ι. διαγέγραπται [14]δὲ καὶ Ἰατροκλεῖ εἰς χάρτας τοὺς συντελουμένους ἐν Τάνει ὥστε [15]Ἀπολλωνίωι

13. [να]ῦ[λ]ο[ν] E.-H., [τὸ μ]ύ[ρ]ο[ν] Edd.

surprised at my not understanding that all these things are subject to toll. I know it, but you are well able to arrange for them to be sent in perfect security.[a] (Addressed) To Zenon. (Docketed) Hierocles about Pyrrhus. Year 29, Xandicus 3, at Memphis.

[a] That is, by using his influence as an agent of the financial minister.

89. FROM PROMETHION TO ZENON

256 B.C.

Promethion[a] to Zenon greeting. I suffered anxiety when I heard of your long protracted illness, but now I am delighted to hear that you are convalescent and already on the point of recovery. I myself am well. I previously gave your agent Heraclides 150 drachmae in silver from your account, as you wrote to me to do, and he is bringing you now 10 *hins* of perfume in 21 vases which have been sealed with my finger-ring. For though Apollonius[b] wrote to me to buy and give him also 300 wild pomegranate wreaths, I did not manage to give him these at the same time, as they were not ready, but Pa . . . will bring them to him at Naucratis; for they will be finished before the 30th. I have paid the price both of these and of the perfume from your account, as Apollonius wrote. I have also paid a charge of 10 drachmae in copper for the boat in which he is sailing up. And 400 drachmae in silver have been paid to Iatrocles for the papyrus rolls which are being manufactured in Tanis for

[a] A banker in Mendes.

[b] The dioecetes.

ἀργυρίου (δραχμαὶ) υ. ταῦτα μὲν οὖν ἐπίστω οὕτως [16]διοικημένα. σὺ δὲ καλῶς ἂν ποιοῖς ἐπιστέλλων, ἐάν τινος τῶν [17]καθ' ἡμᾶς χρείαν ἔχηις. [18]ἔρρωσο. (ἔτους) κθ Χοίαχ κη̄.

Verso: [19]Ζήνωνι. (To left, in small hand) (ἔτους) κθ Περιτίου γ. [20]Προμηθίων ὧν [21]δέδωκεν.

90. FROM APOLLONIUS THE DIOECETES

P. Cairo Zen. 59154. 256 B.C.

[1]Ἀπολλώνιος Ζήνωνι χαίρειν. τῶν ξηρῶν ξύλων [2]ἐμβαλόμενος εἰς πλοῖον κορμοὺς ὅ τι πλείστους καὶ [3]παχυτάτους ἀπόστειλον τὴν ταχίστην εἰς Ἀλεξάνδρεια[ν] [4]ὅπως ἔχωμεν ἀποχρήσασθαι εἰς τὴν ἑορτὴν τῶν Εἰσιείω[ν]. [5]ἔρρωσο. (ἔτους) λ Δίου γ Φαῶφι κγ.

Verso: [6]Ζήνωνι. (Behind the address) ἤδη. (To left of address, 2nd hand) (ἔτους) λ Δίου ιη Ἁθὺρ ιη. [7]Ἀπολλώνιος ξύλων [8][εἰ]ς τὰ Εἰσιεῖα. (In the adjoining fold, 3rd hand) [9][ξύ]λων εἰς τὰ [10][Εἰσιεῖ]α.

91. FROM DROMON TO ZENON

P. Cairo Zen. 59426. 260–250 B.C.

[1]Δρόμων Ζήνωνι χαίρειν. τοῖς θεοῖς πᾶσιν χάριν ἔχομεν, [2]εἰ αὐτός τε ὑγιαίνεις καὶ τὰ λοιπά σοι κατὰ λόγον γέγονεν. [3]ἐρρώμεθα δὲ καὶ αὐτός, καὶ καθότι μοι ἔγραψας τὴν πᾶσαν ἐπι-[4]μέλειαν

3. *l.* αὐτοί.

Apollonius. Take note then that these affairs have been settled thus. And please write yourself if ever you need anything here. Goodbye. Year 29, Choiach 28. (Addressed) To Zenon. (Docketed) Year 29, Peritius 3. Promethion about what he has paid.

90. FROM APOLLONIUS THE DIOECETES

256 B.C.

Apollonius to Zenon greeting. From the dry wood put on board a boat as many of the thickest logs as possible and send them immediately to Alexandria that we may be able to use them for the festival of Isis. Goodbye. Year 30, Dius 8, Phaophi 23. (Addressed) To Zenon. At once.[a] (Docketed by Zenon) Year 30, Dius 18, Hathur 18. Apollonius about wood for the Isis festival. (Docketed by sender) Wood for the Isis festival.

[a] An admonition to the persons concerned to send the letter immediately. In fact, it arrived too late, for the festival began on the 17th of Hathur and ended on the 20th.

91. FROM DROMON TO ZENON

260–250 B.C.

Dromon to Zenon greeting. I give thanks to all the gods if you are in good health yourself and everything else has been satisfactory. I too am well, and in accordance with what you wrote to me

ποιοῦμαι ὅπως ἂν μηθεὶς ἐνοχλῆι τοὺς παρὰ σοῦ. [5]ὡς δ' ἂν ἀναπλέηις ὑγιαίνων, σύνταξόν τινι τῶν παρὰ σοῦ [6]ἀγοράσαι μέλιτος Ἀττικοῦ κοτύλην· χρείαν γὰρ ἔχω πρὸς [7]τοὺς ὀφθαλμοὺς κατὰ πρόσταγμα τοῦ θεοῦ. [8]εὐτύχει.

Verso: Ζήνωνι.

92. FROM PLATON TO ZENON

P. Cairo Zen. 59192. 255 B.C.

[1]Πλάτων Ζήνω[νι χαί]ρειν. Δημητρίου τοῦ ἀποδιδόντος σοι τὴν [2]ἐπιστολήν, ὡς ἔοικ[εν, ὁ πα]τὴρ τυγχάνει τὰς διατριβὰς ποιούμενος ἐν τ[ῶι] [3]Ἀρσινο[ΐτ]ηι νομ[ῶι. βούλε]ται οὖν κα[ὶ αὐ]τὸς ὁ νεανίσκος ἐκεῖ πράττε[ι]ν τ[ι]. [4]πυνθανόμενος δέ σε εἶναι ἐπιε[ι]κῆ ἠξίωσάν τινές με τῶν φίλων γράψαι [5][σο]ι περ[ὶ αὐ]τ[οῦ], ἵνα κατατάξηις που αὐτὸν π[[.]]αρὰ σοί. καλῶς [οὖν ποι-][6]ήσεις εὐχαριστήσας ἡμῖν καὶ φροντίσας ἵνα πράττηι τι, ὃ ἂν σὺ δοκιμάζηις [7]ἐπιτήδειον εἶναι, καὶ τὰ λοιπὰ ἐπιμελόμενος αὐτοῦ, ἐάμπερ σοι ἦι χρήσιμ[ος]. [8]σημεῖον δὲ ὅτι σοι ἀπέστειλα παρὰ Σώσου ἐρεβίνθου κριοῦ ἀρ(τάβας) β ἠγορασμένας ἀνὰ (δραχμὰς) ε, [9]πειράσομαι δὲ καὶ ἐγ Ναυκράτεως, ἐὰν ἦι, προσαγοράσαι σοι εἰς ἀρ(τάβας) κ[[. .]] [10]καὶ αὐτός σοι ἀναγαγεῖν. [11]ἔρρωσο. [12](ἔτους) λα μηνὸς Δίου ιβ.

Verso: Ζήνωνι.

4. *l.* πυνθανόμενοι.

I am taking the utmost care that no one troubles your people. When you are ready to sail up in good health, order one of your people to buy a cotyla of Attic honey; for I require it for my eyes by order of the god.[a] Farewell. (Addressed) To Zenon.

[a] Probably the Memphite Sarapis, who prescribed for the sick by means of dreams.

92. FROM PLATON TO ZENON

255 B.C.

Platon to Zenon greeting. The father of Demetrius the bearer of this letter happens, it seems, to be residing in the Arsinoite nome, and the lad therefore wishes to find employment there himself. On hearing of your kindly disposition some of his friends asked me to write to you about him, begging you to give him a post in your service. Please then do me a favour and provide some employment for him, whatever you may think suitable, and otherwise look after him, if you find him useful. As a token (of goodwill) I have sent you, from Sosus, 2 artabae of chick-peas bought at 5 drachmae each, and if there are any at Naucratis, I will try to buy you about 20 artabae more and bring them up to you myself. Goodbye. Year 31, Dius 12. (Addressed) To Zenon.

93. FROM ARTEMIDORUS TO ZENON

P. Cairo Zen. 59251. 252 B.C.

1Ἀρτεμίδωρος Ζήνωνι χαίρειν. εἰ ἔρρωσαι, εὖ ἂν ἔχοι· ἔρρωμαι δὲ καὶ ἐγὼ καὶ Ἀπολλώνιος ὑγίαινεν καὶ 2τἆλλα ἦν κατὰ γνώμην. ὅτε δέ σοι ἔγραφον, παρεγινόμεθα εἰς Σιδῶνα, συμπεπορευμένοι τῆι βασιλίσσηι 3ἕως τῶν ὁρίων, καὶ ὑπελαμβάνομεν ταχέως παρέσεσθαι πρὸς ὑμᾶς. χαριεῖ οὖμ μοι σαυτοῦ τε ἐπιμελόμενος 4ἵνα ὑγιαίνηις καὶ ἡμῖν γράφων ἐάν τί σοι βούληι γίνεσθαι ὧν ἡμεῖς δυνάμεθα. καλῶς δ' ἂμ ποιήσαις ἀγοράσας 5ἡμῖν ἵνα ὡς ἂμ παραγενώμεθα ἔχωμεν μέλιτος τοῦ βελτίστου μετρητὰς γ καὶ κριθῶν ὥστε εἰς τὰ κτήνη (ἀρτάβας) χ, 6τὴν δὲ τιμὴν ἀπὸ τοῦ σησάμου καὶ τοῦ κρότωνος δοὺς εἰς ταῦτα, καὶ τῆς οἰκίας δὲ τῆς ἐμ Φιλαδελφείαι 7ἐπιμελόμενος ἵνα ὡς ἂμ παραγενώμεθα καταλάβωμεν αὐτὴν ἐστεγασμένην. καὶ τὰ ζευγάρια δὲ καὶ τὰ ἱερ{ι}εῖα καὶ τοὺς χῆνας 8[κ]αὶ τὰ λοιπὰ τὰ ἐνταῦθα ὡς ἂν ἐκποιῆι πειρῶ ἐπισκοπεῖν· οὕτως γὰρ ἡμῖν μᾶλλον ἔσται τὰ δέοντα. 9καὶ τὰ γενημάτια δὲ ἵνα τρόπωι τινὶ συγκομισθῆι ἐπιμελές σοι ἔστω, καὶ ἐάν τι δέηι εἰς 10ἀνήλωμα, τὸ ἀναγκαῖον δοῦναι μὴ ὀκνήσηις. 11ἔρρωσο. (ἔτους) λγ Περιτίου ἐμβολίμου ς̄.

Verso: 12[εἰς Φιλ]αδέλφειαν. Ζήνωνι. (2nd hand) (ἔτους) λγ Φαμενὼθ ς. 13Ἀρτεμίδωρος.

93. FROM ARTEMIDORUS TO ZENON

252 B.C.

Artemidorus[a] to Zenon greeting. If you are well, it would be excellent. I too am well and Apollonius is in good health and other things are satisfactory. As I write this, we have just arrived in Sidon after escorting the princess[b] to the frontier, and I expect that we shall soon be with you. Now you will do me a favour by taking care of your own health and writing to me if you want anything done that I can do for you. And kindly buy me, so that I may get them when I arrive, 3 metretae of the best honey and 600 artabae of barley for the animals, and pay the cost of them out of the produce of the sesame and croton,[c] and also see to the house in Philadelphia in order that I may find it roofed when I arrive. Try also as best you can to keep watch on the oxen and the pigs and the geese and the rest of the stock there ; I shall have a better supply of provisions if you do. Also see to it that the crops are harvested somehow, and if any outlay is required, do not hesitate to pay what is necessary. Goodbye. Year 33, intercalary Peritius 6. (Addressed) To Zenon. To Philadelphia. (Docketed) Year 33, Phamenoth 6. Artemidorus.

[a] A physician in the service of the dioecetes.

[b] The princess Berenice, who was escorted to Syria by Apollonius on the occasion of her marriage to Antiochus II.

[c] The two oils chiefly used in Egypt at this period were made from sesame and croton (= castor-oil plant), the former for food and the latter for lamps.

94. FROM PHILONIDES TO CLEON

P. Petr. ii. 13, 19. About 255 B.C.

[2]]αις, οὕτω γὰρ [ἔστα]ι τυχεῖν καὶ τὸν [3][ὕστερον χ]ρόνον εὐιλάτου τοῦ βασιλ[έως. οὐ] μὴν οὐθὲν ἐμοὶ [4][ἔσται με]ῖζον ἢ σοῦ προστατῆσα[ι τὸν] ἐ[π]ίλοιπον βίον, ἀξίως [5][μὲ]ν σοῦ, ἀξίως δ' ἐμοῦ, καὶ ἐάν τι τῶν κατ' ἄνθρωπον γίνηται, [6]τυχεῖν σε πάντων τῶν καλῶν· ὃ ἐμοὶ [μ]έγιστον ἔσται καλ{λ}ῶς σου [7]προστατῆσαι καὶ ζῶντός σου καὶ εἰς θεοὺς ἀπελθόντος. μάλιστα [8]μὲν οὖν τὴν πᾶσαν σπουδὴν πόησαι [το]ῦ ἀφεθῆναί σε διὰ τέλους· [9]εἰ δ' ἄρα μὴ ὁρᾶις ὂν δυνατόν, αὐτήν γ[ε τὴ]ν ἀνα[χώ]ρησιν τοῦ [10]ποταμοῦ, καθ' ὃν χρόνον οὐθείς ἐστιν κίνδυνος, ἀ[λλ' ἐ]ξέσται καὶ [11]Θεύδωρον καταλειφθέντα ταὐτὸ ποεῖν, ὅπως τ[οῦτό]ν γε [12]τὸν χρόνον παρεπιδημῆις. τοῦτο δ' ἔχε τῆι δια-[νοία]ι ὅτι [13]οὐθέν σοι μὴ γενηθῆι λυπηρόν, ἀλλὰ πᾶν ἐ[μοὶ ἔστ]αι πεφρον-[14]τισμένον τοῦ σε γενέσθαι ἄλυπον. [ἔρρωσο.

9. ⟨κατ'⟩ αὐτήν Wilcken. 10. ἐ]ξέσται revised reading.

95. FROM DEMOPHON TO PTOLEMAEUS

P. Hib. 54. About 245 B.C.

[1]Δημοφῶν Πτολε-[2]μαίωι χαίρειν. ἀπό[σ-][3]τειλον ἡμῖν ἐκ παν-[4]τὸς τρόπου τὸν αὐ-[5]λητὴν Πετῶυν ἔχοντ[α] [6]τούς τε Φρυγίους αὐ-[7]λ[ο]ὺς καὶ τοὺς λοιπούς, κ[αὶ] [8]ἐάν τι δέηι ἀνηλῶσαι [9]δός, παρὰ δὲ ἡμ[ῶ]ν κομι-[10]εῖ. ἀπόστειλον δὲ

94. FROM PHILONIDES TO CLEON [a]

About 255 B.C.

. . . for in this way you will be able to win the king's grace for the future also. Nothing truly will be dearer to me than to protect you for the rest of your life in a manner worthy of you and of myself, and if the fate of mankind befalls you, to see that you enjoy all due honours ; this will be my chief desire, honourably to protect you both while you live and when you have departed to the gods. If possible, then, make every effort to obtain your release for good, or if you see no chance of that, for at least the time of low Nile, at which season there is no danger [b] and Theodorus can be left to take your place, in order that you may spend this season at least with us. Lay this to heart, that nothing painful shall befall you, but that every care will be taken by me to see that you are untroubled. Goodbye.

[a] Chief engineer in the Fayum. Philonides was his son, living in Alexandria.

[b] That is, no danger of the water bursting the dykes. If Cleon was not allowed to resign his post, he could safely take a holiday at that season.

95. FROM DEMOPHON TO PTOLEMAEUS

About 245 B.C.

Demophon to Ptolemaeus [a] greeting. Send me by hook or crook the flute-player Petous with both the Phrygian and the other flutes ; and if any expenditure is necessary, pay and you shall recover from me.

[a] Ptolemaeus was a minor government employee, subordinate to Demophon.

ἡ[μ]ῖν [11]καὶ Ζηνόβιον τὸν μαλα-[12]κὸν ἔχοντα τύμπανον καὶ [13]κύμβαλα καὶ κρόταλα, χρεί-[14]α γάρ ἐστι ταῖς γυναιξὶν πρὸς [15]τὴν θυσίαν. ἐχέτω δὲ [16]καὶ ἱματισμὸν ὡς ἀσ-[17]τειότατον. κόμισαι δὲ [18]καὶ τὸν ἔριφον παρὰ Ἀρισ-[19]τίωνος καὶ πέμψον ἡμῖν. [20]καὶ τὸ σῶμα δὲ εἰ συνεί-[21]ληφας, παράδος ⟦αὐτὸ⟧ [22]Σεμφθεῖ, ὅπως αὐτὸ δι-[23]ακομίσηι ἡμῖν. ἀπόσ-[24]τειλον δὲ ἡμῖν καὶ τυ-[25]ροὺς ὅσους ἂν δύνηι καὶ [26]κέραμον κενὸν καὶ λά-[27]χανα π[αντ]οδαπὰ καὶ [28]ἐὰν ὄψον τι ἔχηι[ς]. [29]ἔρρ[ωσο]. [30]ἐμβαλοῦ δὲ αὐτὰ καὶ φυ-[31]λακίτας οἳ συνδιακομιοῦ-[32]σιν ⟦α⟧ τὸ πλοῖο[ν].

Verso: Πτολεμαίωι.

26. κενόν or κα[ι]νόν. **30.** αυτα not certain: ? ἅμα.

96. FROM ANDRON TO MILON

P. Eleph. 13. 222 (or 223) B.C.

[1]Ἄνδρων Μίλωνι τἀδελφῶι χαίρειν. εἰ ἔρρω[σ]αι καὶ τὰ λοιπά σοι κατὰ λόγον ἐστίν, εἴη ἂν ὡς ἐγὼ [2]θέλω· ὑγίαινον δὲ καὶ αὐτός. παραγενομένου Σανῶτος ἐκομισάμην τὴν παρὰ σοῦ ἐπιστολήν, [3]ἣν ἀναγνοὺς ἐχάρην ἐπὶ τῶι με αἰσθέσθαι τὰ κατὰ σέ. ἐγὼ οὖν ἐπυνθανόμην τοῦ Σανῶτος [4]εἴ τι βούλοιτο ἐν τοῖς καθ' ἡμᾶς τόποις, ὁ δὲ ἐπήινει μόνον, ἐπέταξεν δ' οὐθέν. περὶ δὲ τῶν εἴκοσι [5]δραχμῶν οὔπω ἐκεκόμιστο Φίλων, Πιστοκλῆς [γ]ὰρ οὐχ εὑρήκειμεν. περὶ δὲ τοῦ οἰναρίου Πρα-[6]ξιάδης οὔπω εἰσελήλυθεν ἐξ ἀγροῦ, οὐκ οἶμαι [δ'] αὐτὸν ἔχειν ἐξ ὧν ἡ μήτηρ αὐτοῦ ἀνήγγελλεν.

5. *l.* Πιστοκλῆν.

Send me also Zenobius the effeminate dancer with a drum and cymbals and castanets, for the women want him for the sacrifice; and let him be dressed as finely as possible. Get the kid also from Aristion and send it to me. And if you have arrested the slave, hand him over to Semphtheus to bring to me. Send me also as many cheeses as you can, empty jars, vegetables of all sorts, and any delicacies that you may have. Goodbye. Put them on board with policemen who will help to bring the boat along. (Addressed) To Ptolemaeus.

96. FROM ANDRON TO MILON

222 (or 223) B.C.

Andron to his brother Milon[a] greeting. If you are well and everything else is to your mind, it would be as I desire. I myself am in good health. On the arrival of Sanos I received your letter, and it was a pleasure to read it and hear your news. I inquired of Sanos whether he wanted anything in our district, but he merely thanked me and did not give any order. About the twenty drachmae, Philon has not yet received them, for we have not found Pistocles. About the wine, Praxiades has not yet come in from the country, but from what his mother tells me I do

[a] Milon was a government controller of the finances of temples in Upper Egypt, Andron probably a manager of a temple bank.

7εὐχαριστήσεις οὖμ μοι σαυτοῦ τε ἐπιμελόμενος καὶ μὴ ὀκνῶν γράφειν ἡμῖν καὶ τί ἂν σοι ποιοῦντες 8χαριζοίμην. (2nd hand) 9ἔρρωσο. (ἔτους) κε Μεσορεὶ ιη.

Verso: Μίλωνι.

8. *l.* χαριζοίμεθα.

97. FROM ISIAS TO HEPHAESTION

P. Lond. 42 (=U.P.Z. 59). 168 B.C.

1Ἰσιὰς Ἡφαιστίωνι τῶι ἀδελφῶ[ι χαί(ρειν)]. 2εἰ ἐρρωμένωι τἆλλα κατὰ λόγον 3ἀπαντᾶι, εἴηι ἂν ὡς τοῖς θεοῖς εὐχο-4μένη διατελῶ· καὶ αὐτὴ δ' ὑγίαινον 5καὶ τὸ παιδίον καὶ οἱ ἐν οἴκωι πάντες, 6σοῦ διὰ παντὸς μνείαν ποιούμενοι. 7κομισαμένη τὴν παρὰ σοῦ ἐπιστολὴν 8παρ' Ὥρου, ἐν ἧι διεσάφεις εἶναι 9ἐν κατοχῆι ἐν τῶι Σαραπιείωι τῶι 10ἐν Μέμφει, ἐπὶ μὲν τῶι ἐρρῶσθα[ί] σε 11εὐθέως τοῖς θεοῖς εὐχαρίστουν, 12ἐπὶ δὲ τῶι μὴ παραγίνεσθαί σε [π]ά[ντ]ων 13τῶν ἐκεῖ ἀπειλημμένων παραγεγο[νό]των 14ἀηδίζομαι ἕ[νε]κα τοῦ ἐκ τοῦ το<ιο>ύτου 15καιροῦ ἐμαυτήν τε καὶ τὸ παιδί[ον σ]ου 16διακεκυβερνηκυῖα καὶ εἰς πᾶν τι 17ἐληλυθυῖα διὰ τὴν τοῦ σίτου τιμὴν 18καὶ δοκοῦσα νῦγ γε σοῦ παραγενομένου 19τεύξεσθαί τινος ἀναψυχῆς, σὲ δὲ 20μηδ' ἐντεθυμῆσθαι τοῦ παραγενέσθαι 21μηδ' ἐνβεβλοφέναι εἰς τὴν ἡμετέραν περί-22στασιν, ὡς ἔτ[ι] σοῦ παρόντος πάντων ἐπεδεόμην, 23μὴ ὅτι γε

8. ειναι corr. from γεγονεναι.

[a] Hephaestion was the husband of Isias, but according to Wilcken the term "brother" is to be taken literally.

not think he has got it. Now you will do me a favour if you take care of yourself and do not hesitate to write and tell me what I could do to please you. Goodbye. Year 25, Mesore 18. (Addressed) To Milon.

97. FROM ISIAS TO HEPHAESTION

168 B.C.

Isias to her brother [a] Hephaestion greeting. If you are well and other things are going right, it would accord with the prayer which I make continually to the gods. I myself and the child and all the household are in good health and think of you always. When I received your letter from Horus, in which you announce that you are in detention [b] in the Serapeum at Memphis, for the news that you are well I straightway thanked the gods, but about your not coming home, when all the others who had been secluded there have come, I am ill-pleased, because after having piloted myself and your child through such bad times and been driven to every extremity owing to the price of corn I thought that now at least, with you at home, I should enjoy some respite, whereas you have not even thought of coming home nor given any regard to our circumstances, remembering how I was in want of everything while you were still here, not to mention

[a] Marriage between brother and sister was not uncommon in Egypt.

[b] Probably not through human agency, but in obedience to the will of the god Sarapis, manifested in some way to the person concerned. The recluse was "possessed" by the god, whether for a short period or for many years.

τοσούτου χρόνου ἐπιγεγονότος [24]καὶ τοιούτων καιρῶν καὶ μηθὲν σοῦ ἀπεσταλκότος. [25]ἔτι δὲ καὶ Ὥρου τοῦ τὴν ἐπιστολὴν παρακεκο-[26]μικότος ἀπηγγελκότος ὑπὲρ τοῦ ἀπολελύσθαι σε [27]ἐκ τῆς κατοχῆς παντελῶς ἀηδίζομαι. [28]οὐ μὴν ἀλλ[ὰ] ἐπεὶ καὶ ἡ μήτηρ σου τυγχάνει [29]βαρέως ἔχουσα, καλῶς ποιήσεις καὶ διὰ ταύτην [30]καὶ δι' ἡμᾶς παραγ[ε]νόμενος εἰς τὴν πόλιν, εἴπερ μὴ [31]ἀναγκαιότερόν σ[ε] περισπᾶι. χαριεῖ δὲ καὶ τοῦ [32]σώματος ἐπιμελ[ό]μενος ἵν' ὑγιαίνηις. [33]ἔρρωσο. (ἔτους) β Ἐπεὶφ λ̅.

Verso: Ἡφαιστίωνι.

98. FROM DIONYSIUS TO PTOLEMAEUS

P. Par. 49 (=U.P.Z. 62). About 160 B.C.

[1]Διονύσι[ος Πτολε]μαίωι χαίρειν καὶ [2]ἐρρῶσθα[ι]. τοι[αύ]την ἐμαυτοῦ [3]ἐλευθερ[ιότ]η[τ]α, [ο]ὐ βαναυσίαν [4]ἐκτέθεικα πᾶσιν ἀνθρώποις, [5]μάλιστα δὲ σοὶ κ[α]ὶ τῷ σῷ ἀδελφῶι [6]διά τε τ[ὸν] Σάραπιν καὶ τὴν σὴν [7]ἐλευθε[ρία]ν καὶ πεπείραμαι, [8]ἀφ' οὗτε συνεστάθης μοι, εἰς πᾶν [9]τό σοι χρήσιμον ἐμαυτὸν ἐπιδιδόναι. [10]τοῦ δὲ ἀδελφοῦ σου συμπεσόντος μοι [11]τῆι ιζ τοῦ Μεχεὶρ [12]καὶ ἀξιώσαντός με ὅπως, ἐὰν ἐνέγκηι [13]τρίτομον, μεταλάβωσιν αὐτῶι οἱ πα-[14]ρ' ἐμοῦ γραμματεῖς πάντας τοὺς [15]χρηματισμούς, εἶπα αὐτῶι μὴ ἐμὲ [16]ἀξιοῦν, ἀλλὰ δόξαντα ἀδελφὸν αὐτοῦ [17]ἐν τῆι αὐλῆι εἶναι παραγίνεσθαι, [18]μονο-

ll. 11 and 35 interpolated. Paragraphi below ll. 9, 15, 17, 24, 26, 28, 30, 32. Colons in ll. 15, 17, 24, 26, 28, 30.

[a] Perhaps a minor official in Memphis, but not, as formerly supposed, the strategus (see Wilcken on *U.P.Z.* 62).

this long lapse of time and these critical days, during which you have sent us nothing. As, moreover, Horus who delivered the letter has brought news of your having been released from detention, I am thoroughly ill-pleased. Notwithstanding, as your mother also is annoyed, for her sake as well as for mine please return to the city, if nothing more pressing holds you back. You will do me a favour by taking care of your bodily health. Goodbye. Year 2, Epeiph 30. (Addressed) To Hephaestion.

98. FROM DIONYSIUS TO PTOLEMAEUS

About 160 B.C.

Dionysius[a] to Ptolemaeus[b] greeting and good health. You know what a liberal, not vulgar, spirit I have displayed towards all men and particularly towards you and your brother on account of Sarapis and your own liberal spirit, and ever since you were introduced to me I have sought to devote myself to all your interests. And when your brother met me on the 17th of Mecheir and asked me to allow my clerks, if he brought a third section of a roll,[c] to undertake the transcription of all his documents, I told him not to ask me, but to come, looking on me as his brother at court,[d] and give nothing to

[b] A recluse in the Serapeum (see No. 97, note *b*).

[c] The Greek word has not yet been explained, but it probably means a certain quantity of papyrus. *Cf.* P. Grenf. ii. 38. 5-6 [ὀ]κταδώμου χάρτου and [τετ]ραδώμου χάρτου (revised reading).

[d] Or, according to Wilcken, "but as he supposed that he had a brother at court, to go to him."

γράφοις δὲ μηθὲν διδόναι γράφειν [19]μηδὲ ἀναλίσκειν χαλκοῦς, καὶ ἀπέλυσα [20]εἴπας αὐτῶι ὀρθρίτερον ἐλθεῖν, ὅπως [21]λαβὼν παρ' ἐμοῦ ἐν Μέμφει σησάμου [22]τέταρτον τρίψῃ μοι {ἐν Μέμφει}τρίμμα [23]διὰ τὸ εἰς τὴν πόλιν με θέλειν δοῦναι [24]ἀπενεγκεῖν. ὁ δέ, φαίνεται, τὴν [25]ἡμέραν ἐκείνην ἀσχοληθεὶς ἤσχυνται [26]συμμεῖξαί μοι. εἴπερ οὖν ἐστιν αὕτη [27]ἡ αἰτία καὶ διὰ τοῦτο οὐκέτι ἥκει πρὸς ἐμὲ [28]αἰσχυνθείς, παρακαλέσας αὐτὸν [29]ἀπόστειλον πρὸς ἐμέ· γίνεται γὰρ [30]ἐντραπῆναι. ἐγὼ γὰρ νὴ τοὺς θεοὺς [31]ἀγωνιῶ μή ποτε ἀ[ρ]ρωστεῖ τὸ παιδάριον [32]καὶ οὐκ ἔχω σχολὴν ἀναβῆναι πρὸς ὑμᾶς. [33]εἰ δὲ δι' ἄλλο τι οὐκ ὀπτάνεταί μοι, γίνωσκε [34]σαφῶς ὅτι, ἐὰν ἀναβῶ κἀγὼ προσκυνῆσαι, [35]πρὸς σὲ οὐ μὴ εἰσέλθω, εἰς δὲ [36]⟦εἰς⟧ τὰ Πρωτάρχου καταλύσω. ὑγίαινε [37][δὲ - - -

Verso: Πτολεμαίωι.

25. Wilcken <ἧ> ἤσχυνται.

99. FROM SARAPION TO HIS BROTHERS

P. Par. 43 (=U.P.Z. 66). 154 B.C.

[1]Σαραπίων Πτολεμαίωι καὶ Ἀπολλωνίῳ τοῖς ἀδελφοῖς χαίρειν. εἰ ἔρρωσθαι, ἔρρω-[2]μαι δὲ καὐτοί. συγγέγραμμαι τῆι Ἑσπέρου θυγατρί, μέλλω δὲ ἰσάγειν [3]ἐν τῷ Μεσορὴ μηνί. καλῶς ποιήσεις ἀποστεῖλαί μοι ἱμίχουν [4]ἐλαίου. γέγραφ' ἱμεῖν ἵνα εἰδῆται. [5]ἔρρωσο. (ἔτους) κη Ἐπεὶφ κα. (Added on left) παραγε<νομε>νοῦ δὲ εἰς τὴν ἡμέραν [6]Ἀπολλώνιος.

Verso: [7]Πτολεμαίωι, [8]Ἀπολλωνίωι.

1. *l.* ἔρρωσθε, and understand εὖ ἂν ἔχοι. 2. *l.* καὐτός. 3. *l.* ἡμίχουν. 4. *l.* ὑμῖν, εἰδῆτε.

professional scribes to write nor spend any money on them; and I sent him off telling him to come early next morning in order to get from me in Memphis a quarter of an artaba of sesame and pound me a paste, as I wished to give it to someone to take to the city. But apparently as he had no time that day he has been ashamed to approach me[a] If that is the reason then and it is because of that matter that he has not come to me any more, being ashamed, reassure him and send him to me; for anyone may feel embarrassment. For by the gods I am anxious to know that the boy is not ill and I have no time to come up to you. But if he is keeping out of my sight for some other reason, understand clearly that if I come up to worship, I will not enter your door, but will lodge with Protarchus. Keep well . . . (Addressed) To Ptolemaeus.

[a] According to Wilcken, "*or* he has been ashamed," because his request had been rejected.

99. FROM SARAPION TO HIS BROTHERS

154 B.C.

Sarapion to his brothers Ptolemaeus[a] and Apollonius greeting. If you are well, (it would be excellent). I myself am well. I have made a contract with the daughter of Hesperus and intend to marry her in the month of Mesore. Please send me half a chous of oil. I have written to you to let you know. Goodbye. Year 28, Epeiph 21. Come for the wedding-day, Apollonius. (Addressed) To Ptolemaeus and Apollonius.

[a] The recipient of No. 98 and of the following letter also.

00. FROM APOLLONIUS TO PTOLEMAEUS

P. Par. 47 (=U.P.Z. 70). About 152 B.C.

[1]Ἀπολλώνιος Πτολεμαίωι [2]τῶι πατρὶ χαίρειν. ὀμνύ-[3]ο τὸν Σάραπιν, ἰ μὴ μικρόν [4]τι ἐντρέπομαι, οὐκ ἄν με [5]ἶδες τὸ πόρσωπόν μου [6]πόποτε, ὅτι ψεύδηι [7]πάντα καὶ οἱ παρὰ σὲ [8]θεοὶ ὁμοίως, ὅτι ἐν-[9]βέβληκαν ὑμᾶς εἰς ὕλην [10]μεγάλην καὶ οὗ δυνάμε-[11]θα ἀποθανεῖν κἂν ἴδης [12]ὅτι μέλλομεν σωθῆναι, [13]τότε βαπτιζώμεθα. [14]γίνωσκε ὅτι πιράσεται [15]ὁ δραπέ[τ]ης μὴ ἀφῖναι [16]ἡμᾶς ἐπὶ [τ]ῶν τόπων [17]ἶναι· χάριν γὰρ ἡμῶν [18]ἠζημίοται εἰς χαλκοῦ [19](τάλαντα) ιε. ὁ στρατηγὸς ἀνα-[20]βαίνει αὔριον εἰς τὸ Σαραπι-[21]ῆν καὶ δύο ἡμέρας ποι-[22]εῖ ἐν τῷ Ἀνου-βιείωι [23]πίνων. οὐκ ἔστι ἀνακύ-[24]ψαι με πόποτε ἐν τῇ Τρικομίαι [25]ὑπὸ τῆς αἰσχύνης, ἰ καὶ [26]αὐτοὺς δεδώκαμεν [27]καὶ ἀποπεπτώκαμεν [28]πλανόμενοι ὑπὸ τῶν [29]θεῶν καὶ πιστεύοντες [30]τὰ ἐνύπνια. εὐτύχει.

Verso: [31]Πτολεμαί-[32]ωι χαίρε[ι]ν. (To left, in small hand) [31]πρὸς τοὺς [32]τὴν ἀλή-[33]θειαν λέγοντες.

2. *l.* ὀμνύω. 5. *l.* πρόσωπον. 7. σέ corr. from σοί. 9. *l.* ἡμᾶς. 13. *l.* βαπτιζόμεθα. 18. *l.* ἐζημίωται. 20. *l.* Σαραπιεῖον. 24. *l.* Τρικωμίαι. 28. *l.* πλανώμενοι. 33. *l.* λέγοντας.

101. FROM ESTHLADAS TO HIS PARENTS

Revillout, *Mélanges*, p. 295 (=W. Chrest. 10). 130 B.C.

[1]Ἐσθλάδας τῶι πατρὶ καὶ τῆι μητρὶ χαί(ρειν) [2]καὶ ἐρρῶσθαι. ἐπεὶ πλειονάκις σοι γρά-[3]φω

1. καὶ τῆι μητρί inserted later.

100. FROM APOLLONIUS TO PTOLEMAEUS

About 152 B.C.

Apollonius to Ptolemaeus his father [a] greeting. I swear by Sarapis that if I had not a little compunction, you would never have seen my face again; for you utter nothing but lies and your gods likewise, for they have plunged us into a deep mire in which we may die, and when you have a vision that we are to be rescued, then we sink outright. Know that the runaway [b] will try to prevent us remaining in the place; for because of us he has suffered a loss of 15 talents. The strategus is coming up to-morrow to the Serapeum and will spend two days in the Anubieum [c] drinking. Never again can I hold up my head in Tricomia for shame that we have given ourselves away and been deluded, misled by the gods and trusting in dreams.[d] Farewell. (Addressed) To Ptolemaeus greeting. (Added at the side) A reply to the soothsayers.

[a] Ptolemaeus was really the writer's elder brother.

[b] The writer is referring to an enemy called Menedemus.

[c] A temple of Anubis situated near the avenue of the Serapeum.

[d] The Serapeum was a favourite haunt of persons seeking divine revelations through dreams, and Ptolemaeus was a devout believer in this superstition. Many of his papers refer to the same subject.

101. FROM ESTHLADAS TO HIS PARENTS

130 B.C.

Esthladas to his father and mother greeting and good health. As I have often written to you to keep

περὶ τοῦ διανδραγαθήσαντα [4]σαυτοῦ ἐπιμέλεσθαι μέχρι τοῦ [5]τὰ πράγματ' ἀποκαταστῆναι, [6]ἔτι καὶ νῦν καλῶς ποιήσεις παρα-[7]καλῶν σαυτὸν καὶ τοὺς παρ' ἡμῶν. [8]προσπέπτωκεν γὰρ Παῶν ἀνα-[9]πλεῖν ἐν τῶι Τῦβι μ(ηνὶ) μετὰ δυνάμεων [10]ἱκανῶν πρὸς τὸ καταστεῖσαι τοὺς [11]ἐν Ἑρμώνθει ὄχλους, χρήσασθαι δ' αὐτοῖς [12]{αὐτοῖς} ὡς ἀποστάταις. ἐπισκοποῦ δ[ὲ] [13]καὶ τὰς ἀδελφὰς ⟦αδ⟧ καὶ Πέλοπα [14]καὶ Στάχυν καὶ Σεναθῦριν. [15]ἔρρωσο. (ἔτους) μ Χοίαχ κγ.

Verso: [1]ἀπόδος [ε]ἰς [2]Παθῦρ(ιν) [3]τῶι πατρί.

10. *l.* καταστεῖλαι (Wilcken) rather than καταστῆσαι.

102. FROM PETESOUCHUS TO MARRES

P. Tebt. 56. Late 2nd cent. B.C.

[1]Πετεσοῦχος Μαρρήους γ[εωρ]γὸς [2]τῶν ἐκ Κερκεσήφεως {[εω]ς} [3]Μαρρῆτι Πετοσείριος τῶ[line 4 missing] [5]καὶ ἀδελφῷ χαίρειν. γείν[ωσ]κε δὲ [6]περὶ τοῦ κατακεκλῦσθαι τὸ πεδίον [7]ὑμῶν καὶ οὐκ ἔχομεν ἕως τῆς [8]τροφῆς τῶν κτηνῶν ἡμῶν. [9]καλῶς οὖν ποήσῃς εὐχαριστῆσαι [10]πρῶτον μὲν τοῖς θεοῖς, δεύτερον [11]δὲ σῶσαι ψυχὰς πολλὰς ζητή[σ]α[ς] [12]μοι περὶ τὴν κώμην σου εἰς τὴν [13]τροφὴν ἡμῶν γῆς ἀρούρας πέ[ν-][14]τε ὡς ἕξομεν ἐξ αὐτῶν τὴ[ν] [15]τροφὴν ἡμῶν. τοῦτο δὲ ποήσας [16]ἔσῃ μοι κεχαρισμένος εἰς τὸν [17]ἅπαντα χρόνο[ν]. [18]ἔρρωσο.

7. *l.* ἡμῶν.

a stout heart and take care of yourself until things settle down, once again please exhort yourself and our dependants to take courage. For news has come that Paos is sailing up in the month of Tubi with abundant forces to subdue the mobs at Hermonthis[a] and deal with them as rebels. Look after my sisters also and Pelops and Stachys and Senathuris. Goodbye. Year 40, Choiach 23. (Addressed) Deliver at Pathyris to my father.

[a] A reference to the conflict between Euergetes II. and his sister Cleopatra. Paos was the king's general.

102. FROM PETESOUCHUS TO MARRES

Late 2nd cent. B.C.

Petesouchus son of Marres, cultivator at Kerkesephis,[a] to Marres son of Petosiris . . . his brother greeting. Know that our plain has been flooded and we have not so much as food for our cattle. Please therefore first of all to give thanks to the gods and secondly to save many lives by seeking out in the neighbourhood of your village five arurae of land for our maintenance, in order that we may thence obtain food for ourselves. If you do this, you will oblige me for all time. Goodbye.

[a] A village in the Fayum.

103. FROM PETOSOUCHUS TO HIS FRIENDS

P. Grenf. ii. 36. 95 B.C.

[1]Πετοσοῦχος Πανεβχούνιος Πετεαρσεμθεῖ [2]καὶ Παγάνει Πανεβχούνιος καὶ [3]Παθήμει Παρᾶ καὶ Πετεαρσεμθεῖ [4]Ἁρσενούφ[ι]ος καὶ Πετεαρσεμθεῖ [5]Ψεννήσ[ι]ος καὶ Ὥρωι Πατῆτος χαίρειν [6]καὶ ἐρρῶσθαι· ἔρρωμαι δὲ καὶ αὐτὸς [7]καὶ Ἐσθαῦτις καὶ Πατοῦς καὶ Ἀλμέντις [8]καὶ Φίβις καὶ Ψενοσῖρις καὶ Φάφις [9]καὶ οἱ παρ' ἡμῶν πάντες. μὴ λυ-[10]πεῖσθε ἐπὶ τοῖς χωρισθεῖσι. ὑπε-[11]λαμβάνοσαν φονευθήσεσθαι. οὐθὲν [12]ἡμῖν κακὸν ἐπύησεν, ἀλλ' ἐκ τῶν [13]ἐναντίων ἐπιμεμέληται. [14]περὶ ὧν ἐὰν αἱρῆτε γράψατέ [15]μοι. ἠκούσαμεν τὸν μῦν κατα-[16]βεβρωκέναι τὸν σπόρον. καλῶς [17]ἡμῖν ὧδε, ἢ ἐν Διὸς πόλει ἐὰν [18]αἱρῆσθε, πυρὸν ἀγοράσαι ἥκατε. [19]τὰ δ' ἄλλα χαρίζοισθ' ἑαυτῶν ἐπι-[20]μελόμενοι ἵν' ὑγιαίνητε. [21]ἔρρωται Ὧρος καὶ Πετοσῖρις. [22]ἔρρωσθε. (ἔτους) ιθ Παχὼν η.

Verso: [23]Πετεαρσεμθεῖ Νεβχούνιος. (On left side) παρὰ [24]Πετοσούχου [25]τοῦ Νεβχούνιος.

3. Παρᾶ E. H., παρά Edd. 7. Ἐσθαῦτις, Ἀλμέντις: revised readings. 12. *l.* ἐποίησεν.

104. FROM THE CHIEF PHYSICIAN

B.S.A.A. xiv. p. 194. 1st cent. B.C.

[1]Ἀθηναγόρας ὁ ἀρχίατρος τοῖς ἱερεῦσι τῶν [2]ἐν τῶ[ι] Λαβυρίνθωι στολιστῶν καὶ τοῖς [3]στολ[ισ]ταῖς

[a] Head of the public physicians who were maintained by the state.

[b] Temple attendants whose office was to clothe the images

103. FROM PETOSOUCHUS TO HIS FRIENDS

95 B.C.

Petosouchus son of Panebchounis to Peteharsemtheus and Paganis sons of Panebchounis and Pathemis son of Paras and Peteharsemtheus son of Harsenouphis and Peteharsemtheus son of Psennesis and Horus son of Pates, greeting and good health. I myself am well and Esthautis and Patous and Almentis and Phibis and Psenosiris and Phaphis and all our men. Do not grieve over the departed. They were expecting to be killed. To us he[a] did no harm, but on the contrary has taken care of us. Write to me about any matter that you choose. We heard that mice have eaten up the crop. Pray come to us and buy wheat here, or, if you prefer, at Diospolis.[b] For the rest please do us a favour by taking care of your own health. Horus and Petosiris are well. Goodbye. Year 19, Pachon 8. (Addressed) To Peteharsemtheus son of Nebchounis. From Petosouchus son of Nebchounis.

[a] In another letter the writer mentions a certain strategus as his protector, but whether he is here referring to the same person is quite uncertain.

[b] The Egyptian Thebes.

104. FROM THE CHIEF PHYSICIAN

1st cent. B.C.

Athenagoras the chief physician[a] to the priests of the stolistae[b] at the Labyrinth[c] and to the stolistae

of the gods, though in the present case they seem to have been employed as mummy-dressers. It appears from this passage that only certain of them held the title of priest.

[c] The temple of Amenemhet III. at Hawara in the Fayum.

χαίρειν. ἐπεὶ Ἡρακλείδης [4]ὁ πα[ρ' ἐ]μοῦ ἐπὶ τῶν τόπων τετελεύτηκ(εν) [5]καὶ ἔ[σ]τιν ἐν ταῖς παρ' ὑμεῖν νεκρίαις, [6]τού[τ]ου δὲ χάριν πέπομφα Νικίαν καὶ Κρόκ(ον), [7]καλῶς ποιήσετε προέμενοι τὸ σω-[8]μάτι[ο]ν μηθὲν πράξαντες καὶ συν-[9]καταστήσατε αὐτοῖς ἕως Πτολεμαΐδος. [10]γέγραφαν δὲ ὑμεῖν καὶ οἱ ἀπ' Ἀλεξανδρείας [11]στολ[ισ]ταὶ περὶ αὐτοῦ. ἐπιμέλεσθε δὲ [12]ἑαυ[τῶ]ν ἵν' ὑγιαίνητε. [13]ἔρρωσ(θε). (ἔτους) ιδ Ἁθὺρ κε̅.

Verso: [14]τοῖς ἱερεῦσι τῶν στολιστῶν [15]καὶ τοῖς στολιστα[ῖς].

10. γέγραφαν revised reading: ⟦γ⟧ἔγραψαν Ed.

105. FROM HILARION TO ALIS

P. Oxy. 744. 1 B.C.

[1]Ἱλαρίων{α} Ἄλιτι τῆι ἀδελφῇ πλεῖστα χαί-[2]ρειν καὶ Βεροῦτι τῇ κυρίᾳ μου καὶ Ἀπολλω-[3]νάριν. γίνωσκε ὡς ἔτι καὶ νῦν ἐν Ἀλεξαν-[4]δρέᾳ 'σμεν. μὴ ἀγωνιᾷς· ἐὰν ὅλως εἰσ-[5]πορεύονται, ἐγὼ ἐν Ἀλεξανδρέᾳ μενῶ. [6]ἐρωτῶ σε καὶ παρακαλῶ σε, ἐπιμελή-[7]θ⟨ητ⟩ι τῷ παιδίῳ καὶ ἐὰν εὐθὺς ὀψώ-[8]νιον λάβωμεν ἀποστελῶ σε ἄνω. ἐὰν [9]πολλὰ πολλῶν τέκῃς, ἐὰν ᾖ{ν} ἄρσε-[10]νον, ἄφες, ἐὰν ᾖ{ν} θήλεα, ἔκβαλε. [11]εἴρηκας δὲ Ἀφροδισιᾶτι ὅτι μή με [12]ἐπιλάθῃς. πῶς δύναμαί σε ἐπι-[13]λαθεῖν; ἐρωτῶ σε οὖν ἵνα μὴ ἀγω-[14]νιάσῃς. [15](ἔτους) κθ Καίσαρος Παῦνι κγ.

Verso: [16]Ἱλαρίων Ἄλιτι ἀπόδος.

2. *l.* Ἀπολλωναρίῳ. 4. Or ἀγωνιάσ⟨ῃς⟩. 8. *l.* σοι.

greeting. Since Heraclides my employee has died in your district and is lying in the cemetery there and I have therefore sent to you Nicias and Crocus, please deliver the body without charging any fee and help them to transport it as far as Ptolemais. The stolistae of Alexandria have also written to you about him. Take care of your own health. Goodbye. Year 14, Hathur 25. (Addressed) To the priests of the stolistae and to the stolistae.

105. FROM HILARION TO ALIS

1 B.C.

Hilarion to his sister [a] Alis very many greetings, likewise to my lady Berous and Apollonarion. Know that we are still in Alexandria. Do not be anxious; if they [b] really go home, I will remain in Alexandria. I beg and entreat you, take care of the little one, and as soon as we receive our pay I will send it up to you. If by chance you bear a child, if it is a boy, let it be, if it is a girl, cast it out. You have said to Aphrodisias [c] "Do not forget me." How can I forget you? I beg you then not to be anxious. The 29th year of Caesar,[d] Pauni 23. (Addressed) Deliver to Alis from Hilarion.

[a] Alis was Hilarion's wife. "Sister" is often used as a mere term of endearment; but as marriage between brother and sister was permitted, it is not always possible to say whether the word is to be taken literally. *Cf.* No. 97, note *a*.

[b] Probably his companions.

[c] As a message for Hilarion.

[d] That is, the Emperor Augustus. See No. 3, note *b*.

106. LETTER OF RECOMMENDATION

P. Oxy. 292. About A.D. 25

[1]Θέων Τυράννωι τῶι τιμιωτάτωι [2]πλεῖστα χαίρειν. [3]Ἡρακλείδης ὁ ἀποδιδούς σοι τὴν [4]ἐπιστολὴν ἐστίν μου ἀδελφός· [5]διὸ παρακαλῶ σε μετὰ πάσης δυνά-[6]μεως ἔχειν αὐτὸν συνεσταμέ-[7]νον. ἠρώτησα δὲ καὶ Ἑρμί[α]ν [8]τὸν ἀδελφὸν διὰ γραπτοῦ ἀνηγεῖ-[σθαί] [9]σοι περὶ τούτου. χαρίεσαι δέ μοι τὰ μέγιστα [10]ἐάν σου τῆς ἐπισημασίας τύχηι. [11]πρὸ δὲ πάντων ὑγια<ί>νειν σε εὔχ[ο-][12]μαι ἀβασκάντως τὰ ἄριστα [13]πράττων. ἔρρω(σο).

Verso: Τυράννωι διοικ(ητῆι).

9. *l.* χαρίσει. 13. *l.* πράττοντα.

107. FROM SARAPION TO HERACLIDES

B.G.U. 1079. A.D. 41.

[1]Σαραπίων Ἡρακλείδῃ τῷ [2]ἡμετέρῳ χα(ίρειν). ἔπεμψά σοι [3]ἄλλας δύο ἐπιστολάς, [4]διὰ Νηδύμου μίαν, διὰ [5]Κρονίου μαχαιροφόρου [6]μίαν. λοιπὸν οὖν ἔλα-[7]βον παρὰ το(ῦ) Ἄραβος τὴν [8]ἐπιστολὴν καὶ ἀνέ-[9]γνων καὶ ἐλυπήθην. [10]ἀκολούθει δὲ Πτολλ-[11]αρίωνι πᾶσαν ὥραν· τά-[12]χα δύναταί σε εὔλυτ-[13]ον ποῖσαι. λέγε αὐτῷ· ἄ-[14]λλο ἐγώ, ἄλλο πάντες· [15]ἐγὼ παιδάριν εἰμί· παρὰ [16]τάλαντόν σοι πέπρακα [17]τὰ φο[ρτ]ία μου· οὐκ οἶδα [18]τί μ[ε ὁ] πάτρων ποίσει· [19]πολλοὺς δανιστὰς ἔχο-[20]μεν· μὴ

13. *l.* ποιῆσαι. 15. *l.* παιδάριον. 18. *l.* ποιήσει.

106. LETTER OF RECOMMENDATION

About A.D. 25.

Theon to the most honoured Tyrannus very many greetings. Heraclides, the bearer of this letter, is my brother, wherefore I entreat you with all my power to take him under your protection. I have also asked your brother Hermias by letter to inform you about him. You will do me the greatest favour if you let him win your approval. Before all else I pray that you may have health and the best of success, unharmed by the evil eye. Goodbye. (Addressed) To Tyrannus the dioecetes.[a]

[a] A financial administrator, much less important than the Ptolemaic official who bore the same title.

107. FROM SARAPION TO HERACLIDES

A.D. 41.

Sarapion to our Heraclides greeting. I sent you two other letters, one by Nedymus and one by Cronius the sword-bearer. Well, I received your letter from the Arab and I read it with pain. Wait on Ptollarion at all times; perhaps he can relieve you. Say to him: "I am different from all the rest; I am a slave[a]; I have sold you my wares for a talent[b] too little (?); I do not know what my patron will do to me; we have many creditors; pray do not

[a] Or "I am a child."
[b] Or "except for a talent's worth," but the meaning is obscure.

ἵνα ἀναστατώ-[21]σῃς ἡμᾶς. ἐρώτα αὐτὸν [22]καθ' ἡμέραν· τάχα δύνα-[23]ταί σε ἐλεῆσαι. ἐὰν μή, ὡς [24]ἂν πάντες καὶ σὺ βλέ-[25]πε σατὸν ἀπὸ τῶν Ἰου-[26]δαίων. μᾶλλον ἀκολουθῶν [27]αὐτῷ δύνῃ φιλιάσαι αὐτῷ. [28]ἴδε ἡ δύναται διὰ Διοδώρου [29]ὑπογραφῆναι ἡ τάβλα διὰ [30]τῆς γυναικὸς τοῦ ἡγεμ-[31]όνος. ἐὰν τὰ παρ(ὰ) σατοῦ ποί-[32]σῃς, οὐκ εἶ μεμπτός. [33]ἀσπάζου Διόδωρον μεγάλω(ς). [34]ἔρρω(σο). ἀσπάζου Ἁρποχράτιον. [35](ἔτους) α Τιβερίου Κλαυδίου Καίσαρο(ς) [36]Σεβα(στοῦ) Γερμανικοῦ Αὐτοκρά-(τορος) μηνὸ(ς) [37]Καισαρείου ια.

Verso: [38][ἀπόδος εἰς] Ἀλεξά(νδρειαν) [39]εἰς Σεβα-(στὴν) Ἀγορὰ(ν) εἰς τ[ὴν] . . . . [40]. . . θήκην ὥστε Ἡρακλ(είδῃ) πα(ρὰ) Σαραπίω(νος) [41] . . . . ωνος το(ῦ) Σωσιπάτρου.

25. *l.* σαυτόν. 28. *l.* εἰ. 31. *l.* σαυτοῦ.

108. FROM HORUS TO APION

P. Oxy. 299. Late 1st cent. A.D.

[1]Ὧρος Ἀπίωνι τῷ τειμειωτάτωι χαίρειν. [2]Λάμπωνι μυοθηρευτῇ ἔδωκα αὐτῷ διὰ σοῦ ἀρα-[3]βῶνα (δραχμὰς) η ἵνα μυοθηρεύσει ἐν Τόκα. καλῶς ποιήσεις [4]πέμψεις μοι αὐτάς. καὶ Διονυσίῳ προσ[τ]άτῃ Νεμερῶν [5]κέκρηκα (δραχμὰς) η καὶ ταύτας οὐκ ἔπεμψε, ἵνα εἰδῇς. [6]ἔρρωσ(ο). Παῦνι κδ.

5. *l.* κέχρηκα.

ruin us." Entreat him every day; perhaps he may take pity on you. If not, like everybody else beware you too of the Jews. By waiting on him you are better able to make a friend of him. See if with Diodorus's help you can get the tablet signed through the wife of the praefect. If you attend to your business, you cannot be blamed. Salute Diodorus heartily. Goodbye. Salute Harpocration. Year 1 of Tiberius Claudius Caesar Augustus Germanicus Imperator, the 11th of the month Caesareus.[a] (Addressed) Deliver in Alexandria in the Imperial Market in . . . to Heraclides from Sarapion . . .

[a] = Mesore.

108. FROM HORUS TO APION

Late 1st cent. A.D.

Horus to the most honoured Apion greeting. Regarding Lampon the mouse-catcher, I paid him on your account[a] 8 drachmae as earnest money to catch mice in Toka.[b] You will kindly send me this sum. I have also lent 8 drachmae to Dionysius, president of Nemerae, and he has not sent them back; this is to inform you. Goodbye. Pauni 24.

[a] Understanding διὰ σοῦ as a mistake for ὑπὲρ σοῦ.

[b] It was customary to destroy the mice in the vineyards when the grapes were ripening.

109. FROM GEMELLUS TO SABINUS

P. Fay. 114. A.D. 100.

[1]Λούκιος Βελλῆνος Γέμελλος [2]Σαβίνωι τῶι οιείῶι
χαίρειν. [3]εὖ οὖν πυήσας κομισάμε-[4]νός μου τὴν
ἐπιστολὴν [5]πέμσις μυ Πίνδαρον [6]εἰς τὴν πόλιν τὸν
πεδι-[7]οφύλακα τῆς Διονυσιάδο(ς), [8]ἐπὶ ἐρώτησέ με
Ἑρμο͂-[9]ναξ εἵνα αὐτὸν λά-[10]βῃ εἰς Κερκεσοῦχα
[11]καταμαθῖν τὸν [12]ἐλαιῶνα αὐτοῦ, ἐπὶ [13]πυκνός
ἐστιν καὶ [14]θέλι ἐξ αὐτο͂ν ἐκκό-[15]ψαι φυτά, εἵνα
ἐνπί-[16]ρος κοπῇ τὰ μέλλον-[17]τα ἐκκόπτεσθαι· καὶ
[18]τὴν εἰκθυὶν πέμσις [19]τῆι κδ εἴ κε εἰς τὰ [20]γενέσια
Γεμέλλης. [21]μὴ ο<ὖ>ν ληρήσῃς τὸν [22]ἐκτιναγμόν
σου. [23]ἔρρωσο. (ἔτους) δ Αὐτοκράτορος [24]Καίσα-
ρος Νερούα [25]Τραϊαν[οῦ] Σεβαστοῦ [26]Γερμανικοῦ
Χύακ [27]ιη.

2. l. υἱῶι. 3. l. ποιήσας. 5. l. πέμψεις μοι. 8. l. ἐπεί (so in 12), Ἑρμῶναξ. 14. l. αὐτῶν. 15. l. ἐμπείρως. 18. l. ἰχθύν. 19. l. ἤ.

110. FROM HARPOCRATION TO SABINUS

P. Fay. 123. About A.D. 100.

[1]Ἁρποκρατίων Βελλήνωι [2]Σαβείνωι τῶι ἀ-
[3]δελφῶι χα(ίρειν). καὶ ἐκ-[4]θές σοι ἔγραψα διὰ
[5]Μάρδωνος τοῦ σοῦ γ-[6]νῶναί σε θέλων ὅ-[7]τι διὰ
τὸ ἐπηρεᾶσθαι [8]οὐκ ἠδυνήθην κατελ-[9]θεῖν, καὶ ὥς
ἔχωι [10]ὧδε ἡμέρας ὀλίγας [11]ἐὰν δοκῇ σοι πέμψαι
[12]τὸ ἄποχο{ο}ν Ἰσᾶτος καὶ [13]παραλάβωμεν τὸ
ἐλάδιο-[14]ν λυπὸν ἐὰν δόξῃ σοι. [15]ἐλήλυθεν γὰρ
Τεύφι-[16]λος Ἰουδαῖος λέγων [17][ὅ]τι ἤχθην ἰς γεωρ-

109. FROM GEMELLUS TO SABINUS

A.D. 100.

Lucius Bellenus Gemellus [a] to his son Sabinus greeting. On receipt of my letter you will kindly send me Pindarus, the field-guard at Dionysias, to the city, as Hermonax has asked me to let him take him to Kerkesoucha to examine his olive-grove, as it is too dense and he wishes to cut down some of the trees, in order that those to be cut down may be cut skilfully. And send the fish on the 24th or 25th for Gemella's birthday feast. Now do not talk nonsense about gathering your olives.[b] Goodbye. The 4th year of the Emperor Caesar Nerva Trajanus Augustus Germanicus, Choiak 18.

[a] A discharged veteran who owned land at Dionysias and other villages in the Fayum.
[b] Literally "your shaking down."

110. FROM HARPOCRATION TO SABINUS

About A.D. 100.

Harpocration to Bellenus Sabinus [a] his brother greeting. I wrote to you yesterday too by your man Mardon, wishing you to know that because of the annoyance I have been subjected to I was unable to come down, and as I have to spend a few days here, if you think fit send the receipt (?) of Isas and let us take over the rest of the oil, if you approve. Theophilus the Jew has come saying, " I

[a] See No. 109.

3. *l.* ἐχθές. 12. αποχοον: 2nd ο doubtful; for ἀποχον (= ἀποχήν)? 14. *l.* λοιπόν.

γίαν [18]καὶ βούλομαι πρὸς Σαβεῖ-[19]νον ἀπελθεῖ[ν]. οὔτε γὰρ εἴ-[20]ρηχε ἡμ[ῖ]ν ἀγόμενος [21]ἵνα ἀπολυθῇ, ἀλλὰ αἰ-[22]φνιδί⟦.⟧ως εἴρηχεν ἡμῖν [23]σήμερον. γνώσομαι γὰρ [24]εἰ ἀληθῶς λέγι. [25]ἔρρωσ{σ}ο. ἀσπάζου [26]τοὺς ἀδελφοὺς Λύκον [27]κα[ὶ . . . . . .]ν. [28][Με]χεὶρ ιβ.

Verso: [29]ἀπ[ό]δος Βελλήνῳ [30]Σαβείνωι.

111. FROM A RECRUIT IN ITALY

Class. Phil. xxii. p. 243. — 2nd cent. A.D.

[1]Ἀπολινάρις Ταήσι τῇ μητρεὶ καὶ κυρίᾳ [2]πολλὰ χαίρειν. πρὸ μὲν πάντων εὔχομαί σε [3]ὑγειαίνειν, κἀγὼ αὐτὸς ὑγειαίνω καὶ τὸ προσκύνη-[4]μά σου ποιῶ παρὰ τοῖς ἐνθάδε θεοῖς. γεινώσκειν σε [5]θέλω, μήτηρ, ὅτι ἐρρώμενος ἐγενόμην εἰς Ῥώμην [6]Παχὼν μηνὶ κε̅ καὶ ἐκληρώθην εἰς Μισηνούς, [7]οὔπω δὲ τὴν κε<ν>τυρίαν μου ἔγνων· οὐ γὰρ ἀπε-[8]ληλύτειν εἰς Μισηνοὺς ὅτε σοι τὴν ἐπιστολὴν ταύτην [9]ἔγραφον. ἐρωτῶ σε οὖν, μήτηρ, σεαυτῇ πρόσεχε, [10]μηδὲν δίσταζε περὶ ἐμοῦ· ἐγὼ γὰρ εἰς καλὸν τό-[11]πον ἦλθον. καλῶς δὲ ποιήσ<εις> γράψασ{σ}ά μοι ἐπιστο-[12]λὴν πε[ρ]ὶ τῆς σωτηρίας σου καὶ τῶν ἀδελφῶν μου καὶ [13]τῶν σῶν πάντων. καὶ ᾽γὼ εἴ τινα ἐὰν εὕρω γράφω [14]σοι· οὐ μὴ ὀκνήσω σοι γράφιν. ἀσπάζομαι τοὺς ἀ-[15]δελφούς μου πολλὰ καὶ Ἀπολινάριν καὶ τὰ τέ-[16]κνα αὐτοῦ καὶ Καραλᾶν καὶ τὰ τέκνα αὐτοῦ. [17]ἀσπάζ[ο]μαι Πτολεμαῖν καὶ Πτολεμαείδα καὶ τὰ [18]τέκν[α] αὐτῆς καὶ Ἡρακλοῦν καὶ τὰ τέκνα αὐτῆς. [19]ἀσπά-

have been impressed as a cultivator,[a] and I want to go to Sabinus." He did not say anything to me when he was taken, asking to be released, but he has suddenly told me to-day. I will find out whether he is speaking the truth. Goodbye. Salute my brothers Lycus and . . . Mecheir 12. (Addressed) Deliver to Bellenus Sabinus.

[a] Villages and individual peasants could be compelled to undertake the cultivation of state lands.

111. FROM A RECRUIT IN ITALY

2nd cent. A.D.

Apollinarius to Taesis, his mother and lady, many greetings. Before all I pray for your health. I myself am well and make supplication for you before the gods of this place. I wish you to know, mother, that I arrived in Rome in good health on the 25th of the month Pachon and was posted to Misenum,[a] though I have not yet learned the name of my company[b]; for I had not gone to Misenum at the time of writing this letter. I beg you then, mother, look after yourself and do not worry about me; for I have come to a fine place. Please write me a letter about your welfare and that of my brothers and of all your folk. And whenever I find a messenger I will write to you; never will I be slow to write. Many salutations to my brothers and Apollinarius and his children and Karalas and his children. I salute Ptolemaeus and Ptolemais and her children and Heraclous and her children. I

[a] To join the fleet.

[b] The name of his company or *centuria* would be that of the ship.

ζομαι τοὺς φιλοῦντάς σε πάντας κατ᾽ ὄνο-^{20}μα. ^{21}ἐρρῶσθαί σε εὔχομαι.

Verso: ^{22}ἀπόδ(ος) εἰς Καρανίδα Ταήσι ἀπὸ Ἀπολιναρίου υείοῦ ^{23}Μισηνάτου.

112. FROM A RECRUIT AT MISENUM

B.G.U. 423. 2nd cent. A.D.

^{1}Ἀπίων Ἐπιμάχῳ τῶι πατρὶ καὶ ^{2}κυρίῳ πλεῖστα χαίρειν. πρὸ μὲν πάν-^{3}των εὔχομαί σε ὑγιαίνειν καὶ διὰ παντὸς ^{4}ἐρ<ρ>ωμένον εὐτυχεῖν μετὰ τῆς ἀδελφῆς ^{5}μου καὶ τῆς θυγατρὸς αὐτῆς καὶ τοῦ ἀδελφοῦ ^{6}μου. εὐχαριστῶ τῷ κυρίῳ Σεράπιδι ^{7}ὅτι μου κινδυνεύσαντος εἰς θάλασσαν ^{8}ἔσωσε εὐθέως. ὅτε εἰσῆλθον εἰς Μη-^{9}σηνούς, ἔλαβα βιατικὸν παρὰ Καίσαρος ^{10}χρυσοῦς τρεῖς. καὶ καλῶς μοί ἐστιν. ^{11}ἐρωτῶ σε οὖν, κύριέ μου πατήρ, ^{12}γράψον μοι ἐπιστόλιον, πρῶτον ^{13}μὲν περὶ τῆς σωτηρίας σου, δεύ-^{14}τερον περὶ τῆς τῶν ἀδελφῶν μου, ^{15}τρ[ί]τον ἵνα σου προσκυνήσω τὴν ^{16}χέραν, ὅτι με ἐπαίδευσας καλῶς ^{17}καὶ ἐκ τούτου ἐλπίζω ταχὺ προκό-^{18}σαι τῶν θεῶν θελόντων. ἄσπασαι ^{19}Καπίτων[α π]ολλὰ καὶ τοὺς ἀδελφούς ^{20}[μ]ου καὶ Σε[ρηνί]λλαν καὶ το[ὺς] φίλους μο[υ]. ^{21}ἔπεμψά σο[ι εἰ]κόνιν μ[ου] διὰ Εὐκτή-^{22}μονος. ἔσ[τ]ι [δέ] μου ὄνομα Ἀντῶνις Μά-^{23}ξιμος. ἐρρῶσθαί σε εὔχομαι. ^{24}κεντυρί(α) Ἀθηνονίκη.

(On left margin) ^{25}ἀσπάζεταί σε Σερῆνος ὁ τοῦ Ἀγαθοῦ Δαίμονος [καὶ . . . .]ς ὁ τοῦ [. . . -]^{26}ρος καὶ Τούρβων ὁ τοῦ Γαλλωνίου καὶ Δ[. . .]νᾶς ὁ τ[οῦ . . . . . .]σεν[. . . ^{27}. . . .] . [. . .] . [

17. *l.* προκόψαι.

salute all who love you, each by name. I pray for your health. (Addressed) Deliver at Karanis[a] to Taesis, from her son Apollinarius of Misenum.

[a] A small town in the Fayum.

112. FROM A RECRUIT AT MISENUM

2nd cent. A.D.

Apion to Epimachus, his father and lord, very many greetings. Before all else I pray for your health and that you may always be well and prosperous, together with my sister and her daughter and my brother. I thank the lord Serapis that when I was in danger at sea he straightway saved me. On arriving at Misenum I received from Caesar three gold pieces for travelling expenses. And it is well with me. Now I ask you, my lord and father, write me a letter, telling me first of your welfare, secondly of my brother's and sister's, and enabling me thirdly to make obeisance before your handwriting, because you educated me well and I hope thereby to have quick advancement, if the gods so will. Give many salutations to Capiton and my brother and sister and Serenilla and my friends. I have sent you by Euctemon a portrait of myself. My name[a] is Antonius Maximus, my company the Athenonica. I pray for your health. (Postscript) Serenus son of Agathodaemon salutes you, and . . ., and Turbo son of Gallonius, and . . . (Addressed) To Philadelphia, to Epimachus from Apion his son. (Ad-

[a] The name under which Apion, not being a Roman citizen, was enrolled. He adds below the name of his *centuria*, equivalent in the fleet to the name of the ship.

Verso: ^{28}ε[ἰς] Φ[ιλ]αδέλφιαν Ἐπιμάχῳ ἀπὸ Ἀπίωνος υἱοῦ. (Added below) ^{29}ἀπόδος εἰς χώρτην πρῖμαν Ἀπαμηνῶν’ Ἰο[υλι]α[ν]οῦ ἀντ[ι-]^{30}λιβλαρίῳ ἀπὸ Ἀπίωνος ὥστε Ἐπιμάχῳ πατρὶ αὐτοῦ.

29. *l.* Ἰο[υλι]α[ν]ῷ. 29-30. *l.* (as suggested by Ramsay) ἀντ[ι]λιβραρίῳ.

113. A LETTER FROM ROME

B.G.U. 27. 2nd or 3rd cent. A.D.

^{1}[Εἰρηναῖος Ἀπολιναρίωι τῶι ^{2}φιλτάτ]ωι ἀδε[λ]φ[ῶι] πολ[λ]ὰ χαίρει[ν]. ^{3}καὶ διὰ π[α]ντὸς εὔχομαί σε ὑγιένεν, ^{4}καὶ ἐ[γὼ] αὐτὸς ὑγιένω. γινώσ-^{5}{σ}κειν σε θέλω ὅτει εἰς γῆν ^{6}ἐλήλυθα τῇ ς̄ τοῦ Ἐπεὶφ ^{7}μηνὸς καὶ ἐξεκενώσαμεν τῇ ^{8}ιη̄ τοῦ αὐτοῦ μηνός. ἀνέβην ^{9}δὲ εἰς Ῥώμην τῇ κε̄ τοῦ αὐ-^{10}τοῦ μηνὸς καὶ παρεδέξατο ἡ-^{11}μᾶς ὁ τόπος ὡς ὁ θεὸς ἤθελεν, ^{12}καὶ καθ’ ἡμέραν προσδεχόμ[ε-]^{13}θα διμισσωρίαν, ὥστε ἕως ^{14}σήμερον μηδέναν ἀπολε-^{15}λύσθαι τῶν μετὰ σίτου. ^{16}ἀσπάζομαι τὴν σύνβιόν σου ^{17}πολλὰ καὶ Σερῆνον καὶ πάν-^{18}τες τοὺς φιλοῦντάς σε κατ’ ὄνο-^{19}μα. ^{20}ἔρρωσ⟦θ⟧ο. Μεσορὴ θ.

Verso: Ἀπολιναρί(ωι) ἀπὸ Εἰρηναίου ἀδελφοῦ.

3. *l.* ὑγιαίνειν. 17. *l.* πάντας.

114. FROM EUDAEMONIS TO APOLLONIUS

P. Flor. 332. 2nd cent. A.D.

^{1}Εὐδαιμονὶς Ἀπολλωνίωι τῶι ^{2}υἱῶι χαίρειν. ^{3}οὐ

ditional address) Deliver at the camp of the first cohort of the Apameni to Julianus, vice-secretary, this letter from Apion to be forwarded to his father Epimachus.[a]

[a] The letter was sent to the secretary of a cohort stationed at Alexandria and forwarded by him to Philadelphia in the Fayum.

113. A LETTER FROM ROME

2nd or 3rd cent. A.D.

Irenaeus to Apollinarius his dearest brother many greetings. I pray continually for your health, and I myself am well. I wish you to know that I reached land on the 6th of the month Epeiph and we unloaded our cargo on the 18th of the same month. I went up to Rome on the 25th of the same month and the place welcomed us as the god willed, and we are daily expecting our discharge, it so being that up till to-day nobody in the corn fleet[a] has been released. Many salutations to your wife and to Serenus and to all who love you, each by name. Goodbye. Mesore 9. (Addressed) To Apollinarius from his brother Irenaeus.

[a] The fleet which carried the annual tribute of corn from Egypt to Rome.

114. FROM EUDAEMONIS TO APOLLONIUS

2nd cent. A.D.

Eudaemonis to her son Apollonius[a] greeting.

[a] Strategus of the Lesser Apollonopolite nome in Upper Egypt.

λανθάνει σε ὅτι δίμηνος σήμε-[4]ρον ἐστάλην <πρὸς> τὸν ἄτακτον Δισκᾶν [5]μὴ ἐκδεχόμενόν σου τὴν παρουσί-[6]αν. ἀλλ' ἐπιζητεῖ νῦν μετὰ καὶ ἄλ-[7]λων γυμναστικῶν φίλων πῶς ἐ-[8]πιθῆταί μοι ἀπόντος σου, οἰόμε-[9]νος δύνασθαι τυχεῖν ἀδίκως πρα-[10]γμάτων. ἤδη μὲν τὸ ἐμὸν ἐποίησα, [11]καὶ οὔτ[ε ἐ]λουσάμην [οὔ]τε προσε-[12]κύνησα θεοὺς φοβουμένη σου τὸ [13]μετέωρον, εἴπερ ἐστὶ μετέωρον. μὴ [14]τοίνυν γενέσθω μετέωρον, ἵνα κἀ-[15]γὼ μὴ σκυλῶ εἰς τὰ δικαστήρια. πρὸ [16]πάντων εὔχομαί σε ὑγιαίνειν μετὰ [17]καὶ τῶν παιδίων μου καὶ τῆς μητρὸς [18]αὐτῶν. γράφε μοι συνεχῶς περὶ τῆς [19]ὑγίας ὑμῶν, ἵνα ἔχω παραμύθιον τῆς [20]προελεύσεώς μου. ἔρρωσο, κύριε. [21]Φαῶφι γ̄. [22]τοῖς γάμοις σου ἡ γυνὴ Δισκᾶτος τοῦ ἀδελ-[23]φοῦ μου ἤνεγκέ μοι (δραχμὰς) ρ· ἐπεὶ δὲ νῦν Νῖ-[24]λος ὁ υἱὸς αὐτῆς γαμεῖν μέλλει, δίκαι-[25]όν ἐστι καὶ ἡμᾶς ἀνταποδοῦναι, καὶ [26]εἰ [ἐγκ]λημάτιά ἐστι πρὸς αὐτοὺς ἐν μέσωι.

Verso: Ἀπολλωνίωι υἱῶι.

115. FROM TAUS TO APOLLONIUS

P. Giess. 17. 2nd cent. A.D.

[1]Ταῦς Ἀπ[ολλ]ωνίωι τῶι κυρίωι πλεῖστα [2]χαίρειν. [3]πρὸ τῶν ὅλων ἀσπάζομαί σε, δέσποτα, [4]καὶ

You do not forget that two months ago to-day I went to see the intractable Discas as he would not await your arrival. Well, together with some friends from the gymnasium he is now planning how to attack me in your absence, thinking that he can gain his end unjustly. I have already performed my part, and I have neither bathed nor worshipped the gods[a] because of my fear about your unsettled case, if indeed it is unsettled. Let it therefore not remain unsettled, lest I too be driven to the law-courts. Before all I pray for your health and that of my little ones and their mother. Write to me constantly about your health, in order that I may have consolation for my coming hither. Goodbye, my lord. Phaophi 3. (Postscript) At your wedding the wife of my brother Discas brought me 100 drachmae; and now that her son Nilus is about to marry, it is right that we should make a return gift, even if we have grievances against them still pending. (Addressed) To Apollonius my son.

[a] To show them that she is dissatisfied. Another writer actually threatens them (No. 138). Wilcken has pointed out that this primitive mentality is remarked on by Porphyrius as peculiarly Egyptian.

115. FROM TAUS TO APOLLONIUS

2nd cent. A.D.

Taus to Apollonius[a] her lord very many greetings. Before everything I salute you, master, and I pray

[a] See No. 114, p. 307, note *a*.

εὔχομαι πάντοτε περὶ τῆς ὑγιείας σου. [5]ἠγωνίασα, κύριε, οὐ μετρίως ἵνα ἀκούσω [6]ὅτι ἐνώθρευσας, ἀλλὰ χάρις τοῖς θεοῖς πᾶσι [7]ὅτι σε διαφυλάσσουσι ἀπρόσκοπον. πα-[8]ρακαλῶ σε, κύριε, ἐάν σοι δόξῃ, καὶ πέμ-[9]ψαι ἐφ᾽ ἡμᾶς, εἰ δὲ μή, ἀποθνήσκομεν [10]ὅτι οὐ βλέπομέν σε καθ᾽ ἡμέραν. ὤφελον [11]εἰ ἐδυνάμεθα πέτασθαι καὶ ἐλθεῖν καὶ προσ-[12]κυνῆσαί σε· ἀγωνιῶμεν γὰρ μὲ [βλ]έπου-[13]σαί σε. ὥστε διαλλάγηθι ἡμεῖν κα[ὶ π]έμ-[14]ψον ἐφ᾽ ἡμᾶς. ἔρρωσο, κύριε [—] [15]καὶ πάντα ἔχομ[εν —] [16]Ἐφεὶπ κδ̄.

Verso: [17]Ἀπολλωνίωι στρατηγῶι.

12. *l.* μή.

116. ABOUT GIFTS TO TEACHERS

P. Giess. 80. 2nd cent. A.D.

[1][. .] . [. .] . . . . [ἄδε]λφε [. . . . . . . [2]. .]σου. ἀσπάζεταί σε [Ἡρα]ΐδοῦς κα[ὶ] ημου-[3][.] . ητης κα[ὶ] Ἑλένη καὶ Τινοῦτις κα[ὶ ὁ] πάπας [4][α]ὐτῆς καὶ πάντες ἐν οἴκῳ καὶ ἡ μήτηρ [5][τῆς γλυκυ]τάτης Ἡραΐδοῦτος. τὰ [π]εριστερίδι-[6][α καὶ ὀ]ρνυθάρια, ἃ οὐκ ἤωθα ἔσθειν, πέμ-[7][ψον . .] . . . [.] τῷ καθηγητῇ Ἡραΐδο[ῦτ]ος. [8][? παρεκάλεσ]έ σε Ἑλένη ἡ μήτηρ Ἀπολλωνίου [9]διὰ χερ[ὸς] ἔχειν Ἑρμαῖον τὸν υἱὸν αὐτῆς. [10]ὅσα ποτὲ οὐκ ἔφαγον παρὰ σοῦ ἀφ⟦οσ⟧έστια [11][. .] . . [. .]ας, πέμψον τῷ καθηγητῇ τῆς θυγ[ατρό]ς [12]μου, ἵνα φιλοπονήσῃ εἰς αὐτήν. [13]ἐρρῶσθαι σ[ε εὔ]χομαι. [14]Χοίακ ιζ.

always for your health. I was distressed, my lord, not a little to hear that you had been ill, but thanks be to all the gods that they keep you safe from harm. I beg you, my lord, if it please you, to send for me; else I die because I do not behold you daily. Would that I were able to fly and come to you and make obeisance to you; for it distresses me not to behold you. So be friends with me and send for me. Goodbye, my lord . . . Epeiph 24. (Addressed) To Apollonius the strategus.

116. ABOUT GIFTS TO TEACHERS

2nd cent. A.D.

. . . Salutations to you from Heraidous and . . . and Helena and Tinoutis and her papa and all the household and the mother of our sweetest Heraidous. The pigeons and small fowl, which I am not used to eat, send to . . . the teacher of Heraidous. Helena the mother of Apollonius asks (?) you to keep her son Hermaeus under your eye. Whatever things I did not eat when I . . . them from you send to the teacher of my daughter in order that he may be diligent with her. I pray for your health. Choiak 17.

117. LOST DEEDS

P. Giess. bibl. 20. 1st half of 2nd cent. A.D.

- - - ἐ[πι]στολὰς συστατικὰς πρὸς τὸν ἐπιστράτηγον, μή [2]ποτε φθάσῃ παρ᾽ ὑμῖν γενέσθαι. ἐνετειλάμην δὲ [3]κ[αὶ] Ἀντωνείνωι στρατιώτηι, ὃς ἦν ἐν τῆι ἐπι-[4][στ]ρατηγίαι Οὐίνδικος μεθ᾽ ἡμῶν, ἀναπλεύσαν-[5][τι] δὲ καὶ νῦν μετὰ τοῦ ἐπιστρατήγου, ἵνα ἐν ὅλωι [6][τ]ῶι πράγματί σοι παραστῇ. οὐδὲν δ᾽ ἧττον καὶ νῦν [7][ἔπ]εμψά σοι πρὸς αὐτὸν ἐπιστόλιον. τῶν δού-[8][λω]ν τοὺς χρηματισμοὺς ἕως τούτου οὐχ εὗρον, [9]ὅλως γὰρ πα[ρ᾽] ἐ[μ]οὶ οὔτε ἡ ἀπὸ σοῦ εἰς Ἀχιλλέα ὠνὴ [10][ε]ὑρέθη οὔτ[ε] ἡ ἀπὸ Ἀχιλλέως εἰς τὴν εὔμοιρον. [11]καὶ ὁ Ἀχιλλ[εὺ]ς δὲ ἀποδημεῖ, καὶ ἐπὶ τῶι πράγματι [12]ἀμηχανῶ οὐκ εἰωθὼς ῥείπτε[ι]ν οὐδὲν μὲν [13][ἁ]πλῶς β[ι]βλίον, μάλιστα τὰ ἀνα[γ]καιότερα. ἀλλὰ [14][κ]αὶ ὁ ἀγορά[σας] παρὰ σοῦ τὸ ἄλλο σωμάτιον, ῥητο-[15]ρίσκος τις [ἐ]πὶ τοῦ δικαιοδότου λέγων, πολλά-[16]κις ταξάμενος τὸν χρόνον ἡμῖν εἰπεῖν [17]τῆς ὠ[νῆ]ς ἠγνωμόνησεν. εἰ οὖ[ν δύν]ασαι [18]τὸν χ[ρόν]ον εὐμνημονεῦσαι καὶ διὰ ποίου ἀρχείου τετέλεσται, δήλωσόν μοι [19]καὶ ζή[τησ]ον ἐν τοῖς βιβλίοις σου μὴ ἡ εἰς [20]Ἀπολ[λω]νάριον ὠνή ἐστιν, καὶ [ε]ἰ οἶδας [21]διὰ ποίου γραμματέως ἡ εἰς Ἀχιλλέα ἀπὸ σοῦ [22]καταγ[ραφὴ] γέγονεν, γράψον μοι· οὐ γὰρ εὑρέ-[23]θη π[αρὰ Π]οτάμμωνι τῶι γραμματεῖ. ἵνα δὲ [24]ἐν το⟦υ⟧σούτωι ⟦δ⟧ μηδείς σοι διοχλῇ, ἔγραψα [25]τῶι γραμματεῖ τοῦ στρατηγοῦ [σ]υνιστὰς [26]τὸν μεικρὸν Ἡρακλείδην καὶ περὶ τοῦ [27]πράγματος δηλῶν, ἵνα ἄλλ᾽ ἐπινοῇ [28]ἄχρι ἂν πέμψω τοὺς χρηματισμοὺς

117. LOST DEEDS

1st half of 2nd cent. A.D.

. . . letters of recommendation to the epistrategus, in case he should reach you first. I also instructed the soldier Antoninus, who was in the service of the epistrategus Vindex along with me, and who has now sailed up with the epistrategus, to assist you in all the business; but none the less I have now sent you a letter to him. The documents about the slaves I have not found up to the present; for actually neither the deed of sale from you to Achilleus nor that from Achilleus to the lady now at rest has been found with me. Achilleus too is away from home and the thing beats me, as I am not accustomed to throw away any papers at all, especially those of importance. Moreover the person who bought the other slave from you, a petty pleader at the court of the dicaeodotes, after frequently promising to tell us the date of the sale has played us false. If you can remember the date and the office through which it was concluded, let me know, and look among your papers whether the deed of sale to Apollonarion is not there, and if you know by what scribe the conveyance from you to Achilleus was made, write me word; for it has not been found with the scribe Potammon. To prevent anyone from molesting you in the meantime, I have written to the secretary of the strategus, introducing the young Heraclides and explaining the matter, in order that he may devise some other means until I send the documents

[29]ἢ παραγένωμαι. τὴν περὶ Σαραπί-[30]ωνος ἐπιστολὴν ὡς σὸν κατόρθω-[31]μα τοῖς πυνθανομένοις σου καὶ αὐτῶι [32]τῶι Σαραπίωνι διαβεβαίωσαι ἀν-[33]τιλαμβανομένη καὶ τοῦ μεγέ-[34]θους του πράγματος. κἂν ἐπ' ἀγαθῷ [35]καταπλέῃς, κοιτάριον σπουδαῖον [36]ἔνεγκον, ἵνα πέμψωμεν Φίλωι σπουδαίως [37]⟦Φίλω⟧ ἡμῖν προσενεχθέντι, ἢ ὃ ἐὰν [38]ἄλλο δοκιμάσῃς. (2nd hand) ἐρρῶσθαί σε εὔχομαι, [39]ἀδελφή. Ἡρακλείδην, [40][Ἴ]σειν ἀσπάζου. Πτολε-[41]μαῖος πάντας ἀσπάζεται. [42]Μεχεὶρ κη.

36. Φιλωι above the line. 40. [Ἴ]σειν E.-H., σεινασπάζου for συνασπ. Ed.

118. FROM HERON TO HERACLIDES

P. Giess. bibl. 21. 2nd cent. A.D.

[1]Ἥρων Ἡρακλείδῃ τῷ [2]ἀδελφῷ χαίρειν. [3]παρακληθείς, κύριε, μνήσ-[4]θητί μου τῆς δεήσεως ἧς [5]κατ' ὄψιν σοι πεποίημαι. εἰ [6]καὶ ἐμοῦ οὐ φισθήσῃ, μέν-[7]τοι τὴν παῖδα καὶ τὴν θυ-[8]γατέρα σου αἰδέσθητι, καὶ [9]Σατόρνιλον δὲ καὶ τὴν γυναῖ-[10]κα αὐτοῦ ἀνένενκον. (2nd hand) [11]ἐρρῶσθαί σε εὔχ(ομαι), κύριε.

Verso: Ἡρακλείδῃ τῷ ἀδελφῷ.

119. FROM PTOLEMA TO ANTAS

P. Hamb. 86. 2nd cent. A.D.

[1]Πτολέμα Ἀντᾶτι τῶι [2]ἀδελφῶι [χαίρειν. [3]? Λονγί]νῳ γράφεις πρ[οσ]δέ-[4]χεσθαι τὸν ἡγεμόνα. ἰδέ, [5]ὁ ἡγεμὼν ἀνέβη. ἐὰν με-[6]θ' ὑγίας ἐκπλέξῃς σατόν, [7]ταχέως πρὸ τοῦ ἡγεμό-[8]νος παραγενοῦ, ἵνα ἂν

or come myself. Uphold the letter about Sarapion as your justified action to those who question you and to Sarapion himself, appreciating the importance of the matter. And if you sail down auspiciously, bring a good bed to send to Philus for his good behaviour towards us, or any other gift you think proper. I pray for your health, sister. Give my salutations to Heraclides and Isis. Ptolemaeus salutes you all. Mecheir 28.

118. FROM HERON TO HERACLIDES

2nd cent. A.D.

Heron to Heraclides his brother greeting. I beg you, my lord, to remember my request which I have made to you before your face. If on me you will not have mercy, nevertheless respect the girl and your daughter, and recall[a] Saturnilus and his wife. I pray for your health, my lord. (Addressed) To Heraclides my brother.

[a] It is uncertain whether this is to be understood literally or in the sense of call to mind.

119. FROM PTOLEMA TO ANTAS

2rd cent. A.D.

Ptolema to Antas her brother greeting. You write to Longinus (?) to look out for the praefect. Lo, the praefect has gone up. If you extricate yourself successfully, come here quickly before the praefect,

6. *l.* ὑγιείας, σαυτόν.

[9]δυνασθῶμεν τὸν μικρὸν [10]ἐπικρεῖναι. οἱ ἀγροὶ πάν-[11]τες καλῶς διάκεινται. τὸ [12]ἀπὸ νότου περίχωμα τῶν [13]δεκαεπτὰ ταῖς βουσὶ ἐπράθη. [14]αἱ β[όε]ς σου ἔφαγαν ἄρουραν καὶ [15]ἀπῆλθαν ἰς Πανσούη. πάντα [16]τὰ ἐκεῖ ταῖς βουσὶ ἀφέθη. τὸ [17]ἀπὸ λιβὸς τοῦ λαχάνου ἰς χορτ(ο)-[18]κοπίαν ἀφέθη. πεπράκαμεν [19]τὰ ἐν ταῖς κλ(ηρουχίαις) χορτάρια παρὰ πε-[20]ριχώματα ἕξ τὰ ἀπὸ ἀπηλιώτου [21](δραχμῶν) ριβ. εὔωνος ὁ χόρτ(ος) τόνῳ. ἠγορά-[22]σθη σοι ἄρουραι τρεῖς διὰ Οὐετρανί-[23]ου ἰς χόρτ(ον) (δραχμῶν) ρλ, πέπραται δὲ καὶ δι' ἀτοῦ [24]πρόβασι (δραχμῶν) ξη. ἀσπάζεταί σε Λον-[25]γῖνος καὶ Σαραπίων καὶ οἱ ἐν οἴκῳ [26]πάντε[ς]. Οὐίβ[ι]ς ἀπῆλθε ἰς Ψενῦριν [27]τὸν σῖτον πωλῆσαι. οἱ σοὶ καλῶς [28]τέλλουσι (?) πάντες. ἔρρωσ{σ}ο. [29]Μεχεὶρ λ̄.

23. *l.* αὐτοῦ. 28. τελλουσι very doubtful: ἔχουσι?

120. FROM A PENITENT SON

B.G.U. 846. 2nd cent. A.D.

[1]Ἀντώνις Λόνγος Νειλοῦτι [2][τ]ῇ μητρὶ π[λ]ῖστα χαίρειν. καὶ δι-[3]ὰ παντὸ[ς] εὔχομαί σαι ὑγειαίνειν. τὸ προσκύνη-[4]μά σου [ποι]ῶ κατ' αἰκάστην ἡμαίραν παρὰ τῷ [5]κυρίῳ [Σερ]άπειδει. γεινώσκειν σαι θέλω ὅ-[6]τι οὐχ [ἤλπ]ιζον ὅτι ἀναβένις εἰς τὴν μητρό-[7]πολιν. χ[ά]ρειν τοῦτο οὐδ' ἐγὸ εἰσῆ<λ>θα εἰς τὴν πό-[8]λιν. αἰδ[υ]σοπο[ύ]μην δὲ ἐλθεῖν εἰς Καρα-

3. *l.* σε, and so throughout. 4. *l.* καθ' ἑκάστην ἡμέραν. 6. = οὐκ ἤλπιζον. *l.* ἀναβαίνεις. 7. *l.* τούτου ἐγώ. 8. *l.* ἐδ[υ]σωπο[ύ]μην.

in order that we may be able to have the youngster examined.[a] All the fields are in good condition. The southern basin[b] of the 17 arurae has been sold for the use of the cattle. Your cattle have eaten one arura and gone off to Pansoue. All the land there has been given over to the cattle. The west of the vegetable plot has been given over for grass-cutting. We have sold the grass in the cleruchies, excepting the six eastern basins, for 112 drachmae. Grass is exceedingly (?) cheap. Three arurae were bought for you through Vetranius for 130 drachmae for growing grass, and they have been sold through him again for the use of sheep for 68 drachmae. Longinus and Sarapion and all at home salute you. Vibius has gone off to Psenuris to sell the corn. Your people are all well. Goodbye. Mecheir 30.

[a] For entry into a privileged class.
[b] That is, an area surrounded by a dyke, for the purpose of irrigation.

120. FROM A PENITENT SON

2nd cent. A.D.

Antonius Longus to Nilous his mother very many greetings. I pray always for your health; every day I make supplication for you before the lord Serapis. I would have you know that I did not expect that you were going up to the metropolis[a]; for that reason I did not come to the city myself. I was ashamed to come to Karanis,[b] because I go

[a] Arsinoe the capital of the nome.
[b] A village in the Fayum, the home of the writer's mother.

νίδαν [9]ὅτι σαπρῶς παιριπατῶ. αἴγραψά σοι ὅτι γυμνός [10]εἰμει. παρακα[λ]ῶ σαι, μήτηρ, δ[ι]αλάγητί μοι. λοι-[11]πὸν οἶδα τί [ἐγὼ ?] αἰμαυτῷ παρέσχημαι. παιπαί{δ}-[12]δευμαι καθ' ὃν δῖ τρόπον. οἶδα ὅτι ἡμάρτηκα. [13]ἤκουσα παρὰ το[ῦ . . .].υμου τὸν εὑρόντα σαι [14]ἐν τῷ Ἀρσαινοείτῃ καὶ ἀκαιρέως πάντα σοι δι-[15]ήγηται. οὐκ οἶδες ὅτι θέλω πηρὸς γενέσται [16]εἶ γνοῦναι ὅπως ἀνθρόπῳ [ἔ]τ[ι] ὀφείλω ὀβολόν; and fragments of eight more lines.

Verso: [25]Νειλοῦτι] μητρεὶ ἀπ' Ἀντωνίω Λόνγου υείοῦ.

9. *l.* περιπατῶ, ἔγραψα. 11. *l.* ἐμαυτῷ, πεπαίδευμαι. 13. *l.* τοῦ εὑρόντος. 14. *l.* Ἀρσινοΐτῃ, ἀκεραίως. 15-16. *l.* γενέσθαι ἢ γνῶναι. 25. *l.* Ἀντωνίου.

121. FROM SEMPRONIUS TO SATURNILA AND MAXIMUS

Rev. Ég. 1919, p. 204. 2nd cent. A.D.

[1]Σεμπρώνιος Σατουρνίλᾳ τῇ μητρεὶ [2]καὶ κυρίᾳ πλεῖστα χαίρειν. [3]πρὸ τῶν ὅλων ἐρρῶσθέ σε εὔχομαι μετὰ καὶ τῶν [4]ἀβασκάντων μου ἀδελφῶν, ἅμα δὲ καὶ τὸ προσκύ-[5]νημα ὑμῶν ποιοῦμε ἡμερησίως παρὰ τῷ κυρί-[6]ῳ Σεράπιδι. τοσαύτας ὑμεῖν ἐπιστολὰς διεπεμ-[7]ψάμην κοὐδεμείαν μοι ἀντεγράψαται, τοσούτων [8]καταπλευσάντων. ἐρωτηθεῖσ<α>, ἡ κυρία μου, ἀνόκνως [9]μοι γράφειν περὶ τῆς σωτηρίας ὑμῶν ἵνα κἀγὼ ἀμε-[10]ριμνότερα διάγω· τοῦτό μοι γὰρ εὐκτέον ἐστὶν διὰ παν-[11]τός. ἀσπάζομαι Μάξιμον καὶ τὴν σύμβιον αὐτοῦ καὶ Σα-[12]τουρνῖλον καὶ Γέμελλον καὶ Ἑλένην καὶ τοὺς αὐτῆς. μετάδος [13]αὐτῇ ὅτι ἐκομεισάμην Σεμπρωνίου ἐπειστολὴν [14]ἀπὸ Καπποδοκίας. ἀσπά-

about in filth. I wrote to you that I am naked. I beg you, mother, be reconciled to me. Well, I know what I have brought on myself. I have received a fitting lesson. I know that I have sinned. I heard from . . . who found you in the Arsinoite nome, and he has told you everything correctly. Do you not know that I would rather be maimed than feel that I still owe a man an obol? . . . (Addressed) To Nilous his mother from Antonius Longus her son.[a]

[a] This letter has been widely quoted as an illustration of the parable of the prodigal son.

121. FROM SEMPRONIUS TO SATURNILA AND MAXIMUS

2nd cent. A.D.

Sempronius to Saturnila, his mother and lady, very many greetings. Before everything I pray for your health and that of my brothers, unharmed by the evil eye, and withal I make supplication for you daily before the lord Serapis. How many letters have I sent you and not one have you written me in reply, though so many people have sailed down! I beg you, my lady, be not slow to write me news of your welfare that I may live in less anxiety; for your welfare is what I pray for always. Salutations to Maximus and his wife and Saturnilus and Gemellus and Helena and her family. Inform her that I received a letter from Sempronius from

3. *l.* ἐρρῶσθαι. 5. *l.* ποιοῦμαι. 7. *l.* ἀντεγράψατε.
10. *l.* εὐκταῖον? 14. *l.* Καππαδοκίας.

ζομαι Ἰούλιον καὶ τοὺς αὐ-[15]τοῦ κατ' ὄνομα καὶ Σκυθικὸν καὶ Θερμοῦθιν καὶ τὰ [16]πεδία αὐτῆς. ἀσπάζετε ὑμᾶς Γέμελλος. [17]ἔρρωσό μοι, ἡ κυρία μου, διὰ παντός.

[18]Σεμπρώνιος Μαξίμωι τῷ ἀδελφῷ [19]πλ[ε]ῖστα χαίρειν. πρὸ τῶν ὅλων ἐρῶσθέ [20]σε εὔχομαι. μετέλαβον ὅτι βαρέως δουλεύ{ου}ετε [21]τὴν κυρίαν ἡμῶν μητέραν. ἐρωτηθείς, ἄδελφε γλυ-[22]κύταται, ἐν μηδενεὶ αὐτὴν λύπει· εἰ δέ τεις τῶν ἀ-[23]δελφῶν ἀντιλέγει αὐτῇ, σὺ ὀφείλεις αὐτοὺς κολαφί-[24]ζει[ν]· ἤδη γὰρ πατὴρ ὀφίλεις καλεῖσθαι. ἐπείσταμε [25]ὅτι χωρὶς τῶν γραμμάτων μου δυνατὸς εἶ αὐτῇ [26]ἀρέσε, ἀλλὰ μὴ βαρέως ἔχε μου τὰ γράμματα νουθε-[27]τοῦν[τ]ά σε· ὀφίλομεν γὰρ σέβεσθε τὴν τεκοῦσαν ὡς [28]θε[όν,] μάλειστα τοιαύτην οὖσαν ἀγαθήν. ταῦτά σοι ἔ-[29]γραψα, ἄδελφε, ἐπειστάμενος τὴν γλυκασίαν τῶν [30]κυ[ρί]ων γονέων. καλῶς π[ο]ιήσις γράψας μοι περὶ τῆς [31]σ[ωτ]ηρίας ὑμ[ῶ]ν. ἔρρωσό μοι, ἄδελφε.

Verso: [32]ἀπόδ(ος) Μαξίμωι ἀπὸ Σεμπρωνίου [33]ἀδελφοῦ.

16. *l.* παιδία, ἀσπάζεται. 19. *l.* ἐρρῶσθαι. 21-22. *l.* γλυκύτατε. 22. *l.* τις. 24. *l.* ἐπίσταμαι. 26. *l.* ἀρέσαι. 27. *l.* σέβεσθαι.

122. LATIN LETTER TO A MILITARY TRIBUNE

P. Oxy. 32. 2nd cent. A.D.

[1]*I[u]lio Domitio tribuno mil(itum) leg(ionis)* [2]*ab · Aurel(io) Archelao benef(iciario)* [3]*suo salutem ·* [4]*iam*

Cappadocia. Salutations to Julius and his family, each by name, and to Scythicus and Thermouthis and her children. Gemellus salutes you. Fare you well, my lady, always.

Sempronius to his brother Maximus very many greetings. Before everything I pray that you are well. I have been informed that you serve our mother and lady grudgingly. I beg you, sweetest brother, do not grieve her in anything; and if any of our brothers gainsays her, you ought to cuff them; for you ought now to take the name of father. I know that without my writing you are able to humour her, but do not be offenced by my letter of admonition; for we ought to revere our mother as a goddess, especially one so good as ours. This I have written to you, brother, because I know how sweet a possession our revered parents are. Please write me about your welfare. Goodbye, brother. (Addressed) Deliver to Maximus,[a] from his brother Sempronius.

[a] The two letters were written on one sheet, addressed on the outside to Maximus only, as Saturnila was probably unable to read.

122. LATIN LETTER TO A MILITARY TRIBUNE

2nd cent. A.D.

To Julius Domitius, military tribune of the legion, from Aurelius Archelaus, his *beneficiarius*, greeting.

2-36. *The punctuation of the original is reproduced.*

tibi et pristine commen-[5]daueram Theonem amicum [6]meum et mod[o qu]oque peto [7]domine ut eum ant oculos [8]habeas tanquam · me · est e-[9]nim · tales omo ut ametur [10]a te · reliquit · enim su[o]s [e]t [11]rem suam et actum et me [12]secutus est · et per omnia me [13]se[c]urum fecit · et ideo peto [14]a te · ut habeat intr[o]itum · [15]at te · et omnia tibi refere-[16]re potest · de actu[m] nostrum · [17]quitquit m[e d]ixit · [i]l-[18][lu]t et fact[um . . . .] . [. .] [19]amaui h[o]min[e]m [. . . . .] [20]m[. . . . .]set de . [. . . . .] [21]a[. . . . . .] . domin[e . . . .] [22]m[. . . . . .] . . id es[t . . . .] [23]r[. . . . .] hab[. . . . .] [24]h[. . . . . . .] et [. . . . .] [25]tor . t . . [. . .] ico[. . . . .] [26]illum · ut [. . .]upse[. . . . . inter-] [27]cessoris u[t i]llum co[mmendarem] [28]estote felicissi[mi domine mul-][29]tis annis cum [tuis omnibus] [30]ben[e agentes] [31]hanc epistulam ant ocu-[32]los habeto domine puta[t]o [33]me tecum loqui [34]uale.

Verso: [35]*Ioulio Domitio tribuno militum leg(ionis)* [36]*ab · Aurelio · Archelao b(eneficiario).*

9. *l.* talis homo. 15. *l.* ad, referre. 16. *l.* acto nostro. 17. *l.* quicquid, illud.

123. FROM AN AGENT TO HIS MASTER

P. Ryl. 233. 2nd cent. A.D.

- - - [1]πηγίον καὶ διὰ τῆς πλαγίας ἡ εἴσοδός ἐστι καὶ ἡ ἔξοδος [2]τῶν ἐργαζομένων πάντων· ὅταν δὲ ἐπ' ἀγαθῷ ἐκβῶμεν, [3]καὶ τὸ δῶμα ἀσφαλισθήσεται. ἡ διαβάθρα καγγελλωτὴ καὶ [4]τὰ προσκήνια γενήσεται ἅμα ⟦και⟧ τῶι καγγέλλωι τοῦ μει-[5]κροῦ συμποσίου. τὰ μέλαθρα τῶν θυρίδων τοῦ μεγάλου [6]συμποσίου ἐκ μέρους σήμερον ἡρμολόγηται. τὸ

I have once previously recommended to you my friend Theon, and now again, Sir, I beg you to look upon him as if he were myself. He is indeed a man worthy of your affection. He has left his family, his property and business and followed me, and through all he has shielded me from care. I beg you therefore to grant him admittance to your presence. And he can tell you everything about our business. Whatever he has said[a] . . . I loved the man . . . May you, Sir, and all your kindred enjoy felicity and prosperity for many years. Look upon this letter, Sir, and imagine that I am talking with you. Farewell. (Addressed) To Julius Domitius, military tribune of the legion, from Aurelius Archelaus, *beneficiarius*.

[a] Perhaps "said with regard to me, take that for a fact"; or "said to me, that has been performed."

123. FROM AN AGENT TO HIS MASTER

2nd cent. A.D.

. . . stream, and the entrance and exit for all the workmen is by the side way; but when we bring the work to a happy conclusion, then the roof also will be made secure. The stair has been balustered and the portico will have a balustrade made for it along with that of the small dining-hall. The beams of the windows of the large dining-hall have to-day been partly fixed. The second water-cooling

3. *l.* καγκελλωτή. 4. *l.* καγκέλλωι.

ἕτερον ὑδρ[ο-][7]ψυγεῖον αὔριον στεγάζεται. κωμοκάτοικοί εἰσιν οἱ ἔ-[8][χο]ντες πρὸ τοῦ πυλῶνός σου τὸν ψιλὸν τόπον, ἀνενεγκῶ [9]δὲ Ἡρακλείωι ἵνα πέμψῃ πρὸς αὐτούς. τὸν ἐξ ἀρχῆς λόγον [10]μ[έ]χρι ιδ Παῦνι ἔπεμψά σοι ὑφ' ἓν γεγραμμένον, κεχω-[11]ρισμένον δὲ εἰς δ ἐπιδοσίμους πρὸς τὸν ἐπίτροπόν σου, [12]ἵνα ἔχων ὑπογύως ἐν μνήμηι τὰς τιμὰς ὧν ἀγοράζει [13]ἐξαρτισμῶν ἀνύποπτα τὰ πρὸς τὸν λόγον ἔχηι. ἔγραψα γάρ [14]σοι, κύριε, ἄλλοτε μηδὲν χωρὶς ἐπακολουθήσεως αὐτοῦ [15]ἀγοράζεται. εὔχομαί σε τὸν κύριον ἰδεῖν ἐν μείζοσι [16]προκοπαῖς, ἐν ἁδραῖς εὐημερίαις. ἔρρωσο, κύριε. [17]Παῦνι κ.

6. *l.* ὑδροψυχεῖον. 15. *l.* ἀγοράζεσθαι.

124. FROM MORUS TO EPIMACHUS

P. Oxy. 1482. 2nd cent. A.D.

[1]Μῶρος Ἐπιμάχῳ τῶι κυρίωι μου [2]χαίρειν. [3]γράφω σοι ἵν' ἰδῇς ὅτι λελικμήκαμεν [4]τὴν κριθὴν τοῦ Αὐασίτου τῇ η, καὶ οὐ [5]οὕτως αὐτὴν λελικμήκαμεν μετὰ [6]κόπου. ὁ Ζεὺς γὰρ ἔβρεχε καὶ ἀμάχητος [7]ἦν ὁ ἄνεμος, καὶ Πα<νά>ρες οἶδε ὅσα πεπο<ή>κα-[8]μεν ἵνα εἰσχύσωμεν ὅλως μετενέγκαι τὰ ἄλλα [9]σὺν θεοῖς. ἐξέβησαν δὲ τοῦ ὅλου ἀρτάβαι λη χύνικε(ς) δ· [10]τ<ο>ύτων κατέφθακα ἀρτάβας ιβ∠ χύνικα(ς) η. [11]ἐξήτασα δὲ περὶ τῆς θειμῆς τοῦ χόρτου [12]τοῦ ἐφετινοῦ, ἐπράθη δὲ ἐν τῇ κώμῃ ἐξ [13]ἑπτὰ δραχμῶν τὸ ἀγώγιν· καὶ Πα<νά>ρες δὲ [14]οἶδε. πολλὰ δὲ ἐ{κ}ξετάσας εὗρον ξη[ρὰ] [15]καὶ οὐκ εὐθύχαλκα, ἀλλὰ μετὰ τετρά-[16]μηνον. δοκι-

7. *l.* Πα<νά>ρης; so in l. 13. 9. *l.* χοίν-; so in l. 10.
11. *l.* τιμῆς.

closet is to be roofed to-morrow. The owners of the open space in front of your gateway live in the village; I will report to Heraclius in order that he may send to them. I have sent you the account from the beginning to the 14th of Pauni, written continuously but divided into four sections, to be submitted to your guardian in order that he, having fresh in his mind the prices of the fittings which he buys, may feel no suspicion with regard to the account. For I wrote to you, my lord, on another occasion that nothing is being bought without his cognisance. I pray that I may see you, my lord, enjoying further advancement and solid prosperity. Goodbye, my lord. Pauni 20.

124. FROM MORUS TO EPIMACHUS

2nd cent. A.D.

Morus to my lord Epimachus greeting. I write to let you know that we have winnowed the barley of the man from the Oasis on the 8th, and never have we winnowed barley with such trouble. For it rained and the wind was irresistible, and Panares knows what efforts it took to enable us finally to transport the remainder by the gods' leave. The whole yield was 38 artabae 4 choenices, of which I have reserved in advance 12½ artabae 8 choenices.[a] I inquired about the price of the annual grass: it was sold in the village at 7 drachmae the load, as Panares knows. After many inquiries I found some dry and not to be paid for in ready money but after four months. Will you consider how you are

[a] *i.e.* one-third of the whole.

μάσις δὲ ⟦σὺ⟧ πῶς σε βαστά-[17]ζι<ν> καὶ ἄν συ δοκῇ γράψις μοι περὶ τούτων, [18]καὶ πόστον μέρος καταφθάνω τοῦ μεγάλου [19]κλήρου{ς}, καὶ ἡ θέλις μεῖξαι ⟦αυ⟧τὰ τοῦ Αὐασί-[20]του μετὰ τῶν ἄλλων. ἐν τῷ δὲ τόπῳ τοῦ πα-[21]τρός σου ἀποτέθεικα τὴν μερίδαν μου. [22]τὸ προσκοίνημά σ<ο>υ ποιῶ καὶ τῶν τέκνων [23]σου π[ά]ντων [καὶ] τῶν ἀδελφῶ[ν] σου [πάντων] [24]κ[ατ' ὄνομα ?]. [25]ἐρρῶ]στέ σ' εὔ[χομαι], [26]κύριέ μου.

17. *l.* σοι. 19. *l.* ει for η. 22. *l.* προσκύνημα. 25. *l.* ἐρρῶ]σθαι.

125. FROM SERENUS TO ISIDORA

P. Oxy. 528. 2nd cent. A.D.

[1]Σερῆνος Εἰσιδώρᾳ [τῇ ἀδελ-][2]φῇ καὶ κυρίᾳ πλαῖστ[α χαίρειν]. [3]πρὸ μὲν παντὸς εὔχομ[αί σε ὑγιαί-][4]νει<ν> καὶ καθ' ἑκάστης [ἡμέρα]ς κα[ὶ] [5]ὀψ<ί>ας τὸ προσκύνημά σου πυῶ [6]παρὰ τῇ σε φιλούσῃ Θοήρι. γινόσκειν [7]σε θέλω ἀφ' ὡς ἐ{κ}ξῆλθες ἀπ' ἐμοῦ [8]πένθος ἡγούμην νυκτὸς κλέων [9]ἡμέρας δὲ πενθῶ<ν>. ιβ Φαῶφι ἀφ' ὅτε [10]ἐλουσάμην μετ' ἐσοῦ οὐκ ἐλουσάμην, [11]οὐκ ἤλιμ<μ>ε μέχρει ιβ Ἁθύρ, καὶ ἔπεμ-[12]σάς μυ ἐπιστολὰς δυναμένου λίθον [13]σαλεῦσε, οὕτως ὑ λόγυ σου καικίνη-[14]κάν με. αὐτῇ{ν} τῇ ὅρᾳ ἀντέγρα-[15]ψά συ καὶ ἔδωκα τῇ ιβ μετὰ τῶν [16]σῶν ἐπιστολῶν ἐσ{σ}φραγιζμένα. [17]χωρεὶς δὲ τῶν σῶν λόγων κὲ γρα-[18]μ<μ>άτων ὁ Κόλοβος δὲ πόρνην

2. *l.* πλεῖστ[α. 5. *l.* ποιῶ. 6. *l.* γινώσκειν.
8. *l.* κλαίων. 11. *l.* ἤλειμ<μ>αι, ἔπεμψας; *cf.* 19 and 24.

to convey it and, if you please, write to me about this and say also what proportion I am to reserve in advance from the produce of the large holding, and whether you wish me to mix what belongs to the man from the Oasis with the rest? I have stored my share in the room belonging to your father. I make supplication on behalf of you and all your children and all your brothers, each by name. I pray for your health, my lord.

125. FROM SERENUS TO ISIDORA

2nd cent. A.D.

Serenus to Isidora, his sister and lady,[a] very many greetings. Before all else I pray for your health, and every day and evening I make supplication on your behalf before Thoeris[b] who loves you. I would have you know that ever since you left me I have been in mourning, weeping by night and lamenting by day. Since I bathed with you on Phaophi 12 I have not bathed nor anointed myself until Hathur 12. You have sent me letters that could move a stone, so much have your words stirred me. On the very instant I wrote an answer to you and delivered it on the 12th sealed up along with your letters. Apart from what you say and write, "But Colobus has

[a] Probably the writer's wife.

[b] An Egyptian goddess, usually represented as a hippopotamus.

---

12. *l.* μοι, δυναμένας. 13. *l.* σαλεῦσαι, οἱ λόγοι σου κεκίνηκαν. 14. *l.* ὥρᾳ. 15. *l.* σοι. 17. *l.* καί.

με πεπύ-[19]ηκεν, ἔλεγε δὲ ὅτι ἔπεμσέ μυ φάσειν [20]ἡ γυνή σου ὅτι αὐτὸς πέπρακεν τὸ ἁλυ-[21]σίδιον καὶ αὐτὸς κατέστακέ με ε[ἰ]ς τὸ [22]πλῦν· τούτους τοὺς λόγους λέγεις ἥνα [23]μηκέτι ⟦φ⟧πιστευθῶ μου τὴν ἐνβολ[ήν]; [24]ἐδοῦ ποσά{ρ}κεις ἔπεμσα ἐπὶ σέ. ἔρχῃ [εἴτε] [25]οὐκ ἔρχῃ δήλοσόν μυ. [

Verso: ἀπόδος Εἰσιδόρᾳ π(αρὰ) Σερήνου.

18. *l.* πεποίηκεν. 19. *l.* μοι. 22. *l.* πλοῖον, ἵνα. 24. *l.* ἰδοῦ ποσάκις. 25. *l.* δήλωσόν μοι. 26. *l.* Ἰσιδώρᾳ.

126. FROM SARAPODORUS TO PHANION

B.G.U. 1676. 2nd cent. A.D.

[1]Σαραπόδωρος Φανείωνι τῷ ἀδελ-[2]φῷ χαίρειν. [3]γινώσκειν σε θέλω ὅτι ἀπήλθα-[4]μεν πρὸς τὸν ἑκατ[όν]ταρχον καὶ [5]ἔβαλεν ἡμᾶς ἰς μεσιτίαν κριθῆ-[6]νε μετὰ μαχεροφόρου. καὶ οἱ με-[7]σῖται ἀκούσαντες ἀπὸ τῶν ἀντι-[8]δίκων σου ὅτι τὸ πρᾶγμα ὅλον ἰς σαὶ [9]ἔβαλλειν, ἔδωκα ἐνγύην τῷ μα-[10]χεροφόρῳ ἕως $\overline{\kappa\gamma}$ ἄχρει οὗ πέμ-[11]ψω ἐπὶ σαί. καλῶς οὖν ποιήσις λα-[12]βών μου τὰ γράμματα καὶ ἀναβῆ-[13]νε τῇ προθεσμίᾳ τῆς $\overline{\kappa\gamma}$. ἐὰν δὲ [14]θελήσῃς μὴ ἀναβῆνε, πέμψου-[15]σιν στρατιώτην μετ' ἐμοῦ πρὸς σὲ [16]καὶ δίδωμεν ἄλλο ἐφόδιον. [17]ἐρρῶσθαί σαι εὔχομαι.

Verso: [1]ἀπό(δος) Φανείωνι π(αρὰ) Σαραποδώρου [2]. . . χρατου - - -

5. *l.* κριθῆναι. 6. *l.* μαχαιροφόρῳ (also in l. 9). 8. *l.* σε (also in ll. 10 and 17). 9. *l.* ἔβαλλεν. 12. *l.* ἀναβῆναι (also in l. 14). 16. *l.* δίδομεν.

made me a prostitute," he said to me, " Your wife sent me word saying 'He himself sold the chain and he himself put me in the boat.' " Do you say these things in order that I may no longer be trusted as to what I put on board?[a] See how many times I have sent for you! Whether you are coming or not, let me know. (Addressed) Deliver to Isidora from Serenus.

[a] Owing to the writer's uneducated style, as well as to our ignorance of the circumstances, the second half of this letter is very obscure.

126. FROM SARAPODORUS TO PHANION

2nd cent. A.D.

Sarapodorus to Phanion his brother greeting. I wish you to know that I went to the centurion and he sent me to a court of arbitration for trial in the charge of a sword-bearer. And the arbitrators having heard from your opponents that the matter turned entirely upon you, I gave security to the sword-bearer till the 23rd, to allow me time to send for you. Be good enough then on receiving my letter to come up by the appointed date of the 23rd. If you are minded not to come up, they will send a soldier with me to find you and we shall have a further sum to pay for travelling expenses. I pray for your health. (Addressed) Deliver to Phanion from Sarapodorus. . . .

127. CONCERNING TEMPLE ACCOUNTS

P. Tebt. 315. 2nd cent. A.D.

[1][. . . . .]ω[. .] τῷ φιλτάτωι [2][χαίρ]ειν. [3][διεπεμψ]άμην σοι κα[ὶ] ἕτερα γράμ-[4][ματα δι'] ὧν σου ἐδεόμην περὶ [5][τῶν Πύ]ρρου [ἱ]ματίων ς καὶ [6][. . . . .]ου [π]αλ[λ]ίων β ὅπως μοι [7][πέμψῃς] ὅσου [ἐ]ὰν ᾖ, καὶ νῦν δὲ [8][μετὰ σ]π[ο]υδῆς γράφω ὅπως [9][μὴ μερ]ιμνῇς· ἐγὼ γάρ σε ἄσκυλ-[10][τον] πο[ι]ήσω. γείνωσκε γὰρ [11][ἐξε]ταστὴν [τ]ῶν χειρισμῶν [12][τ]ῶν ἐν τοῖ[ς ἱ]ερ[ο]ῖς εἰσεληλυθέ-[13]ναι καὶ μ[έ]λλ[ι]ν καὶ εἰς τὴν με-[14][ρί]δα σου ἔρχ[ε]σθαι. τοιγαροῦν [15][μη]δὲν ταραχ[θ]ῇς· ἐγὼ γάρ [σ]ε [16][ἀ]παλλάξω. ἐὰν μὲν οὖν σχολὴν [17]ἄγῃς, γράψας [σ]ου τὰ βιβλία ἄνελ-[18]θε πρὸς ἐμέ· ὁ γὰρ ἄνθρωπος λεί-[19]αν ἐστὶ[ν] αὐστηρός. ἐὰν δέ σέ [20]τι κατέχῃ, διάπεμψαί μοι αὐ-[21]τὰ κἀγώ σε ἐκπλέξω· ἐγένετο [22]γάρ μου φίλος. ἐὰν δέ σε περὶ τοῦ δα-[23]πανήματος ⟦σε⟧ ἔχῃ καὶ μὴ ἔχῃς [24]ἐπὶ τοῦ παρόντος, γράψον μοι καὶ-[25][γ]ώ σε τὰ [ν]ῦν ὡς καὶ ἐπὶ τοῦ πρώτου [26][ἀ]παλλάξω. ἔσπευσα δέ σοι γράψαι [27][ὅπ]ως μὴ αὐτ[ὸς] φανῇς· πρὶν γὰρ [28][α]ὐτὸ[ν] π[ρὸ]ς σὲ ἐλθῖν ἐγὼ αὐτὸν ποι-[29][ήσ]ω ἐκπλέξαι σε. ἔχι γὰρ συστατι-[30]κὰς [ὅ]πως τὸν ἀπιθοῦντα μετὰ [31]φρουρᾶς τῷ ἀρχιερῖ πέμπιν. ἀλλὰ [32]μὴ ἀμελήσῃς σαυτοῦ μηδὲ ὧν σοι [33]ἔγραψα ὠνήσασθαί μοι. ἐὰν δὲ καί [34]τινα ἔχῃς [. .] . ιμα, ὅσα ἐὰν ἔχῃς [35]ἀνένεγκέ μοι· χρίαν γὰρ ἔχωι. [36]ἔρρωσό μοι, τιμιώτατε.

31. *l.* πέμψῃ.

127. CONCERNING TEMPLE ACCOUNTS

2nd cent. A.D.

. . . to his dearest . . . greeting. I sent you before another letter about the 6 robes of Pyrrhus and the 2 cloaks of . . ., asking you to send them to me whatever they cost, and I am now writing in haste to prevent your being anxious; for I will see that you are not worried. Know that an inspector of the lists of the temples' property [a] has arrived here and intends to visit your district also. Do not be alarmed then; for I will help you out. Now if you have time, write up your books and come to me; for the man is exceedingly strict. But if anything prevents you, send them on to me and I will see you through; for I have made friends with him. If you are in any difficulty about expense and at present have no funds, write to me and I will help you out now as I did before. I have made haste to write to you to prevent you from appearing yourself; for I will make him let you through before he comes to you. He has a written authorization to send defaulters under guard to the chief priest. But do not neglect yourself nor forget what I wrote to you to buy for me. If you have any . . ., bring me what you have, as I am in need of them. Good-bye, most honoured friend.

[a] Several such inventories have been found among the papyri. Each temple was required to make a regular return of its property and personnel and was liable, as in the present case, to have its books inspected without official warning.

128. FROM DAMAS TO HIS SISTER

P. Tebt. 412. Late 2nd cent. A.D.

1Δαμᾶς ὑπηρέτης Ἀρτεμιδώρᾳ τῇ ἀδελφῇ μου ⟦π⟧ χαίρειν. 2πρὸ μὲν πάντων τὸ προσκύνημά σου κατ' ἑκάστην ἡμέραν ποιῶ. 3καλῶς ποιήσις ἄνελθε εἰς τὴν μητρόπολειν τοῦ νεοῦ ἔτους, 4ἐπὶ καἰγὼ ἀνέρχομε εἰς τὴν πόλιν. ἀσπάζου τὴν μετέρα σου καὶ τὸν πατέρα σου. 5ἐρρῶσθ<α>ι εὔχομαι.

2. For καθ' ἑκάστην. 4. *l.* ἐπεί, ἀνέρχομαι, μητέρα.

129. FROM TASOIS TO DIONYSIUS

P. Oxy. 1295. 2nd or 3rd cent. A.D.

1Τασοῖς Διο[ν]υσίωι τῶι τιμ[ι]ωτά-2τωι χαίρειν. 3ἰδοὺ μὲν ἐγὼ οὐκ ἐμιμησάμην σε 4τοῦ ἀπ<οσπ>ᾶν τὸν υἱόν μου, ἐὰν δὲ μέλ-5λῃς οὕτω αὐτῷ ἐπιτιμᾶν, Πτολε-6μαῖ[ο]ν πέμψασα ἀποσπάσ[ω] αὐτόν. 7ὅτε ὁ πατ[ὴ]ρ αὐτοῦ ἐτελεύτησεν, 8ἔδωκα [ὑ]πὲρ αὐτοῦ (δραχμὰς) Ἀτ καὶ ἀν-9άλωσα αὐτῷ ε[ἰ]ς ἱμάτια (δραχμὰς) ξ. 10δέο<μαι> οὖν, μὴ ἀνάπειθε αὐτὸν τοῦ 11ἐκτός μου ε[ἶ]ναι, ἐπεὶ ἄρασα αὐτὸν 12ἐνέχυρον θήσω εἰς Ἀλεξάνδρι-13αν. καλῶς οὖν ποιήσεις πέμψα[ς] 14μοι διμήνου ὀψώνιον διὰ το[ῦ] 15ἀναδιδόντος σοι τὸ ἐπιστόλιον 16καὶ τὸ ἱμάτιον, καὶ δήλωσόν μοι 17πόσου χαλκοῦ δέδωκες αὐτῶι 18καὶ εἰ ἐκομίσω τὸ ἱμάτιον. 19πέμψον τὸ μαφόρτιον τῷ ἀδελ-20[φ]ῷ σου. 21ἔρρωσο.

Verso: Δ[ιο]νυ[σί]ωι ἀπὸ Τασοῖτος.

17. *l.* πόσον χαλκόν.

128. FROM DAMAS TO HIS SISTER

Late 2nd cent. A.D.

Damas, assistant, to Artemidora my sister greeting. Before all else I make supplication for you every day. Please come up to the metropolis at the New Year, since I also am coming up to the city. Salute your mother and your father. I pray for your health.

129. FROM TASOIS TO DIONYSIUS

2nd or 3rd cent. A.D.

Tasois to the most honoured Dionysius greeting. Look you, I have not imitated your attempt to take away my son, but if you are going to find fault with him in this manner, I will send Ptolemaeus and take him away. When his father died, I paid 1300 drachmae on his behalf and spent 60 drachmae on clothes for him. Pray then cease persuading him to break with me, or I will take him and leave him in Alexandria as a pledge.[a] Now please send me two months' salary by the bearer of the letter and the cloak, and let me know how much money you have given him and whether you received the cloak. Send the shawl to your brother. Goodbye. (Addressed) To Dionysius from Tasois.

[a] Tasois probably means that she will borrow money on the security of her son's labour.

130. TO A SCHOOLBOY FROM HIS MOTHER

P. Oxy. 930. 2nd or 3rd cent. A.D.

. . .^{1}[. . . . . . .]υ μὴ ὄκνι μοι ^{2}[γ]ράφειν καὶ περὶ ὧν ἐ-^{3}[ὰ]ν χρείαν ἔχῃς ἐντεῦ-^{4}θεν. ἐλοιπήθην ἐπιγνοῦ-^{5}σα παρὰ τῆς θυγατρὸς ^{6}τοῦ καθηγητοῦ ἡμῶν ^{7}Διογένους καταπεπλευ-^{8}κέναι αὐτόν· ἠμεριμνουν ^{9}γὰρ περὶ αὐτοῦ εἰδυῖα ὅ-^{10}τι κατὰ δύν[α]μιν μέλλει ^{11}σοι προσέχειν. ἐμέλησε ^{12}δέ μοι πέμψαι καὶ πυθέ-^{13}σθαι περὶ τῆς ὑγίας σου καὶ ^{14}ἐπιγνῶναι τί ἀναγεινώ-^{15}σκεις. καὶ ἔλεγεν τὸ ζῆτα, ^{16}ἐμαρτύρει δὲ πολλὰ πε-^{17}ρὶ τοῦ παιδαγωγοῦ σου. ^{18}ὥστε οὖν, τέκνον, μελη-^{19}σάτω σοί τε καὶ τῷ παιδα-^{20}γωγῷ σου καθήκοντι κα-^{21}θηγητῇ σε παραβάλλειν. ^{22}ἀσπάζονταί σε πολλὰ αἱ ^{23}ἀδελφαί σου καὶ τὰ ἀβάσ-^{24}καντα παιδία Θεωνίδος ^{25}καὶ οἱ ἡμέτεροι πάντες ^{26}κατ' ὄνομα. ἄσπασαι τὸν ^{27}τειμιώτατον παιδαγω-^{28}γόν σου Ἔρωτα. In left margin ^{29}]. ταιδ . . ερρ[. .] . . . [. . .] Ἁθὺρ κ[.]

Verso: ^{30}] Πτολεμαίῳ υἱῷ.

4. *l.* ἐλυπήθην.

131. CONCERNING PROPERTY IN PAWN

P. Oxy. 114. 2nd or 3rd cent. A.D.

- - - ^{1}τὰς μακαλας ο . . . . . ποσ . . . . [. . . .]μα νῦν ^{2}μελησάτω σοι λυτρώσασθαι τὰ ἐμὰ παρὰ Σαρα-^{3}πίωνα. κεῖται πρὸς β μνᾶς· πεπλήρωκα τὸν ^{4}τόκον μέχρι τοῦ Ἐπεὶφ πρὸς στατῆρα τῆς μνᾶς· ^{5}δερματικομαφόρτιν λιβάνινον, δερματικομα-

2. *l.* Σαραπίωνος. 5. *l.* δελματικοφόρτιον; so in ll. 8, 9 μανάκιον, etc.

130. TO A SCHOOLBOY FROM HIS MOTHER

2nd or 3rd cent. A.D.

. . . do not hesitate to write to me about anything which you require from here. I was grieved to learn from the daughter of our teacher Diogenes that he had gone down the river; for my mind was easy with regard to him, as I knew that he intended to look after you to the best of his power. I took care to send and inquire about your health and to learn what you were reading. He said it was the 6th book,[a] and he testified at large to the conduct of your attendant.[b] So now, my child, you and your attendant must take care to have you placed under a suitable teacher. Many salutations from your sisters and the children of Theonis, whom the evil eye shall not harm, and from all our friends by name. Salute from me your esteemed attendant Eros . . . (Addressed) . . . to her son Ptolemaeus.

[a] Of Homer's *Iliad*.

[b] The attendant, παιδαγωγός, was a domestic, generally a slave, who took the boy to school and looked after him in other ways.

131. CONCERNING PROPERTY IN PAWN

2nd or 3rd cent. A.D.

. . . Now make it your business to redeem my property from Sarapion. It is held in pawn for 2 minae, and I have paid the interest up to Epeiph at the rate of a stater the mina.[a] It comprises a Dalmatian shawl of the colour of frankincense, a

[a] That is, 4 drachmae on every 100.

[6]φόρτιν ὀνύχινον, χιτὼν καὶ μαφόρτιν λευκὸν [7]ἀληθινοπόρφυρον, φακιάριον λακωνόσημον, [8]λινούδιον ἐμπόρφυρον, ψέλια $\bar{\beta}$, μανάκιν, [9]λωδίκιν, Ἀφροδίτη, σκάφιν, ληκύθιν κασ-[10]σιτέρινον μέγα καὶ στάμνον. παρὰ Ὀνήτορα [11]κόμισαι τὰ κλάλια τὰ $\bar{\beta}$. πρὸς ὀκτὼ χέρας κεῖτα[ι] [12]ἀπὸ Τῦβι πέρυσι πρὸς στατῆρα τῆς μνᾶς. ἐὰν μὴ [13]ἀρκεσθῇ τὸ κέρμα διὰ τὴν ἀμέλειαν τῆς κυρίας [14]ἡμῶν Θεαγενίδος, ἐὰν οὖν μὴ ἀρκεσθῇ τὸ κέρ-[15]μα, πώλησον τὰ ψέλια εἰς συμ⟦ρω⟧πλήρωσιν τοῦ [16]κέρματος. ἄσπασαι πολλὰ Ἀΐαν καὶ Εὐτυχίαν. [17]ἐρρῶσθαί [σ]ε [ε]ὔχομαι. καὶ Ἀλεξάνδραν. ἀσπάζεται [18]Ἀΐαν Ξανθίλλα καὶ πάντας [19]τοὺς αὐτῆς.

Verso: [20] - - -] ἀπὸ Εὐνοί[ας].

10. *l.* Ὀνήτορος.

132. FROM DIOGENIS TO ALEXANDER

P.S.I. 1080. 3rd cent. (?) A.D.

[1][Δ]ιογενὶς Ἀλεξάνδρῳ τῷ ἀδελφῶι [2]χαίρειν. [3]καθὼς ἐνετίλω Ταамόιτι περὶ οἰκήσεως [ἵ]να [4]μεταβῶμεν, εὕραμεν ἣν προεῖμεν πρὶν [5][με]ταβῶμεν παρὰ Ἀγαθῖνον. ἔστιν δὲ ἡ οἰκία [6][πρ]ὸς τῷ Ἰσίῳ ἐχόμενα οἰκίας Κλαυδ[ι]ανοῦ [7][. . . .]ου. μεταβαίνομεν δὲ ἐκεῖ τ[ῷ Φ]αμενώθ. [8][εἰδέ]ναι δέ σε θέλω ὅτι ἔσχον παρὰ Βόττου [9][δραχ]μὰς ἑκατὸν εἴκοσι. ἔπεμψά σοι δετριον (?) [10][. . . .] πορφύρας διὰ Σαραπιακοῦ. ἃ δὲ διεπέμψω [11][μ]οι γράμματα δῶναι Βολφίῳ, δέδωκα. ἀσπάζου [12][δ]ὲ πολ‹λ›ὰ τὸν μικρὸν Θέωνα. ἠνέχθη δὲ αὐτῷ

6. *l.* ἐχομένη. 11. *l.* δοῦναι.

Dalmatian shawl of the colour of onyx, a tunic and a white shawl with a real purple border, a handkerchief with a Laconian stripe, a garment of purple linen, 2 armlets, a necklace, a coverlet, an Aphrodite, a cup, a large tin flask and a wine-jar. From Onetor recover the 2 bracelets. They have been in pawn since Tubi of last year for eight "hands" [a] at the interest of a stater the mina. If our money is insufficient owing to the carelessness of our lady Theagenis, if, I say, it is insufficient, sell the armlets to make up the money. Many salutations to Aia and Eutychia and Alexandra. Xanthilla salutes Aia and all her people. I pray for your health. (Addressed) . . . from Eunoia.

[a] The meaning of the word is obscure.

132. FROM DIOGENIS TO ALEXANDER

3rd cent. (?) A.D.

Diogenis to her brother Alexander greeting. In accordance with your instructions to Taamois about a house for us to move into, we found the one which we let go before moving over to Agathinus. The house is beside the Iseum, adjoining the house of Claudianus . . . We move into it in Phamenoth. I wish you to know that I received from Bottus a hundred and twenty drachmae. I have sent you . . . of purple dye by Sarapiacus. The letter which you forwarded to me to deliver to Bolphius I have delivered. Many salutations to the little Theon. Eight toys have been brought for him by the lady to

ὑπὸ [13][τῆς] γυναικὸς ἧς μοι ἐδήλωσας ἀσπάσασθαι [14][παί]γνια ὀκτὼ καὶ ταῦτά σοι διεπεμψάμην - - -
Verso: [16]Αὐρ(ηλίῳ) Ἀλεξάνδρῳ.

133. FROM A SCHOOLBOY TO HIS FATHER

Rev. Ég. 1919, p. 201. Early 3rd cent. A.D.

[1]Κυρίῳ μου πατρὶ Ἀρίονι Θῶνις χαίρειν. [2]πρὸ μὲν πάντων τὸ προσκύνημά σου ποι-[3]ῶ καθ' ἑκάστην ἡμέραν καὶ εὐχόμενος [4]ἵνα σε ἀπολάβω ὁλοκληροῦντα καὶ τοὺς ἡ-[5]μῶν πάντας παρ' οἷς ἐπιξενοῦμαι πατρῴ-[6]οις θεοῖς. ἰδοὺ πέμπτον σοι τοῦτο γράφω, [7]καὶ σοὶ εἰ μὴ ἅπαξ μόνον οὐκ ἔγραψάς μοι [8]οὐδὲ περὶ τῆς σῆς ὁλοκληρίας οὐδὲ πρὸς ἐ-[9]μὲ ἦλθας· ταξάμενός μοι ὅτι ἔρχομε οὐ-[10]κ ἦ<λ>θας ἵνα καὶ μάθῃς ἢ προσέχει μοι ὁ δι-[11]δάσκαλος ἢ οὔ. καὶ αὐτὸς οὖν καθ' ἡμέρα<ν> [12]σχεδοῦ τι πυνθάνετε περὶ σοῦ ⟦ἑτοίμως⟧ [13]ὅτι οὔπω ⟦ἦλθεν⟧ ἔρχετε; κἀγὼ οὖν λέγω [14]⟦ὅτι⟧ ἔν· νέ. ⟦ι . . δ⟧ σπούδασον οὖν τάχιον [15]ἐλθεῖν πρὸς ἐμὲ ἵνα με διδάξῃ ὡς πρό-[16]θυμός ἐστιν. ἢ ἧς μετ' ἐμοῦ ἀναβάς, πάλε [17]ἤμην διδαχθείς. μνημόνευσον δὲ [18]ἐρχόμενος ὧν ἔγραψά σοι πολλάκις. ⟦η⟧ τάχιον οὖν [19]ἧκε πρὸς ⟦ἐμὲ⟧ ἡμᾶς πρὶν οὗ εἰς τὰ ἄνω [20]μέρη ἀπέλθῃ. ἀσπάζω πολλὰ τοὺς ἡ-[21]μῶν πάντας κατ' ὄνομα σὺν τοῖς φι-[23]λοῦντι ἡμᾶς. ἀσπάζω δὲ καὶ τοὺς διδα-[22]σκάλους μου. [24]ἔρρωσό μοι, κύριέ μου πάτερ, εὐτυ-[25]χοῦντί μοι σὺν τοῖς ἀβασκάντοις μου [26]ἀδελφοῖς, ὡς εὔχομαι, πολλοῖς χρόνοις. (Postscript) [27]μνημονεύσατε τῶν περιστε-[28]ριδίων ἡμῶν. (Addressed) [29]Ἀρείονι πατρὶ {ιθ} π(αρὰ) - - -

whom you told me to give your salutations, and these I have forwarded to you. . . . (Addressed) To Aurelius Alexander.

133. FROM A SCHOOLBOY TO HIS FATHER

Early 3rd cent. A.D.

To my lord and father Arion from Thonis greeting. Before all else I make supplication for you every day, praying also before the ancestral gods of my present abode that I may find you and all our folk thriving. Look you, this is my fifth letter to you, and you have not written to me except only once, not even a word about your welfare, nor come to see me; though you promised me saying "I am coming," you have not come to find out whether the teacher is looking after me or not. He himself is inquiring about you almost every day, saying "Is he not coming yet?" And I just say "Yes." Endeavour then to come to me quickly in order that he may teach me as he is eager to do. If you had come up with me, I should have been taught long ago. And when you come, remember what I have often written to you about. Come to us quickly then before he goes up country. I send many salutations to all our folk, each by name, together with those who love us. Salutations also to my teachers. Goodbye, my lord and father, and may you prosper, as I pray, for many years along with my brothers whom may the evil eye harm not. (Postscript) Remember our pigeons. (Addressed) To Arion my father from . . .

7. *l.* συ. 9. *l.* ἔρχομαι. 10. *l.* εἰ; so too in l. 16. 12. *l.* σχεδόν, πυνθάνεται. 13. *l.* ἔρχεται. 14. *l.* ναί. 16. *l.* πάλαι. 21. *l.* φιλοῦσιν. 24. *l.* εὐτυχῶν.

134. FROM ISIS TO THERMOUTHION

B.G.U. 1680. 3rd cent. A.D.

[1]Ἶσεις Θερμουθίῳ τῇ μητρὶ πλεῖστα χαίρειν. τὸ προσκύνημά [2]σου ποιῶ καθ᾿ ἑκάστην ἡμέραν παρὰ τῷ κυρίῳ [Σ]αράπιδι καὶ τοῖς [3]συννάοις θεοῖς. γεινώσκειν σε θέλω ὅτι εὖ καὶ καλῶς γέγονα εἰς Ἀλεξάν-[4]δρειαν ἐν τέσσαρσι ἡμέραις. ἀσπάζομαι τὴν ἀδε[λ]φήν μο[υ] [5]καὶ τὰ παιδία καὶ Ἐλουᾶθ καὶ τὴν γυναῖκα αὐτοῦ καὶ Διοσκο-[6]ροῦν καὶ τὸν ἄνδρα αὐτῆς καὶ τὰ παιδία καὶ Τ[ά]μαλιν καὶ τὸν [7]ἄνδρα αὐτῆς καὶ τὸν υἱὸν καὶ Ἥρωνα καὶ Ἀμμωνάριον καὶ τὰ παι-[8]δία αὐτῆς καὶ τὸν ἄνδρα καὶ Σανπὰτ καὶ τὰ παιδία αὐτῆς. [9]καὶ ἐὰν θελήσῃ Ἀΐων στρατεύσασθαι, ἐρχέσθω· στρατεύονται γὰρ [10]πάντες. ἐρρῶσθαι ⟦σε⟧ ὑμᾶς εὔχομαι πανοικί.

Verso: - - - π](αρὰ) Ἴσειτος θυγατρός.

135. FROM APION TO DIDYMUS

P. Tebt. 421. 3rd cent. A.D.

[1]Ἀπίων Διδύμῳ χαίρειν. πάντα [2]ὑπερθέμενος ἐξαυτῆς ἅμα τῷ [3]λαβεῖν σε ταῦτά μου τὰ γράμματα [4]γενοῦ πρὸς ἐμέ, ἐπεὶ ἡ ἀδελφή σου [5]νωθρεύεται. καὶ τὸ κιτώνιον [6]αὐτῆς τὸ λευκὸν τὸ παρὰ σοὶ ἔνιγ-[7]κον ἐρχ[ό]μενος, τὸ δὲ καλλάινον [8]μ[ὴ] ἐνίγκῃς, ἀλλὰ θέλις αὐτὸ πωλῆ-[9]σα[ι] πώλησον, θέλις αὐτὸ ἀφεῖναι [10]τῇ θυγατρί σ[ου] ἄφες. ἀλλὰ μὴ ἀμελή-[11]σῃς τι αὐτῆς [κ]αὶ μὴ σκύλῃς τὴν

6. *l.* ἔνεγκον. 8. *l.* ἐνέγκῃς.

134. FROM ISIS TO THERMOUTHION

3rd cent. A.D.

Isis to Thermouthion her mother very many greetings. I make supplication for you every day before the lord Sarapis and his fellow gods. I wish you to know that I have arrived in Alexandria safe and sound in four days.[a] I send salutations to my sister and the children and Elouath[b] and his wife and Dioscorous and her husband and children and Tamalis and her husband and son and Heron and Ammonarion and her children and husband and Sanpat[b] and her children. And if Aion wishes to join the army, let him come; for everyone is in the army. I pray for the health of all your household. (Addressed) . . . from Isis her daughter.

[a] Presumably from Philadelphia in the Fayum, where the letter was found.
[b] Semitic name.

135. FROM APION TO DIDYMUS

3rd cent. A.D.

Apion to Didymus greeting. The instant you receive this letter of mine put off everything and come to me, for your sister is ill. And when you come, bring the white tunic of hers which is with you. Do not bring the turquoise one, but if you wish to sell it, sell it, or if you wish to let your daughter have it, do so. But do not neglect her in any sort, and do not worry your wife or the children. And when

[12]γ[υνα]ῖκά σου ἢ τὰ παιδία. ἐρχόμε-[13]ν[ο]ς δὲ ἔρχου ἰς Θεογενίδα. [14]ἐρρῶσθαί σε εὔχομαι.

136. FROM SERENUS TO DIOGENES

P. Oxy. 935. — 3rd cent. A.D.

[1]Σερῆνος Διογέν[ε]ι [2]τῷ ἀδελφῷ χαίρειν. [3]θεῶν συνλαμβανόν-[4]των ἡ ἀδελφὴ ἐπὶ τ[ὸ] [5]κομψότερον ἐτράπη, [6]καὶ ὁ ἀδελφὸς δὲ Ἁρπο-[7]κρατίων σώζεται [8]καὶ [ὑγι]αίνει, συνλαμβ[ά-][9]νο[υσι] γὰρ ἡμεῖν ἀεὶ ο[ἱ] [10]π[άτ]ριοι θεοὶ ἡμῶν [11]δ[ιδό]ντες ἡμεῖν ὑγία[ν καὶ] [12]σω[τ]ηρίαν. ἔμελλον δ[ὲ] [13]καὶ α[ὐτὸ]ς ἀναβῆναι τ[ῇ .], [14]ἐπε[ὶ οἱ παρὰ] Σαραπίω[νος] [15]εἶπον [κακ]ῶς ἔχειν α[ὐ]τ[όν], [16]διὸ γ[ράφ]ω σοι ὅπως δι' ο[ὗ] [17]ἐὰν [ἔχῃς] διὰ ὥρας γράφ[ῃς] [18]μο[ι] π[ε]ρὶ τούτου. ἡ μεταφ[ορὰ] [19]τῶν ἀνκαλῶν ἔστε εὐθ[έ-][20]ως ὑπὸ τοῦ πατρός· ἔφθανε [21]γὰρ προβαστάξας τὰς ἐν ταῖς (ἀρούραις?) ι . [22]ἄσπασαι πολλὰ τὸν γλυκύτα-[23]τον ἀδελφὸν Ἁρποκρατίωνα [24]καὶ Θεανοῦν καὶ Θέωνα [25]καὶ Διογένην καὶ Ἡλιόδωρον. [26]πολλὰ ὑμᾶς πάντας ἀσπά-[27]ζεται Ἱ[ερ]ακίαινα καὶ ἡ [28]θυγάτ[ηρ] Τσενῆσις. [29]ἐ[ρ]ρῶσθ(αί) σε εὔχομ(αι) [30]πανοικεί.

19. *l.* ἔσται.

137. FROM A STUDENT TO HIS FATHER

P. Oxy. 1296. — 3rd cent. A.D.

[1]Αὐρήλιος Δῖος Αὐρηλίῳ Ὡρείω-[2]νι τῷ γλυκυτάτῳ πατρί μου πολλὰ [3]χαίρειν. [4]τὸ προσκύνημά

you come, come to Theogonis.[a] I pray for your health.

[a] A village in the Fayum.

136. FROM SERENUS TO DIOGENES

3rd cent. A.D.

Serenus to Diogenes his brother greeting. With the help of the gods our sister has taken a turn for the better, and our brother Harpocration is safe and well; for the gods of our fathers help us at all times, giving us health and safety. I had been intending to come up myself on the [·]th, as Sarapion's people said that he was ill, wherefore I am writing to you to write me news of him from time to time by anyone you can send. The transport of the sheaves will be seen to immediately by my father; he has already carried in those in the 1[·] arurae. Many salutations to my sweetest brother Harpocration and to Theanous and Theon and Diogenes and Heliodorus. Many salutations to all of you from Hieraciaena and her daughter Tsenesis. I pray for the health of you and all the household.

137. FROM A STUDENT TO HIS FATHER

3rd cent. A.D.

Aurelius Dius to Aurelius Horion, my sweetest father, many greetings. I make supplication for

σου ποιῶ καθ' ἑκάστην [5]ἡμέραν παρὰ τοῖς ἐνθάδε θεοῖς. ἀμερί-[6]μνη οὖν, πάτερ, χάριν τῶν μαθημάτων [7]ἡμῶν· φιλοπονοῦμεν καὶ ἀναψύχομεν, [8]καλῶς ἡμε[ῖ]ν ἔσται. ἀσπάζομαι τὴν μη-[9]τέρα μου Ταμιέαν καὶ τὴν ἀδελφήν μου [10]Τνεφεροῦν καὶ τὴν ἀδελφήν μου Φιλοῦν, [11]ἀσπάζομαι καὶ τὸν ἀδελφόν μου Πατερμοῦ-[12]θιν καὶ τὴν ἀδελφήν μου Θερμοῦθιν, [13]ἀσπάζομαι καὶ τὸν ἀδελφόν μου Ἡρακ(λ) [14]καὶ τὸν ἀδελφόν μου Κολλοῦχ(ιν), ἀσπάζομαι [15]τὸν πατέραν μου Μέλανον καὶ τὴν μητέ-[16]ραν μου Τιμπεσοῦρ(ιν) καὶ τὸν υἱὸν αὐτῆς. [17]ἀσπάζαιται ἡμᾶς πάντες Γαΐα, [18]ἀσπάζαιται ἡμᾶς πάντες ὁ πατήρ μου [19]Ὡρείων καὶ Θερμοῦθις. [20]ἐρρῶσθαί σαι εὔχομαι, πάτερ.

Verso: ἀπόδ(ος) Α(ὐρηλίῳ) Ὡρείωνι ἀπὸ Δίου υἱοῦ.

5. *l.* ἀμερίμνει. 17. *l.* ἀσπάζεται ὑμᾶς πάντας; so in l. 18. 20. *l.* σε.

138. FROM HEPHAESTION TO STEPHANUS

P. Oxy. 1065. 3rd cent. A.D.

[1]Στεφάνῳ παρὰ Ἡφαιστίωνος. [2]λαβὼν τὰ γράμματα τοῦ υἱοῦ [3]μου Θέωνος ἐξαυτῆς πάντα ὑπερ-[4]θέμενος ἐλθέ μοι εἰς τὸ ἐποίκιον [5]διὰ τὰ συμβάντα μοι. ἐὰν δὲ [6]ὀλιγωρήσῃς, ὥσπερ [ο]ἱ θεοὶ οὐκ ἐ-[7]φίσαντό μ[ο]υ, οὕτως κἀγὼ [8]θεῶ[ν] οὐ φί[σ]ομαι. [9][ἔρρωσ]ο.

you every day before the gods of this place. Now do not be uneasy, father, about my studies; I am working hard and taking relaxation; I shall do finely. I salute my mother Tamiea and my sister Tnepherous and my sister Philous, I salute also my brother Patermouthis and my sister Thermouthis, I salute also my brother Heracl . . . and my brother Kollouchis, I salute my father Melanus and my mother Timpesouris and her son. Gaia salutes you all, my father Horion [a] and Thermouthis salute you all. I pray for your health, father. (Addressed) Deliver to Aurelius Horion from his son Dius.

[a] Not the Horion to whom the letter is addressed. "Father," "mother," "brother," and "sister" were used very loosely of persons with whom the writer had no kinship.

138. FROM HEPHAESTION TO STEPHANUS

3rd cent. A.D.

To Stephanus from Hephaestion. On receipt of the letter of my son Theon put off everything and come at once to the homestead because of what has happened to me. If you take no heed, as the gods have not spared me, so will I not spare the gods.[a] Goodbye.

[a] For the sentiment *cf.* No. 114, l. 11.

139. TO THEON FROM AN AGENT

P. Oxy. 1220. 3rd cent. A.D.

[1]Τῷ κυρίῳ μου Θέωνι [2][῾Εβ]δόμου χαίρειν. [3][ἀ]νέπεμψά σοι διὰ σημι-[4][ώ]σεως τὸ καθ᾿ ἡμέρα<ν> τοῦ ἀν-[5]αλώματος ἥν᾿ εἰδῇς. ἡ δο-[6]κῖ σοι, κύριέ μου, πέμψε μοι [7]κέρμα εἰς τὰ γινόμενα [8]παρ᾿ ἐμοὶ ἔργα τῆς κοφορίας [9]καὶ ἄλλων ἔργων. καὶ περὶ τῆς [10]λέξις τοῦ οἴνου οὗ ἔγραψές [11]μοι οὐδὲν βλέπω φαύλου παρ᾿ ἐ-[12]μοί. περὶ γὰρ τοῦ πάκτονος [13]ἐπισκευάζεται εἵνα με-[14]τενέγκω τὸν οἶνον τοῦ [15]Σιληνοῦ. πέμψις μοι τοὺς [16]ἐκχυσιαίους ἥλους καὶ γλυοῦ [17]κεράμιον α εἰς τὰ ἐργαλῖα [18]τῶν μηχανῶν· καὶ τοῦτο [19]συνφέρι εἵνα μὴ ἀπόληται [20]ἀμελίᾳ. οὐδὲν ἠφάνισεν [21]ὁ ἱπποποτάμις· ἤ τι γάρ ἐστιν [22]περιέργου, ἐφίσταμε αὐτῶν. [23]καὶ περὶ τῶν χωρίων, ἐὰν παρα-[24]γένῃ σὺν θεῷ, μαθήσι τὴν [25]διάθησιν αὐτῶν. [26]ἐρρῶσθαί σοι εὔχομαι, [27]κύριέ μου, εὐτυχοῦντα. [28]μαθήσεται διὰ τῶν λόγων τὸ [29]καθ᾿ ἓν ὡς περιέχι τὸ πι[τ-][30]τάκιον.

2. *l.* [῞Εβ]δομος? 5. *l.* ἵν᾿, εἰ. 6. *l.* πέμψαι.
8. *l.* χωφορίας. 10. *l.* λέξεως. 12. *l.* πάκτωνος.
16. *l.* γλοιοῦ. 21. *l.* εἴ τι. 22. *l.* ἐφίσταμαι.
25. *l.* διάθεσιν. 26. *l.* σε.

140. FROM ALYPIUS TO HERONINUS

P. Flor. 127. A.D. 256.

[1]Π(αρὰ) [᾿Α]λυπίου. [2]σὺν θεῷ φάναι προσδόκα ἡμᾶς τῇ $\overline{κγ}$ πρὸς σὲ γεινο-[3]μένους. ἧς ὥρας

[a] A large landowner in the Fayum, many of whose letters are preserved. They consist of orders on various subjects

139. TO THEON FROM AN AGENT

3rd cent. A.D.

To my lord Theon from Hebdomus greeting. I have sent you in a statement the details of our daily expenditure for your information. If you please, my lord, send me money for the work of carrying earth which is going on here and for other works. With regard to the collection of the wine about which you wrote to me, I see no carelessness on my part; for as to the boat, I am having it repaired to transport the wine of Silenus. You will please send me the nails for the gutters and a jar of gum for the parts of the machines[a]; this serves to prevent them being ruined by neglect. The hippopotami have done no destruction; for if they show any meddlesomeness, I attend to them.[b] About the fields, if by God's grace you come, you will learn their condition. I pray, my lord, for your health and prosperity. The accounts will show the details as contained in the memorandum.

[a] Probably water-wheels.

[b] The translation assumes that *ὁ ἱπποπόταμ<ο>ς* is a collective singular (*cf. τὸν μῦν* in No. 103, l. 15) and that *αὐτῶν* = *αὐτοῖς*. But the meaning is doubtful.

140. FROM ALYPIUS TO HERONINUS

A.D. 256.

From Alypius.[a] God permitting, expect us to pay you a visit on the 23rd. As soon therefore as you

addressed to a certain Heroninus, entitled *φροντιστής* or "caretaker," who was commissioned to look after the interests of Alypius in one of the villages in which he owned property, and who, as we see from No. 141, was employed in a similar capacity by other landowners as well.

οὖν λαμβάνεις μου τὰ γράμματα [4]τὸ βαλανεῖον παντὶ τρόπῳ ποίησον ὑποκαυθῆ-[5]ναι, καὶ δοκοὺς εἰς αὐτὸ παρενεχθῆναι ποιήσας [6]καὶ ἄχ[υρ]ον πανταχόθεν συλλέξας, ἵνα θερ-[7]μῶς λουσώμεθα χειμῶνος ὄντος. καὶ γὰρ προη-[8]ρήμεθ[α] παρὰ σοὶ καταχθῆναι, ἐπεὶ καὶ τὰ ὑπόλοι-[9]πα χω[ρ]ίδια ἐπιθεωρεῖν μέλλομεν καὶ τὰ παρὰ [10]σοὶ διατ[άξ]αι. καὶ τὴν [ἄλλην] μέντοι π[ᾶ]σαν ὑπη-[11]ρεσίαν φρόντισον ἔχειν, πρὸ δὲ [π]άντων [12]χοιρίδιον καλὸν διὰ τοὺς σὺν ἡμεῖν ὄντας, [13]ἀλλὰ καλὸν πάλιν ἔστω, μὴ ὡς πρώην καὶ [14]λεπτὸν καὶ ἄχρηστον. πέμψον δὲ καὶ ἐπὶ [15]τοὺς ἁλεεῖς ἵνα ἰχθὺν κομίσωσι ἡμῖν. [16]ἀπέστειλα δέ σοι γράμματα πρὸς Ὡρείωνα [17]ἵνα σοι ἀποστείλῃ χόρτου [18]δέσμας πεντακοσίας, καὶ [19]πάλιν αὐτῷ τὸν ἴσον ἀπο-[20]δώσεις· τὰ γὰρ ἐργατικά [21]μου κτήνη χλωρὸν ἐσθί-[22]ει· καὶ πάντως περισσό-[23]τερον χλωρὸ[ν χ]όρτον [24]ποίησον ἐνεχθῆ-ναι, [25]ἵνα καὶ αὐτὰ τὴν [α]ὐτάρκη [26]τροφὴν ἔχῃ. (2nd hand) πέμψον οὖν [27]ἐπὶ τὸν χόρτον πάντως [28]σήμερον. ἐρρῶσθαί σε εὔχο(μαι), [29]τ(ιμιώτατ)ε. (1st hand) [30]Ἡρωνείν[ῳ] φροντ(ιστῇ). [31](ἔτους) γ′ Τῦβι κβ.

15. *l.* ἁλιεῖς.

141. FROM APPIANUS TO HERONINUS

P. Flor. 176. A.D. 256.

[1]Π(αρὰ) Ἀπιανοῦ. [2]κἂν τὸ βραχύτατόν τις ἀνα-[3]πέμπῃ, ὀφείλει μετὰ γραμμά-[4]των ἀναπέμπειν καὶ δηλοῦν [5]τί ἀνεπέμφθη διὰ τίνος. ἃ δὲ [6]ἀν-έπεμψας οὐκ ἦν τοσαῦτα ὥσ-[7]τε καὶ ἄνθρωπον

receive my letter be sure to have the bathroom heated, getting logs carried in and collecting chaff from everywhere, in order that we may bathe in warmth in this wintry weather. For we have chosen to stay at your place, as we intend both to inspect the remaining farms and to arrange the work of your district. See, however, that we are provided with every attention, and above all with a good pig for our party, but, again, let it be a good one, and not lean and unfit to eat like the last. Send word also to the fishermen to bring us some fish. I have sent you a letter for Horion telling him to send you 500 bundles of grass, and you will give him back the same amount; for my working animals are eating green fodder; and at all events have abundance of green grass brought in, in order that they too may have sufficient food. So send for the grass to-day without fail. I pray for your health, most honoured Sir. To Heroninus, steward. Year 3, Tubi 22.

141. FROM APPIANUS TO HERONINUS

A.D. 256.

From Appianus.[a] When one dispatches even the smallest load, he ought to send it with a letter stating what has been sent and by what carrier. And the goods which you dispatched were not so many as to

[a] Another of the landowners who employed Heroninus as agent.

καὶ ὄνον κα-[8]*ταργηθῆναι διὰ τέσσαρα κερ-*[9]*τύλλια συκαρίων σαπρῶν. ἐνε-*[10]*φαίνετο δὲ ἐκ τῆς τῶν σύ-*[11]*κων κακίας καὶ ξηρότη-*[12]*τος καὶ δίψης ἡ τοῦ χωρίου* [13]*ἀμελία. ἀλλὰ περὶ μὲν τού-*[14]*των θήσομέν ποτε λογάριον* [15]*πρὸς αὐτούς. καὶ ὁ τῆς Εὐημε-*[16]*ρίας δὲ ἄλλον ἀνέπεμψε με-*[17]*θ' ὀλίγων, καὶ δύνασθαι ἀμφό-*[18]*τεροι διὰ τοῦ ἑνὸς ἀναπέμ-*[19]*ψαι μηνύσαντες εἷς τῷ ἑνί.* [20]*Ἡρωνείνῳ φρ(οντιστῇ).*

Verso: *Ἡρωνείνῳ φρ(οντιστῇ).*

17. *l.* *μετ' ὀλίγων* and *δύνασθε.*

142. FROM ALYPIUS TO HERONINUS

P. Flor. 162. About A.D. 260.

[1]*Π(αρὰ) Ἀλυπίου.* [2]*εἴ τι δύνασε τῶν μετρη-*[3]*μάτων, π[α]ράδος τῷ* [4]*δεκαπρώτῳ διὰ τοῦ* [5]*σοῦ σ[ι]τομέτρου καὶ τὸ* [6]*σύμβολον αὔθωρον* [7]*κόμισαι εἰδὼς ὅτι, ἐὰν* [8]*ἀμελές τι ποιήσῃς* [9]*καὶ τὰ σύμβολα μὴ λάβῃς,* [10]*καὶ τὰ παλαιά σου ἁμαρ-*[11]*[τ]ήματα ἐπεξελεύσε-*[12]*[ω]ς τεύξεται. ἐρρῶσθαί* [13]*σε εὔχομαι,* [14]*. . .*

Verso: *π(αρὰ) Ἀλυπίου Ἡρωνείνῳ [*

2. *l.* *δύνασαι.*

143. FROM ALYPIUS TO HERONINUS

P. Ryl. 238. A.D. 262.

[1]*Π(αρὰ) Ἀλυπίου.* [2]*φροντίς σοι γενέσθω τοῖς κυνηγοῖς* [3]*οὓς ἀπέστειλα ἀγρεῦσαι συάγρους* [4]*διὰ*

require a man and a donkey to leave their work for them, only four baskets of rotten figs. And it was evident from the poorness and dryness and parched appearance of the figs that the estate has been neglected. But about this we shall have an account to settle between ourselves. Again, the agent at Euhemeria has sent another carrier with a few things, though both of you could send by the same man after notifying each other. To Heroninus, steward. (Addressed on back) To Heroninus, steward.

142. FROM ALYPIUS TO HERONINUS

About A.D. 260.

From Alypius. Deliver any corn-dues that you can to the *decemprimus* through your corn-measurer and take the receipt immediately, understanding that if you are guilty of any negligence and do not get the receipts, your old offences also will come in for punishment. I pray for your health, . . . (Addressed) From Alypius to Heroninus . . .

143. FROM ALYPIUS TO HERONINUS

A.D. 262.

From Alypius. Take heed to supply to the hunters whom I have sent to hunt wild boars everything

πολλὰς χρείας παρασχεῖν τὰ [5]ἐπιτήδια πάντα, τοῦτ᾽ ἔστιν ὅσα [6]ἔθος ἔχουσι λαμβάνειν καὶ τὰ κτήνη [7]αὐτῶν καὶ αὐτοί, ἵνα ἀγρεύσωσι [8]μετὰ πάσης σπουδῆς, καὶ κτηνύ-[9]δριον δὲ αὐτοῖς ἓν γοργὸν τῶν [10]ὑπὸ σὲ παράσχες, ἐπειδήπερ [11]τὸ αὐτῶν ὃ εἶχαν βουρδωνά-[12]ριον εἰς ἐμὴν ὑπηρεσίαν κα-[13]τέσχον. [14](2nd hand) ἐρρῶσθαί σε εὔχομαι, [15]τ(ιμιώτατ)ε. [16](1st hand) Ἡρωνείνῳ φρο(ντιστῇ) Θρασώ. [17](ἔτους) θ Παχὼν κε.

144. FROM ALYPIUS TO HERONINUS

P. Flor. 137*. A.D. 264.

[1]Π(αρὰ) Ἀλυπίου. [2]καὶ ἄλλοτε ὑμῖν ἐγράφη τὴν περιποίη-[3]σιν τοῦ σείτου καὶ τὴν ἀναπομπὴν [4]δηλῶσαι, ὑμεῖς δὲ ἠμελήσατε ἴσως [5]οὐ καλῷ συνειδότι χρώμενοι· [6]ὃ κἂν νῦν ποιήσατε, ἵνα [7]μὴ μετὰ στρατιώτου ἀναγκασθῆ-[8]τε τοῦτο ποιῆσαι. [9]ἐρρῶσθαι σε εὔχ(ομαι), [10]τ(ιμιώτατ)ε. [11]Ἡρω-νείνῳ φρ(οντιστῇ) Θρασώ. [12][(ἔτους) ι]β′ Θὼθ $\overline{κϛ}$.

145. FROM ALYPIUS TO HERONINUS

P. Flor. 142. A.D. 264.

[1]Π(αρὰ) Ἀλυπ[ίου]. [2]ἐπειδήπερ ἐντολικὸν ἔχω [3]ἀναγκαίου φίλου, φροντίς σοι [4]γενέσθω ὄνους δύο θηλείας [5]ὑψηλὰς ἀσινεῖς συνωνήσασθαι [6]τῆς ἀξίας τιμῆς, ὡς μήτε τὸν πι-[7]πράσκοντα ζημιοῦσθαι μή-[8]τε ἡμᾶς ζημίαν πλείονα [9]ὑπομένειν, τῆς τιμῆς ὅταν [10]αὐτὰς ἐπιθεωρήσω εὐθέως [11]σοι ἐξοδια-

necessary for their many requirements, that is, everything that they and their animals are accustomed to receive, so that they may hunt with all zeal. Give them also a mettlesome donkey from those in your charge, since I have retained for my own use the mule which they had. I pray for your health, honoured friend. To Heroninus, steward of Thraso.[a] Year 9, Pachon 25.

[a] A village in the Fayum.

144. FROM ALYPIUS TO HERONINUS

A.D. 264.

From Alypius. You were ordered once before to report the quantities of corn stored up and dispatched, but you neglected the order, having perhaps a bad conscience. Do it this time, however, lest you be compelled to do it in the presence of a soldier. I pray for your health, most honourable Sir. To Heroninus, steward of Thraso. Year 12, Thoth 26.

145. FROM ALYPIUS TO HERONINUS

A.D. 264.

From Alypius. As I have received an order from an intimate friend, make it your care to buy two female asses, tall and without blemish, for the price which they are worth, so that neither does the vendor lose nor do we suffer any serious loss, the price being payable to you immediately after I have inspected

ζομένης. (2nd hand) 12ἐρρῶσθαί σε εὔχ(ομαι), τ(ιμιώτατ)ε. (1st hand) 14Ἡρωνείνῳ φροντ(ιστῇ) Θρασώ. 15(ἔτους) ιβ′ Ἀθὺρ κθ̄.

146. FROM HORION TO CELEAS

P. Flor. 338. 3rd cent. A.D.

1Ὡρείων Κηλέᾳ τῷ ἀδελφῷ χαίρειν. 2εὐσεβὲς τὸ πρᾶγμα ποιεῖς ἐὰν 3ποιήσῃς τὸ βιβλίδιον ἐκεῖνο ὡς 4ἐγύμνασα αὐτὸ σὺν σοὶ ἐν τῇ πόλει· 5ἔχω γὰρ Ἡραπίωνα νῦν ἐξερχό-6μενον διὰ τοῦ Μαρεώτου ἵνα 7αὐτὸ πράξῃ ἐν Ἀλεξανδρείᾳ γενά-8μενος· ἄλλον γὰρ σπουδαῖον οὐκ ἔ-9χωμεν μετὰ τοῦτον. ὥστε, ἄδελ-10φε, σπούδασον· καὶ νῦν τάχα ἡ σὴ 11σπουδὴ καὶ φιλοστοργεία καταινει-12κήσῃ τὴν ἐμὴν ⟦ακ . . . [.]⟧ ἀκαιρείαν. 13καὶ περὶ τῶν βοηθῶν τῶν δεκαπρώ-14των καὶ Ἀσκληπιάδου οὐκέτι 15ἐδήλωσάς μοι. κἂν ν[ῦ]ν οὖν, κύ-16ριέ μου ἄδελφε, δήλωσόν μοι· 17οἶδα γὰρ ὅτι συνειδήσι σπουδάζεις 18ἐμοί· ἐμιάνθην γὰρ παρὰ πᾶσι. 19ἐρρῶσ(θαί) σ' εὔχο(μαι).

9. *l.* ἔχομεν. 11. *l.* κατανικήσει.

147. FROM THEONINUS TO DIDYMUS

P. Flor. 367. 3rd cent. A.D.

1Αὐρήλ(ιος) Θεωνεῖνος Διδύμω[ι τῶι] 2τιμιωτάτωι χαίρε[ιν]. 3ἐγὼ δὲ οὐ μειμήσομαί σε οὐδὲ τ[ὰς ἀ-]4πανθρώπους σου ἐπιστολάς, ἀλλ[' ἐπι-]5στέλλω ὡς Θεωνεῖνος πάλιν Δ[ιδύ-]6μῳ. καὶ γὰρ καὶ πολλάκις μου ἐπιστεί-7λαντός σοι καὶ

them. I pray for your health, most honoured Sir. To Heroninus, steward of Thraso. Year 12, Hathur 29.

146. FROM HORION TO CELEAS

3rd cent. A.D.

Horion to his brother Celeas greeting. It will be a pious act if you prepare that petition as I drafted it with you in the city. For I have Herapion now ready to set out through the Mareotic nome in order to put it in execution when he reaches Alexandria; for we have no zealous man except him. So, brother, exert yourself; and now perhaps your zeal and affection will triumph over my mischance. About the assistants of the *decemprimi* and Asclepiades you have not informed me further. Inform me then, my lord brother, even now, as I know that you are exerting yourself for me conscientiously; for I have been besmirched before all men. I pray for your health.

147. FROM THEONINUS TO DIDYMUS

3rd cent. A.D.

Aurelius Theoninus to the most honourable Didymus greeting. I will not imitate you nor your inhuman letters, but am writing in the old way as Theoninus to Didymus. For though I have often written to you and sent you papyrus for letter-

χάρτας ἐπιστολικο[ὺς ἀπο-]8στείλαντος, ἵν' εὐπορῇς τοῦ γρά[φειν] 9μοι, σὺ οὐδὲ ὅλως ἠξίωσας καθ' ὅ[ντι-]10νοῦν τρόπον μεμνῆσθαί μο[υ· ἀλ-]11λὰ δηλονότι πλούτῳ γαυρωθεὶς [καὶ] 12πολλῇ χρημάτων περιουσίᾳ ὑπ[ερη-]13φανεῖς τοὺς φίλους. μὴ δὴ πρὸς Θε[ω-]14νεῖνον τὸν ἀδελφὸν τοιοῦτος γί-15νου, ἀλλ[ὰ γράφε σ]υνεχέστερον ἡ-16μεῖν ἐ[πιστολάς, ἵν]α καὶ διὰ τῶν 17γραμ[μάτων ὁ φίλος εὐ]πορῇ μανθά-18νων [τὰ σοῦ (?)· ὅτι γὰρ π]αρὰ τῶν πρὸς 19ἡμᾶς [ἐρχομένων πολυπ]ραγμονῶν 20ἑκάστ[ο]τε [πε]ρὶ τῆ[ς ὑγ]είας σου πυνθά-21νομαι, τοῦτο οὐδὲ σὺ ἀγνοεῖς. τὸν πα-22τέρα ἡμῶν Σουχίωνα προσαγορεύ[ω].

Verso: *Διδύμωι φίλωι.*

148. FROM PHILOSARAPIS TO APION

P. Oxy. 1664. 3rd cent. A.D.

1*Χαῖρε, κύριέ μου Ἀπίων, Φιλοσάραπίς 2σε προσαγορεύω εὐχόμενός σε σώζεσθαι 3πανοικησίᾳ καὶ εὖ διάγειν. 4ὅτι οὐ μόνοι ἡμεῖς μεμνήμεθά σου, ἀλλὰ 5καὶ αὐτοὶ ἡμῶν οἱ πάτριοι θεοί, τοῦτο 6δῆλον ἅπασιν, ⟦ἁ⟧πᾶσα γὰρ ἡμῶν ἡ ἡλι-7κία ἐν τοῖς στέρνοις σε περιφέρει, με-8μνημένη τῆς ἀγαθῆς σου προαιρέ-9σεως. περὶ τῶν ἀπὸ πατρίδος σοι χρειω-10δῶν, κύριέ μου, ἐπίστελλέ μοι ἡδέ-11ως ἔχοντι, τὰς γὰρ ἐντολάς σου ἥδιστα 12ἔχων ὡς χάριτας λήμψομαι. προσαγο-13ρεύω τὸν ἀξιολογώτατον γυμνασίαρ-14χον Ὡρίωνα.* (2nd hand) *ἐρρῶσθαί σε εὔχομαι, 15κύριέ μου χρηστὲ καὶ εὐγενέστατε 16Ἀπίων, διὰ βίου εὖ διάγοντα 17μεθ' ὧν ἡδέως διάγεις.*

writing to enable you to write to me, you have never deigned to remember me in any way; but evidently your pride in your wealth and the great abundance of your possessions makes you look down on your friends. Now do not behave in this sort towards your brother Theoninus, but write to me more frequently that by means of your letters your friend [a] may be fully informed about your affairs; for that on every opportunity I make a business of interrogating our visitors about your health, even you are not unaware. I salute our father Souchion. (Addressed) To my friend Didymus.

[a] That is, Theoninus himself.

148. FROM PHILOSARAPIS TO APION

3rd cent. A.D.

Hail, my lord Apion, I, Philosarapis, salute you, praying for the welfare and prosperity of you and all your household. That not only we but also our ancestral gods themselves remember you is manifest to all; for all our young men carry you in their hearts, remembering your goodwill. Do me the pleasure, my lord, of writing to me about anything you need from home; for I shall be most pleased to accept your commands as favours. I salute the most estimable gymnasiarch Horion. I pray for your health, my kind and most noble lord Apion, and lifelong prosperity with those with whom it pleases

Verso: (1st hand) [18]Ἀπίωνι γυμνασιάρχῳ στρατηγήσαντι Ἀνταιοπολείτου (2nd hand?) [19][π(αρὰ)] Φιλοσαράπιδος ἐνάρχου [20][ἱερ]οποιοῦ Ἀνταίου πόλ(εως).

149. FROM PAUSANIAS TO HERACLIDES

P. Oxy. 1666. 3rd cent. A.D.

[1]Παυσ{σ}ανίας Ἡρακλείδῃ τῶι ἀδελφῶι χαίρειν. [2]οἴομαι τὸν ἀδελφὸν Σαραπάμμωνα μεταδεδωκέναι ὑμεῖν [3]δι' ἣν αἰτίαν κατῆλθον εἰς Ἀλεξάνδρειαν, φθάνω δὲ ὑμεῖν [4]πρότερον γεγραφηκὼς περὶ τοῦ μεικροῦ Πανσανίου [5]ὡς εἰς λεγιῶνα στρατευσάμενον. ὡς οὖν ἐβουλήθη μη-[6]κέτι εἰς λεγιῶναν ἀλλὰ εἰς εἶλαν, μαθὼν ἀναγκαίως ἔσχον [7]πρὸς αὐτὸν καταντῆσαι, καίτοι μὴ βουλόμενος. δεηθεὶς [8]οὖν πολλὰ ὑπὸ τῆς μητρὸς αὐτοῦ καὶ τῆς ἀδελφῆς εἰς Κό-[9]πτον αὐτὸν μετενεγκεῖν, κατελθὼν εἰς Ἀλεξάνδρειαν [10]πολλαῖς ἀφορμαῖς ἐχρησάμην ἄχρι οὗ ⟦υ⟧μετενέχθη [11]εἰς τὴν ἐν Κόπτῳ εἶλαν. ἐπιθυμῶν οὖν πρὸς ὑμᾶς [12]τῷ ἀναπλόῳ καταντῆσαι περιεκλείσθημεν ἀπὸ τοῦ [13]δοθέντος [τῷ παι]δίῳ ὑπὸ τοῦ λαμπροτάτου ἡγεμόνος [14]κομεάτ[ου], κ[αὶ δ]ι[ὰ τ]αύτην τὴν αἰτίαν οὐκ εἴσχυσα πρὸς [15]ὑ[μ]ᾶς [κ]αταντῆσαι. θεῶν οὖν βουλομένων πρὸς τὴν [16][ἑορ]τὴν [τῶ]ν Ἀμεσυσίων πειράσομαι πρὸς ὑμᾶς γενέ-[17][σθ]αι. μ[ελη]σάτ[ω] σοι οὖν, ἄδελφε, περὶ τοῦ γράμματος τῆς [18][ὑ]ποθήκ[ης ὥ]στε αὐτὸ ἀπαρτισθῆναι καθὼς ἔθος ἐστίν. [19]παρακαλῶ οὖ[ν], ἄδελφε, γράψαι μοι περὶ τῆς ὑμῶν σω-[20][τ]ηρίας,

5. *l.* στρατευσαμένου.

you to live. (Addressed) To Apion, gymnasiarch and ex-strategus of the Antaeopolite nome, from Philosarapis, holding office as sacrificial magistrate[a] of Antaeopolis.

[a] The magistrate responsible for the proper performance of the public sacrifices.

149. FROM PAUSANIAS TO HERACLIDES

3rd cent. A.D.

Pausanias to his brother Heraclides greeting. I think our brother Sarapammon has informed you of the reason why I went down to Alexandria, and I have written to you before about my boy Pausanias taking service in a legion. As however he wished no longer to serve in a legion but in a squadron,[a] I was obliged on learning of this to go and see him, although I did not want to. So after many entreaties from his mother and sister to transfer him to Coptos,[b] I went down to Alexandria and used many ways and means until at last he was transferred to the squadron at Coptos. Though I longed to pay you a visit on the voyage up, we were limited by the furlough granted to the boy by the most illustrious praefect, and for that reason I did not manage to visit you. I will try therefore, if the gods will, to be with you for the feast of the Amesysia.[c] So, brother, take charge yourself of the deed of mortgage, to have it prepared in the customary way. I beg you, brother, to write to me about your being

[a] The recruit wished to join the cavalry, probably in order to be nearer his family.
[b] An important military centre in Upper Egypt.
[c] An Egyptian festival in honour of the god Amsu.

ἐπεὶ ἤκουσα ἐν τῇ Ἀντινόου ὅτι παρ' ὑμεῖν λοιμὸς [21][ἐγ]ένετο. μὴ οὖν ἀμελήσῃς, ἵνα κἀγὼ περὶ ὑμῶν εὐθυ-[22]μότερον διάξω. [23]ἀσπάζου πολλὰ τὴν κυρίαν μου μητέρα καὶ [τὴν ἀδελ-][24]φήν μου καὶ τὰ ἀβάσκαντα ἡμῶν παιδ[ία. ἀσπά]ζε-[25]ται ὑμᾶς Παυσανίας. ἐρρῶσθαί [σ]ε [εὔχ(ομαι)] πανο[ικ]εί.

Verso: [26]εἰς Ὀξυρυγχείτην Ἡρακλ[ε]ί[δῃ . .] . δ . μν[. .] [27]π(αρὰ) Παυσανίου ἀδελφοῦ.

150. FROM CHARMUS TO SOPATRUS

P. Oxy. 1668. 3rd cent. A.D.

[1]Χάρμος τοῖς ἀδελφοῖς πλ[εῖστα] [2]χαίρειν. πρὸ μὲν πάντων [3]εὔχομαι ὑμᾶς ὁλοκληρεῖν. [4]συνέβαλον τῷ Σκωρὺ χάριν [5]τῶν ἐργαστηρίων, καὶ πρότε-[6]ρον μὲν ἔλεγεν ὅτι ἢ δός μοι [7](ἀρτάβας) ιβ, ἢ λαβὲ (ἀρτάβας) ιβ, καὶ περὶ [8]τούτου διὰ προτέρας ἐπιστολῆς [9]ἐδήλωσά σοι, νῦν δέ μοι ἔλε-[10]γεν ὅτι τὸ ἐφήμισυ ἐδώ-[11]καμεν τοῖς ἐργαζομένοις. [12]οὔπω οὖν ἐγὼ αὐτῷ συνε-[13]θέμην περὶ τούτου, ἄχρι οὗ [14]σοι δηλώσω· εἶπεν γάρ μοι ὅτι οὐ-[15]δ' οὕτως συνέθεντο οἱ ἐρ-[16]γαζόμ[ε]νοι, ἐπὶ ἡ τειμὴ τοῦ [17]σείτου ὀλίγη ἐστίν. ὁ ἡγε-[18]μὼν ἀμνησίαν ἔπεμψεν [19]ἐνθάδε, καὶ οὐκέτι φόβος οὐ-[20]δὲ εἷς ἑνεί· ἐὰν οὖν [21]θέλεις, ἴσελθε καταφρονῶν, [22]⟦ἐπὶ⟧ ἡμεῖς γὰρ οὐκέτι δυνόμεθα ἔσω [23]μεῖναι. πολλὰ γὰρ Ἀννόῃ [24]παρατρείβεται ἀναβάσει, [25]καὶ τὴν

16. ἐπεί. 20. *l.* ἐνί rather than ἔνι.

all well, as I heard at Antinoopolis that there has been plague in your neighbourhood. So do not neglect to write, that I may feel more cheerful about you. Many salutations to my lady mother and my sister and our children, whom the evil eye shall not harm. Pausanias salutes you. I pray for the health of you and all your household. (Addressed) To the Oxyrynchite nome, to Heraclides son of . . . from his brother Pausanias.

150. FROM CHARMUS TO SOPATRUS

3rd cent. A.D.

Charmus to his brothers[a] very many greetings. Before all else I pray for your prosperity. I had a meeting with Skoru about the workshops; and while formerly he said, "Either give me 12 artabae or take 12 artabae," as I told you in a previous letter, he now said to me, "We have given the workmen half as much again." I have not yet, however, agreed to his proposal, waiting till I could inform you; for he said to me that the workmen did not accept an agreement even on these terms, since the value of the corn is small. The praefect has sent an amnesty here, and there is no longer any fear for anyone[b]; so if you will, come back boldly, for we are no longer able to remain in the house. For Annoe is much opposed to our going up, and we are

[a] The writer sometimes addresses one person and sometimes several persons, presumably Sopatros and one or more of his other brothers.

[b] Sopatros had apparently been involved in some political disturbance.

ὑμῶν παρουσί-[26]αν ἐγδεχόμεθα, ἵνα μὴ [27]ἀλόγως ἀποστῶμεν· [28]νομίζει γὰρ ὅτι αὐτὴ [29]μόνη οἰκίαν ἔχει ἐν-[30]θάδε. ἀσπάζεται ὑμᾶς [31]Ἡρακλέα καὶ ἡ μήτηρ αὐ-[32]τῆς. ἀσπαζόμεθα τὰ [33]παιδία, μεθ' ὧ(ν) ἐρρῶ[σθ]αι [34]ὑμᾶς εὔχομ(αι) ε[ὖ διάγ]ον-[35]τας.

Verso: [36]ἀ(πόδος) Σωπάτρῳ π(αρὰ) τοῦ ἀδελφοῦ.

151. FROM HERCULANUS TO APLONARION

P. Oxy. 1676. 3rd cent. A.D.

[1]Φλαούιος Ἡρκουλανὸς Ἀπλωναρίῳ [2]τῇ γλυκυτάτῃ καὶ τειμιωτάτῃ [3]πλεῖστα χαίρειν. [4]ἐχάρην μεγάλως κομισάμε-[5]νός σου ἐπιστολήν, δόντος [6]μοι αὐτὴν τοῦ μαχαιρᾶ· ἣν [7]δὲ γράφεις δ[ι]ὰ Πλάτωνος [8]τοῦ τοῦ ὀρχηστοῦ πεπομ-[9]φέναι μοι οὐκ ἐκομισάμην. [10]ἀλλὰ λείαν ἐλυπήθην ὅτι [11]οὐ παρεγένου ἰς τὰ γενέσια [12]τοῦ παιδίου μου καὶ σὺ καὶ ὁ ἀ-[13]νήρ σ[ο]υ, εἶχες γὰρ ἐπὶ πολλὰς [14]ἡμέρας εὐφ[ρ]ανθῆναι σὺν [15]αὐτῷ. ἀλλὰ πάντως κρείττο-[16]να εἶχες· διὰ τοῦτο ὑπερη-[17]φάνηκας ἡμᾶς. ἐγὼ θέ-[18]λω σε πάντοτε καλῶς [19]ἔχειν ὡς ἐμαυτόν, ἀλλὰ [20]καὶ λυποῦμαι πάλιν ὅτι [21]ἐκτός μου ε[ἶ]. ἐὰν δὲ ἐκ-[22]τός μου οὐκ ἀκάλως ἔχῃς, [23]χαίρω ὅτι καλῶ[ς] ἔχεις μέν, [24]κἀγὼ δὲ πάλι καταξύομαι [25]μὴ ὁρῶν σε. τὸ σύνφορόν [26]σου ποίει· ὅταν γὰρ θέλῃς [27]ἡμᾶς πάντοτε ἰδεῖν, ἥδισ-[28]τά σε παραδεξόμεθα. [29]καλῶς οὖν ποιήσεις ἐλ-[30][θοῦσ]α τῷ Μεσορὴ πρὸς [31][ἡμᾶ]ς ἵνα ὅλως ἴδωμέν σε. [32][ἄσπα]σαι τὴν μητέρα σου [33][καὶ τὸ]ν πατέρα σου καὶ Καλ-[34][λίαν]. ἀσπάζεταί σε ὁ υἱός [35][μου] καὶ ἡ μήτηρ

awaiting your arrival to have an excuse for leaving; for she thinks herself the solitary householder here. Heraclea and her mother salute you. We salute the children, and I pray that you with them may have health and prosperity. (Addressed) Deliver to Sopatros from his brother.

151. FROM HERCULANUS TO APLONARION

3rd cent. A.D.

Flavius Herculanus to the sweetest and most honoured Aplonarion[a] very many greetings. I rejoiced greatly on receiving your letter which was given to me by the cutler, though I have not received the one which you say you have sent me by Platon the dancer's son. But I was exceedingly grieved that you did not come for my boy's birthday, both you and your husband, for you could have enjoyed yourself for many days along with him. But doubtless you had more important business; that is why you have disdained us. I wish you, as much as myself, to be always happy, but yet again I grieve that you are away from me. If you are not unhappy away from me, I rejoice in your happiness, though I myself again fret at not seeing you. Do what suits you; for when any time you wish to see us, we shall be most glad to receive you. Please then come to us in Mesore, in order that we may really see you. Give my salutations to your mother and your father and Callias.[b] My son salutes you,

[a] A shortened form of Apollonarion.
[b] Probably the husband.

αὐτοῦ [36][καὶ Δι]ονύσιος ὁ συναγωνισ-[37][τής μο]υ, ὃς ὑπηρετεῖ με ἐν [38][τῷ στ]αβλαρίῳ. ἄσπασαι τοὺς [39][φιλοῦ]ντάς σε πάντας. (2nd hand) [40]ἐρ-ρῶσθαί σε εὔχομαι.

Verso: (1st hand) [41]ἀπόδος Ἀπλωναρίῳ παρὰ Ἡρκουλανοῦ [-][42]πάτρωνος. παρὰ Φλαουίου Ἡρ-κουλανοῦ.

152. FROM AMMONIUS TO JULIUS AND HILARUS

P. Oxy. 1681. 3rd cent. A.D.

[1]Ἀμμώνιος Ἰουλίῳ [2]καὶ Ἱλάρῳ το[ῖ]ς ἀδελ-[3]φοῖς πλεῖστα χαίρειν. [4]ἴσως με νομίζετε, [5]ἀδελ-φ[ο]ί, βάρβαρόν τι-[6]να ἢ Αἰγύπτιον ἀνάν-[7]θρω-πον εἶναι. ἀλλὰ ἀ-[8]ξιῶ μὴ οὕτως [ἔ]χειν, [9]πρῶτον μὲν ἀπὸ μέ-[10]ρους πεῖραν λαβόν-[11]τας τῆς ἡμετέ-ρας [12]γνώμης, πολλὰ δέ [13]με ἤπειξε πρὸς τοὺς [14]ἐμοὺς γενέσθαι, πρῶ-[15]τον μὲν τὸ δι' ἐνιαυ-[16]τ[ο]ῦ αὐτοὺς θεάσασθαι, εἶ-[17]τα τὸ βούλεσθαι πρὸ [18]χειμῶνος καταλῖ-[19]ψαι τὴν Αἴγυπτον. [20]ἐλπίζω οὖν μετὰ [21]τρεῖς καὶ ἐγὼ πρὸς [22]ὑμᾶς ἐλθεῖν καὶ [23]τὰ περὶ ἐμοῦ ὑμῖν [24]ἐξηγήσασθαι. ἀσπά-[25]σ<ασ>θαι τὴν ἀδελφὴν [26]Ἱερων[ί]δα μετὰ Ἰου-[27]λίου το[ῦ συ]μβίου καὶ [28]Ἰσιδώ[ραν?] μετὰ τῶν [29][. .] . . [

Verso: [30]ἀπ(όδος) Ἰουλίῳ καὶ Ἱλάρῳ ἀδελφοῖς [31]π(αρὰ) Ἀμμωνίου.

24. *l.* ἀσπάσασθε.

and his mother, and Dionysius my fellow-worker, who helps me at the stable. Salutations to all who love you. I pray for your health. (Addressed) Deliver to Aplonarion from her patron[a] Herculanus. From Flavius Herculanus.

[a] The word suggests that Aplonarion was an emancipated slave of Herculanus.

152. FROM AMMONIUS TO JULIUS AND HILARUS

3rd cent. A.D.

Ammonius to his brothers Julius and Hilarus very many greetings. Perhaps, brothers, you think me a sort of barbarian or inhuman Egyptian. But I beg you not to be of this mind, because first you have to some degree had proof of my sentiments, and also many things urged me to visit my family, first the fact that I had not seen them for a year and next my desire to leave Egypt[a] before winter. I hope then in three days' time to come to you myself and tell you my news. Salute my sister Hieronis with Julius her husband and Isidora (?) with her . . . (Addressed) Deliver to my brothers Julius and Hilarus from Ammonius.

[a] This does not necessarily mean that the writer went abroad; for inhabitants of Alexandria, and even of the Fayum, spoke of going "to Egypt."

153. TO APOLLO FROM HIS SON

P. Oxy. 1680. 3rd or 4th cent. A.D.

[2]- - - φίλ]τατε [3]πάτερ, καὶ ε[ὔχομ]αι τῷ θεῷ ὁλοκλη-[4]ρεῖν σε καὶ εὐοδο[ῦ]σθαι καὶ ὑγιαίνον-[5]τί σε ἀπολαβεῖν ἐν τοῖς ἰδίοις. καὶ [6]γὰρ πρὸ τούτου σοι ἐδήλωσα λυπού-[7]μενος ἐπὶ τῇ ἐν ἡμῖν σου ἀπουσίᾳ, [8]μήπως ὃ μὴ εἴοι σοι γένοιτο καὶ μὴ [9]εὕρωμέν σου τὸ σῶμα. κα[ὶ γὰρ] [10]πολλάκις σοι δηλῶσαι {σοι} βού[λομαι ὅτι] [11]βλέπων εἰς τὸ ἀσύστατον σῆ[μα ἠ-][12]θέλησα ἐνχαράξαι σοι. καὶ νῦν γὰρ ἀκού-[13]ω ὅτι σφόδρα Ἡράκλειος ὁ νῦν ἐπίτρο-[14]πος ζητεῖ σε, καὶ ὑπονοοῦμαι ὅτι πάν-[15]τως πάλιν τί ποτε ἔχει πρὸς σέ. [16][εἴ τ]ί ποτε αὐτῷ χρεωστεῖς, καὶ τοῦτό [17][γε βο]ύλομαί σοι γνῶναι ὅτι ἐκόμισα [18][πρ]ὸς Γάειν σίτου ἀρτάβας δύο καὶ - - -

Verso: [19][τῷ κυρίῳ] καὶ ἀγαπητῷ πατρὶ Ἀπόλλωνι [

4. *l.* ὑγιαίνοντα. 8. *l.* εἴη. 17. *l.* σε. 18. *l.* Γάιον.

154. FROM SARAPAMMON TO PIPERAS

P. Tebt. 424. Late 3rd cent. A.D.

[1]Σαραπάμμων Πιπερᾶτι. [2]ἔπεμψά σοι ἐπιστολὴν διὰ τοῦ ἀρτο-[3]κόπου καὶ εἴσως οἶδας τί σοι ἔγραψα. [4]καὶ εἰ μὲν ἐπιμένις σου τῇ ἀπονοί-[5]ᾳ, συνχέρω σοι· εἰ δὲ μετανοεῖς, σὺ οἶ-[6]δας. ἴσθι δὲ ὅτι ὀφίλις φόρους καὶ ἀπο-[7]φορὰς ἑπτὰ ἐτῶν, ὡς ἐὰ⟨ν⟩ μὴ ἀποκα-[8]ταστασίας {[μ]ὴ} πέμψῃς [ο]ἶδάς σου τὸ[ν] [9]κίνδυνον.

5. *l.* συγχαίρω.

153. TO APOLLO FROM HIS SON

3rd or 4th cent. A.D.

. . . dearest father, and I pray to God[a] that you are prosperous and successful and that we may receive you home in good health. I have indeed told you before of my grief at your absence from among us, my fear being that something dreadful might happen to you and that we may not find your body. Indeed I have often wished to tell you that in view of the unsettled state of things I wanted to stamp a mark on you.[b] And now I hear that Heraclius the present overseer is vigorously searching for you, and I suspect that he must have some new claim against you. If you owe him anything, I wish you to know this, that I have taken to Gaius two artabae of corn and . . . (Addressed) To my lord and beloved father Apollo.

[a] Or " to the god," but the address rather suggests that the writer was a Christian.

[b] As it was customary to do on camels and other animals as a means of reclaiming them if stolen. In the present case the writer's idea was that he should be able to identify his father's body and give it proper burial.

154. FROM SARAPAMMON TO PIPERAS

Late 3rd cent. A.D.

Sarapammon to Piperas. I sent you a letter by the baker, and perhaps you know what I wrote to you. If you persist in your folly, I wish you joy; if you are repenting, you yourself know. Let me tell you that you owe me seven years' rents and revenues, so unless you send remittances you know the risk you run.

155. FROM PANISCUS TO HIS WIFE

J.E.A. xiii. p. 61. About A.D. 293.

1Πανίσκο[ς] τῇ σοιμβ[ί]ῳ μου 2Πλουτογενίᾳ μητρὶ τῆς θυγατρός 3μου πλῖστα χαίρειν. 4πρὸ μὲν ‹πάντων› εὔχομέ σοι τὴν ὁλοκληρία[ν] 5καθ' ἑκάστην ἡμέραν παρὰ τοῖς 6θεοῖς πᾶ⟦τρ⟧σι. γινώσκειν σε οὖν 7θέλω, ἀδελφή, ὅτι ἐν Κόπτωι 8αἰ⟦ε⟧μίναμεν ἐνγὺς τῆς ἀδελφῆς 9⟦μου⟧ σου καὶ τῶν τέκνων αὐτῆς, 10ὅπως μὴ λυπηθῇς ἐρχομένη 11ἐν τῇ Κόπτῳ· εἰσὶ γὰρ ἐνθάδε οἱ ἀδελφοί σου. ὅπερ καὶ σὺ 13πάντως βούλῃ αὐτὴν ἀσπά-14σαστε {αὐτὴν} πολλά, τοῖς θεοῖς 15εὔχετ[ε] καθ' ἡμέραν βουλομένη 16σε ἀσπάζε[σ]θαι μετὰ τῆς μητρός 17σου. δ[ε]ξαμ[έ]νη οὖν μου τὰ γράμ‹μα›-18τα ταῦτα ποίησόν σου τὰ ‹κατὰ› χέρα, 19ὅπως, ἐὰν πέμψω ἐπὶ σέν, 20ταχέως ἔλθῃς. καὶ ἔνεγκον 21ἐρχομένη ποκάρια ἐριδίων 22δέκα, ἐλεῶν κεράμια ἕξ, 23στά⟦υ⟧γματος κεράμια τέσσερα, 24καὶ τὸ ὅπλον μου τὸ κενὸν μόνον, 25τὸ κασίδιόν μου. φέρε καὶ τὰ λογχία 26μου. φέρε καὶ τὰ τοῦ παπυλίω-27νος σκεύη. ἐὰν εὕρητε εὐκερί-28αν, μετὰ ἀνθρώπων καλῶν 29δεῦτε. ἐρχέστω μεθ' ἡμῶν 30Νόννος. ἔνεγκον ἡμῶν πάν-31τα τὰ ἡμάτια ἐρχομένη. ἔνεγκον 32ἐρχομένη σου τὰ χρυσία, ἀλλὰ 33μὴ αὐτὰ φορέσῃς ἐν τῷ πλο[ί]ῳ. (continued on verso) 34ἀσπάζομε τὴν κυρίαν μου θυγατέραν Ἡλιοδώραν. ἀσπάζετε ὑμᾶς 35Ἑρμίας.

Verso: 36ἀπόδ(ος) τῇ σοιμβίῳ μου καὶ τῇ θυγατρί μου π(αρὰ) Πανίσκου πατρ[ός].

1. *l.* συμβ[ί]ῳ (so in 36). 4. *l.* εὔχομαι. 8. *l.* ἐμείναμεν. 13. *l.* ἀσπάσασθαι. 18. ‹κατὰ› χέρα

155. FROM PANISCUS TO HIS WIFE

About A.D. 293.

Paniscus to my wife Plutogenia, mother of my daughter, very many greetings. Before all I pray for your prosperity daily before all the gods. I would have you know, sister, that we have been staying in Coptos [a] near your sister and her children, so do not be grieved about coming to Coptos; for your kinsfolk are here. And just as you desire above all to greet her with many greetings, so she prays daily to the gods desiring to greet you along with your mother. So on receiving this letter of mine make your preparations in order that you may come at once if I send for you. And when you come, bring ten fleeces of wool, six jars of olives, four jars of liquid honey, and my shield, the new one only, and my helmet. Bring also my lances. Bring also the fittings of the tent. If you find an opportunity, come in good company. Let Nonnus come with you. Bring all our clothes when you come. Bring with you your gold ornaments, but do not wear them on the boat. Salutations to my lady and daughter Heliodora. Hermias salutes you. (Addressed) Deliver to my wife and my daughter, from Paniscus her father.

[a] The letter was sent from Coptos in Upper Egypt to Philadelphia in the Fayum.

E.-H.: *τὰ χ<ρέ>α* Ed. 22. *l.* *ἐλαιῶν*. 24. *l.* *καινόν*. 27. *l.* *εὐκαιρίαν*. 29. *l.* *ὑμῶν*. 31. *l.* *ἱμάτια*. 34. *l.* *ἀσπάζομαι, ἀσπάζεται*.

156. FROM SATURNILUS TO APOLLONIUS

P. Oxy. 1068. 3rd cent. A.D.

[1]Σατορνῖλος κυρίῳ μου Ἀπολλωνίου [2]χαίρειν. [3]μὴ εὐπορήσας πλοῖον ἐν τῷ Ἀρσενοείδῃ [4]ἔγραψα τῷ κυρίῳ μου Κληματίῳ τῷ ἀρχ‹ι›ε-[5]ρῖ εἵνα μοι πλοῖον διαπέμψεται εἵνα δυ-[6]νηθῶ τὸ σωμάτιν κατενενκῖν ἐν Ἀλε-[7]ξάνδριαν, καὶ διαπέμψετό μοι σκαφίδι-[8]ον ἀρταβῶν ἑξήκοντα. οἱ ἀδελφοὶ οὖν [9]οἱ ἐνέγκαντες αὐτὸ ἔλαβαν καὶ γρ‹ά›μ-[10]ματα ἀπ' αὐτοῦ Κληματίου ἐφ' ᾧ μη-[11]δὶς ἐνοχλήσι αὐτῷ κατὰ τόπον. [12]ἀνελθόντες οὖν ἐν τῷ Ἀρσενοεί-[13]τῃ εὗρον τὸ σωμάτιν μήπου δυνά-[14]μενον κηδευθῆναι, ἀλλὰ ἡμερῶν [15]ἀνοχὴν ἔχω. ἔδοξεν οὖν αὐτοῖς [16]χάριν ἀναγκέας χρίας γενέσθαι [17]εἰς Τοού. παρακαλῶ οὖν, κύριέ μου, ὑπάρ-[18]ξε αὐτοῖς καὶ τὰ τῆς σῆς σπουδῆς, [19]εἵνα μοι μαρτυρήσουσιν ἀνελθόν-[20]τες, καὶ εἴ τι ἂν ἄλλου σου χρίαν σκῶ-[21]σιν· σιμίου χάριν ὅτι ἔπεμψας ἐπὶ [22]τὸν ὄνον καὶ κατέσχον αὐτὸν ἕως [23]γένωμε πρὸς σέ. ἀξιῶ σω οὖν, κύρε μου, [24]εἵνα δῷς αὐτοῖς γράμματα εἵνα μη-[25]δὶς ἐνοχλήσι αὐτοῖς καθ' ὁδόν, [26]εἵνα δυνηθῶ κηδεύσας τὸ σωμά-[27]τιν ἐλθῖν πρὸς σέ. [28]ἐρρῶσθαί σοι εὔχομαι [29]πολλοῖς χρόνοις.

Verso: [30]ἀπόδος Ἀπολλωνίου παρὰ Σατορνίλου.

1. *l.* Ἀπολλωνίῳ; so in l. 30. 3. *l.* Ἀρσινοΐτῃ; so in l. 12. 6. *l.* Ἀλεξανδρίᾳ or εἰς. 7. *l.* διεπέμψατο. 16. *l.* ἀναγκαίας. 17. *l.* ὑπάρξαι. 20. *l.* ἄλλο, σχῶσιν. 21. *l.* σημείου (so Crönert) or Σιμίου. 23. *l.* γένωμαι, ἀξιῶ σε. 28. *l.* σε.

156. FROM SATURNILUS TO APOLLONIUS

3rd cent. A.D.

Saturnilus to my lord Apollonius greeting. Finding no boat available in the Arsinoite nome I wrote to my lord Clematius the chief priest to send me a boat in order that I might be able to carry the body down to Alexandria; and he sent me a skiff of sixty artabas' burden. The brethren who brought it got also a letter from Clematius to the effect that no one should interfere with it locally. Now on going up to the Arsinoite nome they found the body not yet ready to be buried,[a] but I have a delay of some days. So they resolved to go to Toou[b] for an urgent business. I pray you then, my lord, to let them have proofs of your interest, that they may testify of it to me on their return, and anything else that they may need from you; for instance, you sent for the ass and I have kept him until I come to you. I beg you then, my lord, to give them a letter in order that no one may interfere with them on the road and so I may be able to bury the body and come to you. I pray for your lasting health. (Addressed) Deliver to Apollonius from Saturnilus.

[a] It was no doubt being embalmed in the Egyptian manner.

[b] A village in the Heracleopolite nome.

157. FROM MELAS TO SARAPION AND SILVANUS

P. Grenf. ii. 77. 3rd-4th cent. A.D.

[1][Μέλας . . . .] Σαραπίωνι καὶ Σιλβανῷ [2][. . . . . χ]αίρειν. ἀπέστειλα ὑμῖν [3][διὰ τοῦ ν]εκροτάφου τὸ σῶμα τοῦ [4][ἀδελφοῦ] Φιβίωνος καὶ ἐπλήρωσα [5][αὐ]τὸν [το]ὺς μισθοὺς τῆς παρακομι-[6]δῆς τοῦ σώματος ὄντας ἐν δραχμαῖς [7]τριακοσίαις τεσσαράκοντα παλαιοῦ [8]νομίσματος. καὶ θαυμάζω πάνυ [9][ὅτι] ἀλόγως ἀπέστητε μὴ ἄραντες [10][τὸ σ]ῶμα τοῦ ἀδελφοῦ ὑμῶν, ἀλλὰ [11]σ[υ]νλέξαντες ὅσα εἶχεν καὶ οὕτως [12]ἀπέστητε. καὶ ἐκ τούτου ἔμαθον [13]ὅτι οὐ χάριν τοῦ νεκροῦ ἀνήλθατε, [14]ἀλλὰ χάριν τῶν σκευῶν αὐτοῦ. [15]φροντίσατε οὖν τὰ ἀναλωθέντα ἑτοι-[16]μάσαι. ἔστι δὲ τὰ ἀναλώματα [17]τιμ(ὴ) φαρμάκου παλ(αιαὶ) (δραχμαὶ) ξ, [18]τιμ(ὴ) οἴνου τῇ πρώτῃ [19]ἡμέρᾳ χό(ες) β παλ(αιαὶ) (δραχμαὶ) λβ, [20][ὑπ(ὲρ)] δαπάνης ἐν ψω-[21]μίοις καὶ προσφαγίοις (δραχμαὶ) ιϛ, [22][τ]ῷ νεκροτάφῳ εἰς τὸ ὄρος [23]με[τ]ὰ τὸν γεγραμμένον [24]μισθὸν χο(ῦν) ἕνα (δραχμαὶ) κ, [25]ἐλαίου χό(ες) β (δραχμαὶ) ιβ, [26]κρ[ι]θῆς (ἀρτάβη) α (δραχμαὶ) κ, [27]τιμ(ὴ) σινδόνος (δραχμαὶ) κ, [28]καὶ μισθοῦ ὡς πρόκ(ειται) (δραχμαὶ) τμ, [29](γίνονται) ἐπὶ τοῦ λ[όγο]υ τῆς [30]ὅλης δα[πά]νης παλαιοῦ [31]νομίσματος δραχμαὶ [32]πεντακόσιαι εἴκοσι, [33]γί(νονται) (δραχμαὶ) φκ. [34][π]ᾶν οὖν ποιήσετε ὑπηρετῆσαι τὸν [35]μέλλοντα ἐνεγκ[εῖ]ν τὸ σῶμα [36]ἐν ψωμίοις καὶ [οἰ]ναρίῳ καὶ ἐλαίῳ [37]καὶ ὅσα δυνατὸν ὑ[μῖ]ν ἐστιν, ἵνα μαρ-[38]τυρήσῃ μοι. μη[δ]ὲν δὲ δράσητε (along left margin) [39]]ων . . [. . . . .]

157. FROM MELAS TO SARAPION AND SILVANUS

3rd-4th cent. A.D.

Melas[a] . . . to Sarapion and Silvanus . . . greeting. I have sent you by the grave-digger the body of your brother Phibion and have paid him the fee for transporting the body, being 340 drachmae of the old coinage.[b] And I am much surprised that you departed for no good reason without taking the body of your brother, but collected all that he possessed and so departed. And from this I see that you did not come up for the sake of the dead, but for the sake of his effects. Now take care to have ready the sum spent. The expenses are : cost of preservatives 60 old drachmae ; cost of wine on the first day, 2 choes 32 old dr. ; for expenditure on loaves and relishes 16 dr. ; to the grave-digger for the desert journey, besides the above-mentioned fee, 1 chous of wine 20 dr., 2 choes of oil 12 dr., 1 artaba of barley 20 dr. ; cost of linen 20 dr. ; and fee as aforesaid of 340 dr. ; total on reckoning the whole expenditure five hundred and twenty drachmae of the old coinage, total 520 dr. You will therefore make every effort to serve the person who will bring the body by providing loaves and wine and oil and whatever you can, in order that he may testify to me. Do nothing . . . I pray for your health.

[a] On the verso he is styled decadarch, which in Ptolemaic papyri denotes a foreman of workmen or other employees, but in Roman times is usually a military title. The letter comes from the Great Oasis (*cf.* Nos. 8 and 50).

[b] The Imperial coinage of Egypt prior to the reform of Diocletian.

μένων ἐν ἀργυρί[ῳ] διὰ τὸ ἐμὲ - - - 40 - - - Παχὼν κη 41 - - - ἐρρῶσθ[αι ὑμᾶς εὔχομαι].

Verso: 42[Σαρ]απί[ωνι] καὶ 43[Σι]λβανῷ ἀδελφοῖς 44Φιβίωνος 45Μέλας (δεκάδαρχος).

158. FROM TITIANUS

P.S.I. 299. End of 3rd cent. A.D.

1Τῇ κυρίᾳ [ἀ]δελφῇ Τιτιανὸς εὖ πράττειν. 2τυχὼν [τοῦ ἀ]νερχομένου πρὸς ὑμᾶς προήχθην 3γράψαι σο[ι τ]ὰ συμβάντα μοι ὅτι κατεσχέθην 4νόσῳ ἐπὶ πολὺ ὡς μὴ δύνασθαι μηδὲ σαλεύεσθαι. 5ὡς δ' ἐκουφίσθη μοι ἡ νόσος, ἐπύθετό μοι ὁ ὀ-6φθαλμὸς καὶ τραχώματα ἔσχον καὶ δεινὰ 7πέπονθα ἔτι τε καὶ ἕτερα μ[έρ]η τοῦ σώματος 8ὡς καὶ ἐπὶ τομὴν ἥκειν μ[ε] ὀλίγου, ἀλλὰ θεῷ χά-9ρις. ὁ δὲ πατήρ μου ⟦μέχρι⟧ {τ[ο]ύτου}, δι' ὃν καὶ νο-10σῶν παρ[έ]μεινα ⟦μέχρι τούτου⟧, νοσεῖ· καὶ δι' αὐτὸν 11ἔτι ἐνταῦθά εἰμι. μακροψ[ύ]χ[ει] οὖν, ἀδελφή, ἄχρεις 12οὗ ἄν με θεὸς εὐοδώσῃ [πρὸς] ὑμᾶς. καὶ συνε-13χῶς τούτου ἕνεκεν ε[ὔχομαι τ]ῷ θεῷ ἕως οὗ ἄν με 14πάλιν πρὸς ὑμᾶς εὐοδώσῃ. ἐνόσησαν δὲ πάν-15τες οἱ κατὰ τὴν οἰκίαν, ἥ τε μήτηρ καὶ τὰ παιδί-16α πάντα, ὡς μηδὲ ἔχειν ἡμᾶς ὑπηρεσίαν, ἀλλὰ 17τὰ πάντα [σ]υνεχῶς τοῦ θεοῦ δέε[σ]θαι. καὶ αὐτὸς 18δὲ πειρῶμαι, ἐπὰν πλοίου εὐπορηθῶ, καταλα-19βεῖν ὑμᾶς. ἀσπάζεται ὑμᾶς ὁ κύριός μου 20πατὴρ καὶ ἡ μήτηρ. ἀσπάζονται ὑμᾶς οἱ κα-21τὰ τὴν οἰκίαν πάντες. ἀσ[π]άζομαι τὸν κύρι-22[όν] μου [ἀδελφὸ]ν καὶ [. . . . . . κ]αὶ Κυρίλλαν 23 - - -

(Addressed) To Sarapion and Silvanus, brothers of Phibion, from Melas, decadarch.

158. FROM TITIANUS

End of 3rd cent. A.D.

To my lady sister[a] from Titianus, prosperity. Having chanced on someone going up to you I have been moved to write and tell you of my plight, how I was afflicted with illness for a long time so that I could not even stir. When the illness abated, my eye began to suppurate and I had granulations and suffered greatly, and other parts of my body were also affected, so that I nearly had to submit to surgery; but thanks be to God! My father, on whose account I have stayed on till now in spite of illness, is also ill; and it is for his sake that I am still here. Be patient then, sister, until God brings me safely to you. And for this end I unceasingly pray to God until he brings me safely back to you. Everyone in the house was ill, my mother and all the children, so that we had no one to serve us, but besought God for everything unceasingly. For myself, I am seeking to rejoin you as soon as I can find a boat. My lord and father and my mother salute you. Everyone in the house salutes you. I salute my lord and brother and . . . and Cyrilla . . .

[a] Probably the wife of Titianus.

---

2. *τυχὼν* [*τοῦ* E.-H.: *Τύχων*[*ος* Edd. 8. *μ*[*οι*] Edd. 9. Illegible letter above *μεχρι*; so in l. 10. 10. *μεχρι τουτου* cancelled inadvertently. 12. Or *ευοδωσει*.

(Postscript along left margin) [24]ἐπιστολὴ τοῦ ἡγεμόνος μοι ἐπέμφθη· καὶ εἰ μὲν ἠνέχθη σοι, εὖ ἂν [ἔχοι, — — λα-][25]βεῖν ἢ ἀξιωσάτω Μῶρον τὸν ἐπιστολέα τὸν φίλον καὶ ἐγλαβέτω [

25. Μῶρον E.-H.: μωρὸν Edd.

159. FROM A NOTARY TO HIS SON

P. Oxy. 123. 3rd or 4th cent. A.D.

[1]Κυρίῳ μου υἱῷ Διονυσοθέωνι [2]ὁ πατὴρ χαίρειν. [3]εὐκαιρητὶς καὶ νῦν τοῦ ἀνερχομένου πρὸς ὑμᾶς [4]ἀναγκαῖόν μοι ἐγένετο προσαγορεῦσαι ὑμᾶς. [5]πάνυ θαυμάζω, υἱέ μου, μέχρις σήμερον γράμ-[6]ματά σου οὐκ ἔλαβον τὰ δηλοῦντά μοι τὰ περὶ τῆς [7]ὁλοκληρίας ὑμῶν. κἂν ὥς, δέσποτά μοι, ἀντί-[8]γραψόν μοι ἐν τάχει· πάνυ γὰρ θλείβομαι διότι [9]οὐκ ἐδεξάμην σου γράμματα. γενοῦ πρὸς τὸν ἀδελφόν [10]μου Θεόδωρον καὶ ποίησον αὐτὸν σκυλῆναι [11]πρὸς Τιμόθεον καὶ μεταδῶναι αὐτῷ τὸ ἕτοιμον [12]αὐτοῦ ποιῆσαι εἶνα⟦ι⟧ εἰσβῇ προσεδρεῦσαι. ἤδη γὰρ [13]οἱ τῶν ἄλλων πόλεων συνείδησιν εἰσήνεγκαν [14]τοῖς κολλήγαις αὐτῶν, εἰσῆλθαν. εἰσβαίνων οὖν [15]μετὰ τῆς αἰσθῆτος γνώτω ὁ ἐρχόμενος, ἵνα ἕτοι-[16]μος εἰσβῇ. μὴ οὖν θελήσουσιν ἀσυνειδήτως [17]ἡμᾶς φέριν πρὸς ἀλλήλους ὡς ε[ἰ]δότας ὅτι τὸ αὐ-[18]τὸ ἡμᾶς πάντας καταλαμβάνει; ἐκ[ε]λεύσθημεν γὰρ [19]μετὰ τῶν χλαμύδων εἰσβῆναι, ὅθεν ὁ ἐρχόμενος [20]ἕτοιμος ἐλθάτω ὡς προσεδρεῦσαι μέλλων. [21]ἀσπάζομαι τὴν γλικυτάτην μου θυγατέρα

3. l. εὐκαιρηθείς. 7. l. μου. 11. l. μεταδοῦναι.

A letter was sent to me from the praefect; if it was brought to you, that will serve; if not, . . . or let him ask our friend Morus the letter-carrier and receive . . .

159. FROM A NOTARY TO HIS SON

3rd or 4th cent. A.D.

To my lord and son Dionysotheon greeting from his father. Having had the luck to find someone going up to you I felt obliged to address you. I am much surprised, my son, that till to-day I have received from you no news of your welfare. Nevertheless, my master, reply to me promptly; for I am quite distressed at having had no letter from you. Go to my brother Theodorus and make him betake himself to Timotheus and tell him to make his preparations for going in to attend the sitting.[a] For the notaries of the other cities have already apprised their colleagues before they went in. So let the one who goes be informed that when he enters he must do so in proper dress, in order that he may prepare himself before entering. Surely they will not wish to let us meet each other uninformed, when we know that the same rule applies to us all. For we were ordered to enter in our cloaks, wherefore let the one who goes go prepared to attend the sitting. I salute my sweetest daughter Macaria

[a] The nature of the meeting is not definitely known, and some points in the letter are rather obscure; but the writer's chief object was apparently to have Timotheus notified that he must present himself in the prescribed costume.

12. *l.* ἵνα. 14. *l.* <οἳ> εἰσῆλθαν? 15. *l.* ἐσθῆτος.
21. *l.* γλυκυτάτην.

Μακ{κ}αρίαν [22]καὶ τὴν δεσποίνην μου μητέραν ὑμῶν καὶ ὅλους [23]τοὺς ἡμῶν κατ' ὄνομα. ἐρρῶσθαί σε εὔχομαι πολλοῖς [24]χρόνοις, κύριε υἱέ. [25]Ἐπεὶφ κβ. Verso: [26]κυρίῳ μου υἱῷ Διονυσοθέωνι Ἰσχυρίων ταβουλάριος.

160. FROM A MELETIAN

P. Lond. 1915. A.D. 330–340.

[1]- - - ἀδελ]φ[ῷ] [2]Π[αιηοῦτι Ἑριηοῦς ἐν] κ(υρί)ῳ χαίρειν. [3]τοῖ[ς . . . . . .]ηφθονει συμφορᾷ παραπεσοῦσιν [4]βοη[θεῖ]ν π[α]ρ[α]γγέλ<λ>εται ἡμῖν ὁ θεῖος λόγος πᾶσι, μάλιστα [5]τοῖς ἀδελφοῖς ἡμῶν. ἐπειδὴ οὖν ὁ ἀδελφὸς ἡμῶν [6]Παμώνθεις περιστάσεσι <οὐ> τὲς {σ}τυχούσαις παρα-[7]πεσὼν ἔσχιστα πέπονθεν ὑπὸ ἀνθρώπων ἀνε-[8]λεημόνων καὶ ἀθέων, ὥσ[τ]ε ὡς ἔπως εἰπεῖν ἀναγ-[9]κασθῆναι τῆς μακαρίας ἐλπίδος ἡμῶν ἀποστερη-[10]θῆναι, ὅθεν ἐδέησεν ἡμᾶς ἐπιθεῖνε δι' αὐτὰ [11]ταῦτα τὰ γράμματα πρὸς τὴν ἀδελφώτητα [12]ὑμῶν, δηλώσας τὴν τούτου πᾶσιν πρᾶξιν, [13]ἵν<α> καὶ ὑμῖς γνώντες συμβάλλεσθε αὐτῷ μεμνη-[14]μένοι [το]ῦ μακαρίου ἀποστό[λ]ου λέγοντες τοὺς [15]ἀσθενοῦντας μὴ παρορᾶν [ο]ὐ μόνον [ἐ]ν τῇ πίστι [16]ἀλλὰ κα[ὶ ἐ]ν ταῖς κο<σ>μικαῖς π[ρ]άξεσι. οὗτος γὰρ ὁ ἀδελφὸς [17]ἡμῶν ἔτυχέν ποτε οἰνοπράτης καὶ ἐπὶ πολ{λ}ὺ [18]ἐνοχληθεὶς ὑπὸ τῶν ἐν τῇ αὐτοῦ πατρίδι ἀρχώντων [19]⟦παρα⟧ παρὰ τὴν δύναμιν αὐ[το]ῦ εἰσπράτ<τ>εσθαι καὶ ἐκ [20]τούτου ὄγκον ἀργυρίου δαν[ει]σάμενος καὶ ταῦτα [21]ἀπετηθεὶς καὶ μὴ δυνάμενος ἀπαντᾶν πρὸς τὰ

6. *l.* Παμώνθις (=-θιος), ταῖς. 7. *l.* αἴσχιστα.

and my mistress your mother and all the family, each by name. I pray for your lasting health, my lord and son. Epeiph 22. (Addressed) To my lord and son Dionysotheon from Ischyrion, *tabularius*.

160. FROM A MELETIAN [a]

A.D. 330–340.

To . . . brother Paieous from Herieous, greeting in the Lord. The word of God exhorts us to succour all those who have met with misfortune, and especially our brethren. Since therefore our brother Pamonthius has met with no ordinary reverses and has suffered most shameful treatment from pitiless and godless men, so that, one might say, he has perforce been bereft of our blessed hope, it behoved us to make application to your brotherliness by this present letter, exposing all his circumstances, in order that you being informed may help him, remembering the blessed apostle who tells us not to neglect those who are weak, not only in the faith but also in the affairs of this world. For this brother of ours was once a wine-dealer, and having for long been importuned by the magistrates in his native place with exactions beyond his means he consequently borrowed a great sum of money and being summoned to repay it and failing to meet his lia-

[a] The Meletians were a Christian sect called after Meletius the bishop of Lycopolis, whose quarrel with his fellow bishops in Egypt over a question of discipline produced a schism that lasted for several centuries.

8. *l.* ἔπος. 10. *l.* ἐπιθεῖναι. 11. *l.* ἀδελφότητα. 12. *l.* δηλώσαντας, πᾶσαν. 13. *l.* ὑμεῖς γνόντες. 14. *l.* λέγοντος. 18. *l.* ἀρχόντων. 21. *l.* ἀπαιτηθείς.

22χρεωστούμενα ἠναγκάσθη ὑπὸ τῶν δανιστῶν 23πάντα τὰ ἑαυτοῦ ἄχρι καὶ τῶν ἱματίων τῶν 24τὴν ἀσχημοσύνην αὐτοῦ περισκεπασμένων 25πολῆσαι· καὶ τούτων πραθέντων μόγις τὴν ἡμισίαν 26τῶν ἀργυρίων τεδύνηται περινοῆσαι τοῖς δανίσταις, 27οἵτινες οἱ ἀνελεήμονες ἐκεῖνοι καὶ ἄθεοι ἀπέσπα-28σαν τὰ πάντα τὰ ἑαυτοῦ τέκνα νήπια κομιδῇ. 29ὅθεν ἐπιτίνωμεν πρὸς ὑμᾶς ταυτηνὶ τὴν ἐπιστο-30λήν, ἀξιοῦντες ὑμ[ᾶς σ]υμβαλέσθαι αὐτῷ εἰς ὃ ἐὰ[ν] 31δύνασθε [δοῦν]ε ἵν[α] παρ' αὐτῶ[ν αὐ]τὰ [ἀπολάβῃ . . . On left margin 32]εσθαι υἱοὶ τοῦ οὐρανίου πατρὸς ἡμῶν. Verso: 33 - - - 34[. . . .] . ων πάνυ αὐτῷ βοήθησον ἐπιδὴ μάλιστα 35[. . . . .] . νβη ὁ ἀδελφὸς ὅτι ἥρπασαν τὰ τέκν[α 36αὐτοῦ εἰ]ς δου[λ]ίαν. μὴ οὖν ἀμ[έ]λη-σ[ο]ν τὸ 37[. . . . . . .] . καὶ παντὶ τρόπῳ. Lower down, two lines of Coptic. (Addressed) 40ἀπόδ(ος) Παιηοῦτι πρεσβ(υτέρῳ) π(αρὰ) Ἑριηοῦς ἀδελφός.

25. *l.* πωλῆσαι. 26. *l.* δεδύνηται. 29. *l.* ἐπιτείνομεν. 31. *l.* [δοῦν]αι. 40. *l.* Ἑριηοῦτος ἀδελφοῦ.

161. TO ABINNAEUS FROM KAOR

P. Lond. 417. About A.D. 346.

1Τῷ δεσπότῃ μου καὶ ἀγαπητῷ 2ἀδελφῷ Ἀβιννέῳ πραι(ποσίτῳ) 3Καὸρ πάπας Ἑρμοῦ πόλεως χαί<ρ>ειν. 4ἀσπάζωμαι τὰ πεδία σου πολλά. 5γινώσκιν σε θέλω, κύριε, 6π[ερὶ] Παύλω τοῦ στρατιότη 7περὶ τῆς φυγῆς, συνχωρῆσε 8αὐτοῦ τοῦτω τὸ ἅβαξ, 9ἐπειδὴ ἀσχολῶ ἐλθῖν πρὸς 10σὲν αὐτὲ ἡμέρε. καὶ πάλειν, 11ἂμ μὴ παύσεται, ἔρχεται

bilities he was compelled by his creditors to sell all his possessions down to the very garments that cloaked his shame ; and even when these were sold, barely half the money could he scrape together for his creditors, who, those pitiless and godless men, carried off all his children, mere infants as they were. Wherefore we direct to you this letter, requesting you to help him as far as your means allow, in order that he may recover the children from them. P.S. . . . sons of our Heavenly Father. P.P.S. . . . by all means help him, since . . . our brother, because they carried off his children into slavery. Therefore do not neglect . . . by all means. (Addressed) Deliver to Paieous, presbyter, from his brother Herieous.

161. TO ABINNAEUS FROM KAOR

About A.D. 346.

To my master and beloved brother Abinnaeus,[a] praefect, from Kaor, priest of Hermopolis,[b] greeting. Many salutations to your children. I wish you to know, my lord, about Paul the soldier, about his running away, praying you to pardon him this one time, as I am too busy to come to you these present days. And another time, if he will not give over,

[a] A military officer stationed at Dionysias in the Fayum.
[b] Not the great Hermopolis, but a village near Dionysias.

2. *l.* Ἀβινναίῳ. 4. *l.* ἀσπάζομαι, παιδία. 6. *l.* Παύλου, στρατιώτου. 7. *l.* συνχωρῆσαι. 8. *l.* αὐτῷ, τοῦτο, ἅπαξ. 10. *l.* αὗται ἡμέραι.

[12]εἰς τὰς χεῖράς σου ἄλλω ἄβαξ. [13]ἐρρῶσθαί σε εὔχο-[14]μαι πολλοῖς χρό-[15]νοις, κύριέ μου [16]ἄδελφε.

12. *l.* ἄλλο ἅπαξ.

162. TWO LETTERS FROM HERMIAS

P. Oxy. 120. 4th cent. A.D.

[1]Τῇ ἀδελφῇ Ἑρμείας χαίρειν. [2]λοιπὸν τί σοι γράψω οὐκ οἶδα, ἀπαίκα-[3]{κα}μον γάρ σοι αἵκαστον λέγων καὶ [4]οὐκ αἰνακούεις. χρὴ γάρ τινα ὁρῶν-[5]τα αἱαυτὸν ἐν δυστυχίᾳ κἂν ἀνα-[6]χωρῖν καὶ μὴ ἁπλῶς μάχαισθαι τῷ [7]δεδογμένῳ. μετρίων γὰρ καὶ δυσ-[8]τυχῶν γένεσιν αἴχοντες οὐδὲ [9]οὕτω αἱαυτοῖς προσαίχομεν; τέως [10]μὲν οὖν οὐδὲν οὐδέπω παίπρακται. [11]κἂν ὥς, εἴπερ μέλι σοι, ἀπόστιλόν [12]μοί τινα ἢ Γοῦνθον ἢ Ἀμμώνιον [13]παραμένοντά μοι ἄχρις ἂν γνῶ [14]πῶς τὰ κατ' αἰμαὶ ἀποτίθαιται. μὴ ἄρα [15]παρέλκομαι ἢ καὶ εἴργομαι ἔστ' ἂν [16]ὁ θεὸς ἡμᾶς αἰλαιήσῃ; καὶ γὰρ Ἑρμεία[ς] [17]αἰπείγεται ἐλθεῖν πρὸς ὑμᾶς, ἀλλὰ αὐ-[18]τὸν ἀξιώσας παραμῖναι οὐκ αἰβου-[19]λήθη, λέγων ὅτι ἀναγκαῖόν τι αἴχω [20]καὶ δῖ μαι ἀνελθεῖν, καὶ υἱὸς δὲ Γεννά-[21]διος οὐκ ὗός τέ ἐστιν προσαι-δρεύειν [22]κτήσι, μάλιστα ἐπεὶ ξένης καὶ [23]παρὰ τῇ τάξι ὄντα. τὰ κατὰ σὲ διοίκη-[24]σον ὡς πρέπον ἐστίν, μὴ τέλεον ἀνα-[25]τραπῶμεν. οὐ δέδοκται γὰρ ἡμῖν αἴχιν [26]τι δυστυχοῦντες. ἔ[ρ]ρωσό μοι διὰ παντὸς εὖ πράσ[σ]ουσα.

Verso: [1]Ἑρμείας Γούνθῳ υἱῷ χα(ίρειν). [2]εἰ μὴ

Recto: 2. *l.* ἀπέκαμον. 3. *l.* ἕκαστον. 4. *l.* ἐν-ακούεις. 5. *l.* ἑαυτόν. 6. *l.* μάχεσθαι. 8. *l.* ἔχοντες. 9. *l.* ἑαυτοῖς προσέχομεν. 10. *l.* πέπρακται.

he shall be left in your hands.[a] I pray that you may have health for many years, my lord and brother.

[a] That is, left to the commander to punish without any further intercession.

162. TWO LETTERS FROM HERMIAS

4th cent. A.D.

Hermias to his sister greeting. Well now, what to write to you I know not, for I have talked and talked to you till I am tired, and yet you pay no heed. When a man finds himself in misfortune, he ought to draw back and not simply fight against fate. Though lowly and unfortunate by birth, are we not even so to give heed to ourselves? So far then nothing at all has been done. Notwithstanding, if you really care, send me someone, either Gunthus or Ammonius, to remain with me until I know how my affairs stand. Am I to be delayed or even obstructed until God takes pity on us? For Hermias is anxious to return to you; though I asked him to remain, he refused, saying that he has pressing business and must return and that his son Gennadius is unable to attend to the property, especially now that he has left home and is at his post. Manage your local affairs properly, or our disasters will be complete. For we are resolved not to continue in misfortune. Goodbye and may you prosper always.

Hermias to his son Gunthus greeting. Unless

14. *l.* ἐμὲ ἀποτίθεται. 16. *l.* ἐλεήσῃ. 17. *l.* ἐπείγεται. 18. *l.* ἐβουλήθη. 19. *l.* ἔχω. 20. *l.* δεῖ με. 21. *l.* οἷός τε, προσεδρεύειν. 22. *l.* ἐπί. 23. *l.* ὤν for ὄντα. 25. *l.* ἔχειν.

Ἀμμώνιος πάραυτα 3ἔρχαιται πρός μαι, σὺ αὐτὸς 4πάντα ὑπερθέμενος 5ἧκαι αἰκείνου τὸ σὸν ἔργον 6ποιοῦντα. ἀλ<λ>' ὅρα μὴ κα-7ταλίψῃς μαι θλιβόμενον. 8καὶ δήλωσόν μοι πῶς ἔσ-9χεν Δίδυμος. μὴ ἄρα αἱ ἡ-10μέραι τὰ πάντα διατελοῦσι; 11ἐρρῶσθαί σε εὔχο(μαι).

Verso: 3. *l.* ἔρχεται πρός με. 5. *l.* ἧκε (rather than ἢ καί) ἐκείνου. 6. *l.* ποιοῦντος. 7. *l.* με.

163. FROM DEMETRIUS TO FLAVIANUS

P. Oxy. 939. 4th cent. A.D.

1[Τῷ κυρίῳ] μου Φλαβιανῶι 2[Δημήτ]ριος χαίρειν. 3[ὡς ἐν ἄλ]λοις πλείστοις νῦν ἔτι μᾶλλον ἡ πρὸς σὲ 4[τοῦ δεσπό]του θεοῦ γνῶσις ἀνεφάνη ἅπασιν ἡμῖν 5[ἐν τῷ τὴν] κυρίαν ἀνασφῆλαι ἐκ τῆς καταλαβούσης 6[αὐτὴν νόσ]ου, καὶ εἴη διὰ παντὸς ἡμᾶς χάριτας ὁμο-7[λογοῦντα]ς διατελεῖν ὅτι ἡμῖν ἵλεως ἐγένετο 8[καὶ ταῖς εὐ]χαῖς ἡμῶν ἐπένευσεν διασώσας ἡμῖν 9[τὴν ἡμῶν] κυρίαν· ἐν γὰρ αὐτῇ πάντες τὰς ἐλπίδας 10[ἔχομεν]. συνγνώμην δέ, κύριέ μου, σχοίης μοι 11[καὶ εὔνους] ἀποδέξει με εἰ καὶ ἐς τηλικαύτην σε 12[ἀγωνία]ν ἄκων ἐνέβαλον γράψας περὶ αὐτῆς ὅσα 13[ἐκομίσω]. τὰ μὲν γὰρ πρῶτα ἐν θλίψει αὐτῆς 14[πολλῇ οὔ]σης οὐκ ὢν ἐν ἐμαυτῷ ἀπέστειλα 15[γράμματα], εἴ πως ἐκ παντὸς τρόπου δυνηθείης 16[πρὸς ἡμᾶς] ἀφικέσθαι, τοῦτο τοῦ καθήκοντος 17ἀπ[α]ι[τοῦντ]ος· ὡ[ς δὲ ἐπὶ τ]ὸ ῥᾷον ἔδοξεν τετράφθαι, 18ἕτερά σε γράμματα ἐπικαταλαβεῖν ἐσπούδασα διὰ 19Εὐφροσύνου, ἵνα σε εὐθυμότερον καταστήσω. 20νὴ γὰρ τὴν σὴν σωτηρίαν,

Ammonius is coming to me at once, put everything aside and come yourself, letting him do your work. But see that you do not fail me in my straits. And let me know how Didymus has been. Does time really bring everything to fulfilment? I pray for your health.

163. FROM DEMETRIUS TO FLAVIANUS

4th cent. A.D.

To my lord Flavianus from Demetrius greeting. As on many other occasions, but now more than ever, the mind of the Lord God regarding you has been revealed to us all by the recovery of our mistress from the illness which overtook her, and may we never cease to profess our thanks that He has been gracious to us and assented to our prayers, preserving for us our mistress; for she is the object of all our hopes. Grant me pardon, my lord, and take my action in good part, even if I have unwillingly thrown you into such distress by writing about her the news which you have received. For I was out of my mind, seeing her in great affliction, when I sent the first message asking if by any means you could come to us, for so my duty demanded. But as she seems to have taken a turn for the better, I have made haste to have another letter brought to you by Euphrosynus, in order to cheer you. For by your welfare, my lord,

5. [ἐν τῷ E.-H.: [ὥστε Edd. 15. [γράμματα] or [Πλούταρχον] Wilcken: [σπουδάζων] Edd.

κύριέ μου, ἧς μάλιστά [21]μοι μέλει, εἰ μὴ ἐπινόσως ἐσχήκει τὸ σωμάτιον [22]τότε ὁ υἱὸς Ἀθανάσιος, αὐτὸν ἂν ἀπέστειλα πρὸς σὲ [23]ἅμα Πλουτάρχῳ ἡνίκα ἐβαρεῖτο τῇ νόσῳ. νῦν δὲ [24]πῶς πλίονα γράψω περὶ αὐτῆς ἀπορῶ, ἔδοξεν [25]μὲν γὰρ ὡς προεῖπον ἀνεκτότερον ἐσχηκέναι ἀνακαθεσθεῖ-[26]σα, νοσηλότερον δὲ ὅμως τὸ σωμάτιον ἔχει. παρα-[27]μυθούμ[ε]θα δὲ αὐτὴν ἑκάστης ὥρας ἐκδεχόμε-[28]νοι τὴν [σ]ὴν ἄφιξιν. ἐρρῶσθαί σε, κύριέ μου, [29]διὰ παντὸς τῷ τῶν ὅλων [30]δεσπότῃ εὔχομαι. [31]Φαρμοῦθι ϛ.

Verso: [32]Φλαβιανῷ [33]Δημήτριος.

164. FROM HERMIAS TO HORION

P. Oxy. 1223. Late 4th cent. A.D.

[1]Κυρίῳ μο[υ ἀδελφῷ Ὡρίων]ι [2]Ἑρμείας. [3]θαυμάζω εἴπερ ὁ ἀποστελλό-[4]μενος πρὸς σὲ τὸ πλοῖον [5]τὸ τοῦ γεούχου καταλαμβάνει [6]παρὰ σοί. πλὴν ἐὰν διὰ [7]ἀμελίαν τινὰ καταλάβῃ, [8]σπούδασον πάραυτα τὸν [9]ναύτην ἐπὶ τὴν πόλειν [10]ἅμα τῷ πεμφθέντι συμμάχῳ [11]ἐκπέμψαι. ἀλλ' ὅρα μὴ [12]ἀμελήσῃς. ἡ καὶ εὐδία ἐστὶ [13]καὶ τὸ πλοῖον ἀνενέγκε οὐ [14]δύναται ἐν τῇ σήμερον, [15]αὐτὸς ὁ ναύτης ἀπαντήσῃ [16]πρὸς χιρογραφίαν, οὐκ ὀλίγως [17]γὰρ ἐνοχλούμεθα. ἐὰν δὲ ἀμελή-[18]σῃς, ὁ οἶκος ἡμῶν περιστάσι [19]κοινωνεῖν μέλλει διὰ τὴν [20]ἀπουσίαν τοῦ γεούχου ὑπὸ τοῦ [21]φορτικοῦ Ἀμμωνίου σπεκουλά-[22]τορος καὶ τοῦ ἐπαρχικοῦ. εἰ τι δὲ [23]ἀργύρια ἔχεις παρὰ σοὶ ἢ ὁλο-[24]κόττινα, ἐν τάχει ἀπόστιλον· [25]τοσαύτας γὰρ προσδοχὰς

which is my chief concern, I protest that if my son Athanasius had not then been ailing, I should have sent him to you with Plutarchus when her illness lay heavy on her. And now what more to write about her I do not know ; for though, as I said before, she seems to be in more tolerable case, having sat up, she is nevertheless rather ill. We comfort her by looking forward to your arrival every hour. I pray, my lord, to the Master of all to give you lasting health. Pharmouthi 6. (Addressed) To Flavianus from Demetrius.

164. FROM HERMIAS TO HORION

Late 4th cent. A.D.

To my lord and brother Horion from Hermias. I shall be surprised if my messenger finds the boat of the landlord with you. If, however, owing to some carelessness he finds it there, make haste at once to dispatch the sailor to the city along with the assistant whom I have sent. Now see that you do not neglect this. If there is a calm and he cannot bring up the boat to-day, let the sailor come himself to make a bond ; for I am being worried not a little. If you neglect this, owing to the absence of the landlord our house is like to join company with misfortune through that pestilent Ammonius the *speculator* and the praefect's agent. If you have by you any silver coins or solidi, send them in haste ;

χρε-[26]ωστοῦμεν, καὶ οὐκέτι πιστευ-[27]όμεθα, ἐὰν μὴ εὐγνωμονή-[28]σωμεν. πέμπων δὲ δήλωσον [29]τοῖς σοῖς παρασχεῖν μοι τὴν ὑπ(ο)-[30]λοιπάδα⟦ν⟧ τοῦ οἴνου καὶ τῆς καθό-[31]λου μονάδα μίαν ἥμισυ. ὁ [32]ὁλοκόττινος νῦν μυ(ριάδων) ͵βκ [33]ἐστίν· κατέβη γάρ. μὴ ἀμελή-[34]σῃς ἐν τῇ σήμερον τὸ πλοῖον [35]ἢ τὸν ναύτην ἀποστῖλαι. ἐρ-[36]ρῶσθαί σε εὔχομαι [37]πολλοῖς χρόνοις, ἄδελφε.

Verso: κυρίῳ ἀδελφῷ Ὡρίωνι Ἑρμεία[ς].

165. FROM AN ORPHAN ABROAD

P. Bour. 25. 4th cent. A.D.

[1]Κυρίᾳ μου καὶ ἐπιποθήτῃ θείᾳ Τάρη [2]θυγάτηρ ἀδελφῆς σου Ἀλλοῦτος [3]ἐν θ(ε)ῷ χαίρειν. [4]πρὸ παντὸς εὔχομε τῷ θ(ε)ῷ ὑγιένουσάν [5]σε καὶ εὐθυμοῦσαν ἀπολαβῖν τὰ παρ' ἐμοῦ [6]γράμματα· αὕτη γάρ μού ἐστιν εὐχή. γεί-[7]νωσκε δέ, κυρία μου, ὅτι ἀπὸ τῶν Πάσχων [8]ἡ μήτηρ μου, ἡ ἀδελφή σου, ἐτελε[ύτη]σεν. [9]ὅ[τ]ε δὲ τὴν μητέρα μου εἶχα μεθ' [ἑ]αυτῆς, [10]ὅλον τὸ γένος μου αὕτη ἦν, ἀφ' οὗ δ[ὲ] ἐτε-[11]λεύτησεν, ἔμινα ἔρημος μ[η]δένα ἔχουσα [12]ἐπὶ ξένοις τόποις. μνημόνευε οὖν, [13]θεία, ὡς ζώσης τῆς μητρός μου, εἶνα εἴ τι-[14]να εὑρίσκις πέμπε πρὸς ἐμέ. προσα-[15]γόρευε πᾶσαν τὴν συγγένιαν ἡμῶν. [16]ἐρρωμένην σε ὁ κ(ύριο)ς διαφυ-[17]λάττοι μακροῖς καὶ εἰρη-[18]νικοῖς χρόνοις, κυρία μου.

Verso: [19][ἀπό]δος τὴν ἐπιστολὴν [20]Ὡρείνᾳ ἀδελφῇ Ἀπολλωνίου Κοπτιτίσᾳ, παρὰ [21]Τάρης θυγατρὸς ἀδελφῆς αὐτῆς ἀπὸ Ἀπαμίας.

for I have incurred so many obligations and I shall be trusted no longer if I do not deal fairly. Send and tell your people to deliver to me the remainder of the wine and one and a half units of the general amount.[a] The solidus now stands at 2020 myriads[b]; it has fallen. Do not neglect to send the boat or the sailor to-day. I pray for your lasting health, brother. (Addressed) To my lord and brother Horion from Hermias.

[a] The meaning is quite obscure.
[b] Of denarii. See p. xvii.

165. FROM AN ORPHAN ABROAD

4th cent. A.D.

To my lady and beloved aunt from Tare, daughter of your sister Allous, greeting in God. Before all I pray to God that my letter finds you well and cheerful; such is my prayer. Know, dear lady, that my mother, your sister, has been dead since Easter. When I had my mother with me, she was all my family, and since her death I have been left in solitude without a companion in a strange land. Remember me then, aunt, as if my mother were still alive, and if you find someone, send him to me. Salute all our kinsfolk. May the Lord guard you in health for long and peaceful years, my lady. (Addressed) Deliver the letter to Horina sister of Apollonius, of Coptos, from Tare daughter of her sister, of Apamea.[a]

[a] Probably Apamea in Syria.

---

4. *l.* εὔχομαι, ὑγιαίνουσαν. 13. ζώσης revised reading, ζητούσης Ed. 20. *l.* Κοπτιτίσσῃ.

166. FROM CONSTANTINE

P. Oxy. 1872. 5th or 6th cent. A.D.

[1]Π(αρὰ) . [2]καταξιώσῃ <ἡ σὴ> διάθεσις συνηθôς καταξυοῦσα φιλῖν συνκροτῆσε τὸν [3]εὐγε[ν]ῆ Παῦλον ἀποσταλέντα παρ' ἐμοῦ συνονήσασθαι οἶνον ἐμοί, καὶ μὶ συν-[4]χορησάτωι βαρεθε̂ναι τὸ πλοῖον ο<ἴ>νου εἰς τὸ τελόνιν. θαρôν γὰρ τῇ σε̂ ἀρετῇ καὶ [5]τῇ με<τα>ξὺ φιλίᾳ γεγράφεκα· θεὸς γὰρ ὖδεν ὁ ἅγιος οὐ προστασίας ἕνεκεν [6][γ]ε[γ]ράφεκα, ἀλλὰ ἐμοὶ φέρετη ὁ ὖνος. τὰ δὲ ἀποσταλέντα παρ' ἐμοῦ [7]εὐτελέστατα καταξιόσατη ὁς πολλὰ δέξασθαι. τὴ<ν> δὲ σεμνοπρεπεστάτη<ν> [8]ἐλευθέραν καὶ τὰ φίλτατα ὑμῶν πεδία ἐξ ἐμοῦ προσειπῖν καταξίοσον, [9]καὶ ἐν οἷς χρία τôν ἐνταῦθα καταξιώσατη κελεύειν.

Verso: [10]ἐπίδ(ος) τῷ δεσπό(τῃ) διὰ πάντα θαυμασ(ιωτάτῳ) ἐναρέτῳ ἀδελφῷ . [.]αδ . [.]ῳ φίλῳ [11]π(αρὰ) Κωνσταντίνο[υ].

2. *l.* συνηθῶς καταξιοῦσα, συγκροτῆσαι. 3. *l.* συνωνήσασθαι, μὴ συγχωρησάτω. 4. *l.* βαρεθῆναι, τελώνι(ο)ν, θαρρῶν, σῇ. 5. *l.* γεγράφηκα (so in l. 6), οἶδεν. 6. *l.* φέρεται, οἶνος. 7. *l.* καταξιώσατε (so in l. 9) ὡς. 8. *l.* παιδία, καταξίωσον. 9. *l.* τῶν.

167. FROM VICTOR TO A FELLOW ADVOCATE

P. Oxy. 1165. 6th cent. A.D.

[1]Π(αρὰ) . [2]ἔδει τὴν ὑμετέραν ἀδελφικὴν λ[α]μπρὰν παίδευσιν ἀντιποιηθῆναι τῆς εὐτελείας μου [3]καὶ μὴ ἐᾶσαί με ἐπὶ το{υ}σοῦτον λυθῆναι καὶ

166. FROM CONSTANTINE

5th or 6th cent. A.D.

From[a] . Will your discretion, deigning as usual to be amiable, deign to assist the noble Paul sent by me to purchase wine for me, and do not allow the boat of wine to be overtaxed at the custom-house. For I have written in reliance on your virtue and the friendship between us. For the holy God knows I have not written to protect another person, but the wine is being brought for myself. The most mean gifts which I have sent deign to accept as though they were much. Deign to greet from me your most revered wife and your dearest children, and in whatever you need here deign to command me. (Addressed) Deliver to my master, my most wholly admirable virtuous brother . . . my friend, from Constantine.

[a] The name of the writer has not been filled in ; compare No. 167.

167. FROM VICTOR TO A FELLOW ADVOCATE

6th cent. A.D.

From[a] . Your illustrious brotherly erudition ought to have assisted my insignificance and not allowed me to be so upset, and ought not only to re-

[a] See No. 166, note.

οὐ μόνον μὴ ἐπηρεάζειν αὐτῇ καὶ τοῖς διαφέρουσίν μοι [4]εὐτελέσιν πράγμασιν, ἀλλὰ καὶ κωλύειν ἄλλους ἐπηρεάσαι βουλομένους. ταῦτα δέ μοι εἴρηται [5]διὰ τοὺς γεωργούς μου τοὺς ἐν τῷ Ἀμούλῃ ἐν τοιαύτῃ διαστροφῇ γενέσθαι διὰ δέκα μῆλα ἄξια [6]εἴκοσι νουμμίων. καὶ εἰ μὲν ἐς δικαιολογίας χωροῦμεν καὶ λέγει ἡ ὑμετέρα ἀδελφικὴ σοφία ὡς ἡ [7]παραφυλακὴ τοῦτο ἐποίησεν, καὶ κύριοι ἐστὲ τῆς παραφυλακῆς καὶ ἀντιπ[οι]ηθῆναι μᾶλλον ἢ ἐπεξελθεῖν [8]ὀφείλετε καὶ τὸ ὅλον καταλεῖψαι τῇ εὐτελείᾳ μου. καὶ θεὸς οἶδεν, ἐδυνάμην καὶ ἐγὼ ἐπηρεάσαι [9]κτήματι πλησίον τοῦ Μύρμυκος τῆς δεσποίνης τῆς παραφυλακῆς ἐκείνης, ὡς καὶ ἐποίησα [10]ἄλλοτε ἐπὶ τοῦ ἐνδόξ(οτάτου) κόμιτος Παύλου ἐπηρεασθεὶς πάλιν παρὰ τῶν ἀπὸ Τερύθεω[ς]. . . . [. δ]ὲ εἴπω τὸ δέον· [11]παρακληθῆτε οὖν, εἴτε ἔπταισαν εἴτε οὐκ ἔπταισαν, ποιῆσαι αὐτοὺς ἀπολυθῆναι, ἵνα μὴ εἰς ἐκε[ῖ]νο ἔλ[θ]ω [12]ἢ καὶ εἰς ἄλλα δυνάμενα λυπῆσαι ἀλλήλους. ταῦτα γράφω μετὰ τῆς ἐποφειλ[ο]μένης π[ρ]οσκυνήσεως.

Verso: [13]+ δεσπό(τῃ) ἐμῷ πά(ντων) λαμπρ(οτάτῳ) σοφ(ωτάτῳ) π(άσης) προσκ(υνήσεως) ἀξ(ίῳ) [14]π(άντων) φιλ(τάτῳ) ἀδελφ(ῷ) λαμπροτάτῳ σχολ(αστικῷ) + Βίκτωρ σὺν θ(ε)ῷ σχολ(αστικός).

5. δέκα μῆλα E.-H. : δὲ κάμηλα Ed.

168. LETTER OF CONDOLENCE

P. Oxy. 1874, ll. 12-21. 6th cent. A.D.

- - - ὅ-[12]τι ἔπαθες ὁμοίος ἄμμα Εὔ‹α›, ὁμοίος Μαρία, κα[ὶ] ζ[ῇ] θεός, δέσποτά μου, οὔτε δίκιε

frain from injuring me and my insignificant possessions, but to prevent others who wish to do so. This I have said because my cultivators at Amoules have been subjected to such annoyance on account of ten apples worth a score of denarii.[a] If we proceed to litigation and your brotherly wisdom says that this was done by the guard, why, you control the guard and you ought to assist rather than attack me and leave the whole matter to my insignificance. God knows, I too could have injured an estate near Murmux belonging to the mistress of that guard, as I did on another occasion in the time of the honourable *comes* Paul, when once before I was injured by the people of Teruthis. Let me tell you what you ought to do: whether they were at fault or not, grant my request to have them released, lest I have recourse to that step or to others that might cause us mutual pain. I write this with due reverence. (Addressed) To my master, the most illustrious, most wise, worthy of all reverence, my dearest brother, the most illustrious advocate, from Victor, by the grace of God advocate.

[a] That is, worth next to nothing.

168. LETTER OF CONDOLENCE

6th cent. A.D.

. . . that you suffered like mother Eve, like Mary; and, as God lives, my master, neither righteous women

12. *l.* ὁμοίως, δίκαιαι.

οὔτε 13ἑμαρτολὲ οὐτέποτε ἔπαθαν τὸ ἔπαθες· ὅμος δὲν ἑ ἁμαρτίε ὑμôν ε<ἰ>σιν. ἀλλὰ 14δωξάζωμεν τὸν θεὸν ὅτι αὐτὸς ἔδωσεν καὶ αὐτὸς ἔλαβεν· ἀλλὰ εὖξε ἕνα ὁ κύριος 15ἐναπαύσι αὐτοῖς καὶ καταξιώσι ὑμᾶς ἐδῖν ἐν αὐτοῖς εἰς τὸν παράδισον ὅτι κρίνον-16τε ἑ ψυχὲ τôν ἀνθρώπων· αὐτοὶ{ς} γὰρ ἀπêρθαν εἰς κώρφον τ[ο]ῦ Ἀβρ{ρ}αὰμ καὶ 17τοῦ Ἰσαὰκ καὶ τοῦ Ἰακώ<β>. ἀλλὰ παρακαλῶ σε, κύριέ μου, μὲ βάλῃ̣ς [? λύπη]ν εἰς τὸ ψυ-18χί σου καὶ ἀπολήσις τὸ πράγματά σου, ἀλλὰ εὖξε ἕνα ὁ κύριος [ἀποσ]τίλῃ̣ ἐπὶ [σ]αὶ 19τὶν εὐλωγίαν αὐτοῦ. πολλὰ γὰρ καλὰ ἔχι ὁ κύριος καὶ ἀθυμοῦν-[τας] εὐθύμ[ο]υς 20εἴσστιν τοὶς θέλοντες ἀπ' αὐτοῦ εὐλογία<ν>, καὶ ἐλπίζομεν εἰς τὸ[ν] θεὼν ὅταν διὰ 21τῖς λο[ί]πις ταύ[τ]ης χαρὰν πέμ{μ}πι ὑμαυ ὁ κύριως καὶ τὸν κύ[ριον] τὸν ἀδε[λ]φὸν ὑμôν - - -

13. *l.* ἁμαρτωλαὶ οὐδέποτε, ὅμως, αἱ ἁμαρτίαι ὑμῶν. 14. *l.* δοξάζωμεν, εὖξαι ἵνα. 15. *l.* ἀναπαύσῃ αὐτούς, ἰδεῖν or ᾄδειν,

169. FROM VICTOR TO THEODORE

P. Oxy. 1849. 6th or 7th cent. A.D.

1+ Καταξιώσῃ ἡ ὑμετέρα γνησία ἀδελφότης μίαν ὑπὲρ μίαν πέμψαι μοι ἐλεοσπάρακα, 2ἐπειδὴ τὸ λάχανον ὃδε σαπρόν ἐστι καὶ σιαίνομε. ἀλλὰ πάντως τοῦτο πράξῃ̣ ἡ σὴ 3γνησία ἀδελφότης.+

Verso: δεσπό(τῃ̣) τὰ πά(ντα) λαμπρο(τάτῳ̣) πά(σης) τιμ(ῆς) ἀξίῳ̣ γνη(σίῳ̣) ἀδελφῷ̣ Θεοδώρῳ̣ μειζ(ο)τ(έρῳ̣) + Βίκτωρ σὺν θ(εῷ̣) ἀντιγε(οῦχος).+ +

1. *l.* ἐλαιοσπάραγα. 2. *l.* ὧδε, σιαίνομαι.

nor sinners ever suffered what you suffered; nevertheless your sins are nought. But let us glorify God because it was He who gave and He who took away; but pray that the Lord may give them rest and may vouchsafe to behold[a] you among them in Paradise when the souls of men are judged; for they are gone to the bosom of Abraham and of Isaac and of Jacob. But I exhort you, my lord, not to put grief into your soul and ruin your fortunes, but pray that the Lord may send you his blessing. For the Lord has many good things and makes the sorrowful to be of good cheer if they desire a blessing from him; and we hope in God that through this grief the Lord may send joy to you and the lord your brother. . . .

[a] Or "vouchsafe to you to sing among them."

ὅτε κρίνονται. 16. *l.* αἱ ψυχαὶ τῶν, ἀπῆλθαν εἰς κόλπον. 17. *l.* μή. 18. *l.* ἀπολέσῃς τά, εὔξαι ἵνα, σέ. 19. *l.* τὴν εὐλογίαν. 20. *l.* ἵστησιν (?) τοὺς θέλοντας, θεὸν ὅτι. 21. *l.* τῆς λύπης, ὑμῖν ὁ κύριος, ὑμῶν.

169. FROM VICTOR TO THEODORE

6th or 7th cent. A.D.

Will your true brotherliness have the goodness to send me day by day some asparagus, for the vegetables here are rotten and disgust me? Will your true brotherliness be sure to do this? (Addressed) To my master, in all things most illustrious, worthy of all honour, my true brother Theodore, steward, from Victor, by God's grace land-agent.

VI. MEMORANDA

170. TO ZENON FROM AN INVALID

P.S.I. 413. 259–257 B.C.

^{1}Ὑπόμνημα Ζήνωνι ^{2}παρὰ Κυδίππου. ^{3}εἰ μὲν ἦν τι τῶν ὑπο-^{4}γεγραμμένων πράσι-^{5}μον λαβεῖν ἐκ τοῦ ἐμ-^{6}πορίου, καθάπερ οἱ ἰα[τ]ροὶ ^{7}συντάσσουσιν, οὐκ ἂν ^{8}ἐνωχλοῦμεν ὑμᾶς· ^{9}νυνεὶ δὲ γεγράφαμέν σοι ^{10}ὧν χρείαν ἔχομεν, καθά-^{11}περ Ἀπολλώνιος ᾤιετο ^{12}δεῖν. εἰ οὖν παράκειταί σοι, ^{13}ἀπόστειλον ἡμῖν ο[ἴνο]υ τε ^{14}ἢ Λεσβίου ἢ Χίου κεράμιον ^{15}ὡς ἡδίστου, καὶ μέλιτος ^{16}μάλιστα μὲν χοῦν, ^{17}εἰ δὲ μή, ὅσον ἂν ἐνδέ-^{18}χηται· καὶ ταρίχου τὸ ^{19}σταμνίον σύνταξ[ο]ν ἡμῖν ^{20}ἐμπλῆσαι. τούτων γὰρ ἀμ-^{21}φοτέρων πλεί-στην χρείαν ^{22}νομίζουσιν εἶναι. ἐὰγ γὰρ ^{23}ὑγιά-νωμεν καὶ εἰς ^{24}Βυζάντιον ἀποδημή-^{25}σωμεν, ἄξομεν ὑμῖν ^{26}πάλιν σπουδαῖον ^{27}τάριχον.

Verso: ὑπόμνημα Κυδίππου.

171. TO ZENON FROM A HOUSE-PAINTER

P. Cairo Zen. 59445. About 255 B.C.

^{1}Ὑπόμν[ημα Ζήνω]νι παρὰ Θευφί-^{2}λ[ου τ]οῦ . . [. .] . . ου. περὶ τῶν ἔργων ^{3}τῶ[ν ἐ]ν τοῖς Δι[ο]-τίμου· τῆς προστάδος ^{4}[. . . . .]τω ἵνα γραφῆι

VI. MEMORANDA

170. TO ZENON FROM AN INVALID

259–257 B.C.

Memorandum to Zenon from Cydippus. If in accordance with the doctors' orders I could have purchased any of the following things in the market, I should not have troubled you; but as it is I have written you a note of what I require, as Apollonius thought I ought to do. So if you have them in store, send me a jar of wine, either Lesbian or Chian, of the very sweetest, and if possible a chous of honey or, if not, as much as you can; and order them to fill me the vessel with salt fish. For both these things they consider to be most needful. And if my health improves and I go abroad to Byzantium, I will bring you back some excellent salt fish. (On the back) Memorandum from Cydippus.

171. TO ZENON FROM A HOUSE-PAINTER

About 255 B.C.

Memorandum to Zenon from Theophilus the . . . About the work in the house of Diotimus: for the portico, [I undertake] to have the cornice

<κυ>μάτιον περι-[5]πόρφυρον καὶ θρᾶνος ποικίλος καὶ θω-[6]ρακεῖον ὀροβοειδὲς καὶ τὸ ὑποστύλιον [7]φλεβοπεριμέτριον, ἐμαυτῶι πάντα [8]παρέχων, (δραχμῶν) λ, καὶ τοῦ ἑπτακλίνου [9]τὴν καμάραν ποιήσειν οἷον τὸ παρά-[10]δειγμα ἐθεάσεσθε καὶ τὸ θωρακεῖον [11]χρείσει ποθεινῶι καὶ τὸ Λέσβιον γράψαι, [12]ἐμ-[α]υτῶι πάντα παρέχων, (δραχμῶν) κ, [13]καὶ [τ]ῶν πεντακλίνων γράψω τὰ κυ-[14]μάτια, ἐμαυτῶι πάντα παρέχων, (δραχμῶν) γ. [15]εἰς τὸ αὐτὸ γίνεται (δραχμαὶ) νγ. ἐὰν δ' ὑμεῖς παρέχητε πάντα, ποιήσει [17](δραχμὰς) λ. ἔρ<ρ>ωσο.

5. *l.* θωρακεῖον; also in l. 10. 10. *l.* ἐθεάσασθε.

painted with a purple border, the upper part of the wall variegated, the lower course like vetch-seed, and the pediment with circular veining, providing myself with all materials, for 30 drachmae. For the dining-room with seven couches, I will do the vault according to the pattern which you saw, and give the lower course an agreeable tint and paint the Lesbian cornice, providing myself with all materials, for 20 drachmae. And for the dining-rooms with five couches, I will paint the cornices, providing myself with all materials, for 3 drachmae. The sum total is 53 drachmae. But if you provide everything, it will come to 30 drachmae. Goodbye.

VII. INVITATIONS

172. INVITATION TO DINNER

P. Oxy. 1485. 2nd or 3rd cent. A.D.

[1]Ἐρωτᾷ σαι διπν[ῆ-] [2]σαι ὁ ἐξηγητὴ[ς] [3]ἐν τῷ Δημητρίῳ [4]σήμερον ἥτις ἐσ-[5]τὶν θ ἀπὸ ὥρ(ας) ζ.

1. *l.* σε.

173. INVITATION TO DINNER

P. Oxy. 2147. Early 3rd cent. A.D.

[1]Καλεῖ σε Εὐδαίμων δειπνῆ-[2]σαι ἐν τῷ γυμνασίῳ ἐπὶ τ[ῇ] [3]στέψει τοῦ υἱοῦ αὐτ[ο]ῦ Νειλ[ου] [4]τῇ α ἀπὸ ὥρ(ας) η. [5](2nd hand) β.

174. INVITATION TO A WEDDING

P. Oxy. 1487. 4th cent. A.D.

[1]Καλῖ σε Θέων [2]υἱὸς Ὠριγένους [3]εἰς τοὺς γάμους τῆς [4]ἀδελφῆς ἑαυτοῦ [5]ἐν τῇ αὔριον ἥτις [6]ἐστεὶν Τῦβι θ [7]ἀπὸ ὥρ(ας) η.

VII. INVITATIONS

172. INVITATION TO DINNER

2nd or 3rd cent. A.D.

The exegetes requests you to dine at the temple of Demeter to-day, the 9th, at the 7th hour.

173. INVITATION TO DINNER

Early 3rd cent. A.D.

Eudaemon invites you to dine in the gymnasium at the crowning [a] of his son Nilus on the 1st, at the 8th hour. (2nd hand) 2nd. [b]

[a] On entry upon some office.
[b] A revised date; or perhaps the number of the invitation.

174. INVITATION TO A WEDDING

4th cent. A.D.

Theon son of Origenes invites you to the wedding of his sister to-morrow, Tubi 9, at the 8th hour.

175. INVITATION TO A BIRTHDAY FEAST

P. Oxy. 1214. 5th cent. A.D.

[1]Τῷ κυρίῳ [μ]ου Μακαρί[ῳ] [2]Γεννάδιος σπεκ(ουλάτωρ). [3]φεδρύνων τὴν π[α]νήγυριν [4]τῆς γενεθλίου τοῦ υἱοῦ μου Γεννα-[5]δίου καταξίωσον ἅμα ἡμῖν [6]συνδιπνῆσαι τῇ ις ἀπὸ ὥρ(ας) ζ.

3. *l.* φαιδρύνων.

176. INVITATION TO A FESTIVAL

P. Oxy. 112. 3rd or 4th cent. A.D.

[1]Χαίροις, κυρία μου Σερηνία, [2]π(αρὰ) Πετοσείριος. [3]πᾶν ποίησον, κυρία, ἐξελθεῖ[ν τῇ] [4]κ τοῖς γενεθλείοις τοῦ θεο[ῦ, καὶ] [5]δήλωσόν μοι ἢ πλοίῳ ἐξέρχ[ει] [6]ἢ ὄνῳ, ἵνα πεμφθῇ σοι. ἀλ<λ>' ὅρα [μὴ] [7]ἀμελήσῃς, κυρία. ἐρρῶσθ[αί σε] [8]εὔχομαι [π]ολλοῖς [χρόνοις].

4. Or, less probably, Θέω[νος. 5. *l.* εἰ.

175. INVITATION TO A BIRTHDAY FEAST

5th cent. A.D.

To my lord Macarius from Gennadius, adjutant. Deign to gladden the birthday festival of my son Gennadius by dining with us on the 16th at the 7th hour.

176. INVITATION TO A FESTIVAL

3rd or 4th cent. A.D.

Greeting, my lady Serenia, from Petosiris. Make every effort, dear lady, to come out on the 20th, the birthday festival of the god,[a] and let me know whether you are coming by boat or by donkey, in order that we may send for you. Take care not to forget, dear lady. I pray for your lasting health.

[a] Some local deity, whose "birthday" had a place in the calendar.

VIII. ORDERS FOR PAYMENT

177. ORDER ON A BANK

P. Fay. 100. A.D. 99.

[1]Ἀφροδοῦς Σατ[ύ]ρ[ο]υ μέ[τὰ] κυρίου τοῦ συν-[2]γενοῦς Ἀμμωνίου τοῦ Ἡρ[α]κλείδου Σαμβᾶ [3]τῷ καὶ Διδύμῳ τραπ[ε]ζ[ε]ίτῃ χα[ί]ρειν. χρη-[4]μάτισον Χαριτίῳ τῇ καὶ Τασουχαρίῳ [5]Χαριδήμου καὶ Χαρ[ι]τίῳ Διδύμου [6]μετὰ κυρίων ἑκάστ[η]ς τοῦ ἀνδρός, τ[ῇ] [7]μὲν Χαριτίῳ τῆς καὶ Τα[σ]ουχαρίῳ Ἀπολλω-[8]ν[ί]ου τοῦ Ἀπολλω[νί]ου, [τ]ῇ δὲ ἑτέρᾳ Χα-[9]ριτίῳ Ἥρωνος τοῦ Διδύμου, τιμὴν [10]ἡμύσους μέρους οἰκίας καὶ αὐλῆ[ς] καὶ τόπων [11][κ]αὶ τῶν συνκυρόντων πάντων ἐν κώ-[12][μῃ] Θεαδελφείᾳ τῆς Θεμίστου μερίδ(ος) [13][ἀκ]ολ{ολ}ούθως ταῖς γεγονυίαις εἰς αὐ[τὰς [14]. .]. ιαις καταγραφαῖς, ἃς ἔχις μου ἐν [15]θέματι ἀργυρίου δραχμὰς ἑξακοσί-[16][ας], (γίνονται) (δραχμαὶ) χ. (ἔτους) β Αὐτοκράτορος Καίσαρος [17]Νερούα Τραϊανο(ῦ) Σεβαστοῦ Γερμανικοῦ Τῦβ[ι] [18]κη. (2nd hand) Χαρίτιον Διδύμου μετὰ κυρίου τοῦ ἀνδρὸς [19]Ἥρωνος τοῦ Διδύμου καταχώρισον, καὶ ἀνίρημαι [20]τὰς ἐπιβαλλούσας μοι ἀργ(υρίου) (δραχμὰς) τριακοσίας, (γίνονται) (δραχ-

7. *l.* τῇ καί. 8. *l.* Ἀπίωνος as in l. 26. 14. Perhaps [κυ]ρίαις.

VIII. ORDERS FOR PAYMENT

177. ORDER ON A BANK

A.D. 99.

Aphrodous daughter of Satyrus, with her kinsman Ammonius son of Heraclides as guardian, to Sambas also called Didymus, banker, greeting. Pay to Charition also called Tasoucharion daughter of Charidemus and to Charition daughter of Didymus, each with her husband as guardian, Charition also called Tasoucharion with Apollonius son of Apollonius[a] and the other Charition with Heron son of Didymus, as the price of a half share of a house and courtyard and offices and all the appurtenances in the village of Theadelphia in the division of Themistes in accorddance with the . . . deeds of conveyance made with them, the six hundred silver drachmae of mine which you hold on deposit, total 600 dr. The 2nd year of the Emperor Caesar Nerva Trajanus Augustus Germanicus, Tubi 28. (Receipted) I, Charition daughter of Didymus, with my husband Heron son of Didymus as guardian, bid this be filed, and I have received the three hundred silver drachmae falling to my share, total 300 dr. I,

[a] The name should probably be Apion as in the receipt.

μαὶ) τ. [21]Ἥρων *ἔγραψα καὶ ὑπὲρ τῆς γυναικός μου μὴ εἰδυίης* [22]*γράμματα.* (*ἔτους*) *δευτέρου* Αὐτοκράτορος Καίσαρος [23]Νερούα Τραϊανοῦ Σεβαστοῦ Γερμανικοῦ Τῦβι *κη.* (3rd hand) [24]Χαρίτιον *ἡ καὶ* Τασουχ<άρ>ιον Χαριδήμου [25]*μετὰ κυρίου τοῦ ἀνδρὸς* Ἀπολ<λ>ωνίου [26]*τοῦ* Ἀπίωνος *ἀνίρημαι τὰς δραχμὰ-*[27]*ς τριακοσίας,* (*γίνονται*) (*δραχμαὶ*) *τ.* Ἀπολλώνιος [28]*ἔγραψα καὶ ὑπὲρ τῆς γυναικός μου* [29]*μὴ ἰδυείης γράμματα.*

29. *l.* εἰδυίας.

178. ORDER FOR PAYMENT

P.S.I. 784. A.D. 362.

[1]Ζωίλος Ἀγαθοδαίμονι *προνοητῇ χ(αίρειν).* [2]*παράσχου* Ἡρακλείδῃ *ζωγρ<ά>φῳ ὑ(πὲρ) μισθ[οῦ]* [3]*ἰκόνος σίτου ἀρ{α}τάβην μίαν καὶ οἴνου* Κνίδια *δύο μ(όνα).* [4](*ἔτους*) *λη ζ* Τῦβι *κγ. ὁ αὐτὸς σεσημείωμαι.*

Heron, have written for my wife also, as she is illiterate. The 2nd year of the Emperor Caesar Nerva Trajanus Augustus Germanicus, Tubi 28. I, Charition also called Tasoucharion daughter of Charidemus, with my husband Apollonius son of Apion as guardian, have received the three hundred drachmae, total 300 dr. I, Apollonius, have written for my wife also, as she is illiterate.

178. ORDER FOR PAYMENT

A.D. 362.

Zoilus to Agathodaemon, administrator, greeting. Deliver to Heraclides, painter, as fee for a portrait one artaba of wheat and two Cnidian jars of wine only. Year 38 = 7,[a] Tubi 23. Signed by me, the above-named.

[a] See No. 24, p. 71, note *a*.

IX. AGENDA

179. AGENDA WRITTEN BY ZENON

P.S.I. 429. About 250 B.C.

[1]Ἡροδότου πυθέσθαι [2]περὶ τῶν αἰγείων τριχῶν. [3]Ἀμεινίου ὡς ἀπέδοτο τὴν [4]μνᾶν. [5]τὴν πρὸς Διοσκουρίδην ἐπ(ιστολὴν) [6]περὶ τοῦ πλοίου. [7]Τιμαίωι συνθέσθαι περὶ [8]τῶν ἱερείων. [9]τὴν πρὸς Ἀπολλόδωρον [10]συγγραφὴν ὑποτυπώσασ-[11]θαι καὶ γράψαι παραδοῦναι. [12]τὸ πλοῖον γεμίσαι ξύλων. [13]Ἰάσονι γράψαι [14]τὰ ἔρια ἐμβαλέσθαι καὶ [15]καταγαγεῖν Διονύσιον [16]ἐστρουθισμένα· [17]τῶν Ἀραβίων τὸ τέταρ-[18]τὸν μέρος· [19]τὸ ὄξος ⟦ὡσαύτως⟧ κατα-[20]γαγεῖν. [21]Μελίτωνι γράψαι τῆς παρὰ [22]Νεοπτολέμωι βουμάστου (?) [23]ἀμπέλου φυτεῦσαι καὶ Ἀλ-[24]κίμωι ἐὰν δοκιμάζηι. [25]Θεογένει περὶ ταυρικῶν [26]ζευγῶν ιβ. [27]Ἀπολλοδώρωι καὶ Καλλίππωι [28]ἀποδοῦναι . ἐκ τῶν (δραχμῶν) (?)

Verso: [29]παρὰ Μητροδώρου πρὸς [30]Ἀθηναγόραν περὶ τοῦ [31]αὐτοῦ (ἔτους) γενήματος. [32]πρὸς Θεόφιλον φιλάνθρωπον [33]καὶ περὶ τῶν κατὰ τὰ [34]ἔργα. [35]περὶ σίτου Ἰατροκλεῖ καὶ [36]Θεοδώρωι γράψαι πρὸ τοῦ [37]τὸ ὕδωρ ἐκ τῆς διώρυγος [38]καταικυμ . (?)

28. Reading very doubtful; after ἀποδοῦναι Viereck sees λό(γον). 38. Separated from l. 37 by empty space.

IX. AGENDA

179. AGENDA WRITTEN BY ZENON

About 250 B.C.

To ask Herodotus about the goat hair. To ask Aminias at how much the mina he sold it. The letter to Dioscurides about the boat. To make an agreement with Timaeus about the pigs. To draft the contract with Apollodorus and write to him to hand over. To load the boat with wood. To write to Jason to let Dionysius put the wool on board and take it down the river when cleaned; the fourth part of the Arabian wool; to let him take down the sour wine. To write to Meliton to plant shoots of the *bumastus*[a] vine belonging to Neoptolemus, and to Alcimus to do likewise if he approves. To Theogenes about twelve yokes of bulls. To give Apollodorus and Callippus . . . From Metrodorus to Athenagoras about the same year's produce. To Theophilus granting a favour and about the state of the work. To write about corn to Iatrokles and Theodorus before the water from the canal . . .

[a] One of the varieties recorded by Virgil, *Georg.* ii. 102 "tumidis, bumaste, racemis." But the reading of the word in the present passage is not certain.

180. AGENDA OF ZENON

P.S.I. 430. About 250 B.C.

[1]Τὰ γίγαρτα λαβεῖν [2]τῆς ἐλαίας. [3]παρὰ Ἡραγόρου τὸ ἔλαιον. [4][ἀγ]οράσαι τοῖς ἵπποις [5]ψήκτρας δ, σωρακίδας δ, [6]σπάθας δ, καὶ Φατρῆι [7]ψῆκτραν α. [8][κ]ράδας τῶν βασιλικῶν [9]καρυῶν λαβεῖν. [10]τὴν ἀπογραφὴν [11]τοῦ οἴνου τοῦ κατη-[12]γμένου εἰδῆσαι [13]εἰς τίνα νομὸν [14]ἀπογέγραπται. [15]τὸ Ἕρμωνος παιδάριον [16]κομίσασθαι.

180. AGENDA OF ZENON

About 250 B.C.

To get the olive kernels. The oil from Heragoras. To buy for the horses 4 strigils, 4 rubbing cloths, 4 scrapers, and for Phatres 1 strigil. To get shoots of the walnut trees. To ascertain the registration of the wine carried down, for which nome it has been registered. To receive Hermon's boy.

X. ACCOUNTS AND LISTS

181. LIST OF FOREIGN GOODS

P. Cairo Zen. 59069. 257 B.C.

[1]Ἔτους κ̅θ̅ Ξανδικοῦ ι̅α̅, [2]ἐν Ἑρμοῦ πόλει. ἀπολελοίπαμεν [3]ἃ παραδέδωκεν Χάρμος [4]Ἀπολλοδότωι· [5]ἐν θίβει νάρδου μαρσίππια ἐσφρα(γισμένα) ε, [6]καὶ θυλάκιον ἐσφραγισμένον α, [7]δορκαδέων θυλάκιον ἐσφρ(αγισμένον) α, [8]πορφύρα ἐν προσκεφαλαίωι ἑνί, [9]κιρία ποικίλη α, [10]ἡμικίρια [ποικί]λα γ, [11]κιρίαι λευκαὶ β, [12]φοινικαῖ δ, [13]λιβάνου ἐσφραγισμένου [14]μάρσιπποι γ, [15]καὶ μαρσίππιον α, [16]σμύρνης ἐσφραγισμένα [17]μαρσίππια γ, [18]θύλακος δορκαδέων [19]ἀστραγάλων α, [20]πορφύρας θυλάκιον ἐσφραγισ(μένον) α, [21]κρόκου θυλάκιον ἐσφραγισ(μένον) α.

13-15. Opposite each of these lines a small οὐ.

182. LIST OF ZENON'S CLOTHES

P. Cairo Zen. 59092. About 257 B.C.

[1]Ζήνωνος ῥίσκος ἐν ὧι ἔνεστι [2]περίβλημα λινοῦν πεπλυμένον α, [3]χλαμὺς γεωβαφὴς χειμερινὴ πεπλυμένη α, [4]καὶ τριβακὴ α, [5]θερινὴ ἡμιτριβὴς α,

X. ACCOUNTS AND LISTS

181. LIST OF FOREIGN GOODS

257 B.C.

Year 29, Xandicus 11, at Hermopolis.[a] We have left behind these articles which Charmus has handed over to Apollodotus: in a basket 5 small bags of nard sealed and 1 small wallet sealed, 1 small wallet, sealed, containing dice of gazelle bone; purple dye in one pillow-case; 1 strip of variegated cloth; 3 half-strips of variegated cloth; 2 strips of white cloth; 4 strips of purple cloth; 3 bags and 1 small bag of frankincense sealed[b]; 3 small bags of myrrh sealed; 1 wallet containing dice of gazelle bone; 1 small wallet of purple dye sealed; 1 small wallet of saffron sealed.

[a] Hermopolis Parva in the Delta.
[b] Opposite these items "no" in small letters.

182. LIST OF ZENON'S CLOTHES

About 257 B.C.

Zenon's trunk in which are contained: 1 linen wrap, washed; 1 clay-coloured cloak, for winter, washed, and 1 worn, 1 for summer, half-worn, 1

[6]αὐτόχρους χειμερινὴ πεπλυμένη α, [7]καὶ τριβακὴ α, [8]ὀροβοειδὴς θερινὴ καινὴ α, [9]χιτὼν λευκὸς χειμερινὸς [10]χειριδωτὸς πεπλυμένος α, [11]αὐτόχρους χειμερινὸς χειριδωτὸς τριβακὸς α, [12]αὐτόχρους χειμερινὸς τριβακὸς α, [13]λευκοὶ χειμερινοὶ πεπλυμένοι β, [14]καὶ ἡμιτριβὴς α, [15]θερινοὶ λευκοὶ καινοὶ γ, [16]ἄγναφος α, [17]ἡμιτριβὴς α, [18]ἱμάτιον λευκὸν χειμερινὸν πεπλυμένον α, [19]τρίβων α, [20]θέριστρον λευκὸν πεπλυμένον α, [21]καὶ ἡμιτριβὲς α, [22]προσκεφαλαίων Σαρδιανῶν ζε(ῦγος) α, [23]ποδείων γεωβαφῶν καινῶν ζε(ύγη) β, [24]λευκῶν καινῶν ζε(ύγη) β, [25]ζῶναι λευκαὶ καιναὶ β.

Verso: [26]παρὰ Πεισικλέους [27]τῶν Ζήνωνος ἱματίων [28]γραφή.

183. ACCOUNT OF VINE-SHOOTS

P. Cairo Zen. 59736. About 250 B.C.

[1]Ὅσα Ἀνδρόνικο[ς] ἀφέσταλκεν [2]φυτὰ ἀπὸ Ἁθὺρ λ [3]ἕως Χοίαχ $\overline{\iota\alpha}$ ἐν ἡμέ-[4]ραις ιβ, τὰ ὑποζύγια [5]τὰ πηρ' ἡμῶν· [6]τὰ πρῶτα, ὑποζύγια $\overline{\eta}$ [7]ἀνὰ δέσμας η, (γίνονται) δέ(σμαι) ξδ, ἐν τῆι [8]δέσμηι φυτὰ ν, (γίνεται) ͵Γσ· [9]ιη, Ἰναρῶς ὑποζύγια θ [10]ἀνὰ δέ(σμας) η, (γίνονται) δέ(σμαι) οβ, ἐν τῆι [11]δέσμηι φυ(τὰ) ν, (γίνεται) ͵Γχ· [12]κα, τὰ ἡμέ[τερ]α ὑποζύγια - - - [13]καὶ ἄλλας δέ(σμας) ἃς ἤνενκαν ἐγ Μούχεως [14]λς ἀν(ὰ) ν, (γίνεται) ͵Αω. [15]Διονυσοδώρου δὲ παραγενο-[16]μένου καὶ βουλομένου [17]τέμνειν ἐκώλυσεν αὐτὸν [18]⟦ὁρῶν αὐτὸν ἄπειρον ὄντα⟧ [19]Πᾶσις Παιῆτος τέμνειν τὰ φυτὰ [20]φάμενος δεδωκέναι Ἀνδρο-[21]νίκωι ἵνα μὴ τέμνηι

1. = ἀπέσταλκεν. 5. l. παρ'.

natural-coloured, for winter, washed, and 1 worn, 1 vetch-coloured, for summer, new ; 1 white tunic for winter, with sleeves, washed, 1 natural-coloured, for winter, with sleeves, worn, 1 natural-coloured, for winter, worn, 2 white, for winter, washed, and 1 half-worn, 3 for summer, white, new, 1 unbleached, 1 half-worn ; 1 outer garment, white, for winter, washed ; 1 coarse mantle ; 1 summer garment, white, washed, and 1 half-worn ; 1 pair of Sardian pillow-cases ; 2 pairs of socks, clay-coloured, new, 2 pairs of white, new ; 2 girdles, white, new. (Endorsed) From Pisicles, a list of Zenon's clothes.

183. ACCOUNT OF VINE-SHOOTS

About 250 B.C.

The number of shoots[a] which Andronicus has sent in the 12 days from Hathur 30 to Choiach 11 by our donkeys : the first lot, 8 donkeys with 8 bundles each, making 64 bundles, in each bundle 50 shoots, total 3200. 18th, Inaros by 9 donkeys with 8 bundles each, making 72 bundles, in each bundle 50 shoots, total 3600. 21st, by our donkeys . . . and 36 other bundles of 50 shoots which they brought from Mouchis, total 1800. When Dionysodorus arrived and wished to take cuttings, Pasis son of Paies prevented him from doing so, saying that he had given Andronicus

[a] This is one of several documents which show what extensive plantations of vineyards and orchards were made by the Greek settlers in Egypt under the earlier Ptolemies.

ἐκ τοῦ 22ἀμπελῶνος (δραχμὰς) δ, 23ὡσαύτως δὲ καὶ τῶν ῥόδων 24ἵνα μὴ ἐξέληι ἔδωκεν (δραχμὰς) δ, 25τὴν δὲ ὑπόσχεσιν τῶν ὀκτὼ 26δραχμῶν ἔδωκεν αὐτῶι 27ὁρῶν αὐτὸν λυμαινόμενον 28τὰς ἀμπέλους καὶ ἄπειρον 29ὄντα τῆι τομῆι. 30καὶ ἐγ Μούχεως παρὰ τοῦ 31καπήλ[ο]υ Ὥρου φ[.] . . . ος - - - 32καὶ εἷς τῶν ὑποζυγίων τῶν 33μεμισθωμένων ἐπὶ τὰ φυτὰ 34ὥστε ἄγειν ἀπορίψας ἐν τῆι 35ὁδῶι τὰ φυτὰ τὴν γυναῖκα 36ἀνεβίβασεν· καὶ τοὺς κατα-37μηνίους γεωργοὺς ⟦στ . . λ⟧ 38ἀπέστειλεν εἰς τὴν Δικαίου 39καὶ δευτεραῖοι παρεγέ-40νοντο. ὡσαύτως δὲ οἱ 41αὐτοὶ κατέστησαν εἰς 42Φιλαδέλφειαν τὴν γυναῖκα 43αὐτοῦ· καὶ αὐτὸς δὲ κατα-44λιπὼν ἀπῆλθεν. (2nd hand) 45καὶ ἃ ἀπεκόμισεν Διονυσόδωρος Χοίαχ ἀπὸ ια̅ 46ἕως ιϛ̅ ἐν ἡμέραις ϛ̅· 47ια̅, ἡμίονοι ε̅ ἀν(ὰ) δέ(σμας) ι ἀν(ὰ) φυτὰ ν ⟦ιε⟧, (γίνεται) 'Βφ· 48ιϛ̅, ἡμίονοι ε̅ ἀν(ὰ) ιϛ ἑκάστη ν, (γίνεται) 'Γω - - - 49καὶ ὑπάρχει ἐν Ψεοννώφρει δέ(σμαι) μ 50καὶ ἐν Κροκοδίλων πόλει δέ(σμαι) ιβ, (γίνονται) νβ 51ἀν(ὰ) φυτὰ ν, (γίνεται) 'Βχ· 52(γίνεται) τὰ πάντα φυτὰ $\overset{\alpha}{\mathrm{M}}$ 'Βυ.

Verso: 53τῶν δι' Ἀνδρονίκου 54ἀπεσταλμένων φυτῶν.

184. ACCOUNT OF HOUSE RENT

Michigan Inventory 3197 (unpubl.). 177 B.C. (?).

1Ἔτους γ, λόγος ἐνοικίων ὧν ἔχομεν 2ἐκ τῆς ἐν Κροκοδίλων πόλει οἰκίας. 3οἰνῶνος φέροντος τοῦ μηνὸς (δραχμὰς) ρκ 4ἀπὸ Χοίαχ ἕως Φαμενὼθ

4 drachmae not to cut from the vineyard and likewise 4 drachmae not to take cuttings of the roses; and this promise of eight drachmae he gave him because he saw that the man was damaging the vines and was unskilled in the art of cutting. And from Mouchis from the retailer Horus . . . And one of them throwing down on the road the shoots off the donkeys hired to carry them gave his wife a mount. And the monthly-paid cultivators he sent to the village of Dicaeus, and they arrived on the second day. The same persons likewise conveyed his wife to Philadelphia, and he himself left the work and went off. And the shoots which Dionysodorus brought from the 11th to the 16th of Choiach, being 6 days: 11th, 5 mules, each with 10 bundles of 50 shoots, total 2500; 16th, 5 mules, each with 16 bundles, each bundle containing 50 shoots, total 3800 . . . And there are at Pseonnophris 40 bundles and at Crocodilopolis 12 bundles, making 52, each containing 50 shoots, total 2600. Total of all the shoots 12,400. (Endorsed) (Account of) the shoots sent through Andronicus.

---

31. Possibly Φ[ά]βιτος.

184. ACCOUNT OF HOUSE RENT

177 B.C. (?).

The 3rd year. Account of rents which we have received from the house in Crocodilopolis. For a wine-store paying 120 drachmae the month, from

τοῦ αὐτοῦ (ἔτους) (δραχμαὶ) υπ· [5]Φιλουμένης φερούσης τοῦ μηνὸς (δραχμὰς) μ [6]ἀπὸ Χοίαχ ἕως Μεχεὶρ (δραχμαὶ) ρκ· [7]Ἀμμωνίας φερούσης τοῦ μηνὸς (δραχμὰς) μ [8]ἀπὸ Ἁθὺρ ἕως Παχὼν (δραχμαὶ) σξ, λο(ιπὸν) κ· [9]Φιλωτέρα φέρουσα τοῦ μηνὸς (δραχμὰς) ρν [10]ἀπὸ Χοίαχ Εἰρήνη ρ, [11]εἰς γνάπτρα ἱματίου ρν, [12]Ἰθάκη ρ, [13]Ἀπολλωνία πρὸς τὸ<ν> χάρακα ρ, [14]διὰ Σωκλέους υ, [15]ἄλλαι υν, [16]ἄλλας τὸ λοιπὸν τοῦ ἕως Μεσορὴ ν· [17]Δημητρία φέρουσα τοῦ μηνὸς (δραχμὰς) ρ [18]ἀπὸ Ἁθὺρ εἰς τοῦτο ἔχομεν [19]παρ᾽ αὐτῆς ἕως Τῦβι (δραχμὰς) τ, [20]ἄλλας ἕως Μεσορὴ ψ· [21]τοῦ ἄνω οἴκου φέροντος τοῦ μηνὸς (δραχμὰς) τ [22]ἀπὸ Μεχεὶρ εἰς τοῦτο ἔχομεν [23]ἕως Φαρμοῦθι (δραχμὰς) ϡ, [24]ἄλλας Ἄτταλος ἕως Παῦνι (δραχμὰς) χ, [25]ἄλλας διὰ Σωκλέους ἕως [26]Μεσορὴ (δραχμὰς) χ.

Verso: ΑΒΓΔΕΗΘ.

---

[a] Either paid by Irene, Ithaca and Apollonia, or deducted from the rent of Philotera in return for their services. The

185. WINE BILL OF A SOCIAL CLUB

P. Tebt. 118. Late 2nd cent. B.C.

[1]Ἁθὺρ ιζ. περιδίπνου Καλατύτιος [2][ο]ἴνου (ἑξα)χ(όου) α ᾽Β, ἄρτω(ν) δίπνου ϛ ρϙ, [3](γίνονται) ᾽Βρϙ. εἰσὶν ἄνδρες κβ, (τούτων) [4]σύνδει(πνοι) ιη, ξένους

4. *l.* ξένοι; so in l. 12.

---

[a] We possess certain rules of Egyptian clubs, written in demotic, which contain provisions about mourning for the

Choiach to Phamenoth of the said year 480 dr. From Philumene paying 40 dr. the month, from Choiach to Mecheir 120 dr. From Ammonia paying 40 dr. the month, from Hathur to Pachon 260 dr., remainder 20. Philotera paying 150 dr. the month from Choiach: Irene [a] 100; for fulling a mantle 150; Ithaca [a] 100; Apollonia [a] in respect of the stakes 100; through Socles 400, other 450, other 50 being the balance up to Mesore. Demetria paying 100 dr. the month, from Hathur: towards this we have received from her up to Mesore 700. For the upper room paying 300 dr. the month, from Mecheir: towards this we have received up to Pharmouthi 900 dr., up to Pauni other 600 dr. which Attalus paid, up to Mesore through Socles other 600 dr.[b]

(On the back of the account someone has begun to write out the Greek alphabet, omitting the letter Z.)

first two names recall a mistress of Euergetes II., "quam alii quidem Ithacam, alii uero Hirenen denominant" (Josephus, *c. Ap.* ii. 55).

[b] The account is of course in copper drachmae.

185. WINE BILL OF A SOCIAL CLUB

Late 2nd cent. B.C.

Hathur 17. For the funeral feast of Kalatutis [a]: 1 six-chous jar of wine 2000 drachmae,[b] 6 dinner loaves 190 dr., total 2190 dr. 22 persons present, of whom 18 were members and 4 were guests, the

death of a member or of one of his family and sometimes mention a funeral symposium.

[b] Copper drachmae, 2000 of which were worth at this time about 4 silver drachmae.

δ, ὧν Τ . . . [. . .] 5Νουμήνιος, Καμῆς Ἀρφαήσιος, 6Τεῶς Πετεχῶντος, 7Πάπνεβτῦνι{ο}ς Σοκέως, (γίνονται) δ. 8(γίνονται) κβ ἀνὰ ρ Ἐσ, ἐν οἰκο(νόμῳ) [ι]. 9κ. οἴνου (ἑξα)χ(όου) α Ἐ, στεφάνου ρκ, (γίνονται) Ἐ[ρκ]. 10εἰσὶν ἄνδρες σύνδει(πνοι) ιη καὶ [. . . . .] 11Νεφορηγῆς Κερα( ) καὶ Σεν[. . . . .] 12καὶ ξένους Μαρρῆς Πετ[. . . . .] 13Πετεσοῦχος Μέλανο(ς), Χαιρή(μων) Δι[. . . . .] 14(γίνονται) κγ ἀνὰ ρ Ἐτ, 15ἐν οἰκο(νόμῳ) ρπ. 16Τῦβι κε. οἴνου κε(ραμίου) α Ἐ, στ[εφάνου ρκ, (γίνονται) Ἐρκ]. 17εἰσὶν ἄνδρες κα ἀνὰ ρ [Ἐρ], 18ὑπερανή(λωμα) κ.

5. *l.* Νουμηνίου.

186. PRIVATE ACCOUNT

P. Oxy. 736. About A.D. 1.

- - - 1κα. φα[- - -] 2εἰς[- - -] . . (δραχμαὶ) δ, 3βα . [. . .] . . [. .]αφ[. . .] διὰ 4Ζμ[.]. . ς φαινόλ[ο]υ Κοραξοῦ (δραχμαὶ) ι, 5γο[γ]γυλίδος εἰς ταριχείαν (δραχμὴ) α (ὀβολοὶ δύο), 6χαλκίου μισθοῦ εἰς βάψαι (ὀβολοὶ δύο ?), 7ἁλὸς (ὀβολός?), 8ἄλεστρα (πυροῦ) (ἀρτάβης) α ἐπὶ τῆς ιη (τριώβολον ?), 9θρύων εἰς τοὺς ἄρτους (ὀβολοὶ δύο), 10ἤπητρα εἰς φαινόλ(ην) Κοραξοῦ (ὀβολὸς) (ἡμιωβέλιον), 11εἰς κατανθρωπισμὸν γυναικ(ὸς) 12Γεμέλλου (τετρώβολον ?), 13μύρου εἰς ἀποστολὴν ταφῆς 14θυγατρὸς Φνᾶς (τετρώβολον). 15κβ. ἐλαίου χο(ὸς) α (δραχμαὶ) δ (τετρώβολον), 16κηροῦ καὶ γραφείου παιδ(ῶν) (ὀβολός), 17ἄρτου καθαροῦ Πρίμα[ς] (ἡμιωβέλιον], 18εἰς

16. παιδ(ίου), παιδ(ίων) also possible.

latter being T . . . son of Numenius, Kames son of Harphaesis, Teos son of Petechon, Papnebtunis son of Sokeus, total 4. Total 22 at 100 dr. each, 2200 dr.; remaining with treasurer 10 dr. 20th. 1 six-chous jar of wine 2000 dr., a garland 120 dr., total 2120 dr. Persons present, 18 members and . . . Nephoreges son of Kera . . . and Sen . . . son of . . ., and guests Marres son of Pet . . ., Petesouchus son of Melas, Chaeremon son of Di . . ., total 23 at 100 dr. each, 2300 dr.; remaining with treasurer 180 dr. Tubi 25. 1 jar of wine 2000 dr., a garland 120 dr., total 2120 dr. Persons present 21 at 100 dr. each, 2100 dr.; spent in excess 20 dr.

186. PRIVATE ACCOUNT

About A.D. 1.

The 21st: . . . through Zm . . . for a Coraxian cloak,[a] 10 drachmae[b]; turnips for pickling, 1 drachma, 2 obols; hire of a cauldron for dyeing, 2 ob.; salt 1 ob.; cost of grinding 1 artaba of wheat on the 18th 3 ob.; rushes for baking the loaves 2 ob.; cost of mending a Coraxian cloak 1½ ob.; for entertaining the wife of Gemellus 4 ob.; perfume for the dispatch of the mummy of the daughter of Phna 4 ob. The 22nd: 1 chous of oil 4 dr. 4 ob.; wax and stilus for the children 1 ob.; pure bread for Prima ½ ob.; for

[a] *Cf.* No. 187. Line 10 favours the translation "cloak of Coraxus," but Κοραξοῦ may be an error of the scribe for Κοραξόν, or possibly εἰς should be cancelled.

[b] For the value of the drachma in the Roman period see p. xvii.

κ[α]τανθρωπισμὸν Τύχης (τριώβολον). [19]Μεχ(εὶρ) θ. [- - -] (δραχμὴ) α (τριώβολον) - - - [23]ι. ὀλ- [. . .]κο . [.] ἀρίσ[τῳ γ]ερδί(ου) (ὀβολός), [24]κρ[. .] . ν . . . (ἡμιωβέλιον), [25]εἰς τὸ Σαραπιῖον (ὀβολοὶ δύο), [26]ἄρτου καθαροῦ παιδ(ῶν) (ἡμιωβέλιον), [27]ζύτου γ[ε]ρδί(ου) (ὀβολοὶ δύο), [28]πράσων ἀρίστῳ γερδί(ου) (ὀβολός), [29]περιστερᾶς (ὀβολός), [30]Ἀντᾶτι (δραχμαὶ) β, (ὀβολοὶ δύο), [31]ἄνω ἐν τῇ πόλ(ει) ἄλεστρα ἄρτων [32](πυροῦ) (ἀρταβῶν) β διὰ [Ἰ]σᾶτος (δραχμὴ) α (ὀβολοὶ δύο). [33]ια. ἐν παρεμβο[λ]ῇ διὰ Θεοδώρου [34]ἄλεσ[τρα] ἄρ[τ]ω(ν) (πυροῦ) (ἀρτάβης) α (τετρώβολον), [35]ἀρίστῳ [γε]ρ[δί(ου)] (ὀβολός), [36]ἀσπαράγω(ν) [δί]πνῳ Ἀντ(ᾶτος) ὅτ' εἰς [37]τὸ περίδ[ι]πνο(ν) Ἀθη( ) γναφέω(ς) (ἡμιωβέλιον), [38]καὶ παιδαρί[οι]ς δίπνῳ κράμβη(ς) (ἡμιωβέλιον), [39]π . . [.] . . παιδίῳ (ἡμιωβέλιον). - - - [46]ις. προ[σφαγ]ίου (ἡμιωβέλιον), [47]θρύ[ων ε]ἰ[ς] ἄρτους (ὀβολοὶ δύο) (ἡμιωβέλιον). [48]ιζ. γάλακτος παιδ(ῶν) (ἡμιωβέλιον), [49]ἄρτου καθαροῦ (ἡμιωβέλιον). [50]ιη. Σεκουντᾷ παιδ(ῶν) ἰτρίου (ἡμιωβέλιον). [51]ιθ. τισάνης ὁμ(οίως) (ἡμιωβέλιον). [52]κ. ὀψαρίου (ὀβολός), [53]ἄρτου καθαροῦ (ἡμιωβέλιον), [54]εἰς κατανθρωπ(ισμὸν) Ἀντω(νίας ?) (ὀβολοὶ δύο), [55]καὶ εἰς Ταπτολλοῦτος Καικιλ(ίου ?) (τριώβολον), [56]γενεσίοις Τρυφᾶτος στεφά(νων) (ὀβολοὶ δύο), [57]γε<νε>σίοις [.] . [.] . . ω( ) στεφά(νων) (ὀβολοὶ δύο). [58]κα. ῥόας παιδ(ῶν) [ ] (ὀβολός), [59]παιγνίω(ν) καὶ επουριω(ν) παιδ(ῶν) (ἡμιωβέλιον), [60]ζύτου (τριώβολον), [61]ὄψου (ὀβολός). [62]κβ. ὀψαρί[ο]υ (ὀβολός). - - - [68]Θαῆσις [. . . ἡ]με(ρῶν) β, [(πεντώβολον)], [69]μήτηρ [Ἀμ]μωνᾶτο(ς) ἡμε(ρῶν) [ ] [70]Ταарπαῆσις ἡμε(ρῶν) [β] πεντώβολον, [71]Βεροῦς ὁμ(οίως) ἡμε(ρῶν) ι

entertaining Tyche 3 ob. 9th Mecheir : . . . 1 dr. 3 ob. ; . . . the 10th : . . . for the weaver's breakfast 1 ob. ; . . . ½ ob. ; for the Serapeum 2 ob. ; pure bread for the children ½ ob. ; beer[a] for the weaver 2 ob. ; leeks for the weaver's breakfast 1 ob. ; pigeon 1 ob. ; to Antas 2 dr. 2 ob. ; up at the city, cost of grinding 2 artabae of wheat for bread through Isas, 1 dr. 2 ob. The 11th: at the camp through Theodorus, cost of grinding 1 artaba of wheat for bread 4 ob. ; for the weaver's breakfast 1 ob. ; asparagus for the dinner of Antas when he went to the funeral feast of Ath . . . the fuller ½ ob. ; and cabbage for the boys' dinner ½ ob. ; . . . the child ½ ob. . . . The 16th : a relish ½ ob. ; rushes for baking bread 2½ ob. The 17th : milk for the children ½ ob. ; pure bread ½ ob. The 18th : to Secundas for a cake for the children ½ ob. The 19th : barley water for the same ½ ob. The 20th : sauce 1 ob. ; pure bread ½ ob. ; for entertaining Antonia 2 ob. ; and for Taptollous daughter of Caecilius 2 ob. ; on the birthday of Tryphas, for garlands 2 ob. ; on the birthday of . . ., for garlands 2 ob. The 21st : pomegranates for the children 1 ob. ; playthings and . . . for the children ½ ob. ; beer 3 ob. ; sauce 1 ob. The 22nd : sauce 1 ob. . . . Thaesis . . . for 2 days 5 ob. ; the mother of Ammonas for [·] days . . . ; Taarpaesis for 2 days 5 ob. ; Berous likewise for 10

[a] Beer made from barley, the modern *booza*, was a favourite beverage in Egypt from very early times, especially among the lower classes.

(δραχμαὶ) δ (ὀβολός). [72]κδ. ἄλεστρα (πυροῦ) (ἀρτάβης) α (τετρώβολον), [73]ἁλμυρίδος μα(τίων) β (ὀβολοὶ δύο), [74]ἁλὸς (ὀβολός), [75]λίνου καὶ ῥαφίδος (ὀβολός), [76]ἄλεστρα (πυροῦ) (ἀρτάβης) α διὰ Θεοδώ(ρου) (τετρώβολον), [77]κέρκισ[τ]ρα φα[ι]νόλ(ου) (δραχμὴ) α (ὀβολοὶ δύο), [78]ἄρτω(ν) καθαρῶ(ν) Φα[. . .]τω( ) (δραχμὴ) α, [79]περιστερᾶς [πα]ιδ(ῶν) (ὀβολός), [80]ἄρτου κ[αθαροῦ ὁ]μ(οίως) (ἡμιωβέλιον), [81]Σεκούντῳ παιδ(ῶν) ἰτρ[ίου] (ἡμιωβέλιον), [82]καὶ σεμιδάρεως ξηρᾶς (ἡμιωβέλιον), [83]γάλακτος (ἡμιωβέλιον), [84]μύρου ε[ἰ]ς ταφῆς θυγατρὸς [85][Π]άσιτ[ο]ς (δραχμὴ) α - - - Verso: - - - [88]ι. αμ[. . .]γ( ) γυ[ν]αιξὶ συνα[. . . .] (δραχμαὶ) β (τριώβολον), [89]πρ[ο]σφαγί(ων) ταῖς γυναιξὶ [90]ἡμε(ρῶν) β (ὀβολοὶ δύο) (ἡμιωβέλιον), [91]κόλλητρα λυχνίας (ὀβολοὶ δύο) (ἡμιωβέλιον), [92]ἐρεβίνθων [ὅ]τε ὧδε [93]ἐδείπνει . [. . . .]. ι[ο]ς (ὀβολὸς) (ἡμιωβέλιον), [94]εἰς κατανθρωπισμὸν [95]Λα[ο]δίκης (ὀβολοὶ δύο?), [96]⟦.⟧ εἰς τὰ αρτ . [. . .] . . . . (ὀβολοὶ δύο), [97]Στράτου εἰς τὴ[ν .]ε . απ . ς εἰσβολ(ὴν) (δραχμαὶ?) δ, [98][. . . .] δαπανη( ) . . . τα . . . . . ς [ ] [99]Ἥρ[ω]νι εἰς τ . . . ρ . . . κιθῶ(να?) (δραχμ?) [. .], [100]κόλλητρα χαλκ[ίο]υ (ἡμιωβέλιον).

187. LIST OF PERSONAL BELONGINGS

B.G.U. 1666. 1st cent. A.D.

[1]Λόγος σκευῶν τῆς {τῆς} μητρὸς [2]ὃν Ἑλένη· ψέλια ἀργυρᾶ [3]τεσσάρων σ[τ]ατήρων καὶ ἐποί-[4]διον χρ[υ]σοῦν τεταρτῶν τριῶν [5]καὶ στολὴ Συριακὴ λευκὴ (δραχμῶν) ρκ· [6]καὶ Θατρῆς· ψέλια ἀργυρᾶ

days 4 dr. 1 ob. The 24th: cost of grinding 1 artaba of wheat 4 ob.; 2 measures of pickle 2 ob.; salt 1 ob.; thread and needle 1 ob.; cost of grinding 1 artaba of wheat, through Theodorus, 4 ob.; cost of weaving a cloak 1 dr. 2 ob.; pure bread for Ph . . . 1 dr.; pigeon for the children 1 ob.; pure bread for the same ½ ob.; to Secundus for a cake for the children ½ ob., and for dry flour ½ ob.; milk ½ ob.; perfume for the dispatch of the mummy of Pasis's daughter 1 dr. . . . The 10th: . . . for the women 2 dr. 3 ob.; relishes for the women for 2 days 2½ ob.; cost of tinkering a lamp 2½ ob.; chick-peas when . . . dined here 1½ ob.; for entertaining Laodice 2 ob.; . . . cost of tinkering a cauldron ½ obol.

---

82. *l.* σεμιδάλεως.

187. LIST OF PERSONAL BELONGINGS

1st cent. A.D.

Account of the mother's effects: received by Helena, silver armlets weighing 4 staters and a gold ear-pendant weighing 3 quarters[a] and a Syrian robe worth 120 drachmae; and by Thatres, silver

[a] Gold and silver ornaments were weighed on different systems, the former in quarters and mnaiaia (see Glossary) and the latter in drachmae and staters (= tetradrachms).

---

2. *l.* ὧν. 3. *l.* ἐπώτιον or ἐνώτιον (so in l. 7).

τεσσά-^{7}ρων στατήρων καὶ ἐποίδιον χρυ-^{8}[σοῦν] τε[τ]αρτῶν τριῶν καὶ μη-^{9}νίσκον [χ]ρυσοῦν τεταρ-[τῶ]ν τριῶν ^{10}καὶ κοκκ[ί]νη στολὴ (δραχμῶν) ρμ· καὶ ^{11}Ἀφροδ[ο]ῦς· σκάφιν χαλκοῦν καὶ ^{12}πάλλι[ν] Κοραξὸν καὶ ὅλμιν ἀλα-^{13}βάστρινον καὶ χιθῶνα ἰδιώχρω-^{14}[μ]ον ἄ[γ]ναφον (δραχμῶν) ξ καὶ κλείνας β ^{15}καὶ τρά[π]εζα [κ]αὶ ἱμάτιον Συρια-^{16}κὸν (δραχμῶν) π καὶ φέρνην τῆς μητρὸς ^{17}.π(?), γ(ίνονται) (δραχμαὶ) ω.

11-12. *l.* σκάφιον, πάλλιον, ὁλμίον.

188. MONTHLY MEAT BILL OF A COOK

P. Oxy. 108. A.D. 215 (?)

Col. 1. ^{1}Θὼθ δ̄ κδ̄ (ἔτους), ^{2}κρέως μν(αῖ) δ̄, ^{3}ἄκρα β̄, ^{4}γλῶσσα μία, ^{5}ῥυγχίον ᾱ. ^{6}ϛ̄, γλωσσοπωγώνιον. ^{7}ιᾱ, κρέω(ς) μν(αῖ) β̄, ^{8}γλῶσσα μία, ^{9}νεφρία β̄. ^{10}ιβ̄, κρέω(ς) μν(ᾶ) ᾱ, ^{11}στέρνα μία. ^{12}ιδ̄, κρέω(ς) μν(αῖ) β̄, ^{13}στέρνα ᾱ. ^{14}ιϛ̄, κρέως μν(αῖ) γ̄. ^{15}ιζ̄, κρέω(ς) μν(αῖ) β, ^{16}γλῶσσα μία. ^{17}ιη̄, γλῶσσα μία. ^{18}κᾱ, κοιλία.

Col. 2. ^{1}κβ̄, ^{2}κοιλία, ^{3}νεφρία β̄. ^{4}κγ̄, ^{5}κρέω(ς) μν(αῖ) β̄, ^{6}κοιλία ᾱ, ^{7}ἄκρα β̄. ^{8}κϛ̄, ^{9}γλῶσσα μία. ^{10}λ̄, στέρνα μία. (2nd hand) ^{11}καὶ πρὸ τούτων Μεσορὴ ^{12}ιη̄, κρέως μναῖ β, κοιλία α, ^{13}νεφρία β. κᾱ, στέρνα α. ^{14}κγ̄, γλωσσοπωγώνιον α, νε-^{15}φρία β. κδ, μναῖ β, νεφρί-^{16}α β. κε̄, Τρύφωνι μναῖ β, ^{17}ὠτίον α, ἄκρον α, νεφρία β. ^{18}κθ̄, μναῖ β, ἄκρα β, γλῶσ-^{19}σα α. ἐπαγομένων β̄, ^{20}γλῶσσα α. γ̄, στέρνα α.

Verso: ^{1}λόγος ^{2}μαγείρου.

armlets weighing 4 staters and a gold ear-pendant weighing 3 quarters and a gold crescent weighing 3 quarters and a scarlet robe worth 140 dr.; and by Aphrodous, a copper basin and a Coraxian cloak and an alabaster mortar and a tunic, natural-coloured, not fulled, worth 60 dr., and 2 couches and a table and a Syrian mantle worth 80 dr. and her mother's dowry . . ., total 800 dr.

188. MONTHLY MEAT BILL OF A COOK

A.D. 215 (?)

Thoth 4th, 24th year, 4 minae[a] of meat, 2 trotters, 1 tongue, 1 snout. 6th, half a head with the tongue. 11th, 2 minae of meat, 1 tongue, 2 kidneys. 12th, 1 mina of meat, 1 breast. 14th, 2 minae of meat, 1 breast. 16th, 3 minae of meat. 17th, 2 minae of meat, 1 tongue. 18th, 1 tongue. 21st, 1 paunch. 22nd, 1 paunch, 2 kidneys. 23rd, 2 minae of meat, 1 paunch, 2 trotters. 26th, 1 tongue. 30th, 1 breast. And before this on Mesore 18th, 2 minae of meat, 1 paunch, 2 kidneys. 21st, 1 breast. 23rd, 1 half a head with the tongue, 2 kidneys. 24th, 2 minae, 2 kidneys. 25th, for Tryphon 2 minae, 1 ear, 1 trotter, 2 kidneys. 29th, 2 minae, 2 trotters, 1 tongue. 2nd intercalary day, 1 tongue. 3rd, 1 breast. (Endorsed) Cook's account.

[a] Roughly, 4 pounds.

189. INVENTORY OF THE PROPERTY OF A DECEASED HUSBAND

P. Tebt. 406, ll. 8-29. About A.D. 266.

[8]Λόγος ὧν κατάλειψεν Παῦλος γενόμ[ε]νός μου ἀ[ν]ήρ, πατὴ[ρ [9]τ]ῆς ἀφήλικός μου θυγατρὸς Π[αυ]λίνας, ἃ καὶ παρεδόθη [10]Πασιγένῃ ἀδελφῷ τοῦ ἀνδρός μου διὰ Σουχάμμωνος μ[ε-][11]σίτου. ἔστι δέ· [12]λυχνεία τελεία σὺν Ἔρωτι καὶ λυχ[νί]ῳ συντετειμένη (δραχμῶν) .ς, [13]λεκάνη χαλκῆ, τήγανον, [ ]τ[·]απη, [14]καὶ ἐν ἱματίοις κιτώνιον πρ[ωτό]γναφον λακωνόσημον [15]στατηριεῖον, [16]μαφόρτης ὁμοίως λευκὸς λακ[ων]όσημος ἔχων δίδραχμον, [17]ἄλλο κιτώνιον ἱμιτ[ρ]ιβῆ, κολόβιον λινοῦν δ[ί]σημον καινόν, [18]φακιάνον λινοῦν καινόν, λίνα λευκὰ ἀριθμῷ ι[β] ἐκ (δραχμῶν) η (δραχμῶν) ϙς, [19]ξοΐδιον εἰς περικοπήν, ὕνις ὁμ[οί]ως τελεία, κράβακτος ξύλι-[20]νος τέλειος. [21]καὶ ἃ ἔχει πρὸς τοὺς ἀδελφοὺς κοινὰ ὄντα χαλκίον τέλειον [22]μολυβοῦν εἰς ἕψησιν λίνων, σκάφιον τέλειον, χαλκίον [23]μικρόν, κάδος μικρός. [24]καὶ ὧν ἐπικρατῖ δούλων κοινῶν ὄντων {κοινῶν} τοῦ πα-[25]τρὸς τῆς θυγατρός μου ἀριθμῷ ε· [26]Νεικόις, Κωφὴ ἄλλη, καὶ ταύτης ἔγγονα [27]Λακωνίς, Βελλῆς, Σαραπιάς. [28]κα[ὶ ὧ]ν πάλιν ἐπικρατῖ ἀρουρῶν πολλῶν ὄν-[29][τ]ων.

8. *l.* κατέλειψεν. 10. Or Α[ὑα]σίτου (='Οασίτου). 13. *l.* τάπης or [ἀσ]τ[ρ]άβη? 15. *l.* στατηριαῖον. 17. *l.* ἡμιτ[ρ]ιβές. 18. *l.* φακιάλιον. 28. *l.* οὐσῶν.

189. INVENTORY OF THE PROPERTY OF A DECEASED HUSBAND

About A.D. 266.

Account of effects left by Paul, my late husband and father of my daughter Paulina, not yet of age, which have been delivered to Pasigenes the brother of my husband through Souchammon the arbitrator (?).[a] They are: a lamp-stand, perfect, with an Eros and a lamp, valued at [·]6 drachmae; a copper dish; a frying-pan; a . . .; and in clothing a tunic new from the fuller, with a Laconian stripe, worth a stater; a shawl, likewise white and with a Laconian stripe, worth 2 drachmae; another tunic, half worn; a new linen shirt with two stripes; a new linen kerchief; white linen cloths 12 in number, worth, at 8 drachmae each, 96 drachmae; a chisel for planing; a ploughshare, likewise perfect; a wooden bedstead, perfect; and property held in common with his brothers: a leaden cauldron, perfect, for boiling linen; a basin, perfect; a small cauldron; a small jar; and the slaves of my daughter's father, whom he holds as common property, 5 in number: Nicois, another named Cophe, and the children of the latter, Laconis, Belles, Sarapias; and also the arurae held by him, which are many.

[a] Or perhaps "of the Oasis."

190. LIST OF PAYMENTS

P. Oxy. 2144. Late 3rd cent. A.D.

[1]Καὶ ὁμοί(ως) ἐξωδιάσθη ὑπ' ἐμοῦ [2]Ἀμμωνᾶ εἰς λόγ(ον) τῶν γεούχων· [3]δι(ὰ) Σαραπάμμωνος τι(μῆς) πετροσελί-[4]νου Μακεδονικ(οῦ) οὐγκ(ίας) α εἰς καταπό-[5]τιον ἵππων ἀθλητικῶν (δραχμαὶ) ω, [6]τῇ γεούχῳ ὑπ(ὲρ) τι(μῆς) μίλτου ὁλκ(ῆς) μν(ῶν) ε (δρ.) φ, [7]τῇ αὐτ(ῇ) ὁμοί(ως) ὑπ(ὲρ) τι(μῆς) κόλλης τεκτονικ(ῆς) [8]εἰς τὸν κτίστην ὁλκῆς μνᾶς δ' ⟦. . .⟧ (δρ.) ρνβ, [9]τῇ αὐτῇ ὁμοί(ως) ὑπ(ὲρ) τι(μῆς) μίλτου [10]μν(ῶν) ι (δρ.) Ἀ, [11]Θωνίῳ ἰδίῳ ὁμοί(ως) ὑπ(ὲρ) τι(μῆς) μίλτου [12]ὁλκ(ῆς) μν(ῶν) β εἰς τὸ Κόσμου (δρ.) σ, [13]Ἐπαφροδείτῳ ὁμοί(ως) ἰδίῳ ὑπ(ὲρ) κη-[14]ροῦ μν(ᾶς) α δοθείσης τῷ [15]πρίγκιπι (δρ.) ρ, [16]τῷ γεούχῳ Σαραπί[ω]νι κη-[17]ροῦ μν(ῶν) δ (δρ.) υ, [18]Ἡλιοδώρῳ ἰδίῳ ὑπ(ὲρ) τι(μῆς) κόλλης τε-[19]κτονικῆς εἰς τὸ Κόσμου μν(ᾶς) (ἡμίσους) (δρ.) τ, [20]Εὐμενείῃ ἰδίᾳ εἰς γάμους Ἀπολ-[21]λωνίου ὑπ(ὲρ) τι(μῆς) λύχνων (δρ.) μ, [22]Θωνίῳ ὁμοί(ως) κόλλης τεκτονι-[23]κῆς μνᾶς δ' (δρ.) ρνβ, [24]Ζωίλῳ ἰδίῳ ὁμοί(ως) κόλλης τεκτονι-[25]κῆς μν(ᾶς) δ' εἰς τρόχους ἵππων [26]ἀθλητικῶν (δρ.) ρνβ, [27]Σαραπίωνι γεούχῳ ἀγωνοθε-[28]τοῦντι ἐν τῇ Ἀντινόου [29]πλάσματα λιβανωτοῦ ἀρι-[30]θμῷ [δ]έκα (δρ.) ω.

---

[a] Contrast the purchasing power of the drachma in the third century B.C., when red ochre cost 1 dr. the mina,

190. LIST OF PAYMENTS

Late 3rd cent. A.D.

Paid likewise by me, Ammonas, on account of the landlords: through Sarapammon for the price of 1 oz. of Macedonian rock-parsley for a bolus for race-horses, 800 drachmae; to the landlady for the price of red ochre to the weight of 5 minae, 500 dr.; to the same likewise for the price of carpenter's glue for the builder to the weight of ¼ mina, 152 dr.[a]; to the same likewise for the price of 10 minae of red ochre, 1000 dr.; to Thonius of my household likewise for the price of red ochre to the weight of 2 minae for Cosmu,[b] 200 dr.,; to Epaphroditus likewise of my household for 1 mina of wax given to the *princeps*,[c] 100 dr.; to the landlord Sarapion for 4 minae of wax, 400 dr.; to Heliodorus of my household for the price of carpenter's glue for Cosmu, weight ½ mina, 300 dr.; to Eumeneia of my household for the price of lamps for the wedding of Apollonius, 40 dr.; to Thonius likewise for ¼ mina of carpenter's glue, 152 dr.; to Zoilus of my household likewise for ¼ mina of carpenter's glue for the wheels of the racing chariot, 152 dr.; to Sarapion the landlord, who has the office of director of games at Antinoe, 10 cakes of frankincense, 800 drachmae.

carpenter's glue the same, and wax usually less than 1 dr. the mina.

[b] An Oxyrhynchite hamlet.

[c] Both a military and a civil title.

191. LIST OF ARTICLES SHIPPED

P. Oxy. 1924. 5th or 6th cent. A.D.

1 + Λό(γος) εἰδôν βληθέντον 2 εἰς τὼ πλ[οῖ]ον· 3 [ο]ἴνου Ἀσκαλόνεα γ, 4 σαφωνίου κεράμιν α, 5 χεδρίας κεράμια β, 6 ὀμφοκερᾶς γάρου α, 7 ἐλαίου Σπάνου ἀγγῖ[ο]ν α, 8 ταριχίου Γαζίτια ζ, 9 κ[ο]ῦφα ἀγγῖα ε, 10 κοῦφον Ἀσκαλόνιν α, 11 Γαζίτινεν κοῦφον α, 12 ὀμφοκερᾶς κούφ[η] α, 13 χάρτου σφυρύδιν α, 14 ταπήτ(ιον) α.

1. *l.* εἰδῶν βληθέντων. 3. *l.* Ἀσκαλώνια. 4. *l.* σαπωνίου. 5. *l.* κεδρίας. 6. *l.* ὀμφακηρά; so in l. 12. 11. *l.* Γαζίτινον? 13. *l.* σφυρίδι(ο)ν.

192. INVENTORY OF CHURCH PROPERTY

P. Grenf. ii. 111. 5th or 6th cent. A.D.

1 + Ἀναγρ[α]φ(ὴ) τῶν ἁγί(ων) κ[ει]μηλ(ίων) καὶ ἑτέρων σκευῶν 2 τῆς ἁγί(ας) ἐκκλ(ησίας) ἄπα Ψ[α]ΐο(υ) κώμ(ης) Ἰβιῶνος 3 παραδοθ(έντων) τῷ εὐλαβ(εστάτῳ) Ἰωάννῃ πρ(εσβυτέρῳ) καὶ οἰκ(ονόμῳ) 4 Χοίαχ ιε // ιγ ἰνδ(ικτίονος), οὕτ(ως)· 5 ποτήρ(ια) ἀργυρ(ᾶ) γ, 6 ξέστ(ης) ἀργυρ(οῦς) α, 7 καταπετάσμ(ατα) β, 8 ῥάβδ(ος) σιδηρ(ᾶ) α, 9 ὁμοί(ως) μικρ(ὰ) α, 10 τράπεζ(α) μαρμαρ(ᾶ) α, 11 τρίπους χαλκ(οῦς) τῆς τραπέζ(ης) α, 12 μαμπ(άρια) λινᾶ τῆς τραπέζ(ης) κγ, 13 μαμπ(άρια) ἐρεινᾶ ε, 14 οὐηλόθυρα ϛ, 15 ὁμοί(ως) παλαιὸν α, 16 οὐηλάρ(ιον) ἐρειν(οῦν) κρεμ(αστὸν) α, 17 στρῶμ(α) κρεμαστ(ὸν) α, 18 λυχνίαι χαλκ(αῖ) δ, 19 λυχνίαι σιδηρ(αῖ) β, 20 βω<μ>ὸς χαλκ(οῦς) α, 21 {βωμὸς

191. LIST OF ARTICLES SHIPPED

5th or 6th cent. A.D.

List of articles placed on the boat: 3 Ascalon jars of wine,[a] 1 jar of soap, 2 jars of cedar oil, 1 flagon of sauce, 1 vessel of Spanish oil, 7 Gaza jars of pickled fish, 5 empty vessels, 1 empty Ascalon jar, 1 empty Gaza jar, 1 empty flagon, 1 basket of papyrus, 1 rug.

[a] That is, re-used jars in which some commodity had been imported from Ascalon.

192. INVENTORY OF CHURCH PROPERTY

5th or 6th cent. A.D.

Inventory of the holy treasures and other utensils of the holy church of Apa Psaius[a] of the village of Ibion, entrusted to the most discreet John, presbyter and steward, Choiak 15, 13th indiction, being as follows: 3 silver chalices; 1 silver paten; 2 hangings; 1 iron rod; 1 other, small; 1 marble slab; 1 bronze tripod for the slab; 23 linen cloths for the slab; 5 woollen cloths; 6 door-curtains; 1 other, old; 1 hanging woollen curtain; 1 hanging cover; 4 bronze lamp-stands; 2 iron lamp-stands; 1 bronze

[a] The saint to whom the church was dedicated. Apa is an ecclesiastical title.

χαλκ(οῦς) α} [22]λέβης χαλκ(οῦς) α, [23]κοκκούμ(ιον) χαλκ(οῦν) α, [24]λουτήρ(ια) χαλκ(ᾶ) β, [25]χειρολυχν(ίαι) ϛ μύξ(αι) ϛ, [26]πλοιάρ(ια) χαλκ(ᾶ) δ μύξ(αι) δ, [27]βιβλία δερμάτι(να) κα, [28]ὁμοί(ως) χαρτία γ, [29]κοτύλ(η) α, [30]κύαθ(ος) α, [31]μάχαιρ(α) α, [32]κραβάκτ(ιον) α, [33]μαγὶς ξυλ(ίνη) α, [34]τυλάρ(ια) δερμάτ(ινα) β, [35]θυΐα{ν} α, [36]καθέδρ(αι) ξυλ(ίναι) γ, [37]σεμψέλλ(ια) β, [38]ἱστ(ὸς) τριύφ(αντος) α, [39]ἀπαιοθήκ(η) α, [40]λύκηθ(ος) χαλκ(ῆ) α.

Verso: δι' ἐμοῦ Ἡλίου ἀρχιδιακ(όνου) ὑπ(ὲρ) τοῦ ἁγί(ου) ἄπα Γεωργίου.

37. *l.* συμψέλλ(ια). 39. *l.* ἀποθήκ(η). 40. *l.* λήκυθ(ος).

altar; 1 bronze basin; 1 bronze flagon; 2 bronze fonts; 6 hand-lamps with 6 nozzles; 4 boat-shaped lamps with 4 nozzles; 21 parchment books; 3 others of papyrus; 1 cup; 1 ladle; 1 knife; 1 bier; 1 wooden tray; 2 leather cushions; 1 mortar; 3 wooden chairs; 2 stools; 1 triply woven web; 1 cupboard; 1 bronze flask. (Endorsed) Made by me, Elias, archdeacon, on behalf of the holy Apa George.[a]

[a] Apparently as agent for a church of St. George.

XI. QUESTIONS TO ORACLES

193. QUESTION TO AN ORACLE

Oxy. 1148. 1st cent. A.D.

[1]Κύριέ μου Σάραπι Ἥλιε [2]εὐεργέτα. εἰ βέλτειόν [3]ἐστιν Φανίαν τὸν υἱό(ν) [4]μου καὶ τὴν γυναῖκα [5]αὐτοῦ μὴ συμφωνῆσαι [6]νῦν τῷ πατρὶ α(ὐτοῦ), ἀλλὰ [7]ἀντιλέγειν καὶ μὴ δι-[8]δόναι γράμματα· τοῦ-[9]τό μοι σύμφωνον ἔνεν-[10]κε. ἔρρω(σο).

2. ει may = ἦ, but is more probably to be read as εἰ introducing an indirect question, the verb being understood. 6. Schubart α(ὐτῆς).

194. QUESTION TO AN ORACLE

P. Oxy. 1149. 2nd cent. A.D.

[1]Διὶ Ἡλίῳ μεγάλωι [2]Σεράπ[ι]δι καὶ τοῖς [3]συν-νάοις. ἐρωτᾷ [4]Νίκη εἰ σ[υ]μφέρει [5]μοι ἀ[γο]ράσαι παρὰ [6]Τασαρ[α]πίωνος ὃν [7]ἔχει δοῦλον Σαρα-πί-[8]ωνα τ[ὸ]ν κα[ὶ Γ]αΐωνα. [9][τοῦτό μ]οι δός.

195. FROM A LIST OF QUESTIONS TO AN ORACLE

P. Oxy. 1477. About A.D. 300.

[1]οβ, εἰ λήμψομαι τὸ ὀψώνιον. [2]ογ, εἰ μενῶ ὅπου

1-21. ει: see No. 193, note.

XI. QUESTIONS TO ORACLES

193. QUESTION TO AN ORACLE

1st cent. A.D.

O Lord Sarapis Helios, beneficent one. (Say) whether it is fitting that Phanias my son and his wife should not agree now with his father, but oppose him and not make a contract. Tell me this truly. Goodbye.

194. QUESTION TO AN ORACLE

2nd cent. A.D.

To Zeus Helios great Serapis and his fellow gods. Nike asks whether it is to my advantage to buy from Tasarapion her slave Sarapion also called Gaion. Grant me this.

195. FROM A LIST OF QUESTIONS TO AN ORACLE

About A.D. 300.

72, shall I receive the allowance? 73, shall I

ὑπάγω. [3]οδ, εἰ πωλοῦμαι. [4]οε, εἰ ἔχω ὠφελίαν ἀπὸ τοῦ φίλου. [5]οϛ, εἰ δέδοταί μοι ἑτέρῳ συναλλάξαι. [6]οζ, εἰ καταλλάσσομαι εἰς τὸν γόνον (?). [7]οη, εἰ λαμβάνω κομιᾶτον. [8]οθ, εἰ λήμψομαι τὸ ἀργύριον. [9]π, εἰ ζῇ ὁ ἀπόδημος. [10]πα, εἰ κερδαίνω ἀπὸ τοῦ πράγματ[ος]. [11]πβ, εἰ προγράφεται τὰ ἐμά. [12]πγ, εἰ εὑρήσω πωλῆσαι. [13]πδ, εἰ δύναμαι ὃ ἐνθυμοῦμαι ἆρα[ι]. [14]πε, εἰ γίνομαι βιόπρατος. [15]πϛ, εἰ φυγαδεύσομαι. [16]πζ, εἰ πρεσβεύσω. [17]πη, εἰ γίνομαι βουλευτής. [18]πθ, εἰ λύεταί μου ὁ δρασμός. [19]ϙ, εἰ ἀπαλλάσσομαι τῆς γυναικό[ς]. [20]ϙα, εἰ πεφαρμάκωμαι. [21]ϙβ, εἰ λαμβάνω [τ]ὸ ἴδ[ιο]ν.

6. γονον very doubtful; the first letter might be σ, the third κ or μ, and the end may be missing. 14. πρα of βιοπρατος not certain.

remain where I am going? 74, am I to be sold? 75, am I to obtain benefit from my friend? 76, has it been granted me to make a contract with another person? 77, am I to be reconciled (?) with my offspring (?)? 78, am I to get furlough? 79, shall I get the money? 80, is he who left home alive? 81, am I to profit by the transaction? 82, is my property to be put up to auction? 83, shall I find a means of selling? 84, am I able to carry off what I have in mind? 85, am I to become a beggar (?)? 86, shall I be a fugitive? 87, shall I be an ambassador (?)? 88, am I to become a senator? 89, is my flight to be stopped? 90, am I to be divorced from my wife? 91, have I been poisoned? 92, am I to get my own?

XII. CHRISTIAN PRAYERS

196. CHRISTIAN PRAYER

P. Oxy. 925. 5th or 6th cent. A.D.

[1]+ Ὁ θ(εὸ)ς ὁ παντοκράτωρ ὁ ἅγιος [2]ὁ ἀληθινὸς φιλάνθρωπος καὶ [3]δημιουργὸς ὁ π(ατ)ὴρ τοῦ κ(υρίο)υ (καὶ) σω(τῆ)ρ(ο)ς [4]ἡμῶν Ἰ(ησο)ῦ Χ(ριστο)ῦ, φανέρωσόν μοι τὴν [5]παρὰ σοὶ ἀλήθιαν εἰ βούλῃ με ἀπελθεῖν [6]εἰς Χιούτ. ἦ εὑρίσκω σε σὺν ἐμοὶ [7]πράττοντα (καὶ) εὐμενήν; γένοιτο, ϙθ.

197. CHRISTIAN PRAYER

P. Oxy. 1150. 6th cent. A.D.

[1]+ Ὁ θεὸς (+) τοῦ προστάτου ἡμῶν [2]τοῦ ἁγίου Φιλοξένου, ἐὰν [3]κελεύεις εἰσενεγκεῖν [4]εἰς τὸ νοσοκομῖόν σου Ἀνούπ· [5]δεῖξον τὴν δύναμ[ίν σου] [6]καὶ ἐξέλθῃ τὸ πιττ[ά]κ[ιον].

XII. CHRISTIAN PRAYERS

196. CHRISTIAN PRAYER[a]

5th or 6th cent. A.D.

O God almighty, holy, true, benevolent, Creator, Father of our Lord and Saviour Jesus Christ, reveal to me thy truth, whether it is thy will that I go to Chiout. Shall I find thee aiding me and gracious? So be it; Amen.[b]

[a] This type of prayer is directly derived from the questions to pagan oracles (see Nos. 193-195).

[b] Literally "99," as the letters of ἀμήν read as figures and added up make that number.

197. CHRISTIAN PRAYER

6th cent. A.D.

O God of our patron Saint Philoxenus, (say) whether thou biddest us take Anoup to thy hospital; show thy power and let this prayer be accomplished.

XIII. CHARM

198. GNOSTIC CHARM

P. Oxy. 1478. About A.D. 300.

[1]Νεικητικὸν Σαραπάμμωνει υἱῷ Ἀπολ-[2]λωνείου. 10 or 11 magical symbols. [3]δὸς νείκην ὁλοκληρίαν σ<τ>αδίου καὶ [4]ὄχλου τῷ προκειμένῳ Σαραπάμμωνι [5]ἐξ ἀνόματος ΣΥΛΙΚΥΣΗΣΟΥ.

5. *l.* ὀνόματος.

XIII. CHARM

198. GNOSTIC CHARM

About A.D. 300.

Charm for victory for Sarapammon son of Apollonius. . . . Give victory and safety in the race-course and the crowd to the aforesaid Sarapammon in the name of Sulicusesus.[a]

[a] Some mysterious deity.

XIV. HOROSCOPES

199. HOROSCOPE OF PHILOE

P. Oslo 6. A.D. 150.

[1]Γένεσις Φιλόης. ιγ (ἔτους) Ἀντωνίνου [2]Καί-σαρος τοῦ κυρίου Φαμ(ενὼ)θ ιε̅ [3]εἰς ις̅ ὥρας δ νυκτός. Ἥλιος ἐν [4]Ἰχθύσι, Ζεὺς Ἑρμῆς ἐν Κριῷ, [5]Κρόνος ἐν Καρκίνῳ, Ἄρης Λέοντ(ι), [6]Ἀφροδί(τη) Σελήνη Ὑδρηχ[ό]ῳ, [7]ὡροσκώπος Σκωρπ(ίος).

7. *l.* ὡροσκόπος Σκορπ(ίος).

200. HOROSCOPE OF SARAPAMMON

P. Oxy. 1476. A.D. 260.

[1]Α (ἔτους) Μακρ{ιν}ιανοῦ καὶ Κυιήτου [2]Σεβαστῶν Φαῶφι β ἡμέρας [3]ὥρ(ᾳ) ι πεπληρωμένῃ μοι(ρῶν) β. [4]ὡροσκόπος Ὑδροχόῳ μοι(ρῶν) κη, [5]Κρόνον Κρειῷ ια λεπ(τῶν) λβ ἀκρώνυ-[6]κτος ἀφαιρετι[κό]ς, [7]Ἄρης Λέοντι αὐ . [.]τερος, [8]Ζεὺς Παρθένῳ γ λεπτῶν < >, [9]Ἀφροδείτη Παρθένῳ η ις, [10]Ἑρμῆς Παρθένῳ κγ μδ, [11]Ἥλιος Ζυγῷ η, [12]Σελή[νη] <Αἰγόκερῳ> μοι(ρῶν) η λεπ(τῶν) λβ. [13]Σαρα-π[ά]μμωνος.

5. *l.* Κρόνος.

XIV. HOROSCOPES

199. HOROSCOPE OF PHILOE

A.D. 150.

The birth of Philoe. The 10th year of Antoninus Caesar the lord, Phamenoth 15 to 16, 1st hour of the night. Sun in Pisces, Jupiter and Mercury in Aries, Saturn in Cancer, Mars in Leo, Venus and Moon in Aquarius, horoscopus Capricorn.

200. HOROSCOPE OF SARAPAMMON

A.D. 260.

The 1st year of Macrianus and Quietus, Augusti, Phaophi 2, the 10th hour of the day completed, 2°. Horoscopus Aquarius 28° ; Saturn in Aries 11° 32′,[a] in opposition and subtractive ; Mars in Leo at the beginning ; Jupiter in Virgo 3° <·>′ [b] ; Venus in Virgo 8° 16′ ; Mercury in Virgo 23° 44′ ; Sun in Libra 8° ; Moon <in Capricorn> 8° 32′. (Birth) of Sarapammon.

[a] That is, 11 degrees, 32 minutes.

[b] The number of the minutes has been inadvertently omitted.

GLOSSARY OF TECHNICAL TERMS

Actuarius, a military accountant and paymaster
Agoranomus, a government notary through whom publicly made contracts were usually drawn up
Antiblemata, see No. 19, note *b*
Antichresis, substitution of usufruct for interest on a loan
Anubieum, temple of the dog-headed god Anubis
Apa, see No. 192, p. 433, note *a*
Archidicastes, see No. 53, p. 161, note *a*
Artaba, a measure of capacity, equal to about 40 litres, but variable according to the standard employed
Arura, an area of land, about 2025 square metres
As, a Roman coin of small value
Athlophorus, literally "prize-bearer," title of an eponymous priestess at Alexandria
Augustalianus, a person in the service of one of the Byzantine military commanders who bore the title of Dux et Augustalis

Beneficiarius, a soldier attached to the personal suite of his commander, enjoying consequent privileges

Canephorus, literally "basket-bearer," title of an eponymous priestess at Alexandria
Carat, see No. 23, p. 69, note *a*
Catoecic, belonging to catoeci or soldiers to whom parcels of land had been granted under the Ptolemies. This category of land retained the name catoecic in Roman times, though no longer occupied by military holders
Chalcus, $\frac{1}{8}$th of an obol
Choenix, a measure of capacity, about 1 litre
Choi, see No. 34, note *d*
Chous, a liquid measure, about 3 litres
Chrematistae, see No. 53, note *b*
Cleruch, a soldier holding a grant of land
Cleruchy, land which belongs or formerly belonged to cleruchs
Comes, a title of honour borne by various officials, military and civil, in the Byzantine period
Compromissum, see No. 61, note *a*
Cosmetes, holder of one of the municipal offices which the richer men in Graeco-Egyptian towns were obliged to undertake at their personal expense
Cotyla, a liquid measure, about $\frac{1}{4}$ litre

Decadarch, see No. 157, note *a*
Decemprimus, member of a local senate appointed to supervise the collection of corn dues
Decurion, commander of a company of ten men
Defensor, a municipal magistrate in the Byzantine period, whose nominal duty was to protect the citizens against oppression
Deme, a subdivision of the tribes in which the Greek cities in Egypt were organized
Denarius, Roman coin, see p. xvii

GLOSSARY OF TECHNICAL TERMS

Diadochi, literally "successors." "Of the diadochi" was an honorific title under the later Ptolemies

Dicaeodotes, the chief judge in Roman Egypt after the praefect, whom he assisted

Dicast, one who judges

Dies augustus, see No. 69, note *c*

Dioecetes, under the Ptolemies the minister of finance; in Roman times a financial administrator of more restricted scope; but the title was also given to subordinate officials in the provinces

Domain-land, see No. 52, p. 157, note *a*

Drachma, see pp. xvi-xvii

Dromos, see No. 43, note *b*

Epigone, see No. 2, note *b*. Perhaps the term originally denoted sons of foreign soldiers, born in Egypt, but in later times "Persian of the Epigone" was used indiscriminately to signify a certain legal status

Epistrategus, civil governor of a large district

Exegetes, holder of one of the municipal offices (see Cosmetes)

Follis, see No. 23, note *b*

Forum, courts of law

Gymnasiarch, holder of one of the municipal offices (see Cosmetes)

Hin, an Egyptian measure, about ½ litre

Hipparch, commander of cavalry

Imperator, as a title after the name of an Emperor originally signified victorious commander

Indiction, see p. xvi

Iseum, temple of the Egyptian goddess Isis

Maniaces, a necklace of a special kind

Matrona stolata, see No. 36, note *a*

Metretes, a liquid measure, containing usually, but not invariably, 6 choes or about 18 litres

Metropolis, capital of a nome

Mina, as a sum of money = 100 silver drachmae; as a weight about an English pound, but variable according to the standard employed

Mnaiaion, as money a gold piece equal in value to 100 silver drachmae; as a weight about 28 grammes

Nome, an Egyptian district with local administration, like an English county

Numerus, a military force attached to a particular locality

Obol, see p. xvii

Pagarchy, administration of a district, an important office in the later Byzantine period

Parapherna, articles which were brought by a bride along with her dowry, but which remained her special property

Patrician, a title given by Byzantine emperors to distinguished members of the court

Praefect usually denotes the Roman governor of Egypt

Praefect of the praetorium, see No. 56, note *a*

Praetorian fleet = Imperial fleet

Princeps, see No. 190, note *c*

Quarter, a weight used in weighing gold; ¼ of a gold stater or 1/16 of a mnaiaion, about 1⅔ grammes

Sabautia, see No. 43, note *c*

Salotia, see No. 43, note *c*

Schoenion, see No. 52, note *d*

Serapeum, temple of the Graeco-Egyptian god Sarapis or Serapis

Sestertius, a small Roman coin

Solidus, a Byzantine gold coin weighing about 4½ grammes; see p. xvii

Speculator, a military title, adjutant

GLOSSARY OF TECHNICAL TERMS

Stater, either a weight or a sum of money; in silver = 4 drachmae, in gold = 2 drachmae
Stolistae, see No. 104, note *b*
Strategus, civil governor of a nome or other district
Sword-bearer, an armed attendant

Tabularius, an official clerk
Tactomisthus, see No. 37, note *b*
Techerere, see No. 30, p. 91, note *b*
Tetradrachm, see p. xvii
Thebaid, district of Thebes, Upper Egypt
Toparchy, a division of an Egyptian nome
Tribe, see deme

Vicarianus, in the service of a lieutenant-commander

INDEX OF SOURCES

INDEX OF SOURCES

INDEX OF SOURCES